Do just once what others say you can't do, and you will never pay attention to their limitations again.

—James R. Cook

CONTENTS

PREFACE

W. Edwards Deming maintained that real quality improvement isn't possible without *profound knowledge.* According to Deming, profound knowledge comes from an understanding of the theory of knowledge, knowledge of variation, an understanding of psychology, and appreciation for systems.

Most modern organizational systems are considered to be *cybernetic* systems. That is, they are capable of *self-adjustment.* Besides adjusting their components and inputs to control the quality and quantity of their outputs, cybernetic systems can redesignate their goals, too, in response to changes in their environment. So, if we appreciate a system, it would mean that we thoroughly understand how the system's components interact with each other and how the entire system interacts with its environment. Such understanding is indispensable to effective change.

Eliyahu M. Goldratt's Theory of Constraints is a *system* improvement philosophy. How does this differ from more commonly known continuous improvement theories? Nearly all the improvement philosophies focus primarily on improvement of *processes.* The unspoken, underlying assumption seems to be that if all the component processes are improved and refined to their maximum, the entire system will exhibit maximum improvement. Unfortunately, this assumption ignores the effects of *interdependence,* or the linkage, between processes.

Goldratt, however, maintains that organizations live or die as systems, not as processes. Their success or failure is a function of how well the different component processes *interact* with one another. Moreover, he contends that systems are analogous to *chains,* or networks of chains. Like a chain, a system's performance is limited by the performance of its weakest link. This means, by extension, that no matter how much effort you put into improving the processes of a system, only the improvements to the weakest link will produce any detectable system improvement. The weakest link is the system's *constraint.* And Goldratt's Theory of Constraints is the paradigm he's created to manage the living daylights out of these weakest links, with the end result that systems improve much more quickly than they might otherwise. So if you're an executive, a senior manager, or even a lone individual responsible for improving the performance of a system—any system—this book can help you.

The Theory of Constraints (TOC) is really a collection of system principles and tools, or methods for solving the problem of improving overall system performance. Some of these, such as Throughput Accounting and the "Drum-Buffer-Rope" approach to production control, are generic enough to have broad application to many businesses and agencies, well beyond those specific companies in which they were originally developed. Two exceptional books by Goldratt serve as "companion readers" for this one: *The Goal* and *It's Not Luck.*[1]

It's worth pointing out, too, that although the subtitle of this book is "A Systems Approach to Continuous Improvement," the Theory of Constraints is not necessarily limited to continuous improvement, in the traditional meaning of the phrase. "Continuous improvement," to most people, connotes the repetitive refinement and enhancement of an *existing* process. Even using a systems *approach,* the emphasis might be considered still to be on the existing system. But as you get into this book, especially chapter 5, "Future Reality Trees," you'll find that Goldratt's theory is eminently well suited to much more than existing system refinement. It will become obvious that TOC can be used to completely *reengineer* a business or organization as well.

The full scope of TOC methods and applications is much too broad to cover in depth in a book like this. Moreover, there are other books on such discrete topics as Throughput Accounting[2] and "Drum-Buffer-Rope"[3] that better address the financial and production control aspects of TOC. So, except for a brief overview of the theory and its principles in chapter 1, the majority of the book is devoted to explaining Goldratt's logical "Thinking Process": five tools of great power and versatility. When effectively applied, these logical tools empower the user to identify precisely and to execute the one or two focused changes that will produce maximum system improvement with the minimum investment of time, energy, and resources—and do it right the first time, without costly trial and error.

The content of this book constitutes my understanding and interpretation of the TOC Thinking Process, and I've endeavored to describe and apply it as faithfully as possible. Goldratt has not edited this book or provided comments. Readers already familiar with the logical tools will notice that certain elements of this book diverge somewhat from Goldratt's teachings. Almost without exception, these "departures" result from my continuing efforts to make the complexities of the thinking process easier for people to understand and quicker to learn. To paraphrase something Bob Stein has said, for us to merely duplicate the efforts of others is to condemn ourselves to mediocrity. It is time we recognized that we can improve on the current level of understanding.[4]

Some readers may find it easier than others to understand and appreciate the logical methodology and concepts embodied in the TOC Thinking Process. As a general rule, about 70 percent of the population falls into the category of the "sensing" type personality, while only 30 percent qualify as "intuitive."[5] This means that 7 out of 10 people randomly selected are likely to appreciate the immediate step-by-step nature of the logic, but they may have more difficulty envisioning the wide range of potential applications it offers. On the other hand, the other 30 percent will likely see the ramifications of the applications but may have more difficulty with the rigor of step-by-step logical construction. So be patient. The potential rewards are tremendous if you persevere.

I am grateful to Dr. Goldratt for the opportunity to learn about his philosophy, and especially how to use the powerful logical tools that are described in detail in this book. These tools have the capability to change lives. I know this firsthand, because they have profoundly changed mine.

NOTES

1. Both books are available at local chain bookstores, or by special order at such stores.
2. Eric Noreen, Debra Smith, and James Mackey, *The Theory of Constraints and Its Implications for Management Accounting* (Great Barrington, Mass.: North River Press, 1995) Also: John A. Caspari, Ch. 8A, "Theory of Constraints," in *Management Accountant's Handbook, 4th ed., 1993 Supplement* (New York: John Wiley & Sons, 1993).
3. Michael A. Umble and M. L. Srikanth, *Synchronous Manufacturing* (Great Barrington, Mass.: North River Press, 1990).
4. Robert E. Stein, *The Next Phase of Total Quality Management: TQM II and the Focus on Profitability* (New York: Marcel Dekker, 1994).
5. Otto Kroeger and Janet M. Thuesen, *Type Talk* (New York: Dell Publishing, 1988).

ACKNOWLEDGMENTS

I'd be remiss if I failed to thank several people for their willingness to help me in writing this book. Karl Cook provided invaluable comments on the clarity and readability of the first draft. Dr. James Holt's insightful suggestions made the first revision even better. Dan Childs posed thoughtful questions about the first draft that enabled me to identify deficiencies in some original explanations and technical errors in diagrams. Phil Adelman's eagle eye caught a number of word usage problems in the text and protocol errors in some of the figures. Mel Anderson suggested editorial changes that improved the flow. My project editor at ASQC Quality Press, Jeanne Bohn, provided expert advice on the publication process, and Annette Wall, the production editor from Editorial Production Specialists, turned the lead I gave her into the gold you hold in your hands. I thank all of you for your conscientious effort and willingness to help me.

I would be remiss, too, if I failed to acknowledge the significant contributions made to my knowledge of the Theory of Constraints and, especially, the Thinking Process by Christie Latona, Alex Klarman, Oded Cohen, Dick Moore, and Dee Keenan. I owe a debt of gratitude that will be difficult to repay to Craig Morgan, who encouraged me to write this book, provided guidance on publishing it, and conceived of the term *Conflict Resolution Diagram* to better characterize the function of the most powerful of the Thinking Process tools. But the most profound contribution of all was that of Dr. Eli Goldratt, the originator of the Thinking Process. I'm indebted to all of these consummate professionals.

H. William Dettmer
gsi@empirenet.com
http://www.empirenet.com/~gsi

Goldratt's Theory of Constraints

Chapter 1
INTRODUCTION TO THE THEORY OF CONSTRAINTS

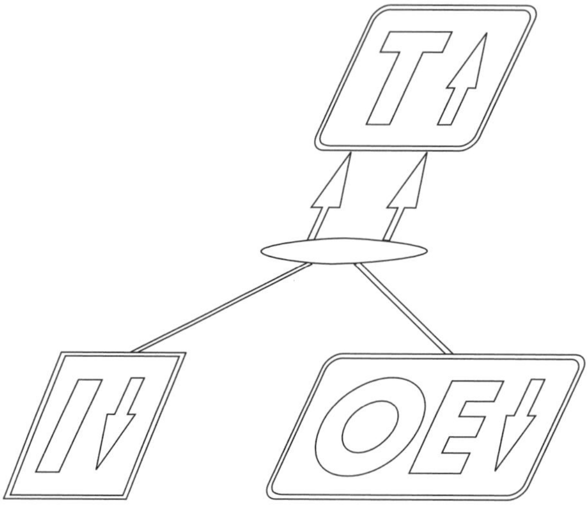

Chapter Outline

Profound knowledge must come from outside the system, and by invitation.

—W. Edwards Deming

SYSTEMS AND "PROFOUND KNOWLEDGE"

W. Edwards Deming maintained that real quality improvement isn't possible without *profound knowledge*.[1] According to Deming, profound knowledge comes from

- An understanding of the theory of knowledge
- Knowledge of variation
- An understanding of psychology
- Appreciation for systems

"Appreciation for systems"—what does that mean? A system might be generally defined as a collection of interrelated, interdependent components or

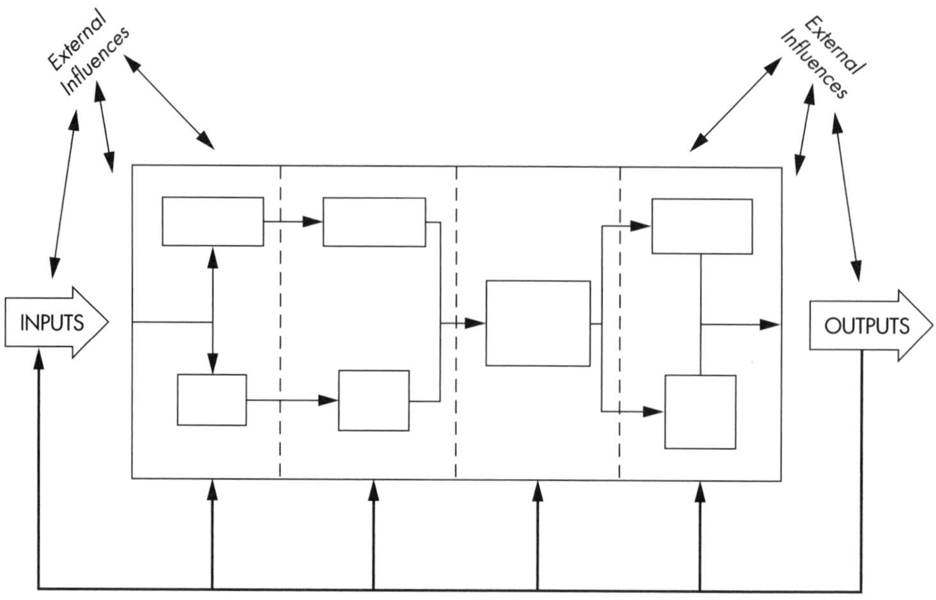

FIGURE 1.1. A Basic System Environment.

processes that act in concert to turn inputs into some kind of outputs in pursuit of some goal (see Figure 1.1). Systems influence, and are influenced by, their external environment. Obviously, quality (or lack of it) doesn't exist in a vacuum. It can only be considered in the context of the system in which it resides. So, to follow Deming's line of reasoning, it's not possible to improve quality without a thorough understanding of how that system works. Moreover, the thinking process that is the subject of this book provides a solid foundation of understanding of the theory of knowledge: *how* we know *what* we know.

THE SYSTEM'S GOAL

Let's look at systems from a broader perspective. Why do we, as human beings, create systems? In the most basic sense, the answer is "To achieve a goal." Okay, if a system's purpose is to achieve some goal, *who gets to decide what that goal should be*? Obviously, the goal-setter ought to be the system's owner—or owners. Let's face it, if you or I paid for the system, we'd expect to be the ones to decide what that system's goal should be. Privately held companies respond to the directions of their owners. Publicly held corporations work toward the goals of their stockholders—or at least they're supposed to. Government agencies are essentially "owned" by the taxpayers and should be doing what the taxpayers expect them to do.

> ***The essence of management is recognizing the need for change, then initiating, controlling, and directing it, and solving the problems along the way. If it were not so, managers wouldn't be needed—only babysitters.***

THE MANAGER'S ROLE

In most complex systems, the responsibility for satisfying the owners' goals rests with the managers of the system—from the chief executive officer down to the frontline supervisor. In a general sense, the Theory of Constraints (TOC) is about management.

> ***1. Anyone can make a decision, given enough facts.***
> ***2. A good manager can make a decision without enough facts.***
> ***3. A perfect manager can operate in perfect ignorance.***
>
> ***—Spencer's Laws of Data***

Who Is a Manager?

Inevitably, some readers will respond, "But I'm not a manager. Why would the Theory of Constraints be important to me?" The truth is, *we're all managers.* Everyone is a manager of something—in different arenas, perhaps, but a manager nonetheless. Whether you're in charge of a large corporation, a department, or a small team, you're a manager. Even if you're "none of the above," you're still a manager. Under ideal circumstances, all individuals manage their lives and careers, though frequently they don't do a very effective job of it.

Some of us have more than one management role. Basically, we differ only in our span of control and the size of our sphere of influence. At the very least you manage (or possibly fail to manage) your personal activities, time, and perhaps your finances. For example, a homemaker manages a household; a lawyer manages legal case preparation and litigation; a student manages time and effort.

One of the hallmarks of effective managers is that they deal less with the present and more with the future. In other words, they concentrate on "fire prevention" rather than "fire fighting." If you're more focused on the present than the future, you'll always be in a time lag following changes in your environment—a *reactive* rather than a *proactive* mode.

> ***It is more important to know where you are going than to get there quickly. Do not mistake activity for achievement.***
>
> ***—Mabel Newcomber***

What Is the Goal?

The Theory of Constraints rests on the admittedly somewhat rash assumption that managers and/or organizations know what their real purpose is, what goal they're trying to achieve. Unfortunately, this isn't always the case. No manager can hope to succeed, however, without knowing three things:

- What the ultimate goal is
- Where he or she currently stands in relation to that goal
- The magnitude and direction of the change needed to move from the status quo to where he or she wants to be (the goal)

This might be considered "management by vector analysis." But in fact that's really what managers do: They determine the difference between what *is* and what *should be,* and they change things to eliminate that deviation.

Average managers are concerned with methods, opinions, and precedents. Good managers are concerned with solving problems.
—Unknown

Goal or Necessary Condition?

If you're a manager, how do you *know* what the system's goal is? Frequently a system's managers—and perhaps even the owners—have different ideas about the system's goal. In a commercial enterprise, the stockholders (owners) usually consider that the system's goal is "to make more money." The underlying assumption here is that a system making money pays dividends to the stockholder who, in turn, makes more money.

The managers in a system might see the goal a little differently. While they acknowledge the need to make money for the stockholders, they also realize that other things are important, too—things like competitive advantage; market share; customer satisfaction; a satisfied, secure workforce; or first-time quality of product or service. Factors like these often show up as goals in strategic or operating plans. But are they goals or necessary conditions?

A goal can be defined as *the result or achievement toward which effort is directed.*[2] A necessary condition is *a circumstance indispensable to some result,* or *that upon which everything else is contingent.*[3] There is a dependent relationship inherent in these definitions. It sounds as if you have to satisfy the necessary conditions in order to attain the goal.

Eliyahu M. Goldratt suggests that the relationship is actually *interdependent.* If this is so, does it matter what you call a goal and what you decide is a necessary condition? Goldratt doesn't think so. He contends that because of this interdependency, no matter what factor you designate to be the goal, all other related factors become conditions necessary to achieving that goal.

For example, your stockholders (represented by the board of directors) might decide that "increased profitability" is the company's goal (see Figure 1.2). In this case, "customer satisfaction," "technology leadership," "competitive advantage," and "improved market share" might all be necessary conditions that you can't ignore without the risk of not attaining the profitability goal. But you might just as easily consider the goal to be "customer satisfaction," as many quality-oriented companies do these days. In this instance, "profitability" becomes a necessary condition without which you can't satisfy customers. Why? Because unprofitable companies don't stay in business very long, and if they're not in business, they can't very well satisfy customers.

The major difference between rats and people is that rats learn from experience.
—B. F. Skinner

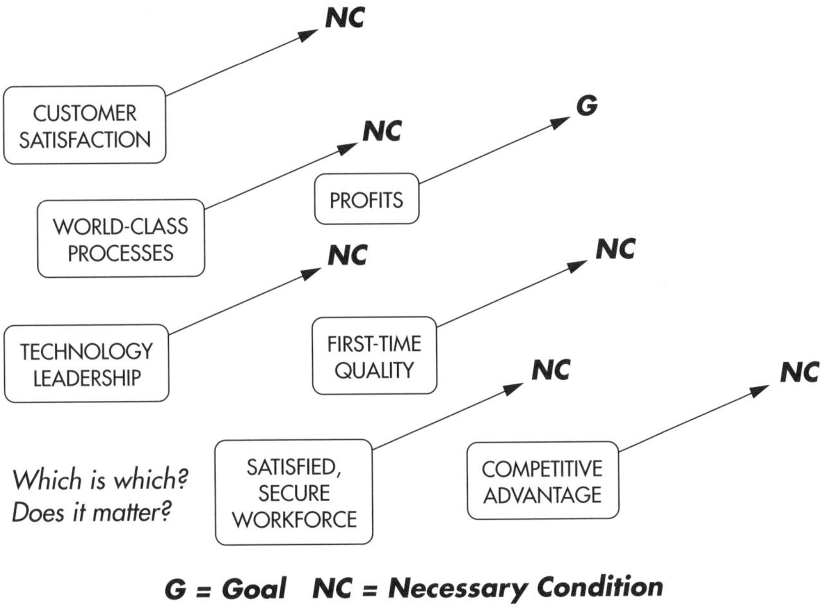

FIGURE 1.2. Goal or Necessary Condition?

THE CONCEPT OF SYSTEM CONSTRAINTS

Let's assume for the moment that you, the manager, have decided what your system's goal is and what the necessary conditions are for attaining it. Are you attaining that goal *right now*? If not, could you be doing better? Most people would agree that they *could* be doing a better job of progressing toward their goal. Okay, what keeps your system from doing better? Would it be fair to say that something is *constraining* your system—keeping it from realizing its maximum potential? If so, what do you think that constraining factor might be? The chances are that everybody in your organization has an opinion about it. But who's right? And how would you *know* if they're right? If you can successfully answer that question, you probably have a bright future ahead of you. Let's see if we can help you with that answer. To do this, let's go back to the concept of a system.

Systems as Chains

Goldratt likens systems to chains, or networks of chains. Let's consider the chain in Figure 1.3 a simple system. Its goal is to transmit force from one end to the other. If you accept the idea that all systems are constrained in some way, how many constraints does this chain have?

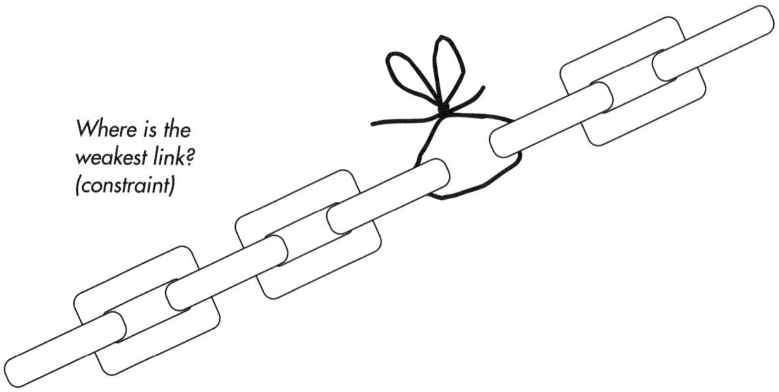
Where is the
weakest link?
(constraint)

FIGURE 1.3. A System: The "Chain" Concept.

The "Weakest Link"

Let's say you keep increasing the force you apply to this chain. Can you do this indefinitely? Of course not. If you do, eventually the chain will break. But where? At what point? The chain will fail at its weakest link (see Figure 1.3). How many "weakest links" does a chain like this have? One—only one. It will fail first at only one point, and that weakest link is the constraint that prevents the chain (system) from doing any better at achieving its goal (transmission of force).

Constraints and Nonconstraints

So we can conclude that our chain has only one link constraining its current performance. How many nonconstraints does it have? An indeterminate number, but equal to the number of remaining links in the chain. Goldratt contends that there is only one constraint in a system at any given time. Like the narrow neck of an hourglass, that one constraint limits the output of the entire system. Everything else in the system, at that exact time, is a nonconstraint.

Let's say we want to strengthen this chain (improve the system). Where would the most logical place be to focus our efforts? Right! The weakest link! Would it do us any good to strengthen anything *except* the weakest link (that is, a nonconstraint)? Of course not. The chain would still break at the weakest link, no matter how strong we made the others. In other words, no efforts on nonconstraints will produce immediate, measurable improvement in system capability.

Now let's assume we're smart enough to figure out which link is the weakest, and let's say we double its strength. It's not the weakest link anymore. What has happened to the chain? It has become stronger, but is it infinitely stronger? No. Some other link is now the weakest one, and the chain's capability is now limited by the strength of that link. It's stronger than it was, but still not as strong as it could be. The system is still constrained, but the constraint has migrated to a different component.

A Production Example

Here's a different look at the chain concept (see Figure 1.4). This is a simple production system that takes raw materials, runs them through five component processes, and turns them into finished products. Each process constitutes a link in the production chain. The system's goal is to make as much money as possible from the sales of its products. Each of the component processes has a daily capacity as indicated. The market demand is 15 units per day.

Where is the constraint in this chain, and why? The answer is Step C, because it can never produce more than six units per day, no matter how many the rest of the components produce. Where are the nonconstraints? Everywhere else.

What happens if we improve the C process so that its daily capacity is now tripled, to 18 units per day? What constrains the system now, and why? The answer is Step D, because it can produce only eight units per day. Where are the nonconstraints? Everywhere else.

Let's continue this improvement process, until Steps D, E, and A are all much better than before. Look at this new version of the production diagram (see Figure 1.5). Where's the system's constraint now? It's in the marketplace, which

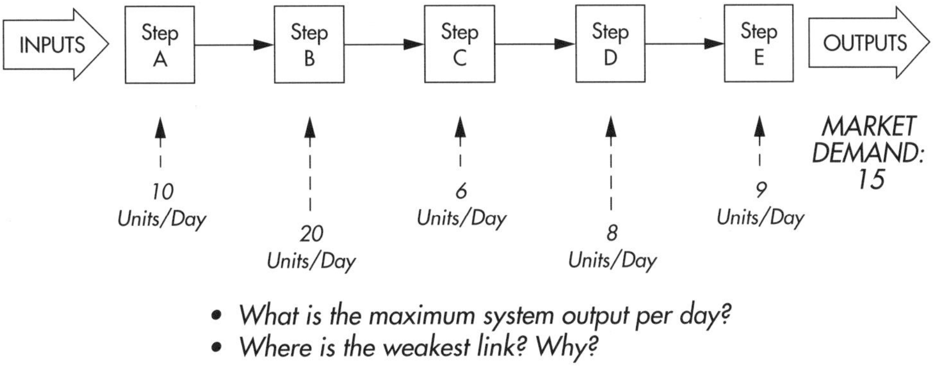

FIGURE 1.4. A Production Example.

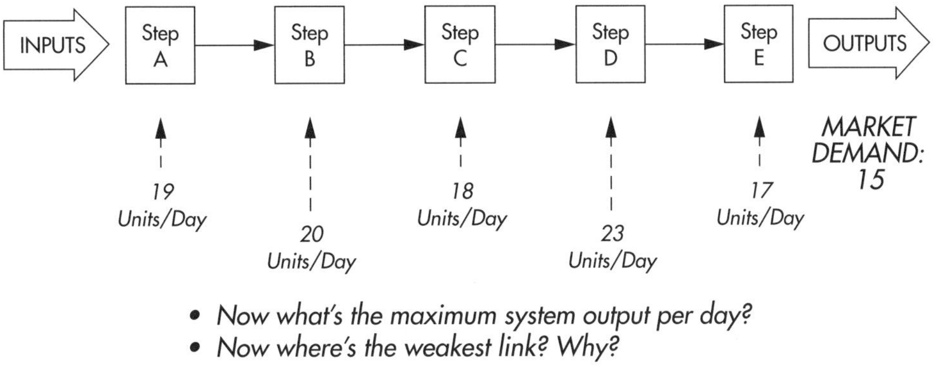

FIGURE 1.5. Another Version of the Production Example.

can accept only 15 units per day. We've finally removed the constraint, haven't we? Well, not really. All we've done is eliminate *internal* constraints. That which keeps our system from doing better in relation to its goal is now outside the system, but it's a constraint nonetheless. If we're going to attack this constraint, however, we'll need a different set of task skills and knowledge. Or will we?

RELATION OF CONSTRAINTS TO QUALITY IMPROVEMENT

Deming developed 14 points that he offered as a kind of "road map to quality."[4] Most other approaches to continuous improvement have comparable prescriptions for success. Deming's 14th point is "Take action to accomplish the transformation." He amplifies this by urging organizations to get everyone involved, train everybody in the new philosophy, convert a "critical mass" of people, and form process improvement teams.[5]

Management in most organizations interprets this point quite literally: Get everyone involved. Employee involvement *is* a very important element of Deming's theory, and of most other total quality philosophies, and for good reason: Success is inherently a cooperative effort. Most organizations having formal improvement efforts include employees, usually in teams, in the process.

Let's assume that these improvement teams are working on things that "everybody knows" need improving. If we accept Goldratt's contentions about constraints and nonconstraints, how many of these team efforts are likely to be working on nonconstraints? Answer: probably all but one (see Figure 1.6). How many of us know *for sure* exactly where in our organizations the constraint lies? If our management isn't even thinking in terms of system constraints, yet they're putting everybody to work on the transformation, how much effort do you think might actually turn out to be unproductive?

"Wait a minute," you're probably thinking, "TQM is a long-term process; it can take years to produce results. We have to be patient and persevere. We'll need all of these improvements someday."

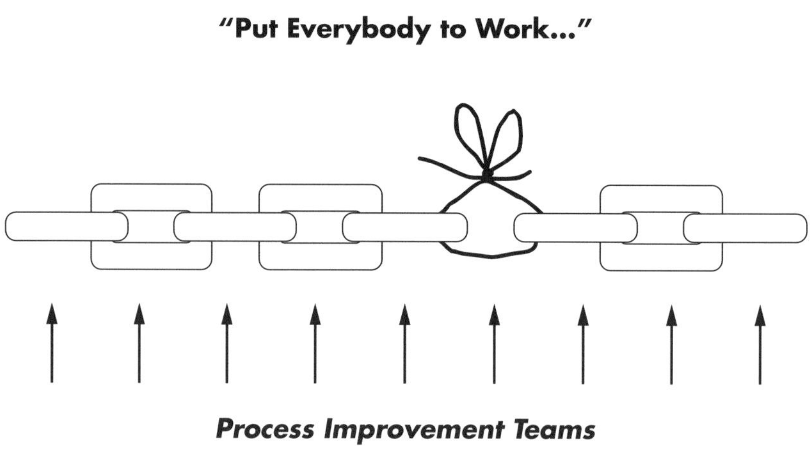

FIGURE 1.6. If All the Teams Are Working on Things, How Many Are Working on Nonconstraints?

That's true. The way most organizations approach it, TQM is a long-term process that may take years to show results. Limited time, energy, and resources are spread across the entire system, instead of being focused on the one part of it that has the potential to produce immediate system improvement: the constraint. Impatience, lack of perseverance, and failure to see progress quickly enough are all reasons why many organizations give up on TQM. People soon get discouraged when they see no tangible system results from the dedicated efforts they've put into process improvement. So interest, motivation, and eventually commitment to TQM die from a lack of *intrinsic reinforcement*. Everybody might be working diligently, but only a few have the potential to really make a difference quickly. For most organizations, the real question is: Will our business environment allow us the luxury of time? Can we wait for the long term to see results?

Does it have to be this way? No! Goldratt has developed the approach to continuous improvement called the Theory of Constraints. He even wrote a book describing this theory, called *The Goal,*[6] and another, entitled *It's Not Luck,*[7] demonstrating how the logical tools of the theory are applied. The Theory of Constraints (TOC) is a prescriptive theory, which means it can tell you not only what's holding your system back, but also what to do about it and how to do it. A lot of theories answer the first question—what's wrong. Some even tell you what to do about it, but those that do usually focus on processes rather than the system as a whole. And they're completely oblivious to the concept of system constraints.

There is no such thing as staying the same. You are either striving to make yourself better or allowing yourself to get worse.
—Unknown

CHANGE AND THE THEORY OF CONSTRAINTS

Deming talks about "transformation,"[8] which is another way of saying "change." Goldratt's Theory of Constraints is essentially about change. Applying its principles and tools answers the three basic questions about change that every manager needs to know:

- *What* to change? (Where is the constraint?)
- What to change to? (What should we *do* with the constraint?)
- *How* to cause the change? (How do we implement the change?)

Remember that these are system-level, not process-level questions. The answers to these questions undoubtedly have an impact on individual processes, but they're designed to focus efforts in system improvement. Processes *are* important, but our organizations ultimately succeed or fail as systems. What a shame it would be to win the battle on the process level, only to lose the war at the system level!

Remember, too, that TOC and TQM are not mutually exclusive. Rather, TOC fills a void that TQM never adequately addresses: how best to channel improvement efforts for maximum immediate effect. In other words, by using TOC in addition to TQM, the problem of taking a long time to show results goes away. Effectively applying TOC in concert with TQM, you're likely to find that TQM and significant short-term results need not be mutually exclusive. So don't think about throwing away your TQM toolbox. If anything, the traditional TQM tools can become more useful than ever, because TOC can suggest when and how to employ each one to best effect.

> ***It is not necessary to change; survival is not mandatory.***
> ***—W. Edwards Deming***

TOC PRINCIPLES

Theories are usually classified as either *descriptive* or *prescriptive*. Descriptive theories, such as the law of gravity, tell us why things happen, but they don't help us to do anything about them. Prescriptive theories both explain why and offer guidance on what to do. TOC is a prescriptive theory, but we'll look at the descriptive part first.

Goldratt submits that several principles converge to make the environment particularly fertile ground for the prescriptive part of his theory. The accompanying chart (see Figure 1.7) lists most of these principles, but a few of them are worth emphasizing because of their striking impact on reality.

- Systems thinking is preferable to analytical thinking in managing change and solving problems.
- An optimal system solution deteriorates over time as the system's environment changes. A process of ongoing improvement is required to update and maintain the effectiveness of a solution.
- If a system is performing as well as it can, not more than one of its component parts will be. If all parts are performing as well as they can, the system as a whole will not be. THE SYSTEM OPTIMUM IS NOT THE SUM OF THE LOCAL OPTIMA.
- Systems are analogous to chains. Each system has a "weakest link" (constraint) that ultimately limits the success of the entire system.
- Strengthening any link in a chain other than the weakest one does NOTHING to improve the strength of the whole chain.
- Knowing what to change requires a thorough understanding of the system's current reality, its goal, and the magnitude and direction of the difference between the two.
- Most of the undesirable effects within a system are caused by a few core problems.
- Core problems are almost never superficially apparent. They manifest themselves through a number of undesirable effects (UDEs) linked by a network of cause and effect.
- Elimination of individual UDEs gives a false sense of security while ignoring the underlying core problem. Solutions that do this are likely to be short-lived. Solution of a core problem simultaneously eliminates all resulting UDEs.
- Core problems are usually perpetuated by a hidden or underlying conflict. Solution of core problems requires challenging the assumptions underlying the conflict and invalidating at least one.
- System constraints can be either physical or policy. Physical constraints are relatively easy to identify and simple to eliminate. Policy constraints are usually more difficult to identify and eliminate, but removing them normally results in a larger degree of system improvement than the elimination of a physical constraint.
- Inertia is the worst enemy of a process of ongoing improvement. Solutions tend to assume a mass of their own that resists further change.
- Ideas are NOT solutions.

FIGURE 1.7. Partial List of TOC Principles.

Systems as "Chains"

This is crucial to TOC. If systems function like chains, weakest links can be found and strengthened.

Local vs. System Optima

Because of interdependence and variation, the optimum performance of a system as a whole is not the same as the sum of all the local optima. We saw this in the production example earlier. If all the components of a system are performing at their maximum level, the system as whole will not be performing at its best.

Cause and Effect

All systems operate in an environment of cause and effect. Something causes something else to happen. This cause-and-effect phenomenon can be very complex, especially in complex systems.

Undesirable Effects and Core Problems

Nearly all of what we see in a system that we don't like is not *problems,* but *indicators*. They are the resultant effects of underlying causes. Treating an undesirable effect is like putting a bandage on an infected wound: It does nothing about the underlying infection. So its remedial benefit is only temporary. Eventually the indication resurfaces, because the underlying problem causing the indication never really goes away. Eliminating undesirable effects gives a false sense of security. Identifying and eliminating the core problem not only eliminates all the undesirable effects that issue from it, but it prevents them from returning.

Solution Deterioration

An optimal solution deteriorates over time, as the system's environment changes. As Goldratt says, "Yesterday's solution becomes today's historical curiosity." ("Isn't that curious?! Why do you suppose they ever did *that*?") A process of ongoing improvement is necessary to update and maintain the efficiency (and effectiveness) of a solution. Inertia is the worst enemy of a process of ongoing improvement. The attitude that "We've solved *that* problem—no need to revisit it" hurts continuous improvement efforts.

Physical vs. Policy Constraints

Most of the constraints we face in our systems originate from policies, not physical things. Physical constraints are relatively easy to identify and break. Policy constraints are much more difficult, but they normally result in a much larger degree of system improvement than elimination of a physical constraint.

> ***An organization must have some means of combating the process by which people become prisoners of their procedures. The rule book becomes fatter as the ideas become fewer. Almost every well-established organization is a coral reef of procedures that were laid down to achieve some long-forgotten objective.***
>
> ***—John W. Gardner***

Ideas Are NOT Solutions

The best ideas in the world never realize their potential unless they are implemented. And most great ideas fail in the implementation stage.

THE FIVE FOCUSING STEPS OF TOC

This is the beginning of the prescriptive part of the Theory of Constraints. Goldratt has developed five sequential steps to concentrate improvement efforts on the component that is capable of producing the most positive impact on the system.[9]

1. Identify the System Constraint

What part of the system constitutes the weakest link? Is it physical or is it a policy?

2. Decide How to Exploit the Constraint

By "exploit," Goldratt means we should wring every bit of capability out of the constraining component as it currently exists. In other words, "What can we do to get the most out of this constraint without committing to potentially expensive changes or upgrades?"

3. Subordinate Everything Else

Once the constraint is identified (Step 1) and we've decided what to do about it (Step 2), we adjust the rest of the system to a "setting" that will enable the constraint to operate at maximum effectiveness. We may have to "de-tune" some parts of the system, while "revving up" others. Once we've done this, we must evaluate the results of our actions: Is the constraint still constraining the system's performance? If not, we've eliminated the constraint, and we skip ahead to Step 5. If it is, we still have a constraint—and we continue with Step 4.

4. Elevate the Constraint

If we're doing this, it means that Steps 2 and 3 weren't sufficient to eliminate the constraint and we have to do something more. It's not until this step that we entertain the idea of major changes to the existing system—reorganization, divestiture, capital improvements, or other substantial system modifications. This step can involve considerable investment in time, energy, money, or other resources, so we must be sure we aren't able to break the constraint in the first three steps. "Elevating" the constraint means that we take whatever action is required to eliminate the constraint. When this step is completed the constraint *is* broken.

5. Go Back to Step 1, But Beware of "Inertia"

If, at Steps 3 or 4, a constraint is broken, we must go back to Step 1 and begin the cycle again, looking for the next thing constraining our performance. If you'll recall the production example (p. 9), this is exactly what we did. After we broke the constraint at process Step C, we went back and found D, then E, then A, and, finally, the marketplace. The caution about inertia reminds us that we must not become complacent; the cycle never ends. We keep on looking for constraints, and we keep breaking them. And we never forget that because of interdependency and variation, each subsequent change we make to our system will have new effects on those constraints we've already broken. We may have to revisit and update them, too.

The Five Focusing Steps have a direct relationship with the three management questions pertaining to change: what to change, what to change to, and how to cause change. They tell us how to answer those questions.

To determine what to change, we look for the constraint. To determine what to change to, we decide how to exploit the constraint and subordinate the rest of the system to that decision. If that doesn't do the complete job, we elevate the constraint. The subordinate and elevate steps also answer the question "how to cause the change."

"This is all well and good," you're probably saying, "but how do we convert these abstract steps into concrete actions we can take? And how do we know when we've had a positive impact on the system?" These are two key questions. Let's look at the second one first.

THROUGHPUT, INVENTORY, AND OPERATING EXPENSE

A burning question we have to address is, "How do we know whether our constraint-breaking has had a positive effect on our overall system?" Another way of asking this same question is, "How do we measure the effects of local decisions on the global system?" Organizations have struggled with this question for years. The Theory of Constraints is particularly useful in this arena.

Part of the answer to the question lies in the TOC emphasis on fixing the weakest link (constraint) and ignoring, at least temporarily, the nonconstraints. Most effective laboratory research involves quantifying the effect of a change in one variable by holding all the others constant—or as nearly so as possible. This is "sensitivity analysis," and it's particularly useful in determining how much of an outcome is attributable to a particular cause.

By doing essentially the same thing in our organizations (that is, working only on the constraint), we achieve two benefits: (1) we realize the maximum system improvement from the least investment in resources, and (2) we learn exactly how much effect improving a specific system component has on overall system performance. I suspect Deming would consider this "appreciation for a system"[10] of the highest order.

- THROUGHPUT: The rate at which the entire system generates money through sales (product or service).
- INVENTORY: All the money the system invests in things it intends to sell.
- OPERATING EXPENSE: All the money the system spends turning Inventory into Throughput.

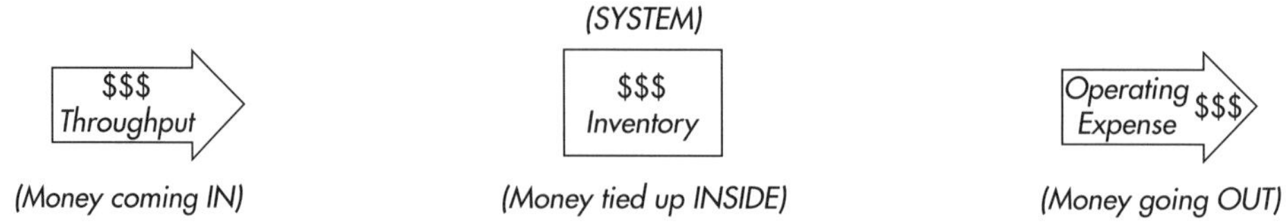

FIGURE 1.8. Definitions of Throughput, Inventory, and Operating Expense.

Goldratt has created a very simple relationship for determining the effect that any local action has on progress toward the system's goal. Every action is assessed by its effect on three system-level dimensions: Throughput, Inventory, and Operating Expense.[11] Goldratt provides some very precise definitions of these terms (see Figure 1.8).

Throughput (T)

Throughput is the rate at which the entire system generates money through sales.[12] Another way of looking at Throughput is "all the money coming into the system." In a nonprofit organization or a government agency, the concept of "sales" may not apply. In cases where an organization's Throughput may not be easily expressed in dollars, it might be defined in terms of the delivery of a product or service to a customer. Another way of thinking about Throughput is

> ***The world is not interested in the storms you encountered, but did you bring in the ship?***
>
> ***—William McFee***

Inventory (I)

Inventory is all the money the system invests in things it intends to sell, or all the money tied up within the system.[13] Obviously, raw materials, unfinished goods, purchased parts, and other "hard" items intended for sale to a customer spring to mind. But Inventory also includes the investment the organization makes in equipment and facilities. Eventually, obsolescent equipment and facilities are intended to be sold, too, even if only at their scrap value. As these assets depreciate, their depreciated value remains in the "I" column, but the depreciation is added to Operating Expense (see the next section).

Operating Expense (OE)

Operating Expense is all the money the system spends turning Inventory into Throughput. In other words, it's the money going out of the system.[14] Direct labor, utilities, consumable supplies, and the like are examples of Operating Expenses. Depreciation of assets is also considered an Operating Expense, because it constitutes the value of a fixed asset expended, or "used up," in turning Inventory into Throughput.

Goldratt contends that all three of these dimensions are interdependent. That is, a change in one will automatically result in a change in one or more of the other two. Let's consider that for a minute. If you increase Throughput by increasing sales, Inventory and Operating Expense will also likely increase. Why? Because you're likely to need more Inventory to support increased sales, and you're likely to spend more, in variable costs, to produce more. But you can also make more money (if that's your goal) without increasing sales. How? If you can produce the same sales revenues with less Inventory and spend less on Operating Expense doing it, you get to keep more of the money coming into the company (net profit).

So, to improve *your* system, what would you, as a manager, try to do? Obviously, increase Throughput, while decreasing Inventory and Operating Expense. And here we have the key to relating local decisions to the performance of the entire system. As you decide what action to take, ask yourself these questions:

- Will it increase Throughput? If so, how?
- Will it decrease Inventory? If so, how?
- Will it decrease Operating Expense? If so, how?

If the answer to these questions is "yes," go ahead with your decision, confident that the overall system will benefit from it. If you're not sure, perhaps you'd better reevaluate. The bottom line is that if it doesn't result in increased Throughput, you're wasting your time—and probably your money.

Which Is Most Important: T, I, or OE?

To improve your system, where should you focus your efforts? On T, I, or OE? Consider the example in Figure 1.9. The choices are to focus on decreasing OE, decreasing I, or increasing T.

As you look at the graph, note that the theoretical limit in reducing OE and I is zero. Obviously, a system can't produce many outputs with no Inventory and no Operating Expense, so the practical limits of I and OE are somewhat above zero. Theoretically, there's no upper limit to how high you can increase T, but from a practical standpoint there is a limit to the size of your market. However, it's highly probable that the potential for increasing T is always likely to be much higher than the potential for decreasing I and OE. So it would make sense to expend as much effort as possible on activities that tend to increase T primarily, and make reduction of I and OE a secondary priority (see Figure 1.10).

But what's the normal priority of most companies in a competitive environment? Cut costs (Operating Expense) first. Then, maybe, reduce Inventory (usually without a lot of consideration for how far it can be reduced without hurting Throughput). And finally, try to increase Throughput directly.

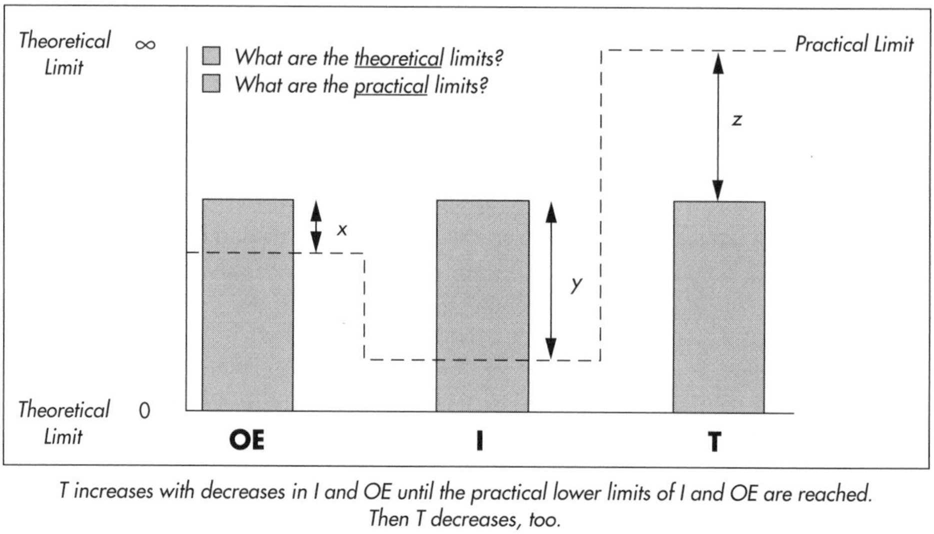

FIGURE 1.9. Limits to T, I, and OE.

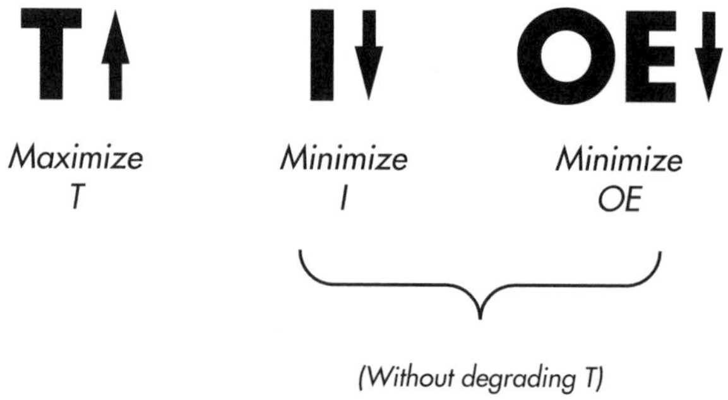

FIGURE 1.10. Management Priorities with T, I, and OE.

T, I, and OE: An Example

A classic example is the American aerospace defense industry. Traditionally these companies have depended on huge government contracts to keep them going. As the defense budget dramatically declined in the early 1990s, fewer contracts were awarded, and for much smaller production runs. In most cases, the remaining defense business of these companies was not enough to keep the organization, as originally structured, afloat. So what was the response of these companies? Most took the traditional approach to some extent: cut Operating Expense. They laid off thousands of workers. Some even reduced Inventory by selling off plants, warehouses, or other physical assets. But even that hasn't been enough for certain companies, so they've merged with others to "strengthen" their capacity to bid for whatever defense business remains. A few companies, however, have seen the handwriting on the wall. With the bottom not yet in sight, they can't continue to cut Inventory or Operating Expense, so they've opted to do what they probably should have done in the first place: look for ways to increase Throughput.

How? By finding new market segments for their core competencies, markets that don't depend on government contracts. One satellite builder found a market for its data technology in credit reporting and for its electronic technology in the automotive industry. Another defense electronics firm diversified into consumer communications: home satellite television and data communication. In both cases, the companies found new ways to increase Throughput, rather than just reducing Operating Expense and Inventory.*

T, I, and OE in Not-for-Profit Organizations

A common question often asked is, "What about organizations in which 'making more money, now and in the future' isn't the goal—as with charitable foundations, government agencies, and some hospitals? How do T, I, and OE apply to them?"

It's true that Goldratt conceived of Throughput, Inventory (or Investment), and Operating Expense as ways to measure an organization's progress toward its goal. However, when he created these measures, he was focusing exclusively on for-profit companies. In such organizations, money is an effective surrogate measure for almost all critical aspects of system-level performance, especially those pertaining to the organization's goal.

But it's clearly different in the case of a not-for-profit. Since the organization's goal is *not* to "make more money, now and in the future," the financial expression of Throughput loses significance. So how can we measure progress toward our goal if we're a not-for-profit organization?

A variety of alternatives has been suggested to modify expressions of T, and the variable elements of I, so that they accurately reflect progress toward a nonmonetary goal. The problem with almost all of these alternatives is that they're contrived—an attempt to fit not-for-profits into a "metrics box" they were never intended to occupy.

Goldratt himself has offered what may be the best solution to the problem of assessing the progress of not-for-profits toward their goals. In July 1995, he made the following observations.[15] Figure 1.11 illustrates his concept.

Universal Measures of Value

In recorded history, money has been the closest thing to a universal measure of value that humankind has ever created. Where it applies completely, it's very effective. But because it's not always a valid measure of value, and since no other universal nonmonetary measure of value has ever been invented, a different scheme for not-for-profits should be employed.

Goldratt suggests a dual approach. Operating expense is still measurable in monetary terms; Inventory, only partially so; and Throughput, not at all. Inventory, he proposes, should be differentiated as either "passive" or "active."

---

*A more detailed treatment of T, I, and OE can be found in three other sources: *The Race* and *The Haystack Syndrome* by Goldratt, and *The Theory of Constraints and Its Implications for Management Accounting* by Eric Noreen, Debra Smith, and James T. Mackey, from North River Press, 1987, 1990, and 1995, respectively.

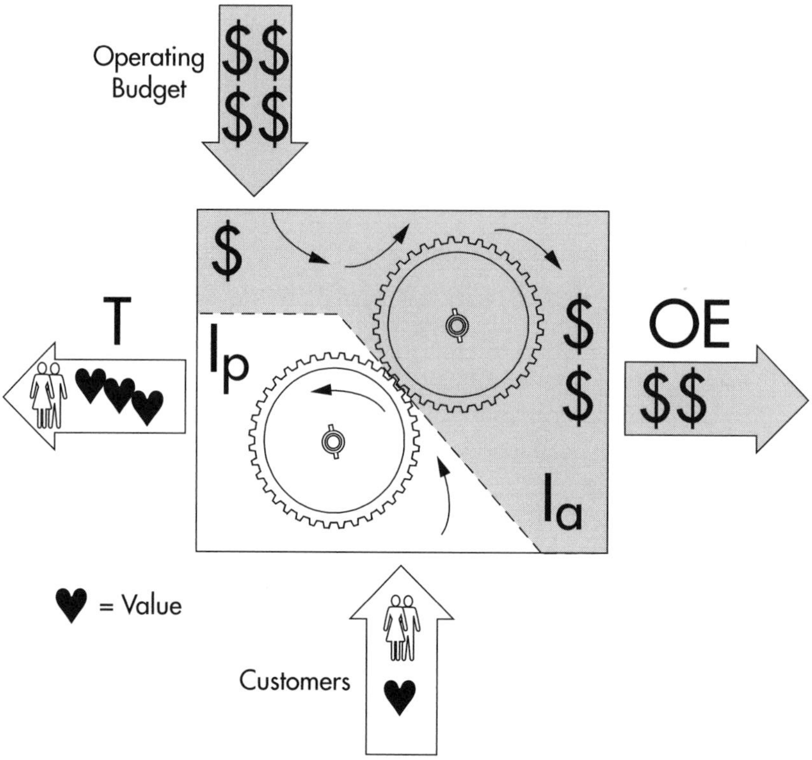

FIGURE 1.11. T, I, and OE in a Not-for-Profit Organization.

Passive Inventory

Passive inventory, as the name implies, is *acted upon*. In the manufacturing model, passive inventory would be the raw materials that are converted into Throughput. But in a not-for-profit (a hospital, for example), passive Inventory isn't measurable in monetary terms, because the "raw materials" are often people. Figure 1.11 shows customers going through the nonmonetary side of the system and becoming "Throughput": well people.

Active Inventory

Active inventory, on the other hand, *is* measurable in monetary terms, because it constitutes the facilities, equipment, and tangible assets that *act upon* the passive inventory. This part of the inventory is shown in the upper right portion of the system in Figure 1.11.

So how should managers of not-for-profits adjust their focus? In principle, the emphasis remains the same: increase Throughput, decrease Inventory, and decrease Operating Expense—in that order. In practice, active Inventory and Operating Expense—both expressed in monetary terms—are managed the same way they are in for-profit companies. The difference arises in how we should manage Throughput and passive Inventory.

Managing T Through Undesirable Effects

Without a universal nonmonetary measure of value, Goldratt suggests, measuring T and passive I in not-for-profits isn't ever likely to be practical. So, he says, don't bother trying to do it. Instead, work on eliminating the undesirable effects (UDE) associated with Throughput. (Refer to chapter 3, "Current Reality Trees," for a thorough discussion of undesirable effects and their relationship to root causes.) Use UDEs as your indicators of progress. As you eliminate them, progress toward the organization's goal can be assumed.

In summary, a not-for-profit should search out and correct the causes of UDEs affecting Throughput, while keeping the costs of active Inventory and Operating Expense down (refer to Figure 1.11). But the primary emphasis should always be on the former, not the latter.

Note: Many people will inevitably ask, "What about the operating budget of a not-for-profit? Where does *that* fit into the T, I, and OE formulation?" It isn't in Throughput, because production efforts aren't aimed at increasing it. And it isn't really an Operating Expense alone, because some part of it is spent on capital improvements, which are really Inventory (investment). The answer, according to Goldratt, is that the annual operating budget should be considered a *necessary condition.* Efforts to reduce active Inventory and Operating Expense will naturally have a beneficial effect on the annual budget. But the budget is the means to an end—a necessary condition—not the goal.

THE TOC PARADIGM

The Theory of Constraints is considerably more than just a theory. In effect, it's a paradigm, a pattern or model that includes not only its concepts, guiding principles, and prescriptions, but its tools and applications as well.

We've seen its concepts (systems as chains; T, I, and OE) and its principles (cause and effect, local vs. system optima, and so on). We've examined its prescriptions (the Five Focusing Steps; what to change, what to change to, how to change). To complete the picture, we need to consider its applications and tools.

Applications

Each application of TOC starts out being unique. As the theory is applied in a new situation, it creates a distinctive solution. Often, however, such solutions are easily transferrable to other circumstances.

For example, in *The Goal,* Goldratt describes a TOC solution to a production control problem in a specific plant of a fictitious company. But this solution became the basis for a generic solution applicable to similar production situations in other industries. Goldratt called this production control solution "Drum-Buffer-Rope."[16] Many companies have applied this solution, originally developed to solve one company's problem, with great success. Consequently, Drum-Buffer-Rope has become an application added to the TOC paradigm.

Another application is called "Throughput Accounting." This is a direct outcome of the use of Throughput, Inventory, and Operating Expense as management decision tools, as opposed to traditional management cost accounting.[17] Throughput Accounting basically refutes the commonly used concept of allocating fixed costs to units of a product or service. While the summary financial figures remain essentially the same, the absence of allocated fixed costs promotes very different management decisions concerning pricing and marketing for competitive advantage. In other words, Throughput Accounting is a much more effective philosophy for supporting good operational decisions than standard cost accounting. As with Drum-Buffer-Rope production control, Throughput Accounting began as a specific solution to one company's competitive pricing problem and ended up applicable to any company's pricing problems.

Tools

The tools Goldratt has developed to apply TOC are logical by nature. They are comprised of five distinct logic trees and the "rules of logic" that govern their construction. The trees include the Current Reality Tree, the "Evaporating Cloud," the Future Reality Tree, the Prerequisite Tree, and the Transition Tree.[18] The rules are called the Categories of Legitimate Reservation. These trees, the Categories of Legitimate Reservation, and how to use them are the subject of this book.

THE CURRENT REALITY TREE

The Current Reality Tree (CRT) is a problem-analysis tool (see Figure 1.12). It helps us examine the cause-and-effect logic behind our current situation. The

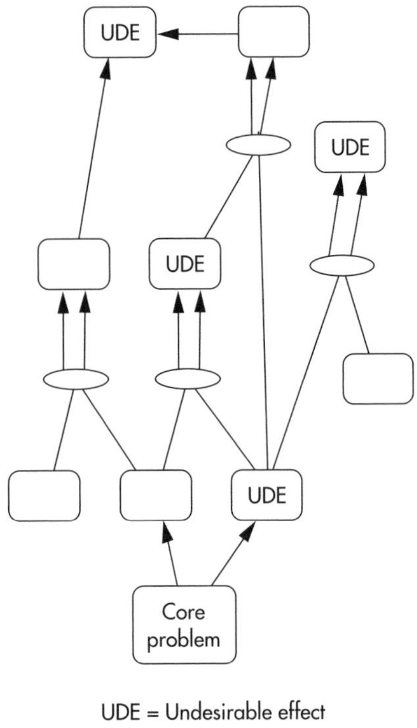
UDE
UDE
UDE
UDE
Core problem
UDE = Undesirable effect

FIGURE 1.12. The Current Reality Tree.

CRT begins with the undesirable effects we see around us and helps us work back to identify a few root causes, or a single core problem, that originate all the undesirable effects we're experiencing. The core problem is usually the constraint we're trying to identify in the Five Focusing Steps. The CRT tells us *what to change*—the one simplest change to make that will have the greatest positive effect on our system. Chapter 3 describes the Current Reality Tree in detail and provides comprehensive instructions and examples on how to construct one.

THE CONFLICT RESOLUTION DIAGRAM: THE "EVAPORATING CLOUD"

Goldratt designed the Conflict Resolution Diagram (CRD) (which he referred to as an "evaporating cloud") to resolve hidden conflicts that usually perpetuate chronic problems (see Figure 1.13). The CRD is predicated on the idea that most core problems exist because some underlying tug-of-war, or conflict, prevents straightforward solution of the problem; otherwise, the problem would have been solved long ago. The CRD can also be a "creative engine," an idea generator that allows us to invent new, "breakthrough" solutions to such nagging problems. Consequently, the CRD answers the first part of the question, *what to change to*. Chapter 4 describes the Conflict Resolution Diagram in detail and provides several approaches for building one.

THE FUTURE REALITY TREE

The Future Reality Tree (FRT) serves two purposes (see Figure 1.14). First, it allows us to verify that an action we'd like to take will, in fact, produce the ultimate results we desire. Second, it enables us to identify any unfavorable new consequences our contemplated action might have, and to nip them in the bud. These functions provide two important benefits. We can logically "test" the effectiveness of our proposed course of action before investing much time, energy, or resources in it, and we can avoid making the situation worse than when we started. This tool answers the second part of the question *what to change to* by validating our new system configuration. The FRT can also be an invaluable

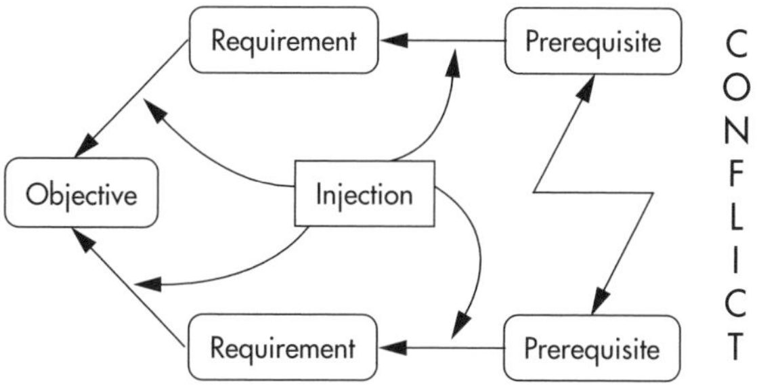

FIGURE 1.13. The Conflict Resolution Diagram: The "Evaporating Cloud."

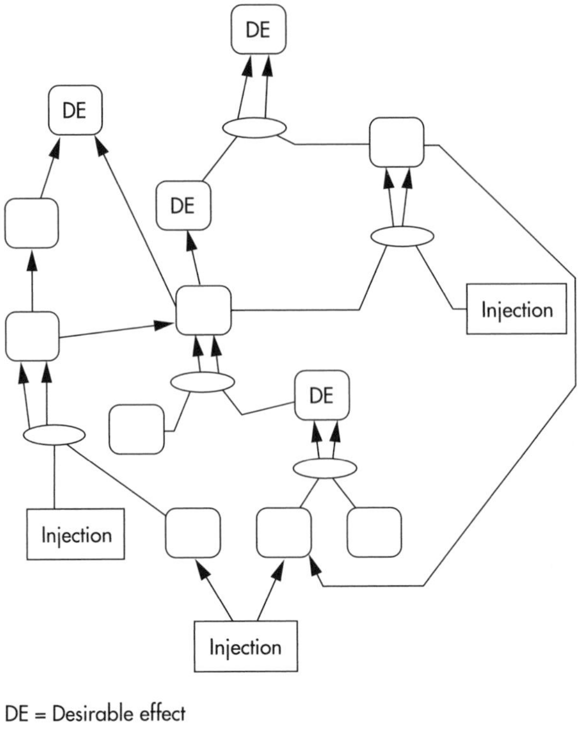

FIGURE 1.14. The Future Reality Tree.

strategic planning tool. Chapter 5 describes the Future Reality Tree in detail, providing examples and comprehensive instructions on how to create one.

THE PREREQUISITE TREE

Once we've decided on a course of action, the Prerequisite Tree (PRT) helps us implement that decision (see Figure 1.15). It identifies obstacles to what we want to do and the best ways to overcome those obstacles. It also tells us in what sequence we need to complete the major milestones in implementing our decision. The PRT provides the first half of the answer to the last question, *how to change*. Chapter 6 describes the Prerequisite Tree in detail and provides both examples and comprehensive procedures for constructing one.

THE TRANSITION TREE

The last of the five logical tools is the Transition Tree (TT) (see Figure 1.16). The TT can give us the detailed step-by-step instructions for implementing a course of action. It provides both the steps to take (in sequence) and the rationale for each step. The TT is essentially the detailed road map to our objective, and it answers the second half of the question, *how to change*. Chapter 7 describes the Transition Tree, gives examples, and provides detailed instructions on how to build one.

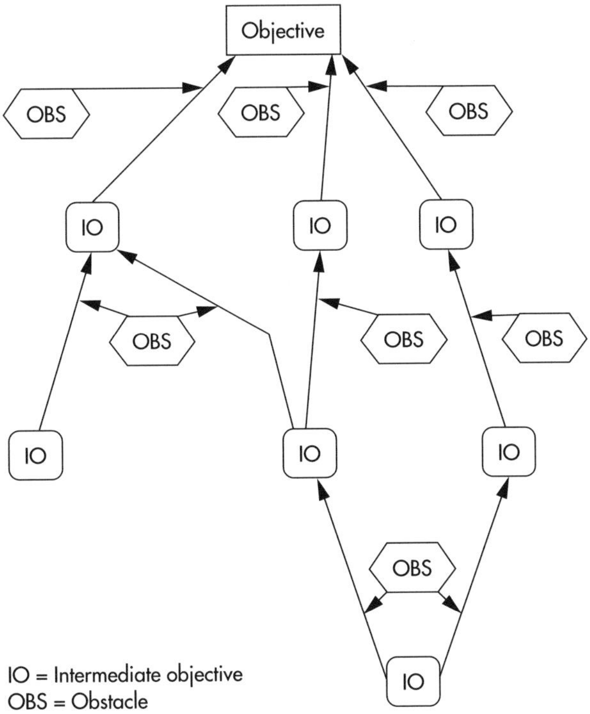
Objective
OBS
OBS
OBS
IO
IO
IO
OBS
OBS
OBS
IO
IO
IO
OBS
IO
IO = Intermediate objective
OBS = Obstacle

FIGURE 1.15. The Prerequisite Tree.

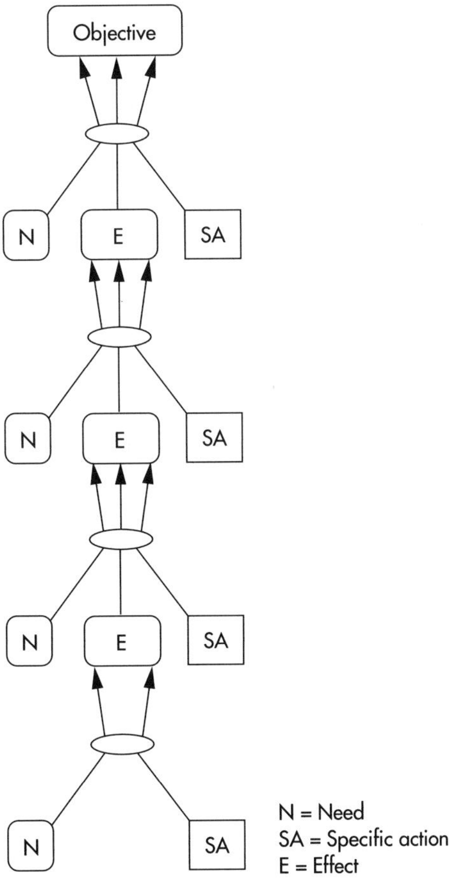
Objective
N
E
SA
N
E
SA
N
E
SA
N
SA
N = Need
SA = Specific action
E = Effect

FIGURE 1.16. The Transition Tree.

THE CATEGORIES OF LEGITIMATE RESERVATION

The Categories of Legitimate Reservation (CLR) are the "logical glue" that holds the trees together. Essentially, they are eight rules, or tests, of logic that govern the construction and review of the trees. To be logically sound, a tree must be able to pass all of these tests. The eight CLR include

- Clarity
- Entity Existence
- Causality Existence
- Cause Sufficiency
- Additional Cause
- Cause-Effect Reversal
- Predicted Effect Existence
- Tautology

We use the CLR as we construct our trees, to be sure our initial relationships are sound. We use the CLR after the tree is built, to review it as a whole. We use the CLR to scrutinize and improve the trees of others (and they to review ours). And, most important, we use the CLR to communicate disagreement with others in a nonthreatening way, which promotes better understanding rather than animosity. Chapter 2 describes the CLR in detail, gives examples of their application, and provides instructions on how to scrutinize your own trees as, or after, you build them. Chapter 8, "Group Dynamics and the TOC Thinking Process," provides guidance on how to use the CLR in groups, to scrutinize the trees of others, and to communicate disagreement amicably.

THE LOGICAL TOOLS AS A COMPLETE "THINKING PROCESS"

Each of Goldratt's five logical tools can be used individually, or they can be used in concert, as an integrated "thinking process." Recall that, earlier, we discussed TOC as a methodology for managing change. The three basic questions a manager must answer about change (*what* to change, what to change *to,* and *how* to cause the change) can be answered using the five logical tools as an integrated package. Figure 1.17 shows the relationship of the logical tools to the three management questions about change.

Figure 1.18, at the end of the chapter, shows a general overview of how each tool fits together with the others to produce an integrated thinking process. Nonquantifiable problems of broad scope and complexity are particularly prime candidates for a complete thinking process analysis. The rest of this book is devoted to explaining how the five logic trees and the Categories of Legitimate Reservation are used.

It is wise to keep in mind that no success or failure is necessarily final.

—Unknown

Stage of Change	**Applicable Logical Tool**
What to change?	Current Reality Tree
What to change *to*?	Conflict Resolution Diagram, Future Reality Tree
How to cause the change?	Prerequisite Tree, Transition Tree

FIGURE 1.17. How the Logical Tools Relate to Three Management Questions About Change.

NOTES

1. W. Edwards Deming, *The New Economics* (Cambridge, Mass.: MIT Center for Advanced Engineering Study, 1993), pp. 94–118.
2. *Webster's New Universal Unabridged Dictionary,* 1989.
3. Ibid.
4. W. Edwards Deming, *Out of the Crisis* (Cambridge, Mass.: MIT Center for Advanced Engineering Study, 1986).
5. Ibid., pp. 86–92.
6. Eliyahu M. Goldratt, *The Goal,* 2nd ed. (Great Barrington, Mass.: North River Press, 1992).
7. Eliyahu M. Goldratt, *It's Not Luck* (Great Barrington, Mass.: North River Press, 1994).
8. Deming, *Out of the Crisis,* p. 24.
9. Goldratt, *The Goal,* pp. 300–308.
10. Deming, *The New Economics,* p. 96.
11. Goldratt, *The Goal,* pp. 58–62. Also, Eliyahu M. Goldratt, *The Haystack Syndrome* (Croton-on-Hudson, N.Y.: North River Press, 1990), pp. 14–30.
12. Goldratt, *The Goal,* pp. 58–62.
13. Ibid., pp. 58–62.
14. Ibid., pp. 58–62.
15. Source: Message posted to the TOC-L Internet Discussion List, July 19, 1995, SUBJ: "T, I, and OE in Not-For-Profit Organizations," summarizing a conversation between Dr. Eliyahu M. Goldratt and the author on July 16, 1995, and posted at Dr. Goldratt's request.
16. Refer to *The Race,* by Eliyahu M. Goldratt and Robert E. Fox (North River Press) for a more detailed understanding of the Drum-Buffer-Rope concept in practice.
17. John A. Caspari, Chapter 8A, "Theory of Constraints," in *Management Accountants' Handbook, 4th ed., 1993 Supplement,* by Donald E. Keller, James Bulloch, and Robert Shultis (New York: John Wiley & Sons, 1993).
18. "Jonah" Course, A.Y. Goldratt Institute, New Haven, Conn., February 1993.

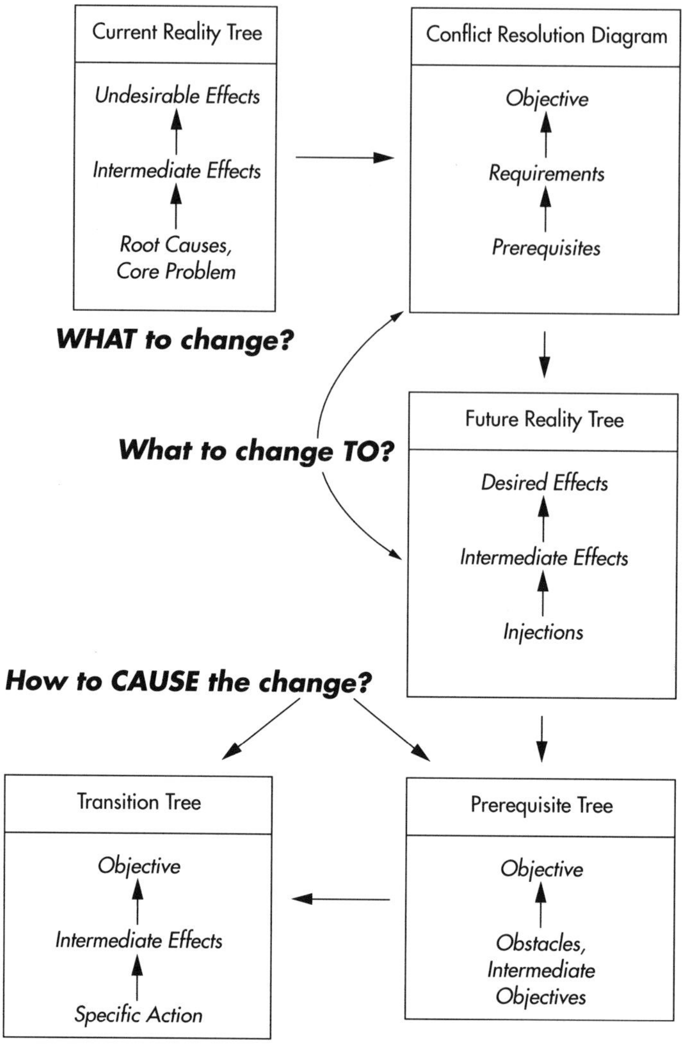

FIGURE 1.18. The Five Logical Tools as an Integrated Thinking Process.

Chapter 2
CATEGORIES OF LEGITIMATE RESERVATION

1. CLARITY

2. ENTITY EXISTENCE

3. CAUSALITY EXISTENCE

4. CAUSE INSUFFICIENCY

5. ADDITIONAL CAUSE

6. CAUSE-EFFECT REVERSAL

7. PREDICTED EFFECT EXISTENCE

8. TAUTOLOGY

Chapter Outline

When both logic and intuition agree, you are always right.
—Unknown

The TOC thinking process is composed of *logical* tools. The emphasis here is on the word "logic" for a good reason. A lot of problem-analysis tools use graphical representations. Flowcharts, "fishbone" diagrams, and tree and affinity diagrams are typical examples. But none of these diagrams are, strictly speaking, logic tools, because they don't incorporate any rigorous criteria for validating the connections between one element and another. In most cases, they're somebody's perception of the relationship.

The most significant difference between the TOC thinking process and traditional problem-analysis tools is a series of rules that govern the acceptability of the connections in each of the trees. As stated in chapter 1, these rules of logic are called the Categories of Legitimate Reservation—often abbreviated as CLR. The CLR are what differentiate somebody's perception from an accurate representation of existing reality.

A thorough understanding of these logical rules is absolutely essential to your success in using the TOC trees. While the rules are not difficult to understand, there are eight of them, and it requires some study and practice to keep them straight in your mind and to know when each one applies. So what, exactly, are these Categories of Legitimate Reservation?

DEFINITION

The CLR constitute a framework of eight specific tests, or proofs, used to verify cause-and-effect logic. The eight proofs include

1. Clarity
2. Entity Existence
3. Causality Existence
4. Cause Insufficiency
5. Additional Cause
6. Cause-Effect Reversal
7. Predicted Effect Existence
8. Tautology

PURPOSE

The Categories of Legitimate Reservation (CLR) are the foundation upon which logic in general, and the Theory of Constraints (TOC) thinking process in particular, is built. The CLR can be used for a number of purposes. Although they were designed to verify the validity of cause-and-effect logic trees, they can be applied in other ways, too. Some of these applications include the following:

- Use by a *tree-builder* to initially construct the five structures of the TOC thinking process (Current Reality Tree, Conflict Resolution Diagram, Future Reality Tree, Prerequisite Tree, and Transition Tree).
- Use by a *tree-builder* to self-check the tree after construction.
- Use by a *scrutinizer* with subject matter knowledge to review and evaluate a tree built and *presented* by someone else.
- Use by a *facilitator* in a group setting to ensure that both *scrutinizers* and *presenters* adhere to the rules of logic.
- Use by a *scrutinizer* or *facilitator* to communicate disagreement with the cause-and-effect logic of a *presenter* of a tree in a way that fosters consensus and discourages confrontation.
- Use by anyone in interactive discussion, not associated with logic trees, to evaluate and challenge or accept the validity of logic in the statements of others without offending or generating animosity.
- Use by anyone in evaluating the validity of logic in written text (books, magazines or journals, newspapers, advertising, and the like).

ASSUMPTIONS

The effectiveness of the Categories of Legitimate Reservation in fulfilling their intended purpose is based on the following assumptions:

1. Tree-builders want to construct logically sound trees.
2. Tree-builders, at some point, will also present their trees to others to communicate and elicit action.
3. Tree-builders/presenters naturally develop an emotional attachment to their own trees ("pride of the inventor").
4. Tree-builders/presenters often express cause-and-effect connections that are intuitive to themselves but not to others (that is, intermediate steps appear to be missing).
5. Tree-builders/presenters don't want to be embarrassed by presenting logically weak trees.
6. Presenters look for affirmation as well as constructive advice on their trees.
7. Presenters are sensitive to criticism of their work.
8. Presenters can accept, even welcome, constructive advice when they solicit it, and if it is offered in a nonthreatening way (that is, not "You against me," but "You and I against the system").
9. Scrutinizers are truly interested in helping presenters to improve their trees and in contributing to the analysis of the subject.
10. Scrutinizers are not interested in humiliating presenters or in bolstering their own egos by their scrutiny.
11. Scrutinizers have substantial intuition in the area of the tree's subject matter.
12. Facilitators concern themselves exclusively with the logical process and not with subject matter content.

HOW TO USE THIS CHAPTER

This chapter is composed of text with accompanying illustrations, with two figures emphasized at the end. Figures 2.31 and 2.32 are designed to summarize the content of the chapter and to be used as checklists or quick references, after the entire chapter has been read.

- Read all of chapter 2 and the accompanying examples to understand the circumstances in which each applies.
- Review Figure 2.31, "Categories of Legitimate Reservation." Figure 2.32, "Categories of Legitimate Reservation: Self-Scrutiny Checklist," provides a concise checklist that you can use for constructing and scrutinizing your own cause-effect trees.
- Refer to chapter 8 for guidance on using the CLR to communicate criticism to others in a nonthreatening way, and to scrutinize logic trees. Review Figure

8.4, "Directions for Communicating Using the CLR." Refer to this when presenting, scrutinizing, or facilitating the review of trees.

> ***The weaker the argument, the stronger the words.***
>
> ***—Unknown***

DESCRIPTION OF THE CATEGORIES OF LEGITIMATE RESERVATION

> ***I know you think you understand what you think I said, but I'm not sure you realize that what you heard is not what I meant.***
>
> ***—Unknown***

Clarity

Clarity is always the first reservation one should consider when questioning the logic of cause and effect. Clarity is not, strictly speaking, a logic-based reservation. Its roots are in communication.

Why Clarity Comes First

Clarity is raised first so that any misunderstandings resulting from inaccurate or incomplete communication of an idea are eliminated before the logic is examined. Most conflict in any situation involves communication breakdown to some extent. The Clarity reservation defuses potential conflict between speaker and listener early in the scrutiny process and helps keep it on a professional rather than a personal level.

Raising the Clarity reservation first establishes the protocol for the use of all the other categories. Stated briefly, in the words of Stephen R. Covey (*The Seven Habits of Highly Effective People*),[1] that protocol is

> *Seek to* understand *before seeking to be* understood.

By following this protocol we ensure that ineffective communication doesn't compromise logic.

What Clarity Means

A Clarity reservation means that a listener doesn't comprehend the speaker. Since the Clarity reservation is the first step in a check of logical validity, be sure that you and the speaker agree on the meaning of the speaker's statement. Whether the listener agrees with the *content* of the speaker's statement is not at issue in a Clarity reservation—just the *meaning*. Validity of logic is not addressed until *mutual understanding* is achieved. Some indications or examples of a breakdown in communication:

- The listener doesn't understand the *meaning* of the speaker's statement.
- The listener doesn't see the *significance* of the speaker's statement.
- The listener doesn't understand the *meaning* or *context* of specific words or phrases in the speaker's statement.
- The listener doesn't recognize a reasonable connection between a stated cause and a stated effect.

- The listener doesn't see some intermediate steps implied by the speaker but not explicitly stated. (In cause-effect trees, this is sometimes referred to as a "long arrow.")

Up to this point, we've spoken of Clarity as though we were referring to conversation among two or more people. Like the other categories, Clarity is certainly useful in this respect. However, the primary focus of this chapter is on using the Categories of Legitimate Reservation in constructing, validating, and streamlining logic trees. As we proceed into more details on logic trees, what we've called "statements" by speakers (or writers, for that matter) will be referred to as *entities* in logic trees. "Entities," as used this way, are defined in the next section. Figure 2.1 presents an abbreviated test and example of the Clarity reservation.

Figure 8.4, "Directions for Communicating Using the CLR," located at the end of chapter 8, provides detailed guidance on how to express a Clarity reservation, as well as how to respond to such reservations when presenting and scrutinizing trees.

> ***The greatest tragedy of science is that you often slay a beautiful hypothesis with an ugly fact.***
>
> ***—Thomas Huxley***

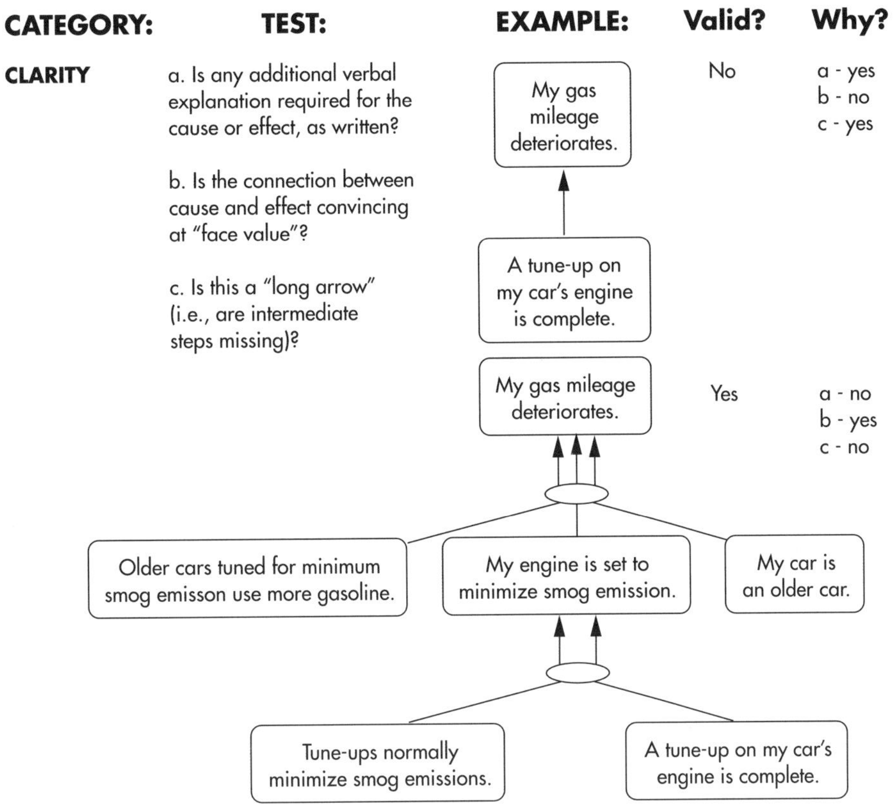

FIGURE 2.1. A Test and Example of the Clarity Reservation.

Entity Existence

For the purposes of logical examination, an *entity* is a complete idea expressed as a statement. Most often this idea is a *cause* or an *effect* represented in a logic tree, but in a broader application of the rules of logic it can also be a statement made in conversation, discussion, lecture, or writing. *Entity Existence* is a reservation raised by a listener when he or she detects one of three conditions affecting the statement:

- The statement is an incomplete idea. Normally this means the statement is not expressed in a grammatically correct sentence.
- The statement is not structurally sound; that is, it expresses multiple ideas in a single entity, or it contains an embedded "if–then" statement within it.
- The statement, at face value, does not seem valid to the listener.

Completeness

A complete idea is normally communicated using a grammatically correct sentence. In building logic trees, complete sentences are essential. At a minimum, there must be a *subject* and a *verb;* frequently there is an *object* as well. Impersonal pronouns (for example, "it," "this," and "those") are not acceptable (see Figure 2.2).

For example, the phrase "economic recession" can't stand alone as an idea. It raises the inevitable question, "What *about* economic recession?" To be effective in a logic tree, the entity must make sense when read with "if" or "then" preceding it. "Economic recession occurs" would be an acceptable entity from the standpoint of completeness.

Structure

An Entity Existence reservation based on structure is concerned exclusively with the mechanics of the entity. Adherence to structural rules for entities is necessary to preclude confusion, ensure simplicity of depiction, and achieve logically tight, or "dry," trees. The two structural rules for entities are

- No compound entities (see Figure 2.3). A single entity must not contain more than one idea. For example, "The sky is falling" is an entity that contains only one idea. If it had read, "The sky is falling and it hits Chicken Little on the head," it would be a *compound entity.* Two different ideas are expressed here, and each merits its own entity statement.

- No embedded "if–then" statements (see Figure 2.4). It's very hard to isolate causes and effects when both are wrapped together in a single statement. It would seem easy to avoid this trap: Just make sure the words "if" and "then" don't appear in your entity statements. But there is an insidious form of "if–then" that is indicated by the phrases "in order to . . ." or ". . . because. . . ." Since "if" or "then" aren't there, it may seem acceptable, but it wouldn't be.

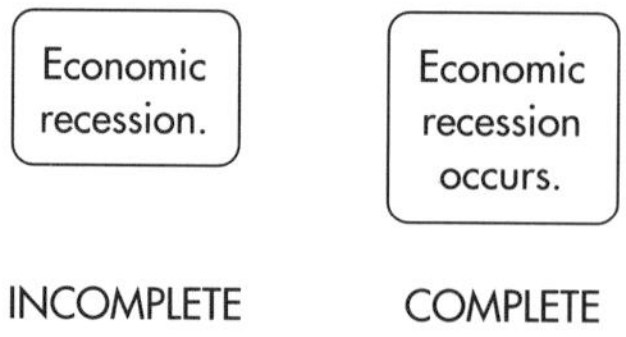

FIGURE 2.2. Completeness.

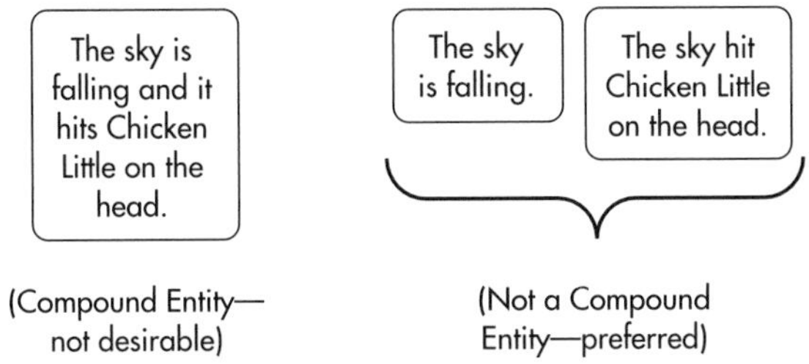

FIGURE 2.3. Structure: Compound Entity.

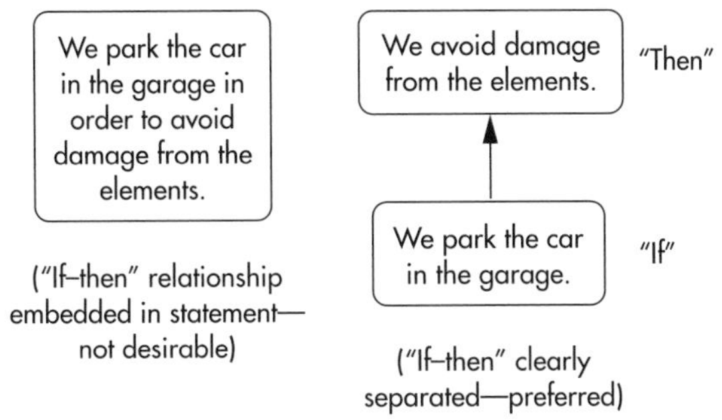

FIGURE 2.4. Structure: Embedded "If–Then."

Let's look at two examples. The entity reads "We park the car in the garage *in order to* avoid damage from the elements." No "if" or "then" appears in this sentence anywhere. But the phrase "in order to" alerts us to the fact that the idea can be conveyed another way: "*If* we park the car in the garage, *then* we avoid damage from the elements." This is an "if–then" expression in disguise. Similarly, a ". . . because . . ." statement may be nothing more than an "if–then" statement reversed. For example, an entity that reads "He insults me *because* he doesn't like me" could just as easily read "*If* he doesn't like me, *then* he insults me."

Note: As a general rule, when building logic trees, the more simply you can state your entities, the better off you'll be.

Validity

Once an idea has passed the Clarity, Completeness, and Structure hurdles (that is, do I understand the presenter, and is it a complete, properly constructed statement?), the next test of Entity Existence is *validity* (see Figure 2.5). For our purposes, validity means that the *content* of the statement is sound, or well-founded. It must have real meaning in the experience of the listener, or it must be a conclusion that the listener can reasonably accept.

For example, "The sky is falling" doesn't exist in most people's reality. So even though it might be a clear, complete, structurally sound statement, it could nevertheless be questioned based on Entity Existence. On the other hand, "Most grass is green" is complete, structurally correct, and a valid statement.

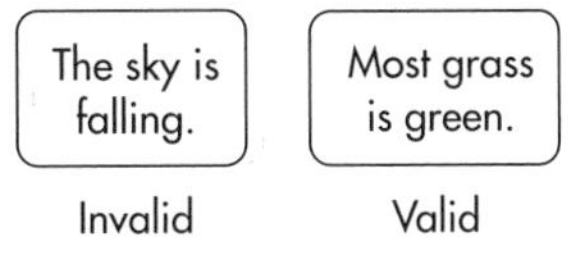

FIGURE 2.5. Validity.

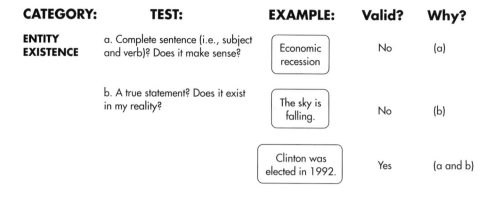

CATEGORY:	TEST:	EXAMPLE:	Valid?	Why?
ENTITY EXISTENCE	a. Complete sentence (i.e., subject and verb)? Does it make sense?	Economic recession	No	(a)
	b. A true statement? Does it exist in my reality?	The sky is falling.	No	(b)
		Clinton was elected in 1992.	Yes	(a and b)

FIGURE 2.6. A Test and Example of the Entity Existence Reservation.

Note: The validity test applies only to *conditions* of reality, not *actions*. For example, a condition of reality might be, "The sun is overhead at noon." An action might be, "I drive my car." In Future Reality and Transition Trees, the completeness and structure of action statements may be challenged, but not their validity, because future actions and their effects don't exist yet.

Figure 2.6 presents an abbreviated test and example of the Entity Existence reservation.

Figure 8.4, "Directions for Communicating Using the CLR," located at the end of chapter 8, provides detailed guidance on how to express an Entity Existence reservation, as well as how to respond to such reservations when presenting and scrutinizing trees.

Beware of half-truths; you may have gotten the wrong half.

—Unknown

Causality Existence

A listener with a Causality Existence reservation has some doubts about whether the stated cause does, in fact, lead to the stated effect. Where Entity Existence focuses on the validity of the statements themselves, Causality Existence challenges the validity of the *arrows,* or *connections,* between entities. Causality Existence addresses the following concerns:

- **Does the cause really result in the effect?** Does an "if–then" connection really exist? Verbalizing the arrow often helps to clarify any doubts about the causality: "If [cause], then we *must* have [effect]." The cause-effect relationship must make sense when read aloud exactly using "if–then" (see Figure 2.7).

Caution: Scrutinizers and other listeners must be careful to read or hear only what is written or said, not what they read into what is written or said. Raising the Clarity reservation should preclude this problem most of the time.

- **Is the cause intangible?** To be "tangible," a cause must be measurable or observable. Frequently an effect may be directly measurable or observable, but the cause is not (see Figure 2.8). For example, "My boss is dissatisfied with me" is not really observable in and of itself (unless the boss happens to tell you so). But "I stop watering the lawn" is observable. In both cases, the effects are

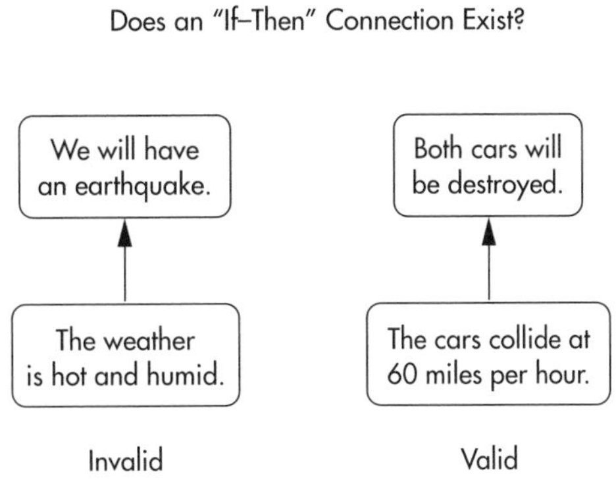

FIGURE 2.7. Causality Existence.

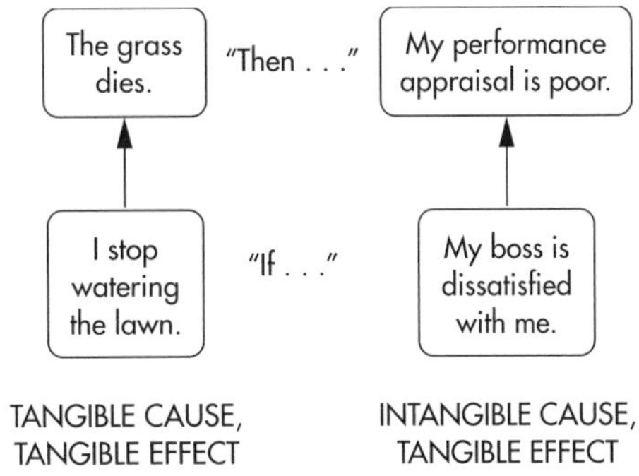

FIGURE 2.8. Tangible vs. Intangible Causes.

measurable or observable, but in the first case, the cause is not. Verifying the cause-effect relationship in this instance requires identifying the presence of at least one other directly measurable effect attributable to the same cause. Discussion of the CLR "Predicted Effect Existence," p. 50, contains a more detailed discussion of this technique of verification.

Figure 2.9 presents an abbreviated test and example of the Causality Existence reservation.

Figure 8.4, "Directions for Communicating Using the CLR," located at the end of chapter 8, provides detailed guidance on how to express a Causality Existence reservation, as well as how to respond to such reservations when presenting and scrutinizing trees.

Cause Insufficiency

Because the world is a network of intricate, complex systems, Cause Insufficiency is the most common deficiency found in logic trees or human dialogue. In complex interactions, relatively few effects are likely to have a single, unequivocal cause. Most of the time, a given effect will have either multiple dependent factors causing it, or perhaps more than one completely independent cause. In this section, we see how several dependent factors combine to produce cause sufficiency, and how to know when there is a Cause Insufficiency. Additional Cause is discussed in the next section.

The Cause Insufficiency reservation is raised when a listener believes that a presenter's stated cause is not enough, by itself, to produce the stated effect. As with Causality Existence, Cause Insufficiency focuses more attention on the *arrow* than

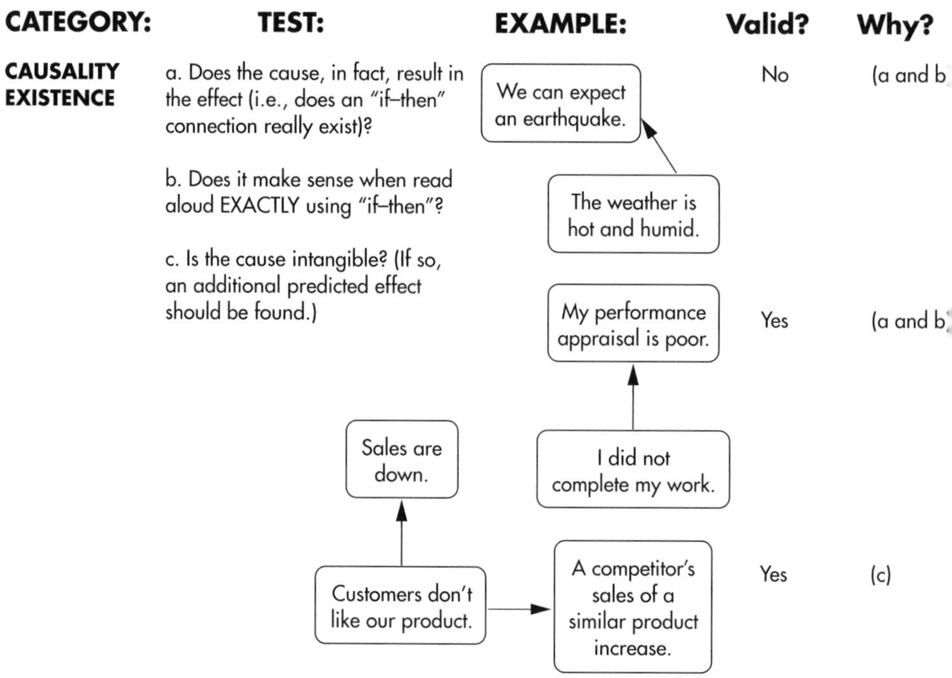

FIGURE 2.9. A Test and Example of the Causality Existence Reservation.

on the entity. With a Cause Insufficiency reservation, the listener is tacitly saying, "I agree that your stated cause is *an element* of causality, but it isn't sufficient to create your effect without including some other factor that you haven't stated."

The Ellipse

How are multiple dependent causes expressed in a logic tree? In portraying such a relationship, contributing entities are linked to their resulting effect with arrows passing through an ellipse (see Figure 2.10). Sometimes this ellipse is described as an "AND" gate, or, because of its shape, a lens or a "banana." Whatever you choose to call it, the ellipse's function is to identify and enclose the major contributing causes that are *sufficient in concert but not alone* to produce the effect.

Relative Magnitude of Dependent Causes

The idea of "relative magnitude" in a true dependency has no real meaning. Both (or all) causes are needed to produce the effect, and removing any one eliminates the effect. So we might say that any one of these causes accounts for all of the effect. But they all need each other, too. The sidebar entitled "Complex Causality," following the section "Additional Cause," discusses some important aspects of causality.

How Many Arrows?

Theoretically, there is no limit to how many arrows can pass through an ellipse. But there is a practical limit. At some point it becomes extremely difficult to depict and keep track of an expanding number of component causes. Also, at some point the number of contributors becomes so large that the effect of any one may be considered negligible.

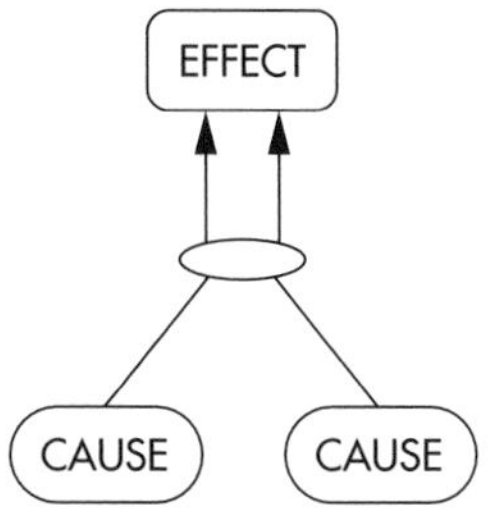

FIGURE 2.10. Indicating Cause Sufficiency with an Ellipse.

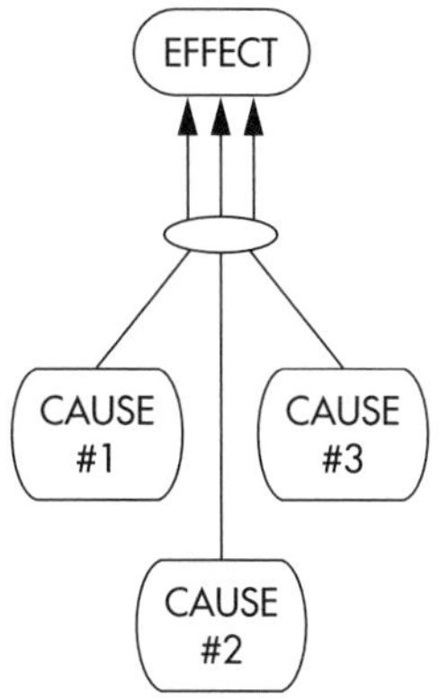

FIGURE 2.11. How Many Contributing Causes?

How many arrows should you include in the ellipse? This is an individual judgment call. Only you can determine the break point between having enough weight of causes to produce the effect or not. As a "rule of thumb," however, try to limit the number of contributing causes to three if possible, or four at most (see Figure 2.11). Beyond four, the relative influence of each contributor becomes so low that it might not be considered "major." Your objective should be to include only those causes without which the effect would either cease to exist or be of such limited magnitude that it would not be consequential to the larger system relationship.

Realistically, most effects are likely to have only a few major causes. If you have to exceed three contributing causes, take a closer look at all the causes. One or more might be an independent, or *additional,* cause. (The following section discusses Additional Cause.)

The Concept of "Oxygen"

One of the most common points of contention concerning Cause Insufficiency is the exclusion of some cause factor that is so basic to the situation that it is "transparent" to the presenter—but maybe not to the listener or scrutinizer. The best way to illustrate this issue is with an example. Consider the following cause-and-effect statement (see Figure 2.12):

If *we have fuel* and *a sufficient heat source,* then *we have a fire.*

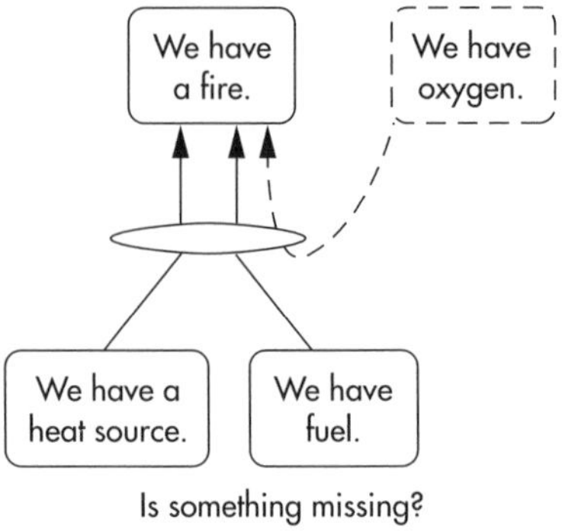

FIGURE 2.12. The Concept of "Oxygen."

Is there something missing? A physicist might say, "You forgot something very important—oxygen. You can't have combustion without it." To that extent, a Cause Insufficiency reservation might be raised about the example statement.

But a presenter might respond, "True, but since oxygen is always present in the situation where my fire might occur, I consider it a constant that doesn't have to be shown." So the concept of "oxygen" connotes a factor that is accepted as present-but-transparent by anyone with intuitive knowledge of the system under examination.

As a presenter, however, you should be prepared for scrutinizers to raise one of two concerns:

- The cause factor you omitted is not obvious ("oxygen") to the scrutinizer.
- The cause factor cannot really be assumed, but rather is a significant variable factor that is neither transparent nor constant in the situation.

In either case, presenters must be prepared to reexamine their cause-effect relationship. Figure 8.4, "Directions for Communicating Using the CLR," located at the end of chapter 8, provides detailed guidance on how to express a Cause Insufficiency reservation, as well as how to respond to such reservations when presenting and scrutinizing trees.

Figure 2.13 presents an abbreviated test and example of the Cause Insufficiency reservation.

Additional Cause

Sometimes more than one completely independent cause can produce a similar effect. A listener who perceives this situation might raise an Additional Cause reservation. For example, an above-normal human body temperature can result from either an internal infection or physical exertion on a hot summer day (see Figure 2.14). The key words are "either" and "or." Whereas a Cause Insufficiency reservation challenges an incomplete "AND" condition, an Additional Cause reservation signifies a missing "or" condition.

With an Additional Cause reservation, the listener or scrutinizer is not contesting the presenter's stated cause. He or she is only suggesting that there is something else that, by itself, might generate the same effect.

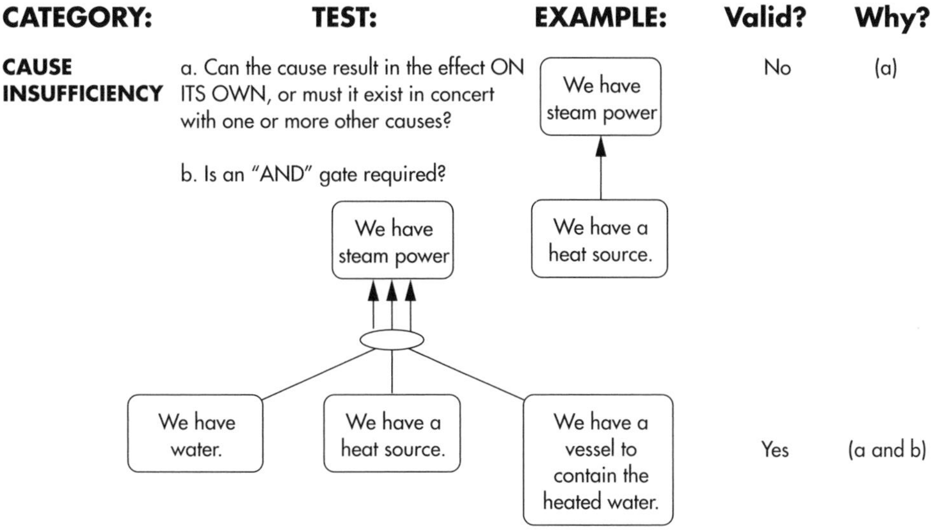

FIGURE 2.13. A Test and Example of the Cause Insufficiency Reservation.

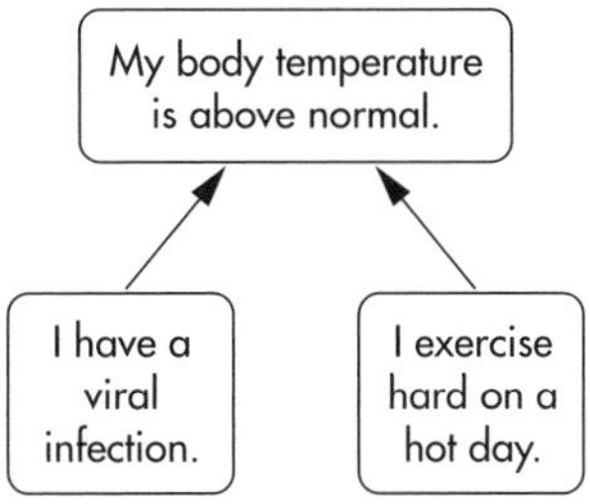

FIGURE 2.14. Additional Cause.

Magnitude

In order for the Additional Cause reservation to be valid, the suggested additional cause must produce the stated effect in *at least as much magnitude* as the presenter's originally stated cause. For example, everyone's sales may drop 10 percent in a declining economy, but if your sales declined 20 percent, there may be an additional cause accounting for the other 10 percent. If the effect produced by the suggested additional cause is relatively small when compared with the original stated cause, it shouldn't be considered an additional cause. As with the Cause Insufficiency reservation, magnitude of effect is a personal judgment call.

Test

The quickest test for an Additional Cause condition is to ask the question, "If I eliminate the stated cause, is there any other circumstance under which the same degree of effect would still occur?"

A Unique Variation of Additional Cause

It is possible, even common, to have multiple independent (additional) causes that are themselves made up of contributing factors. Under some circumstances, three contributing entities with arrows passing through an ellipse to an effect may be considered one independent cause, if that effect can also be caused by something else. That "something else" may, itself, be composed of multiple causes joined by an ellipse (see Figure 2.15). In such cases, each ellipsed group is considered an additional cause, but cause sufficiency rules still apply within the ellipse.

Figure 8.4, "Directions for Communicating Using the CLR," located at the end of chapter 8, provides detailed guidance on how to express an Additional Cause reservation, as well as how to respond to such reservations when presenting and scrutinizing trees.

Figure 2.16 presents an abbreviated test and example of the Additional Cause reservation.

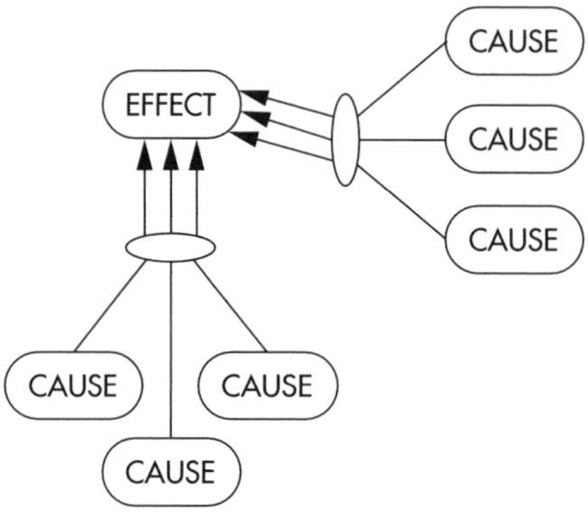
EFFECT
CAUSE
CAUSE
CAUSE
CAUSE
CAUSE
CAUSE

Each ellipsed group is considered an Additional Cause.

FIGURE 2.15. Variation of Additional Cause.

CATEGORY:	TEST:	EXAMPLE:	Valid?	Why?
ADDITIONAL CAUSE	a. Is this the only major cause? b. Are there other INDEPENDENT causes that might result in the same effect? c. If the cause in question is eliminated, are there other circumstances under which the effect might still be present?	Trash litters the yard. Dogs dumped the trash can.	No	a - no b - yes c - yes
		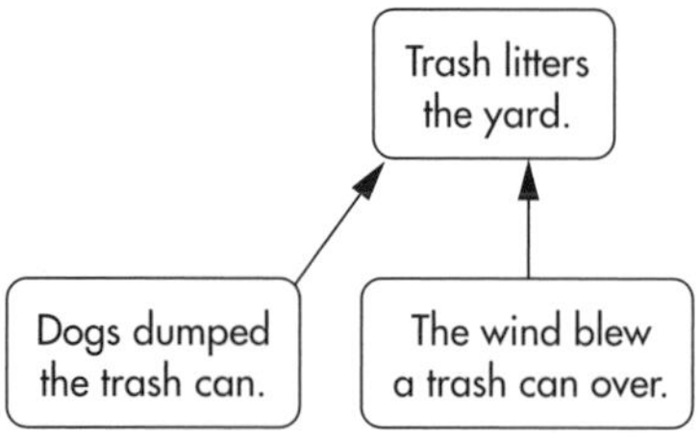Trash litters the yard. Dogs dumped the trash can. The wind blew a trash can over.	Yes	a - yes b - yes* c - yes*

*There are STILL additional causes that might produce this effect.

FIGURE 2.16. A Test and Example of the Additional Cause Reservation.

SIDEBAR

COMPLEX CAUSALITY

WHAT IS IT?

"It's not as simple as that . . ." How many of us have heard that phrase at least once? Most of us, probably. It's an audible indication that *complex causality* might be involved. Simply stated, complex causality is a situation in which a given effect might have more than one cause. Maybe these causes are related to one another somehow, or maybe not. In any case, it's helpful to realize that complex causality is more likely to be the rule than the exception. If you accept this as a basic fact of reality, wouldn't it be nice to know how to handle complex causality when you're building a tree? And wouldn't it make you feel more confident about the logical soundness of a tree when you read it?

Simple causality is represented in a logic tree by a single arrow connecting a single cause with a single effect (see Figure 2.17). It implies that the stated cause alone is enough to produce all of the indicated effect. Complex causality, on the other hand, implies that more than one cause is involved in producing the same effect.

Complex causality occurs two different ways. One is inherent in the Category of Legitimate Reservation known as "Additional Cause," and another in "Cause Sufficiency."

ADDITIONAL CAUSE

The Additional Cause postulates that several independent causes can produce the same effect. In fact, each cause can account for 100 percent of the effect *by itself* (see Figure 2.18). We show this relationship by drawing separate single arrows from each cause to the same effect.

What does this mean to you? Basically, if you want to get rid of the effect, you have to eliminate all the causes. Removing only one or two might not do any good, because any remaining cause can still produce the effect *by itself.*

CAUSE SUFFICIENCY

As we've seen, Cause Sufficiency (or Insufficiency, as used in the Categories of Legitimate Reservation) describes a situation in which two or more causes relate to one another in order to produce an effect. Cause sufficiency comes in two variations.

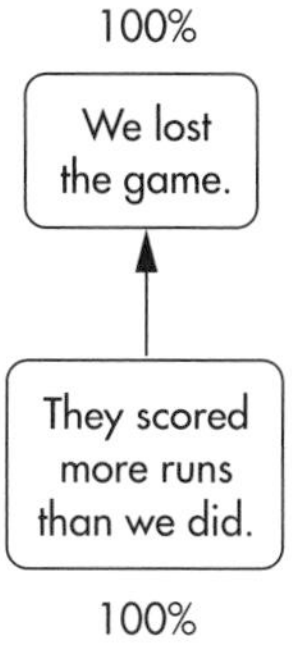

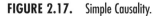

FIGURE 2.17. Simple Causality.

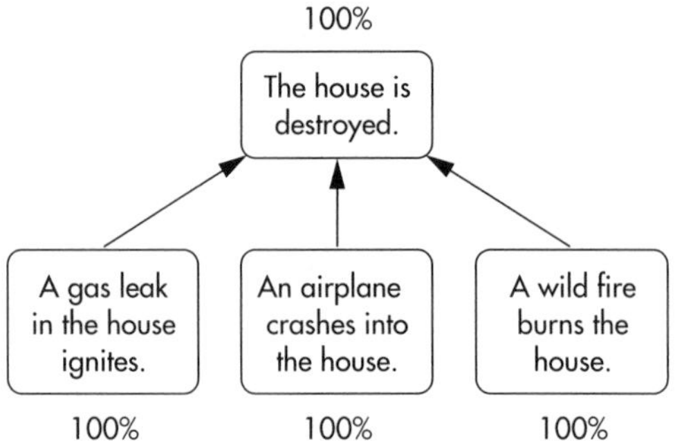

FIGURE 2.18. Additional Cause.

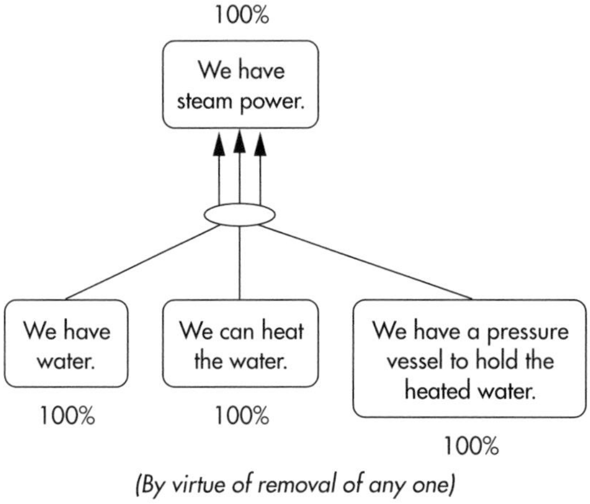

FIGURE 2.19. Conceptual "AND."

Conceptual "AND." This is the Cause Sufficiency situation we see most often. It's represented by arrows from several causes passing through an ellipse to the effect (see Figure 2.19). Each cause is needed, but it can't produce the effect without the help of the other(s). Removal of any one cause completely eliminates the effect. Thus, each cause could be said to be 100 percent responsible for the effect. But unlike the "Additional Cause" scenario, the causes *need each other.* They're interdependent.

Magnitudinal "AND." This Cause Sufficiency situation is less common. It falls somewhere between "Additional Cause" and Conceptual "AND." In a Magnitudinal "AND" condition, each cause contributes to the effect in an *additive* way. In other words, each cause adds progressively more to the effect. Conversely, removing one cause neither leaves the effect completely intact nor completely eliminates it. The effect is proportionately reduced.

Symbols. Because the causes in a "Magnitudinal AND" situation aren't completely independent (that is, any one cause producing all of the effect) or completely dependent (that is, removal of any one eliminates the effect), we have a problem graphically representing the "Magnitudinal AND." Goldratt established

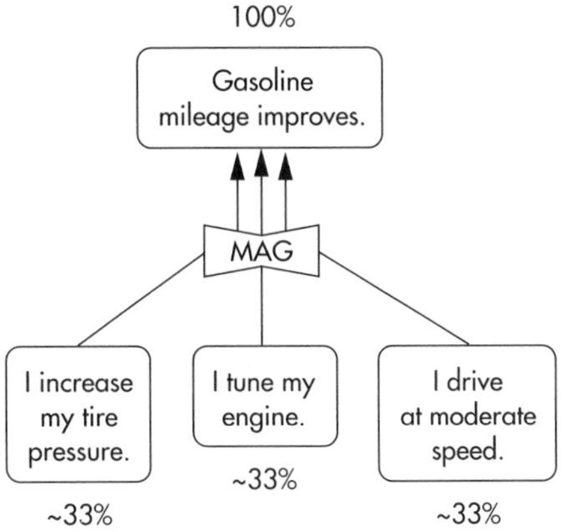

FIGURE 2.20. Magnitudinal "AND."

an ellipse to indicate a Conceptual "AND" (complete dependency), and no symbol at all to indicate an Additional Cause (complete independence).

But the independent arrows of the Additional Cause don't accurately represent the magnitudinal relationship. The ellipse of Cause Sufficiency doesn't highlight the additive nature of the magnitudinal condition, either.

So there's a need for a new symbol to signify that unusual condition—the Magnitudinal "AND." In this book, we'll use a "bow-tie" shape to reflect a Magnitudinal "AND" (see Figure 2.20). You're welcome to use any symbol you like—or none at all, if you prefer. Just remember to differentiate between Conceptual "AND" and the Magnitudinal "AND" somehow, or eventually you're likely to have a logic problem with your trees.

Cause-Effect Reversal

The Cause-Effect Reversal reservation is based on a very subtle distinction: *why* an effect exists versus *how we know* it exists. Sometimes this distinction is lost when a cause-effect relationship is written down or graphically depicted. Another way of verbalizing this concern is to ask the question, "Is the stated cause the *source* of the effect, or is the *effect* really the source of the cause?" It seems as if this should be an obvious error to detect, but that's not always the case.

The "Fishing Is Good" Example

To clarify the difference between why something happens and how we know it happens, consider the following two cause-effect relationships (see Figure 2.21):

#1

"*If* many fishermen are fishing from the river bank, *and* the fishermen's stringers are full of fish, *then* fishing is good."

#2

"*If* the river was stocked with fish yesterday, *and* fishing season opens today, *then* fishing is good."

Which of these statements makes more sense? Was the good fishing *caused* by the fishermen fishing or the stringers full of fish? Or were these the *indications* that led us to conclude that fishing was good? In actuality, the two cause-effect

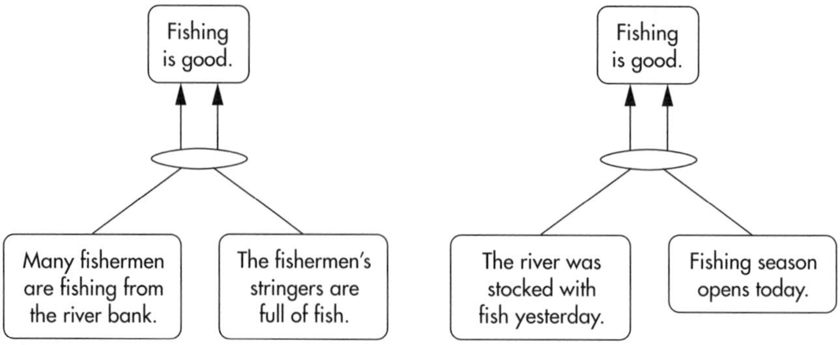

This example created by Charles M. Johnson.

FIGURE 2.21. The "Fishing Is Good" Example.

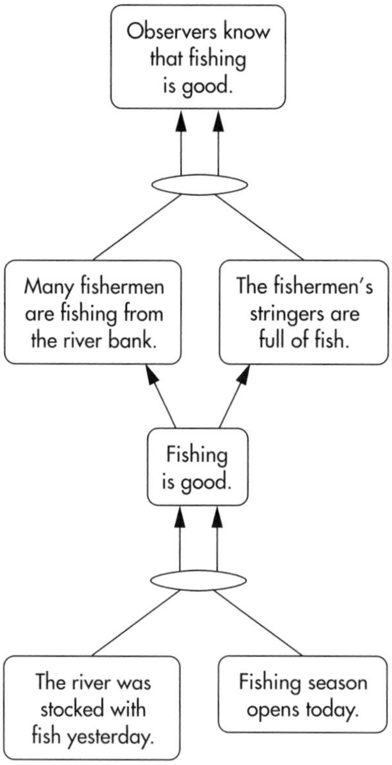

This example created by Charles M. Johnson.

FIGURE 2.22. Combined "Fishing Is Good" Example.

relationships should be combined, with some modification, to present a much more accurate picture of the situation in Figure 2.22.

The Statistical Example

"If standardized test scores are at or below the 50th percentile, *then* the academic qualifications of new students are poor." Are the low test scores the

cause of poor qualifications, or are they the reason *we know* those qualifications are poor? In other words, did the low scores cause the poor qualifications, or are they just an indicator of them?

The Medical Example

"*If* my body temperature is higher than normal and I have a pain in my lower abdomen, *then* I have appendicitis." Did the fever and the pain *cause* the appendicitis, or was it the other way around? As you can see, it's not too difficult to go astray on Cause-Effect Reversal.

Test

There are two ways to detect a Cause-Effect Reversal:

- Does it seem that the arrow between cause and effect is pointing in the wrong direction? This is most likely to be a "gut feeling" and the first inkling you have that something is not quite right.
- Could the stated cause really be an *indicator,* rather than a *source*?

Figure 2.23 presents an abbreviated test and example of the Cause-Effect Reversal reservation.

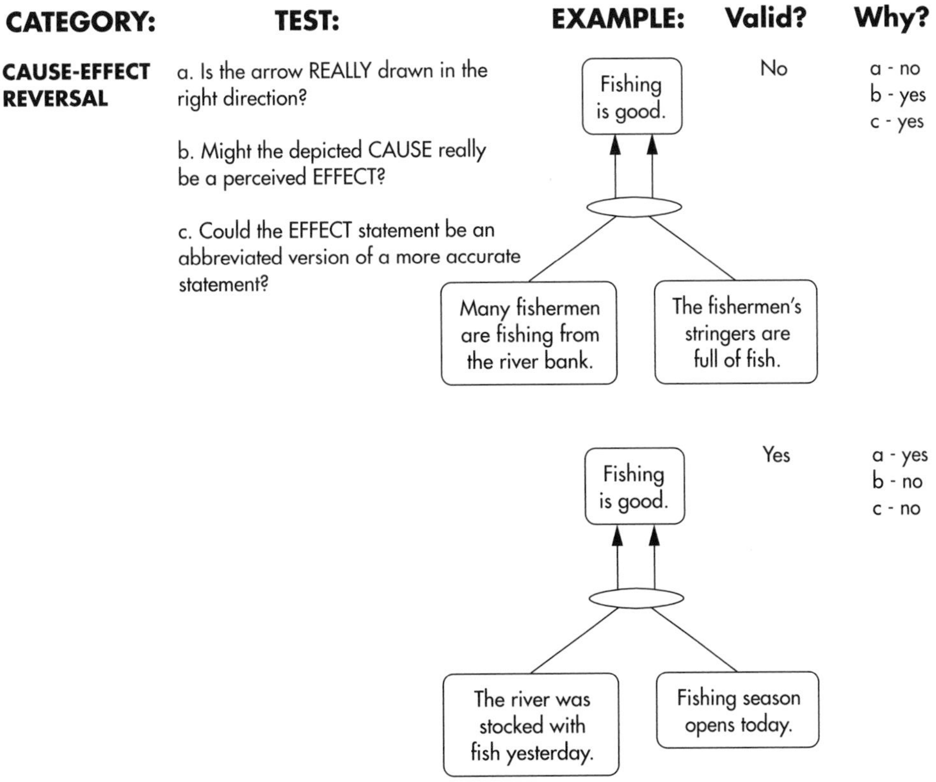

This example created by Charles M. Johnson.

FIGURE 2.23. A Test and Example of the Cause-Effect Reversal Reservation.

Figure 8.4, "Directions for Communicating Using the CLR," located at the end of chapter 8, provides detailed guidance on how to express a Cause-Effect Reversal reservation, as well as how to respond to such reservations when presenting and scrutinizing trees.

Predicted Effect Existence

Predicted Effect Existence means that if the proposed cause-effect relationship is valid, another unstated effect would also be expected. EXAMPLE: "I have appendicitis" might be offered as the cause of the effect "I have a pain in my abdomen." But if the cause is really valid, we might also expect to see a couple of other effects: "I have a fever" and "My white cell count is elevated."

The Predicted Effect Existence reservation does not stand alone. It is always invoked to substantiate a reservation for Causality Existence, Cause Insufficiency, Additional Cause, or Cause-Effect Reversal. Predicted Effect Existence becomes the proof that one of the other causality reservations is—or is not—valid. Consequently, the Predicted Effect Existence reservation can be used either by a presenter to support causality, or by a scrutinizer to refute causality.

Conflict or Differences in Magnitude?

The Predicted Effect Existence reservation recognizes the complex nature of most systems. Most causes in the "real world" result in more than one effect. Even if only one effect is stated or germane to a given situation, if you look hard enough, in most cases additional effects can be identified. Three characteristics of predicted effects make them especially useful in validating or refuting proposed effects:

- *Expectation.* ("Is it there?") Given the proposed effect, one expects to see another related effect; or, one expects not to see a certain effect. It's either there, or it isn't; and its presence or absence will either support or refute the proposed cause-effect relationship.
- *Coexistence.* ("Is it there at the same time?") If the predicted effect is present, proposed effects and predicted effects must be able to coexist. If a case can be made that the two effects can't exist at the same time (or that the cause can't produce both effects), then the proposed cause-effect relationship is suspect. Or, if the proposed cause can be shown to produce the same effect to differing degrees under the same circumstances, the cause-effect relationship is also called into question. EXAMPLE: The same cause, under the same circumstances, can't simultaneously cause a profit and a loss. If you can show that it does, the original cause-effect relationship is refuted.
- *Magnitude.* ("Is it *all* there?") If the predicted effect is present and it can coexist with the proposed effect, the predicted effect may also be expected to exist at a specific magnitude. If the actual magnitude is significantly greater or less than expected, the proposed cause may be refuted as either invalid or insufficient. If the actual magnitude approximates the expected magnitude, the cause-effect relationship is validated.

To determine whether a predicted effect supports or refutes a cause-effect relationship, test it with the following proofs:

	Support	Refute
1. The effect is *there*, but *shouldn't* be.	NO	YES
2. The effect is *not* there, but *should* be.	NO	YES
3. The effect is *there*, and *should* be.	YES	NO
4. It can coexist with the predicted effect.	YES	NO
5. Are the predicted and proposed effects mutually exclusive?	NO	YES
6. Is the predicted effect more or less than expected?	NO	YES
7. Is the predicted effect about the same degree as expected?	YES	NO

Figure 2.24 provides several examples showing how the Predicted Effect Existence reservation is used to support or refute causality.

Tangible or Intangible?

As previously stated in "Causality Existence," p. 38, Predicted Effect Existence can be used to verify the existence of an intangible cause. It can also be used when the cause is tangible. In the latter case, however, the cause doesn't need verification; it's already tangible. But the causality, or arrow, does.

A scrutinizer taking issue with the existence of an intangible cause would use Predicted Effect Existence to show that another expected effect of the same cause is absent. For example, let's assume the presenter says, "*If* customers don't like our product, *then* sales are down." A scrutinizer could challenge the Causality Existence of this relationship by pointing out the absence of *just one other* expected effect of that intangible cause. Figure 2.25 illustrates two such possible collateral effects.

If either of these predicted effects doesn't exist, then the originally stated cause does not exist, and the scrutinizer's reservation is valid. However, if the presenter can demonstrate that both of those collateral effects do exist, then Predicted Effect Existence supports the original cause-effect relationship.

What if the cause *is* tangible? Predicted Effect Existence can also be used to support or refute the logical connection, or arrow, between cause and effect. For example, "Quality has deteriorated" may be a quantitatively verifiable fact (see Figure 2.26). "Sales are going down" may also be substantiated by numbers. But has deteriorated quality necessarily caused decreased sales? One additional predicted effect of poor quality might be "Customers' complaints increase." Does this quantitatively verifiable effect exist? If so, the causality relationship between poor quality and decreased sales is likely to be valid. If not, decreased sales may have another cause—perhaps a general economic downturn—but decreased quality may not be the cause. In fact, if there is no alternative product or service, it isn't likely to be the cause.

Verbalizing Predicted Effect Existence

To avoid confusion, verbalize a Predicted Effect Existence reservation this way:

> *If we accept that [CAUSE] is the reason for [ORIGINAL EFFECT], then it must also lead to [PREDICTED EFFECT(S)], which [do/do not] exist.*

Figure 2.27 provides an abbreviated test and example of the Predicted Effect Existence reservation.

Figure 8.4, "Directions for Communicating Using the CLR," located at the end of chapter 8, provides detailed guidance on how to express a Predicted Effect Existence reservation, as well as how to respond to such reservations when presenting and scrutinizing trees.

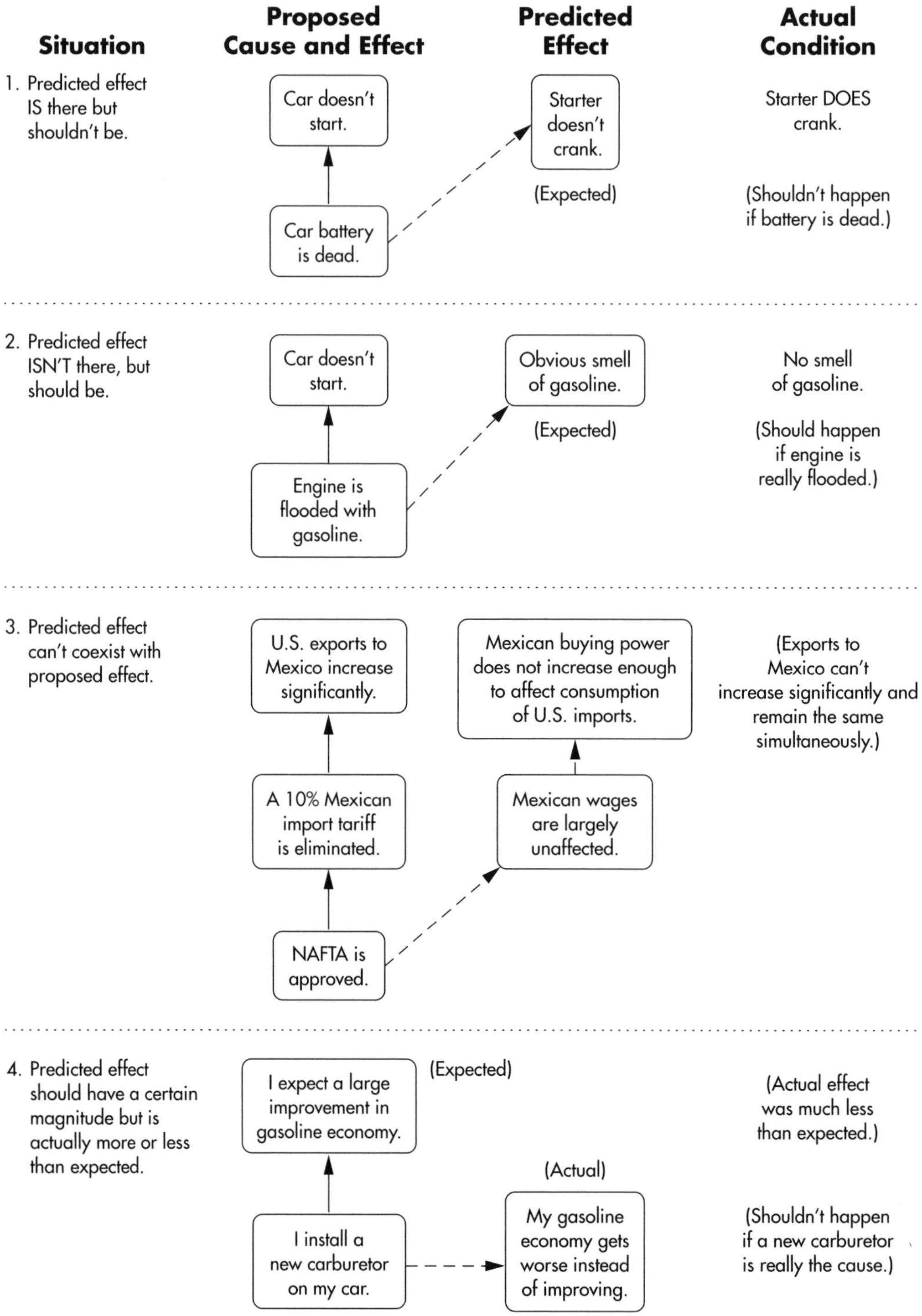

FIGURE 2.24. Example of Applying the Predicted Effect Existence Reservation.

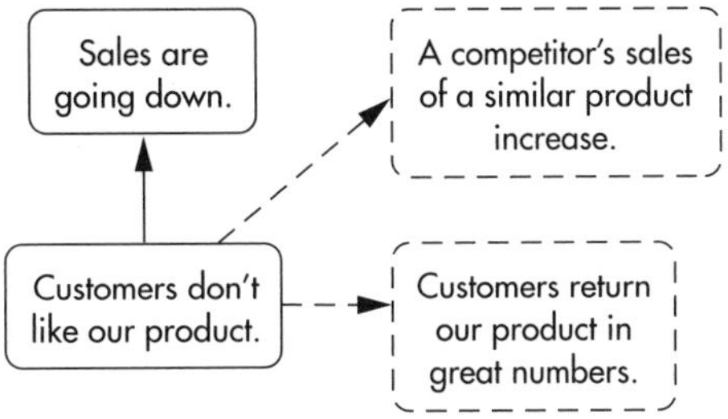

FIGURE 2.25. Predicted Effect: Verifying an Intangible Cause.

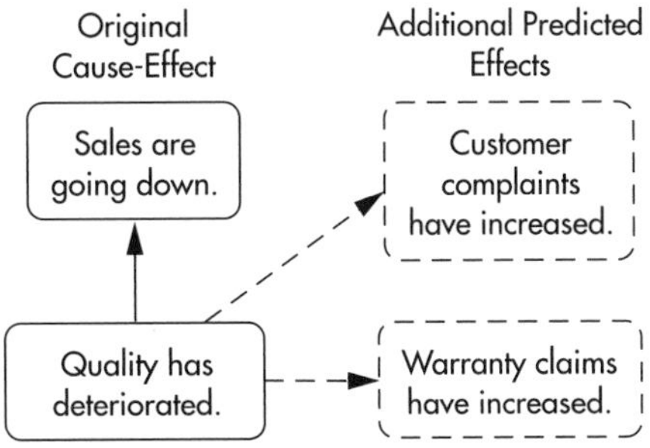

FIGURE 2.26. Another Predicted Effect: Verifying a Tangible Cause.

CATEGORY:	TEST:	EXAMPLE:	Valid? Why?
PREDICTED EFFECT EXISTENCE	a. Is the cause INTANGIBLE? If so, are there one or more additional expected effects that must exist for the cause-effect relationship to be valid?	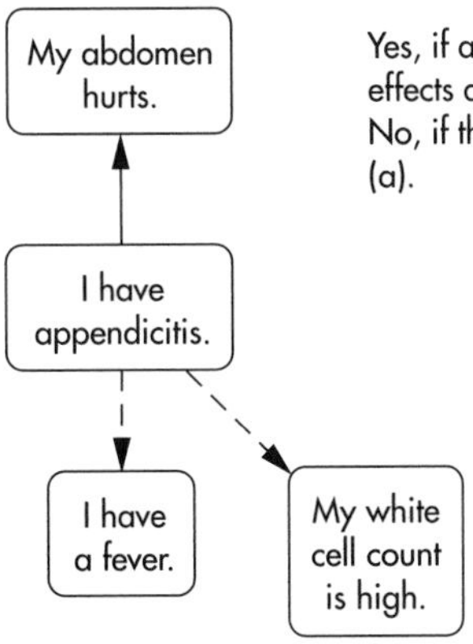	Yes, if additional effects are present. No, if they are not (a).

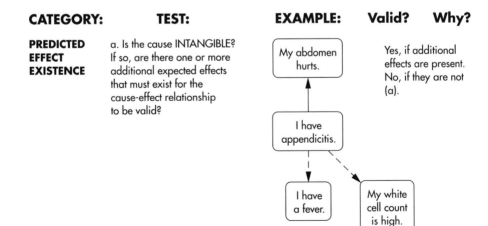

FIGURE 2.27. A Test and Example of the Predicted Effect Existence Reservation.

Tautology

Tautology is another name for circular logic: The effect is offered as a rationale for the existence of the cause. Since causality must be questioned before the issue of Tautology can be raised, like Predicted Effect Existence, Tautology can never stand alone. It must be preceded by another causality reservation—usually Causality Existence.

Tautology is most likely to surface when Causality Existence is questioned and the cause is intangible. If no additional predicted effect is offered, other than the stated one, to substantiate the intangible cause, it becomes very easy to forsake a more rigorous examination of the causality and let the effect provide the rationale for the cause.

Baseball Example

This example, while not presented in "if–then" format, is typical of tautologies common in the electronic and print media (see Figure 2.28).

Statement: "The Dodgers lost the game because they played poorly."
Challenge: *What makes you think they played poorly?*
Rationale: "They lost the game, didn't they?"

Clearly, the effect is offered as a rationale for the existence of the cause. Since causality was not more intensively investigated, additional predicted effects such as number of errors, bases on balls, extra-base hits, and so forth were not offered to substantiate the intangible cause. And totally ignored is the fact that the Dodger pitcher may have had a no-hitter going into the 10th inning when he gave up a solo home run.

Vampire Example

Figure 2.29 is an example in an "if–then" format.

Proposed Cause: "I wear garlic around my neck and sleep with a cross."
Proposed Effect: "Vampires stay away."
Challenge: *How do you know that the garlic and cross really work?*
Rationale: "You don't see any vampires, do you?"

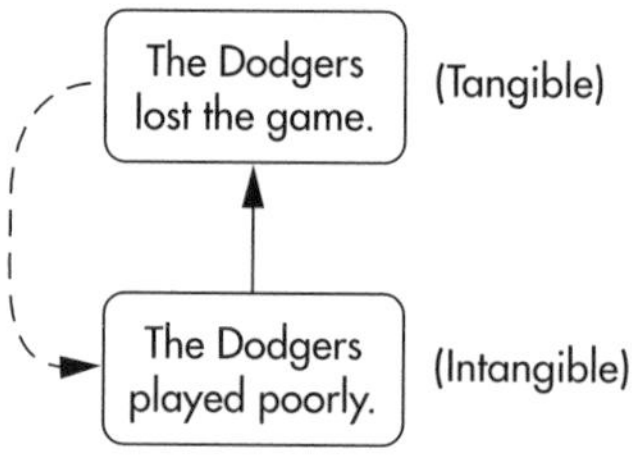

FIGURE 2.28. Tautology (Circular Logic).

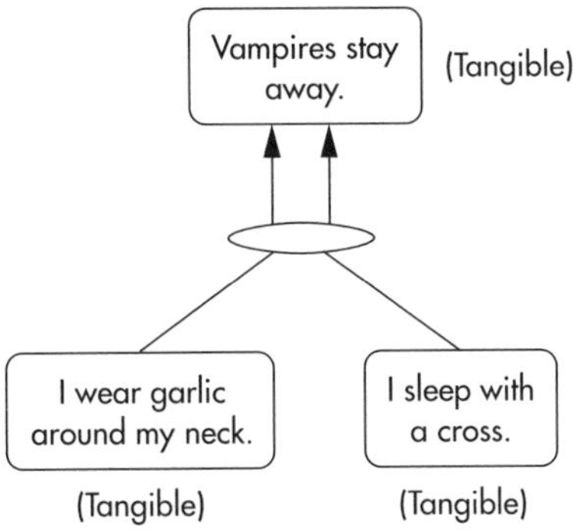

FIGURE 2.29. Tautology (Tangible Cause).

CATEGORY:	TEST:	EXAMPLE:	Valid?	Why?
TAUTOLOGY	a. Is it circular logic (i.e., is the effect offered as a rationale for the cause)? E.g., "You don't see any bite marks on my neck, do you?" b. Is an additional verifiable effect offered?	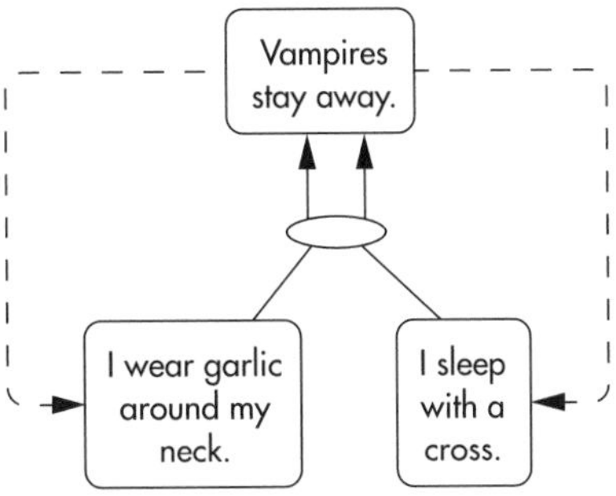	No	(a and b)

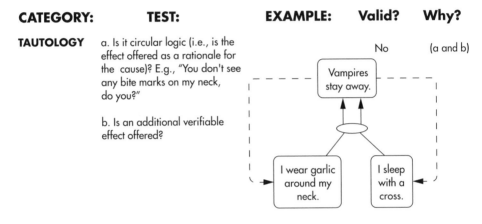

FIGURE 2.30. A Test and Example of the Tautology Reservation.

Test

To avoid the Tautology trap, ask the following questions:

- Is the cause intangible?
- Is the effect offered as a rationale for the existence of the cause?
- Are there any additional predicted effects that could substantiate the intangible cause?

Figure 2.30 presents an abbreviated test and example of the Tautology reservation.

It's a wonderful feeling when you discover some logic to substantiate your beliefs.

—Unknown

SUFFICIENCY-BASED VS. NECESSITY-BASED LOGIC TREES

As we proceed through the five logic trees of the TOC thinking process, you'll notice that two of these trees—the Conflict Resolution Diagram (also called the "Evaporating Cloud") and the Prerequisite Tree—are expressed differently from the Current Reality Tree, Future Reality Tree, and Transition Tree. That's because their foundations are a little different.

The Current Reality Tree, Future Reality Tree, and Transition Tree are considered *sufficiency* trees. They're read in an "if–then" format. The validity of their cause-effect relationships depends on sufficiency. To determine sufficiency, we ask questions like "Is *this* enough (or sufficient) to cause *that*?"

The Conflict Resolution Diagram and Prerequisite Tree are considered *necessity* trees. They're read in an "In order to . . . we must . . . because . . ." format. The validity of their cause-effect relationships depends on meeting *minimum necessary requirements.*

The Categories of Legitimate Reservation were designed to apply primarily to sufficiency trees, but they do have some applicability to necessity trees as well. These distinctions will be explained in more detail in chapter 4, "Conflict Resolution Diagrams," and chapter 6, "Prerequisite Trees."

SUMMARY

We've discussed the Categories of Legitimate Reservation in detail. We've seen how they're used to ensure that the cause-and-effect trees we build are logically sound, and we've seen how to use them to scrutinize the logic trees of others. Now it's time to start using the CLR to build a tree.

There is a mighty big difference between good, sound reasons and reasons that sound good.

—Burton Hillis

NOTE

1. Stephen R. Covey, *The Seven Habits of Highly Effective People* (New York: Simon & Schuster, 1989), pp. 236–260.

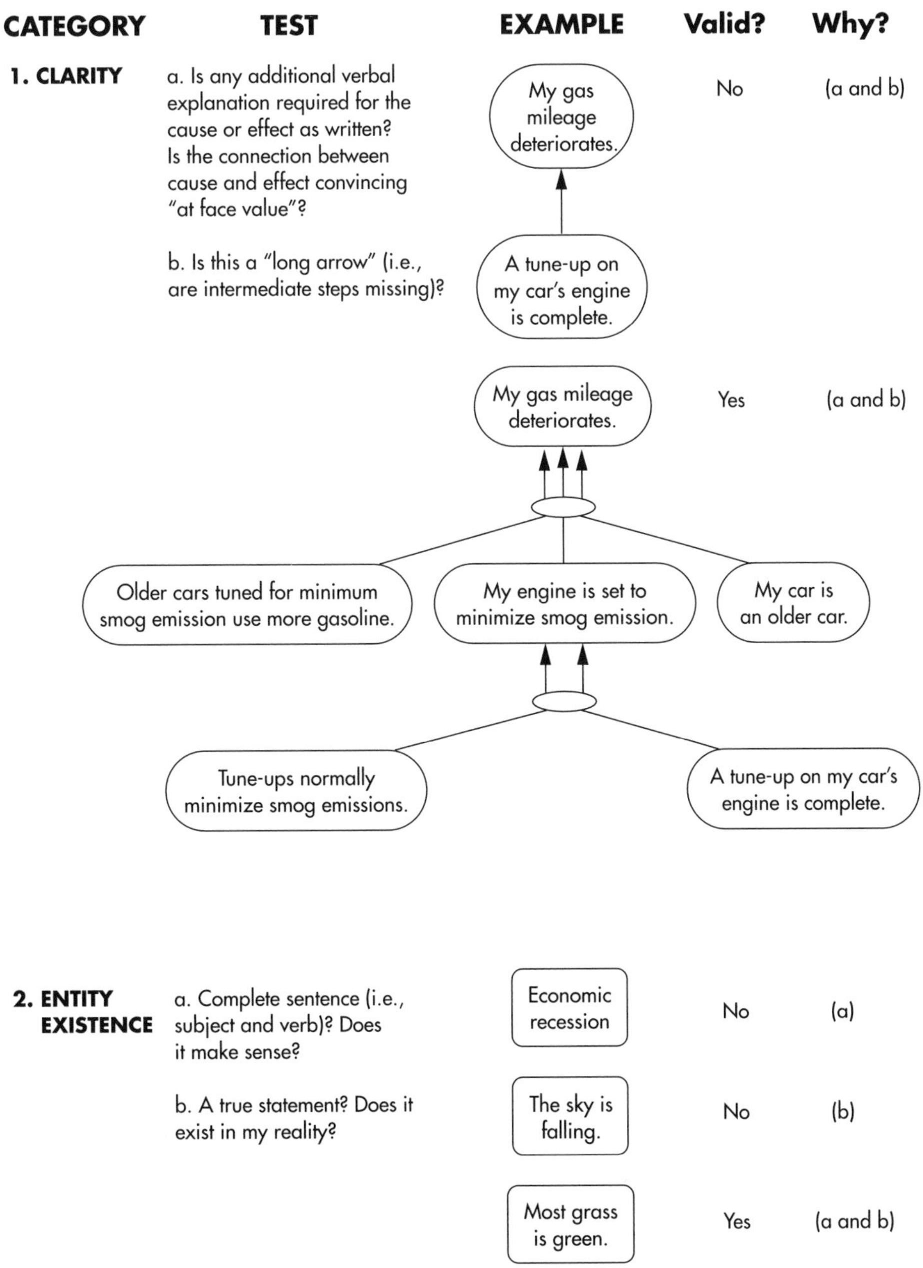
CATEGORY
TEST
EXAMPLE
Valid?
Why?
1. CLARITY
a. Is any additional verbal explanation required for the cause or effect as written? Is the connection between cause and effect convincing "at face value"?
b. Is this a "long arrow" (i.e., are intermediate steps missing)?
My gas mileage deteriorates.
A tune-up on my car's engine is complete.
No
(a and b)
My gas mileage deteriorates.
Yes
(a and b)
Older cars tuned for minimum smog emission use more gasoline.
My engine is set to minimize smog emission.
My car is an older car.
Tune-ups normally minimize smog emissions.
A tune-up on my car's engine is complete.
2. ENTITY EXISTENCE
a. Complete sentence (i.e., subject and verb)? Does it make sense?
b. A true statement? Does it exist in my reality?
Economic recession
No
(a)
The sky is falling.
No
(b)
Most grass is green.
Yes
(a and b)

FIGURE 2.31. Categories of Legitimate Reservation.

CATEGORY | **TEST** | **EXAMPLE** | **Valid?** | **Why?**

3. CAUSALITY EXISTENCE

TEST:

a. Does the cause, in fact, result in the effect (i.e., does an "if–then" connection really exist)?

b. Does it make sense when read aloud EXACTLY using "if–then"?

c. Is the cause intangible? (If so, an additional predicted effect should be found.)

EXAMPLE:

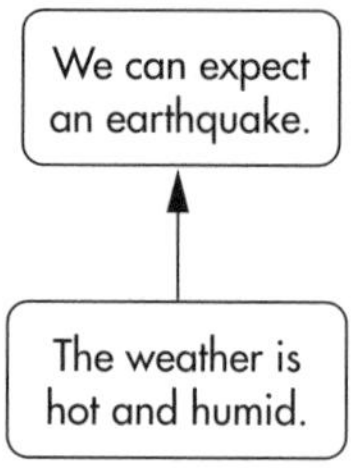

We can expect an earthquake.
The weather is hot and humid.

Valid? No — Why? (a and b)

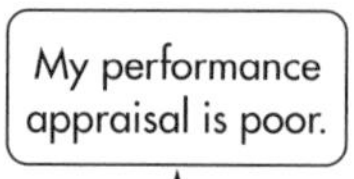

My performance appraisal is poor.
I did not complete my work as promised.

Valid? Yes — Why? (a and b)

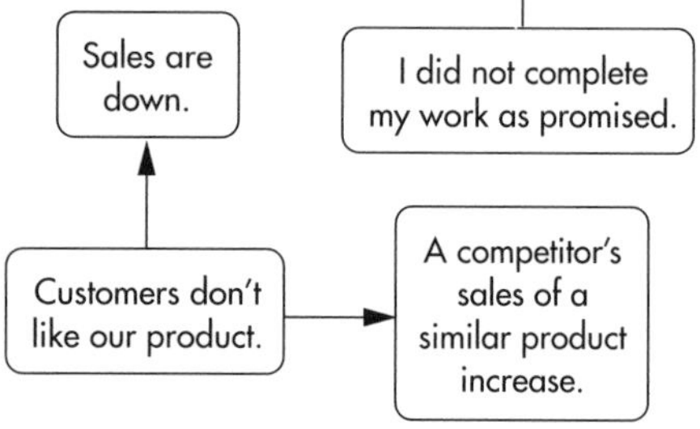

Sales are down.
Customers don't like our product.
A competitor's sales of a similar product increase.

Valid? Yes — Why? (c)

4. CAUSE INSUFFICIENCY

TEST:

a. Can the cause result in the effect ON ITS OWN, or must it exist in concert with one or more OTHER causes?

b. Is an ELLIPSE required?

EXAMPLE:

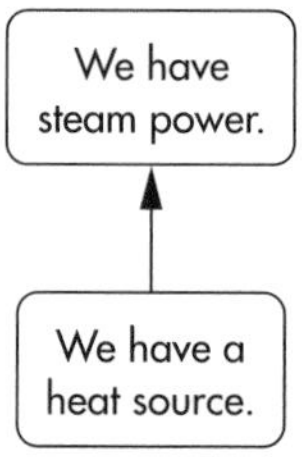

We have steam power.
We have a heat source.

Valid? No — Why? (a)

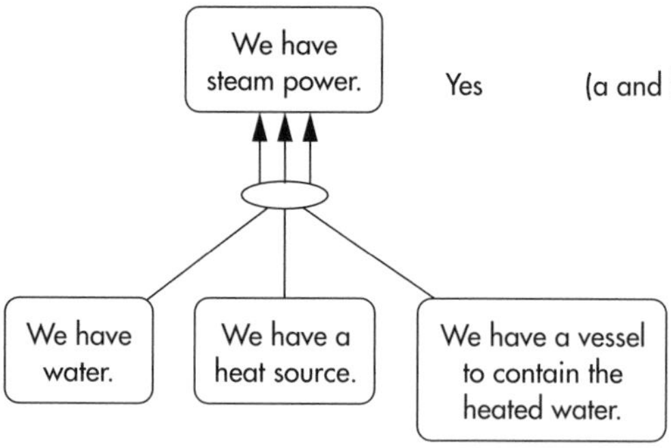

We have steam power.
We have water.
We have a heat source.
We have a vessel to contain the heated water.

Valid? Yes — Why? (a and b)

FIGURE 2.31—*Continued.*

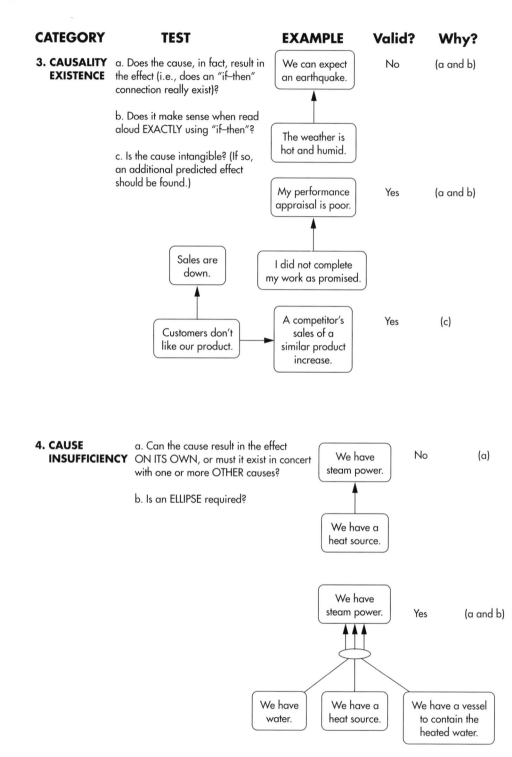

CATEGORY	TEST	EXAMPLE	Valid?	Why?
5. ADDITIONAL CAUSE	a. Is this the only major cause? Are there other INDEPENDENT causes that might result in the same effect? b. If the cause in question is eliminated, are there other circumstances under which the effect would still be present?	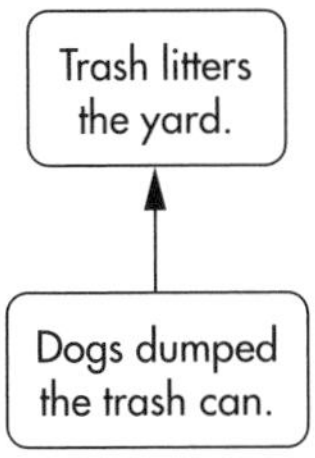	No	(a and b)
		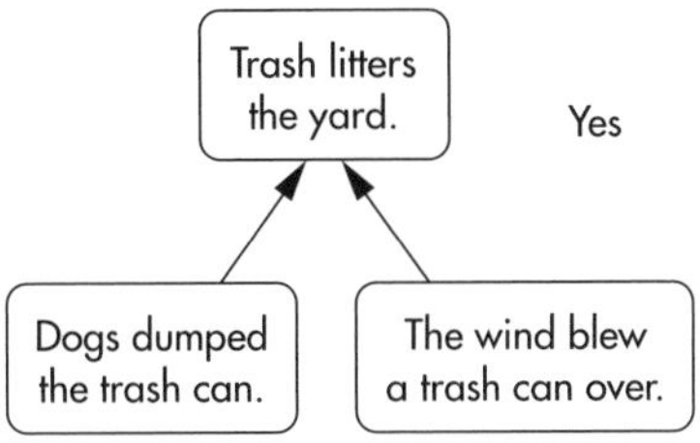	Yes	(a and b)
6. CAUSE-EFFECT REVERSAL	a. Is the arrow REALLY drawn in the proper direction? Is it possible that what is offered as the CAUSE might really be a perceived EFFECT? b. Is the EFFECT statement really an abbreviated version of a more accurate statement?	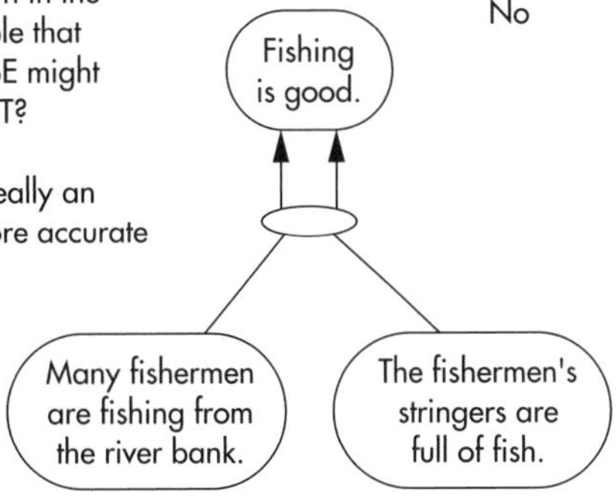	No	(a and b)
		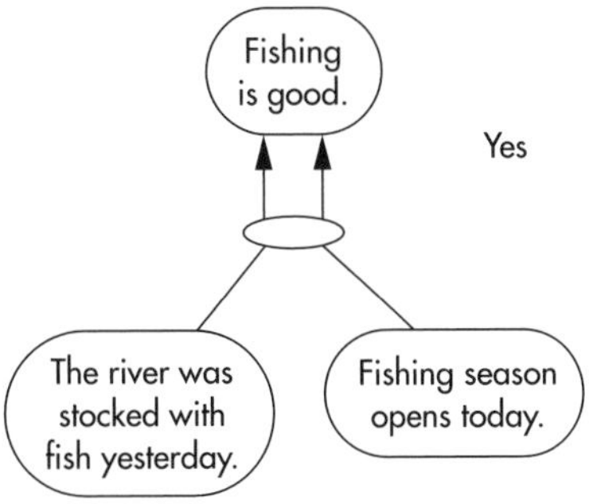	Yes	(a and b)

This example created by Charles M. Johnson.

FIGURE 2.31—*Continued.*

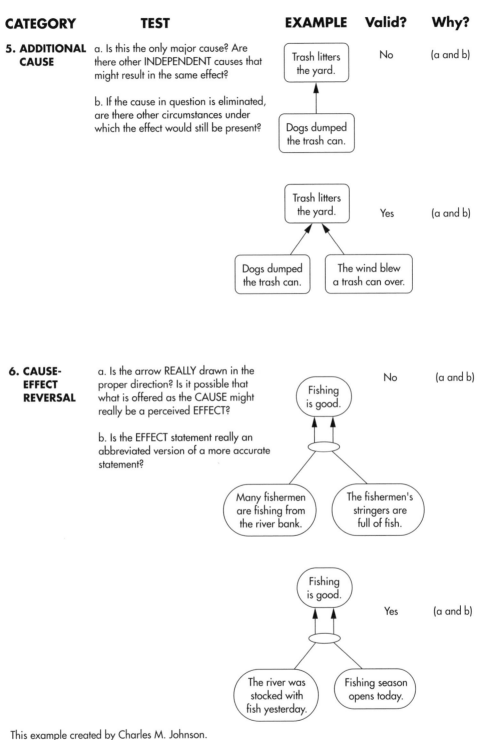

CATEGORY	TEST	EXAMPLE	Valid?	Why?
7. PREDICTED EFFECT EXISTENCE	a. Is the cause intangible? If so, are there one or more additional predicted effects that must exist for the cause-effect relationship to be valid?	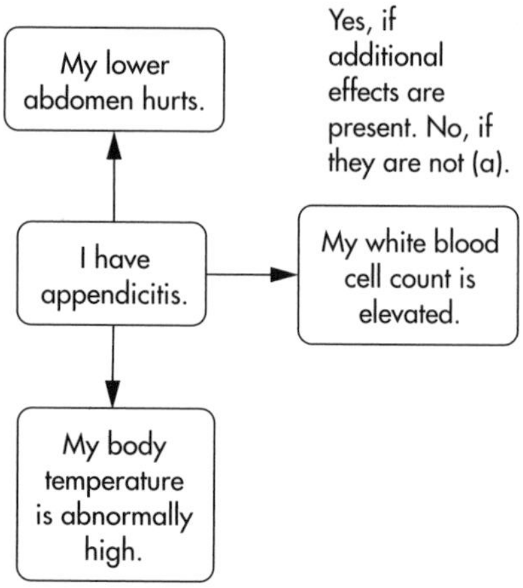	Yes, if additional effects are present. No, if they are not (a).	
8. TAUTOLOGY	a. Is it circular logic (i.e., is the effect offered as a rationale for the cause)? E.g., "You don't see any bite marks on my neck, do you?" b. Is an additional verifiable effect offered?	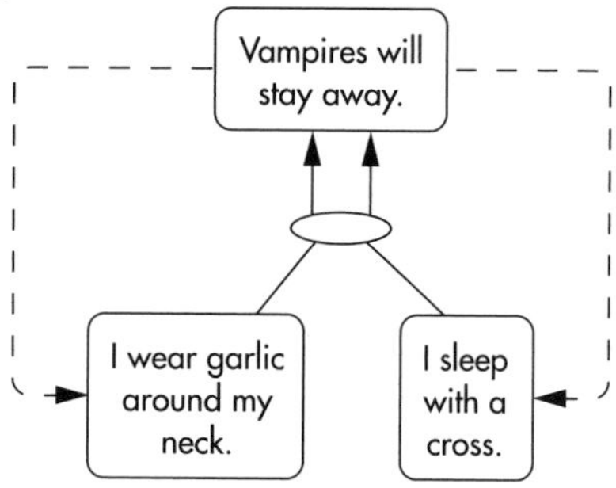	No	(a and b)

FIGURE 2.31—*Continued.*

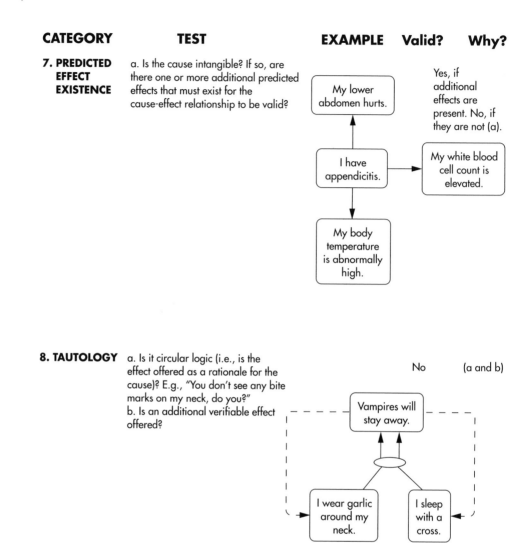

1. **CLARITY.** (Seeking to understand)
    - Would I add any verbal explanation if reading the tree to someone else?
    - Is the meaning/context of words unambiguous?
    - Is the connection between cause and effect convincing "at face value"?
    - Are intermediate steps missing?
2. **ENTITY EXISTENCE.** (Complete, properly structured, valid statements of cause, effect)
    - Is it a complete sentence?
    - Does it make sense?
    - Is it free of "if–then" statements? (Look for ". . . because . . .", ". . . in order to . . .")
    - Does it convey only *one* idea? (I.e., not compound entity)
    - Does it exist in my reality?
3. **CAUSALITY EXISTENCE.** (Logical connection between cause and effect.)
    - Does an "if–then" connection really exist, as written?
    - Does the cause, in fact, result in the effect?
    - Does it make sense when read aloud exactly as written?
    - Is the cause *intangible*? (If so, look for an additional predicted effect.)
4. **CAUSE INSUFFICIENCY.** (A nontrivial dependent element missing)
    - Can the cause, as written, result in the effect on its own?
    - Are any significant cause factors missing?
    - Is/are the written cause(s) sufficient to justify all parts of the effect(s)?
    - Is an ellipse required?
5. **ADDITIONAL CAUSE.** (A separate, independent cause producing the same effect)
    - Is there anything else that might cause the effect *on its own*?
    - If the stated cause is eliminated, will the effect be almost completely eliminated?
6. **CAUSE-EFFECT REVERSAL.** (Arrow pointing in the wrong direction)
    - Is the stated effect really the cause, and vice versa?
    - Is the stated cause the reason *why*, or just *how we know* the effect exists?
7. **PREDICTED EFFECT EXISTENCE.** (Additional corroborating effect resulting from cause)
    - Is the cause intangible?
    - Do other unavoidable outcomes exist besides the stated effect?
8. **TAUTOLOGY.** (Circular logic)
    - Is the cause intangible?
    - Is the effect offered as a rationale for the existence of the cause?
    - Do other unavoidable outcomes exist besides the stated effect?

FIGURE 2.32. Categories of Legitimate Reservation: Self-Scrutiny Checklist.

Chapter 3
CURRENT REALITY TREE

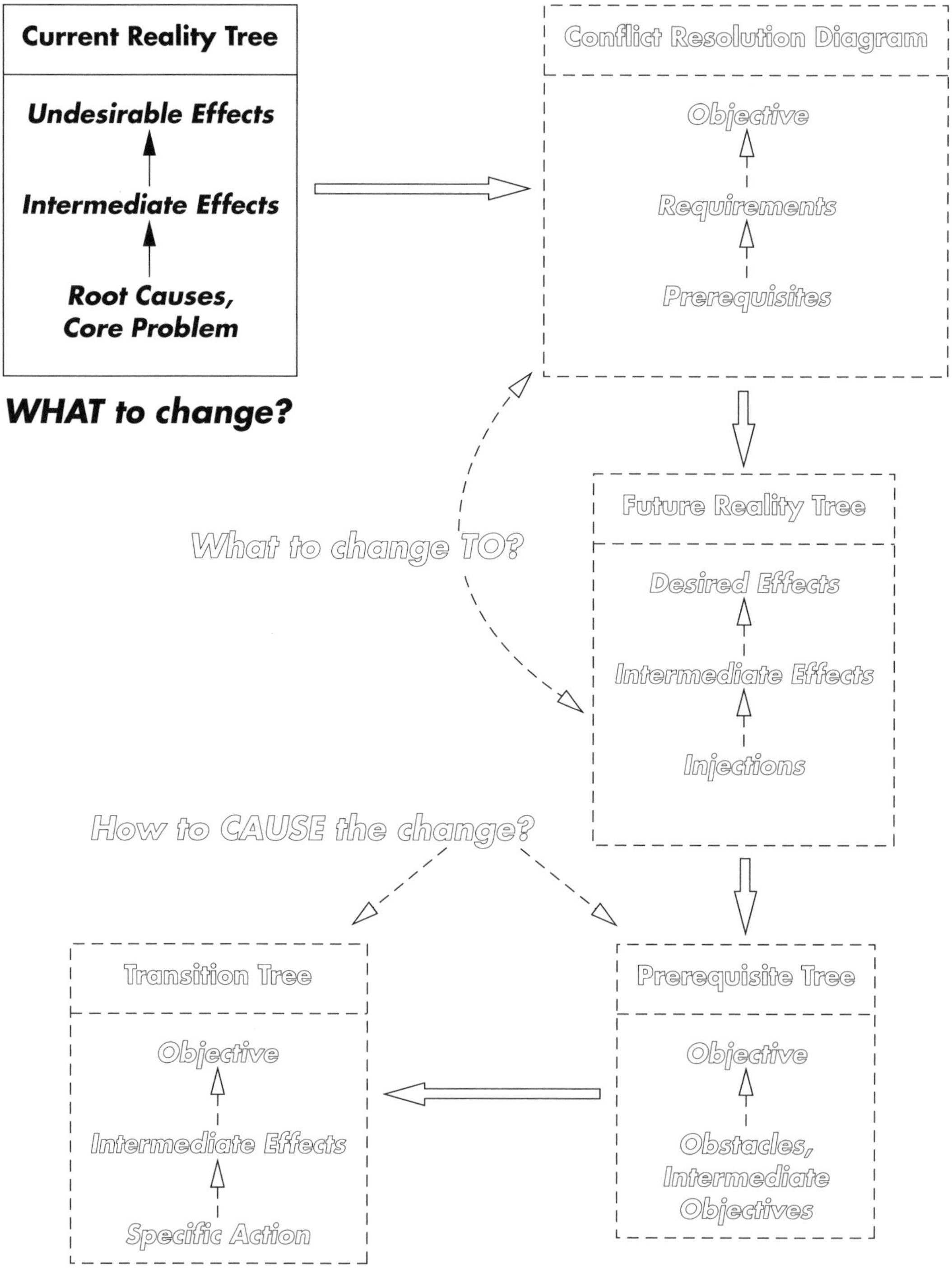
Current Reality Tree
Undesirable Effects
Intermediate Effects
Root Causes, Core Problem
WHAT to change?
Conflict Resolution Diagram
Objective
Requirements
Prerequisites
What to change TO?
Future Reality Tree
Desired Effects
Intermediate Effects
Injections
How to CAUSE the change?
Transition Tree
Objective
Intermediate Effects
Specific Action
Prerequisite Tree
Objective
Obstacles, Intermediate Objectives

Chapter Outline

If you can keep your head when all about you are losing theirs, then you obviously don't understand the problem.

—Evans' Law

"It's not that simple." How many times have we heard someone say that, usually after a simple solution to a complex problem has been suggested? Does this mean that complex problems can only be solved using complex solutions? No, but it does imply that the complexities of the situation probably were not fully visible, or taken into consideration, before a solution was proposed.

Here's a typical example: corporate downsizing. The indications that a problem exists are usually obvious: Profits are down, sales are sluggish, cash flow may be down to a trickle, finished (unsold) inventory is high. What's the most common response of senior management? Cut costs! Lay people off! It's a solution, isn't it? Certainly. But "it's not that simple." The causes of the obvious symptoms of this problem are not as clear-cut as the downsizing solution would have us believe.

What happens if we've identified the wrong problem (that is, costs are too high)? Inevitably, we expend time, energy, and resources solving the wrong problem, which means that the original problem is still with us. And that means the overall situation will probably not improve. Or, if it does, the improvement is likely to be minimal and only temporary.

How can we avoid the pitfall of solving the wrong problem—which not only wastes resources, but may actually create new problems where there were none previously? Clearly, the first, most important step in problem solving is to be certain we've identified the real problem correctly. And there's a funny thing about "real" problems in complex situations: They're not usually visible to the naked eye. So what can we do about that?

One option is to construct a Current Reality Tree—a logic tree Goldratt designed specifically to find hidden system-level problems in complex situations. In this chapter, we'll see what a Current Reality Tree is, what it tells us, and why we can be confident that it's pointed us at the right problem, even though that problem may be hidden beneath many layers of cause and effect.

DEFINITION

A Current Reality Tree (CRT) is a logical structure designed to depict the state of reality as it currently exists in a given system. It reflects the most probable chain of cause and effect, given a specific, fixed set of circumstances. The CRT seeks cause-and-effect connections between visible indications of a system's condition and the originating causes that produce them (see Figure 3.1). It is *functional* rather than *organizational,* blind to arbitrary internal and external system boundaries. Consequently, it can produce a faithful representation of cause and effect.

PURPOSE

The Current Reality Tree is designed to achieve the following objectives:

- Provide the basis for understanding complex systems.
- Identify undesirable effects (UDEs) exhibited by a system.
- Relate UDEs through a logical chain of cause and effect to root causes (RC).
- Identify, when possible, a core problem (CP) that eventually produces 70 percent or more of the system's UDEs.
- Determine at what points the root causes or core problem lie beyond one's *span of control* or *sphere of influence.*
- Isolate those few causative factors (constraints) that must be addressed in order to realize the maximum improvement of the system.
- Identify the one simplest change to make that will have the greatest positive impact on the system.

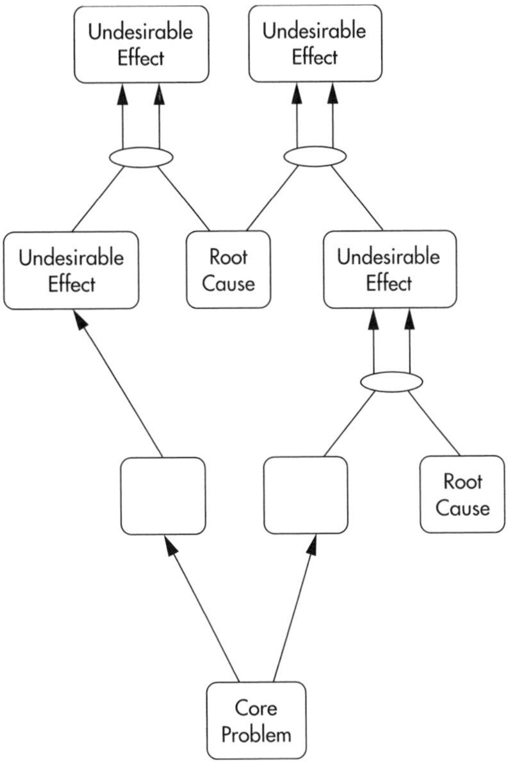

FIGURE 3.1. The Current Reality Tree.

ASSUMPTIONS

The effectiveness of the Current Reality Tree is based on the following assumptions:

- Cause and effect is not the same as correlation.
- All systems are subject to interdependencies among their components; that is, a change in one component will produce collateral changes in one or more other components.
- All processes within a system, including the overall system itself, are subject to variation.
- The operation of a system produces both intended (desirable) and unintended (desirable or undesirable) effects.
- Undesirable effects in a system do not exist in isolation from one another.
- All effects (desirable or undesirable) within a system are the products of root causes that may be several steps removed from these effects.
- Cause and effect is governed by the Categories of Legitimate Reservation (CLR) and is verifiable through the CLR.
- Unstated assumptions about reality underlie all cause-and-effect relationships.
- Events related by verifiable cause and effect will be replicable. Another iteration of the chain should give the same effects if no changes to circumstances or to the system are made.

HOW TO USE THIS CHAPTER

- Read "Description of the Current Reality Tree," the next section. This describes what a Current Reality Tree is and how it works.
- Read "Building a Current Reality Tree," p. 88, and the associated examples. This section explains in detail each of the steps in building a Current Reality Tree and why they're necessary.
- Read "Scrutinizing the Current Reality Tree," p. 100. This section tells how to ensure that your Current Reality Tree is logically sound and accurately depicts "the way things are."
- Review Figure 3.44, "Current Reality Tree Example." This is a complete Current Reality Tree on the subject of why organizations fail at total quality. It illustrates in a typical real-world example just how complex reality can be and how effective the Current Reality Tree is at analyzing complex cause and effect.
- Review Figure 3.45, "Procedures for Building a CRT." This is an abbreviated checklist that you can use to guide you in constructing your own Current Reality Tree. The checklist contains brief instructions and illustrations for each step. Detailed explanations for each step in the checklist are provided in the chapter itself, under "Building a Current Reality Tree," p. 88.
- Practice with a "Current Reality Tree Exercise," provided in Appendix C.

DESCRIPTION OF THE CURRENT REALITY TREE

The objective of the Current Reality Tree is to help you isolate what needs changing in any situation. It does this by helping you identify the things you aren't currently satisfied with and by tracing those "gripes" back to one or more basic causes. As previously discussed, the visible indicators of your dissatisfaction are called undesirable effects; the factors that originate them are known as root causes.

Why do you need a Current Reality Tree to identify the undesirable effects and root causes? In some cases you may not *need* a Current Reality Tree. Some situations are so simple and obvious that the root cause stands out like a sore thumb. But the world is complex, and many (if not most) situations encompass several factors or forces that interact to produce the effects we see around us. In such cases, a complete physical depiction of the situation makes it infinitely easier to visualize the interdependencies in the system.

Plant growth, for instance, is normally thought to be the result of three *necessary conditions:* water, nutrition, and light (see Figure 3.2). If a plant fails to grow properly, you must immediately consider deficiencies in one of those three areas. But the failure of a plant to grow may also be the result of factors beyond those three conditions, because while they may be necessary, they may not be sufficient—a favorable temperature range is needed, too. Diagnosing the problem may not be as simple as it looks, as most gardeners can tell you. Because most situations are complex, often with inconspicuous causes driving the results, it can be difficult deciding what to change to make the situation right. A Current Reality Tree can help reveal complex relationships.

For example, if your house is consistently too hot or cold, a knee-jerk reaction might be to adjust the thermostat in the central heating/air conditioning

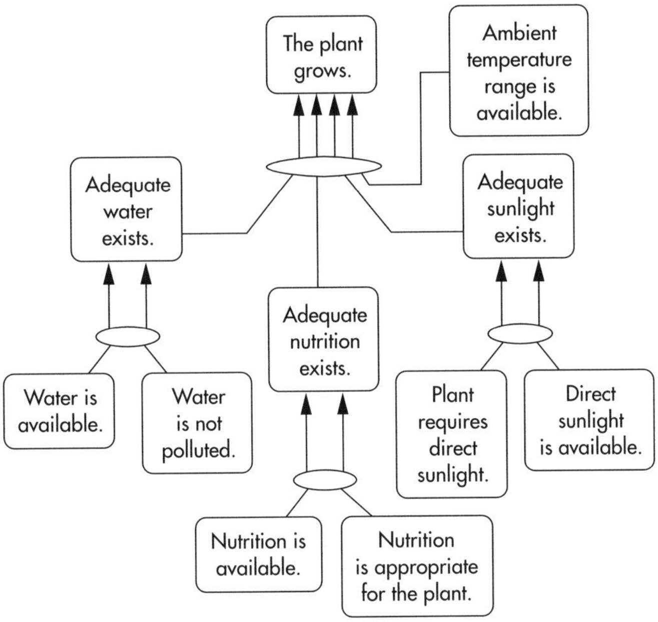

FIGURE 3.2. An Example of Plant Growth.

unit. Seems simple enough. But if the outside temperature fluctuates significantly during the course of a day, you could find yourself making a lot of adjustments. This might make the inside temperature acceptable, but it might also result in higher utility bills. The Current Reality Tree in Figure 3.3 shows how much more complex the situation could be than it actually seems. It also shows some root causes that, if you only adjust the thermostat, remain unaddressed and will allow the problem to continue or surface again at another time.

A Single Tool or Part of a Set

The Current Reality Tree can be used by itself to identify root causes of straightforward problems in your daily life. Or it can be used as the first step in the entire TOC thinking process, to effect major changes in complex systems. In either case, the process is the same. The final section in this chapter discusses the use of the Current Reality Tree with other TOC thinking process tools.

Span of Control and Sphere of Influence

Before we can effectively explain the Current Reality Tree, it's necessary to establish the context in which the CRT will be used.

We all function in complex systems with varying degrees of control over our environment. In some areas we have a high degree of control over parts or functions of that environment. These areas are said to lie within our *span of control.* We enjoy virtually complete authority to change anything within our span of control. Just outside our span of control lies our *sphere of influence,* a region of the environment where we can influence things to varying degrees but don't

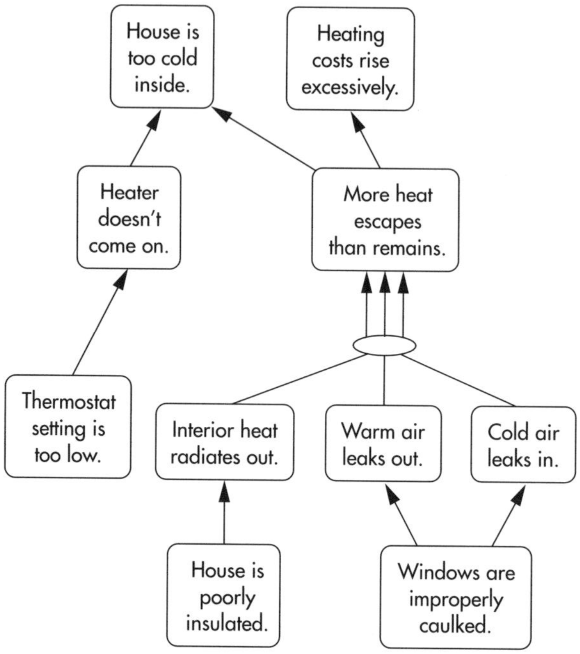

FIGURE 3.3. An Example of Temperature in a House.

enjoy direct control. Beyond our sphere of influence we have neither control nor influence (see Figure 3.4).

Once we understand this concept of reality, a few things about Current Reality Trees become apparent. In a complex situation, a CRT that accurately depicts reality might conceivably overlap all three regions: our span of control, our sphere of influence, and the outside, or uncontrolled, environment (see Figure 3.5). The most significant ramification of this situation is the effect it has on our decisions about what we can change in a system. If the most significant problems lie outside our span of control, we must depend on others for help. This means persuading others to do things they might not be obligated to do. If the problems lie outside our sphere of influence, we may not be able to do anything about them at all.

Keep this concept of span of control and sphere of influence in mind while you're building your Current Reality Tree. Don't let it limit you in its construction: Follow the cause-and-effect chain wherever it may lead you. But after the tree is done, and before you select which problem to attack, revisit the issue of sphere of influence. Use it to help you decide which problems you can reasonably expect effective results on and which ones might be futile to attack. Generally, solving problems, especially big ones, is a game in which you try to see how far toward the outer limits you can stretch your sphere of influence. "Root Causes" and "Core Problems," later in this section, address this subject in greater detail.

Enthusiasm without knowledge is like running in the dark.

—Unknown

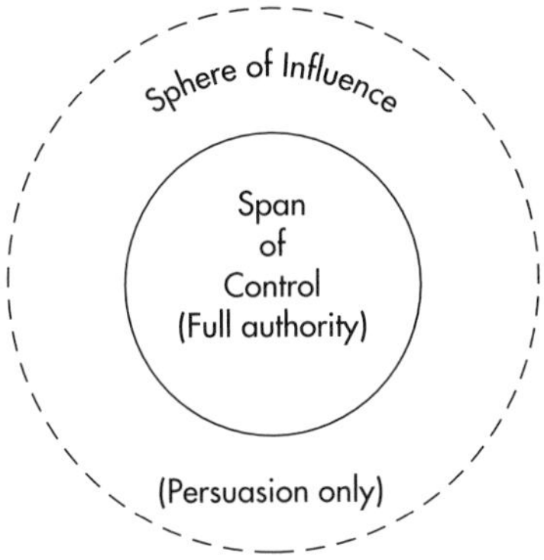

FIGURE 3.4. Span of Control and Sphere of Influence.

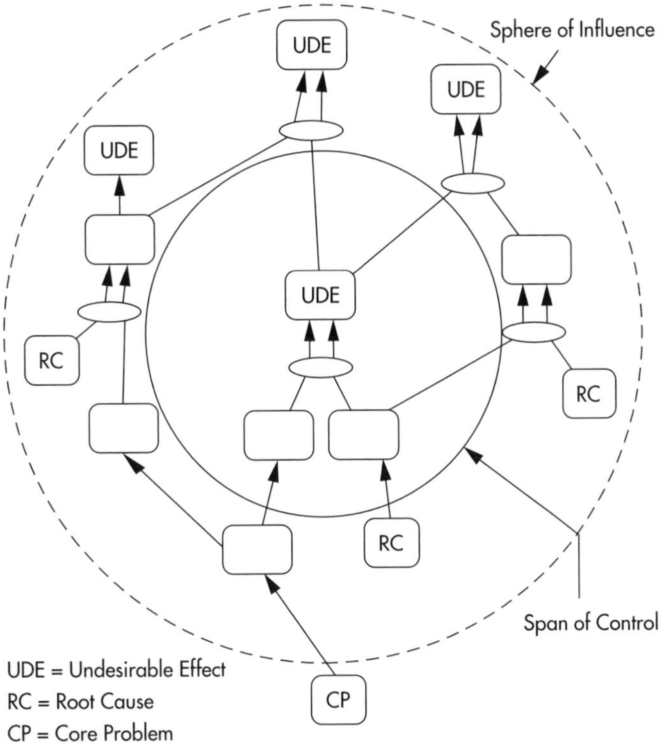

FIGURE 3.5. Span of Control, Sphere of Influence, and the CRT.

Correlation vs. Cause and Effect

The power of the Current Reality Tree comes from its basis in cause and effect. Sometimes people confuse cause and effect with correlation. It's important to understand the difference between the two, because Current Reality Trees with correlations embedded in them are prone to be invalid: They may isolate the wrong root causes, which could cost you time, energy, and resources in trying to solve the wrong problem. The grandest CRT will eventually collapse from an embedded correlation.

The difference between correlation and cause and effect is essentially the difference between *how* and *why*. You have a correlation when you can observe patterns and trends and conclude how one phenomenon behaves in relation to another. But the key element that correlation lacks is the answer to the question "Why?" Without knowing why, you'll never know what makes the correlation exist. This means you'll never be sure whether the correlation depends on other variables you haven't identified. In a problem analysis situation, this could cause you to focus on the wrong problem. It also means that you won't be able to effectively predict future instances of the correlation, because you'll never know whether a key variable is present or not.

The Junk Bond Example

Take, for example, the junk bond "feeding frenzy" among investors in the late 1980s (see Figure 3.6). People with no real understanding of cause and effect observed others buying large quantities of junk bonds making huge profits and concluded, "If I buy junk bonds, then I'll make a lot of money." They erroneously attached cause-and-effect significance to a correlation. Some did make money. But many people who bought the junk bonds incurred large losses, because the correlation depended on other inconspicuous but critical variables that were subject to change without notice. A basic assumption in cause and effect is that, under the same circumstances, an expected effect must be replicable from the same cause (See "Assumptions," p. 65). In the junk bond case, a different outcome resulted from what people assumed to be the same cause, so there really was no cause and effect, only a correlation.

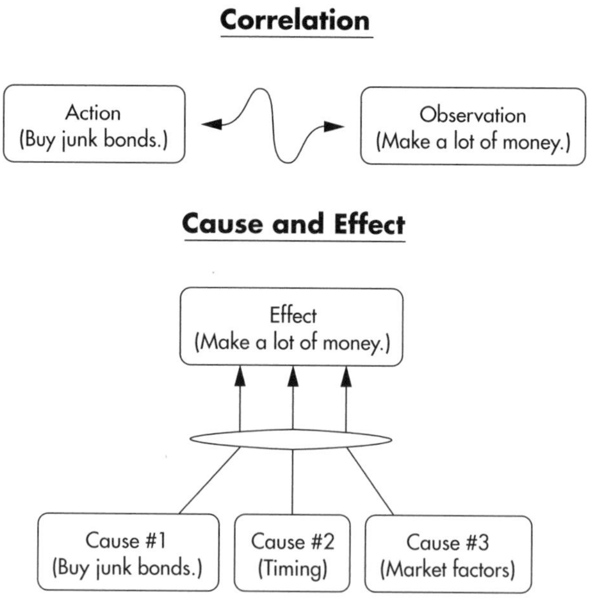

FIGURE 3.6. Correlation vs. Cause and Effect: The Junk Bond Example.

This is why decisions based on correlations are inherently less sound than those based on cause and effect. But how do we ensure that we don't fall victim to correlation in our Current Reality Trees? The answer is the Categories of Legitimate Reservation (CLR). Effective application of the CLR ensures that correlation is not confused with cause and effect. As you proceed through this chapter, it will be helpful to refer periodically to chapter 2, "Categories of Legitimate Reservation." With an understanding of the importance of cause and effect, now let's look at the elements that make up a Current Reality Tree.

Undesirable Effects

One of the first elements of a Current Reality Tree that you will encounter is the undesirable effect (UDE). What is an undesirable effect? Essentially, it's the first indication you have that something might be amiss in a system. A UDE is something that *really exists* and is *negative on its own merits* (see Figure 3.7). You might be aware of many UDEs. Or you might notice just one. In a complex system, there will probably be several. But you can start a Current Reality Tree with as few as one.

Undesirable to Whom?

UDEs are subjective to some degree. What is undesirable for one person may not be for another; it may even be desirable for some people.

Note: An effect that is obviously desirable for one person or group but undesirable for another is a "warning flag" indicating a conflict that must be surfaced and resolved. It is also a likely indication of *suboptimization* in the system—one person

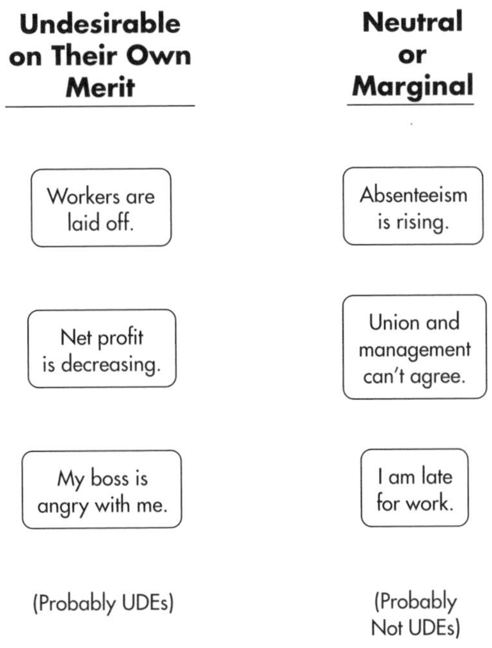
Undesirable on Their Own Merit
Neutral or Marginal
Workers are laid off.
Absenteeism is rising.
Net profit is decreasing.
Union and management can't agree.
My boss is angry with me.
I am late for work.
(Probably UDEs)
(Probably Not UDEs)

FIGURE 3.7. Undesirable Effects.

or group maximizing their own performance at the expense of the entire organization. Don't interrupt building your Current Reality Tree to handle conflict at this early stage. You may miss some critical element of the conflict by not completing the CRT. Instead, make note of the conflict and consider using the Conflict Resolution Diagram to resolve it. Refer to chapter 4, "Conflict Resolution Diagram," for more on how to use this powerful tool to resolve conflict.

Clearly, an individual's own concept of "negative" will influence what might be considered a UDE. Another major consideration might be, "For whom am I constructing this tree?" If you're doing it solely for yourself (that is, you're operating within your span of control), *you* can be the final arbiter of what's negative. But if you're doing it to convince others to take action (you're operating in your sphere of influence), you'll probably have to consider what *they* might define as negative.

How to Identify and Check for Undesirability

To determine whether you've really got a UDE or just a "fact of life," phrase the effect in a complete sentence. Then look for these indications of negativity:

- Are there pejorative words present (words like "punishment," "job loss," "anger," "resentment," and so forth)?
- Are others in my organization or situation likely to agree that these effects are negative in and of themselves (for example, "decreased profits," "excessive time/cost," and the like)?
- Would society at large agree that the effects are negative (for example, "increased crime rate," "health deterioration," and so forth)?
- Is it important to you, the tree-builder, and does it constitute an unacceptable deviation?
- Does it adversely affect the Throughput in your system (however Throughput may be defined)?

If you can answer "yes" to any of these questions, you probably have a UDE. But as a last check, give it the "So what?" test. Read the statement as if someone else were saying it to you, and respond, "So what?" Your first reaction will probably be to come up with a "Because . . .". If you have a valid "because . . .", that may actually be your UDE. If the statement needs no "because . . .", it can probably stand alone as negative.

Existence in Reality

The second test of a valid UDE is *existence*. Does it really exist, or is it someone's negative fantasy? Consider the example in Figure 3.8:

If *I speak my mind* . . . then *my boss fires me.*

The effect is unarguably negative to the tree-builder. But does it really exist? Is the boss really unable to deal objectively and nonpunitively with something he or she may not like to hear? Or is this a worst-case scenario with very little probability of happening? Here's a slightly different example: "Sales are down." Is that a fact, or is it just somebody's perception? Are there verifiable data to confirm that this effect really exists?

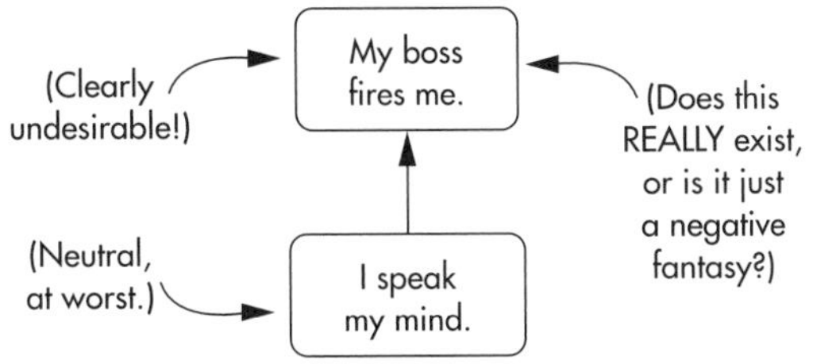

FIGURE 3.8. Undesirable Effects: Do They Really Exist?

Why the Emphasis on UDEs?

Why is effective UDE identification so important to building a good Current Reality Tree? We focus on UDEs for the same reason the media focuses on negative stories—they're higher in visibility, and we want to get rid of them. They're what make us feel bad about our situation. We start with UDEs because doing so speeds our analysis of what's wrong with our system and generally leads to faster improvement. The UDEs are only the most visible results of much more complex interactions and processes, but they're the "gateway" to finding the real problem. If you choose the wrong gateway, you won't find the right problem. So some degree of care in selecting your UDEs is warranted.

Complex problems have simple, easy-to-understand wrong answers.
—Grossman's Misquote of H. L. Mencken

Root Causes

In building a Current Reality Tree, we work our way from UDEs back through the chain of cause and effect to root causes. The root cause is the beginning of the cause-effect relationship. There may be several intermediate effects and causes between the root cause and the UDE. These may not be neutral, or even positive (from a subjective point of view). But when you've worked your way down to a cause and you just can't go any farther, you're at a root cause.

Why might you not be able to go any farther? Theoretically, you could trace cause and effect all the way back to the creation of the world. But from a practical standpoint, you quickly exceed your span of control and soon thereafter your sphere of influence. There's no point in working on something over which you don't have at least *some* influence. So a prime indication that you may have reached a root cause in your tree is finding yourself at the boundary of your sphere of influence. The root cause can be:

- The lowest cause in the chain before passing outside your sphere of influence—the most basic thing you can do something about
- The first cause *beyond* your sphere of influence—something you can't do anything about.

For example, in Figure 3.9 there are two root causes:

1. "The formal reward system doesn't satisfy important individual needs."
2. "People's behavior is motivated by unsatisfied needs."

The first is a condition of the system itself, which you may have some latitude to change; that is, it lies within your sphere of influence. The second is a condition of human nature, which you are unlikely to have any influence over whatsoever—it clearly lies outside your sphere of influence. *Both* can be considered root causes. One you have to live with, the other you don't. And it's the latter one that provides your problem-solving flexibility.

Every Current Reality Tree will have several root causes—maybe even a lot of them. Every cause statement that has arrows coming out of it but no arrows going in is technically considered a root cause (see Figure 3.10). It's worth remembering that a root cause is a *point of origin* in a CRT—no more, no less. The term does not necessarily connote anything negative.

For example, "The sun shines every day" might be a root cause of skin cancer, but it's not necessarily negative in and of itself—it's just a fact of life. A root cause may be positive, negative, or neutral, depending on your perception, but most will have no particular significance. A few, however, will.

Core Problems

One root cause in any Current Reality Tree is likely to be the origin of a substantial number of UDEs (see Figure 3.11). While this is not a hard-and-fast rule, it does apply in the majority of Current Reality Trees. The primary objective of the CRT is to work backward from UDEs through a chain of cause and effect to

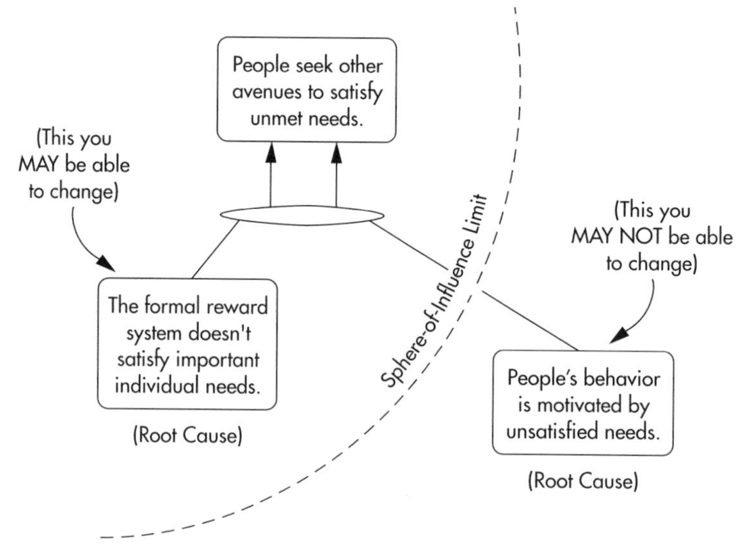

FIGURE 3.9. Root Causes.

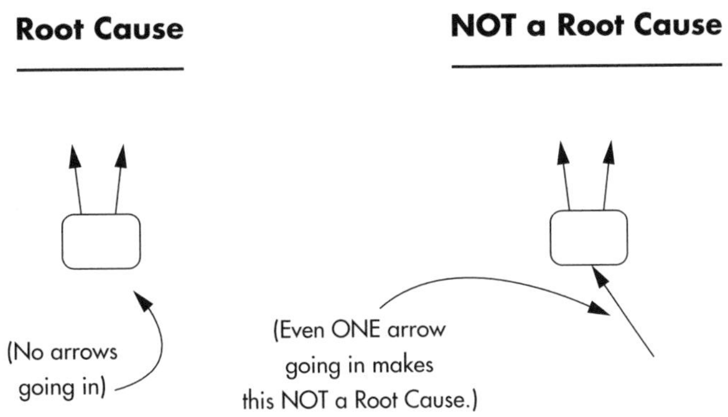
Root Cause
NOT a Root Cause
(No arrows going in)
(Even ONE arrow going in makes this NOT a Root Cause.)

FIGURE 3.10. Identifying Core Problems.

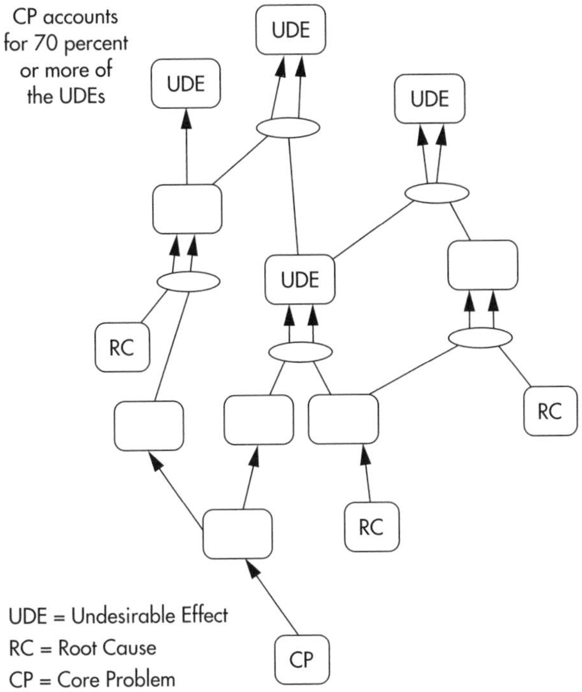
CP accounts for 70 percent or more of the UDEs
UDE
UDE
UDE
UDE
RC
RC
RC
CP
UDE = Undesirable Effect
RC = Root Cause
CP = Core Problem

FIGURE 3.11. Identifying the Core Problem.

identify this root cause. When this cause accounts for 70 percent or more of the UDEs in a CRT, it is considered a *core problem* (CP). Besides accounting for a majority of the UDEs, the core problem should match your intuition about the condition of the system. After you've tentatively identified it, you should feel confident in saying, "This *really is* the big problem in this system."

While every Current Reality Tree can be built downward to a core problem eventually, that core problem may be beyond your sphere of influence (see Figure 3.12). In such a case, for all practical purposes you don't have a core problem. Instead, for a realistic probability of successful application, you'll have to work with a number of root causes rather than a single core problem. None of these root causes may account for 70 percent of your UDEs. But if you don't have much chance of affecting the core problem, you'll have to deal with the root causes you can influence.

For example, if the problem were to concern your local public school system, you might find that an underfunded school budget is the core problem driving most of the UDEs (see Figure 3.13). However, since most of public school funding

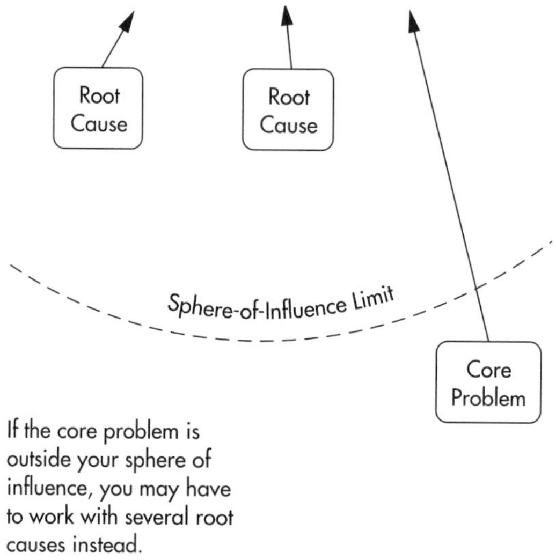

FIGURE 3.12. Stay Within Your Sphere of Influence.

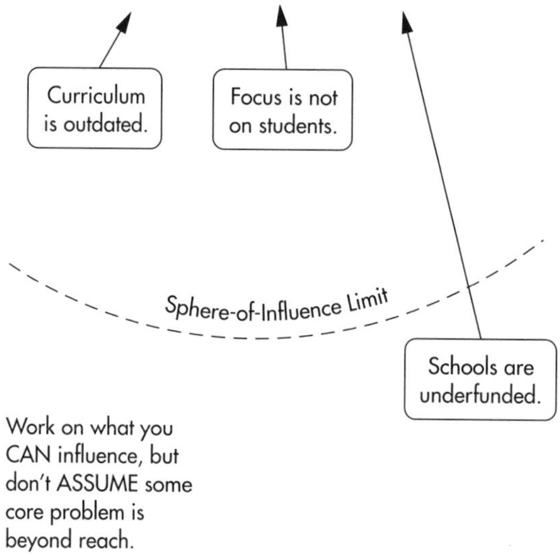

FIGURE 3.13. Sphere of Influence: Education System Example.

is disbursed by the state, rather than by cities, the state department of education is likely to be outside your personal sphere of influence. You may have to work instead with a number of root causes at the local level.

Remember, however, that your purpose in building a Current Reality Tree is to try to find the one problem that, if corrected, will have the greatest positive impact on system improvement—the most "bang for your buck." So, if possible, you should exhaust every possibility before concluding that you'll have to settle for working several root causes rather than reaching a core problem.

> ***At some time in the life cycle of virtually every organization, its ability to succeed in spite of itself runs out.***
>
> ***—Brien's First Law***

Validity Test

How can you be sure a root cause you've picked is really a core problem? Here's a simple test:

- Can you trace a chain of cause and effect *upward* through the CRT to 70 percent or more of the UDEs?
- Does the proposed core problem match your intuition about the source of the difficulties?
- Is it really a big problem? Does it really "burn you up"?
- Will the correction of this difficulty assure that the problem will not occur again—now or in the future?

If you can answer "yes" to these four questions, you've found your core problem.

Missing Elements or Connections

What if you've worked your way back to a number of root causes, most within your sphere of influence, and none seem to qualify as a core problem? This is not a rare occurrence. Often the failure to identify a core problem is the result of missing elements or connections.

A missing element would be a cause that you haven't yet identified at a lower level in the tree. This cause may join two "branches" of your tree in what is known as a V-shaped connection (see Figure 3.14). You should be especially watchful for these connections the closer you get to root causes.

A missing connection is an undiscovered link between parts of the Current Reality Tree you've already finished. It may pass through one or more intermediate effects that you have overlooked (see Figure 3.15).

If you find yourself with a series of root causes but no core problem, perform the following checks:

- Visually compare each root cause, one at a time, with every other root cause. Ask yourself, "Are these two related in some way? What one entity might cause these two to exist?" Continue comparing until all combinations are checked, or until you find a V-shaped connection you can add.
- Scan the existing branches of your Current Reality Tree. Look for entities in different branches that appear to be related. Connect them, if possible. Add intermediate causes/effects as required to solidify the relationship.

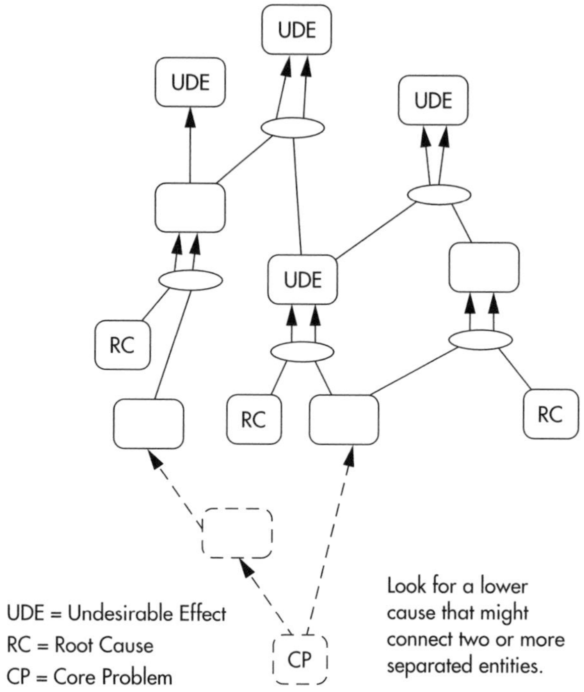
UDE
UDE
UDE
RC
UDE
RC
RC
CP
UDE = Undesirable Effect
RC = Root Cause
CP = Core Problem
Look for a lower cause that might connect two or more separated entities.

FIGURE 3.14. V-Shaped Connections.

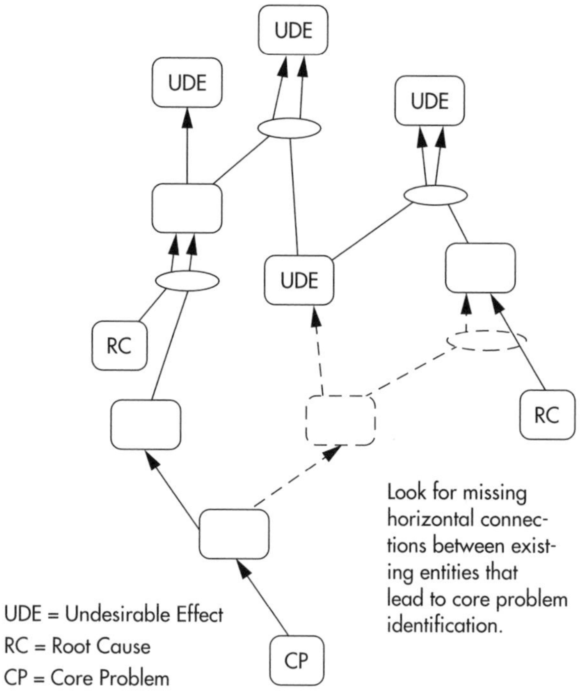
UDE
UDE
UDE
UDE
RC
RC
CP
UDE = Undesirable Effect
RC = Root Cause
CP = Core Problem
Look for missing horizontal connections between existing entities that lead to core problem identification.

FIGURE 3.15. Missing Connections.

In the final analysis, you may not be able to make V-shaped connections or lateral connections between branches, even with outside assistance or scrutiny. You may not be able to isolate a core problem. You may have to work with multiple root causes. But do everything you can to isolate a core problem. Any such effort is a worthwhile investment in time and energy.

Note: Everyone would like to get to a single core problem all the time. Obviously, it makes things neater, and it seems to give us a sense of confidence that a solution can be focused on a single issue. But sometimes "forcing" a Current Reality Tree to a core problem "contrives unnatural connections." In such cases, you're probably better off dealing with several root causes than artificially creating a V-shaped connection just to "wrap" a Core Problem around some diverse causes. Often such core problems must be so vaguely worded (for example, "ineffective corporate policies") that they're almost impossible to deal with in the solution phase. MORAL: Use good judgment. Don't force a V-shaped connection that doesn't seem to occur naturally just to get a single core problem. However, be sure that no UDE is left unconnected, even if you don't identify a single core problem.

Depicting a Current Reality Tree

The symbology used to depict current reality is straightforward (see Figure 3.16). A round-cornered rectangle indicates a cause or effect. Effects that are undesirable are highlighted in some way, through either stars, asterisks, or perhaps drop shadows. Arrows connect causes with effects. And ellipses are used to indicate that two or more causes must combine to produce the effect.

Entities

As you will notice from reading other chapters of this book, all of the TOC logic trees contain statements bordered by some kind of geometric figure. In the Current Reality Tree you will see only round-cornered rectangles. Conflict Resolution Diagrams have both round-cornered and sharp-cornered rectangles. Future

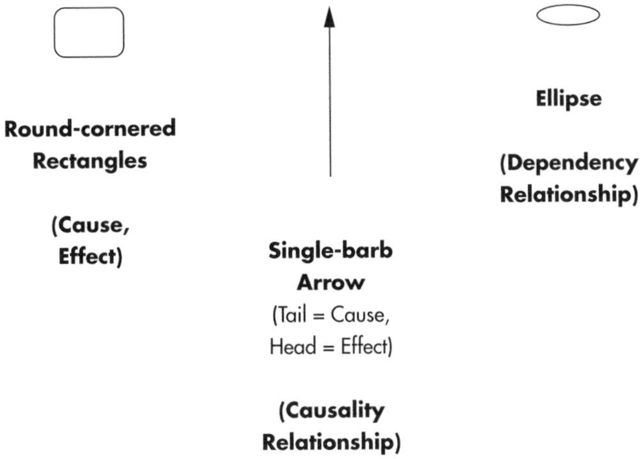
Round-cornered Rectangles
(Cause, Effect)
Single-barb Arrow
(Tail = Cause, Head = Effect)
(Causality Relationship)
Ellipse
(Dependency Relationship)

FIGURE 3.16. CRT Symbology.

Reality Trees have both round and sharp-cornered rectangles, as do Transition Trees. Prerequisite Trees have hexagons and square-cornered rectangles. These figures and the statements they enclose fall into the general category of "entities." The name itself implies that the statement can stand alone, so it must be a complete sentence that conveys a complete idea.

Why an "Entity"?

Why do we need a term like "entity"? If a scrutinizer were to say, "I think there's a missing entity," he or she is telling you that a significant block on your tree has been left out. It may be a cause, effect, injection, objective, obstacle, or intermediate objective. The scrutinizer is trying to give you the maximum opportunity for self-discovery by not giving you the answer—for example, "You left out an Obstacle on your PRT," or "You need another Injection in your FRT." It's much more to your advantage to find your own deficiencies than to have someone else show them to you.

Sometimes a procedure will direct you to "connect the entities," or "develop additional entities." It's referring to these statements enclosed with a geometric figure. But because a "canned" procedure can't always determine what kind of statement is needed in every situation, a term is needed to encompass all possible options. So when you see the word "entity," remember that its use was specifically intended so as not to exclude possibilities by using another, more specific term.

Entities in a Current Reality Tree

With a Current Reality Tree, the issue is simple: An entity is either a cause or an effect. Or it can be both, that is, the effect of one cause and the cause of another. This is what enables us to create chains of cause and effect.

Arrows

Arrows appear in *every* TOC thinking process tool, but they signify different relationships. In the Current Reality, Future Reality, and Transition Trees, they signify sufficiency in a cause-and-effect relationship. In an Evaporating Cloud and a Prerequisite Tree they represent a necessary—but not necessarily sufficient—condition relationship. Refer to the section in chapter 2, "Sufficiency-Based vs. Necessity-Based Logic Trees," p. 56, for more details on this distinction.

In the Current Reality Tree, the arrow implies a sufficiency relationship: The cause, positioned at the tail of the arrow, is sufficient to produce the effect, located at the head of the arrow. To read a cause-effect relationship (two entities connected by an arrow), attach "If . . ." to the beginning of the cause statement and ". . . then . . ." to the beginning of the effect statement.

> If *I turn off the light,* then *the room is dark.*

However, you must be careful in using and reading arrows in a Current Reality Tree. The previous example has a catch to it (see Figure 3.17). It assumes that (a) it's dark (that is, night) outside the room, or (b) there are no windows or other openings that could admit other light. These assumptions aren't stated in the cause-effect relationship, but they're there just the same, and they have a direct bearing on the validity of the cause-effect relationship.

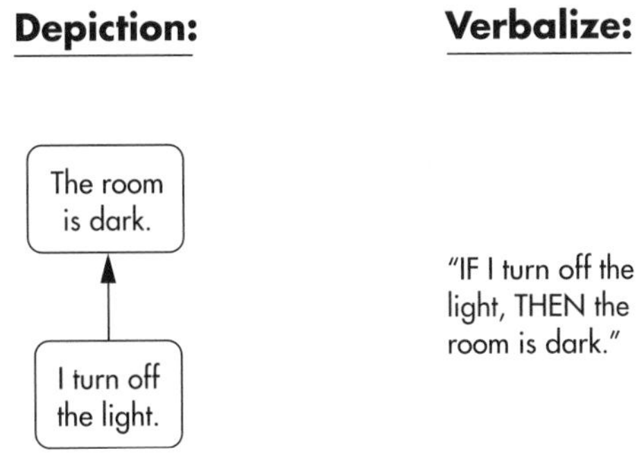

FIGURE 3.17. Cause Sufficiency.

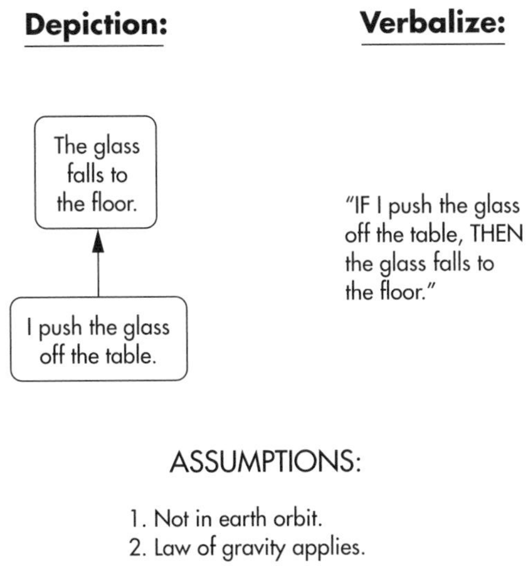

FIGURE 3.18. Underlying Assumptions.

Underlying Assumptions

Every arrow in a Current Reality Tree is based on unstated but underlying assumptions about the situation, environment, or laws of nature. For example, consider this cause-and-effect relationship, depicted with entities and an arrow (see Figure 3.18):

> If *I push the glass off the table, then it falls to the floor.*

There is an unstated but underlying assumption here that the law of gravity applies in this situation. "Well, of course," you're probably thinking, "That's obvious. Gravity *always* applies." Perhaps. But maybe not. Astronauts in orbit around the earth don't need to worry about the glass falling to the floor; they have to worry about it floating away, because the underlying assumption about gravity does not apply in their situation. As a result, when the underlying assumptions change, *the same cause results in a different effect.* Keep this in mind, both when you build your own trees and when you scrutinize someone else's: What are the assumptions underlying the arrows? And the follow-up question is: "In light of these assumptions, does the cause-effect relationship make sense?" Chapter 2, "Categories of Legitimate Reservation," provides more guidance on analyzing cause-effect relationships.

Ellipses

The ellipse is unique to sufficiency-based logic trees (Current Reality, Future Reality, and Transition Trees). Its function is to encompass multiple causes that must all be present to produce the effect in question (see Figure 3.19). The absence of any one cause whose arrow passes through the ellipse is enough to destroy the cause-effect relationship. However, the most common situation you're likely to encounter is a missing ellipse—a contributing cause requiring an ellipse to combine it with the one you've already stated.

Let's recall the example, "*If* I turn off the light, *then* the room is dark." It's conceivable that turning off the light alone is not sufficient to make the room dark (see Figure 3.20). You might add another cause: ". . . and *if* the room has no windows. . . ." Is this sufficient yet? No? How about adding: ". . . and *if* the only door into the room is closed . . . ." Now it's a pretty tight, or "dry," cause-effect relationship.

REMEMBER: We live in a complex world. Most effects result from multiple causes, some independent, some contributing. An independent cause is a single entity, sufficient by itself, to produce the effect. Sometimes, when several independent causes apply, they are referred to as additional causes (see "Additional Cause," p. 42, for a more detailed explanation). A *contributing cause* is one of two or more factors that alone can't produce the effect, but together will. Contributing cause arrows are always enclosed by an ellipse. You should look at every causality arrow critically and ask yourself the question, "Is an ellipse required?"

Note: It isn't necessary to include every underlying assumption or potential contributing cause in your Current Reality Tree. It would quickly get out of hand if you did. Your decision rule should be: "For whom am I building this tree?" If it's for

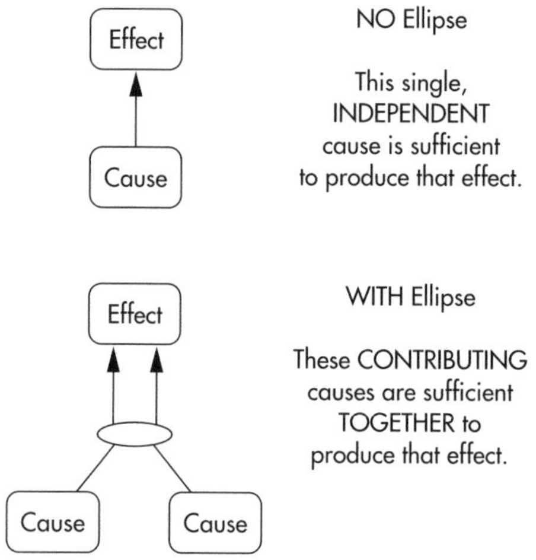

FIGURE 3.19. Ellipses.

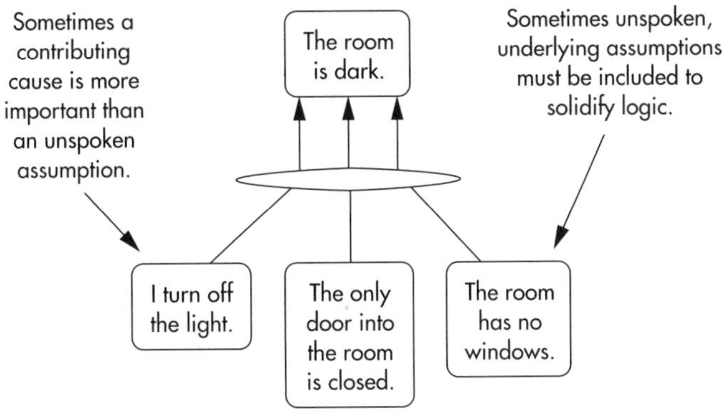

FIGURE 3.20. Cause Sufficiency (with an Ellipse).

yourself alone, and it's about an environment in which you have good intuitive knowledge, you can leave much more unstated but assumed. If you're going to present your tree to someone else, you have to consider how much they might know about the situation. Trees presented to others must usually be more detailed (that is, with fewer unstated assumptions and more contributing causes) to preclude confusion and embarrassment.

Numbering Entities in a Tree

Sometimes logic trees (Current Reality, Future Reality, Prerequisite, and Transition) can become quite complex. Figures 3.44 and 5.35 show just how complex they can be. An extremely complex tree can be both intimidating and frustrating to a reader, especially someone who isn't familiar with the graphical way of presenting cause-and-effect logic. As tree-builders, we have an obligation to make the reader's job as easy as possible. One way to do this is to use an orderly means of numbering entities in a tree. The sidebar, "Numbering Entities in a Tree," describes one such approach. You may elect to use a different one of your own, but the objective should still remain clear in your mind: Keep it simple and easy to follow.

SIDEBAR

NUMBERING ENTITIES IN A TREE

A tree can have as few as 10 to 20 entities, or it might have hundreds. The U.S. Transportation Command, for example, constructed a Current Reality Tree with 170 undesirable effects alone, not to mention the rest of the entities leading to these UDEs. Without some kind of coherent numbering system, tracing the chain of cause and effect from root causes to UDEs could be a nearly impossible task.

So how should the entities in a logic tree by numbered? Whatever method you choose should have three basic characteristics (see Figure 3.21):

1. Numbers should increase in the direction of the arrows.
2. It should be easy to follow connections to other pages.
3. A given page should be easy to locate quickly, without undue searching.

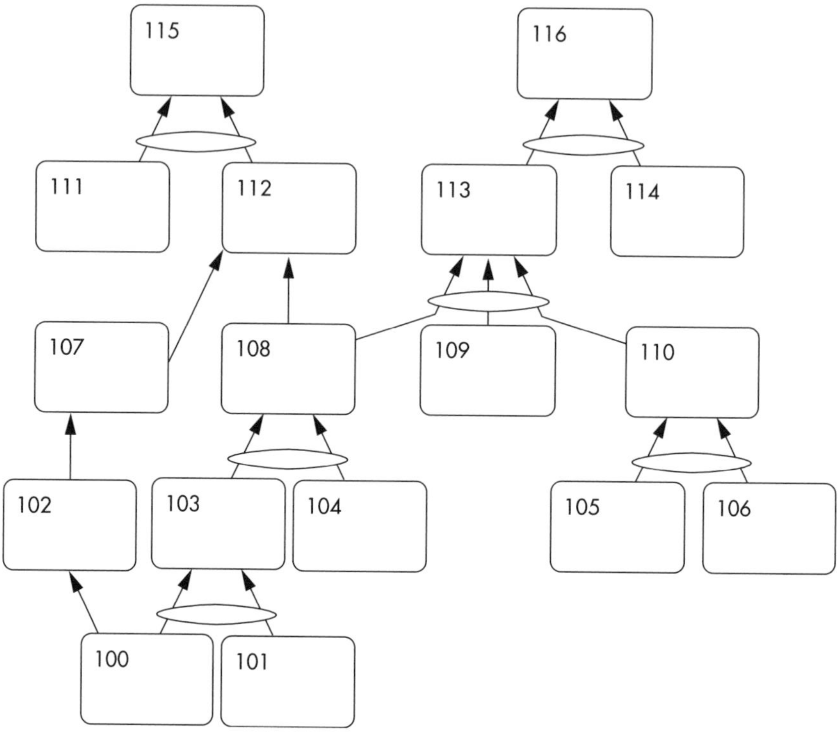

FIGURE 3.21. A Cause-Effect Tree on One Page.

No one numbering method is necessarily the best. The one suggested here meets the characteristics just mentioned, and offers some other benefits as well.

One numbering sequence will probably suffice if your tree can be confined to one $8^1/_2'' \times 11''$ page, or if you're using paper large enough to keep the tree on one page. Once you have a need for two or more pages, start a new sequence for the second page (see Figure 3.22).

- Don't number your entities until you're sure the tree is as logically sound as you can make it (that is, you think all the entities you'll need are present).
- Use a three-digit method, starting with 100. Every time you start a new page, begin a new sequence (for example, 200 on page 2, 300 on page 3, and so forth) (see Figure 3.23).
- Later, if you decide you need to add entities use decimal numbers for the new additions (for example, 217.1, 224.5, 234.7, and so forth).
- When a cause on one page leads to an effect on another page, show the "destination entity number" on the cause page, and the "originating entity number" on the effect page (see Figure 3.24). Replicate the cause on the effect page, with a heavy border for emphasis, to draw attention to the fact that it originated on another page. Beside each off-page connection, indicate the page the connection is going *to* (or the page the entity came *from*).

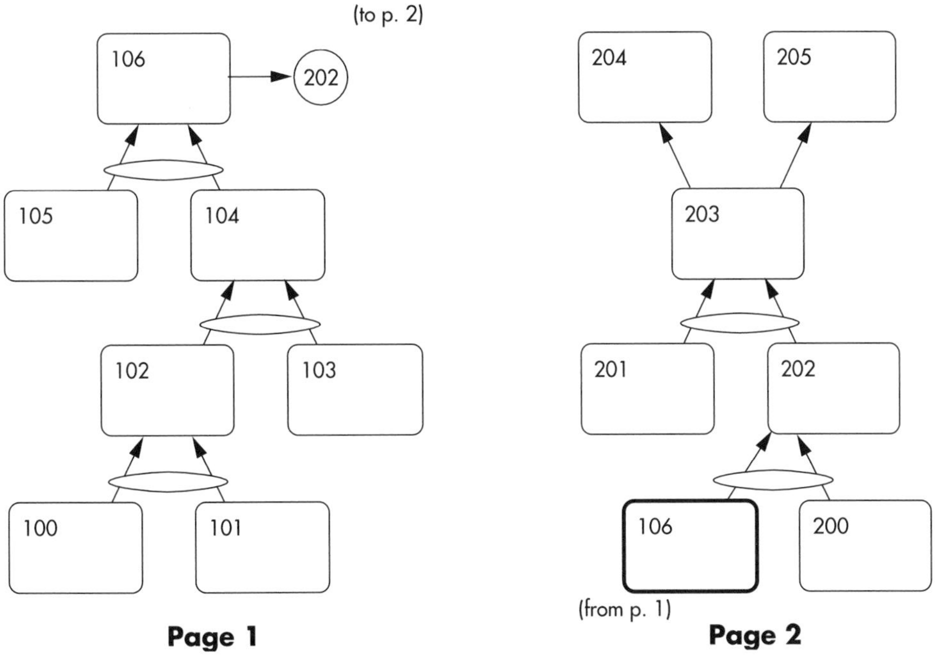

FIGURE 3.22. A Cause-Effect Tree on Two Pages.

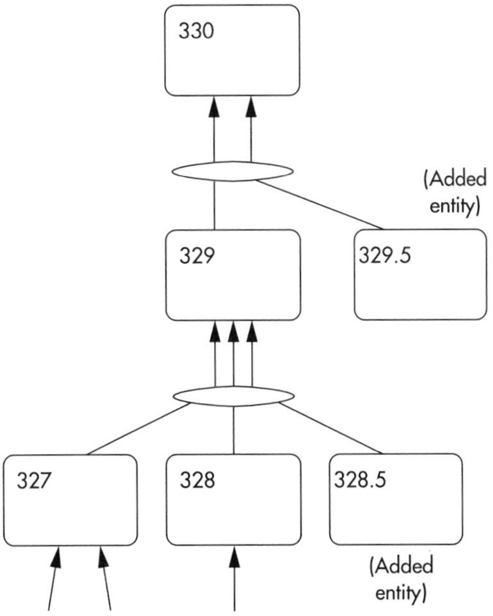

FIGURE 3.23. Adding Entities After Numbers Have Been Assigned.

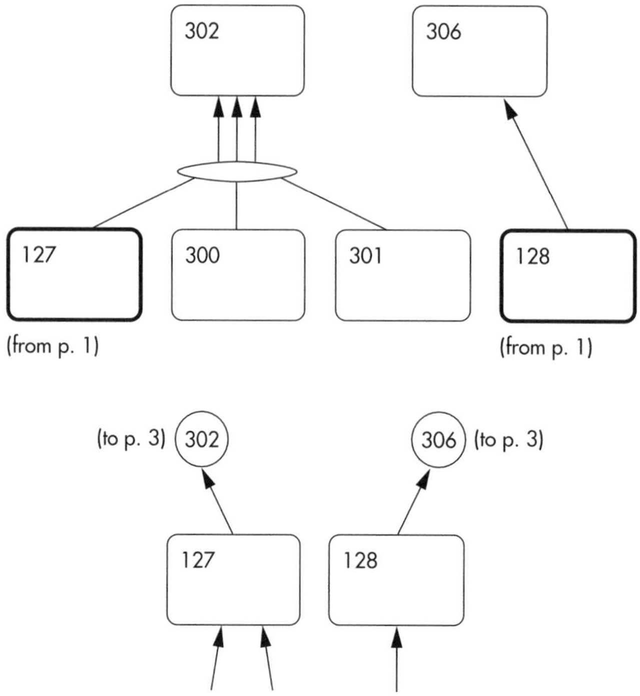

FIGURE 3.24. Off-Page Connections.

Reading a Current Reality Tree

The Current Reality Tree is relatively easy to read. Since every entity must be worded as a complete sentence, each cause or effect can become a comprehensible clause in a complex sentence. Locate the entity at the tail of the arrow, and read it aloud, preceded by the word "If." After that, read the entity at the head of the arrow, preceded by the word "then." If you have several causes joined by an ellipse, read the "If" only once, with the other contributing cause statements joined by "and." For example:

> If *people don't stop for red lights,* then *odds of accidents increase (see Figure 3.25).*
>
> ***or***
>
> If *people have little motivation to apply total quality principles,* and *successful total quality implementation requires major organizational change,* then *people are not likely to be motivated to change as required to successfully implement total quality (see Figure 3.26).*

Negative Reinforcing Loops

As you begin building your Current Reality Tree, connecting the UDEs, and working your way down to root causes, you might occasionally notice a special relationship between a UDE and a cause lower in the tree. Sometimes an undesirable effect actually reinforces the cause that produced it. This is known as a *negative reinforcing loop* (Figure 3.27). It represents both bad and good news.

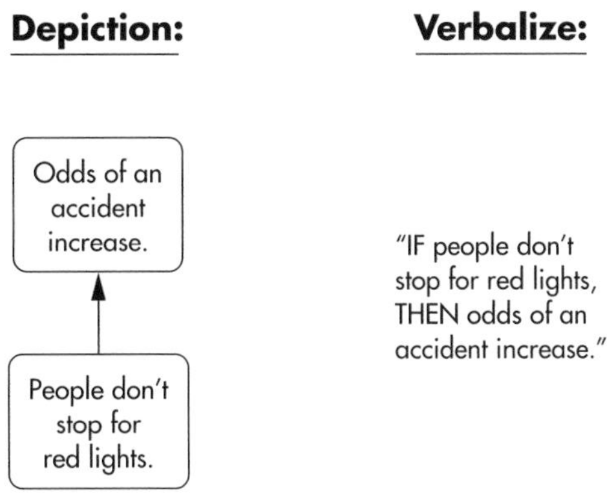
Depiction:
Verbalize:
Odds of an accident increase.
People don't stop for red lights.
"IF people don't stop for red lights, THEN odds of an accident increase."

FIGURE 3.25. Reading a CRT: Single Independent Cause.

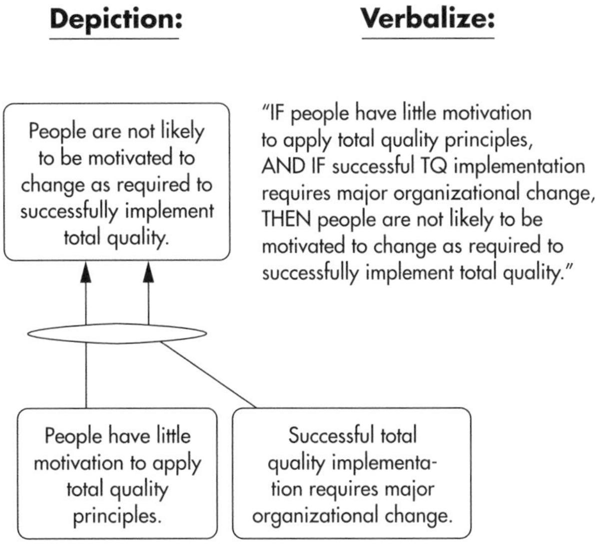
Depiction:
Verbalize:
People are not likely to be motivated to change as required to successfully implement total quality.
People have little motivation to apply total quality principles.
Successful total quality implementation requires major organizational change.
"IF people have little motivation to apply total quality principles, AND IF successful TQ implementation requires major organizational change, THEN people are not likely to be motivated to change as required to successfully implement total quality."

FIGURE 3.26. Reading a CRT: Multiple Dependent Causes.

It's bad news, because if you find such a phenomenon, it means that you have a self-perpetuating bad situation. It may even magnify the undesirable effect with each iteration of the loop. This is a kind of "death spiral," in which the system causes continual deterioration in itself.

However, the fact that you can identify a negative reinforcing loop is good news, because once you know it's there you can take steps to break it. The cause involved in such a loop may or may not be the core problem. But because of the self-perpetuating characteristic of those entities that are part of the loop, you need to examine the loop carefully.

- Will it disappear if the core problem is solved?
- Will you need to take additional specific actions to break the loop?

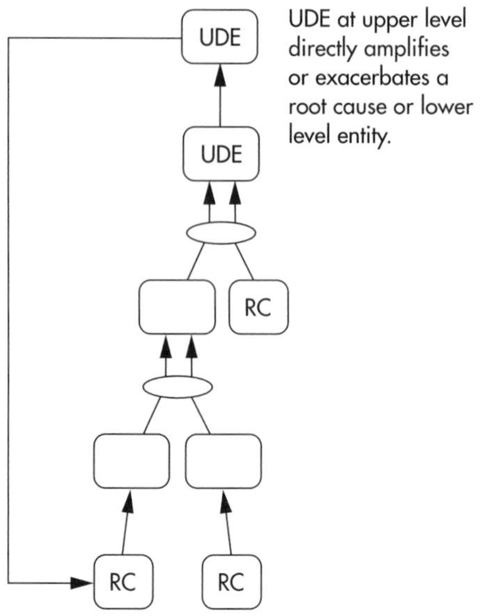

FIGURE 3.27. Negative Reinforcing Loop (Feedback).

- Is it possible that the right corrective action could turn it into a *positive reinforcing loop?* (Refer to chapter 5, "Future Reality Tree," for more on positive reinforcing loops.)

A negative reinforcing loop is such an undesirable condition that correcting it will often significantly reduce the magnitude of undesirable effects even if nothing else is done to alleviate the core problem.

It's a simple thing to make things complex, but a complex task to make them simple.

—Meyer's Law

BUILDING A CURRENT REALITY TREE

Now you're ready to begin constructing your own Current Reality Tree. Before you start, does your situation *qualify* for a CRT?

- Do you have adequate *intuitive knowledge* about the situation? Are you able to recognize and understand patterns and interactions in your system?
- Do you care about finding a solution to the problem? Have you assumed *ownership* of the problem? Do you have a burning desire to fix it?

If you can answer "yes" to these questions, you're ready to proceed. Let's assume that you've already recognized that a Current Reality Tree would be appropriate for your situation. There's something you don't like and want to change about your circumstances. You are able to say, confidently, "It really bothers me that . . ." and put your finger on a few aggravating aspects of the situation. What's the first thing you must do?

1. Identify Your Span of Control and Sphere of Influence

It should be fairly easy to define your span of control—those things you have authority to change. It's a little tougher to delimit your sphere of influence (see Figure 3.28). That will vary, depending on the "direction" you're facing. In some areas, your sphere of influence may not exceed your span of control by very much. In other areas it may be very broad. Moreover, you should not forget that to a great extent *you can determine how far out you want your sphere of influence to be.* People of no particular standing in society often find that their influence can reach all the way to the halls of government in Washington, D.C., if they put their minds to it. This first step is a mental exercise. There's no need to write anything down. Just create a picture in your mind of how far out your influence might extend. And don't forget: It may be a lot farther out than you think.

2. Create a List of Undesirable Effects

Start with a clean sheet of paper. At the top, in the center, write a one-sentence summary of the problem you're dealing with. Write it as a question. Since we're looking for a chain of cause and effect, the key question is "Why?" so build your statement around that. For example, "Why am I not happy with my life?" or "Why does total quality implementation fail?"

Now it's time for a little "reality testing"—is that "why" statement really valid? Below the "why" statement, start listing the reasons you know it to be true. What are the indications you see that tend to confirm your statement of the problem—the undesirable effects? If it really is a problem, you shouldn't have any trouble coming up with some indicators that really exist and that you consider negative on their own merits.

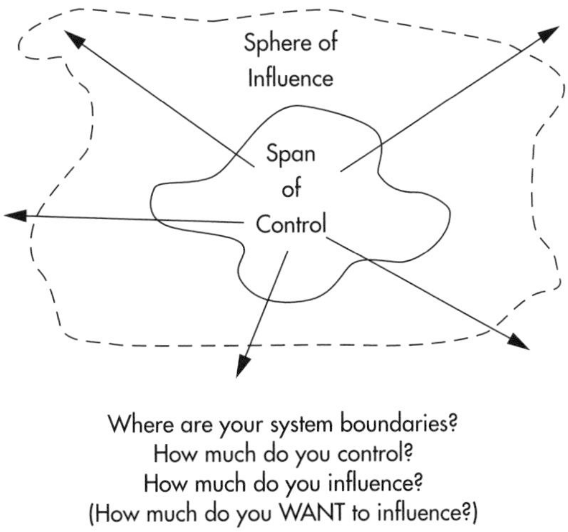
Sphere of Influence
Span of Control
Where are your system boundaries?
How much do you control?
How much do you influence?
(How much do you WANT to influence?)

FIGURE 3.28. Identifying Your Span of Control and Sphere of Influence.

List one to five UDEs. If you can't think of at least one, then forget this exercise. You don't have a problem. In a really bad situation, you may be able to think of 10 or more UDEs. If you can think of this many UDEs, list them all, then select the worst five to start with. Don't discard the rest; set them aside for inclusion in the Current Reality Tree later. Five UDEs is a good, manageable number to start with. *Write the UDEs in complete, grammatically correct sentences.* For example:

Why does total quality implementation fail?

- People resist the changes necessary for TQ to succeed.
- TQ creates more "red tape" and paperwork.
- TQ seems to take too long to generate positive results.
- Credibility of management commitment to TQ is low.
- Quality improvements don't seem to last.

Check each one for "undesirability"—that is, when someone else reads it, will it really stand alone as negative on its own merit, without additional explanation from you about why it's negative? Would another person reasonably knowledgeable about the situation consider it negative, too? If so, it qualifies as a UDE.

Then, using the Categories of Legitimate Reservation (CLR), subject each UDE to the Entity Existence reservation. (Refer to chapter 2, "Categories of Legitimate Reservation," for more on Entity Existence.)

3. Begin the Current Reality Tree

You'll need a large piece of paper (see Figure 3.29). (Standard 8½″ × 11″ paper won't do.) Try to find easel flip-chart paper, or use butcher block paper or the back of a sheet of wrapping paper—as long as it's about 20″ × 30″ or larger. If all you have is standard bond paper, tape sheets together until you've approximated those dimensions.

You'll also need a lot of very small, adhesive-backed notes, such as 3M's Post-it™ notes (the optimum size is 1½″ × 1″). Your tree will be built out of groupings of these notes (entities). Depending on the complexity of your problem, your tree might exceed a hundred entities, so you'll need an ample supply.

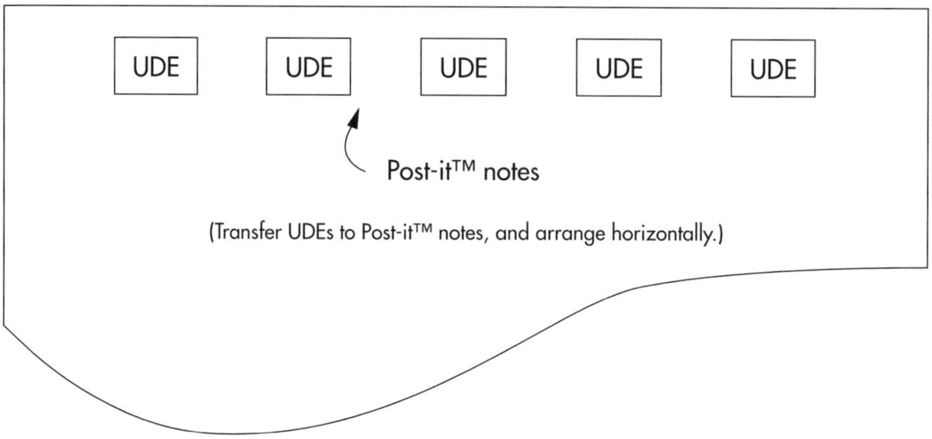

FIGURE 3.29. Beginning the Current Reality Tree.

Start your tree by transferring the five UDEs from your original list onto Post-it™ notes. Distinguish them as UDEs on the notes by writing them in different colors or drawing a prominent star ("★" or "✱"). Line up the UDE Post-it™ notes horizontally in the upper third of your paper. The order is not important.

4. Connect the First Two UDEs

Look for two UDEs among the first five that you intuitively believe to be related to one another in some way (see Figure 3.30).

a. Decide which of the two *leads to*—not necessarily *causes*—the other.

b. Arrange the two vertically, with the "leader" below the "follower." Using a pencil, draw an arrow from the leader pointing to the follower.

c. Keeping the Categories of Legitimate Reservation (CLR) in mind, ask yourself:

- Does the lower one *cause* the upper one?
- Is the upper one the *direct and unavoidable outcome* of the lower one?

If the answer is "no," continue to step d. If the answer is "yes," confirm it using the CLR and skip ahead to step 5.

d. If the answer to either question is "no," determine why the connection you originally perceived doesn't seem to be direct.

- Are there intervening steps missing? (See Figure 3.31.) If so, identify them and write them as entities on Post-it™ notes. If you started with more than five UDEs, take a look at those you put aside. See if any of them fill the gap between the leader and the follower. Insert any "new" entities between the leader and the follower. Connect them with arrows and, if

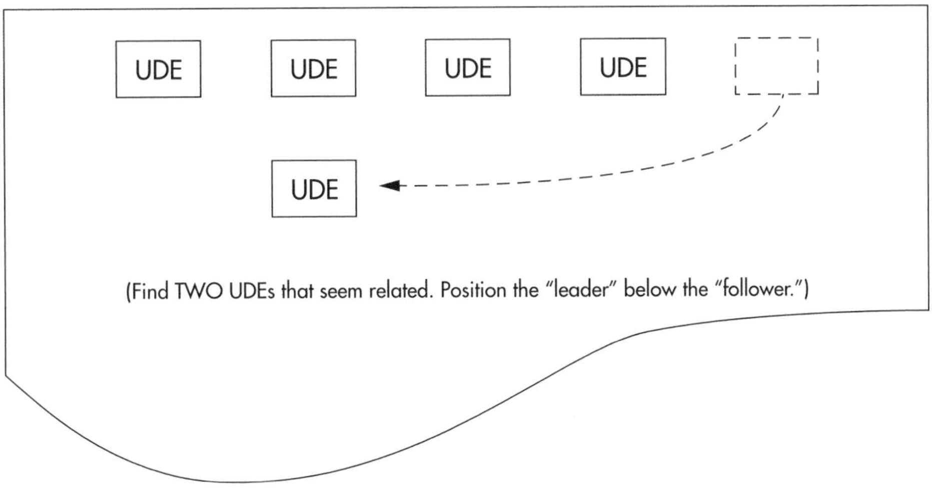
UDE
UDE
UDE
UDE
UDE
(Find TWO UDEs that seem related. Position the "leader" below the "follower.")

FIGURE 3.30. Connecting the First Two UDEs.

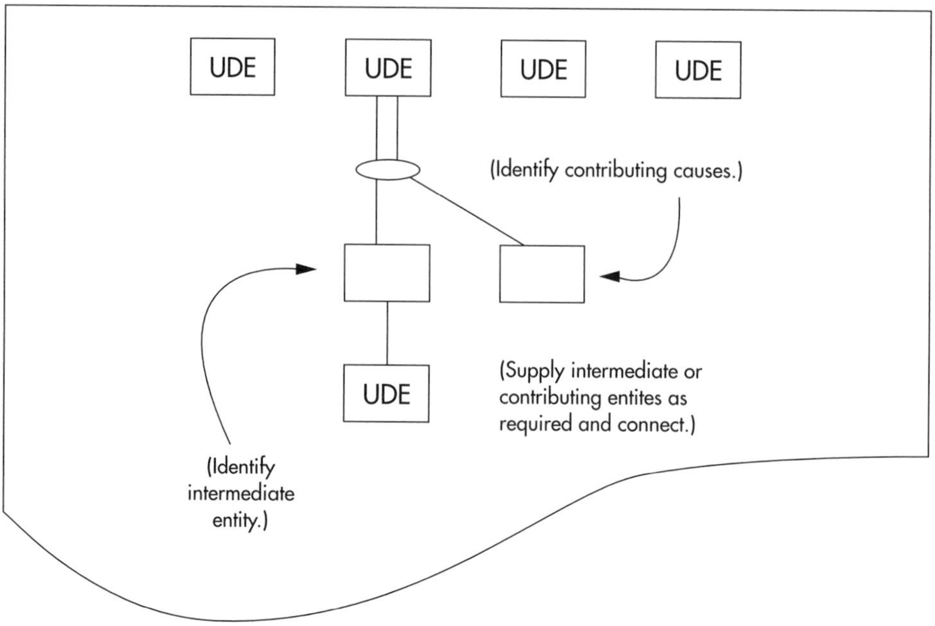

FIGURE 3.31. Are There Intervening Steps Missing?

necessary, ellipses. (Redraw arrows as required.) Subject the new connections to the CLR.

- Are the two UDEs reversed? Does the upper one actually cause the lower one? If so, switch their positions. Apply the CLR to the new arrangement.
- Are there other contributing causes? If you can say "The leader results in the follower, but something else is missing," look for other dependent causes. Here's another place to review, and possibly pick up, the UDEs you set aside in step 2. Write them on Post-it™ notes and insert them between the leader and follower. Redraw arrows and add ellipses where required. Scrutinize all new connections using the CLR.

5. Connect Other UDEs

Repeat this process with the remaining three UDEs (see Figure 3.32).

a. Look for UDEs among the remaining three that should be connected to each other. Use the procedure outlined in step 4.

b. Look for UDEs among the remaining three that should be connected to the first two. Use the procedure outlined in step 4.

c. If you've made all possible connections and don't have all five UDEs connected, go on to step 6.

6. Build the Cause-and-Effect Chain Downward

If you're extremely lucky, by the end of step 5 you've been able to connect all five of your UDEs. In most cases, however, you're likely to have two or more

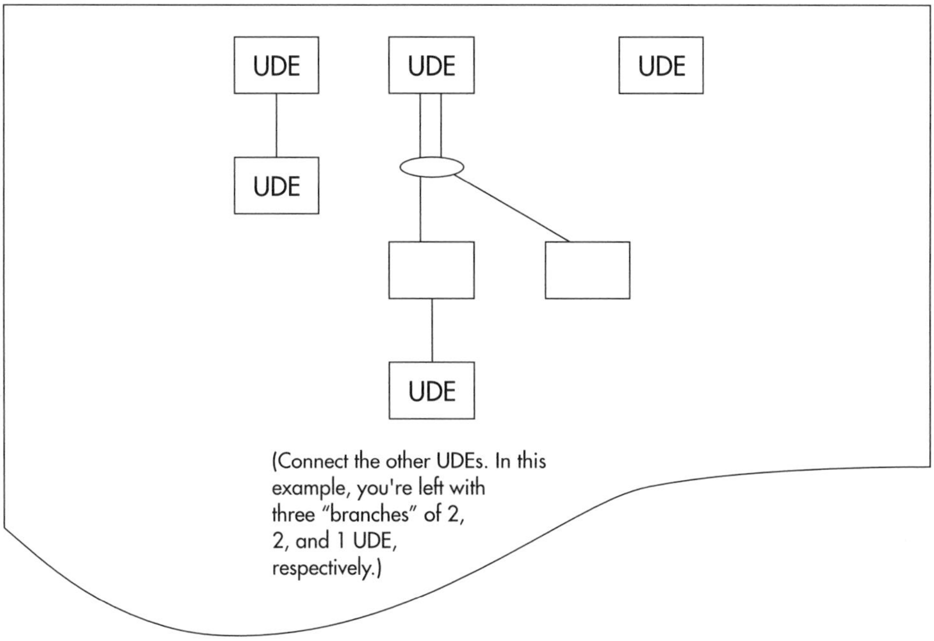

FIGURE 3.32. Connecting the Other UDEs.

groupings of UDEs (for example, 1 and 4; 2 and 3; or 2, 2 and 1). Each of these UDEs or clusters constitutes the beginning of a "branch" in your Current Reality Tree. Your objective is to trace the cause-and-effect chain downward in each branch until the branches meet at a common root cause (see Figure 3.33). If enough branches converge, and if this root cause accounts for at least 70 percent of the UDEs, it will qualify as a core problem. Choose one branch and start building downward. Then do the same for the other branches.

a. To construct each successive level, answer the following questions:

- Why does your lowermost entity exist? The "because . . ." with which you answer this question will be the next lower entity.

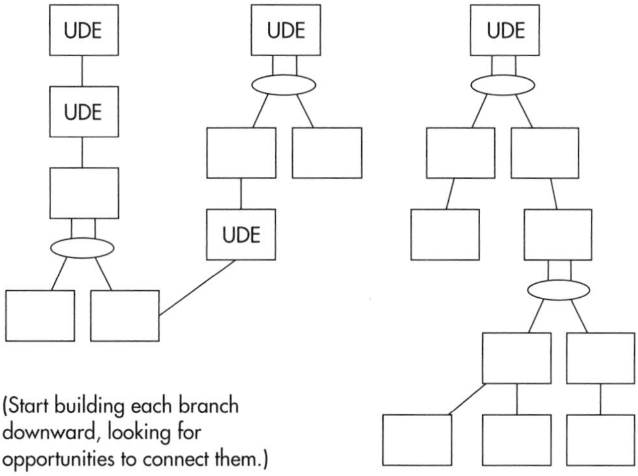

FIGURE 3.33. Building the Cause-and-Effect Chain Downward.

- What is the direct and unavoidable cause of your lowermost entity? This answer should be the same as the "because . . ." for the preceding question. If it's not, keep looking for an appropriate "because. . . ."
- Is that the only cause? Could something else cause or contribute to the same effect (the lowermost entity)?

b. Use the CLR as you go along to confirm each new level. If the CLR check isn't conclusive, look for another cause that satisfies the "why" question.

c. As you add each successively lower level, compare that new level with all adjacent branches of your tree. Look for lateral connections that may enable you to merge branches (see Figure 3.34). Be alert to the fact that you may have to create an intermediate entity or two in order to complete an effective lateral connection. Some of these intermediate entities may come from the excess UDEs you set aside in step 2.

d. Stop when you have all branches (that is, the original five UDEs) connected. Review the entire tree, from top to bottom. Ask yourself, "Does this tree, as a whole, reflect my intuition about the system?" This is a "gut check." If the answer is "no," recheck each arrow for additional causes and cause sufficiency using the CLR.

e. Look for negative reinforcing loops in your tree. Examine each UDE and, using the CLR, determine whether it might possibly reinforce or amplify an entity at a lower level in the tree. If you find such situations, depict the loop by drawing an arrow from the UDE back down to the entity it reinforces. (It may be necessary for you to insert an intermediate entity or two between the UDE and the reentry point.)

7. Redesignate UDEs

Although you may have started your tree with only five UDEs, if the problem is complex, chances are that more will have cropped up. If you were working with only five from an original list of several more, by this point you will probably have found places in the tree to insert the ones you set aside in step 2

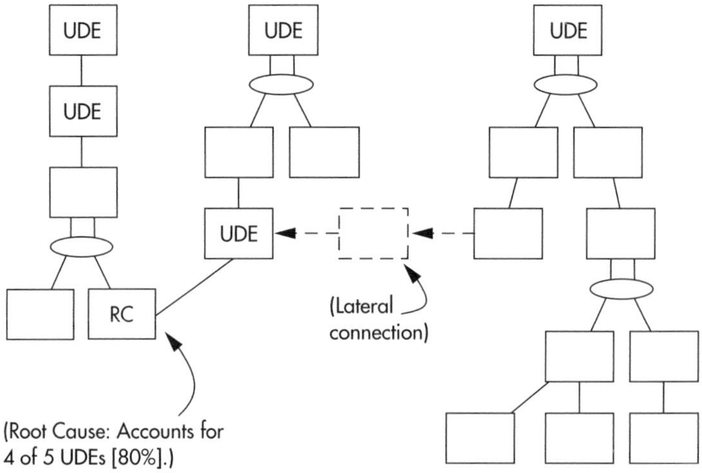

FIGURE 3.34. Looking for Lateral Connections.

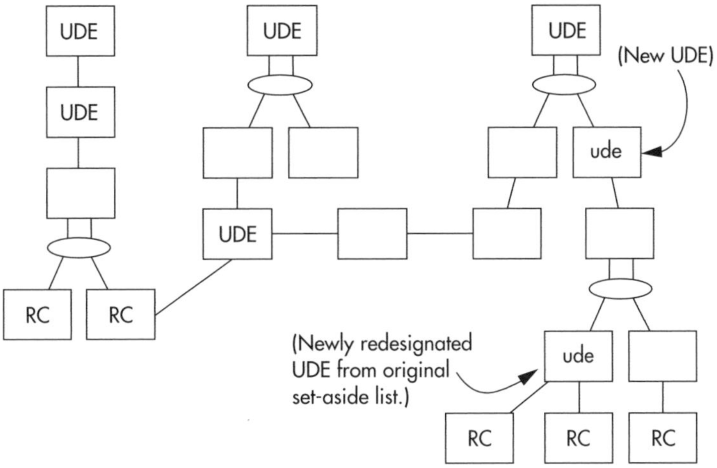

FIGURE 3.35. Redesignating UDEs.

(see Figure 3.35). If there are any from step 2 left, recheck them for Entity Existence and find appropriate places for them in the tree. Then update the UDEs throughout the entire tree by redesignating, as appropriate.

a. Look at each of the original five UDEs. Do they still qualify as UDEs in the context of the rest of the tree? If not, delete the distinguishing marks you placed on the Post-it™ notes in step 3. They may still be necessary for a chain of logical cause and effect, but if they don't qualify as UDEs anymore, their distinguishing marks should be deleted.

b. Locate any UDEs you set aside in step 2 and incorporated later. In the context of the whole tree, are they still undesirable? If so, make sure they're appropriately marked. If not, remove any distinguishing marks they may have.

Note: Some of the UDEs you set aside, or others that occur to you as you're building the tree, may actually lie higher in the tree than your original five UDEs. It may be necessary for you to build upward from your original five to encompass them all. This is why we located the original five in the upper third of the page in step 3, leaving some space to expand upward.

c. Review each entity on the tree, especially the ones you created to fill gaps, to tighten logic and to make lateral connections. Could any of *these* be considered UDEs? If so, mark them appropriately.

d. "Prune" from the tree any entities that are not required to connect all the UDEs—but don't delete any root causes! (See Figure 3.36.)

e. Also "prune" from the top and bottom of the tree any extraneous entities that aren't necessary to support either root causes or UDEs.

Note: This is a judgment call on your part. The reason for doing this is to keep your tree from becoming a "picture of the world" that goes down too deeply or up too high. Such a tree begins to include parts of reality that may be interesting but not related to solving the problem. The acid test: "Are these entities really needed to paint a complete picture of the UDEs or the core problem?" If not, trash 'em!

f. Count up all the UDEs, the originals and any that you added. Make a mental note of the total.

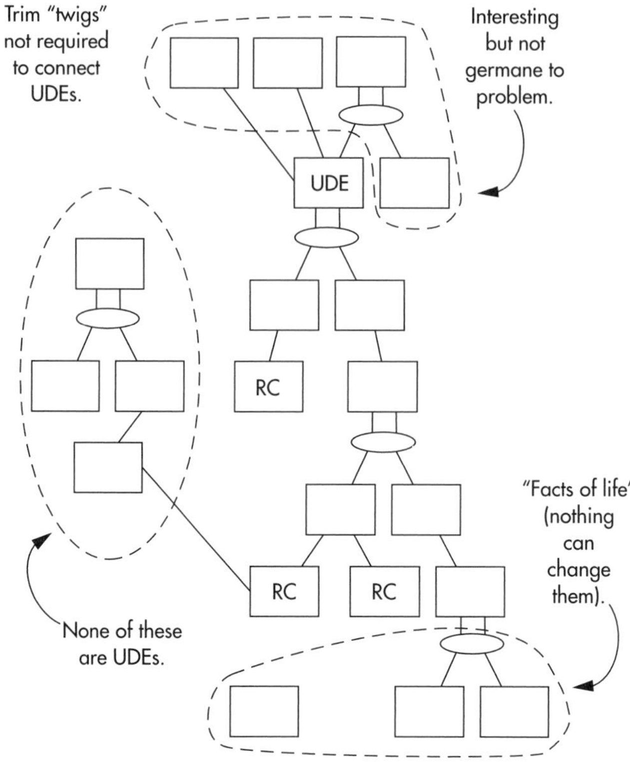

FIGURE 3.36. Pruning the Entities That Are Not Needed.

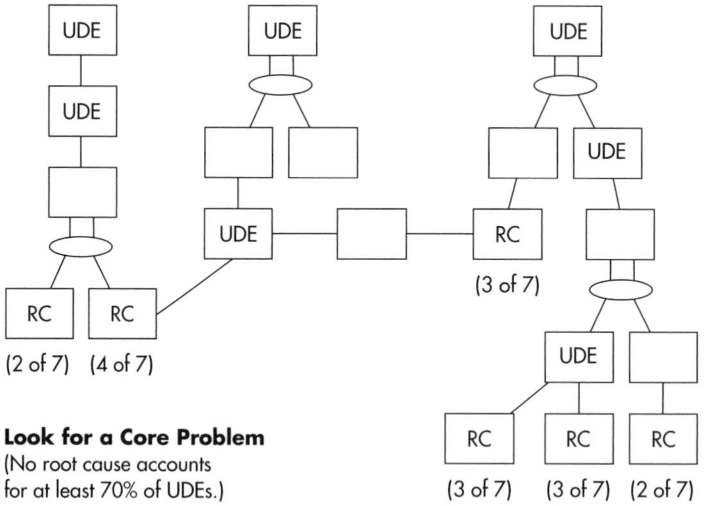

FIGURE 3.37. Identifying Root Causes and the Core Problem.

8. Identify Root Causes and the Core Problem

Now it's time to find, if possible, the system's constraint—the core problem that produces most of the undesirable effects (see Figure 3.37).

a. First locate all the root causes (entities with arrows coming out, but none going in).

b. Determine whether any root cause accounts for 70 percent or more of the UDEs. Keep track of how many UDEs result from each root cause and compare that number to the total you counted in step 7. If one root cause results in 70 percent or more, designate that the core problem. To confirm this, start with each root cause and trace the arrows back up through the tree to the UDEs. Verbalize it this way:

If I remove [root cause], then [next effect] disappears. If that effect doesn't exist, then the following effect disappears, and so on until the UDE is gone.

Note: As you go through this check, remember the significance of the ellipse. If you've built your tree effectively using the CLR, you don't have to eliminate all the causes whose arrows pass through an ellipse. Removing just one should be enough to destroy the cause-effect relationship leading to the UDE. This is why the TOC thinking process is a *minimalist* approach: it helps you to solve the problem with the least investment in time and resources that will do the job effectively. By working down to the core problem, which is really the system's *constraint,* you identify the one thing to change that will do the most good—that will achieve the most "bang for your buck."

c. If you can't identify a core problem among your root causes, go on to step 9. If you can identify a core problem, skip ahead to step 10.

9. Look for V-Shaped or Missing Connections

If you've come this far and haven't reached a core problem yet, you may have to build down farther, even though all UDEs are connected above. At this point you probably have several "branches" ending at the bottom in root causes (see Figure 3.38).

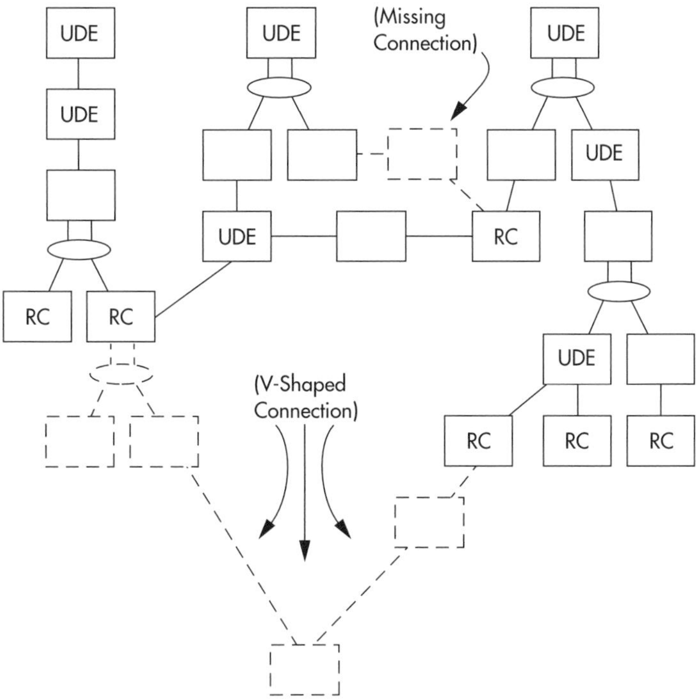

FIGURE 3.38. Looking for V-Shaped or Missing Connections.

a. Examine all root causes and compare them with each other, one at a time.

b. Try to find two that might be related, much as you did when you began connecting your first two UDEs in step 4. If you find two, continue building one or both downward, just as you did in step 6, until you reach a common cause that logically (that is, following the CLR) produces both branches, above. This is known as a V-shaped connection. If this connection provides you with a new root cause that accounts for 70 percent or more of your UDEs, you now have a core problem (constraint).

c. Alternatively, compare the different branches of your tree, at the level of the root cause or above. See if you may have overlooked any lateral connections, perhaps through an intermediate entity you haven't shown on your tree yet. Make the connection, verifying it with the CLR, and reevaluate your root causes to see if one now qualifies as a core problem (the "70 percent" check). One of these two steps (b or c) will eventually produce a core problem.

10. Decide Which Root Cause(s) to Attack

Normally, this would seem like a straightforward decision: Go for the core problem. But let's revisit step 1 of this procedure. Where does your span of control end? How far out does your sphere of influence extend? The answers to these questions will direct you toward your point of attack (see Figure 3.39).

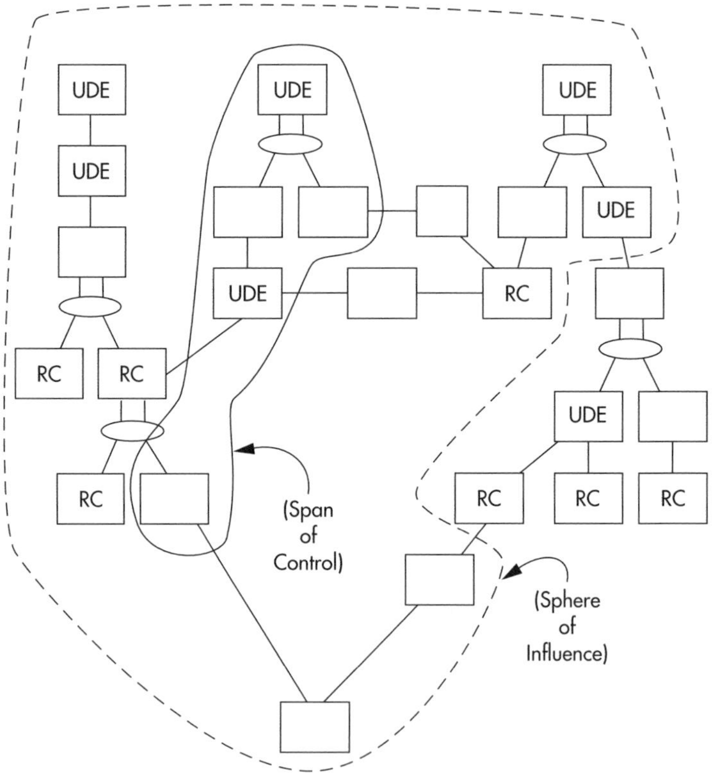

FIGURE 3.39. Deciding Which Root Cause(s) to Attack.

a. With your entire tree fully displayed before you, begin to scribe your span of control, enclosing the entities you have authority over. If possible, close the line completely. It's probably not going to be a true circle; more likely, it'll look like an amoeba. The physical layout of your tree may be such that you can't encompass all of your authority in a single closed figure. So draw as many smaller closed lines as you have to. Use a distinctive color that you can associate with your span of control.

b. Repeat step 10a for your sphere of influence, using a different color line. But for your sphere of influence, open your imagination to what might be possible. Influence varies by degree. Your influence may be indirect. For instance, you may not be able to change public law, but you may be able to muster enough support through persuasion to convince lawmakers to do so. The Brady Bill and Mothers Against Drunk Driving are two such examples. Encompass as much as you dare in your sphere of influence, even if you're not quite sure how you'll go about doing the influencing.

c. With your span of control and sphere of influence lines drawn, see where your core problem lies with respect to them. If the core problem is within your sphere of influence, go for it! If it's outside, select two or more root causes, according to your subjective liking, that can account for a majority of the UDEs. These will be the problems you'll work on cracking.

Note: Even if you can work with a core problem rather than multiple root causes, what if it doesn't account for all the UDEs? We've demanded only 70 percent coverage to qualify—what about the other 30 percent? Remember the Five Focusing Steps. Our purpose is to identify the weakest link in the chain. This is the core problem, whether it accounts for all the UDEs or not. In order to continually improve a system, eventually you'll have to address the "other 30 percent." But try to start with the core problem, for reasons previously stated. In correcting that problem, you will essentially be changing the system, maybe significantly. Afterward, the "other 30 percent" may no longer be UDEs in the context of the new configuration. And if they are, you'll probably find it more effective to build a new Current Reality Tree for the remaining 30 percent, because the new system configuration may point you toward different root causes the second time around. This constitutes the fifth of the Five Focusing Steps: When a constraint is broken, go back to the beginning and work on the next weakest link.

Be thankful for your problems. If they were less difficult, someone with less ability might have your job.

—Unknown

Core Problems and "Really Bad" UDEs

What if you go through this whole procedure, identify a core problem, and it doesn't account for the one UDE that "burns" you the most? UDEs are not all created equal. Some are clearly more undesirable than others—but to whom? The Current Reality Tree procedure gives you quantitative guidelines (that is, 70 percent) in deciding what to attack, but not qualitative. Common sense tells you that you shouldn't ignore the UDE that bothers you the most, even if it isn't among the 70 percent. In a situation like this, ask yourself the following questions:

- Will solving the core problem result in the greatest improvement in system Throughput?

- If the UDE that bothers me most isn't among the 70 percent resulting from the core problem, will I be suboptimizing (that is, sacrificing overall system benefits to maximize my own part of it) if I work on it?
- Can I do justice to system Throughput *and* to myself by working on both the core problem and the root cause of my "burning" UDE at the same time?

Only you can answer these questions. As with anything else, this thinking process *can* be subverted for personal gain. True ongoing improvement depends on your ethical use of these tools. If you can't work on a core problem, you're going to have to deal with multiple root causes anyway. It's up to you to decide which ones to work on, but the one that leads to your "burning" UDE would certainly be a good candidate.

> ***One gauge of success is not whether you have a tough problem to handle, but whether it is the same problem you had last year.***
>
> ***—Unknown***

SCRUTINIZING THE CURRENT REALITY TREE

Scrutinizing is the process of critically examining a logic tree and strengthening it as much as possible. It involves locating and eliminating any weaknesses in logic at any point in the tree. As you've probably noticed, you do a lot of scrutinizing during the building process—so much, in fact, that you'll probably have a hard time making yourself go back over it again after it's completed.

Moreover, we are all blind to our own mistakes. Despite your best efforts, your tree, while it looks "dry" to you, will undoubtedly have sufficiency and additional cause errors, at the very least. No matter how many times you go over the tree, you probably will see right through them. That's why it's important to have someone else look at your tree. Clearly, if you plan to present the tree to someone else for the purpose of persuading him or her to do something, it's absolutely critical to have an independent set of eyes review it for you.

The Categories of Legitimate Reservation

Outside scrutinizers need not be well versed in the Categories of Legitimate Reservation, though it certainly helps if they are. All that's really necessary for effective scrutiny of a Current Reality Tree is that the person have intuitive knowledge of the tree's subject matter. If *you* understand the CLR, you'll be able to translate questions and comments into reservations from one of the eight categories. Refer to chapter 2, "Categories of Legitimate Reservation," chapter 8, "Group Dynamics and the TOC Thinking Process," and Figure 8.4, "Directions for Communicating Using the CLR," for more detail on how to scrutinize your Current Reality Tree with the help of others.

Common Logic Pitfalls

While the Categories of Legitimate Reservation will provide you with all the help you need to "dry out" your tree, it's worth knowing what mistakes are most commonly found in Current Reality Trees. These are the ones you'll run into most frequently, in your own trees or those of others. Any one of them is enough to ruin a tree.

Entity Existence

A common shortcoming with many logic trees is the "all or none" problem. The accompanying sidebar, "When 'All' or 'None' Are Not Acceptable," describes this problem in detail and ways to deal with it.

> ***Beware of half-truths; you may have gotten the wrong half.***
>
> ***—Unknown***

Causality Existence

The most frequent logic trap most people fall into is accepting causality when it doesn't really exist, or confusing it with correlation. You can avoid this trap by staying close to the CLR. (Refer to chapter 2, "Categories of Legitimate Reservation.")

"Lack of Oxygen"

Oxygen is a vital but invisible presence in our lives. As we mentioned in chapter 2, "oxygen" in logic trees represents the elements we take for granted or assume to be present, even though we don't reflect them in our trees. What is frequently "oxygen" to one person may not be so inherent to another that it can remain unstated. You can expect to be questioned on the "lack of oxygen" issue, perhaps more so than any other reservation except Causality Existence.

SIDEBAR

WHEN "ALL" OR "NONE" ARE NOT ACCEPTABLE

Consider this statement: "People are naturally paranoid." Would you agree with it if somebody else said it? It's pretty inclusive. Without any qualifying adjectives, it implies that *everybody* is paranoid. What about you? Are you paranoid? If not, you might take exception with such an inclusive statement: "I think that's wrong. Not everybody is paranoid."

What if the person who made that statement had, instead, said: "*Some* people are naturally paranoid." Could you agree with that? Most of us probably could. What's the difference between the one you might accept and the one you'd contest? Clearly, it's the presence of the word "some." It's a "qualifier."

INCLUSIVE AND EXCLUSIVE

In this world, very little is all "black" or all "white" (except maybe for a couple colors of paint). This means that in building logic trees, we have to take into consideration the possibility that our statements may not be valid if they're completely *inclusive* or *exclusive*. We may have to qualify our statements, especially if we intend to present our trees to others. Otherwise, we risk compromising our own credibility.

QUALIFYING WORDS

Qualifying words can save our credibility. Words like "some," "many," "most," "few," and "a majority" acknowledge the fact that very few situations are "all or none." But how do you know which to use, and when? The scale in Figure 3.40 provides a possible benchmark. Consider it a starting point. You may choose to redesign it, or modify it in any way you like. Its sole function is to permit you to evaluate your situation and put some kind of logical limit on your statement, a limit that will make it more acceptable to the average reader.

FEW OR SOME?

For example, if you think that 10 percent or fewer (but more than zero) people are paranoid, you might say, "a *few* people are naturally paranoid." If you think the number is closer to 25 percent, you might say, "*Some* people are naturally paranoid."

MANY, A MAJORITY, OR MOST?

If you think that 45 percent of the population likes baseball, you might say, "*Many* people like baseball." If you think that 60 percent are displeased with a baseball strike, it might translate to "A *majority* of fans oppose the strike." Once you get above 75 percent, you might be safe in saying that "*Most* fans oppose the strike." (Technically, 51 percent or more could constitute "most." You're free to establish your own thresholds for each of these qualifiers, but you should consider using them to add credibility to your logic.)

COMBINING "QUALIFIERS" IN EFFECTS

Once you've decided how to qualify a statement that is to be an entity in your tree, you have to decide how the combination of two or more "qualified"

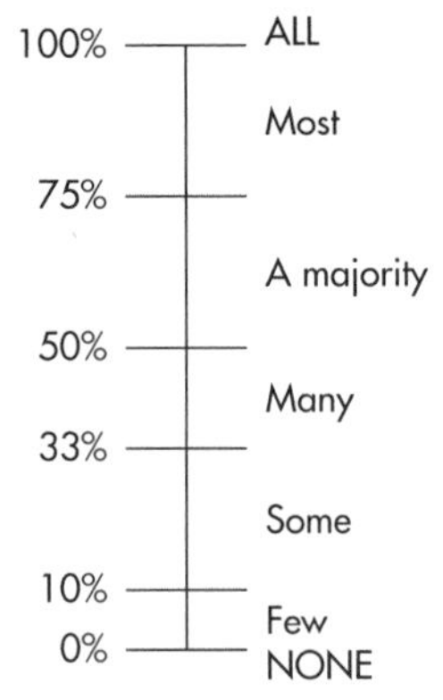

FIGURE 3.40. A Scale for Qualifying Your Statements.

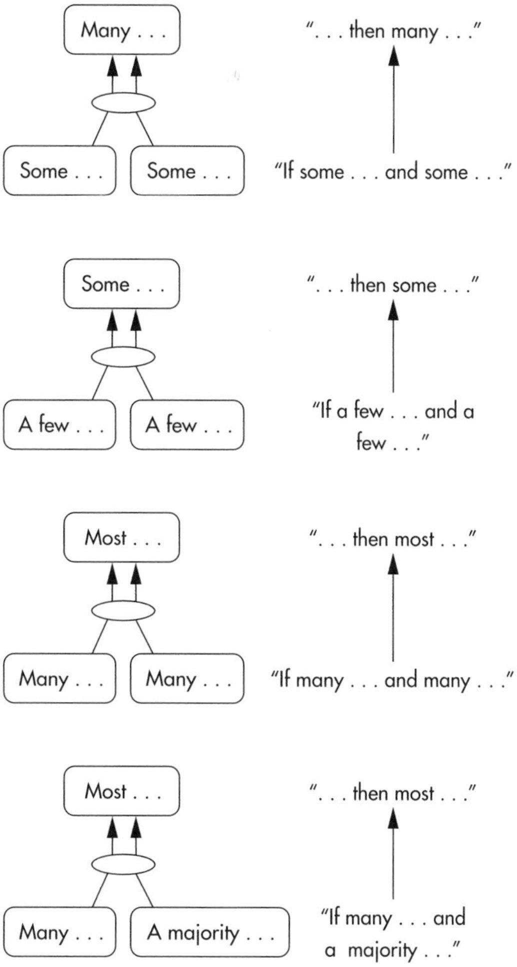

FIGURE 3.41.
Combining "Qualifiers" in Effects.

statements will play out in the effect. Are "some" and "some" sufficient to produce "many"? Will "many" and "some" produce "a majority"? How about "many" and "many"—will they give you "most"? Figure 3.41 shows some possible combinations and their proposed effects. Undoubtedly you'll be able to think of others. Experiment with "qualifiers" until you're certain the logic of your cause-and-effect connections is as tight as you can make it.

Cause Insufficiency

This is different from "oxygen," but it's often related to it, at least in the eyes of the tree-builder. What one person considers "oxygen" could, in fact, be a significant contributing cause that can't be ignored without risking the validity of the tree. Also, because of personal "blind spots," we're more likely to overlook contributing causes than almost any other pitfall except "oxygen." Adding such contributors and "ellipsing" them with other causes is the most frequent correction you'll make. The reverse of this problem is also common: having several causes improperly joined through an ellipse, when one of the causes is sufficient alone to result in the effect. Another Cause Insufficiency pitfall can be indicated by having too many arrows going through an ellipse. If you seem to have four or more causes contributing to a single effect, look very closely to see if some of them might not be better grouped in a second ellipse, as a separate cause.

Additional Cause

After Cause Insufficiency, you're most likely to overlook a completely independent cause that might produce the same effect. Of the three pitfalls mentioned here, this is the one on which you're most likely to have a mental block—that is, you probably won't find it without outside help.

Cause-Effect Reversal

This involves mistaking an effect for a cause. "*If* firefighters are hosing down the house, *then* the house is on fire." Is the house on fire *because* the firefighters are hosing it down, or are they hosing it down because the house is on fire? You won't see this problem as frequently as the previous ones; but it will occasionally come up.

USING THE CURRENT REALITY TREE WITH OTHER PARTS OF THE TOC THINKING PROCESS

The Current Reality Tree is a superb tool by itself. But it really becomes invaluable when used in concert with other parts of the TOC thinking process. Moreover, the times when you'll use it in isolation are likely to be few. After all, what good does it do you to identify a core problem or root causes if you're not going to press on and do something about them? While the other logical tools have great utility by themselves as well, the Current Reality Tree really is designed to lead into two other parts of the thinking process: the Conflict Resolution Diagram and the Future Reality Tree.

Why do core problems exist? If they're such a constraint on a system's performance, you'd expect that someone would have stepped up to them and solved them before. There are two possible reasons why this hasn't happened: The problem has gone unrecognized, or there is hidden conflict underlying the situation.

The Current Reality Tree and the Conflict Resolution Diagram

The core problem may be perpetuated by some hidden conflict. This may not be as obvious as animosity between two people or organizations. The conflict may merely be a conflict of interests between people or groups. Sometimes those involved are tacitly aware of the conflict, but often they are not. However, the possibility of conflict should always be investigated before moving on to the solution stage. Failure to address hidden conflict will undermine any solution you might develop. The same "infection" will cause the patient (system) to relapse if the underlying conflict is not resolved. This is the function of the Conflict Resolution Diagram

When conflict is present, the Current Reality Tree leads into the Conflict Resolution Diagram. If you want to solve the core problem, what you're essentially trying to do is achieve a condition that is opposite to that core problem. For example, if your core problem is (see Figure 3.42):

Personnel policy limits our ability to reach our goal.

then the opposite condition might be:

Personnel policy supports and optimizes our ability to achieve our goal.

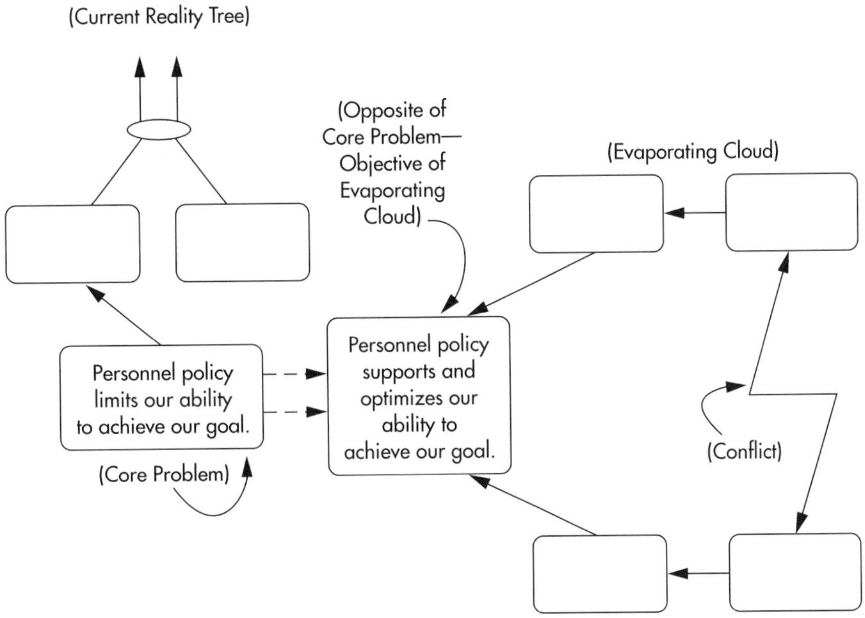

FIGURE 3.42. The Current Reality Tree and the Conflict Resolution Diagram.

This opposite condition now becomes the objective, or entering argument, for the Conflict Resolution Diagram.

The Conflict Resolution Diagram also offers exceptional potential as a "creative engine" for developing new ideas and approaches for solving problems. Refer to chapter 4, "Conflict Resolution Diagram," for more on how to use it to resolve conflict by inventing win-win solutions, and how to create new ways to solve problems.

The Current Reality Tree and the Future Reality Tree

If the core problem doesn't result from a conflict, the other possibility is that it hasn't been recognized or its impact appreciated. If this is the case, merely completing and presenting an effective Current Reality Tree might be enough to prompt action to solve the core problem. Once the emperor recognizes that he has no clothes, he's likely to move smartly to find some. In this case, it's probably possible to move directly to a Future Reality Tree (see Figure 3.43), if:

- You know exactly what action(s) to take to solve the core problem.
- You don't have to invent some completely new approach to solving the problem.

If you can't meet either of these conditions, you're probably going to need the Conflict Resolution Diagram to help you. Once the core problem is identified and you can formulate its *diametrically opposite condition*—a situation that will cause the core problem to go away—it can be translated over into the Future Reality Tree. It becomes an intermediate step in converting the Current Reality Tree's UDEs into the Future Reality Tree's desirable effects. The actions needed to achieve the core problem's opposite condition will appear below it as injections. The desirable effects will result from it, above.

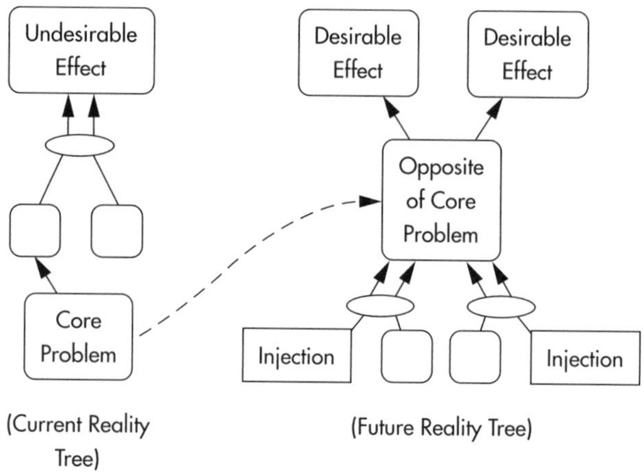

FIGURE 3.43.
The Current Reality Tree and the Future Reality Tree.

Refer to chapter 5, "Future Reality Tree," for more details on how to restructure the current situation, test the new solution for effectiveness, and avoid creating new undesirable effects.

SUMMARY

We've seen how a Current Reality Tree can help us find the hidden, underlying root causes that produce our system's problems—*what* to change in our system. Now it's time to start the second phase of problem solution: what to change *to*. The first part of that phase is the Conflict Resolution Diagram—the subject of chapter 4.

The greatest obstacle to discovering the shape of the earth, the continents, and the ocean was not ignorance but the illusion of knowledge.

—Daniel J. Boorstin, "The Discoverers"

"Why Organizations Fail at TQ" Undesirable Effects (UDE) List

- Organizational resources are inefficiently employed. (112)
- Employees perceive TQ to create more "red tape" and paperwork. (204)
- TQ seems to take too long to generate positive system-wide results. (213)
- Many employees resist the changes necessary for TQ to succeed. (607)
- The organization's goal is not achieved. (611)
- Quality improvement efforts cost more than they produce. (711)
- Credibility of management commitment to TQ is low. (702)
- The same problems keep cropping up. (704)
- Employees become disillusioned with TQ. (811)
- Employees pay lip service to TQ but don't practice it. (810)
- Many people put personal agendas ahead of organizational objectives. (903)

FIGURE 3.44. Current Reality Tree Example: "Why Organizations Fail at Total Quality."

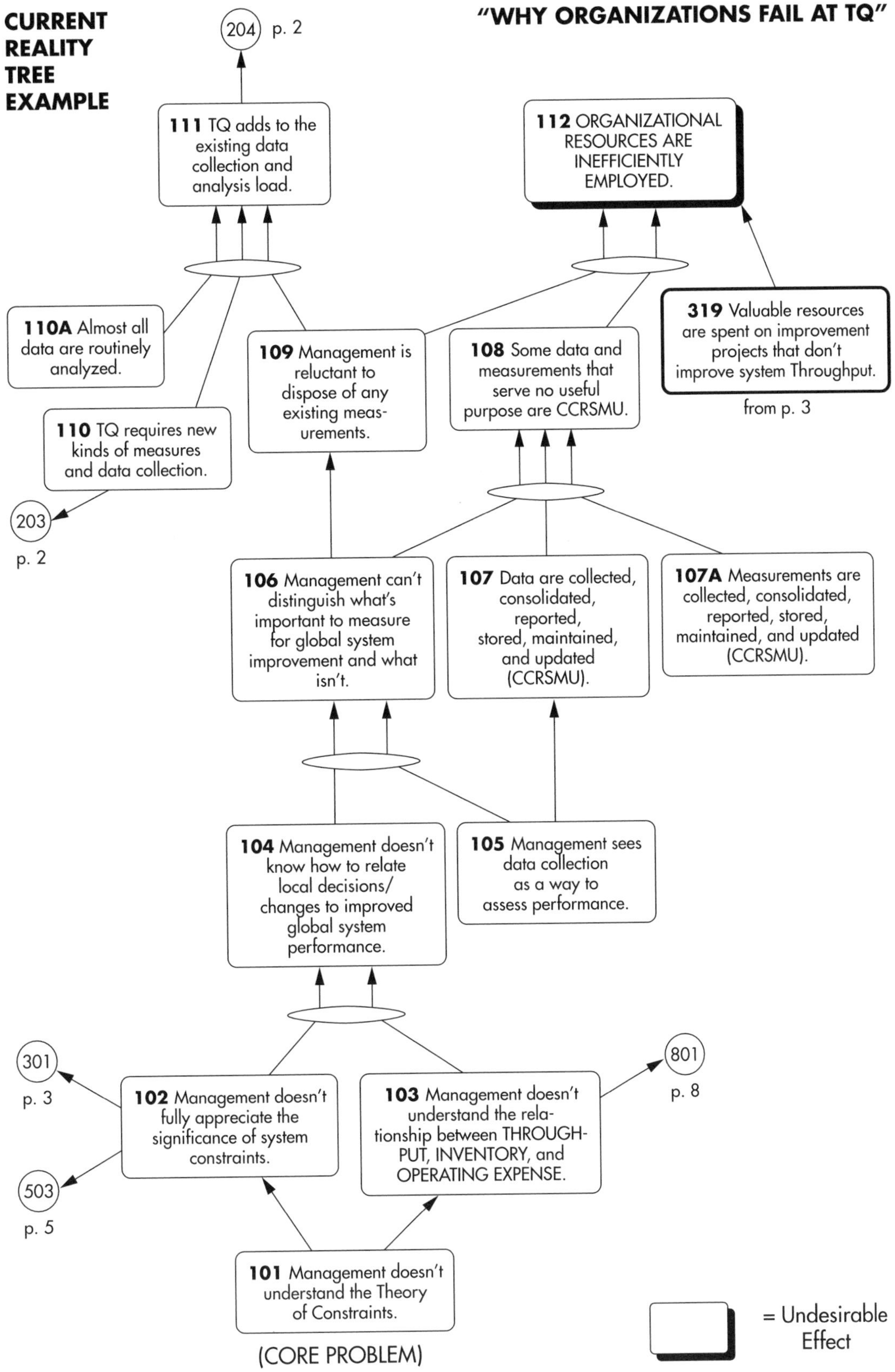
CURRENT REALITY TREE EXAMPLE
"WHY ORGANIZATIONS FAIL AT TQ"
204 p. 2
111 TQ adds to the existing data collection and analysis load.
112 ORGANIZATIONAL RESOURCES ARE INEFFICIENTLY EMPLOYED.
110A Almost all data are routinely analyzed.
109 Management is reluctant to dispose of any existing meas-urements.
108 Some data and measurements that serve no useful purpose are CCRSMU.
319 Valuable resources are spent on improvement projects that don't improve system Throughput.
from p. 3
110 TQ requires new kinds of measures and data collection.
203 p. 2
106 Management can't distinguish what's important to measure for global system improvement and what isn't.
107 Data are collected, consolidated, reported, stored, maintained, and updated (CCRSMU).
107A Measurements are collected, consolidated, reported, stored, maintained, and updated (CCRSMU).
104 Management doesn't know how to relate local decisions/ changes to improved global system performance.
105 Management sees data collection as a way to assess performance.
301 p. 3
503 p. 5
801 p. 8
102 Management doesn't fully appreciate the significance of system constraints.
103 Management doesn't understand the rela-tionship between THROUGH-PUT, INVENTORY, and OPERATING EXPENSE.
101 Management doesn't understand the Theory of Constraints.
(CORE PROBLEM)
= Undesirable Effect

FIGURE 3.44—*Continued.*

CURRENT REALITY TREE, p. 2

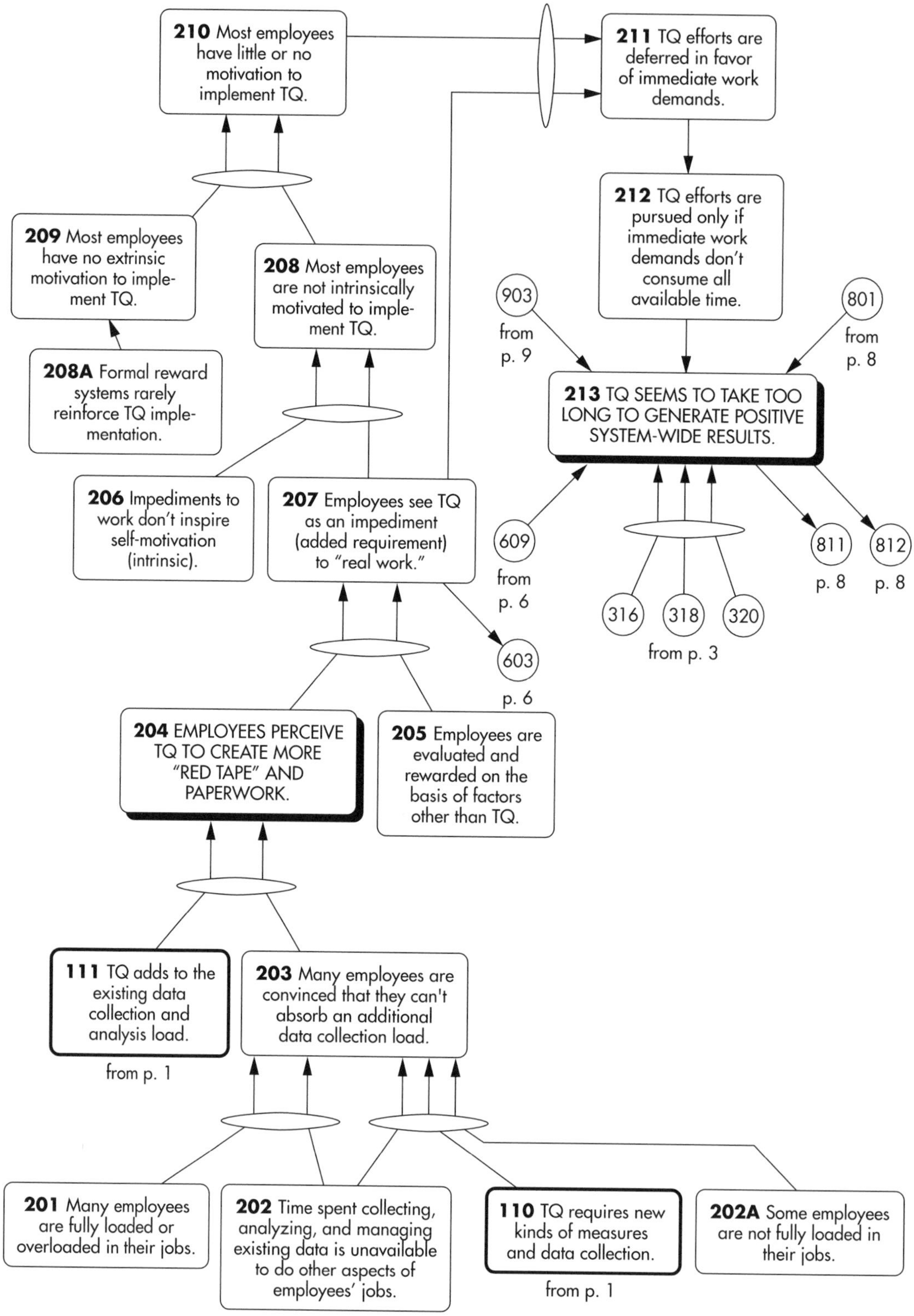

FIGURE 3.44—*Continued.*

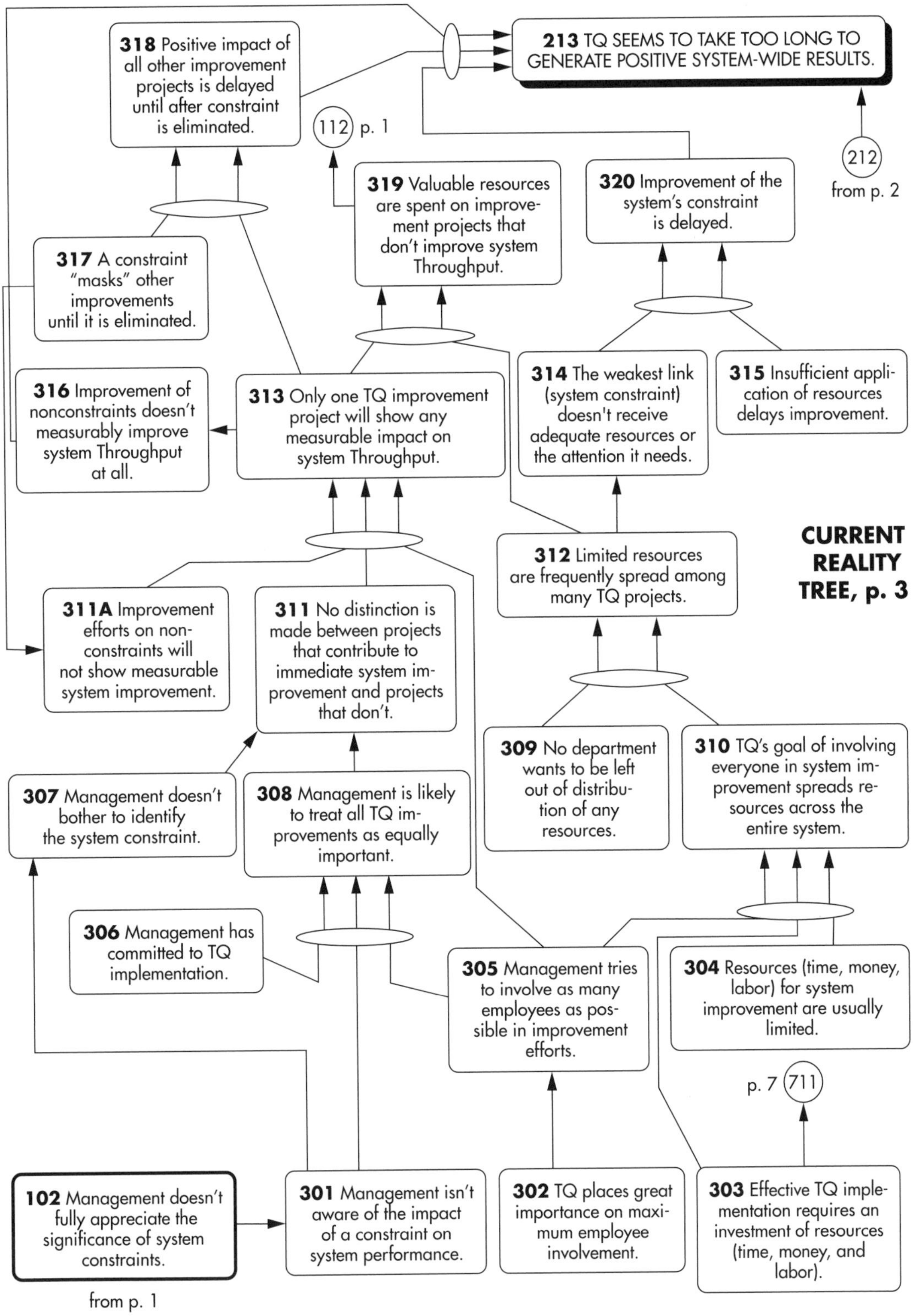

213 TQ SEEMS TO TAKE TOO LONG TO GENERATE POSITIVE SYSTEM-WIDE RESULTS.
318 Positive impact of all other improvement projects is delayed until after constraint is eliminated.
112 p. 1
212 from p. 2
319 Valuable resources are spent on improvement projects that don't improve system Throughput.
320 Improvement of the system's constraint is delayed.
317 A constraint "masks" other improvements until it is eliminated.
316 Improvement of nonconstraints doesn't measurably improve system Throughput at all.
313 Only one TQ improvement project will show any measurable impact on system Throughput.
314 The weakest link (system constraint) doesn't receive adequate resources or the attention it needs.
315 Insufficient application of resources delays improvement.
CURRENT REALITY TREE, p. 3
312 Limited resources are frequently spread among many TQ projects.
311A Improvement efforts on nonconstraints will not show measurable system improvement.
311 No distinction is made between projects that contribute to immediate system improvement and projects that don't.
309 No department wants to be left out of distribution of any resources.
310 TQ's goal of involving everyone in system improvement spreads resources across the entire system.
307 Management doesn't bother to identify the system constraint.
308 Management is likely to treat all TQ improvements as equally important.
306 Management has committed to TQ implementation.
305 Management tries to involve as many employees as possible in improvement efforts.
304 Resources (time, money, labor) for system improvement are usually limited.
p. 7 711
102 Management doesn't fully appreciate the significance of system constraints.
from p. 1
301 Management isn't aware of the impact of a constraint on system performance.
302 TQ places great importance on maximum employee involvement.
303 Effective TQ implementation requires an investment of resources (time, money, and labor).

FIGURE 3.44—*Continued.*

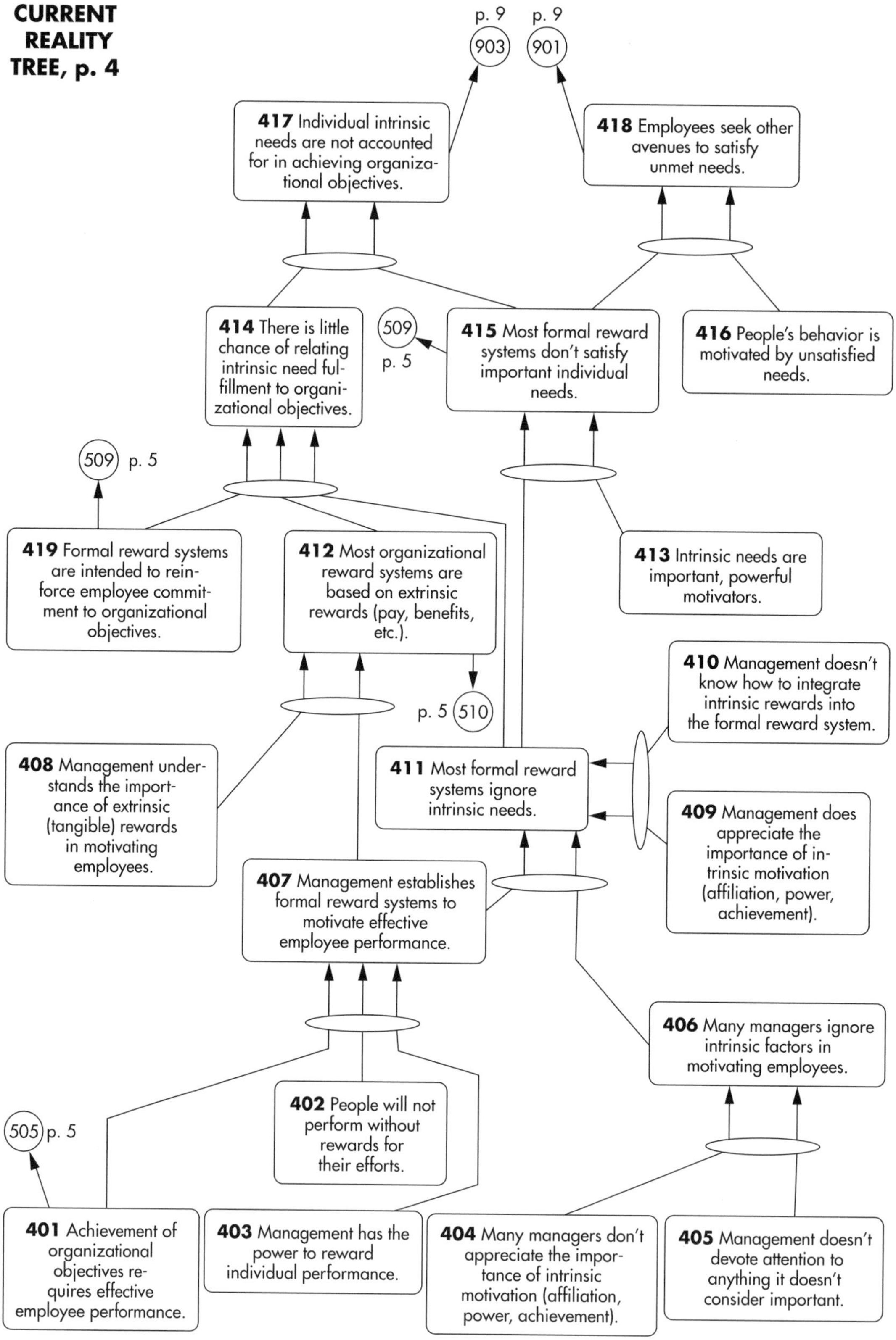

FIGURE 3.44—*Continued.*

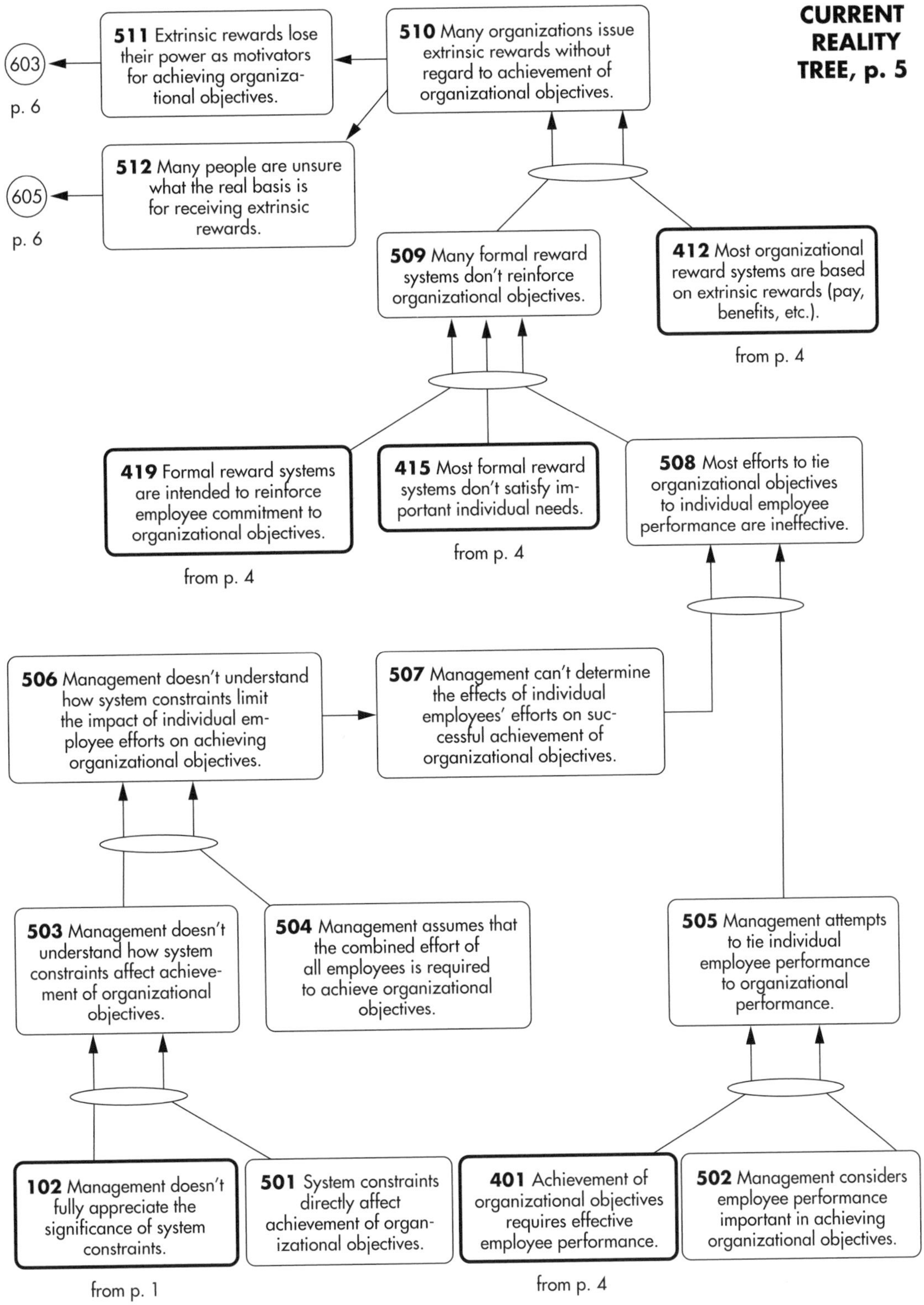
CURRENT REALITY TREE, p. 5
603
p. 6
605
p. 6
511 Extrinsic rewards lose their power as motivators for achieving organizational objectives.
510 Many organizations issue extrinsic rewards without regard to achievement of organizational objectives.
512 Many people are unsure what the real basis is for receiving extrinsic rewards.
509 Many formal reward systems don't reinforce organizational objectives.
412 Most organizational reward systems are based on extrinsic rewards (pay, benefits, etc.).
from p. 4
419 Formal reward systems are intended to reinforce employee commitment to organizational objectives.
from p. 4
415 Most formal reward systems don't satisfy important individual needs.
from p. 4
508 Most efforts to tie organizational objectives to individual employee performance are ineffective.
506 Management doesn't understand how system constraints limit the impact of individual employee efforts on achieving organizational objectives.
507 Management can't determine the effects of individual employees' efforts on successful achievement of organizational objectives.
503 Management doesn't understand how system constraints affect achievement of organizational objectives.
504 Management assumes that the combined effort of all employees is required to achieve organizational objectives.
505 Management attempts to tie individual employee performance to organizational performance.
102 Management doesn't fully appreciate the significance of system constraints.
from p. 1
501 System constraints directly affect achievement of organizational objectives.
401 Achievement of organizational objectives requires effective employee performance.
from p. 4
502 Management considers employee performance important in achieving organizational objectives.

FIGURE 3.44—*Continued.*

CURRENT REALITY TREE, p. 6

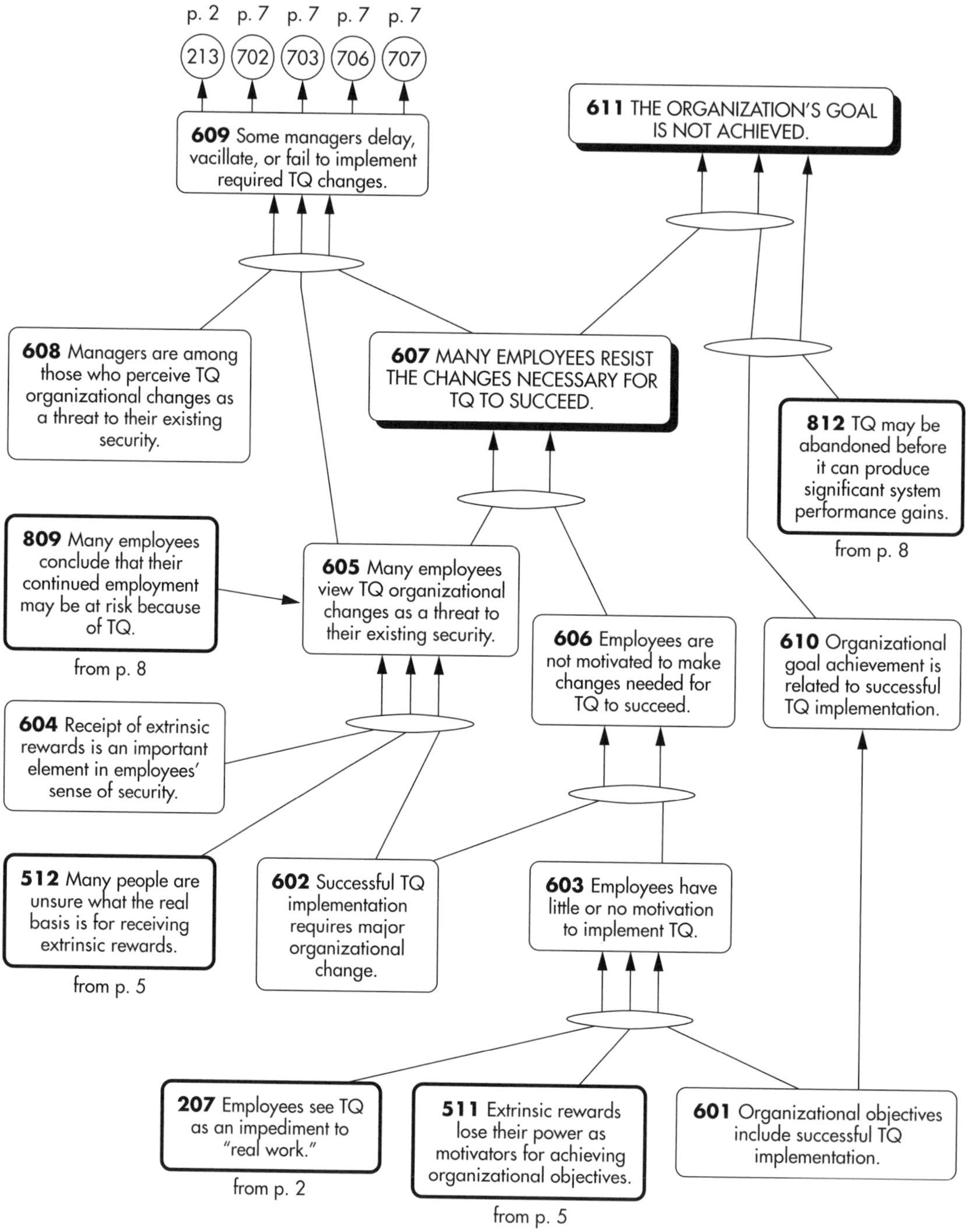
p. 2
p. 7
p. 7
p. 7
p. 7
213
702
703
706
707
609 Some managers delay, vacillate, or fail to implement required TQ changes.
611 THE ORGANIZATION'S GOAL IS NOT ACHIEVED.
608 Managers are among those who perceive TQ organizational changes as a threat to their existing security.
607 MANY EMPLOYEES RESIST THE CHANGES NECESSARY FOR TQ TO SUCCEED.
812 TQ may be abandoned before it can produce significant system performance gains.
from p. 8
809 Many employees conclude that their continued employment may be at risk because of TQ.
from p. 8
605 Many employees view TQ organizational changes as a threat to their existing security.
606 Employees are not motivated to make changes needed for TQ to succeed.
610 Organizational goal achievement is related to successful TQ implementation.
604 Receipt of extrinsic rewards is an important element in employees' sense of security.
512 Many people are unsure what the real basis is for receiving extrinsic rewards.
from p. 5
602 Successful TQ implementation requires major organizational change.
603 Employees have little or no motivation to implement TQ.
207 Employees see TQ as an impediment to "real work."
from p. 2
511 Extrinsic rewards lose their power as motivators for achieving organizational objectives.
from p. 5
601 Organizational objectives include successful TQ implementation.

FIGURE 3.44—*Continued.*

CURRENT REALITY TREE, p. 7

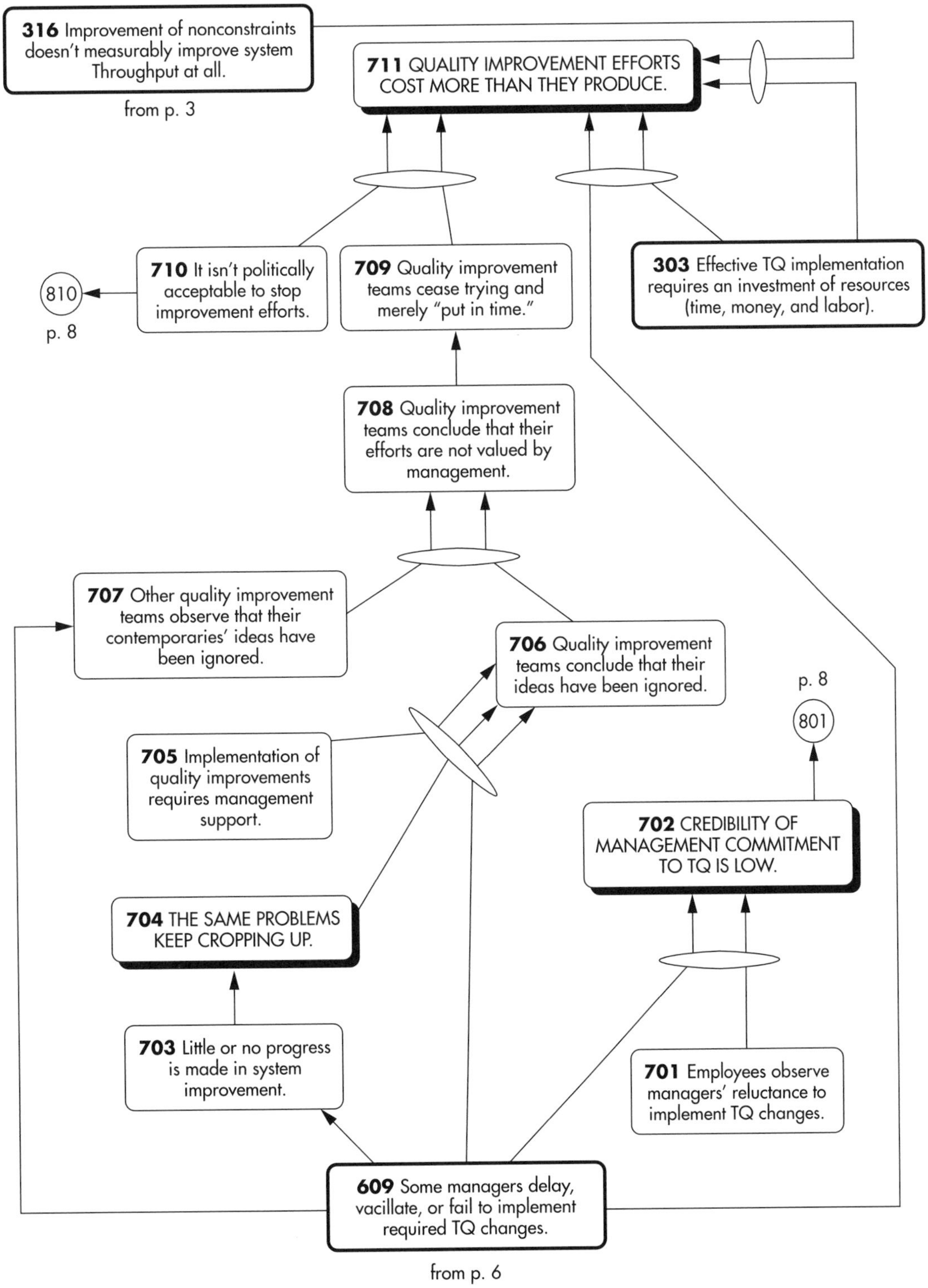
316 Improvement of nonconstraints doesn't measurably improve system Throughput at all.
from p. 3
711 QUALITY IMPROVEMENT EFFORTS COST MORE THAN THEY PRODUCE.
710 It isn't politically acceptable to stop improvement efforts.
810
p. 8
709 Quality improvement teams cease trying and merely "put in time."
303 Effective TQ implementation requires an investment of resources (time, money, and labor).
708 Quality improvement teams conclude that their efforts are not valued by management.
707 Other quality improvement teams observe that their contemporaries' ideas have been ignored.
706 Quality improvement teams conclude that their ideas have been ignored.
p. 8
801
705 Implementation of quality improvements requires management support.
702 CREDIBILITY OF MANAGEMENT COMMITMENT TO TQ IS LOW.
704 THE SAME PROBLEMS KEEP CROPPING UP.
703 Little or no progress is made in system improvement.
701 Employees observe managers' reluctance to implement TQ changes.
609 Some managers delay, vacillate, or fail to implement required TQ changes.
from p. 6

FIGURE 3.44—*Continued.*

CURRENT REALITY TREE, p. 8

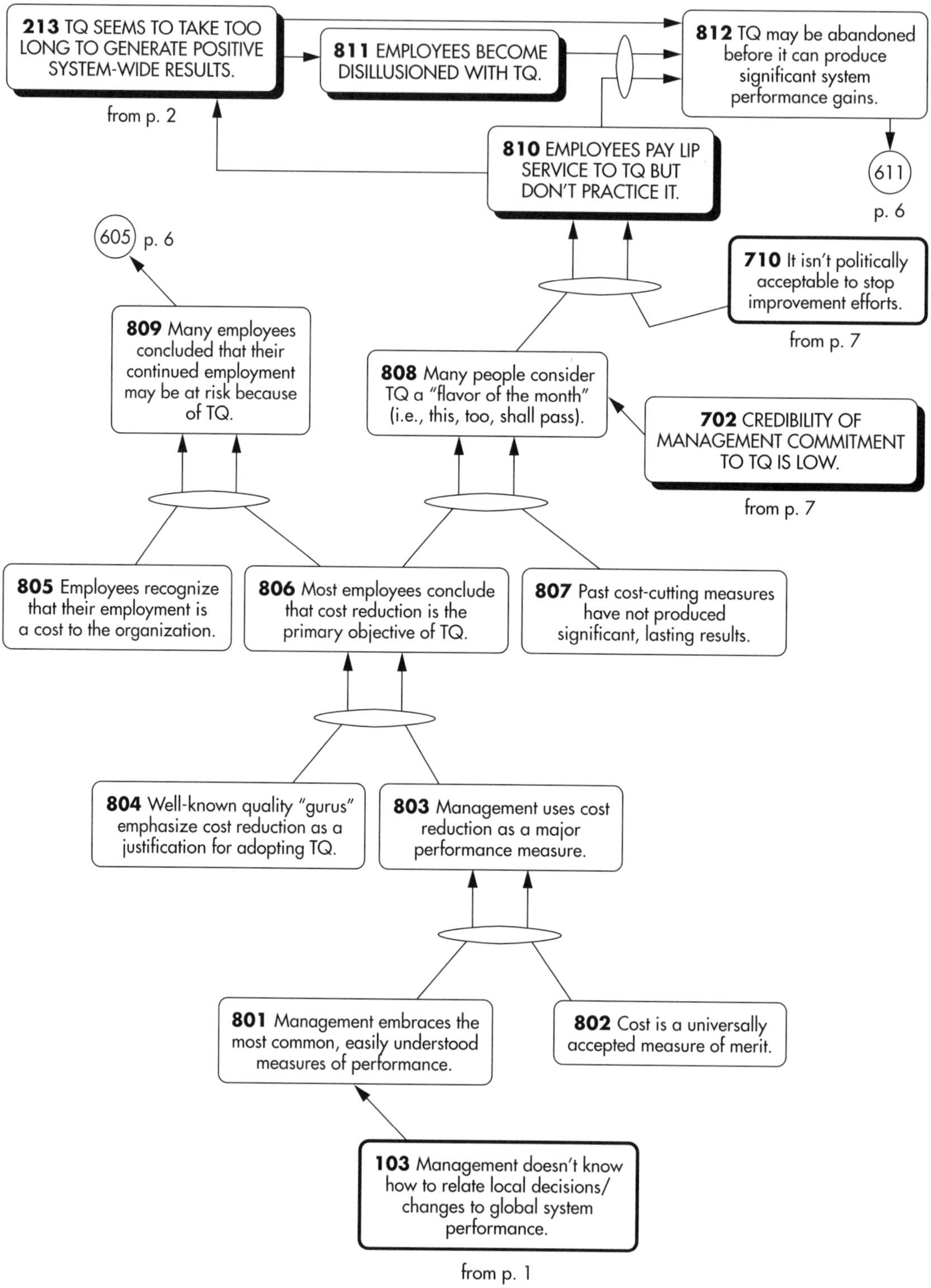

213 TQ SEEMS TO TAKE TOO LONG TO GENERATE POSITIVE SYSTEM-WIDE RESULTS.
from p. 2
811 EMPLOYEES BECOME DISILLUSIONED WITH TQ.
812 TQ may be abandoned before it can produce significant system performance gains.
611
p. 6
810 EMPLOYEES PAY LIP SERVICE TO TQ BUT DON'T PRACTICE IT.
605
p. 6
710 It isn't politically acceptable to stop improvement efforts.
from p. 7
809 Many employees concluded that their continued employment may be at risk because of TQ.
808 Many people consider TQ a "flavor of the month" (i.e., this, too, shall pass).
702 CREDIBILITY OF MANAGEMENT COMMITMENT TO TQ IS LOW.
from p. 7
805 Employees recognize that their employment is a cost to the organization.
806 Most employees conclude that cost reduction is the primary objective of TQ.
807 Past cost-cutting measures have not produced significant, lasting results.
804 Well-known quality "gurus" emphasize cost reduction as a justification for adopting TQ.
803 Management uses cost reduction as a major performance measure.
801 Management embraces the most common, easily understood measures of performance.
802 Cost is a universally accepted measure of merit.
103 Management doesn't know how to relate local decisions/changes to global system performance.
from p. 1

FIGURE 3.44—*Continued.*

CURRENT REALITY TREE, p. 9

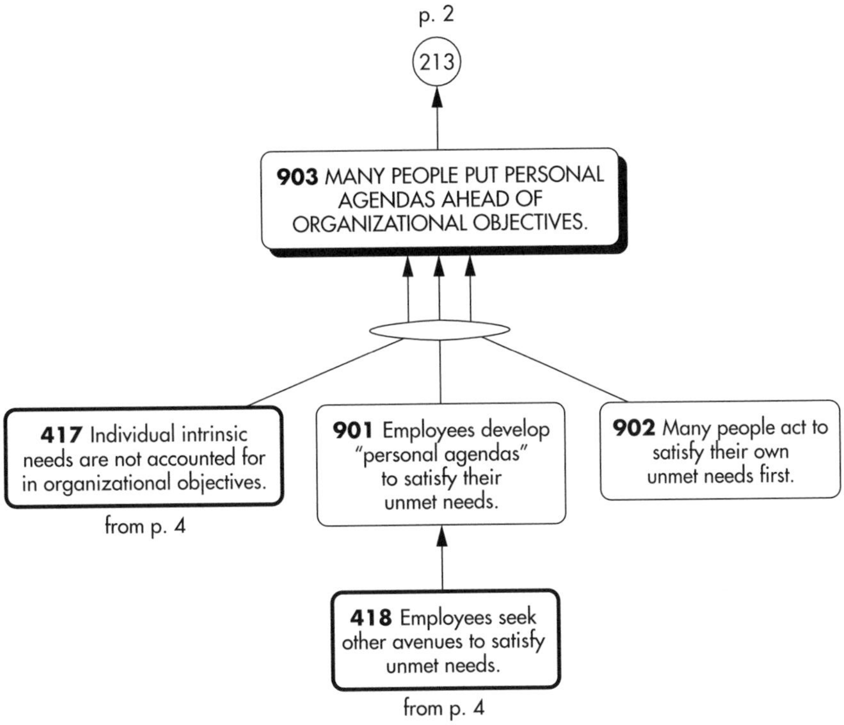
p. 2
213
903 MANY PEOPLE PUT PERSONAL AGENDAS AHEAD OF ORGANIZATIONAL OBJECTIVES.
417 Individual intrinsic needs are not accounted for in organizational objectives.
from p. 4
901 Employees develop "personal agendas" to satisfy their unmet needs.
902 Many people act to satisfy their own unmet needs first.
418 Employees seek other avenues to satisfy unmet needs.
from p. 4

FIGURE 3.44—*Continued.*

1. **IDENTIFY YOUR SPAN OF CONTROL AND SPHERE OF INFLUENCE.**
   - What are the boundaries of your system?
   - Create a mental picture of the limits of your control and influence.

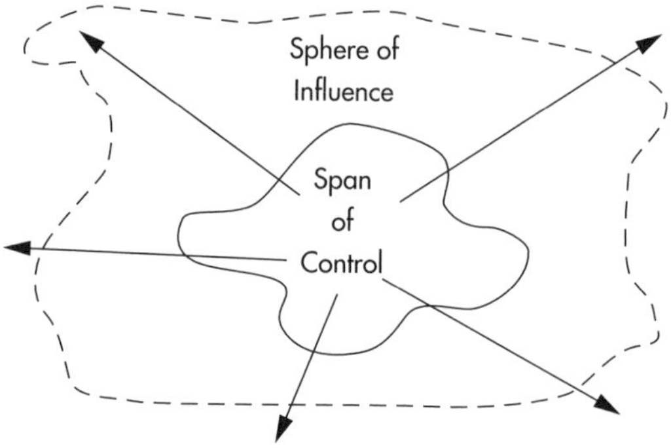

2. **CREATE A LIST OF UNDESIRABLE EFFECTS.**
   - Write a question, beginning with "why," that succinctly states the problem.
   - List as many undesirable effects (UDE) as you can that confirm the existence of the problem.
   - Write UDEs in grammatically correct sentences.
   - Check your UDEs for "undesirability."
   - Verify that the UDE *really* exists (Entity Existence).
   - Choose the "worst" five; set the rest aside.

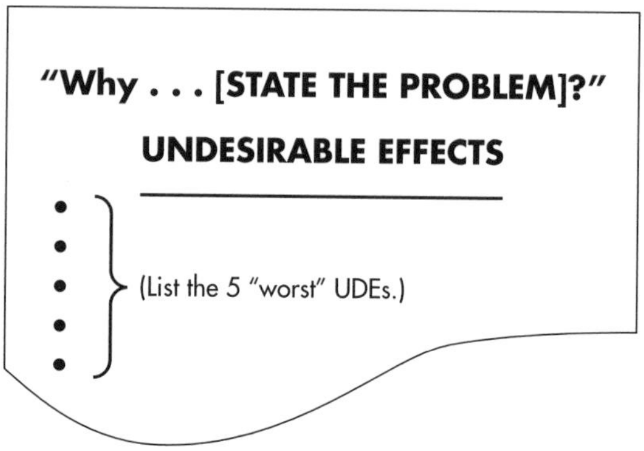

3. **BEGIN THE CRT.**
   - Transfer the five "worst" UDE statements to Post-it™ notes
   - Distinguish these Post-it™ notes with a star, asterisk, or different color ink.
   - Arrange them horizontally on a large sheet of paper.

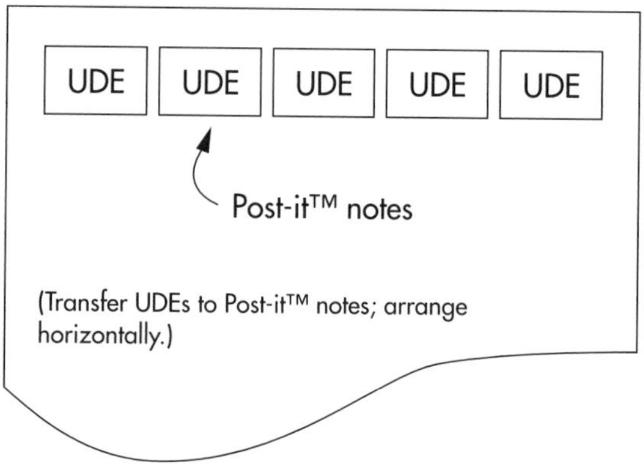

4. **CONNECT THE FIRST TWO UDEs.**
   - Find two among the five that seem related.
   - Position the one that seems to *lead* below the one that seems to *follow* and connect with an arrow (use a pencil).
   - Use the CLR to determine Cause Sufficiency and whether additional cause applies.
   - Identify any intervening entities needed to solidify the cause-effect relationship.
   - Write additional Post-it™ notes and insert where required, with ellipses if necessary.

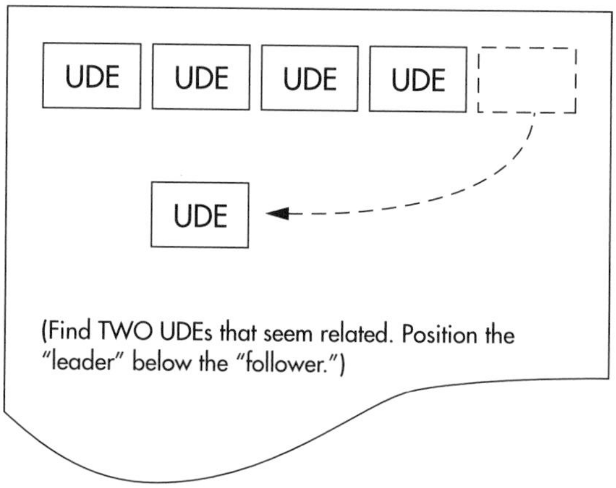

FIGURE 3.45. Procedures for Building a Current Reality Tree.

5. CONNECT OTHER UDEs.

- Repeat step 4 with the other three UDEs.
- Connect them with each other or with the original two.

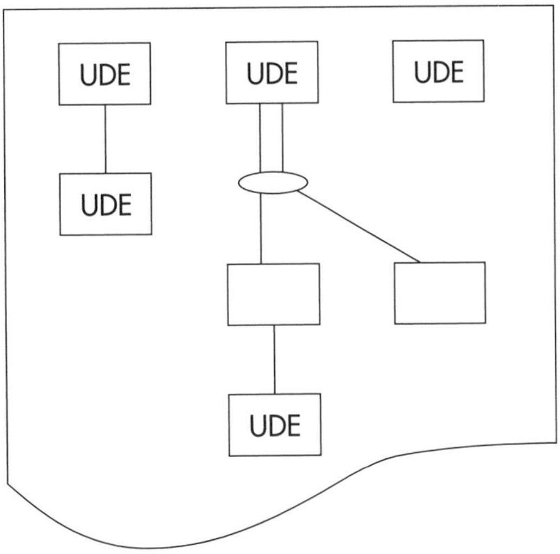

6. BUILD THE CAUSE-AND-EFFECT CHAIN DOWNWARD.

- Link each "branch" with the others.
- Build each branch downward until a logical lateral connection presents itself.
- Add entities as required to tighten logic.
- Incorporate "leftover" UDEs from step 2 when possible.
- Stop when all of the original five UDEs have been connected.
- Recheck all connections using the CLR.
- Watch carefully for connections that may actually be *correlations,* rather than *cause and effect.*

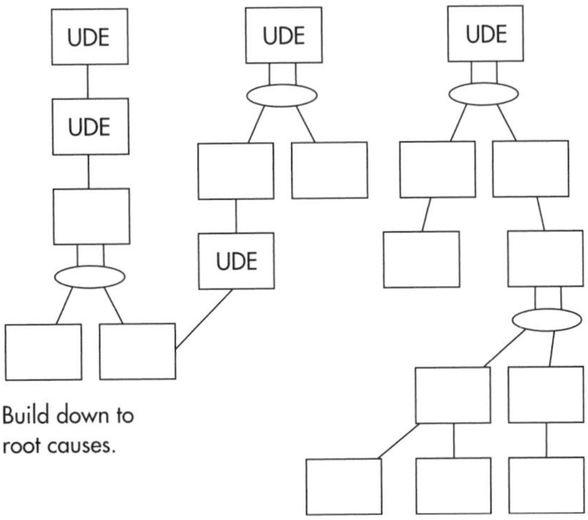

7. REDESIGNATE UDEs.

- Recheck the original five UDEs: do they still qualify as UDEs? If not, remove their distinguishing marks.
- Reexamine every other entity in the tree. Identify and mark any you believe to be additional UDEs.
- Trim from the tree any branches or "twigs" not required to connect all UDEs. (Do NOT delete any root causes.)

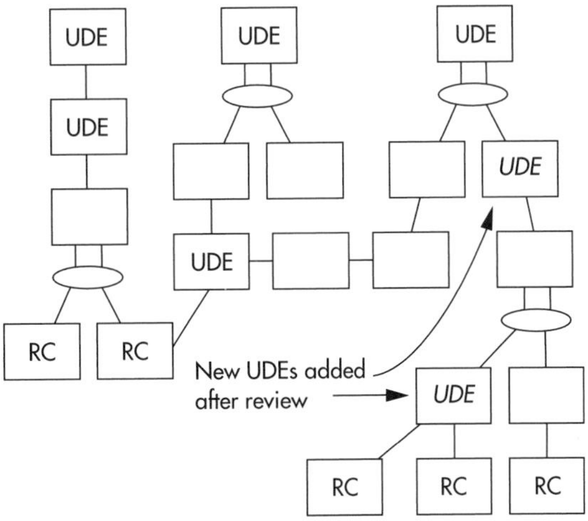

FIGURE 3.45—*Continued.*

8. IDENTIFY ROOT CAUSES AND CORE PROBLEMS.

- Locate all root causes (entities with outbound arrows only).
- Determine how many UDEs each root cause produces.
- Determine whether any one root cause produces 70 percent or more of the UDEs. If so, designate that the core problem. If not, go to step 9.

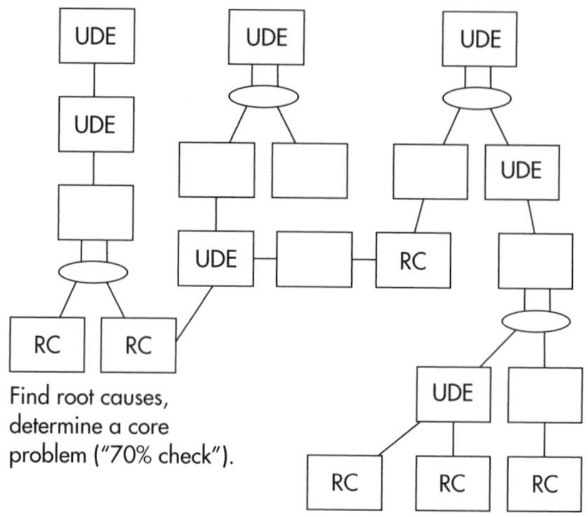

9. LOOK FOR V-SHAPED OR MISSING CONNECTIONS.

- Compare root causes; look for two that might be related (see step 4).
- Build one or both downward, per step 6, until the two branches converge below the root causes.
- Look for previously missed lateral connections above the root causes; connect per step 6.
- Determine core problem ("70 percent" rule).

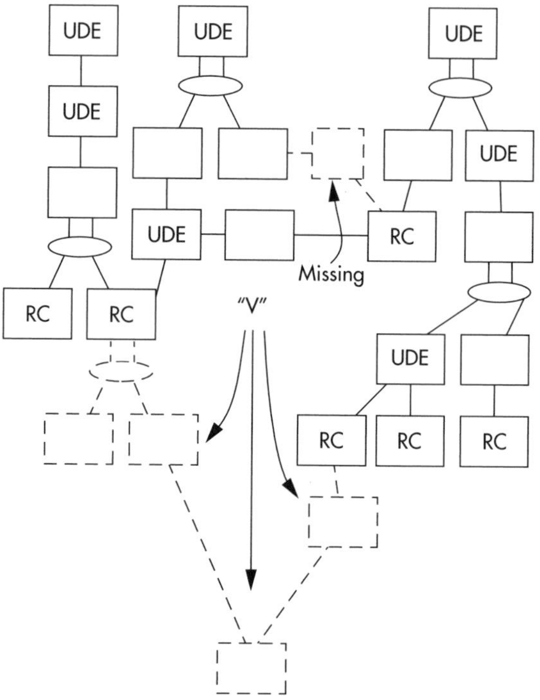

FIGURE 3.45—*Continued.*

10. DECIDE WHICH ROOT CAUSE(S) TO ATTACK.

- Draw your span of control to enclose all entities over which you have authority.
- Draw your sphere of influence to enclose all entities outside your span of control that you can influence.
- Select the core problem, if it lies within your sphere of influence.
- If the core problem is not within your sphere of influence, select one or more root causes within your sphere of influence.

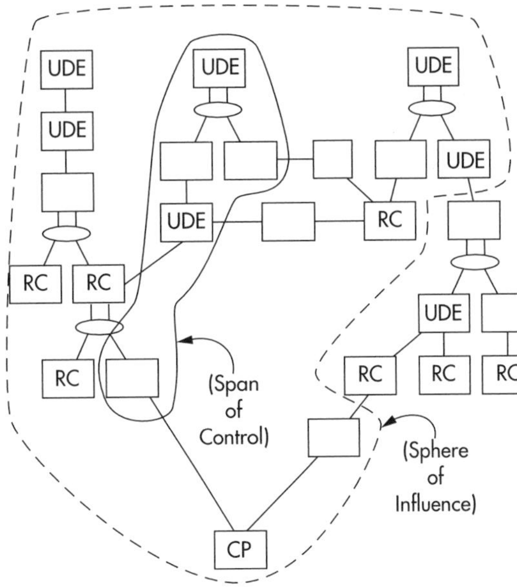

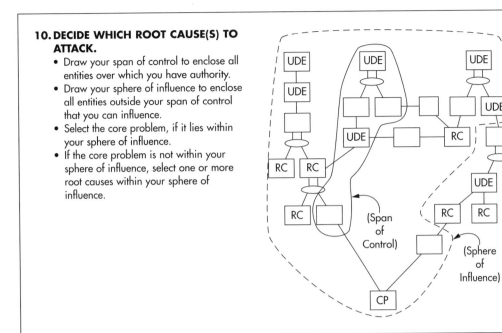

FIGURE 3.45—*Continued.*

Chapter 4
CONFLICT RESOLUTION DIAGRAM

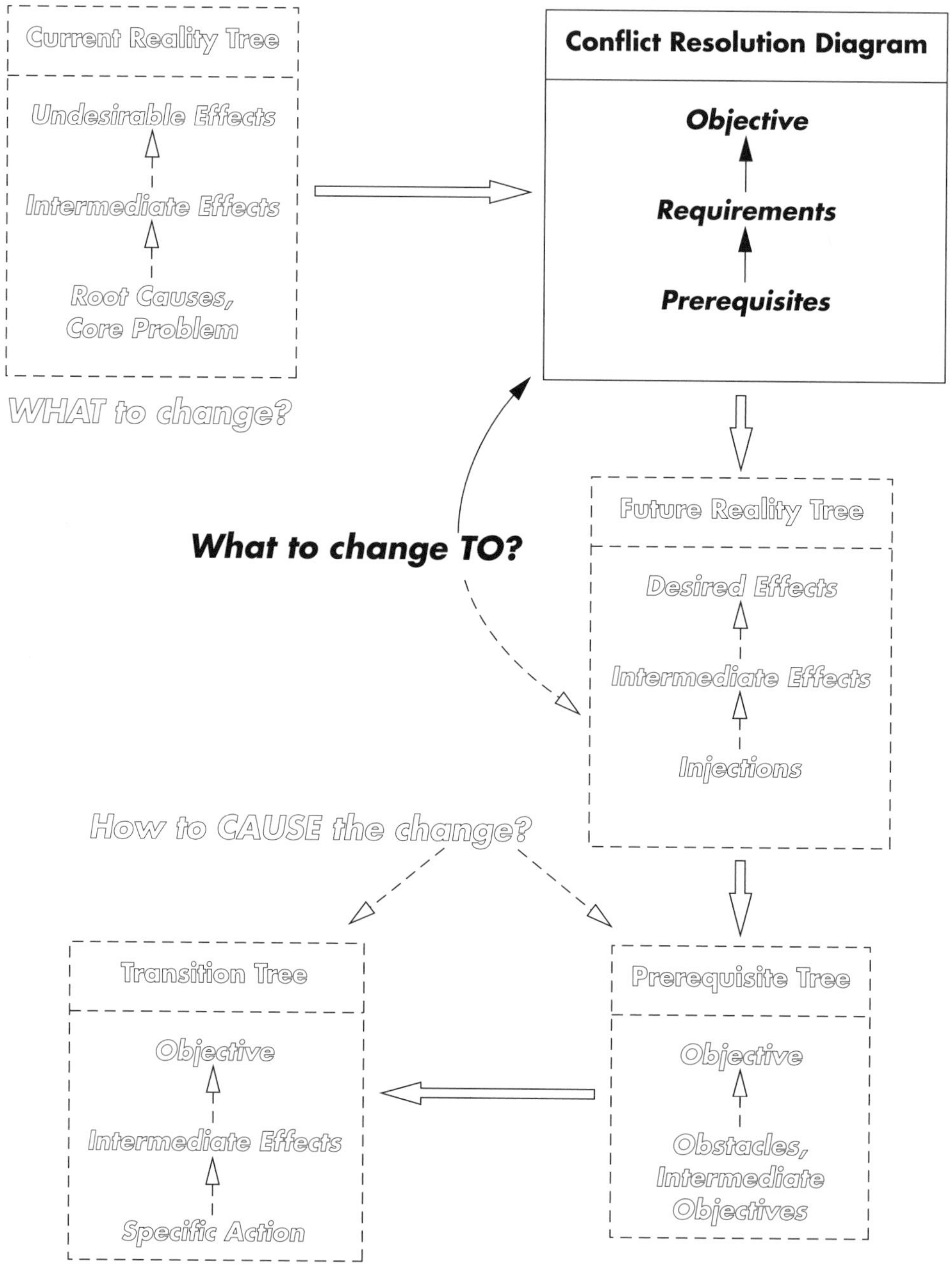

Chapter Outline

Just as most issues are seldom black or white, so are most good solutions neither black nor white. Beware of the solution that requires one side to be totally the loser and the other side to be totally the winner. The reason there are two sides to begin with usually is because neither side has all the facts.

—Stephen R. Schwambach

Why do root causes of problems exist? Often it's because some hidden conflict stagnates or thwarts efforts to change the status quo. This isn't always the case, but it happens frequently enough to justify a concerted effort to search for an underlying conflict that might be perpetuating a particularly persistent problem.

Like root causes or a core problem in a Current Reality Tree, conflict is not always obvious. In most complex situations, it's usually insidious. So how can we determine if some hidden conflict is the culprit? How can we "ferret out" the contending elements that keep us from a prompt solution to our problem? Goldratt has developed an ingenious tool for resolving conflict in a way that leaves both sides "winners"—the Conflict Resolution Diagram (CRD).

DEFINITION

Some people refer to the Conflict Resolution Diagram as an "evaporating cloud" because of its capacity to "evaporate" conflict. It's a *necessary condition* structure designed to identify and display all elements of a conflict situation and suggest ways to resolve it. The diagram includes the system objective, necessary-but-not-sufficient requirements that lead to it, and the conflicting prerequisites that satisfy them (see Figure 4.1). The Conflict Resolution Diagram surfaces hidden underlying assumptions that, though accepted as valid, are actually questionable and subject to invalidation, rendering the conflict moot. The CRD produces ideas that can be converted into solutions to complex problems.

PURPOSE

The Conflict Resolution Diagram is intended to achieve the following purposes:

- Confirm that conflict actually exists.
- Identify the conflict perpetuating a major problem.
- Resolve conflict.
- Avoid compromise.
- Create solutions in which both sides win.
- Create new, "breakthrough" solutions to problems.
- Explain in depth why a problem exists.
- Identify all assumptions underlying problems and conflicting relationships.

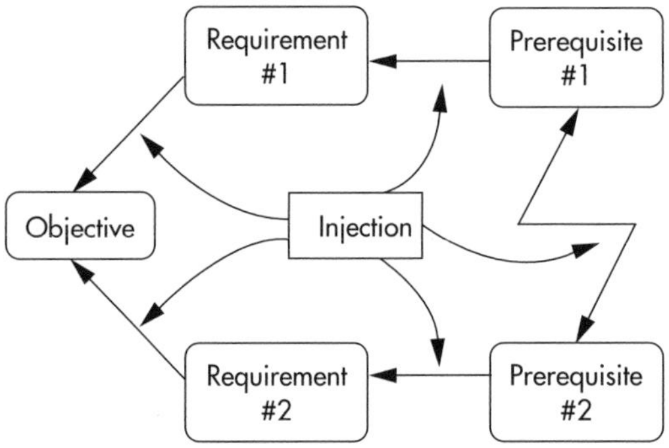

FIGURE 4.1. The Conflict Resolution Diagram.

ASSUMPTIONS

The effectiveness of the Conflict Resolution Diagram is based on the following assumptions:

- Problems exist because strong, competing forces perpetuate them.
- Competition at some point becomes conflict.
- Conflict within a system is an indication of suboptimization.
- Conflict may not be visible, obvious, or overtly confrontational.
- Accomplishment of system objectives usually means satisfying more than one underlying requirement, each of which is necessary but not sufficient alone. These requirements may not be in conflict with one another.
- Underlying requirements are driven by prerequisites, which is the real level at which conflict usually occurs.
- Conflicting forces can exist at several levels, both functionally and organizationally.
- Conflicts may originate from either policies or from human relationships.
- Conflict results from one or more underlying assumptions.
- Assumptions underlying conflict can be identified and their validity successfully assessed.
- Successful conflict resolution depends on effectively breaking, or invalidating, one or more assumptions underlying opposing or competing positions.
- Conflict frequently involves complex interaction among several factors; it is not always bipolar.
- Most conflicts cannot be resolved with "silver bullets" (that is, single actions or changes that make the entire problem go away).
- "Breakthrough" ideas are not solutions.

HOW TO USE THIS CHAPTER

- Read "Description of the Conflict Resolution Diagram."
- Read "Building a Conflict Resolution Diagram."
- Read "Scrutinizing a Conflict Resolution Diagram."
- Review Figure 4.33, "Conflict Resolution Diagram Example." This is a complete Conflict Resolution Diagram on an issue related to "Why Organizations Fail at Total Quality." It illustrates in a typical real-world example how a Conflict Resolution Diagram can be used to resolve hidden conflict.
- Review Figures 4.34 through 4.36, "Procedures for Building a Conflict Resolution Diagram." These are abbreviated checklists that you can use to guide you in constructing your own Conflict Resolution Diagrams. The checklists contain brief instructions and illustrations for each step. Detailed explanations for each step in the checklist are provided in the chapter itself, under "Building a Conflict Resolution Diagram," pp. 137 to 148.

- Practice the "Conflict Resolution Diagram Exercise" provided in Appendix D.
- For your convenience, blank Conflict Resolution Diagram worksheets are provided in Figure 4.37. You may reproduce or reconstruct this format for use in building your own Conflict Resolution Diagrams.

We are all faced with great opportunities . . . brilliantly disguised as impossible situations.

—Unknown

DESCRIPTION OF THE CONFLICT RESOLUTION DIAGRAM

As the name implies, the Conflict Resolution Diagram (also sometimes referred to as an "evaporating cloud") is designed to surface and resolve conflict. "Resolve" does not mean compromise. A compromise has been described as a solution with which everybody is equally unhappy because nobody really gets what they want. True conflict resolution, however, requires a "win-win" solution—that is, both sides feel as though they've come out winners.

The compromise will always be more expensive than either of the suggestions it is compromising.

—Juhani's Law

Another function of the Conflict Resolution Diagram is to generate new ideas—"breakthrough" solutions to difficult problems. Obviously, there is some overlap here with conflict resolution. "Win-win" solutions often require us to come up with new ways of doing things, new solutions to old problems that might also be described as "breakthroughs." But even if a conflict is not obvious in solving a problem, the Conflict Resolution Diagram can serve as a "creative engine," stimulating ideas. In other words, there's more than one way to skin a cat, and you don't necessarily have to throw away the skin, or the cat, afterward.

The Nature of Conflict

Conflict is often painfully obvious. Some of its indicators may include loud voices, angry words, hard feelings, or clearly opposing positions. A classic example of conflict is rancorous labor negotiations leading to a strike. But conflict is even more often likely to be subtle—more like different opinions on the same subject, the difference between what you need to do and what you're allowed to do, or two different parties competing for exclusive use of the same resources (for example, time, money, labor, and equipment).

Conflict Is Not Always Obvious

In the former case, the conflict is so obvious that special techniques, especially designed for the purpose, are trotted out to help resolve it: collective bargaining, negotiation, and binding arbitration. But in the latter case, the conflict frequently goes unrecognized, so nobody is aware that an underlying conflict, with a life of its own, is even affecting the situation. As a result, the problem may be difficult or even impossible to effectively resolve.

The obvious is that which is never seen until someone expresses it simply.

—Kahlil Gibran

Two Types of Conflict

Because "conflict" has such a pejorative connotation, most people tend to think only of the overt indications of conflict mentioned earlier. But for the purpose of identifying and solving problems, it's sometimes better to think in terms of "competing forces." These competing forces are usually of two types:

- *Opposite Conditions.* In this situation, one force pushes us to "do this." The other force pushes us to "not do this" (or to do something which is the polar opposite). For example, one side of the conflict might tell us to "save money," while the other side might say "spend money." This particular conflict is inherent in the problem of reducing the federal budget, where one school of thought says "Spend money to stimulate the economy," while the other says "Reduce federal spending to cut the deficit."
- *Different Alternatives.* This kind of conflict forces us to choose between two alternatives that are not opposite conditions, but are, for some reason, mutually exclusive. This kind of conflict is inherent in any resource shortage. For example, "We only have so much money; we can do either 'A' or 'B,' but we can't do both." This is a classic conflict condition: the choice between equally desirable alternatives that we can't do at the same time. Any "either-or" situation implies a hidden conflict of this type.

Compromise, "Win-Lose," or "Win-Win"?

When it comes to resolving conflict, there are three basic paths: compromise, "win-lose," and "win-win." Only one of these is truly desirable, though the other two may be necessary at times. In a compromise, neither side gets everything it expected. In "win-lose," one side gets what it expected—maybe more—while the other side doesn't get what it expected—and maybe gets nothing. In a "win-win," both sides get more than they expected.

Compromise The first idea that almost everybody thinks of when a conflict or contention arises is, "Let's split the difference—you take half, and I'll take half." If both sides are willing to live with a compromise, it's probably the easiest and fastest way to resolve differences. But what if the conflict doesn't have an acceptable compromise? That leaves two other alternatives.

"Win-Lose" This type of resolution assumes that the situation is a zero-sum game: One side must win and the other side must lose. If I win, you can't win, and vice-versa. This is okay—maybe even desirable—for athletic contests. But in big business, careers, interpersonal relationships—the "games of life"—it's neither necessary nor desirable. All it does is create hard feelings and lasting resentment.

"Win-Win" This is an ideal situation. When both sides win, nobody feels exploited. Both sides probably get more than they'd hoped for. And most important of all, good will is generated on both sides, which bodes well for the future of the relationship.

An Indication of Hidden Conflict

If the conflict isn't obvious, how do we know we really have one? A principal indication of an underlying, hidden conflict is a sense of stagnation: "We have a problem, and, despite our best efforts, we haven't been able to make any headway on it." This situation forces us to ask the question, "What's keeping us from solving this problem?"

One way to confirm that a conflict may be causing a core problem is to look closely at how management spends its time. Typically, a hidden conflict can eat up as much as 50 percent of senior management's time and energy. If you see this happening, you can be reasonably sure a hidden conflict is perpetuating the problem.

How can we be sure a conflict is involved? In truth, this may not always be the case. Maybe the only reason we can't resolve our problem is that we just don't have enough intuitive knowledge about it to work it out—and if we did, we would. But if it's a serious, nagging problem that knowledgeable people have tried unsuccessfully to solve, the chances are that a conflict is perpetuating the problem's existence. If inadequate knowledge was really the roadblock, good minds and better intentions should have overcome this obstacle and solved the problem already. The only way to know for sure whether the problem is perpetuated by a conflict or inadequate knowledge is to try to build a Conflict Resolution Diagram. If a conflict is really present, it will show up in the CRD.

"Breakthrough" Solutions

The Conflict Resolution Diagram helps explain why a problem exists and what perpetuates it. It serves as a kind of template or environment in which to develop various "breakthrough" solutions. The key word here is "breakthrough," because it implies the challenging of traditional assumptions—the ones associated with the phrase "but that's the way we've always done it."

> ***Creative thinking may simply mean that there's no particular virtue in doing things the way they have always been done.***
>
> ***—Rudolph Flesch***

When the problem has you at a standstill, "the way we've always done it" probably isn't going to be good enough anymore. Or, as Goldratt would say, "yesterday's solution is tomorrow's historical curiosity." ("Isn't that the funniest thing you ever saw? Why on earth do you suppose they did it *that* way?")

Elements of the Conflict Resolution Diagram

The typical Conflict Resolution Diagram has seven elements, six of them connected by arrows:

- One objective
- Two necessary, but not sufficient, requirements
- Two conflicting prerequisites
- Underlying assumptions
- One or more injections

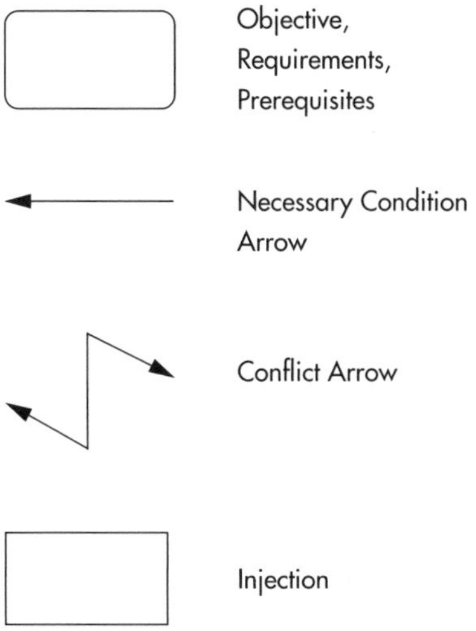
Objective,
Requirements,
Prerequisites
Necessary Condition
Arrow
Conflict Arrow
Injection

FIGURE 4.2. CRD Symbology.

Symbology

The symbols used to depict a Conflict Resolution Diagram are relatively straightforward (see Figure 4.2).

- Since objectives, requirements, and prerequisites are essentially conditions of existing or desired reality, a round-cornered rectangle encloses their respective statements. These entities are arranged in a five-sided figure that resembles baseball's "home plate" lying on its side (refer to Figure 4.1).
- The objective, requirements, and prerequisites are connected by necessary condition arrows. These differ significantly from the sufficiency arrows used in the Current Reality, Future Reality, and Transition Trees (more on this in a moment). The most important thing to remember about the arrows is that they signify the presence of hidden underlying assumptions about the relationship between the entities they connect. (See "Assumptions," p. 131.)
- Between the two prerequisites the arrow has a "zig-zag" and barbs on either end to indicate the presence of a conflict or competing conditions.
- In the center of the Conflict Resolution Diagram is a sharp-cornered rectangle indicating an injection, the idea developed to break the conflict. Sometimes the injection is drawn as a parallelogram purely for the convenience of layout; it fits better within the CRD than does a standard rectangle.

Objective

The objective of a Conflict Resolution Diagram is essentially a *common purpose.* In a negotiation, for example, even though both sides may be at odds over some things, there is an elemental reason they are both in the same room, at the same table, attempting to negotiate. Labor and management basically want the same thing—a profitable company—because that's essential to the well-being of both sides. That's their common purpose, or objective (see Figure 4.3).

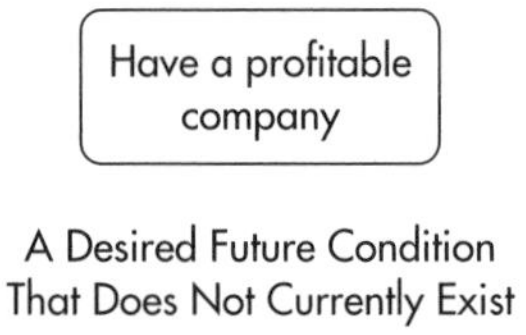
Have a profitable company
A Desired Future Condition That Does Not Currently Exist

FIGURE 4.3. An Example of an Objective.

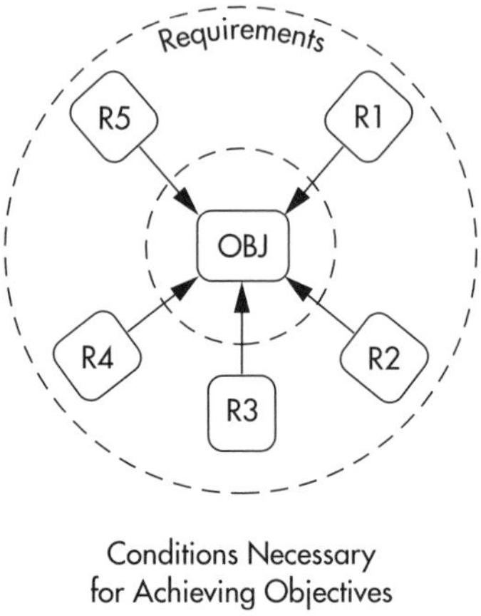
Requirements
R5
R1
OBJ
R4
R3
R2
Conditions Necessary for Achieving Objectives

FIGURE 4.4. Requirements.

Requirements

A requirement is a *necessary condition*—something that must be satisfied in order to achieve the objective. Each requirement is necessary but not sufficient alone to achieve the objective. There may be many of these requirements, like spokes in a wheel, and in most cases, these requirements don't conflict with each other. They may even seem so benign that they are often not noticed (see Figure 4.4).

For example, in order to have a profitable company, we might need to have satisfied customers, a popular product or service, low operating costs, stabilized production, effective sales and marketing, or other conditions. There is no direct conflict here, and each of these requirements can be considered necessary, though not sufficient alone. In the accompanying example, the objective "Have a profitable company" depends on many requirements, two of which are "Reduce inventory costs" and "Stabilize production" (see Figure 4.5).

Prerequisites

Satisfying the necessary conditions, or requirements, usually demands some actions on our part that are better defined and more specific. In the preceding example, the requirement "Stabilize production" might require the specific action "Run large batches." This specific action is called a prerequisite, because it is considered a necessary condition for satisfying the requirement "Stabilize production" (see Figure 4.6).

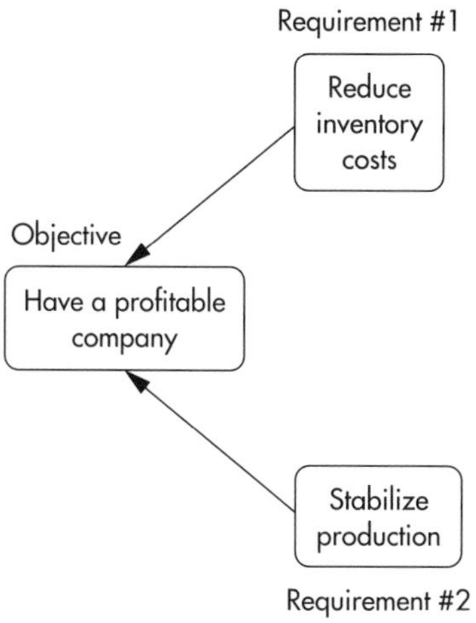

FIGURE 4.5. Objectives Depend on Requirements.

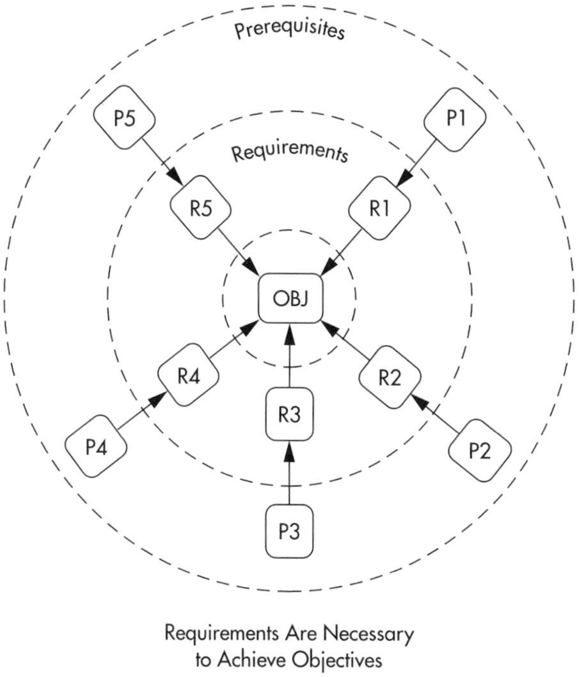

FIGURE 4.6. Prerequisites Satisfy Requirements.

It is at the prerequisite level that conflict, or competing forces, usually occur. While the requirements may not conflict, the prerequisites may (see Figure 4.7). Remember, not all prerequisites conflict; perhaps only two or three do. But these are usually enough to stall progress toward satisfying the requirements, or necessary conditions, that they support. And since *all* the requirements are necessary to achieve the objective, failure to satisfy any one can prevent achievement of the objective. So as few as two prerequisites in conflict with one another can shortstop the objective.

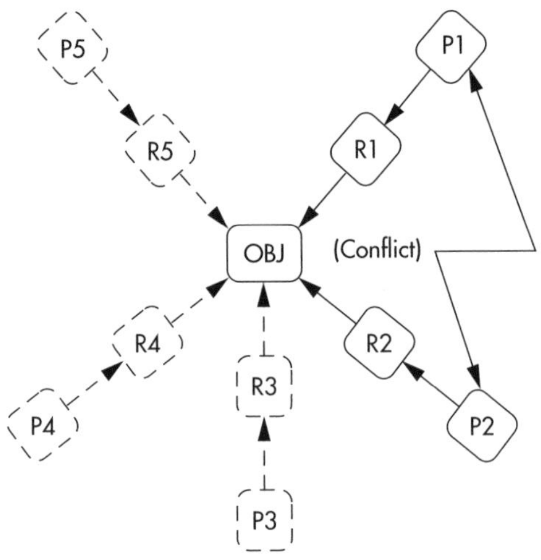

FIGURE 4.7. Some Prerequisites Conflict.

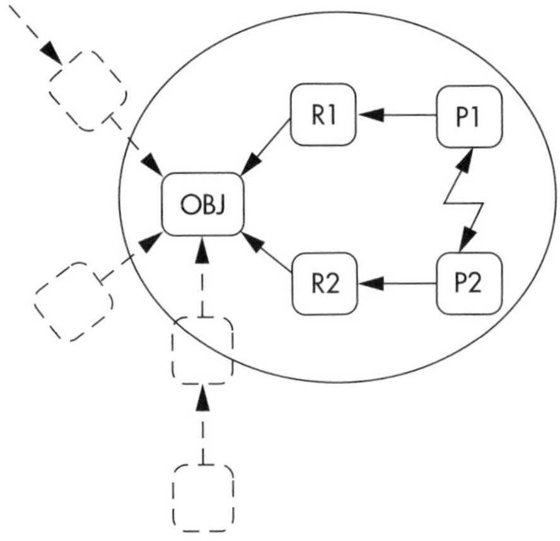

FIGURE 4.8. CRD: A Small Part of the Whole.

Even though there may be many requirements and an equal number of prerequisites, it's the ones in conflict with one another that we're most interested in. That's why the "pie" configuration pictured in Figure 4.6, though it effectively illustrates the whole objective/requirement/prerequisite situation, is not as useful to us in resolving the conflict as is the "slice," which we configure to resemble "home plate" (see Figure 4.8). So when you see the Conflict Resolution Diagram, keep in mind that it's really a piece of a larger structure, most of which we're not immediately concerned about because it doesn't pose a problem.

In our continuing example, the requirement "Reduce inventory costs" generates the prerequisite "Run small batches." Immediately the conflict becomes apparent. On the one hand, we have to run large production batches to satisfy one necessary condition. On the other hand, we have to run small batches to satisfy another equally necessary condition. Even though both conditions are necessary, they are not directly in conflict with one another—but the prerequisites they generate are (see Figure 4.9).

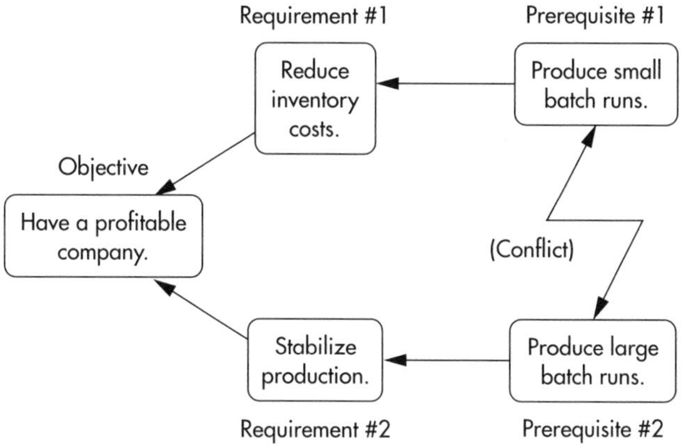

FIGURE 4.9. An Example of Conflicting Prerequisites.

Assumptions

As with any of the TOC Thinking Process tools, the presence of an arrow in a diagram or tree indicates the existence of hidden, underlying assumptions about the relationship between elements, or entities, of the diagram. These assumptions are the key to unlocking the conflict. An assumption is a statement about reality that is accepted as true or valid without question or demand for proof.

Invalid Assumptions What makes assumptions so important to the conflict resolution process is that invariably some of these assumptions are not valid. They may never have been valid. Or, if they were, changes in the environment may have rendered them invalid. Resolving conflict, or solving problems, with a Conflict Resolution Diagram calls upon us to surface all the underlying assumptions we possibly can about the entire prerequisite-requirement-objective relationship and identify the ones that are invalid.

Assumptions That Can Be Invalidated In some situations it may seem to you that all the assumptions you identify are valid. If you haven't been able to come up with any invalid assumptions, try evaluating the valid ones you already have. Maybe you can *make* one invalid. Doing so will usually involve finding a substitute for the entity at the tail of the connecting arrow. (Refer to "injections," following.)

When we find invalid assumptions, we create injections (actions or conditions) to break them. Each invalid assumption may require a different injection to break it. Or, if the situation is simple enough, perhaps one injection (a "silver bullet") will, in fact, be enough. It's also possible that one injection may break several assumptions, or, conversely, that several injections may be necessary to break one assumption. The lesson here is to avoid locking your thinking into a one-to-one relationship.

In the case of our continuing example, some invalid assumptions we might identify could underlie the relationship (arrow) between the requirement "Stabilize production" and the prerequisite "Run large batches." One assumption might be "Only large batch runs can reduce setups." Another might be "Only fewer setups can stabilize production" (see Figure 4.10). Both of those assumptions fairly beg to be challenged.

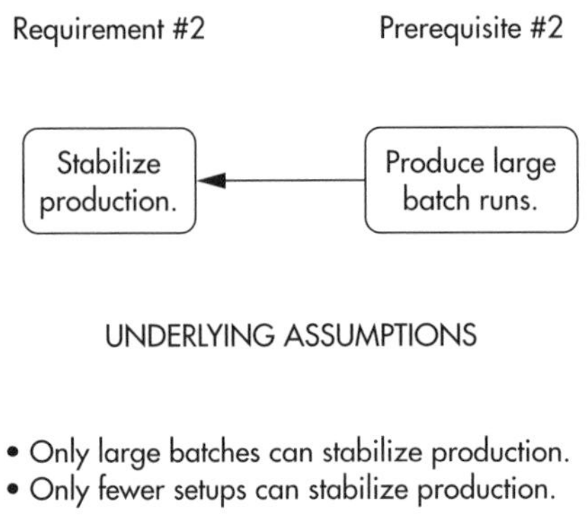
Requirement #2
Prerequisite #2
Stabilize production.
Produce large batch runs.
UNDERLYING ASSUMPTIONS
• Only large batches can stabilize production.
• Only fewer setups can stabilize production.

FIGURE 4.10. Assumptions.

Injections

An injection is a change you initiate, or "inject," into existing reality to break the conflict or solve the problem. This change may be a specific action that you take, but if you're in "breakthrough" territory, you may not know exactly what action you need to take. You may only have an idea of the condition you're trying to achieve. If so, write this condition as your injection; the action(s) necessary to achieve it can be developed later. (Refer to chapter 6, "Prerequisite Trees.")

So an injection can be either an action or a condition. The distinction that makes injections important is that they are something that doesn't exist now—something *you* have to make happen. In our example, the injection is "Differentiate between transfer batches and process batches."

Injections and Assumptions How are injections related to assumptions? Remember that the conflict exists because of the assumptions each side makes about reality. The odds are high that one or more of these assumptions are erroneous—or invalid—in the first place. An injection is an alternative way (an action or a condition) to achieve the entity at the head of the connecting arrow without needing to have the entity at the tail. The injection basically bypasses the invalid assumption—that is, makes it not even necessary to consider.

Injections can also be formulated to invalidate an apparently valid assumption. In other words, you can also bypass (make nonrelevant) valid assumptions with the right "breakthrough" injection.

"Silver Bullets"

Injections are not usually "silver bullets." In most situations, especially complex ones, it's unlikely that one single "mother of all injections," whether an action or a condition, will suffice to completely eliminate the conflict. (That happens only in the movies.) What is more likely is that it may take several injections to do the job. However, the Conflict Resolution Diagram is equal to the task of identifying them all.

Multiple Conflicts

The Conflict Resolution Diagram may seem overly simplistic to some people. Very few situations can be totally reduced to a bipolar condition: A versus B,

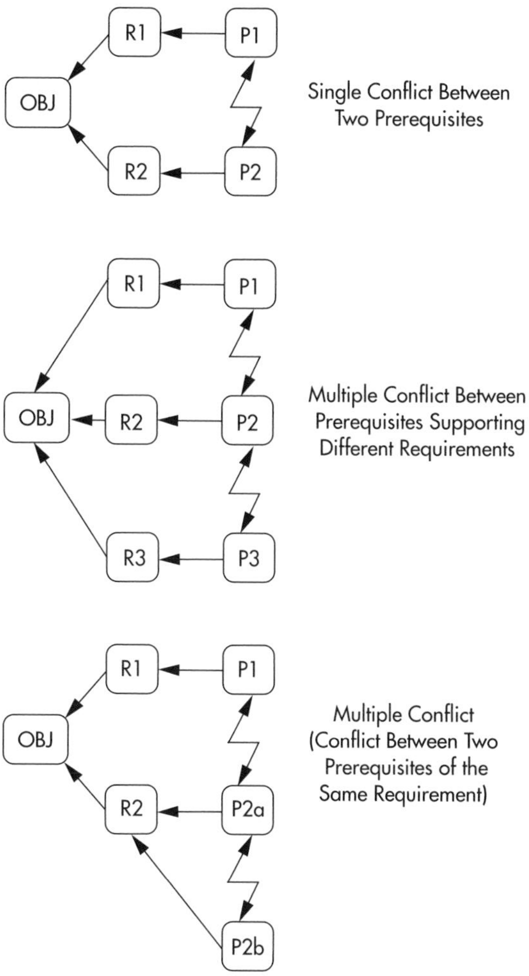

FIGURE 4.11. Various Conflict Configurations.

doing this versus that. Not much of our world is purely black or purely white. But remember: The Conflict Resolution Diagram is a tool for partitioning complex situations into manageable pieces.

Figure 4.11 illustrates several kinds of complex conflict situations, which are probably closer to the kinds of situations encountered in the real world. But to keep us from being overwhelmed by complexity, the Conflict Resolution Diagram allows us to attack complex conflicts two factors at a time.

Reading a Conflict Resolution Diagram

We read the Conflict Resolution Diagram from left to right, starting with the objective and working toward the conflicting prerequisites. Because the CRD is a necessity-based logic structure, verbalizing the relationship of its components is different from the traditional "if–then" format. Necessary conditions are expressed in an "In order to . . . we must . . ." form. And instead of reading

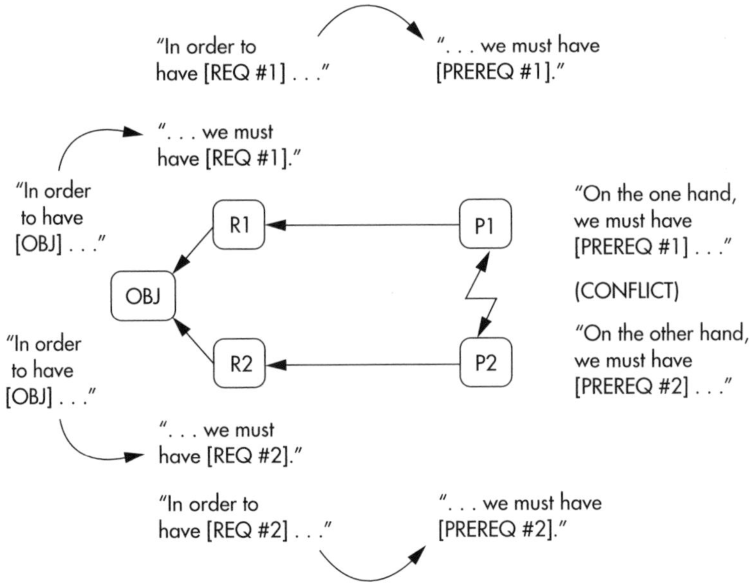

FIGURE 4.12. Reading a Conflict Resolution Diagram.

in the direction the arrow is pointing (from tail to barb), we read the Conflict Resolution Diagram the opposite way. For example (see Figure 4.12):

- "In order to have [OBJECTIVE], we must have [REQUIREMENT]."
- "In order to have [REQUIREMENT], we must have/do [PREREQUISITE]."

Both legs of the Conflict Resolution Diagram are read this way before getting to the conflict relationship.

Verbalizing the Conflict

When it comes to conflicting prerequisites, indicated by the zig-zag arrow with barbs at each end, read them this way:

- "On the one hand, we must have/do [PREREQUISITE #1]. On the other hand, we must have/do [PREREQUISITE #2]."

Verbalizing Assumptions

The conflict we're expressing with the Conflict Resolution Diagram results from assumptions that underlie the arrows throughout the diagram. Our job is to expose those assumptions and challenge their validity where possible. In so doing, we open new doors to conflict resolution.

Assumptions are verbalized as part of the "In order to have . . ." statements of the Conflict Resolution Diagram. They follow the ". . . we must . . ." phrase and are linked to it by the word ". . . because. . . ." For example:

- "In order to have a beautiful yard [REQUIREMENT], we must plant grass [PREREQUISITE], because grass is essential to beautiful landscaping [ASSUMPTION]."

This is an example of a complete necessary condition statement, but it may not be a complete statement of the relationship between the two elements connected by an arrow. In all probability, there will be several assumptions underlying the arrow between two entities in the Conflict Resolution Diagram.

Exposing All Assumptions

It's absolutely critical to effective problem solving and conflict resolution that as many underlying assumptions as possible be exposed and considered. You can do this by brainstorming, or by some other means of idea generation. Why are assumptions so critical? Consider the following example. The assumptions provide the hidden rationale for *why* the "In order to have . . . we must . . ." relationship exists. For example (see Figure 4.13):

- "In order to have high-quality federal construction [REQUIREMENT], Congress must change the existing contracting law [PREREQUISITE], because:

ASSUMPTIONS

1. Existing law always favors the lowest bidder above all other considerations.
2. Existing law always drives contractors to cut costs to the bone.
3. Heavy cost-cutting always encourages cutting corners on quality.
4. Use of inexpensive, low-quality materials is the only way to cut costs.
5. Low-quality materials never last as long as customers expect.
6. Low-cost materials never last as long as customers expect.
7. Contractors are never required to guarantee their work.

In this example there are seven assumptions underlying the arrow. There may be more: Can you think of any others? Are these all valid assumptions? At first

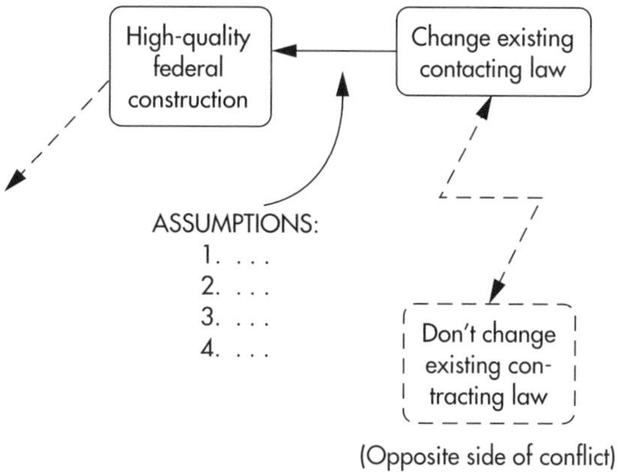

FIGURE 4.13. Federal Contracting Example.

cut they all look reasonable, and some undoubtedly are, but there are probably one or two whose validity might be challenged.

Are the Assumptions Valid?

For the sake of argument, let's assume that all the assumptions are valid except numbers 5 and 6. If low-cost, high-quality, durable materials were possible, the construction would last much longer, even if all of the other assumptions remained valid and unchallenged. If such a "miracle material" could be found, assumptions 5 and 6 would no longer apply, but it might not be necessary to eliminate the prerequisite (change the existing law), because the requirement (high-quality federal construction) might have been satisfied without having to do so. Finding high-quality, low-cost building materials becomes the injection we use to break the conflict between prerequisites.

> ***If the assumptions are wrong, the conclusions aren't likely to be very good.***
>
> ***—Burns's Balance***

"Win-Win" vs. "Win-Lose"

Consider the implications of this kind of problem resolution. Obviously, the other side of the conflicting relationship is the opposite of our stated prerequisite, that is, "Don't change existing contracting law." Somebody is certainly going to be entrenched in that position. But by invalidating the key assumptions that we did (numbers 5 and 6), we have eliminated the need to choose one prerequisite over the other—a "win-lose" situation. Instead, we found a way to satisfy the requirement (high-quality federal construction) without making anyone a loser—the essence of a "win-win" solution.

Is the Idea Feasible?

Notice, however, that we have not considered the feasibility of our idea (injection). That's not the purpose of the Conflict Resolution Diagram. There are other tools, namely the Future Reality Tree and the Prerequisite Tree, whose function it is to test feasibility and identify paths around obstacles to implementing the idea. The CRD is an "idea generator"—a breakthrough idea generator. As with brainstorming, Crawford Slip, and other idea-generating methods, if we let feasibility enter into the equation during the creative stage of problem solving, we dramatically *decrease* the chance of inventing breakthrough solutions.

All Arrows Are Fair Game

In the federal construction example, Figure 4.13, we examined the assumptions underlying just one arrow in the Conflict Resolution Diagram: the one between a prerequisite and a requirement. But remember, there are five arrows in each CRD, and assumptions underlie them all. You need not confine yourself to trying to break the assumptions between only prerequisites and requirements.

The world is constantly changing. It may be that an assumed requirement is no longer a valid necessary condition to attaining the objective, but if you never examine the assumptions underlying that arrow, you'll never know it. If that particular relationship in the conflict situation turns out to be easier to eliminate than any other, failing to examine it may cost you unnecessary aggravation as you work on a more difficult assumption perpetuating the conflict. And who needs *that?*

What to Remember About Conflict Resolution Diagrams

The key points to remember about Conflict Resolution Diagrams are:

- In any conflict situation, there are usually five arrows indicating underlying assumptions.
- Each arrow implies the existence of at least one, but probably more, assumptions.
- Expose as many assumptions underlying each arrow as you can to:
  - (a) improve your chances of finding an easy one to invalidate, and
  - (b) open the range of potential solutions as wide as possible.
- The injections you develop to invalidate assumptions are ideas, not solutions. They should not be constrained by premature considerations of feasibility.
- In complex conflict situations, injections are likely to be conditions you want to create, rather than actions you expect to perform. Many separate actions may be necessary to achieve these conditions.

Changing things is central to leadership. Changing them before anyone else does is creativeness.

—Jay's First Law of Leadership

BUILDING A CONFLICT RESOLUTION DIAGRAM

Now that we've examined the Conflict Resolution Diagram in detail, it's time to start learning how to build one of your own.

How to Begin

Since every situation is different, there are several approaches to constructing a Conflict Resolution Diagram. Your first choice is to decide which approach is most suitable for you. This is not an irrevocable decision. If you try one you think might be best, but it turns out not to be, you can always begin again with a different approach (see Figure 4.14).

- *Right-to-Left.* If the conflict is obvious to everyone, the easiest approach is to start by articulating the opposing positions (prerequisites). Then work left to determine what requirements each of the prerequisites is trying to satisfy. These will be the necessary-but-not-sufficient conditions for achieving the objective. Once the requirements have been established, you develop the objective they're both trying to satisfy; that is, "What can we agree is our larger purpose for trying to resolve the conflict?" This is a classic way to approach negotiated disputes, such as labor-management issues.
- *Left-Right-Center.* This is usually a little more difficult, but it's particularly useful when you already know the objective but the conflict obstructing it isn't open or obvious—that is, it's hidden. You begin by stating your objective. Then you jump over to delineating the conflicting prerequisites that prevent progress toward that objective. Once you have the conflict identified,

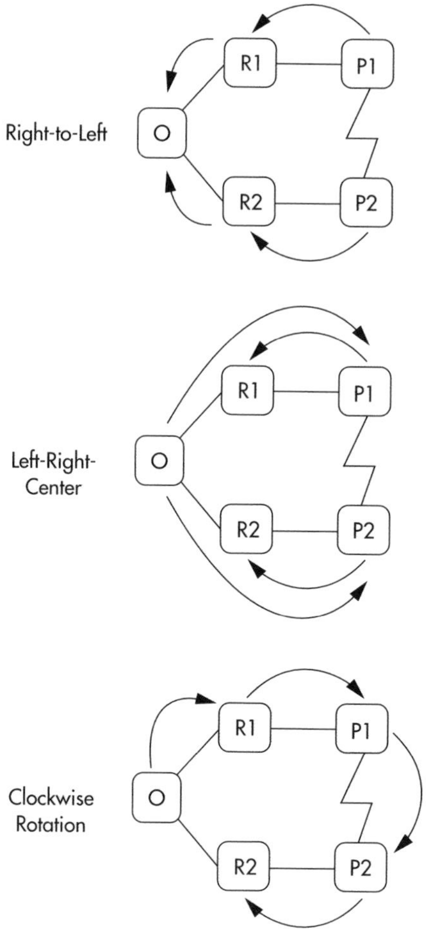

FIGURE 4.14. Different Approaches to Building a CRD.

you work back toward the left to fill in the requirements that the prerequisites are trying to satisfy.

- *Clockwise Rotation.* The clockwise rotation is useful if you know the objective and can articulate the prerequisites, but you're having some difficulty in identifying the requirements. To use this approach, start by stating the objective. Then move to the right, stating the necessary-but-not-sufficient requirement on the upper leg of the Conflict Resolution Diagram, and the prerequisite that supports it. Then work down to the conflicting prerequisite on the lower leg and, finally, left to determine what requirement it's supporting.

The following sections describe the steps to each of these approaches in detail. Some of the later steps remain the same in the sections on the Left-Right-Center and Clockwise Rotation variations. These steps are not duplicated. Instead, you'll be directed to pick up the appropriate steps in the Right-to-Left section. **Rather than reading all three sections through consecutively, you might find it less confusing to decide ahead of time which approach suits your situation best, then go directly to that section.**

The Right-to-Left Approach

In most daily applications of the Conflict Resolution Diagram, you'll probably be able to zero in on the conflict without much difficulty. In these situations, you'll be trying to answer the questions "Why do we have this conflict, and what can we do about it?" In this approach you'll identify the requirement that each side of the conflict is trying to satisfy, then the common objective of both sides.

Keep in mind that, in some instances, the requirement of one side may not be mandated by the organization. It may be driven by personal agendas. Don't overlook this possibility in determining the requirements.

1. Construct a Blank Conflict Resolution Diagram

Create five empty round-cornered boxes in the "home plate" configuration, as shown in Figure 4.15. Label the boxes, left to right, "objective," "requirements 1 and 2," and "prerequisites 1 and 2." Create a sharp-cornered box for the center of the diagram and label it "injection." Connect the round-cornered boxes with appropriate arrows, as shown. Alternatively, you could reproduce the first part of Figure 4.37 and use it instead.

2. Articulate the Conflicting Prerequisites

The next step is to explicitly state the positions that oppose one another (see Figure 4.16). These will usually be either opposite conditions or different alternatives (see "Two Types of Conflict," p. 125).

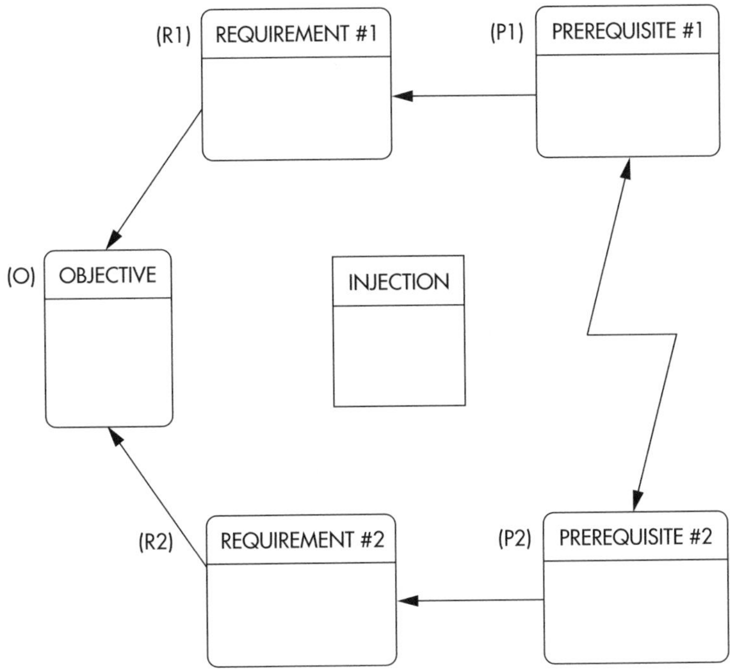

FIGURE 4.15. Constructing a Blank CRD.

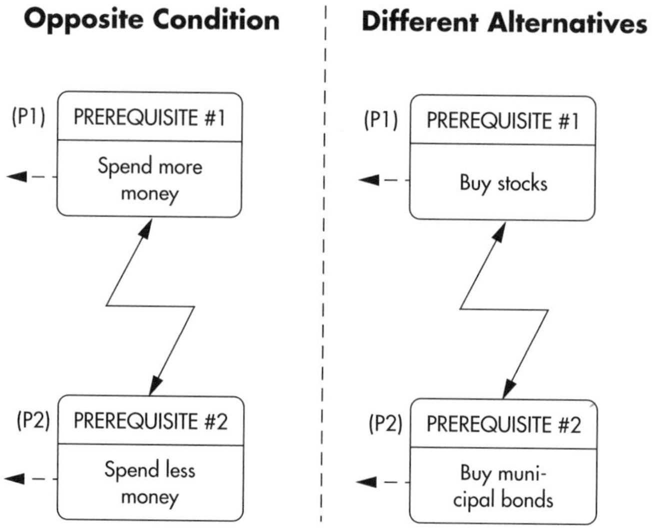

FIGURE 4.16. Articulating the Conflicting Prerequisites.

To help articulate the prerequisites, verbalize them using "On one hand . . . on the other hand. . . ." Adjust the wording of the prerequisites until they make sense when read this way. Write the final prerequisite statements in the round-cornered boxes (P1 and P2) created in step 1.

If you find that you can define one side of the conflict but have trouble articulating the other, you may need to "come in through a back door." Starting with the side of the conflict you prefer, ask yourself the question, "What stops me from doing (or having) my side?" The answer to this question can form the basis of the other side of the conflict.

3. Determine the Requirements

What are the necessary conditions that each prerequisite is trying to satisfy? Why do we need the prerequisites? Read the "In order to . . . we must . . ." statement backwards, and try to fill in the blank (see Figure 4.17). For example,

We must have/do [PREREQUISITE] in order to have/satisfy [REQUIREMENT].

State both requirements succinctly. Assess the accuracy of each requirement statement: Is this *really* the reason we're doing the prerequisite? Adjust the wording of the requirements until they make sense when read in the "In order to have . . ." form. For example,

In order to have/satisfy [REQUIREMENT], we must have/do [PREREQUISITE].

Write the final requirement statements in the round-cornered boxes (R1, R2) created in step 1.

4. Formulate the Objective

This may be the most difficult part of constructing a Conflict Resolution Diagram using the Right-to-Left approach (see Figure 4.18). It should be relatively easy to determine the immediate reason *why* we need a certain prerequisite (that is, the requirement). But in moving on, the next level, the objective, may

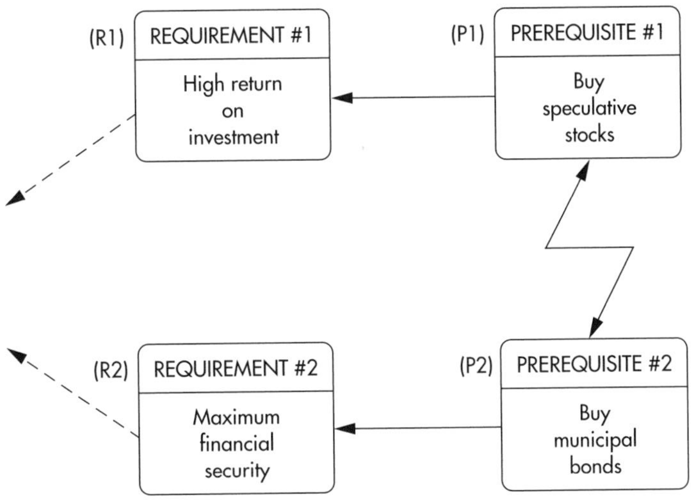

FIGURE 4.17. Determining the Requirements.

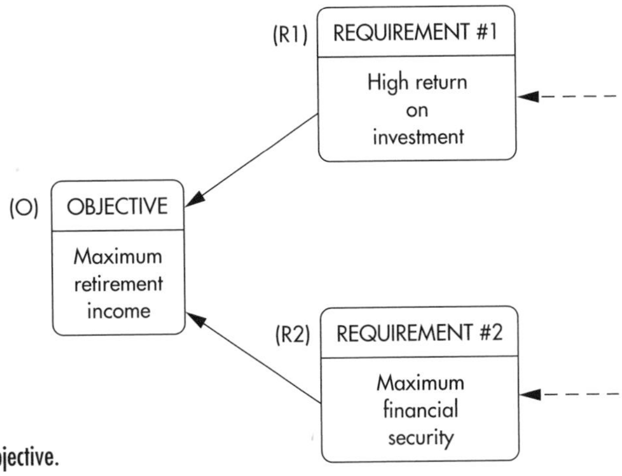

FIGURE 4.18. Formulating the Objective.

be less clear. Ask yourself the question, "These requirements are necessary conditions for achieving *what* objective?" *Both requirements* must be considered together to come up with the objective.

Note #1: It is unlikely that requirements (necessary conditions) will be in conflict with one another, since conflict is inherently absent in a necessary condition relationship. If you think you have conflicting requirements, recheck your construction very carefully. One or both of the requirements are probably really prerequisites. You may actually have a multiple conflict in your situation. (Refer to "Multiple Conflicts," pp. 132–133, and Figure 4.11.)

Note #2: In some circumstances, there may be an intermediate level of additional requirements between R1/R2 and the objective (see Figure 4.19). You should consider them in formulating the objective, but they need not be depicted in the diagram as long as

a. They are necessary but not sufficient alone,
b. They *do not,* themselves, conflict with each other, and

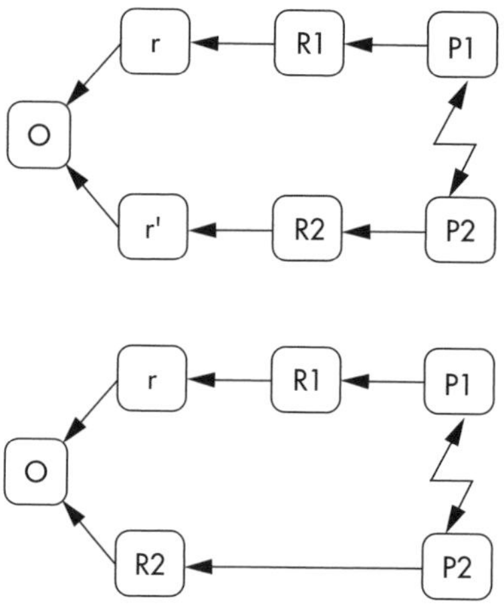

FIGURE 4.19. Intermediate Requirements: Two Variations.

c. Their existence is likely to be understood and accepted, without being explicitly expressed, by anyone else to whom you might show the Conflict Resolution Diagram.

If you can't meet these three criteria, for the sake of clarity include the additional requirements in your Conflict Resolution Diagram. Figure 4.19 shows two variations on how this might be done. However, this should be a last resort. Whenever possible, adhere to the KISS principle: "Keep It Simple, Stupid!"

Adjust your objective statement until it makes sense when read in the "In order to . . ." form with your requirements. When you have an objective statement that seems to mesh well, write it in the box (O) you created in step 1.

5. Evaluate the Conflict Resolution Diagram Relationship

Read the entire Conflict Resolution Diagram aloud, from objective to prerequisites, using the "In order to . . . we must . . ." form. EXAMPLE:

- "In order to have maximum retirement income (O), I must have a high return on investment (R1)."
- "In order to have maximum retirement income (O), I must have maximum financial security (R2)."
- "In order to have a high return on investment (R1), I must buy speculative stocks (P1)."
- "In order to have maximum financial security (R2), I must buy municipal bonds (P2)."
- "On the one hand, I must buy speculative stocks (P1). On the other hand, I must buy municipal bonds (P2). I can't do both."

As a whole, does this construction accurately reflect your intuition on the issue? If not, go back to the parts that seem weak and refine them; enlist help from others knowledgeable in the issue, if necessary. If so, go on to step 6.

6. Develop Underlying Assumptions

Make a list of assumptions underlying each arrow of the Conflict Resolution Diagram. Set your goal at 10 assumptions per arrow. You may not achieve that many, but if you strive for that number, you'll probably be assured of nailing the most important ones. Use the format in the second part of Figure 4.37 to array your assumptions for effective review.

a. Annotate the arrow relationship you're about to express in the left margin, for example, "R1 → O:"

b. Then write "In order to . . . we must . . ." statements for each segment of each leg of the Conflict Resolution Diagram. But instead of closing the ". . . we must . . ." part of the statement with a period, attach a ". . . because:". For example:

R1-to-O: *In order to have [OBJECTIVE], we must have [REQUIREMENT #1], because:*

P1-to-R1: *In order to have [REQUIREMENT #1], we must have [PREREQUISITE #1], because:*

Repeat this action for the arrows on the opposite side of the diagram (that is, R2→O and P2→R2).

c. Write the conflict statement a little differently.

P1-to-P2: *On the one hand we must [PREREQUISITE #1]. On the other hand, we must [PREREQUISITE #2]. We can't do both, because:*

d. Beneath each statement, begin listing all the "becauses" (assumptions) for each statement. When your creative well is dry on one statement, go on to the next.

The "Outrageous" Approach. There is a technique to writing assumption statements that will later help you zero in on the invalid ones—the ones you'll want to challenge. Instead of writing a fairly bland statement, word the assumption in the most extreme, outrageous way you can think of. For example:

Instead of: *We can't eat without having money.*
Try: *Of course, there's absolutely no way we can eat without having money.*

The latter wording virtually invites challenge: "Oh yeah? Well, I can eat without having money. I can . . ." We'll address the rest of this line of thought in the discussion of injections, following. Suffice it to say that through the use of the "outrageous" approach, the invalid assumptions will fairly jump off the page at you when you get to step 7.

Here are some typical phrases you might use to convert neutral expression to extreme:

- "*Of course* we must . . ."
- "*Of course* we can't . . ."
- "We can *never* . . ."
- "We must *always* . . ."
- "There's *absolutely no way* . . ."
- "It's *absolutely impossible to* . . ."

Assumptions Underlying the Conflict Arrow. These are usually the most difficult assumptions to articulate. Since each end of the arrow is a competing, rather than a supporting, position, assumptions are generally limited to factors directly related to the conflict itself (that is, "We can't do both, because . . . [why?]." The most common assumptions underlying the "opposite condition" conflict are

- "They absolutely have to be done at the same time," and
- "They are always mutually exclusive."

One underlying the "different alternatives" conflict is

- "There are never enough resources to do both."

Don't be complacent, though; try to come up with others of your own.

Note: Here's another way to surface assumptions under the arrows connecting the prerequisites with the requirements. Try turning the Conflict Resolution Diagram on its side, so the objective is at the top and the prerequisites are at the bottom. Below each prerequisite make two columns, one labeled "PRO" and the other labeled "CON." Then in each "PRO" column begin listing as many advantages to having each prerequisite as you can. Do the same with the drawbacks for each side. The PROs might become assumptions why each prerequisite is needed to satisfy each requirement. The CONs might become assumptions for the opposite side of the conflict (see Figure 4.20).

e. After your first pass through all the assumptions, go back through each one again, looking for any you might have missed and possible duplicate entries (that is, the same assumption that might apply to more than one statement).

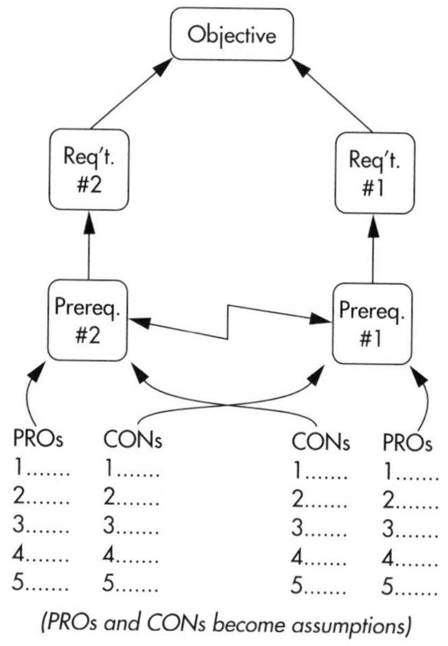

FIGURE 4.20. Another Way to Surface Assumptions.

After you think you've accounted for all the assumptions, ask another knowledgeable person to review your work and suggest assumptions you might have missed.

> **Note:** Don't be afraid to list the same assumption more than once under the same statement, but worded differently. This may help you more clearly identify the Assumption that is critical to the necessary condition ("arrow") relationship. Remember, too, that you're looking for *all* assumptions, but your purpose is to find the invalid ones—the ones that can be attacked with an injection.
>
> *Don't* fall into the trap of building a "bulletproof" Conflict Resolution Diagram—one that has only valid assumptions listed. If your only assumptions are valid, then you have an *unbreakable conflict,* and that's not why we build Conflict Resolution Diagrams. We want to *resolve* conflict, not set it in stone. Consequently, to the best of your ability be sure that your assumptions reflect current reality. Doing so should help ensure that the invalid assumptions, as well as the valid ones, are exposed.

After you're relatively certain you have all the assumptions listed, begin at the top and number them consecutively for ease in differentiating them.

7. Evaluate Assumptions

Now it's time to find the invalid assumptions. If you used the "outrageous" approach described in the previous step, this should be a relatively easy task. Reread each assumption and mark the invalid ones with a "★" or other distinguishing mark beside the number of the assumption. The second part of Figure 4.33 shows a complete list of assumptions with potentially invalid ones highlighted by a "★."

It may be that you have some arrows for which all the assumptions are completely valid. When it's time to start formulating injections, you'll be better off focusing your attention on the other arrows—the ones that *do* have invalid assumptions underlying them.

8. Create Injections

The key word here is "create," and this is the most creative part of the Conflict Resolution Diagram process. You now have to come up with the best not-yet-existing condition or action that will neutralize the conflict. In other words, the injection will constitute a change that will render the competing positions irrelevant. Coming up with a "best" injection implies that you have a number of options to choose from. How do we go about doing this? A tall order! It isn't possible, or even desirable, to reduce the creative process to a set of restrictive, rote steps. However, two general approaches can help make the job of creating Injections a little easier.

a. Validate the Requirements Let's resolve not to waste our efforts unnecessarily. Remembering that the whole purpose of the Conflict Resolution Diagram is to eliminate conflict, we can save ourselves a lot of trouble by first checking to see if either of the requirements is really essential. Maybe one of the requirements was established under other conditions that no longer pertain to the current environment—in other words, it may have outlived its usefulness. If so, the conflict may really be a mirage.

So the first thing we must do is verify that the two requirements in question are actually necessary to achieving the objective (see Figure 4.21). If one of the requirements isn't really necessary, it can be eliminated, thus voiding the

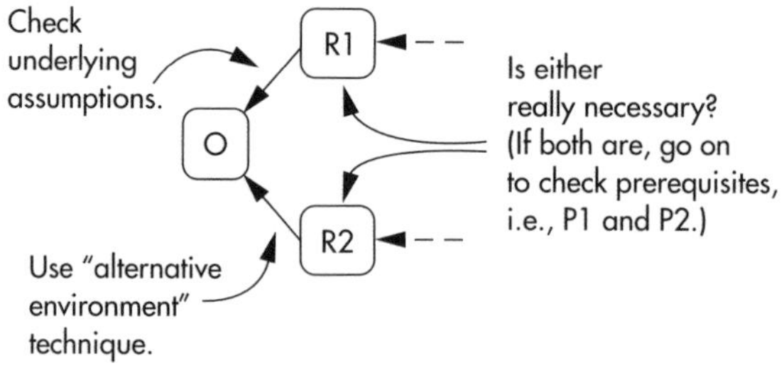

FIGURE 4.21. Validate the Requirements.

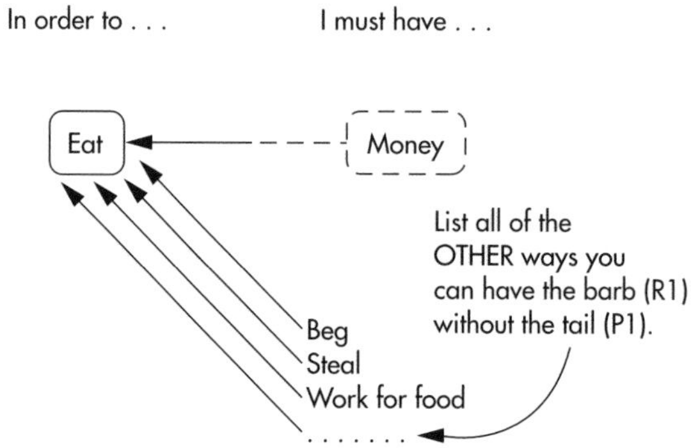

FIGURE 4.22. Alternate Environment.

conflict outright. In this case, an injection might not even be necessary. Or a requirement might be modified in such a way that it still leads to the objective but eliminates the need for the contentious prerequisite that supports it. In either case, validating each requirement requires that you look first at the assumptions underlying the requirement-to-objective arrows. You may use the "alternative environment" technique described below to work on vulnerable assumptions in these parts of the Conflict Resolution Diagram.

b. Alternative Environment Since requirements are usually necessary conditions for good, valid reasons, it may be more difficult to attack the conflict on the left side of the Conflict Resolution Diagram. In most cases, it'll more likely be within your span of control or sphere of influence to effect changes to the way the requirement is satisfied—that is, the prerequisites on the right side of the diagram. A good technique to use for this purpose is called the "alternative environment" (see Figure 4.22).

With alternative environment, you ask yourself "How can I have the requirement without needing its prerequisite?" (Applied to the left side of the Conflict Resolution Diagram, the question would be "How can I have the objective without needing the requirement?") Then, using brainstorming, Crawford Slip, or some other idea-generation method, develop as many different ways as possible to have the barb of the arrow without having to be saddled with the tail.

In the example on p. 143, we responded to the "outrageous" wording of the assumption about eating by saying, "Oh yeah? Well, I can eat without having money. I can. . . ." Now it's time to finish that sentence. What are all the different ways you can think of to eat without having any money? Figure 4.22 lists a few. Can you think of any others?

Once you've collected all the ideas you can think of to have the requirement (or objective) without needing the prerequisite (or requirement), you essentially have a list of injections.

c. Conditions or Actions? Remember that injections can be either conditions or actions. If you know exactly what action you need to take to have the "barb without the tail," make it easy on yourself: Choose the action ("do" rather than "have"). But if you don't know exactly what action to take, or if there might be a complex set of actions necessary, try wording your injection as a condition ("have" rather than "do").

For example, in Figure 4.23, "Have a $1,000,000 retirement fund" is a condition-type injection you might create to satisfy the requirement of "Financial security in declining years." You may later have to develop specific steps needed to realize that injection, but for the moment it's enough to state it as a condition of desired future reality. An injection formulated as an action in this example might look like "Con Mom and Dad out of $1,000,000." But if your parents aren't rich (or gullible), the condition wording might be more appropriate until you can figure out what specific steps you need to take.

9. Select the Best Injection

Now you have a list of injections to choose from. If you repeated the alternative environment technique for every assumption you marked as invalid, you may be like the cat who happens on a nest of mice in the basement: You may not know which injection to chase first. In a situation like this, it helps to have a few "decision rules." Some helpful ones might be:

- Choose the easiest injection to do that breaks the most critical assumption (obviously, some value judgments must be applied here).
- Choose the injection that breaks the assumption that appears most often (if the same assumption shows up under more than one arrow).

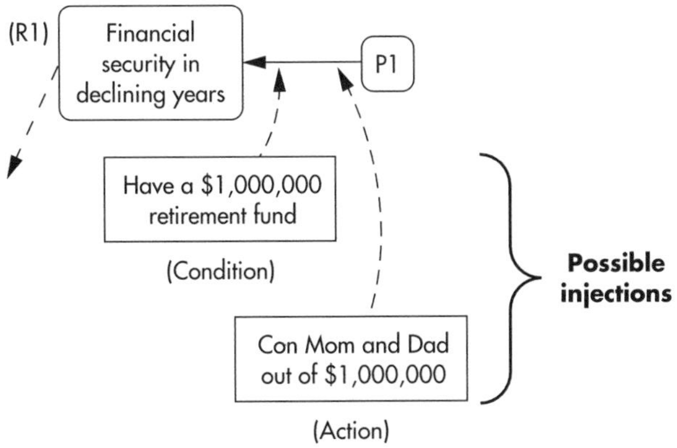

FIGURE 4.23. Conditions or Actions?

- Choose the least expensive injection that shows promise of doing the job.
- Choose several injections (if you can't make up your mind, or if it seems clear that more than one must happen to break the conflict).

Helpful hint: Don't discard any injections that you decide not to use immediately. There are two reasons for this.

a. You may find later that you'll have to go back to resurrect one or two of them if the original ones you chose don't do the job you expected, or
b. You may find that several injections are required, and you may not have originally chosen them all (remember the "silver bullet" warning!). If you've retained the injections you didn't immediately use, you can save a lot of time you might otherwise waste if you had to develop the additional injections from scratch.

Your Conflict Resolution Diagram is now complete. You've identified the objective, the requirements, and the conflicting prerequisites. You've exposed the assumptions and identified the invalid ones. You've created injections to break the invalid assumptions. Now you're ready to think about implementing change.

The Left-Right-Center Approach

The Left-Right-Center approach begins with formulating the objective, then jumps to the conflicting prerequisites that prevent attainment of that objective. Finally, it works backward to establish the requirements needed to achieve the objective.

Because this is somewhat more difficult than the Right-to-Left approach, it's probably advisable to use it only when you need to. One such situation might happen during problem solving, when you are fairly certain what the objective is to start with, and you need to figure out what conflict may be keeping you from attaining it.

The Conflict Resolution Diagram and the Current Reality Tree

In a typical example of such a problem-solving situation, you might use a Current Reality Tree to get you into the Conflict Resolution Diagram. The purpose of a Current Reality Tree is to expose a core problem that results in a number of undesirable effects observed within a system. Unseen conflict can often perpetuate the core problem. This is often why such problems never seem to get solved, and their resulting undesirable effects either remain or are only temporarily abated.

1. Construct a Blank Conflict Resolution Diagram

Create five empty round-cornered boxes in the "home plate" configuration (refer to Figure 4.15 or use the first part of Figure 4.37). Label the boxes, left to right, "Objective," "Requirements 1 and 2," and "Prerequisites 1 and 2." Create a sharp-cornered box for the center of the diagram and label it "Injection." Connect the round-cornered boxes with appropriate arrows, as shown.

2. Formulate the Objective

Common sense tells us that if we can identify a core problem, what we should aspire to is probably the diametric opposite of that problem. In essence, that opposite condition becomes the objective of our Conflict Resolution Diagram

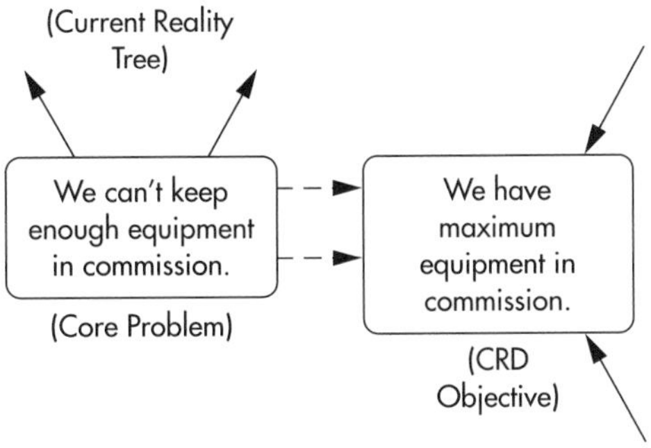

FIGURE 4.24. Formulating the Objective.

(see Figure 4.24). Since the core problem of a Current Reality Tree points the way, it's a lot easier to establish an objective this way than developing one using the Right-to-Left method.

Define the Diametric Opposite In formulating the objective, we should be striving for something better than "not the core problem." That is, if the core problem is "Cash flow is inadequate," the objective should not be "Cash flow is not inadequate." That's not an opposite; at best, it's a neutral condition: not "inadequate," but not "adequate" either. Rather, the objective should be worded in the most positive way possible, for example, "Cash flow is outstanding."

To come up with an effectively stated objective, create a mental picture of the core problem. Then envision what the situation would be like under the best possible circumstances. Reduce that positive vision of the future to a succinct statement. Write the objective statement in the space (O) created in step 1.

3. Articulate the Conflicting Prerequisites

The next step is to explicitly state the positions that oppose one another. These will usually be either opposite conditions or different alternatives (see "Two Types of Conflict," p. 125).

This is sometimes a tough jump to make. It's what usually makes the Left-Right-Center approach more difficult than the Right-to-Left approach. Figure 4.25 is an example of the Left-to-Right jump.

To help articulate the prerequisites, verbalize them using "On one hand . . . on the other hand. . . ." Adjust the wording of the prerequisites until they make sense when read this way. Write the final prerequisite statements in the round-cornered boxes (P1 and P2) created in step 1.

4. Determine the Requirements

What are the necessary conditions that each prerequisite is trying to satisfy? Why do we need the prerequisites? Read the "In order to . . . we must . . ." statement backwards, and try to fill in the blank (see Figure 4.26). For example, "We must have/do [PREREQUISITE] in order to have/satisfy [REQUIREMENT]." State both requirements succinctly. Assess the accuracy of each requirement statement: Is this really the reason we're doing the prerequisite? Adjust the wording of the requirements until they make sense when read in the "In order

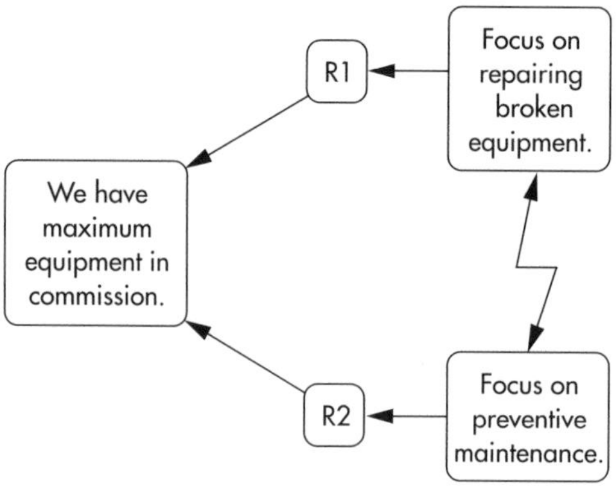

FIGURE 4.25. Articulating the Conflict.

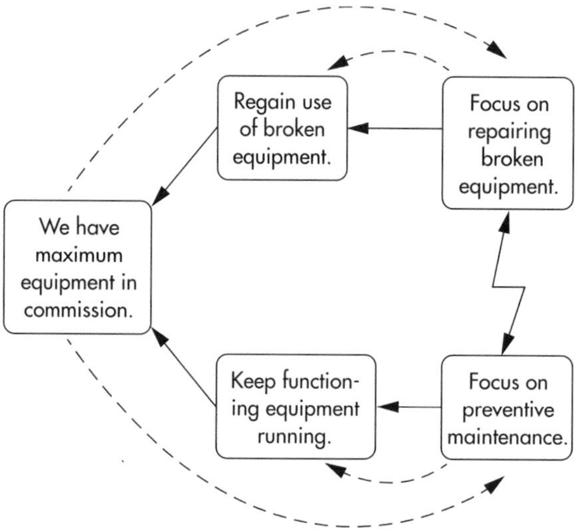

FIGURE 4.26. Determining Requirements.

to have . . ." form. For example, "In order to have/satisfy [REQUIREMENT], we must have/do [PREREQUISITE]." Write the final requirement statements in the round-cornered boxes (R1 and R2) created in step 1.

> **Note #1:** It is unlikely that requirements (necessary conditions) will be in conflict with one another, since conflict is inherently absent in a necessary condition relationship. If you think you have conflicting requirements, recheck your construction carefully. One or both the requirements are probably really prerequisites. You may actually have a multiple conflict in your situation. (Refer to "Multiple Conflicts," pp. 132–133, and Figure 4.11).

> **Note #2:** In some circumstances, there may be an intermediate level of additional requirements between R1/R2 and the objective (see Figure 4.27). You should consider them in formulating the objective, but they need not be depicted in the diagram as long as

a. They are necessary but not sufficient alone.
b. They do not, themselves, conflict with each other.

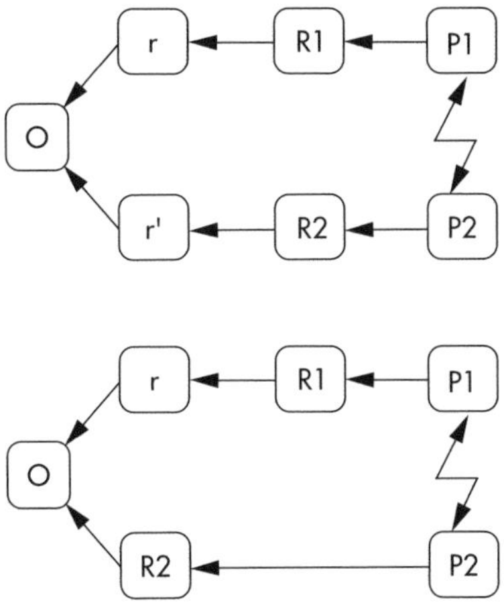

FIGURE 4.27. Intermediate Requirements: Two Variations.

c. Their existence is likely to be understood and accepted, without being explicitly expressed, by anyone else to whom you might show the CRD.

If you can't meet these three criteria, for the sake of clarity include the additional requirements in your Conflict Resolution Diagram. Figure 4.27 shows two variations on how this might be done. However, this should be a last resort. Whenever possible, adhere to the KISS principle: "Keep It Simple, Stupid!"

5. Evaluate the Conflict Resolution Diagram Relationship

Read the entire Conflict Resolution Diagram *aloud,* from Objective to Prerequisites, using the "In order to . . . we must . . ." form. EXAMPLE:

- "In order to have maximum equipment in commission (O), we must regain the use of broken equipment (R1)."
- "In order to have maximum equipment in commission (O), we must keep functioning equipment running (R2)."
- "In order to regain the use of broken equipment (R1), we must focus on repairing broken equipment (P1)."
- "In order to keep functioning equipment running (R2), we must focus on preventive maintenance (P2)."
- "On the one hand, we must focus on repairing broken equipment (P1). On the other hand, we must focus on preventive maintenance (P2). We can't do both."

As a whole, does this construction accurately reflect your intuition on the issue? If not, go back to the parts that seem weak and refine them; enlist help from others knowledgeable in the issue, if necessary. If so, go on to step 6.

From this point, the steps are the same as steps 6 through 9 in "The Right-to-Left Approach." Refer to pp. 143 through 147.

The Clockwise Rotation Approach

The Clockwise Rotation is really a variation on the Left-Right-Center approach. You start by defining the objective, but instead of jumping directly to the prerequisites, you work from left to right to the first requirement, then to prerequisite #1. After that you establish the conflict (prerequisite #2) and work back to the left to determine the second requirement.

This approach is useful if you've tried and failed with the Left-Right-Center approach. It's particularly helpful if you can immediately nail down the objective, one of the requirements, and its supporting prerequisite. You can then build the other requirement/prerequisite pair much as you would using the Right-to-Left approach.

1. Construct a Blank Conflict Resolution Diagram

Create five empty round-cornered boxes in the "home plate" configuration (refer to Figure 4.15 or use the first part of Figure 4.37). Label the boxes, left to right, "Objective," "Requirements 1 and 2," and "Prerequisites 1 and 2." Create a sharp-cornered box for the center of the diagram and label it "Injection." Connect the round-cornered boxes with appropriate arrows, as shown.

2. Formulate the Objective

Common sense tells us that if we can identify a core problem, what we should aspire to is probably the diametric opposite of that problem (see Figure 4.28). In essence, that opposite condition becomes the objective of our Conflict Resolution Diagram. Since the core problem of a Current Reality Tree probably points the way, it's a lot easier to establish an objective as such an opposite than to develop one using the Right-to-Left method.

Define the Diametric Opposite In formulating the objective, we should be striving for something better than "not the core problem." That is, if the core problem is "Cash flow is inadequate," the objective should not be "Cash flow is not inadequate." That's not an opposite; at best, it's a neutral condition: not "inadequate," but not "adequate" either. Rather, the objective should be worded in the most positive way possible, for example, "Cash flow is outstanding."

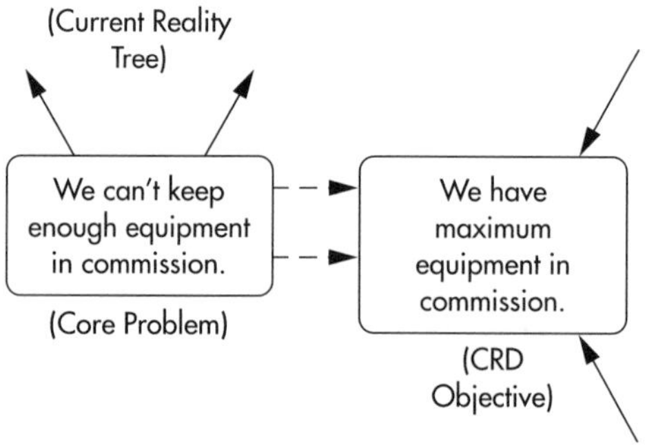

FIGURE 4.28. Formulating the Objective.

To come up with an effectively stated objective, create a mental picture of the core problem. Then envision what the situation would be like under the best possible circumstances. Reduce that positive vision of the future to a succinct statement.

Write the objective statement in the space (O) created in step 1.

3. Determine Requirement #1

What is the first *necessary* condition that must be met in order to achieve the objective? Obviously, it should be one that you intuitively believe to be a player in the conflict. Read the "In order to . . . we must . . ." statement, and try to fill in the blank (see Figure 4.29). For example,

"In order to achieve [OBJECTIVE], we must meet [REQUIREMENT #1]."

Assess the accuracy of the requirement. Is this really necessary to achieving the objective? Adjust the wording of the requirement until it makes sense when read in the "In order to have . . ." form.

Write the final requirement statement in the space (R1) created in step 1.

4. Articulate the Conflicting Prerequisites

The next step is to explicitly state the positions that oppose one another (see Figure 4.30). These will usually be either opposite conditions or different alternatives (see "Two Types of Conflict," p. 125). Start with prerequisite #1. Then determine what action or condition is in direct opposition to the first prerequisite.

To help articulate the prerequisites, verbalize them using "On one hand . . . on the other hand. . . ." Adjust the wording of the prerequisites until they make sense when read this way.

Write the final prerequisite statements in the round-cornered boxes (P1 and P2) created in step 1.

5. Determine Requirement #2

What is the necessary condition that prerequisite #2 is trying to satisfy? Why do we need the prerequisite? Read the "In order to . . . we must . . ." statement backwards, and try to fill in the blank (see Figure 4.31). For example,

"We must have/do [PREREQUISITE] in order to have/satisfy [REQUIREMENT]."

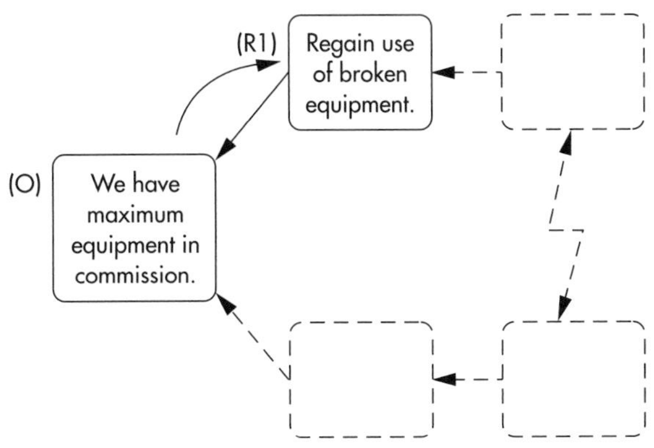

FIGURE 4.29. Determining Requirement #1.

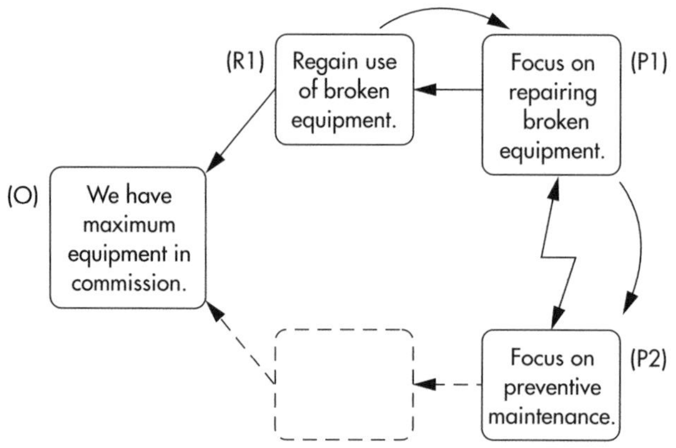

FIGURE 4.30. Articulating the Conflict.

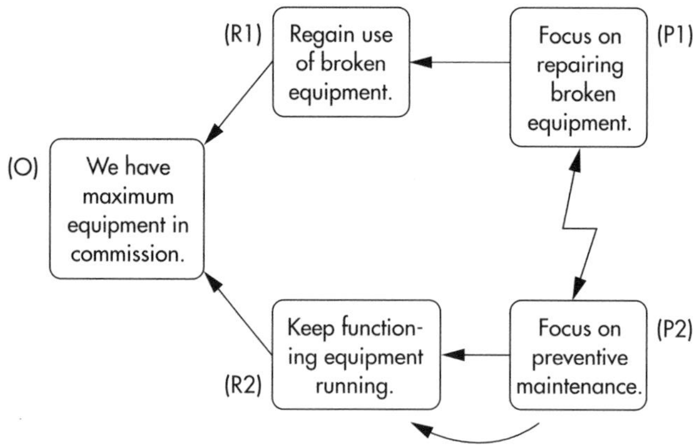

FIGURE 4.31. Determining Requirement #2.

State requirement #2 succinctly. Assess the accuracy of the requirement statement: Is this really the reason we're doing the prerequisite? Adjust the wording of the requirements until they make sense when read in the "In order to have . . ." form. For example,

"In order to have/satisfy [REQUIREMENT], we must have/do [PREREQUISITE]."

Write the final requirement statement in the space (R2) created in step 1.

Note #1: It is unlikely that requirements (necessary conditions) will be in conflict with one another, since conflict is inherently absent in a necessary condition relationship. If you think you have conflicting requirements, recheck your construction carefully. One or both of the requirements are probably really prerequisites. However, in rare cases you may actually have a multiple conflict in your situation. (Refer to "Multiple Conflicts," pp. 132–133, and Figure 4.11.)

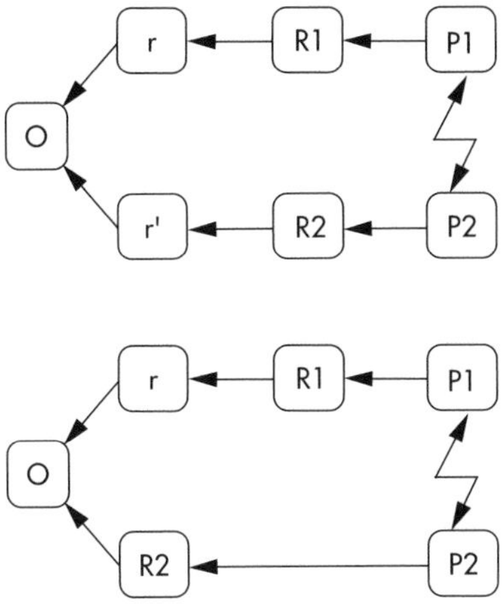

FIGURE 4.32. Intermediate Requirements: Two Variations.

Note #2: In some circumstances, there may be an intermediate level of additional requirements between R1/R2 and the objective (see Figure 4.32). You should consider them in formulating the Objective, but they need not be depicted in the diagram as long as

a. They are necessary but not sufficient alone.
b. They do not, themselves, conflict with each other.
c. Their existence is likely to be understood and accepted, without being explicitly expressed, by anyone else to whom you might show the Conflict Resolution Diagram.

If you can't meet these three criteria, for the sake of clarity include the additional Requirements in your CRD. Figure 4.32 shows two variations on how this might be done. However, this should be a last resort. Whenever possible, adhere to the KISS principle: "Keep It Simple, Stupid!"

6. Evaluate the Conflict Resolution Diagram Relationship

Read the entire Conflict Resolution Diagram *aloud,* from objective to prerequisites, using the "In order to . . . we must . . ." form. EXAMPLE:

- "In order to have maximum equipment in commission (O), we must regain the use of broken equipment (R1)."
- "In order to have maximum equipment in commission (O), we must keep functioning equipment running (R2)."
- "In order to regain the use of broken equipment (R1), we must focus on repairing broken equipment (P1)."
- "In order to keep functioning equipment running (R2), we must focus on preventive maintenance (P2)."
- "On the one hand, we must focus on repairing broken equipment (P1). On the other hand, we must focus on preventive maintenance (P2). We can't do both."

As a whole, does this construction accurately reflect your intuition on the issue? If not, go back to the parts that seem weak and refine them; enlist help from others knowledgeable in the issue, if necessary. If so, go on.

From this point, the steps are the same as steps 6 through 9 in "The Right-to-Left Approach." Refer to pp. 143 through 147.

SCRUTINIZING A CONFLICT RESOLUTION DIAGRAM

Scrutiny of a Conflict Resolution Diagram is substantially different from scrutiny of a sufficiency-based tree, such as a Current Reality or Future Reality Tree. There are really only two tests of a Conflict Resolution Diagram's validity.

Reflection of Current Reality

The Conflict Resolution Diagram is essentially a depiction of what is happening now—not what we think should be happening. Consequently, the Conflict Resolution Diagram must reflect current reality with reasonable accuracy. This is purely a subjective judgment on your part, based on your intuitive knowledge of the situation.

Perception

Unlike the Current Reality Tree, however, your worst enemy is a "dry," solid, logical Conflict Resolution Diagram. Why? Remember that the purpose of the CRD is to identify faulty logic in an existing situation so as to expose an opportunity to break a conflict, not entrench it. The entity at the tail of each arrow should be perceived by most people to be necessary to achieve the entity at the barb. The word "perceived" is key. It may not actually be necessary—but if it's generally accepted as necessary, the Conflict Resolution Diagram is sound.

If you build your Conflict Resolution Diagram in such a way that you include only the valid assumptions, you'll end up with an unbreakable CRD. So be sure that your CRD actually reflects the general perception of the existing situation. After the CRD is complete, you should be able to look at and ask yourself "Is this what we *see?*" rather than "Is this what *is?*"

Figure 4.33 provides some examples of Conflict Resolution Diagrams. Figures 4.34, 4.35, and 4.36 provide abbreviated checklists for building a CRD, using the Right-to-Left, Left-Right-Center, and Clockwise Rotation methods, respectively. Figure 4.37 contains blank forms that may be reproduced and used to build your CRD.

SUMMARY

As we've seen, success in using the Conflict Resolution Diagram is based on surfacing the underlying assumptions we make about current reality—assumptions whose validity is questionable. Once we've determined that our conflict is based on invalid assumptions, the door to new ways of satisfying our requirements is opened, ways that completely bypass the original conflict. And the Conflict Resolution Diagram helps us to creatively assemble new alternatives.

But new ideas are *not* solutions. Until they're tested and implemented, they're just ideas. Now that we have an idea for a solution, it's time to verify it. Will it really do what we want it to do? And will it do so without creating more problems than it solves? Verifying the effectiveness of our idea is the job of the second part of determining what to change *to:* the Future Reality Tree. This is the subject of chapter 5.

It is not because things are difficult that we do not dare. It is because we do not dare that they are difficult.

—Seneca

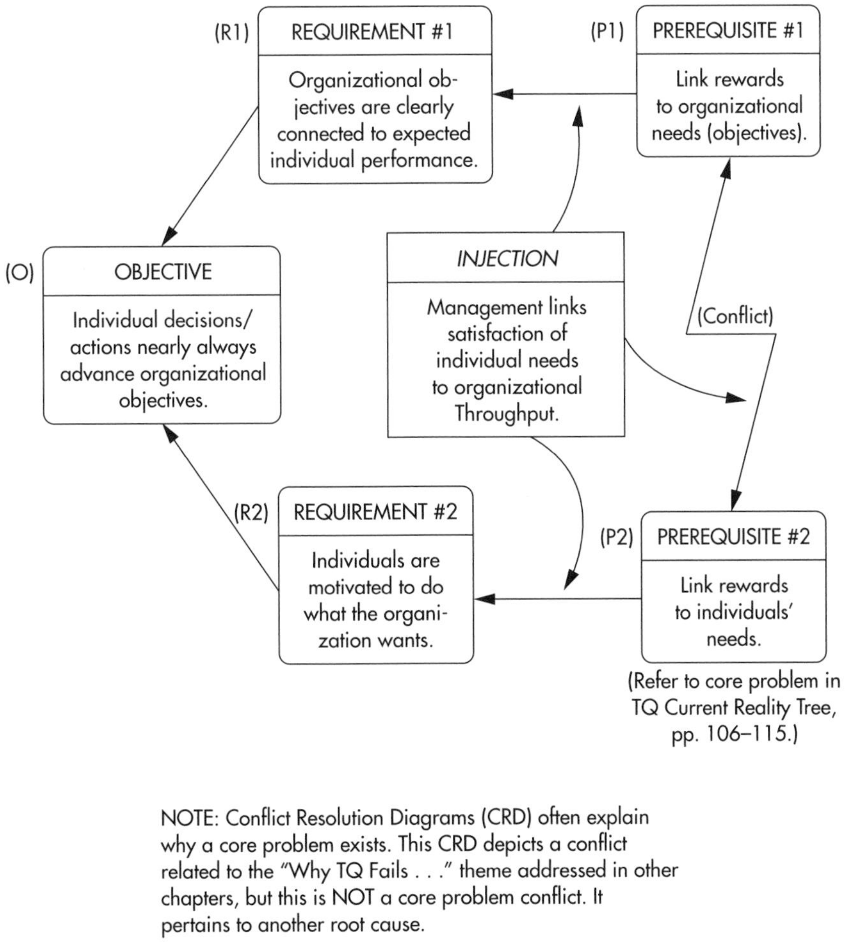

FIGURE 4.33. Conflict Resolution Diagram Example: "Why Organizations Fail at Total Quality."

CONFLICT RESOLUTION DIAGRAM
EXAMPLE: Total Quality (Assumptions)

R1 → O: In order for individual decisions/actions to nearly always advance organizational objectives (O), organizational objectives must be clearly connected to expected individual performance (R1), because:

★ 1. Organizations always know how individual performances affect system performance.
★ 2. The organization always knows what its system-level objectives are.
★ 3. The organization always knows what its supporting (subordinate) objectives are.
4. Local decisions/actions always affect system-level performance.

R2 → O: In order for individual decisions/actions to nearly always advance organizational objectives (O), individuals must be motivated to do what the organization wants (R2), because:

5. Individuals will never behave the way the organization wants them to without some motivation to do so.
★ 6. Organizational objectives and individuals' motives never naturally coincide.
★ 7. Local decisions/actions always affect system-level performance.
8. Individuals are never motivated except by extrinsic rewards.

P1 → R1: In order for organizational objectives to be clearly connected to individuals' performance (R1), rewards must be linked to organizational needs [objectives] (P1), because:

9. People will never work toward organizational objectives without rewards.
10. Linking rewards to organizational objectives is the only way to connect objectives to individuals' performance.
★ 11. Only traditional organizational rewards can reinforce organizational objectives.
★ 12. Organizational rewards always satisfy all individual needs.

P2 → R2: In order for individuals to be motivated to do what the organization wants (R2), rewards must be linked to individual needs (P2), because:

13. People act to satisfy their own needs above all others.
14. Individuals need rewards to be satisfied.
★ 15. Formal (extrinsic) rewards are the only kind that satisfy individual needs.
16. The value of rewards always rests in the eye of the beholder (individual).
★ 17. Management always knows what rewards motivate individual behavior.

Pa ↯ P2: On one hand, we must link rewards to organizational needs [objectives] (P1); on the other hand, we must link rewards to individuals' needs (P2). We can't do both, because:

★ 18. The same rewards can't simultaneously reinforce organizational objectives and individuals' needs.
★ 19. Organizational objectives and individual needs always collide.
★ 20. Management doesn't know how to link the two.

★ = Assumptions vulnerable to invalidation

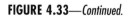

FIGURE 4.33—*Continued.*

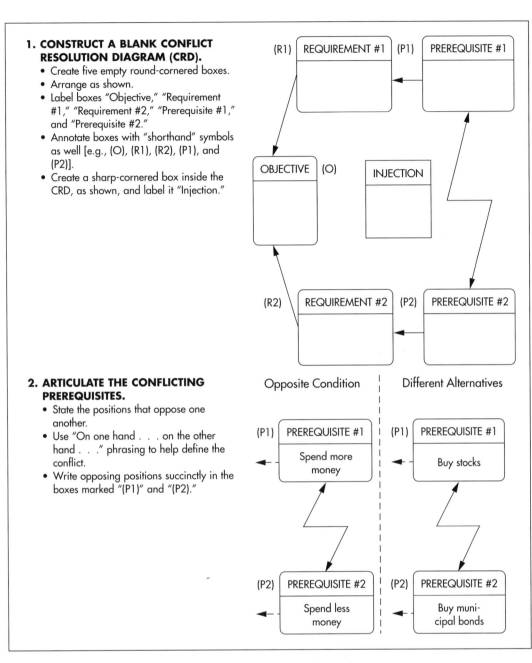

1. CONSTRUCT A BLANK CONFLICT RESOLUTION DIAGRAM (CRD).

- Create five empty round-cornered boxes.
- Arrange as shown.
- Label boxes "Objective," "Requirement #1," "Requirement #2," "Prerequisite #1," and "Prerequisite #2."
- Annotate boxes with "shorthand" symbols as well [e.g., (O), (R1), (R2), (P1), and (P2)].
- Create a sharp-cornered box inside the CRD, as shown, and label it "Injection."

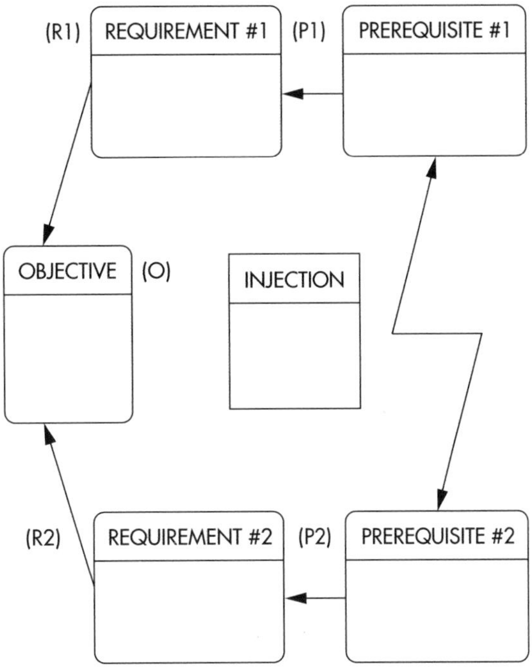

2. ARTICULATE THE CONFLICTING PREREQUISITES.

- State the positions that oppose one another.
- Use "On one hand . . . on the other hand . . ." phrasing to help define the conflict.
- Write opposing positions succinctly in the boxes marked "(P1)" and "(P2)."

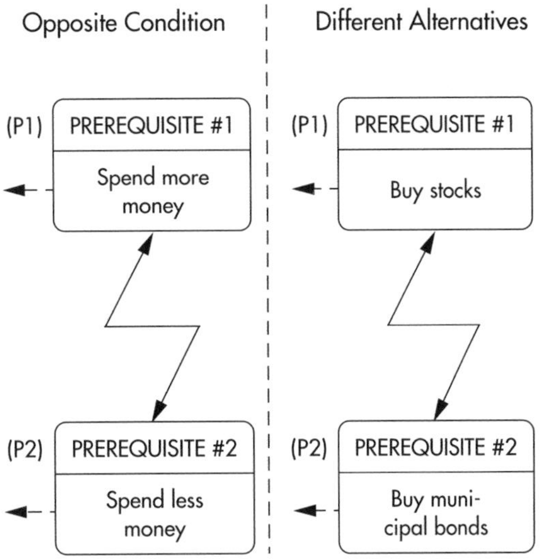

FIGURE 4.34. Procedures for Building a Conflict Resolution Diagram (Right-to-Left).

3. DETERMINE THE REQUIREMENTS.

- Identify the conditions, guidelines, or criteria that the prerequisites are intended to satisfy.
- Use "We must . . . in order to . . ." phrasing to help develop the requirements that drive the prerequisites.
- Write the requirements in the boxes marked "(R1)" and "(R2)."

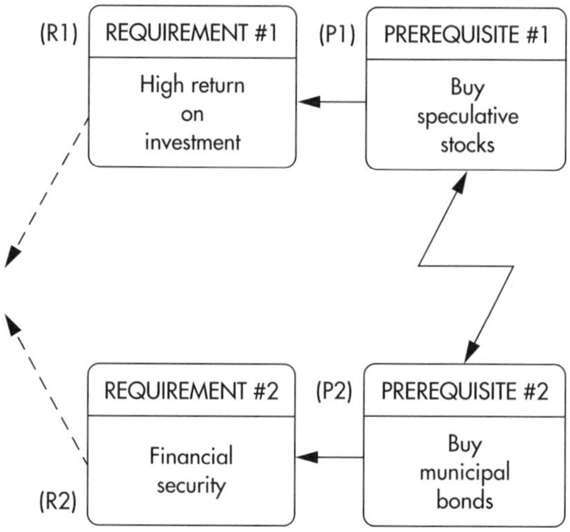

4. FORMULATE THE OBJECTIVE.

- Determine what purpose the requirements are intended to serve.
- Ask the question "These Requirements are necessary conditions for achieving *what* objective?"
- Develop an objective statement that effectively answers the preceding question for both requirements.
- Write the objective statement succinctly in the box marked "(O)."

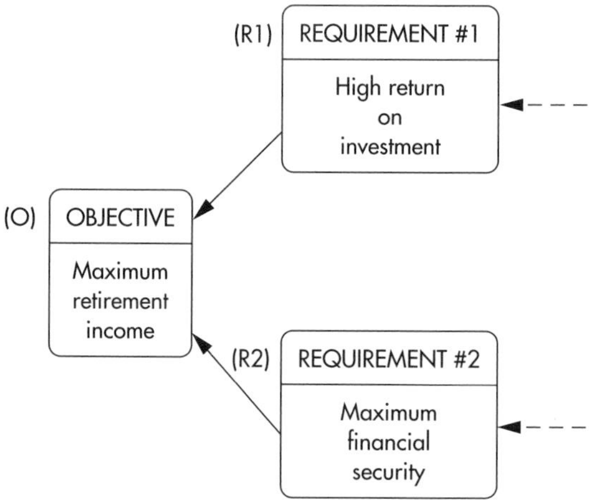

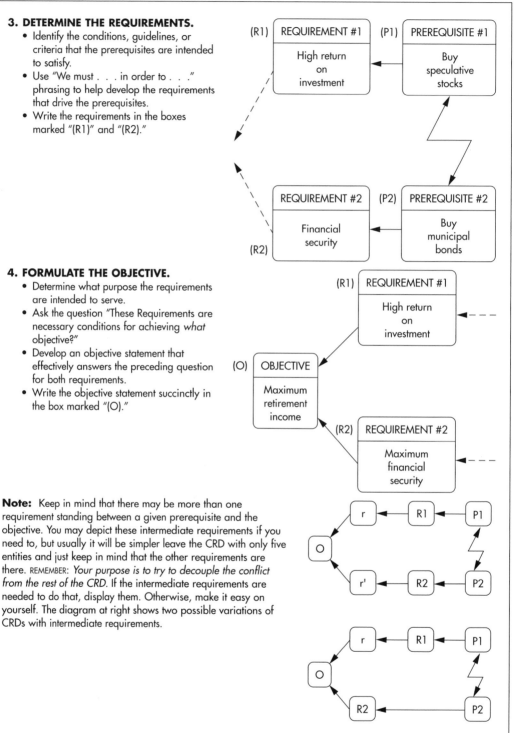

Note: Keep in mind that there may be more than one requirement standing between a given prerequisite and the objective. You may depict these intermediate requirements if you need to, but usually it will be simpler leave the CRD with only five entities and just keep in mind that the other requirements are there. REMEMBER: *Your purpose is to try to decouple the conflict from the rest of the CRD.* If the intermediate requirements are needed to do that, display them. Otherwise, make it easy on yourself. The diagram at right shows two possible variations of CRDs with intermediate requirements.

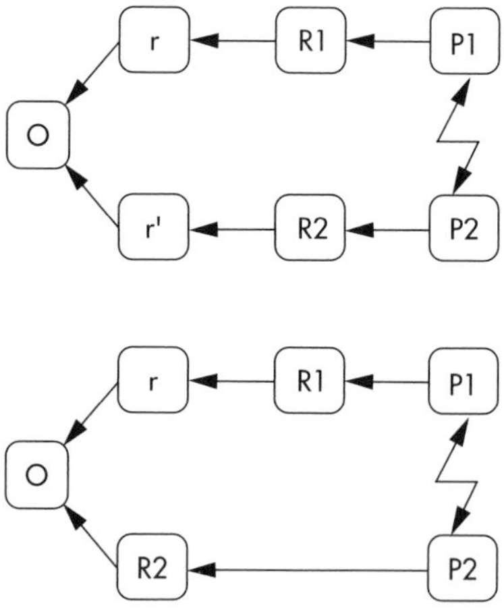

FIGURE 4.34—*Continued.*

5. EVALUATE THE CRD RELATIONSHIP.

- Read the entire CRD *aloud,* from left to right.
- Use "In order to . . . we must . . ." phrasing.
- Decide whether the entire CRD reflects your intuition on the issue.
- Does it "sound right"?
- If not, refine the weak parts until they are satisfactory to you.
- If so, go on to step 6.

- "In order to have maximum retirement income (O), I must have a high return on investment (R1)."
- "In order to have maximum retirement income (O), I must have maximum financial security (R2)."
- "I order to have high return on investment (R1), I must buy speculative stocks (P1)."
- "In order to have maximum financial security (R2), I must buy municipal bonds (R2)."
- "On one hand, I must buy speculative stocks (P1). On the other hand, I must buy municipal bonds (P2). I can't do both."

6. DEVELOP UNDERLYING ASSUMPTIONS.

- Make a list of assumptions underlying each arrow.
- Aim for 10 assumptions per arrow.
- Annotate the arrow relationship (e.g., **R1 → O**) in the left margin.
- Beside the annotation, write "In order to . . . we must . . ." statement for each horizontal segment of the CRD.
- Write the conflict statement in "On one hand . . . on the other hand. . . . We can't do both." form.
- Identify assumptions (the "because" part of the relationship statement).
- Use the "outrageous" technique to develop the assumptions under each relationship statement.
- Duplicate entries are acceptable.
- After assumptions are all identified, number them consecutively.

R1→O:	"In order to have . . . I must . . . because:"
P1→R1:	"In order to have . . . I must . . . because:"
P1 ↯ P2:	"On one hand, I must . . . On the other hand, I must . . . I can't do both, because:"

- "*Of course* we must . . ."
- "*Of course* we can't . . ."
- "We can *never* . . ."
- "We must *always* . . ."
- "There's *absolutely no way* . . ."
- "It's *absolutely impossible* to . . ."

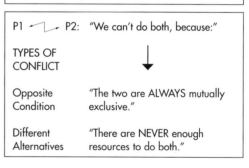

P1 ↯ P2:	"We can't do both, because:"
TYPES OF CONFLICT	↓
Opposite Condition	"The two are ALWAYS mutually exclusive."
Different Alternatives	"There are NEVER enough resources to do both."

FIGURE 4.34—*Continued.*

7. EVALUATE ASSUMPTIONS.

- Review all assumptions underlying each arrow relationship.
- Determine which might be weak or invalid.
- Mark weak or invalid assumptions beside their assigned number.

P1→R1: "In order to . . . we must . . . because:"
1- . . . .
★ 2- . . . .
3- . . . .
★ 4- . . . .

8. CREATE INJECTIONS.

- Develop ideas to break the assumptions you marked as weak or invalid.
- Start by validating the requirements—are they really needed, as written?
- Use the "alternative environment" technique to create new ideas.
- Attempt to satisfy the valid requirements without having to have one of the conflicting prerequisites.
- If you can't come up with a specific action to break an assumption, use a desired condition.

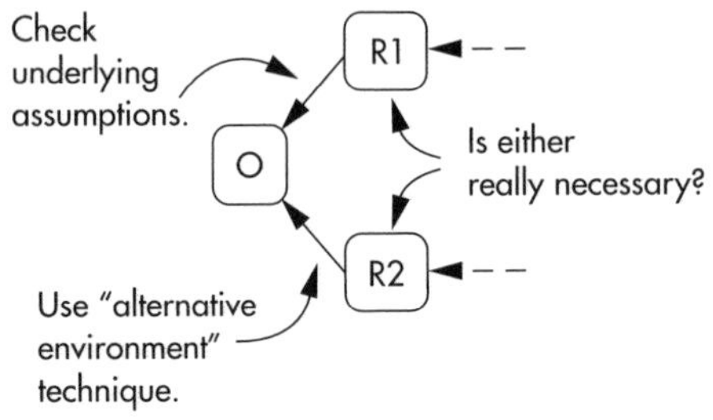

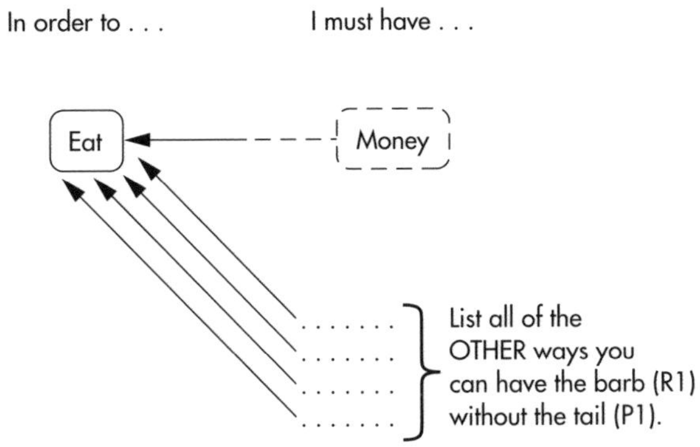

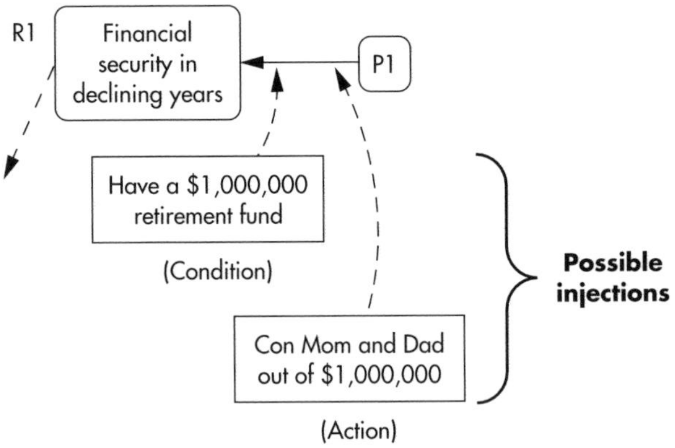

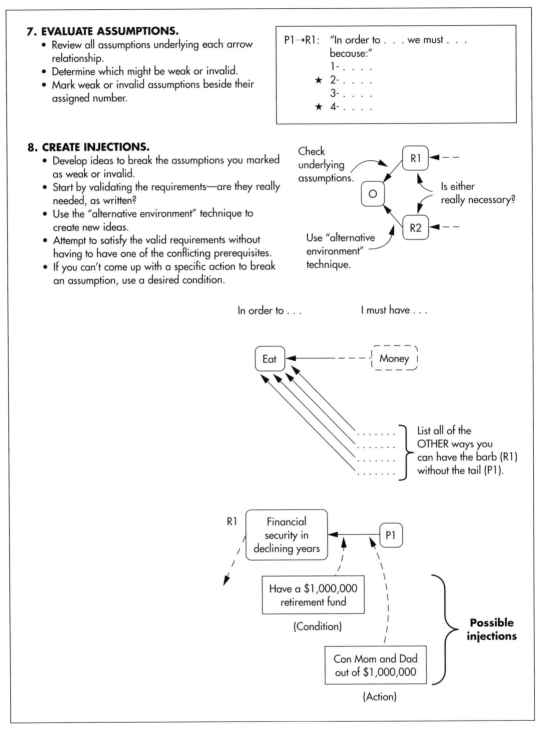

FIGURE 4.34—*Continued.*

9. SELECT THE BEST INJECTION.

- Decide on a "decision rule" by which to select the "best" injection.
- Some examples might be:
  - Easiest to do
  - Breaks the most frequent assumption
  - Least expensive
  - Several injections (if you can't choose only one)
- Save all unused injections for later use, as required.

- EASIEST to do
- One that breaks the most CRITICAL Assumption
- One that breaks the MOST FREQUENT Assumption
- LEAST expensive
- SEVERAL injections

FIGURE 4.34—*Continued.*

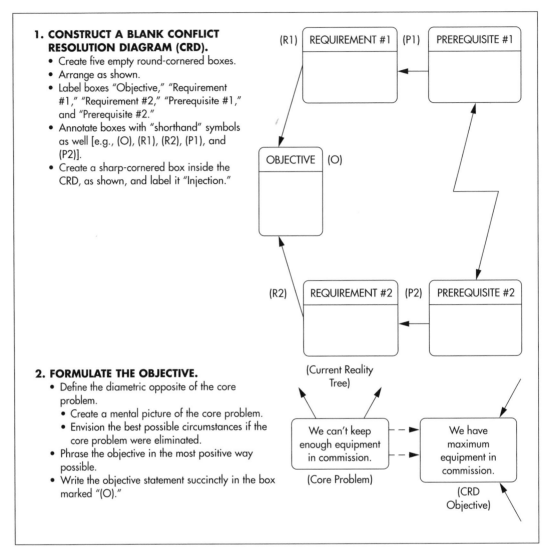

1. CONSTRUCT A BLANK CONFLICT RESOLUTION DIAGRAM (CRD).

- Create five empty round-cornered boxes.
- Arrange as shown.
- Label boxes "Objective," "Requirement #1," "Requirement #2," "Prerequisite #1," and "Prerequisite #2."
- Annotate boxes with "shorthand" symbols as well [e.g., (O), (R1), (R2), (P1), and (P2)].
- Create a sharp-cornered box inside the CRD, as shown, and label it "Injection."

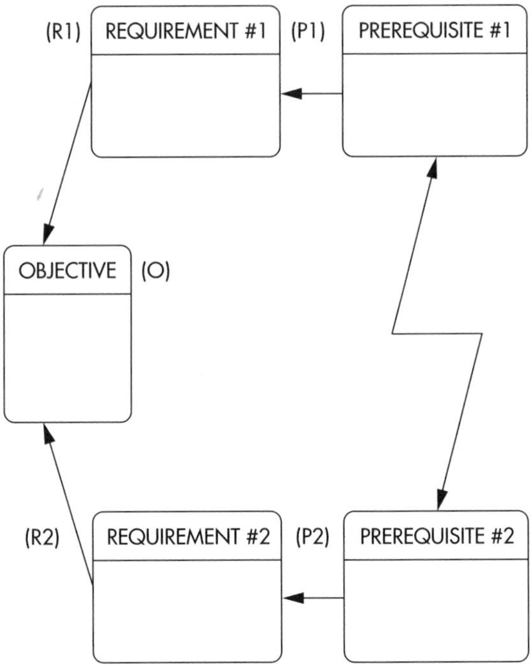

2. FORMULATE THE OBJECTIVE.

- Define the diametric opposite of the core problem.
  - Create a mental picture of the core problem.
  - Envision the best possible circumstances if the core problem were eliminated.
- Phrase the objective in the most positive way possible.
- Write the objective statement succinctly in the box marked "(O)."

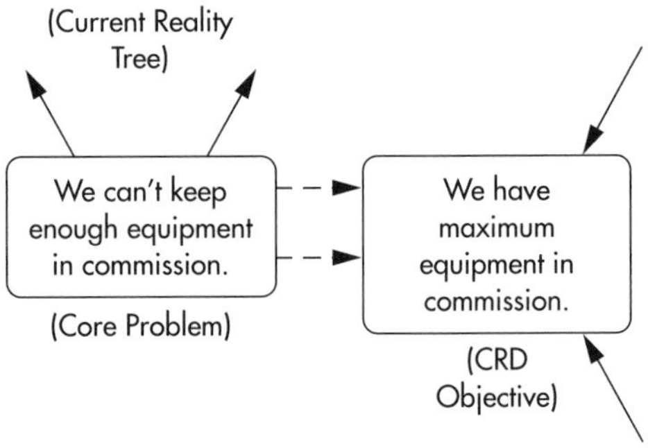

FIGURE 4.35. Procedures for Building a Conflict Resolution Diagram (Left-Right-Center).

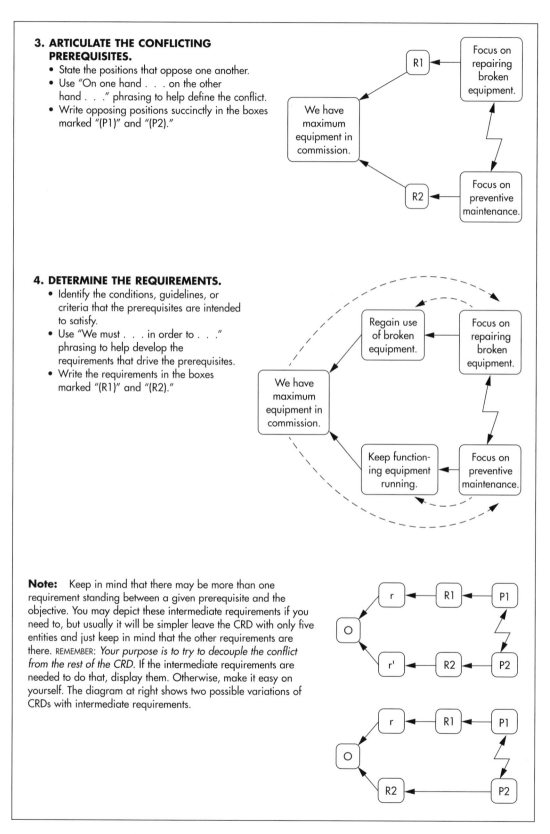

3. ARTICULATE THE CONFLICTING PREREQUISITES.

- State the positions that oppose one another.
- Use "On one hand . . . on the other hand . . ." phrasing to help define the conflict.
- Write opposing positions succinctly in the boxes marked "(P1)" and "(P2)."

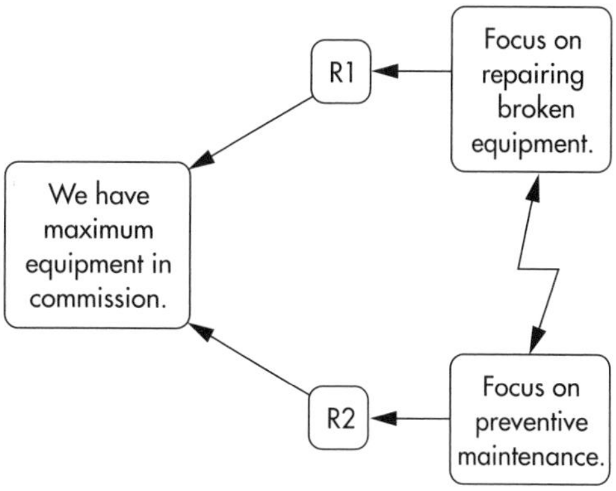

4. DETERMINE THE REQUIREMENTS.

- Identify the conditions, guidelines, or criteria that the prerequisites are intended to satisfy.
- Use "We must . . . in order to . . ." phrasing to help develop the requirements that drive the prerequisites.
- Write the requirements in the boxes marked "(R1)" and "(R2)."

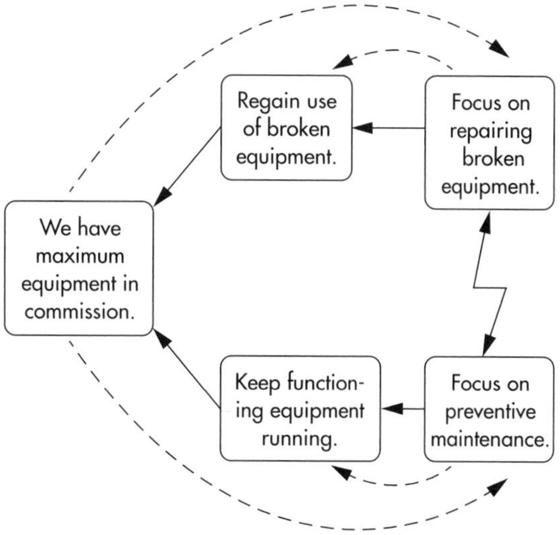

Note: Keep in mind that there may be more than one requirement standing between a given prerequisite and the objective. You may depict these intermediate requirements if you need to, but usually it will be simpler leave the CRD with only five entities and just keep in mind that the other requirements are there. REMEMBER: *Your purpose is to try to decouple the conflict from the rest of the CRD.* If the intermediate requirements are needed to do that, display them. Otherwise, make it easy on yourself. The diagram at right shows two possible variations of CRDs with intermediate requirements.

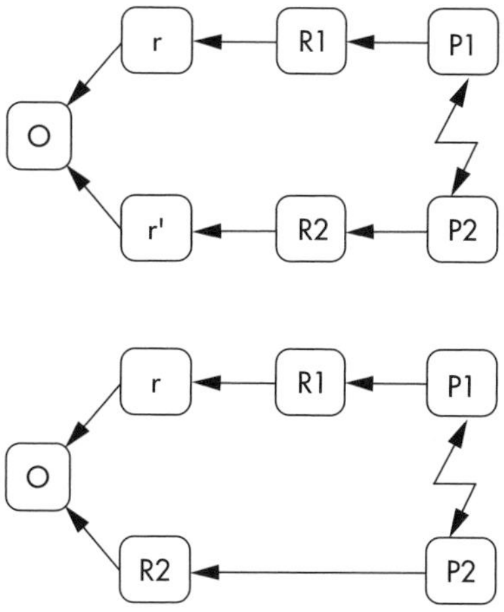

FIGURE 4.35—*Continued.*

5. EVALUATE THE CRD RELATIONSHIP.

- Read the entire CRD *aloud,* from left to right.
- Use "In order to . . . we must . . ." phrasing.
- Decide whether the entire CRD reflects your intuition on the issue.
- Does it "sound right"?
- If not, refine the weak parts until they are satisfactory to you.
- If so, go on to step 6.

> - "In order to have maximum retirement income (O), I must have a high return on investment (R1)."
> - "In order to have maximum retirement income (O), I must have maximum financial security (R2)."
> - "In order to have high return on investment (R1), I must buy speculative stocks (P1)."
> - "In order to have maximum financial security (R2), I must buy municipal bonds (R2)."
> - "On one hand, I must buy speculative stocks (P1). On the other hand, I must buy municipal bonds (P2). I can't do both."

6. DEVELOP UNDERLYING ASSUMPTIONS.

- Make a list of assumptions underlying each arrow.
- Aim for 10 assumptions per arrow.
- Annotate the arrow relationship (e.g., **R1 → O**) in the left margin.
- Beside the annotation, write "In order to . . . we must . . ." statement for *each* horizontal segment of the CRD.
- Write the conflict statement in "On one hand . . . on the other hand . . . We can't do both." form.
- Identify assumptions (the "because" part of the relationship statement).
- Use the "outrageous" technique to develop the assumptions under each relationship statement.
- Duplicate entries are acceptable.
- After assumptions are all identified, number them consecutively.

R1 → O:	"In order to have . . . I must . . . because:"
P2 → R1:	"In order to have . . . I must . . . because:"
P1 ↯ P2:	"On one hand, I must . . . On the other hand, I must . . . I can't do both, because:"

> - "*Of course* we must . . ."
> - "*Of course* we can't . . ."
> - "We can *never* . . ."
> - "We must *always* . . . "
> - "There's *absolutely no way* . . ."
> - "It's *absolutely impossible* to . . ."

P1 ↯ P2:	"We can't do both, because:"
TYPES OF CONFLICT	↓
Opposite Conditon	"The two are ALWAYS mutually exclusive."
Different Alternatives	"There are NEVER enough resources to do both."

FIGURE 4.35—*Continued.*

7. EVALUATE ASSUMPTIONS.

- Review all assumptions underlying each arrow relationship.
- Determine which might be weak or invalid.
- Mark weak or invalid assumptions beside their assigned number.

P1→R1: "In order to . . . we must . . . because:"
1- . . . .
★ 2- . . . .
3- . . . .
★ 4- . . . .

8. CREATE INJECTIONS.

- Develop ideas to break the assumptions you marked as weak or invalid.
- Start by validating the requirements—are they really needed, as written?
- Use the "alternative environment" technique to create new ideas.
- Attempt to satisfy the valid requirements without having to have one of the conflicting prerequisites.
- If you can't come up with a specific action to break an assumption, use a desired condition.

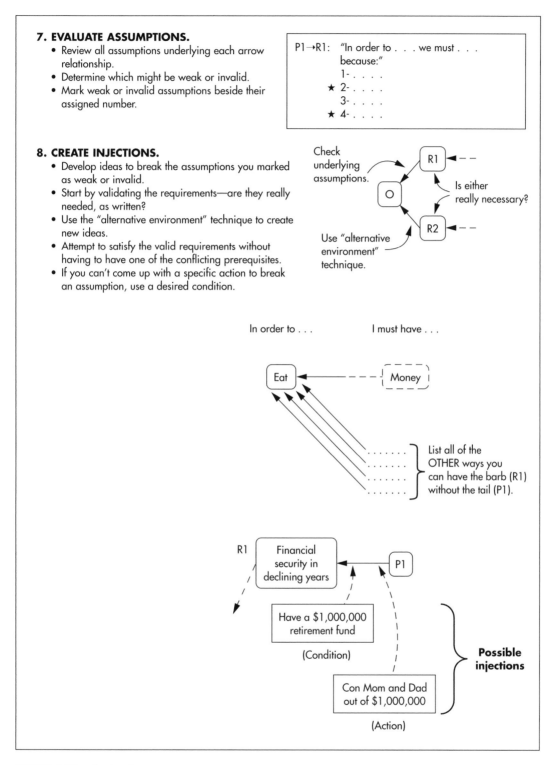

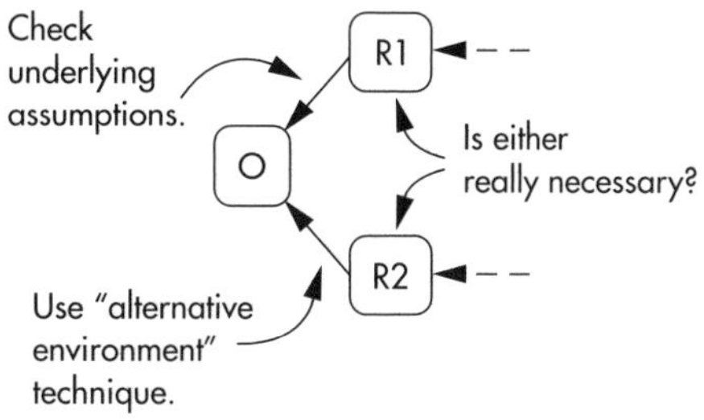
Check underlying assumptions.
R1
O
R2
Is either really necessary?
Use "alternative environment" technique.

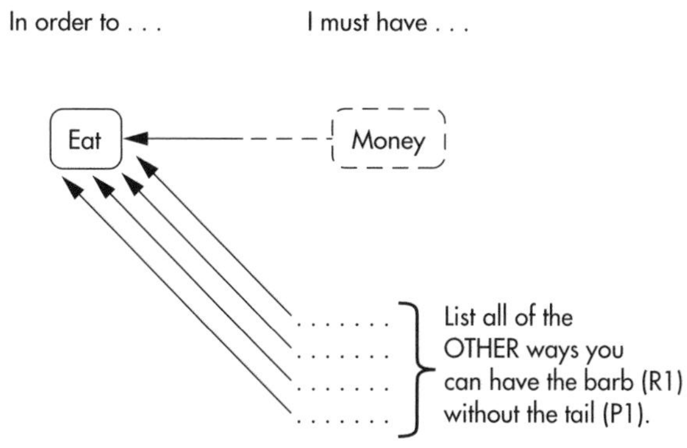
In order to . . .
I must have . . .
Eat
Money
List all of the OTHER ways you can have the barb (R1) without the tail (P1).

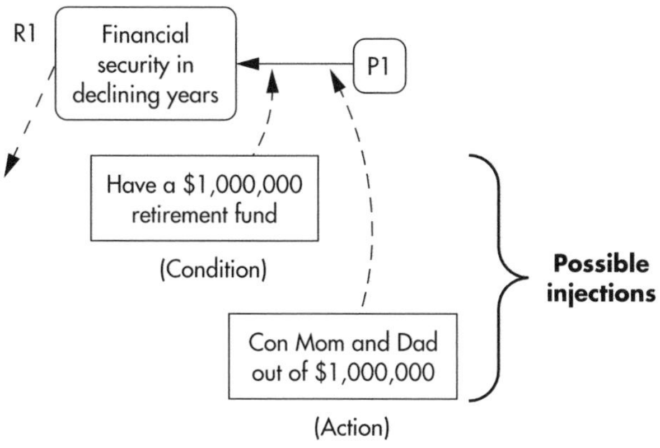
R1
Financial security in declining years
P1
Have a $1,000,000 retirement fund
(Condition)
Con Mom and Dad out of $1,000,000
(Action)
Possible injections

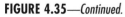

FIGURE 4.35—*Continued.*

9. SELECT THE BEST INJECTION.

- Decide on a "decision rule" by which to select the "best" injection.
- Some examples might be:
  - Easiest to do
  - Breaks the most frequent assumption
  - Least expensive
  - Several injections (if you can't choose only one)
- Save all unused injections for later use, as required.

- EASIEST to to
- One that breaks the most CRITICAL assumption
- One that breaks the MOST FREQUENT assumption
- LEAST expensive
- SEVERAL injections

FIGURE 4.35—*Continued.*

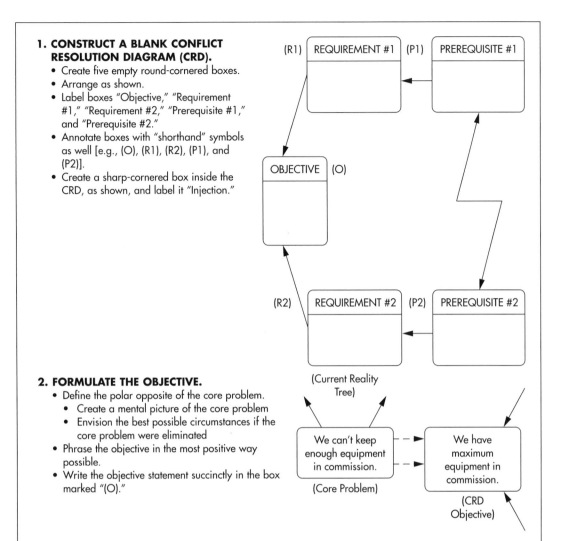

1. CONSTRUCT A BLANK CONFLICT RESOLUTION DIAGRAM (CRD).

- Create five empty round-cornered boxes.
- Arrange as shown.
- Label boxes "Objective," "Requirement #1," "Requirement #2," "Prerequisite #1," and "Prerequisite #2."
- Annotate boxes with "shorthand" symbols as well [e.g., (O), (R1), (R2), (P1), and (P2)].
- Create a sharp-cornered box inside the CRD, as shown, and label it "Injection."

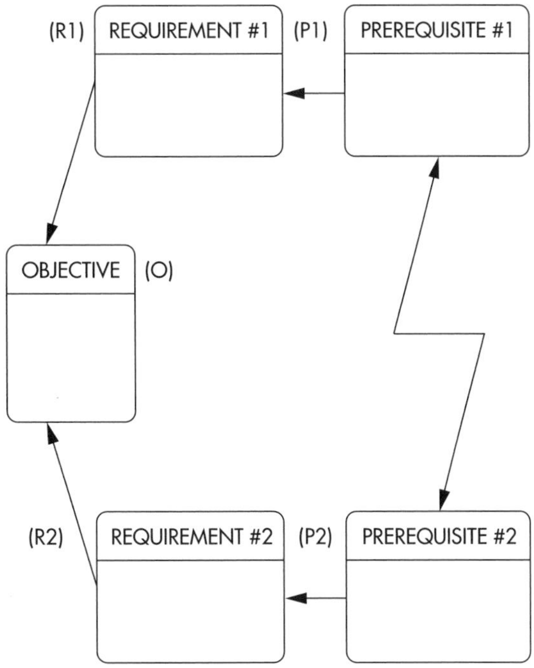

2. FORMULATE THE OBJECTIVE.

- Define the polar opposite of the core problem.
  - Create a mental picture of the core problem
  - Envision the best possible circumstances if the core problem were eliminated
- Phrase the objective in the most positive way possible.
- Write the objective statement succinctly in the box marked "(O)."

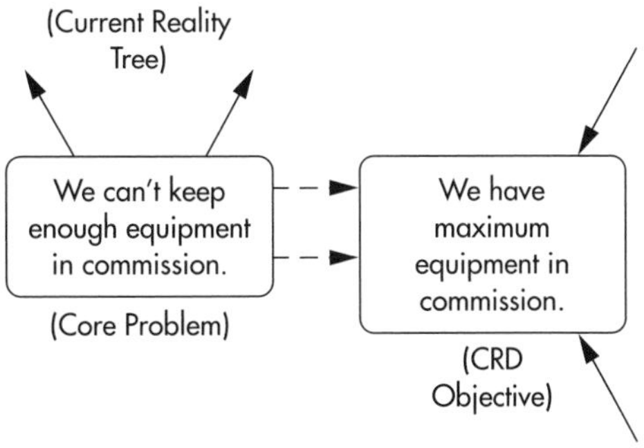

FIGURE 4.36. Procedures for Building a Conflict Resolution Diagram (Clockwise Rotation).

3. DETERMINE REQUIREMENT #1.

- What is the first necessary condition to meet in order to achieve the objective?
- This requirement should be something you believe to be inherently involved in the conflict in some way.
- Verbalize the "In order to . . . we must . . ." statement to help fill in the requirement blank.
- Is your verbalized requirement really necessary to achieving the objective?
- Write the requirement #1 statement succinctly in the space marked "(R1)."

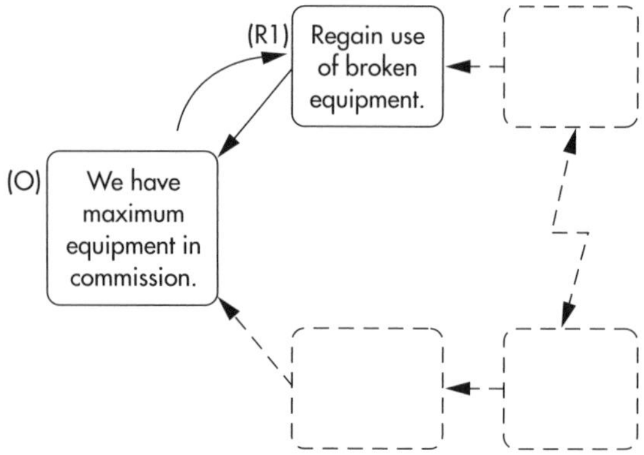

4. ARTICULATE THE CONFLICTING PREREQUISITES.

- State the positions that oppose one another.
- Use "On one hand . . . on the other hand . . ." phrasing to help define the conflict.
- Write opposing positions succinctly in the boxes marked "(P1)" and "(P2)."

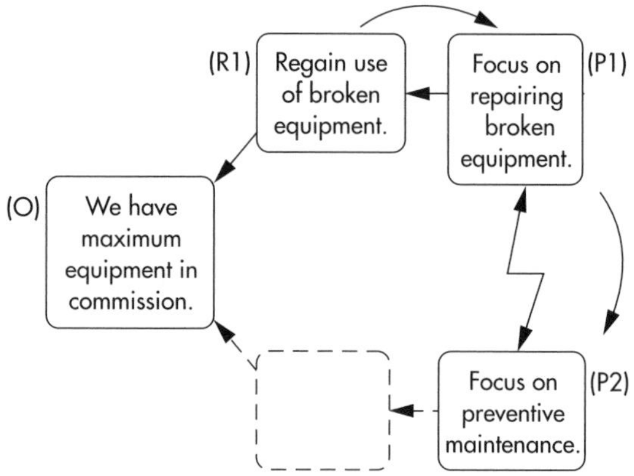

5. DETERMINE REQUIREMENT #2.

- What is the necessary condition that prerequisite #2 is trying to satisfy?
- Why do we need prerequisite #2?
- Verbalize the relationship "We must have/do [PREREQUISITE #2] in order to have/satisfy . . . ," and develop the end of that statement.
- When you have a requirement #2, "wordsmith" it until it makes sense when verbalized in the "In order to . . . we must . . ." form.
- Assess your new requirement #2; is this really the reason you need prerequisite #2?
- If so, write it in the space marked "(R2)."

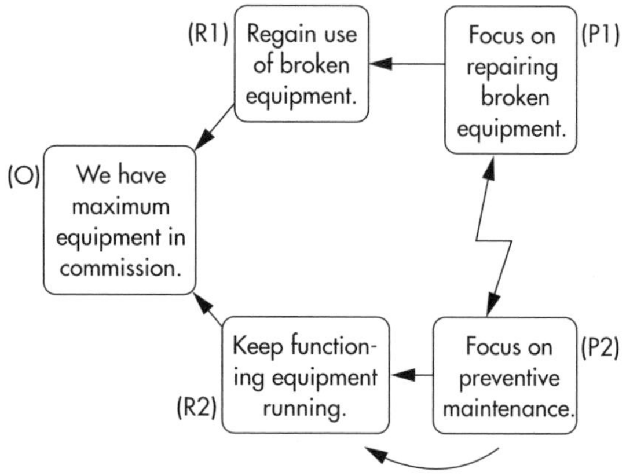

FIGURE 4.36—*Continued.*

Note: Keep in mind that there may be more than one requirement standing between a given prerequisite and the objective. You may depict these intermediate requirements if you need to, but usually it will be simpler leave the CRD with only five entities and just keep in mind that the other requirements are there. REMEMBER: *Your purpose is to try to decouple the conflict from the rest of the CRD.* If the intermediate requirements are needed to do that, display them. Otherwise, make it easy on yourself. The diagram at right shows two possible variations of CRDs with intermediate requirements.

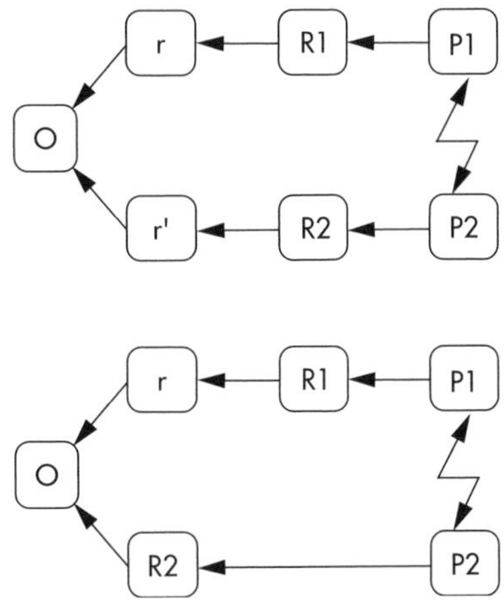

6. EVALUATE THE CRD RELATIONSHIP.
- Read the entire CRD *aloud,* from left to right.
- Use "In order to . . . we must . . ." phrasing.
- Decide whether the entire CRD reflects your intuition on the issue.
- Does it "sound right"?
- If not, refine the weak parts until they are satisfactory to you.
- If so, go on to step 7.

> - "In order to have maximum retirement income (O), I must have a high return on investment (R1)."
> - "In order to have maximum retirement income (O), I must have maximum financial security (R2)."
> - "In order to have high return on investment (R1), I must buy speculative stocks (P1)."
> - "In order to have maximum financial security (R2), I must buy municipal bonds (R2)."
> - "On one hand, I must buy speculative stocks (P1). On the other hand, I must buy municipal bonds (P2). I can't do both."

7. DEVELOP UNDERLYING ASSUMPTIONS.
- Make a list of assumptions underlying each arrow.
- Aim for 10 assumptions per arrow.
- Annotate the arrow relationship (e.g., **R1 → O**) in the left margin.
- Beside the annotation, write "In order to . . . we must . . ." statement for each horizontal segment of the CRD.
- Write the conflict statement in "On one hand . . . on the other hand . . . We can't do both." form.
- Identify assumptions (the "because" part of the relationship statement).

R1 → O:	"In order to have . . . I must . . . because:"
P1 → R1:	"In order to have . . . I must . . . because:"
P2 ↯ P2:	"On one hand, I must . . . On the other hand, I must . . . I can't do both, because:"

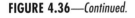

FIGURE 4.36—*Continued.*

- Use the "outrageous" technique to develop the assumptions under each relationship statement.
- Duplicate entries are acceptable.
- After assumptions are all identified, number them consecutively.

> - "*Of course* we must . . ."
> - "*Of course* we can't . . ."
> - "We can *never* . . ."
> - "We must *always* . . ."
> - "There's *absolutely no way* . . ."
> - "It's *absolutely impossible* to . . ."

P1 ↯ P2: "We can't do both, because:"

TYPES OF CONFLICT	↓
Opposite Condition	"The two are ALWAYS mutually exclusive."
Different Alternatives	"There are NEVER enough resources to do both."

8. EVALUATE ASSUMPTIONS.

- Review all assumptions underlying each arrow relationship.
- Determine which might be weak or invalid.
- Mark weak or invalid assumptions beside their assigned number.

P1→R1: "In order to . . . we must . . . because:"
1- . . . .
★ 2- . . . .
3- . . . .
★ 4- . . . .

9. CREATE INJECTIONS.

- Develop ideas to break the assumptions you marked as weak or invalid.
- Start by validating the requirements—are they really needed, as written?

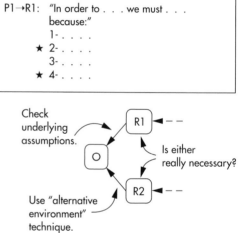

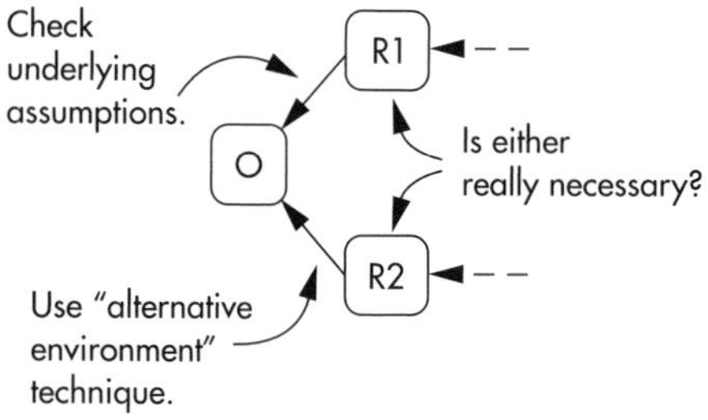
Check underlying assumptions.
R1
O
R2
Is either really necessary?
Use "alternative environment" technique.

FIGURE 4.36—*Continued.*

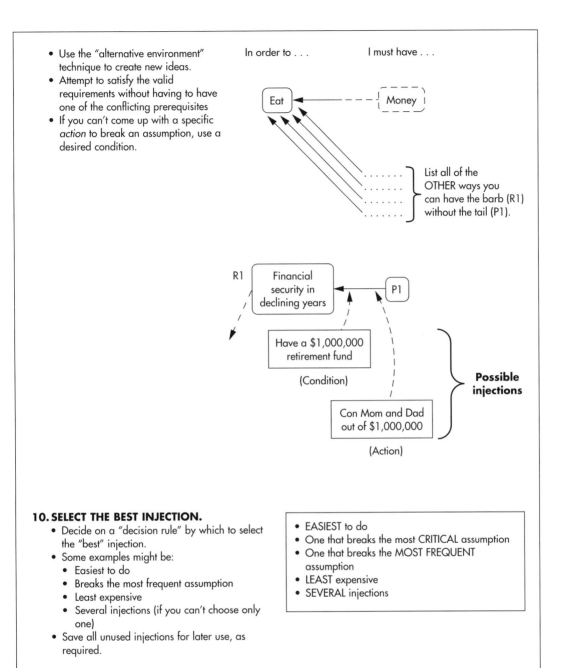

- Use the "alternative environment" technique to create new ideas.
- Attempt to satisfy the valid requirements without having to have one of the conflicting prerequisites
- If you can't come up with a specific *action* to break an assumption, use a desired condition.

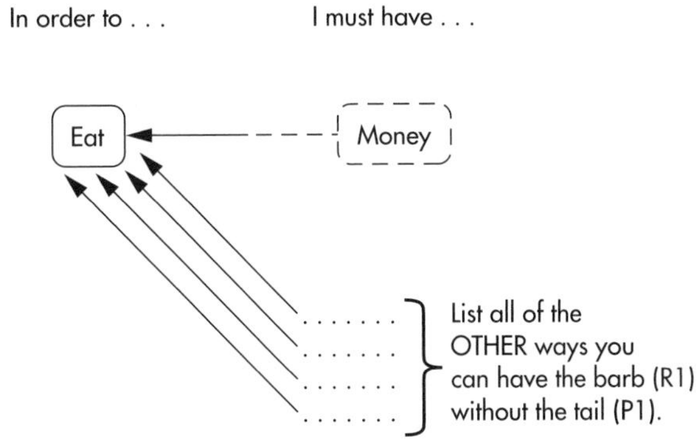
In order to . . .
I must have . . .
Eat
Money
List all of the OTHER ways you can have the barb (R1) without the tail (P1).

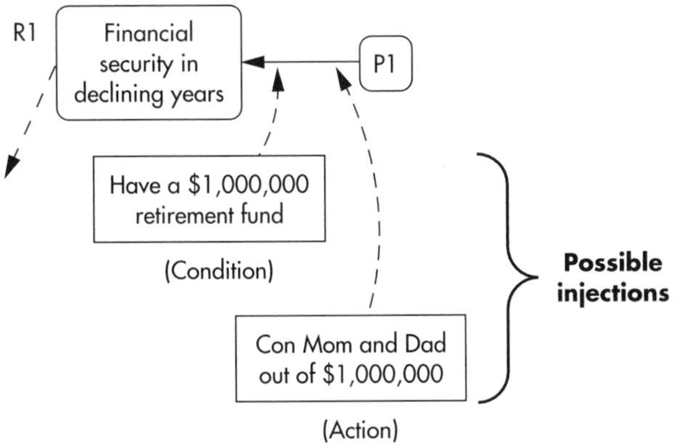
R1
Financial security in declining years
P1
Have a $1,000,000 retirement fund
(Condition)
Con Mom and Dad out of $1,000,000
(Action)
Possible injections

10. SELECT THE BEST INJECTION.

- Decide on a "decision rule" by which to select the "best" injection.
- Some examples might be:
  - Easiest to do
  - Breaks the most frequent assumption
  - Least expensive
  - Several injections (if you can't choose only one)
- Save all unused injections for later use, as required.

- EASIEST to do
- One that breaks the most CRITICAL assumption
- One that breaks the MOST FREQUENT assumption
- LEAST expensive
- SEVERAL injections

FIGURE 4.36—*Continued.*

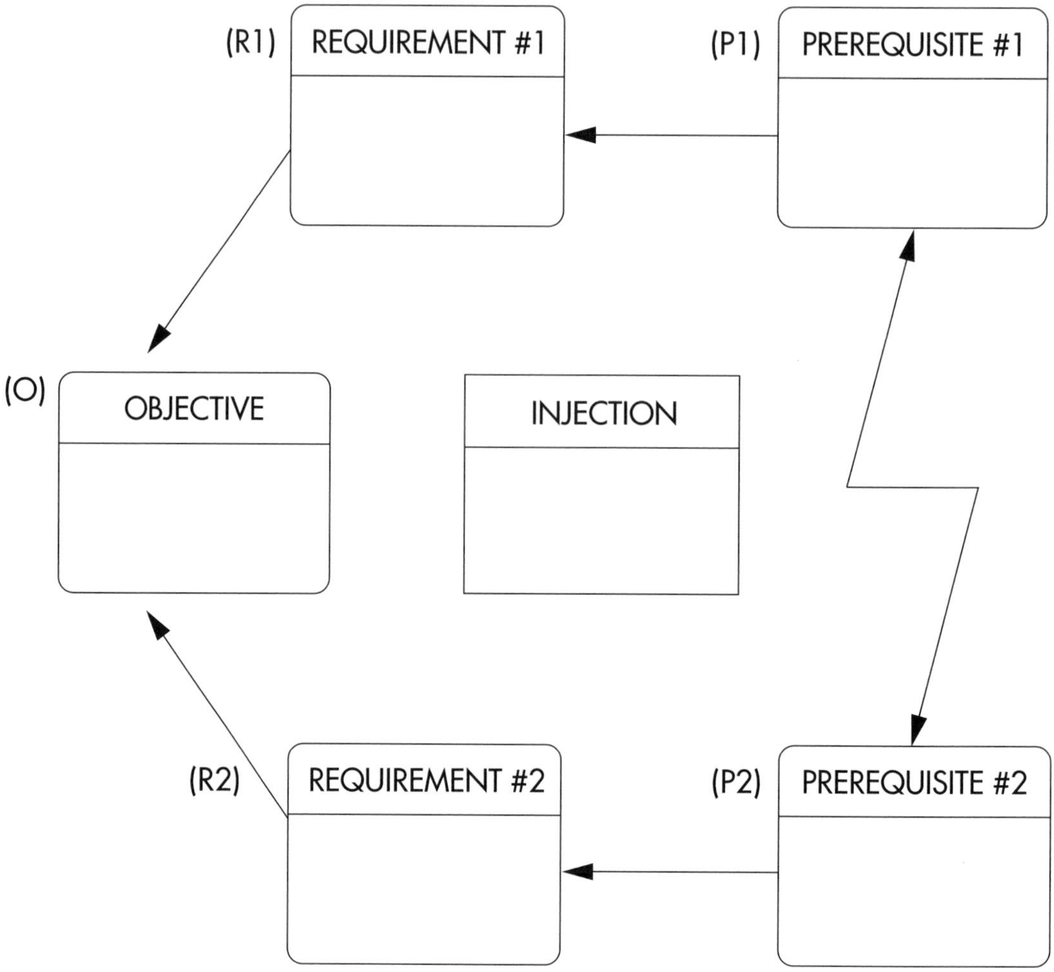

(Reproduce this page as a worksheet, or reconstruct a form like this.)

FIGURE 4.37. Conflict Resolution Diagram Worksheets.

Conflict Resolution Diagram Worksheet
ASSUMPTIONS

R1 → O: In order to ____________________

We must ____________________ because:

-

-

-

-

R2 → O: In order to ____________________

We must ____________________ because:

-

-

-

-

P1 → R1: In order to ____________________

We must ____________________ because:

-

-

-

-

P2 → R2: In order to ____________________

We must ____________________ because:

-

-

-

-

P1 ↯ P2: On the one hand ____________________

On the other hand ____________________

We can't have both, because:

-

-

-

FIGURE 4.37—*Continued.*

Conflict Resolution Diagram Worksheet
INJECTIONS

Some ways we can have (O) ____________________

without having (R1) ____________________ are:

-
-
-
-
-
-
-
-
-
-

Some ways we can have (O) ____________________

without having (R2) ____________________ are:

-
-
-
-
-
-
-
-
-
-

Some ways we can have (R1) ____________________

without having (P1) ____________________ are:

-
-
-
-
-
-
-
-
-
-

Some ways we can have (R2) ____________________

without having (P2) ____________________ are:

-
-
-
-
-
-
-
-
-
-

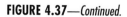

FIGURE 4.37—*Continued.*

Chapter 5
FUTURE REALITY TREE

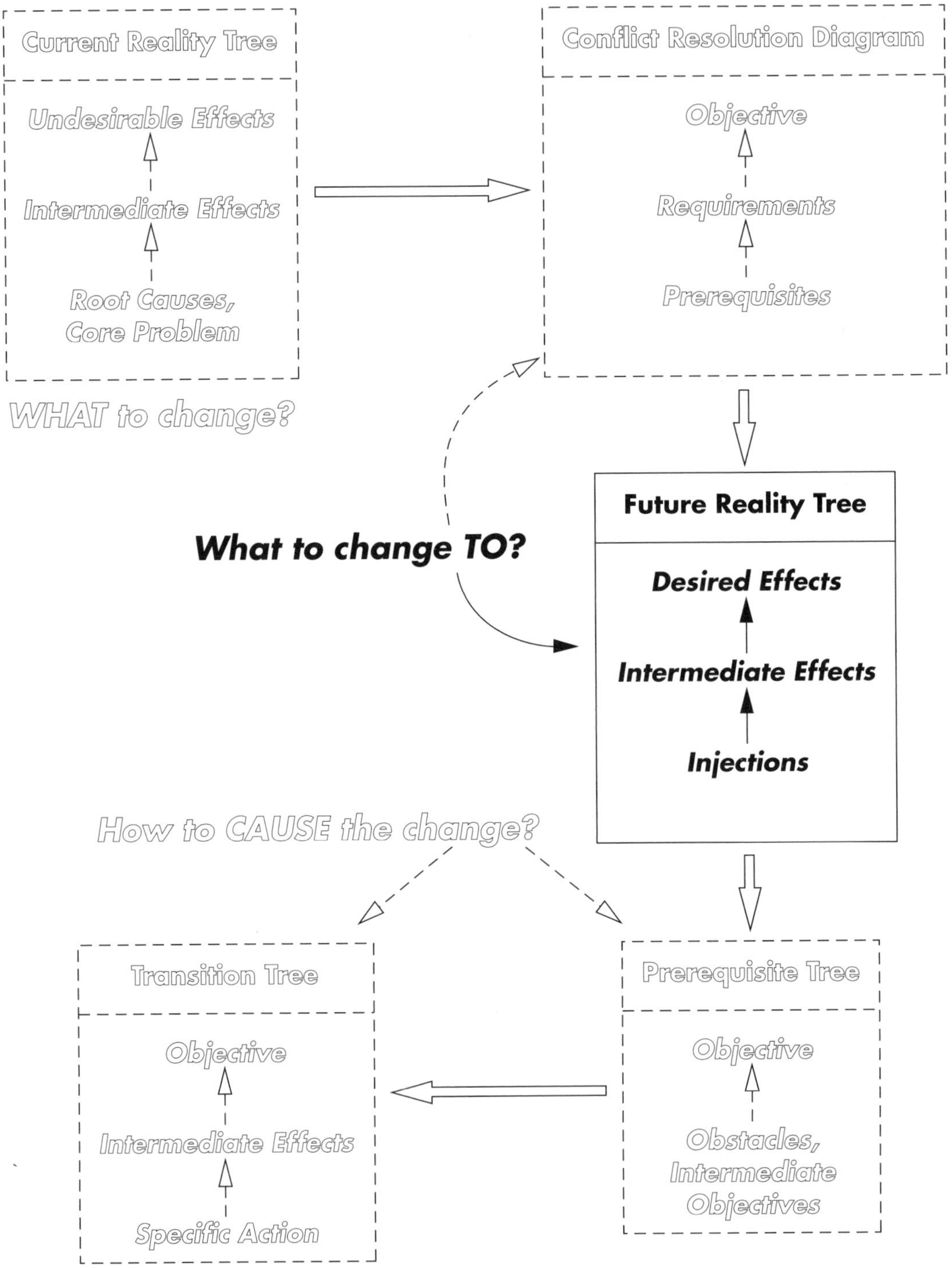

Chapter Outline

To introduce something altogether new would mean to begin all over, to become ignorant again, and to run the old, old risk of failing to learn.

—Isaac Asimov

Picture yourself responsible for the performance of a complex system—say, a state education system, for example. For the sake of argument, let's say it's failing the students it's charged with educating. You know you have to make changes to it or watch it collapse completely. And you have no shortage of people telling you what you should do to "fix" the system. But this is not a decision to be entered into lightly. You know it's likely to cost millions of dollars to put the system back on track again, and you really have only one chance to get it right. What are you going to do?

Would you just choose a course of action that feels good and say, "That looks about right!"? Or would you rather have some confidence that the decision you're about to make will actually deliver the results you expect—and not dig the hole you're in any deeper in the process?

Naturally, most of us would choose the latter, rather than the former. But guess what? Many of us make big decisions in our professional and personal lives, with no better assurance that we're doing the right thing than "that feels right!" What if we had a way to "bench test" an idea before we commit a lot of time, energy, and resources to executing it? Wouldn't that be preferable to a "by-guess-and-by-gosh" approach?

The Future Reality Tree can give us the confidence that our chosen path is the right one. In fact, Goldratt specifically designed it to do just that.

DEFINITION

The Future Reality Tree (FRT) is a sufficiency-based logic structure designed to reveal how changes to the status quo would affect reality—specifically to produce desired effects (DE) (see Figure 5.1). It's an expression of a reality that does not yet exist. The Future Reality Tree visually unfolds the cause-and-effect relationship between changes we make to existing systems and their resulting outcomes. It's a simulation model of the future. Since the Future Reality Tree is a projection of the

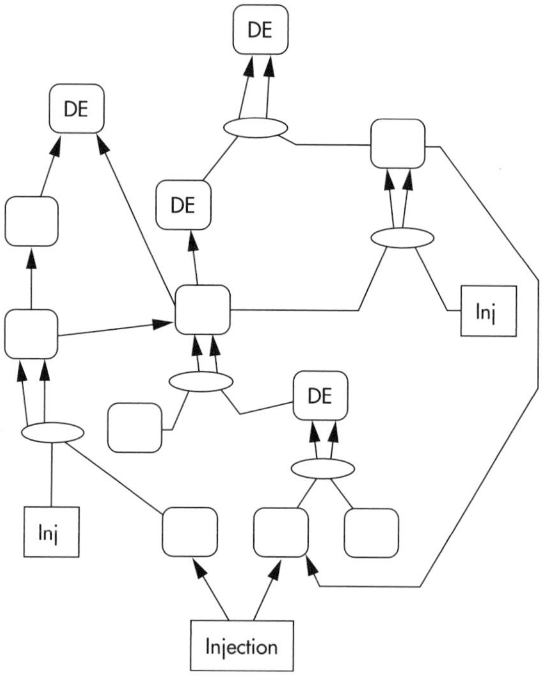

FIGURE 5.1. The Future Reality Tree.

future from the starting point of the present, it is constructed from the bottom upward, rather than from the top downward, the way a Current Reality Tree is.

PURPOSE

The Future Reality Tree serves seven basic purposes.

- Enables effectiveness testing of new ideas before committing resources (time, money, people) to implementation.
- Determines whether proposed system changes will, in fact, produce the desired effects without creating devastating new side effects.
- Reveals, through negative branches, whether (and where) proposed changes will create new or collateral problems as they solve old problems.
- Provides a means of making beneficial effects self-sustaining through the deliberate incorporation of positive reinforcing loops.
- Provides a means of assessing the impacts of localized decisions on the entire system.
- Provides an effective tool for persuading decision makers to support a desired course of action.
- Serves as an initial planning tool for changing the course of the future.

ASSUMPTIONS

The effectiveness of the Future Reality Tree is based on the following assumptions.

- System components are interdependent. A change in one affects others.
- A definite chain of cause-and-effect governs the functioning of all systems.
- Change has both intended and unintended effects.
- Unintended effects of changes can be anticipated.
- Unintended effects can be beneficial, neutral, or detrimental.
- Some changes can cause more problems than they solve.
- It is possible to determine, with reasonable confidence, what effects, both intended and unintended, a change will have on a system.
- Negative effects can be anticipated, located, and prevented before they happen.
- Cause-and-effect logic applies equally effectively to the future as it does to the present or past.
- Ideas do not become solutions until they have been validated as effective and implemented.
- All processes within a system, including the overall system itself, are subject to variation.

- Cause and effect is regulated by the Categories of Legitimate Reservation (CLR) and is verifiable through the CLR.
- Unstated assumptions about reality underlie all cause-and-effect relationships

HOW TO USE THIS CHAPTER

- Read "Description of the Future Reality Tree," p. 182. This section describes what a Future Reality Tree is and how it works.
- Read "Building a Future Reality Tree," p. 202, and the associated examples. This section explains in detail each of the steps in building a Future Reality Tree and why they're necessary.
- Read "Scrutinizing a Future Reality Tree," p. 216. This section tells how to ensure that your Future Reality Tree is logically sound and accurately depicts "the way things will be" after you make a change.
- Review Figure 5.35, "Future Reality Tree Examples." This is a complete Future Reality Tree on the subject "How Organizations Can Succeed at Total Quality." It illustrates in a typical real-world example just how complex reality can be and how effective the Future Reality Tree is at mapping the route from proposed changes to the effects that are desired from them.
- Review Figure 5.36, "Procedures for Building a Future Reality Tree." This is an abbreviated checklist that you can use to guide you in constructing your own Future Reality Tree. The checklist contains brief instructions and illustrations for each step. Detailed explanations for each step in the checklist are provided in the chapter itself, under "Building a Future Reality Tree," p. 202.
- Practice the "Future Reality Tree Exercise" provided in Appendix E.

Repetition does not establish validity.

—Souder's Law

DESCRIPTION OF THE FUTURE REALITY TREE

How many times have you heard the term "computer simulation model"? Simulation modeling is used extensively in complex, high-technology design processes. New airplane designs, such as the B-2 bomber, are exhaustively tested for stability, airworthiness, and flight-handling characteristics long before the first real airplane rolls down the runway. Why are simulation models so valuable? Aside from the cost of losing an expensive prototype in a crash (not to mention danger to the pilot), consider the risk of committing $70 billion to a production program such as the B-2 without knowing until too late whether it will do what it was intended to do.

Is it conceivable that this same approach—the simulation model—can apply to other complex situations? That, in essence, is what the Future Reality Tree does. While it isn't an interactive computer model, the Future Reality Tree's greatest potential value lies in its capability to simulate the future: to identify "bright ideas" that are, in reality, not very bright (that is, they won't get the job done or, worse yet, they'll create more problems than they solve).

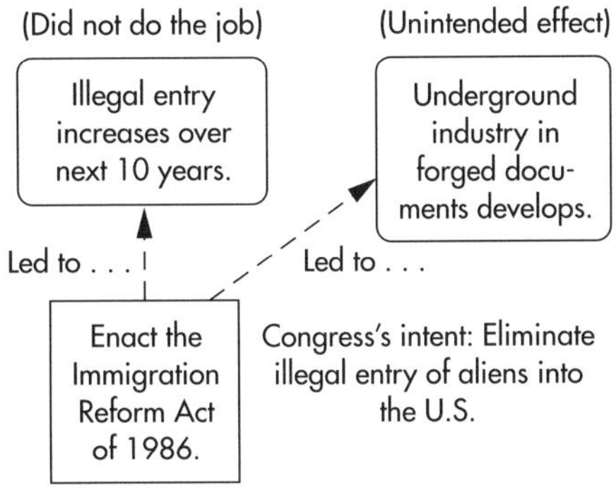

FIGURE 5.2. A Real-World Example: The Immigration Reform Act of 1986.

A Real-World Example

Consider the Immigration Reform Act of 1986. The U.S. Congress committed no small amount of time, energy, money, and agony trying to get this legislation passed—in spite of political gridlock and over the objections of special interests. The intent of the law was simple: to end illegal entry of aliens into the United States.

Did it succeed? Ten years after its passage, the influx of illegal aliens is higher than ever. Clearly, the legislation did not do the job it was designed to do. Worse yet, it created at least one collateral problem that didn't previously exist. The law's requirement for employers to verify residency status before hiring spawned a cottage industry in forged documents of all kinds: drivers' licenses, ID cards, Social Security cards, and—worst of all—birth certificates that are virtually indistinguishable from legitimate ones except by close professional examination. The net result of this forgery is a drain on Social Security, Medicaid, and other entitlement resources by people not legally authorized to have them. Surely the U.S. Congress did not anticipate or intend for this to happen (see Figure 5.2).

The chief cause of problems is solutions.

—Sevareid's Law

How much of this outcome might have been foreseen and precluded before the fact? By making good use of a Future Reality Tree, virtually all of it. An effective Future Reality Tree can give you a measure of assurance that your idea will work before you invest time, energy, and money trying to make it happen.

A Framework for Change

The Future Reality Tree provides you with a framework in which to design and refine change. It combines elements of existing reality with injections (actions or conditions) that you create to produce new outcomes, or expected reactions.

For example, one element of existing reality is Bernoulli's Principle, which describes the relationship between air flow over a surface and pressure on that surface. What if we combine that bit of reality with an injection that we create? That injection is to make a device that enables us to sustain and control air flow over a specially designed surface. The immediate outcome is an airfoil, or wing; the ultimate effect is powered flight (see Figure 5.3). This is essentially how the

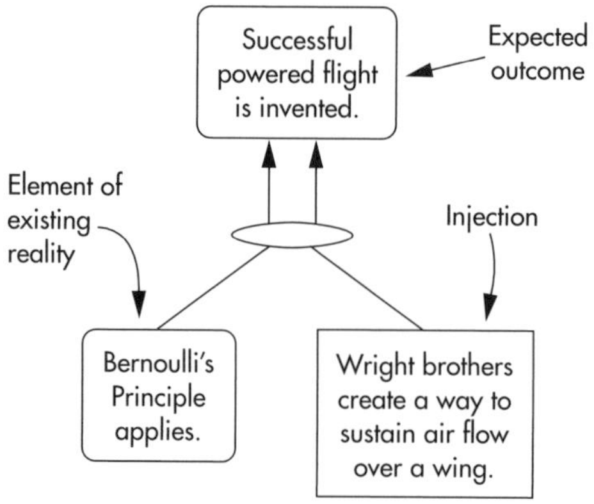

FIGURE 5.3. A Framework for Change.

Wright brothers changed the world as we know it: They combined existing reality with an injection of their own creation to produce an expected reaction that did not currently exist. The rest, as they say, is history.

The Wright brothers didn't have the benefit of a Future Reality Tree to help them, but you do. You can take an existing situation, combine it with changes you initiate, and plot the outcome as a chain of cause and effect leading to a future configuration of reality that you particularly desire. The Future Reality Tree gives you the ability to map the future.

Nothing is ever so bad that it can't get worse.
—Gattuso's Extension of Murphy's Law

Negative Branches

Anytime you change the status quo, one of three possibilities will occur: things will get better, stay the same, or get worse. The first is eminently desirable. The second may be acceptable. The third is to be avoided at all costs—unless, of course, it was your intent to make things worse in the first place.

But if your intent is *not* to make things worse, the negative branch is an aspect of the Future Reality Tree that will prove invaluable to you. In fact, the negative branch is so powerful you can use it by itself, in daily applications, without needing a complete Future Reality Tree. The negative branch enables you to surface the hidden undesirable outcomes that might proceed from any action you're contemplating (see Figure 5.4). Moreover, using the procedures to identify negative branches, you can locate the exact point in your Future Reality Tree where the chain of cause and effect begins to turn sour. And if you decide to proceed in the face of possible negative consequences, the negative branch will help you decide on ways to minimize or eliminate the negative consequences. The upcoming section, "Negative Branches," p. 195, will show you how to take advantage of this powerful tool.

The Positive Reinforcing Loop

Another powerful aspect of the Future Reality Tree in designing the future is the positive reinforcing loop (see Figure 5.5). Nothing is more frustrating than to

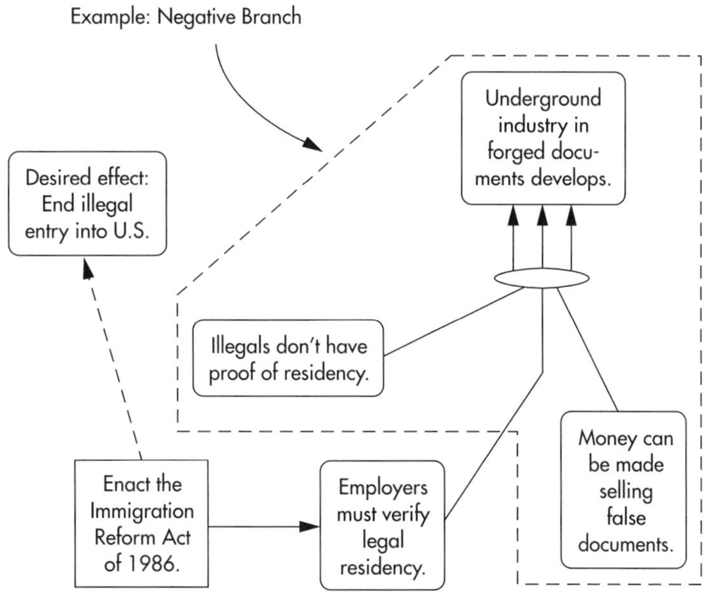

FIGURE 5.4. Example of a Negative Branch.

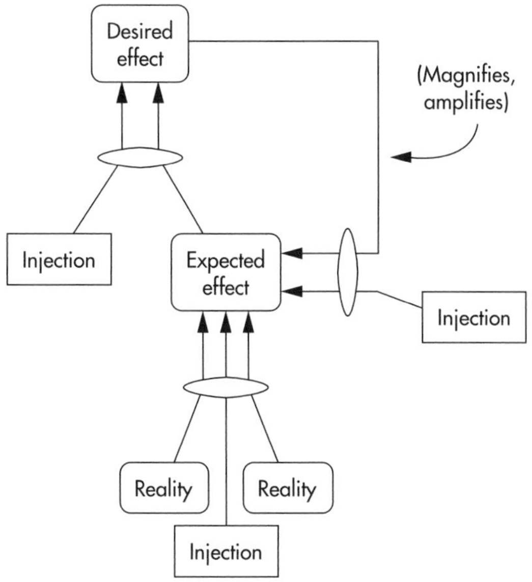

FIGURE 5.5. The Positive Reinforcing Loop.

initiate a change for the better, only to have it fall apart because it wasn't continually monitored and reinforced. Wouldn't it be ideal to implement a solution that was self-sustaining—a solution that reinforced its own existence? The function of the positive reinforcing loop is to do precisely that. In a Future Reality Tree, a desirable effect is routed back down toward one of its causes, perhaps combined with another element of reality or a subsequent injection, and the original desirable effect is ultimately magnified. This loop relationship reinforces the stability of the new reality and helps make it self-sustaining. Moreover, you

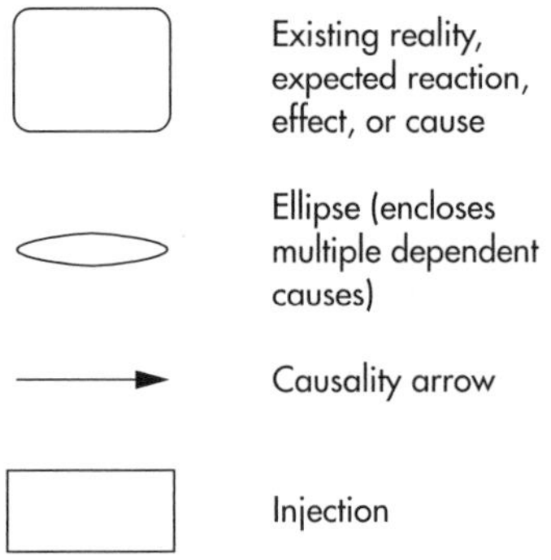

FIGURE 5.6. FRT Symbology.

need not depend on chance to have a positive reinforcing loop. You can design one into your Future Reality Tree. "5. Build in Positive Reinforcing Loops," p. 209, will show you how to do this.

Future Reality Tree Symbology

The symbols used in a Future Reality Tree are similar to those used in a Current Reality Tree (see Figure 5.6). A round-cornered box indicates a condition of existing reality, an expected reaction, or an effect. Expected reactions or effects may be desirable or undesirable. An ellipse encompasses several dependent causes contributing to an effect. And a cause-effect arrow indicates causality, with the cause lying at the tail and the effect at the barb.

The significant new symbol in the Future Reality Tree is a sharp-cornered box, which represents an injection.

Injections

The entity that gives the Future Reality Tree its flexibility and unlimited potential is the injection. In essence, an injection is a new condition or action that does not exist in current reality. It's something you must make happen in order for future reality to unfold the way you want it to. The Future Reality Tree's flexibility comes from the fact that injections are not fixed. You have many choices, and by changing injections, you can redesign the way the future develops.

Consider, for example, how differently your personal future might turn out if you substitute one of these injections for another:

- "I go directly from high school to college."
- "I enlist in the Marine Corps directly from high school."

Remembering that a Future Reality Tree is like a computer simulation of the future, injections become the variables you can change to see how differently the subsequent simulations turn out. Don't lose sight of the fact that injections are not solutions—they're *ideas* for solutions. The difference between the two is that solutions have been tested, the kinks have been worked out, obstacles have been overcome, and implementation has been thoroughly planned.

Where Do Injections Come From?

If you've previously constructed a Conflict Resolution Diagram (refer to chapter 4), injections might come from there. But the Future Reality Tree can also be used alone, without the other trees. So injections may originate from anywhere—your imagination or someone else's.

Actions as Injections

Visualize yourself starting the steps necessary to change current reality into desired future reality. Under ideal conditions, you'll know exactly *what* you should do and *how* to do it. If this is the case, consider yourself fortunate, and structure your injection as a specific action.

For example, let's say your desired effect is to realize long-term financial independence. But right now you don't have much money. If you know exactly how to get it, you can make an injection out of the action you'll need to take. In chapter 4, we saw that one injection might be to con a million dollars out of your parents (see Figure 5.7).

Even if you know how to get the money, it may require several major steps, in sequence, on your part. Each step, or action, will be an injection. In this situation, the first action becomes the first of several injections. Conning the money out of your parents, for example, may have to be done in several discrete steps. The first step becomes your first injection, which, when combined with a fact of existing reality, leads to an expected reaction that didn't exist before. That reaction, combined with your second step (injection), results in still another reaction.

At some point you may find that you can't proceed any farther without some new injection, one that you hadn't previously foreseen. In this event, you must incorporate that new injection into your Future Reality Tree (see Figure 5.8). Each added injection is like a course correction keeping you on track toward your ultimate desired effect.

How will you know when to add a new injection? The Categories of Legitimate Reservation will tell you. When you encounter a cause insufficiency in a Future Reality Tree between one level and the next, *you* have to add the not-yet-existing injection (condition or action) needed to complete the logical causality.

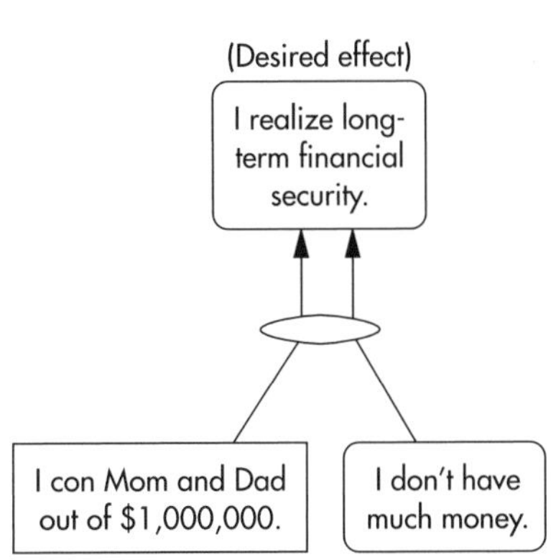

FIGURE 5.7. Actions as Injections.

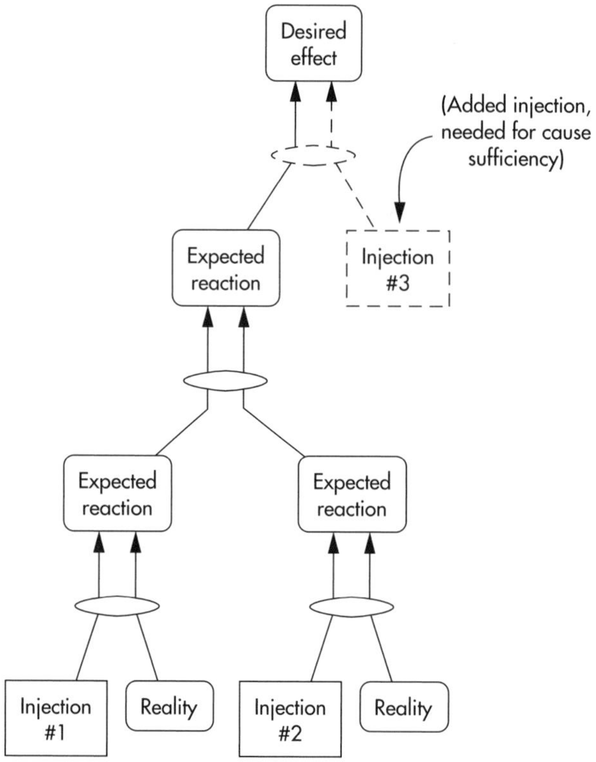

FIGURE 5.8. A Complex Action Requiring Several Steps.

The Danger of Actions as Injections

There are two potential pitfalls associated with making your injections actions.

- By settling too quickly on a specific action, you may foreclose other possibilities that might turn out to be less expensive, easier to do, or more effective. For example, "*Build* a central warehouse" forecloses some less expensive options such as renting space. "*Have* a central warehouse" is a condition, rather than an action, which opens options other than construction. Remember that designing future reality is a creative exercise. Don't constrain your creativity unnecessarily with preconceived solutions by zeroing in on any specific action too soon.
- By focusing too soon on a specific action, there's a tendency to start worrying about implementation before the overall solution is completely and effectively tested for its ability to do the job without creating unacceptable adverse effects. Don't forget the purpose of the Future Reality Tree. If you jump too quickly to specific actions, you risk missing the FRT's benefits.

Conditions as Injections

As mentioned earlier, under ideal circumstances you'll know exactly what to do and how to do it. But how often do we have "ideal circumstances"? More frequently we're sure about the state of the new reality we want, but we're less sure of the steps needed to achieve it.

In our continuing example, we decided to try to con Mom and Dad out of $1,000,000. That's an action we might know how to do. But what if we don't have rich parents? Or parents who can be conned, for that matter? In this case, we

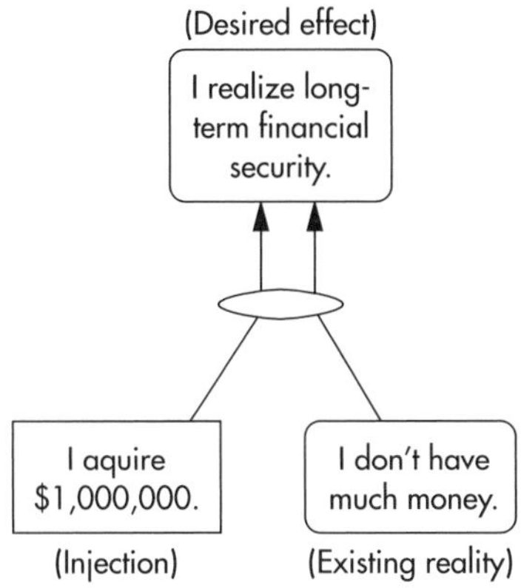
(Desired effect)
I realize long-term financial security.
I aquire $1,000,000.
(Injection)
I don't have much money.
(Existing reality)

FIGURE 5.9. Conditions as Injections.

have to expand our horizon of possible choices beyond one specific action (see Figure 5.9). Rather than say, "Do *this* to get $1,000,000," we phrase our injection as a condition that opens the door to other possible ways of realizing it—earning the $1,000,000 instead of defrauding someone, for example. So our injection phrased as a condition becomes "I acquire $1,000,000," rather than "I con somebody out of $1,000,000" (an action).

Remember that the Future Reality Tree is a simulation model of the future. As such, it may not contain a lot of detail. Injections may be worded as desired future conditions. If you expect to implement your model of the future, however, these "condition" injections will eventually have to be translated into effects. The specific actions needed to realize these effects can be developed in Prerequisite Trees (chapter 6) and Transition Trees (chapter 7).

Multiple Injections: The "Silver Bullet" Fallacy

In building a Future Reality Tree, your aim should be to make the simplest change to existing reality that will produce the future conditions you desire. Unfortunately, because most situations in which you'd need a FRT are complex, it's not likely that you'll find a single "mother of all injections" that will do the job for you. A lone "silver bullet" may kill a vampire in the movies, but such neat solutions don't usually exist in reality. Let's say, for example, that a major injection in your FRT is to change a broad policy. You may find several discrete faulty parts of that policy that need to be addressed separately in order to ensure the elimination of different undesirable effects.

Consequently, you'll need multiple injections to realize most conditions of desired future reality. You may start with only one injection, but you'll undoubtedly need to add others as you go along. Where do these injections come from?

- *The Current Reality Tree.* If you've begun your analysis with a Current Reality Tree, it can be a source of possible injections. Look for root causes in the Current Reality Tree: They may suggest the injection(s) necessary to eliminate them. In any case, they are likely to be elements in the Future Reality Tree because they're conditions of existing reality. If they lead to an undesirable effect in the Current Reality Tree, they may need to be combined with an injection in the FRT to favorably modify the future (see Figures 5.10 and 5.11). The injection may replace the root cause, but it is more likely to be in addition to it, as in Figure 5.10. If the root cause also generates positive effects, you probably won't want to replace it.

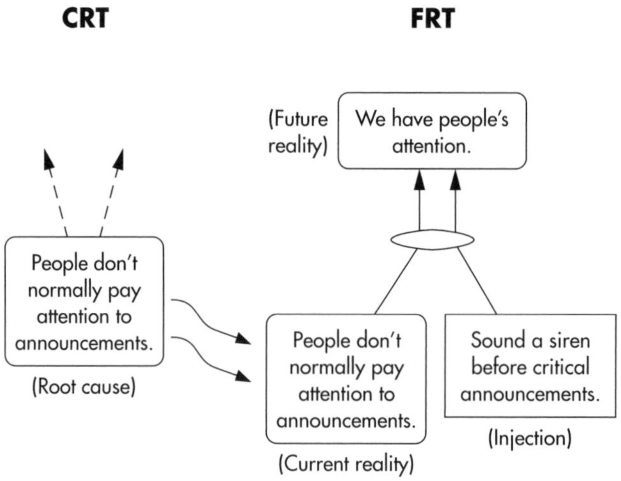

FIGURE 5.10. CRT: A Source of Injections.

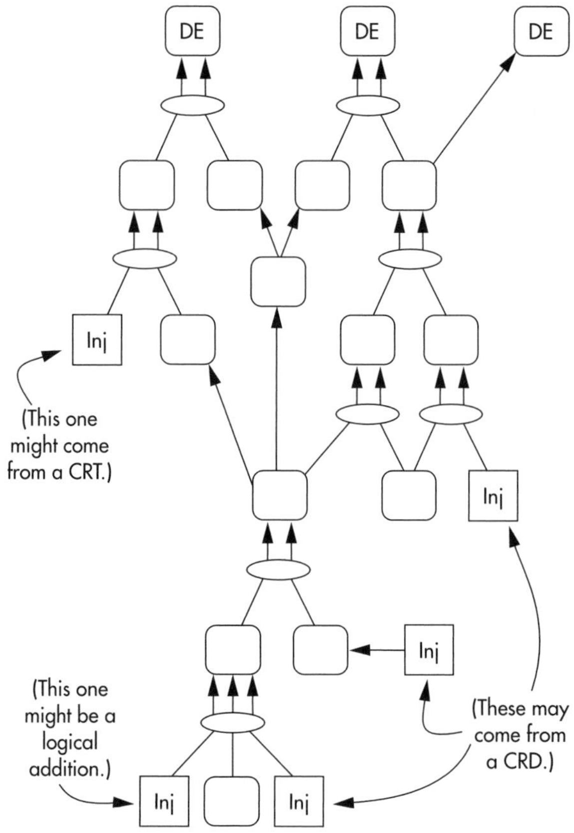

FIGURE 5.11. Where Injections Might Originate in an FRT.

• *The Conflict Resolution Diagram.* If you used a Conflict Resolution Diagram to help solve your problem, the injections you developed in it will form the foundation layers of your Future Reality Tree (remember, FRTs are built from the bottom up) (see Figure 5.11). Refer to chapter 4, "Conflict Resolution Diagram," for more on how to use a CRD to develop injections.

• *Spontaneous Creativity.* If you haven't used a CRD, you might use some other structured idea generation method (brainstorming, Crawford Slip, Delphi, or other technique) to create your initial injections.

• *Logical Additions.* We alluded to this approach previously, under "Actions as Injections." Using this technique, you essentially start with existing reality and your expected reaction or desired effect, then ask the question, "What do I need to add to existing reality to produce the desired effect?" (See Figure 5.12.) After you create an action or condition to add to the relationship, check the connection using the Categories of Legitimate Reservation. They should immediately tell you if your cause is insufficient.

Note: As your Future Reality Tree begins to take shape, most of the causality arrows should be passing through ellipses—substantially more than you might expect to find in a Current Reality Tree. Because injections constitute changes, they must always be combined with existing reality entities to produce a new expected effect. By definition, then, single arrows from injections to effects should be extremely rare. Moreover, the same is generally true of new effects created by combining injections with existing reality. The expected reactions will also need to merge with realities or other effects to produce the ultimate desired effect. So if you see a single arrow in a Future Reality Tree, examine it carefully. An additional injection or unstated reality might be needed. Use the cause insufficiency test: "Can all parts of the effect be accounted for in the cause?" If not, determine what's missing and include it.

The Future Reality Tree and Other System Thinking Tools

You can build a Future Reality Tree from scratch, without the help of the other TOC system thinking tools, but in most cases you're likely to find that to be a "brute force" approach. After all, why would you be trying to change the future unless you're dissatisfied with the present? And if you're dissatisfied with the present, how will you know *what* to change about the present—or what to change it *to* for the future?

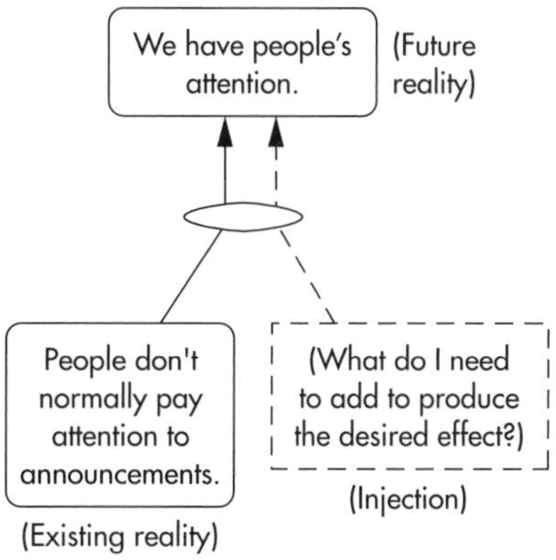

FIGURE 5.12. Logical Additions.

The Future Reality Tree and the Current Reality Tree

Even if you're strategically planning the future, rather than solving a specific problem, you'll be starting from a reference point in the present that will probably need to be clearly expressed. This is the essential function of the Current Reality Tree. Whatever you define as the core problem in a Current Reality Tree, the chances are that your future objective is the diametric opposite of that situation. If you have undesirable effects in existing circumstances, you probably want them converted into their opposites, desired effects, in your future (see Figure 5.13).

Moreover, it's often very difficult to plan the future unless you're intimately familiar with the causes and effects of the present. The Current Reality Tree can be, in effect, the road map to the Future Reality Tree. If you've already constructed a CRT, you'll find that much of that structure may be usable in building your FRT. Basic relationships in reality are not likely to change very much, so the same logical causes and effects you developed in your CRT will probably show themselves in the FRT. This means that parts of the CRT may be transferrable directly to the upper level of your FRT. These transferred parts may have to be modified slightly to reflect positive wording, and they will lead to desirable effects instead of undesirable effects. But the general relationship will remain the same. Refer to chapter 3, "Current Reality Tree," for more on how Current Reality Trees interact with Future Reality Trees.

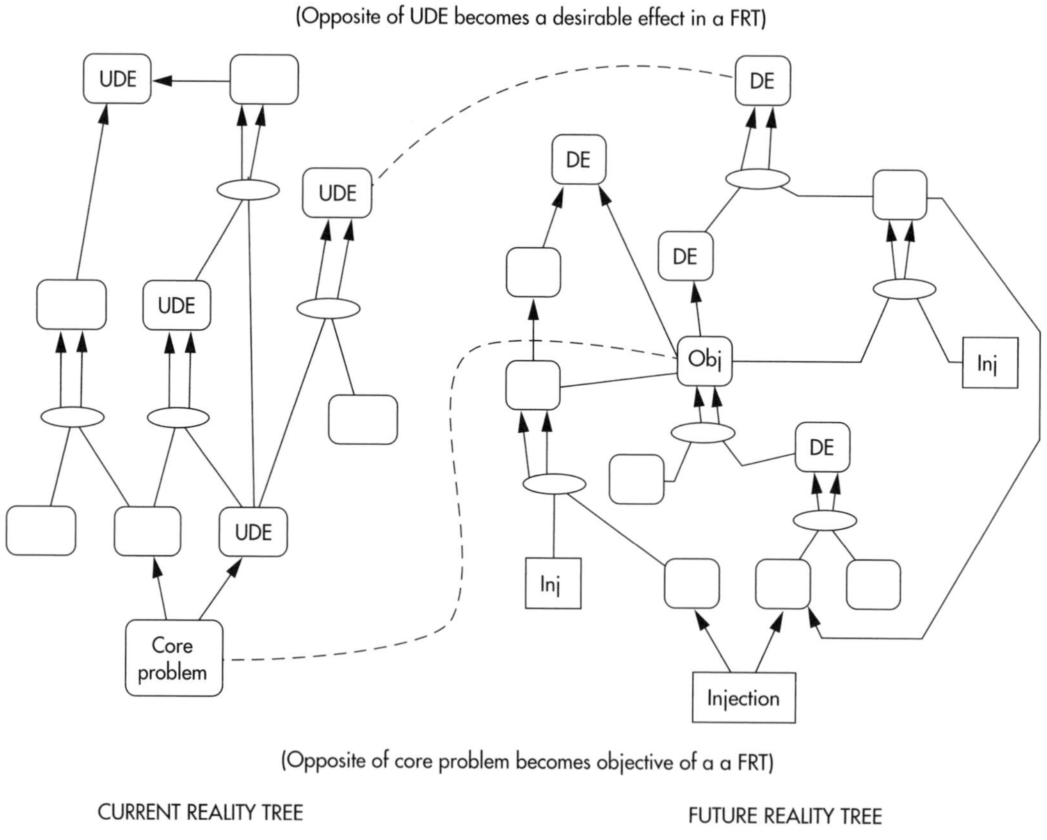
(Opposite of UDE becomes a desirable effect in a FRT)
UDE
UDE
UDE
UDE
Core problem
DE
DE
DE
Obj
Inj
DE
Inj
Injection
(Opposite of core problem becomes objective of a a FRT)
CURRENT REALITY TREE
FUTURE REALITY TREE

FIGURE 5.13. The Future Reality Tree and the Current Reality Tree.

The Future Reality Tree and the Conflict Resolution Diagram

Effectively changing future reality demands that you know what to change it *to*. The Conflict Resolution Diagram provides the first half of the answer to that question by suggesting injections to break assumptions about existing reality. The Future Reality Tree then answers the second half of the question through validation testing of the effectiveness of those injections (see Figure 5.14). So if you use both the Current Reality Tree and the Conflict Resolution Diagram to help structure your Future Reality Tree, you will have some very important elements already in place as you begin to make logical connections.

Figures 5.13 and 5.14 show how essential elements of the Conflict Resolution Diagram and Current Reality Tree provide the framework for your Future Reality Tree. Refer to chapter 4, "Conflict Resolution Diagram," for more on how CRDs interact with FRTs.

The Future Reality Tree and the Prerequisite Tree

You'll recall that injections can be either actions or conditions. The Future Reality Tree is basically a simulation model with which to test the effectiveness of an idea, or ideas. It's the second half of the process that answers the question of "what to change *to*." As such, it's not intensively concerned with implementation. That's the purpose of the Prerequisite Tree and the Transition Tree. But the Prerequisite Tree serves an important purpose for the FRT. It can identify how to execute the injections developed in the CRD and the FRT (see Figure 5.15).

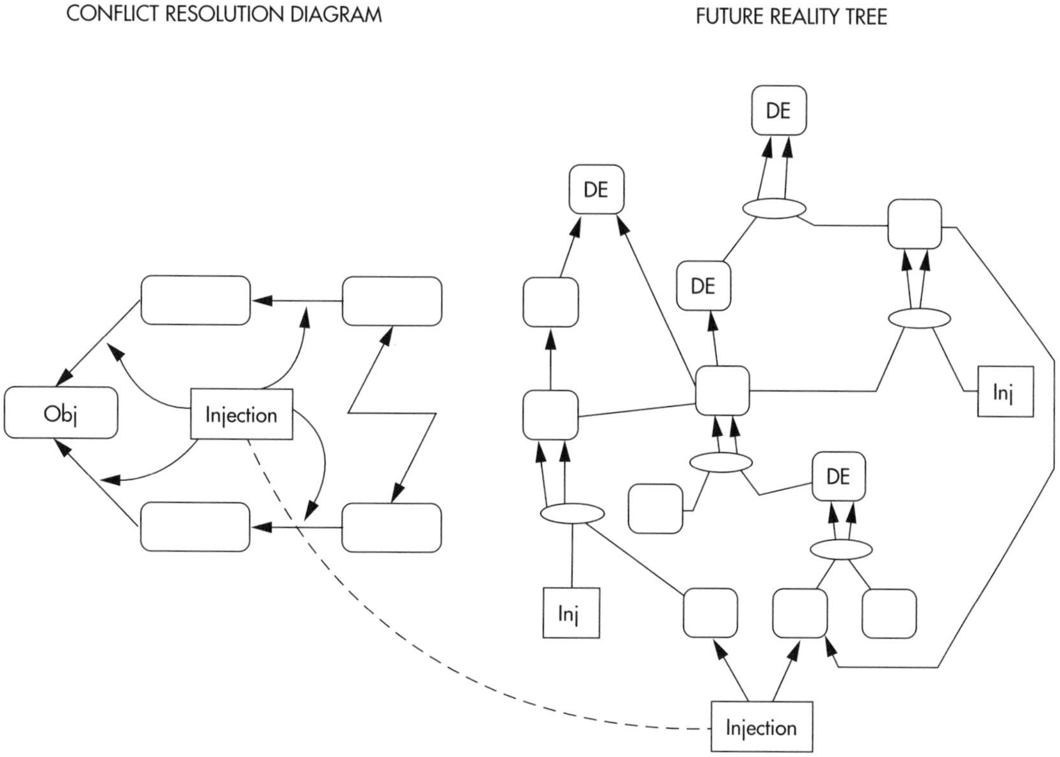

FIGURE 5.14. The Future Reality Tree and the Conflict Resolution Diagram.

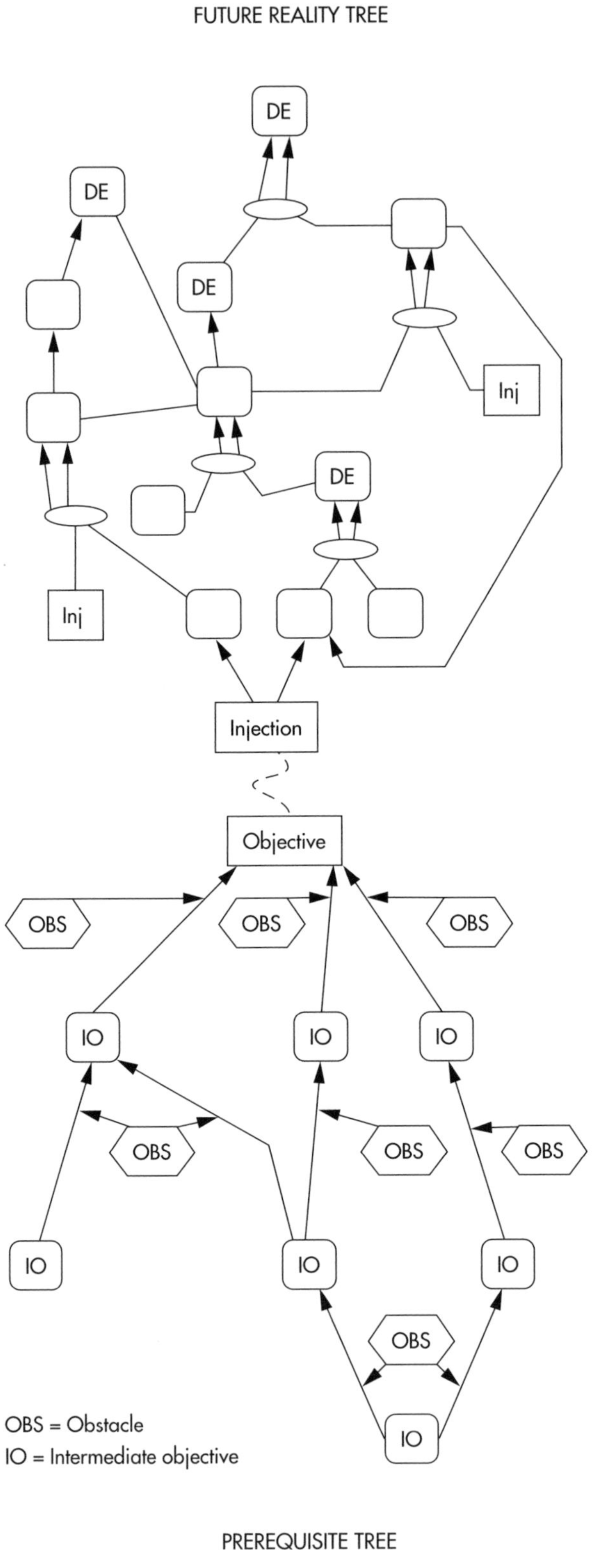

FIGURE 5.15. The Future Reality Tree and the Prerequisite Tree.

In most cases, these injections should be conditions, because you probably won't want to limit your options by settling too soon on a specific action. But at some point, you need to determine what must be done to achieve that desired future condition. If you aren't sure how to achieve that condition, the Prerequisite Tree can do two things for you.

- It can identify all the component actions to be completed in order to achieve the desired injection (condition).
- Even if you're reasonably certain of all the steps needed to achieve the injection, the Prerequisite Tree can help you sequence them in the proper order.

The injection you want to introduce into the Future Reality Tree becomes the Objective of the Prerequisite Tree. Refer to chapter 6, "Prerequisite Tree," for more on how the Prerequisite Tree interacts with the Future Reality Tree.

The Future Reality Tree as a "Safety Net"

Although it can be used by itself, one of the strengths of the Future Reality Tree lies in its capacity as a safety net for the Current Reality Tree and the Conflict Resolution Diagram. What this means is that you don't have to have a perfect Current Reality Tree or CRD to have an effective FRT.

If you don't precisely identify the core problem in the Current Reality Tree, it's not critical—you only need the Current Reality Tree to get you into the *area* of the core problem. If you don't identify all the assumptions that need to be broken in the CRD, don't worry. As long as you have a major invalid assumption to attack, you have enough to get started. The Future Reality Tree will catch any omissions from the CRD or inaccuracies in the Current Reality Tree through negative branches. As Goldratt has said, "It's better to be approximately correct than precisely incorrect." So don't agonize over unnecessary precision in the Current Reality Tree or CRD. The FRT is the one to be precise on. If you're thorough and conscientious with your logic in the FRT, you'll catch any deficiencies overlooked with the other two tools.

> ***In our haste to deal with the things that are wrong, let us not upset the things that are right.***
>
> ***—Unknown***

Negative Branches

The negative branch is one of the most powerful features of the Future Reality Tree. It can save planners and problem solvers much heartache and aggravation during implementation.

The negative branch is a variety of Predicted Effect Existence reservation. (Refer to chapter 2, "Categories of Legitimate Reservation," for more on the Predicted Effect Existence reservation.) However, instead of using it to prove the existence of an intangible cause, we use predicted effects to expose any possible undesirable outcomes associated with an injection we're thinking of using (see Figure 5.16). For example, let's say that your injection is "I lend you my car." The outcome I desire is "You drive my children to school." (See Figure 5.17.)

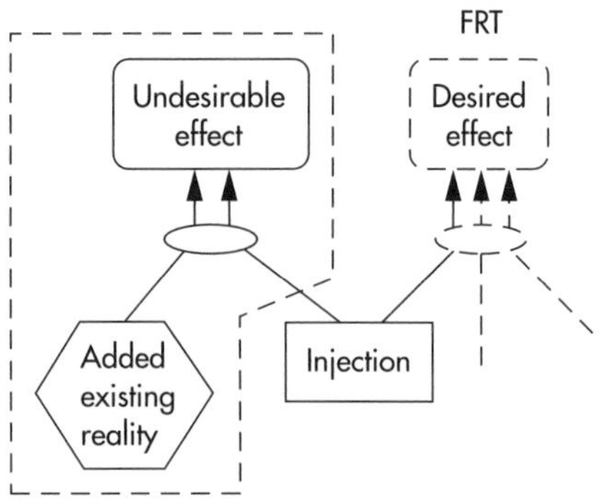

FIGURE 5.16. Negative Branch.

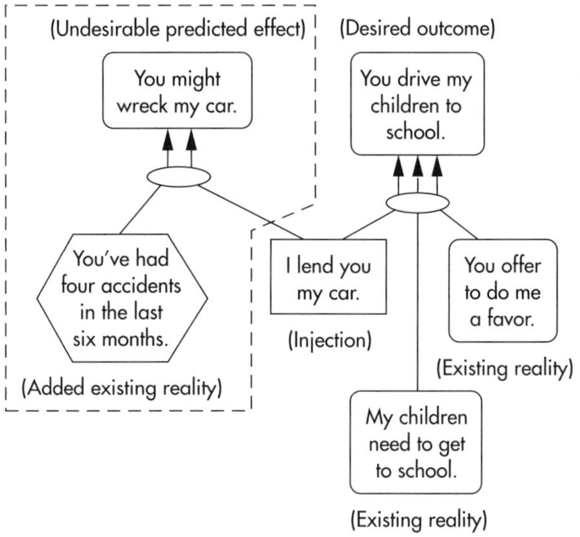

FIGURE 5.17. Example of a Negative Branch.

My desired outcome is probably entirely reasonable. But some other conditions of reality might be considered (for example, "You've had four accidents in the last six months"). In a situation like this, the following negative branch then becomes a real possibility: "You wreck my car."

Using the Negative Branch as a "Stand-Alone"

The preceding example also illustrates a feature of negative branches that makes them extremely useful in daily application: You don't need any of the other Thinking Process tools to make good use of negative branches, not even a Future Reality Tree. If you're called upon to render a decision that seems questionable, ask for some time to consider the issue: "Let me think about that for a few minutes." Then see if you can construct a quick negative branch. If you decide there are no realistic negative consequences, you'll be more confident about your decision. If there are undesirable outcomes, the negative branch may help you do one of two things:

- Decline the request tactfully, without incurring animosity, or
- Find an alternative means (injection) of satisfying the original intent without incurring the risk of an undesirable outcome.

For example, if you had come to me and asked to borrow my car, I could have begun with the injection "I lend you my car," and developed a negative branch all by itself, without resorting to a Future Reality Tree. If I really perceive a risk of your wrecking my car, the negative branch might steer me to this response: "If you can wait until lunchtime, I'll drop you by your appointment on my way out, and pick you up on my way back." The negative branch helps make your response "palatable" for others to accept without incurring ill feelings.

Day-to-day decisions can be effectively analyzed this way. Figure 5.38 shows how this particular negative branch might be completely developed and suggests possible actions to trim it. Figure 5.37, "Procedures for Building and Trimming a Stand-Alone Negative Branch," provides abbreviated steps for using a negative branch without a complete Future Reality Tree.

Added Realities

If your negative branch is a growth on a Future Reality Tree, you may sometimes have to add some conditions of reality that were not in the original FRT. In the car example, when introducing the injection "I lend you my car," we have to consider your history of accidents. This may always have been a factor, but it might not have been explicitly stated in the FRT because it wasn't needed—until we introduced the injection, at which time it became an important factor to consider. Such added conditions that become parts of negative branches can be represented by hexagons with the label "added reality."

Assumptions

Remember that, as with Current Reality Trees and Conflict Resolution Diagrams, the arrows in a negative branch also imply the presence of underlying assumptions. The ones that are particularly important in a negative branch are those associated with the arrows connecting neutral entities or injections to the negative entity. It is at this point that the Future Reality Tree begins to turn "sour," and this is where trimming needs to be done.

You must identify as many assumptions as possible underlying these crucial arrows, and develop new injections to break them, much as you would do with a Conflict Resolution Diagram (CRD). In fact, you can use a CRD to help you develop injections to trim negative branches.

"Trimming" Negative Branches

Once you have the added realities and the additional injections needed to break the assumptions that turn the branch negative, you're on the verge of trimming the negative branch.

Incorporate the added reality and the new injection(s) into your Future Reality Tree at the point where the branch had begun to turn from positive or neutral to negative. Then recheck the entire tree downstream from (that is, above)

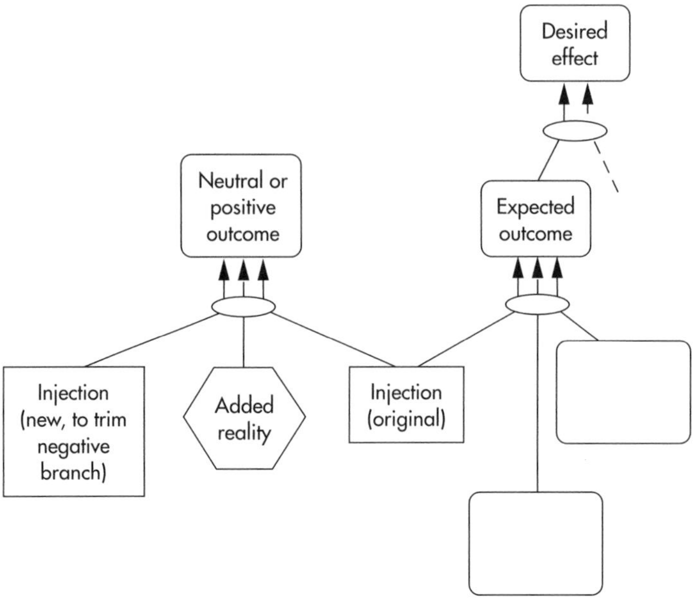

FIGURE 5.18. Incorporating a "Trimmed" Negative Branch into an FRT.

the trim point. Make any subsequent logical adjustments required to meet CLR requirements, not just at the trim point (see Figure 5.18).

When to Raise Negative Branch Reservations

In many situations as you're building a Future Reality Tree, you'll notice places where it's highly probable that a negative branch might develop. These places may be very obvious. As the builder of the tree, if you see such indications, it's always a good idea to deal with them immediately, even before you finish building the Future Reality Tree. Always make your FRT as logically tight as you can during construction. However, because of the inventor's inherent "blindness" to logical deficiencies, you may not see many negative branches until after someone else scrutinizes your tree.

If you present your tree to others for scrutiny, ask them to make note of any negative branch they might see but to wait to tell you about it until after the entire tree has been presented. Figure 5.37, "Procedures for Building and Trimming a Stand-Alone Negative Branch," provides detailed directions for constructing negative branches. Figure 5.38 provides a typical example.

Positive Reinforcing Loops

In building a Future Reality Tree, you'll occasionally notice situations where a desired effect feeds back and amplifies another entity lower in the tree. That lower entity is usually neutral or positive on its own merit, but the outcome of the desired effect higher up is to reinforce or increase the magnitude of the entity below (see Figure 5.19).

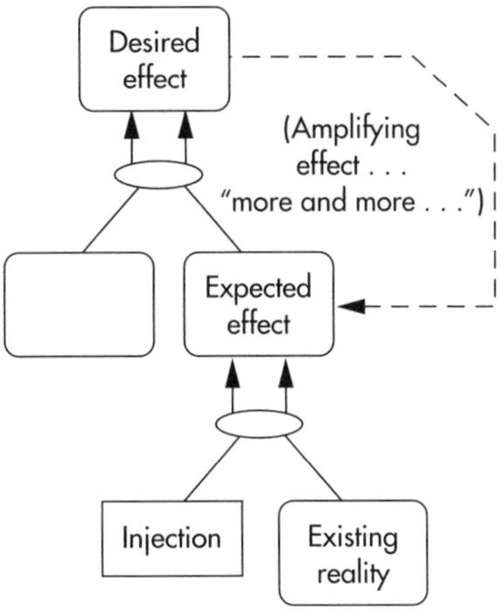

FIGURE 5.19. Positive Reinforcing Loop.

As we've seen earlier, this effect is called a positive reinforcing loop, and it's highly desirable in any Future Reality Tree. In fact, it's so desirable that if you don't notice one occurring naturally, you should actively search for ways to *make* the ultimate desired effects reinforce their causes lower in the tree. By doing so you can frequently make your desirable condition self-sustaining and synergetic. The more positive loops you have, the greater the probability of a self-sustaining solution.

Figure 5.35 presents a more detailed example, part of a Future Reality Tree on implementing TQM. Figure 5.36, "Procedures for Building a Future Reality Tree," includes a specific step prompting you to create positive reinforcing loops.

Strategic Planning with a Future Reality Tree

So far we've examined the Future Reality Tree in a problem-solving role as a "solution tester"—a way of validating the effectiveness of ideas for solutions and exposing any undesirable collateral effects of these ideas. This is probably the mode in which you'll most frequently use the it. But the Future Reality Tree's capability as a strategic planning model is potentially its most valuable application. The FRT is no substitute for a well-written, thoroughly documented strategic plan, but like the blueprint for a complex design, it can visually represent what needs to be done.

In chapter 1 we established one interpretation of a manager's mission: Identify the goal, ascertain where we stand in relation to it, and determine the magnitude and direction of the difference between the two. This is the essence of strategic planning. Most organizations can, with careful thought, settle on a feasible goal. With more effort, they can also determine the conditions necessary to its attainment. The difficulties arise, first, in deciding what to do to reach the goal and, second, in verifying whether those actions will really result in goal attainment. In other words, "I know what I want, but I'm not entirely sure how to get it."

A Current Reality Tree might tell you where you stand in relation to the goal, and a Conflict Resolution Diagram might help you decide what initial actions (injections) to take. But the Future Reality Tree can help you establish the road map to your goal and overlay upon it the actions you've decided to take. You can then logically trace the effectiveness of your actions all the way to the goal, and any undesirable side effects (negative branches) can be clearly exposed. Moreover, as you execute your plan, you can refer regularly to a Future Reality Tree, just as you might a road map, to keep yourself (or your system) on course. Few, if any, other strategic planning methodologies incorporate a "self-test" function that logically tests effectiveness and anticipates potential pitfalls.

To use the Future Reality Tree as a strategic planning tool, you must start by formulating your goal statement (see Figure 5.20). Place the goal statement where the very top of the tree will eventually be. Then identify all the necessary conditions that must be satisfied in order to realize the goal. Depending on the nature and scope of your plan, this may be no small task. An individual preparing a strategic career plan may spend many hours figuring out the necessary conditions and how they lead to the goal. Corporate executives might spend weeks doing the same thing for a company. Once the necessary conditions are all identified, locate them horizontally immediately below the goal. In your strategic Future Reality Tree, these necessary conditions would be represented as desired effects you're trying to achieve. They might be considered "critical success factors."

The necessary conditions will suggest the kinds of general programs you'll need to initiate to satisfy them. Each program may be composed of one or more closed-ended project or initiatives. Successful completion of these subordinate projects will constitute continuing effective support of the larger program. A completed program might be an objective of a preceding Conflict Resolution Diagram (CRD). The subordinate projects might be requirements from the same CRD. The lowest level of the strategic Future Reality Tree will be the conditions of current reality that you want to change and the injections (that is, project initiations) you'll need to effect the changes. The injections (actions or new reali-

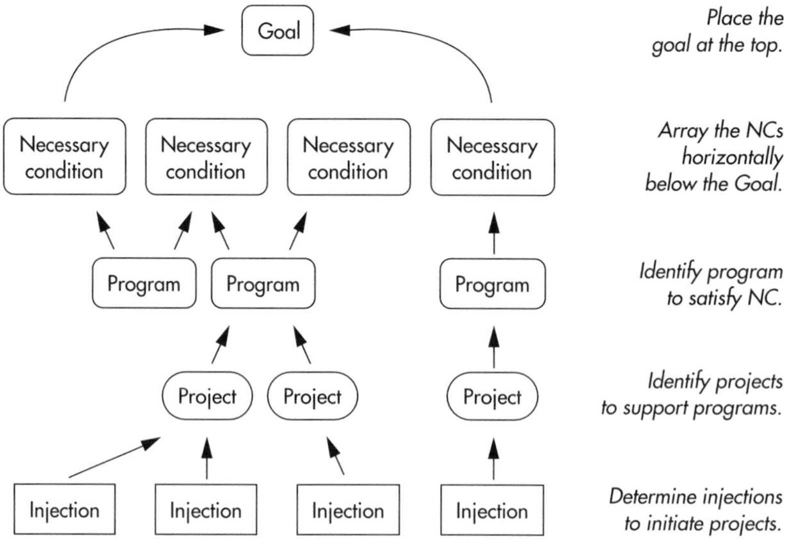

FIGURE 5.20. FRT: The Strategic Planning Model.

ties you'll create) might be the breakthrough ideas from preceding CRDs. You now have the framework upon which to flesh out your strategic plan. "Building a Future Reality Tree," p. 202, and Figure 5.36 specify the procedures to follow in constructing a FRT. Detailed stages of project planning (how to complete projects) are the domain of a Prerequisite Tree. Refer to chapter 6, "Prerequisite Tree," for more on how to use it in strategic and project planning.

When your strategic Future Reality Tree is completed, it should look something like Figure 5.21, with your ultimate goal at the top, the programs and

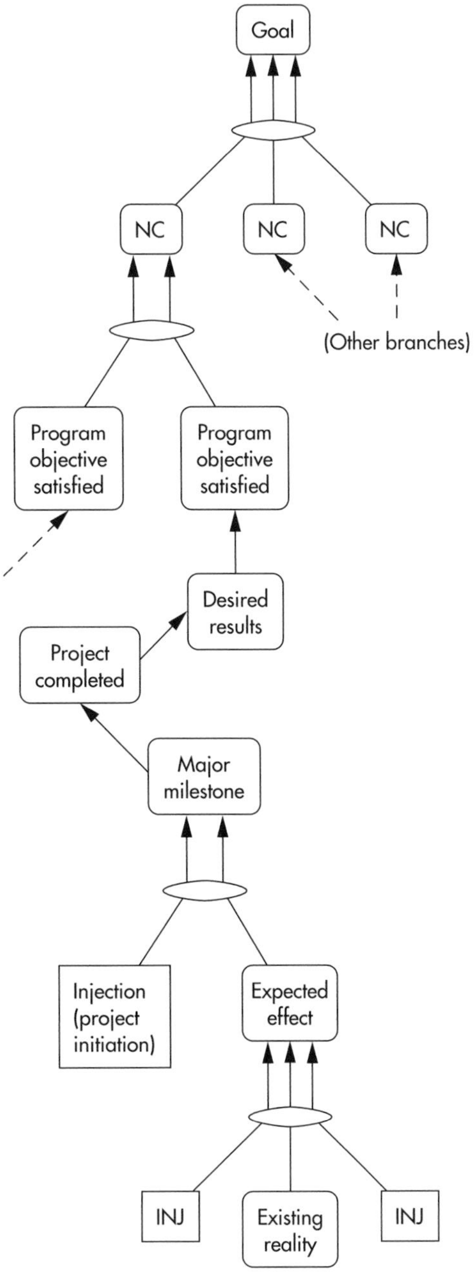

FIGURE 5.21. Strategic Plan FRT.

projects in the middle, and the actions (injections) you'll need to take to start the ball rolling at the bottom.

The discrete programs, projects, or initiatives you engage in to reach your goal will each constitute a different branch on the tree. These branches may cross-connect at some points, because the components of a system are interdependent. But if you've properly identified all the necessary conditions, the completed tree will represent the totality of your strategic plan. Anything you're already doing that doesn't appear in the tree should be questioned: "Does this *really* contribute to my stated goal?" If it does, it should already be incorporated into the tree. If not, consider not wasting any more resources on it and focusing exclusively on the elements of the Future Reality Tree.

Once the tree is completed, all that remains is the writing of the strategic plan itself and any subordinate or supporting plans. Bear in mind that the Future Reality Tree isn't limited to strategic planning alone; smaller, more limited FRTs could be constructed to help in designing the projects or programs needed to satisfy necessary conditions enroute to the goal.

BUILDING A FUTURE REALITY TREE

Now you're ready to begin building a Future Reality Tree. The following procedures will lead you through the process. An abbreviated checklist of these same procedures may be found in Figure 5.36, "Procedures for Building a Future Reality Tree."

1. Gather All Necessary Information and Materials

Are you starting your Future Reality Tree from scratch, or are you leading into it with a Current Reality Tree or Conflict Resolution Diagram? If the latter, make sure your Current Reality Tree and CRD are close at hand. From the Current Reality Tree, make a list of undesirable effects, the core problem, and significant root causes. From the CRD, make a list of the objective and any injections you have developed. Keep your list of assumptions close at hand, too. If you aren't leading into the FRT from other Thinking Process tools, go on to the next step.

You'll need an oversized sheet of paper, a pencil, and small Post-it™ notes, just as you did for the Current Reality Tree.

2. Formulate Desired Effects

Begin your tree by writing on Post-it™ notes statements of the desired effects you're trying to achieve (see Figure 5.22). If you haven't already completed a Current Reality Tree, you'll have to compose the desired effects from scratch. If you have a Current Reality Tree to start from, extract all of the undesirable effects (UDE) from it. Then rephrase each one in an opposite, or desirable, way. For example, if the UDE reads "The company is losing money," the opposite (desirable) phrasing might be "The company makes money." These desired effects will be the ultimate targets of the Future Reality Tree.

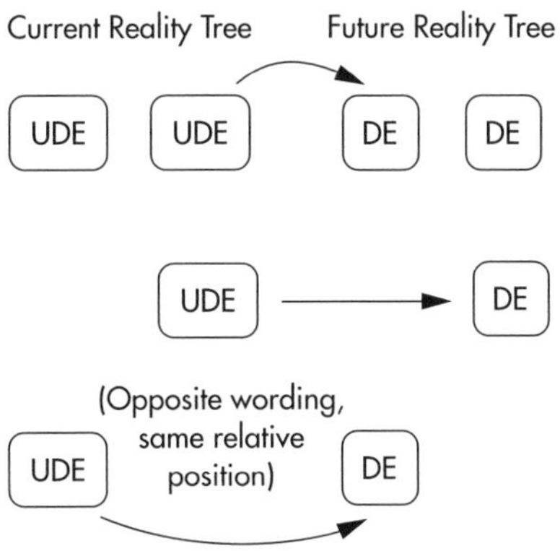

FIGURE 5.22. Formulating Desired Effects.

Positive, Not Neutral

Make sure the opposite statement of the UDE that you use to word your desired effect is truly positive and not merely neutral (that is, be sure it reads "good," and not just "not bad").

Use Present Tense

Avoid future tense in wording all entities in your Future Reality Tree. Consider the FRT a real-time computer simulation—it's happening right now. So use present tense wording (for example, "is," "are," and "can," not "will be").

Lay Out Desired Effects

Arrange the desired effect Post-it™ notes horizontally across the top of your paper. Because the basic relationships of reality should remain the same, if your desired effects came from UDEs in a Current Reality Tree, they will occupy the same relative positions in the Future Reality Tree.

3. Add the Injection(s)

Place your injection Post-it™ notes at the bottom of the page (see Figure 5.23). For the future to unfold differently from the present, some change in what's currently happening must be initiated. You have to do something differently, or create conditions favorable to the development of the future along your intended path. The changes you make will constitute injections.

Where Do I Find Injections?

If you're starting your Future Reality Tree without having completed a Current Reality Tree or Conflict Resolution Diagram, you'll have to be creative in deciding what to change and what form the changes should take. Traditional idea generation methods such as brainstorming, nominal group technique, and Crawford Slips can be useful in developing injections.

However, if you have a Current Reality Tree or CRD, you'll have done much of the creative work already. In fact, the CRD, besides helping resolve conflict, is a natural "idea generator." Chances are, if you've built a CRD, you'll already

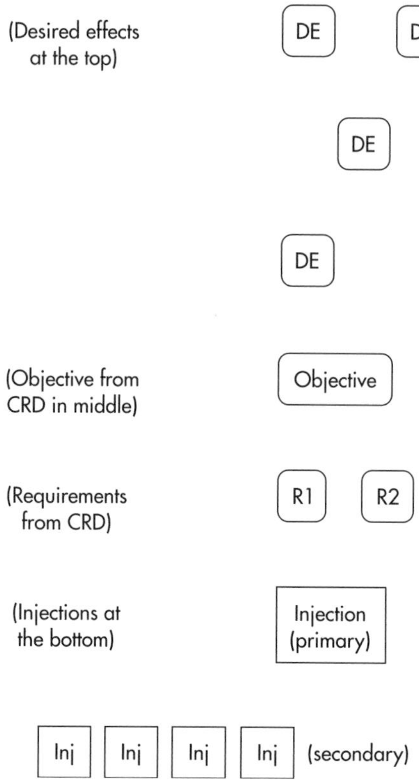

FIGURE 5.23. Adding Injections and the Objective.

have one primary injection and a host of secondary ones. Write your injections on Post-it™ notes. Distinguish them from effect entities by using different color notes or by outlining the edges.

Injections at the Bottom

Put your primary injection at the bottom of the paper, in the center. If you have additional injections you expect to use, arrange them temporarily in a horizontal "holding pattern" to one side along the bottom edge of the paper (see Figure 5.23).

> **Note:** If you already have a Current Reality Tree or CRD relating to your problem, you can add a few more elements. One is the opposite of the core problem (the CRD's objective). On a Post-it™ note, draft an effect entity that replicates the CRD's objective or the opposite of the Current Reality Tree's core problem. Place it approximately in the center of the page, between the primary injection and the desired effects. Two others may be the requirements from the CRD. The latter would show up as effects of the primary injection, positioned above it but below the CRD's Objective (see Figure 5.23).

4. Fill in the Gaps

You now have a framework in which to build your Future Reality Tree.

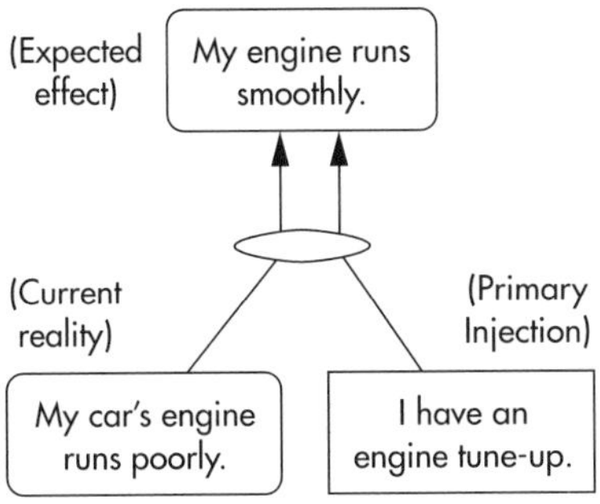

FIGURE 5.24. Building Upward.

Build Upward

Starting with your primary injection, at the bottom, build upward toward the desired effects (see Figure 5.24). Adhere to the requirements of the Categories of Legitimate Reservation, with special attention to cause insufficiency and additional cause. Combine your injection with an entity of current reality, using an ellipse, to produce an expected effect (one that does not yet exist). For example, let's assume that your current reality is "My car's engine runs poorly." Your injection is "I have an engine tune-up." The expected effect of these two entities would be "My engine runs smoothly."

Continue Building on the Expected Effect

The expected effect may be enough, when combined with another current reality, to produce a subsequent expected effect. If not, you may have to help the process along with another injection (see Figure 5.25).

Add Injections as Necessary

Each expected effect should move you another step toward your desired effects. If you reach a point where the momentum of your original injection runs out, you may need to add another injection. In the previous example, a tune-up smoothed out your engine performance. This led to decreased gasoline expenses. However, no further progress is possible without taking some additional action—that is, adding another injection. In this case, the additional injection, "Increase tire pressure," is combined with another current reality, "Higher tire pressures decrease gasoline consumption." The expected effect, "Gasoline consumption is reduced," is combined with "Gasoline expenses go down" to produce a new expected effect, "Gasoline expenses go down even more."

Where do you get these additional injections? You may have a small collection of secondary injections on Post-it™ notes in a "holding pattern" at the bottom of your Future Reality Tree. Check first to see if any of these are appropriate. If not, create a new one specifically for this situation.

Incorporate the Objective

If you built a Current Reality Tree, the opposite of the core problem became an objective that you prepositioned near the middle of your Future Reality Tree. If you built a CRD, its objective is probably what you inserted into your FRT. (See

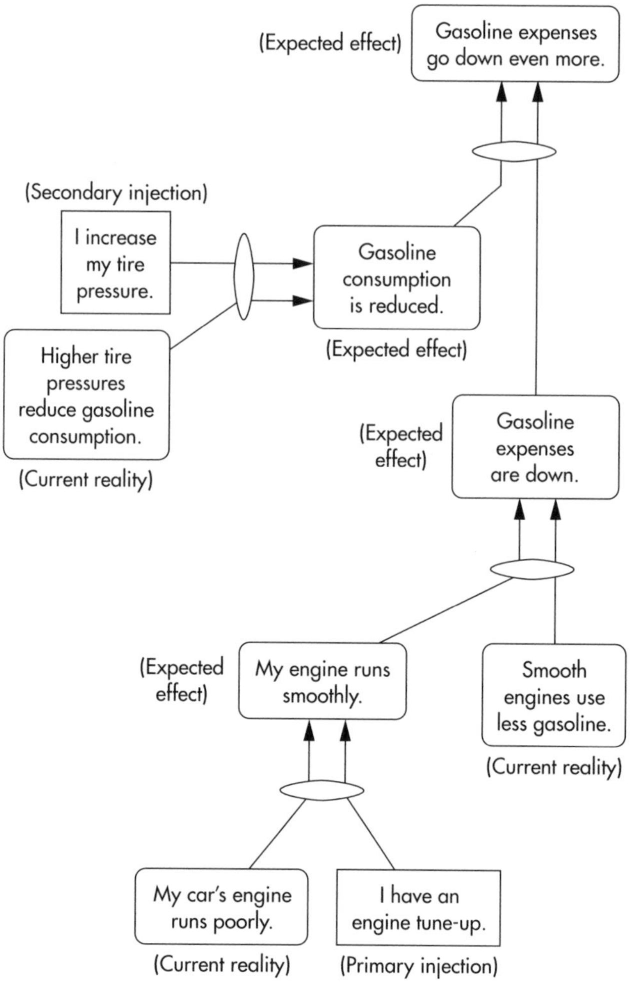

FIGURE 5.25. Building and Adding Injections.

Note in step 3.) As you build your FRT upward from the primary injection, keep trying to get closer to this objective. At some point you should be able to make one last connection of an expected effect and a current reality entity directly to the objective. In other words, this objective becomes the unavoidable effect of all injections and their outcomes introduced up to this point (see Figure 5.26).

Note: Remember that an injection from a CRD is intended to resolve conflict by allowing us to realize both of the CRD's requirements. Consequently, you should probably depict one or both of these requirements in your Future Reality Tree. Logically, they should appear just below the objective of the CRD, but above the primary injection.

Continue Building Toward the Desired Effects

At this point you should be considerably closer to reaching your desired effects. The procedure for continuing remains the same: Combine expected

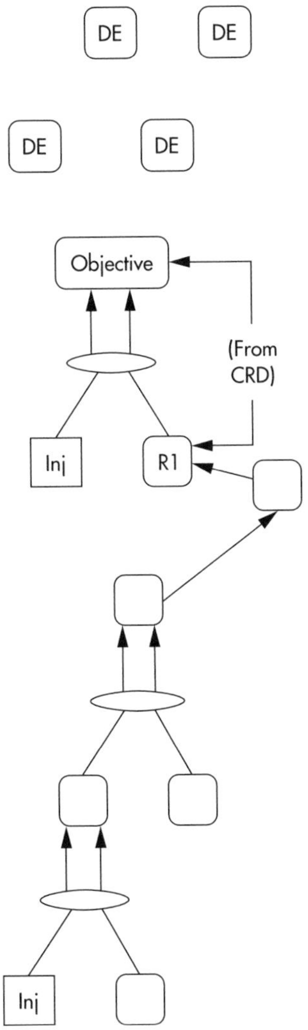

FIGURE 5.26. Incorporating the Objective.

effects with current realities to produce other expected effects. Add injections when required to maintain progress toward the desired effects.

> **Note:** If you have a Current Reality Tree to work from, you have a big advantage. The essential relationships in the Current Reality Tree can be superimposed on the upper part of the Future Reality Tree, between the objective and the desired effects. Some of the same reality entities may be directly transferrable. Even though you're working with opposite conditions in the Future Reality Tree, the structure will be similar (see Figure 5.27).
>
> The reason for this is that the basic cause-effect relationships you constructed in the Current Reality Tree still exist, even though the effects you're trying to achieve are desirable rather than undesirable. The part of the Future Reality Tree that does not exist in the CRT is the part you add in building the FRT: the injections and their effects, which lead you to the upper part of the FRT.

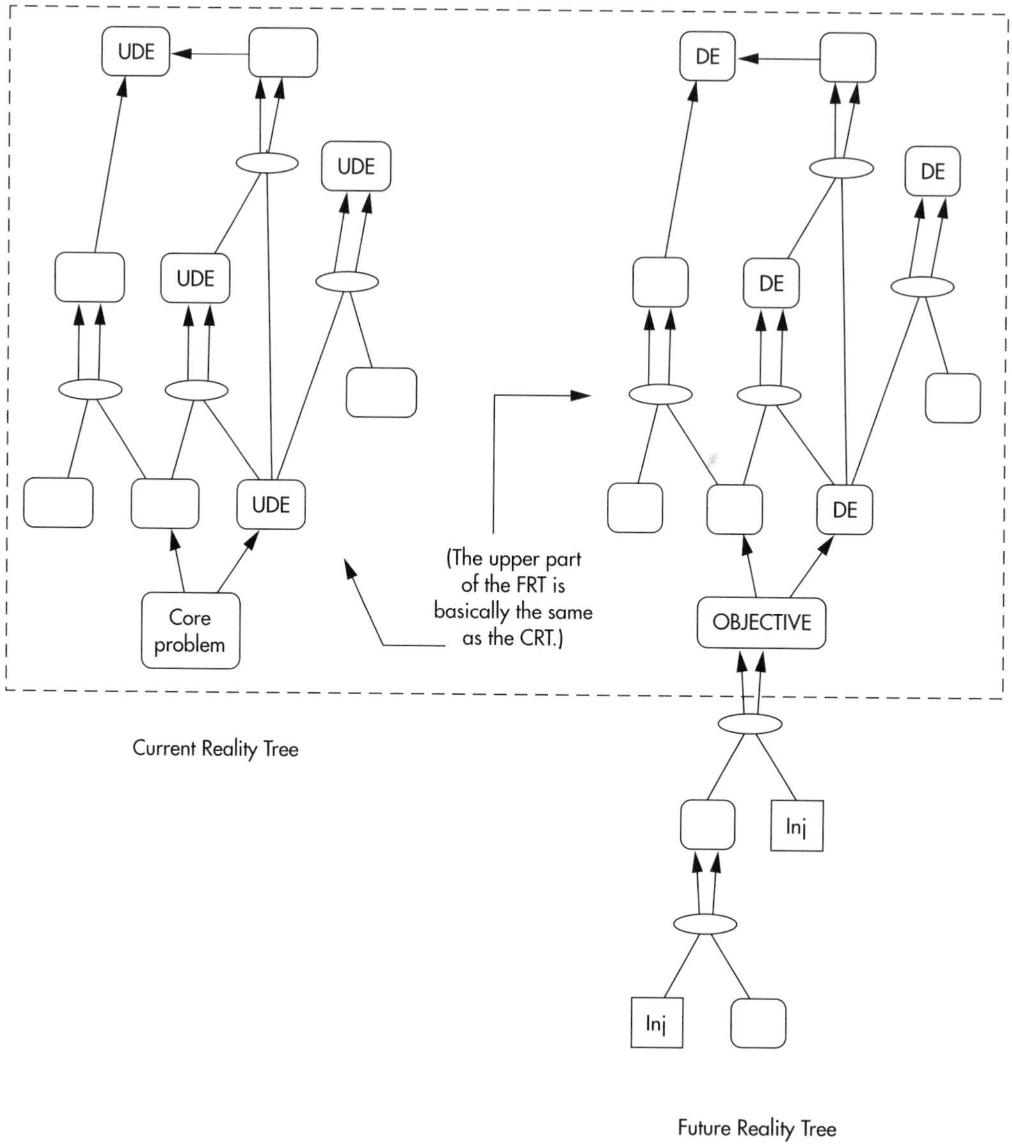

FIGURE 5.27. Continuing to Build Toward the Desired Effects.

> **Caution:** You probably won't be able to transfer your Current Reality Tree "lock, stock, and barrel" to your Future Reality Tree. Some modifications will undoubtedly be necessary, because you've changed the future environment to some extent with your injections. But the Current Reality Tree can provide you a general pattern for the upper part of your tree (above the objective).

This is why we say the Current Reality Tree provides a map to the Future Reality Tree. If you don't have a CRT to work from, you may have to "hack your way through the jungle" a bit to reach your desired effects.

5. Build in Positive Reinforcing Loops

Examine each desired effect (DE) as a possible candidate for a positive reinforcing loop. Then, starting at the bottom of the tree, try to find an effect entity below the desired effect that the DE will amplify or reinforce.

If none present themselves naturally, add entities and injections as necessary to create a positive loop (see Figure 5.28). The arrow from the DE may have to be combined with the added entity using an ellipse.

Make sure that the entity at the reentry point of the loop will withstand an additional cause reservation. In other words, be sure that the entity the loop leads to can't be produced by any other independent cause. If it can be produced by another cause, you'll never know whether your loop is the cause of the reinforcement. You may think it is, but if that additional cause suddenly goes away, you could lose your reinforcing effect and not understand why.

> ***What we anticipate seldom occurs. What we least expected usually happens.***
>
> ***—Benjamin Disraeli***

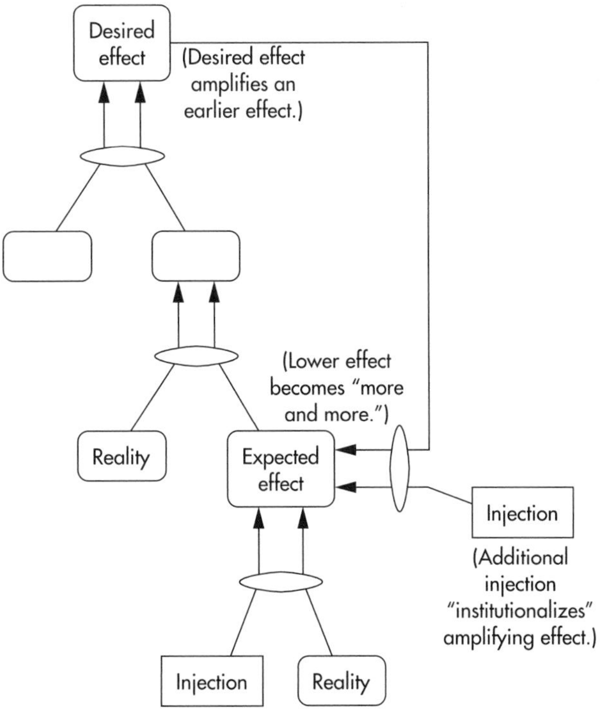

FIGURE 5.28. A Positive Reinforcing Loop.

6. Look for Negative Branches

Starting at the bottom of the Future Reality Tree, systematically examine each expected effect of every injection for possible negative outcomes (see Figure 5.29). Ask yourself, "Besides this desired outcome, what else could result from this injection that I would not like?"

Since negative branches can develop at any subsequent point above the injection, don't become complacent if you don't find one immediately above the injection. Work upward from the injection along each branch to the top of the Future Reality Tree. Don't overlook negative outcomes associated directly with the desired effects, either. It's so easy to focus on the desirable outcomes of a FRT that the adverse impacts may be overlooked. There's a tendency to breathe a sigh of relief when you reach the desired effects and ignore their downsides. What are the possible undesirable effects of your reaching that pot of gold at the end of the rainbow?

Why should we be concerned about negative branches? Other than the obvious reason (that is, we may not like the outcome), we might have to consider other people as well. Frequently we have to work outside our span of complete control to change things. What if you need the assistance of other people to achieve the desired effects? And what if those people can see downsides to your proposed course of action, maybe disadvantages that affect them directly? How can we expect their support, unless we can demonstrate that we've already identified those disadvantages and taken steps to neutralize them? Part of the persuasion process in such cases involves addressing negative branches

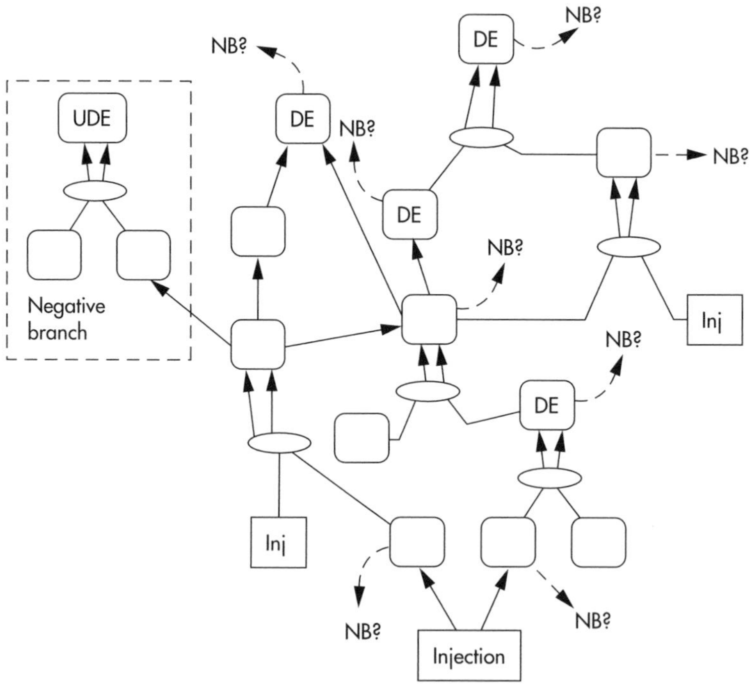

FIGURE 5.29. Looking for Negative Branches.

in the presentation of the Future Reality Tree to others. (Refer to the section in chapter 8, "Persuading Others with Your Logic," p. 343.)

Note #1: Don't start looking for negative branches before your Future Reality Tree is complete. It's too easy to become sidetracked, and the tree may never develop its basic shape. In pursuit of negative branches, you may be diverted from your original purpose, which is to build up to the desired effects. So save work on negative branches until after the Future Reality Tree is done, even if you're certain you know where some might pop up.

Note #2: Remember that, as with any personal creation, you have "pride of authorship" in your tree. To some extent, this can blind you to its deficiencies. Moreover, it's likely that you'll be unable to see all the negative possibilities associated with it. Even if you find a few negative branches, you'll probably need the help of "outside eyes" to locate them all. Before acting on your tree, you're well advised to have someone else scrutinize your tree—someone with intuitive knowledge of your situation. Even if he or she doesn't point out any more negative branches, the additional review is likely to help you clarify and strengthen the logic of your Future Reality Tree.

7. Develop the Negative Branch

If you find possible negative branches, write the entities on Post-it™ notes and place them in their proper positions. To preclude confusion, you may want to develop your negative branch on a separate piece of paper. Include additional reality entities and ellipses if required. Continue building the negative branch upward until you reach effects that are undesirable on their own merit (see Figure 5.30).

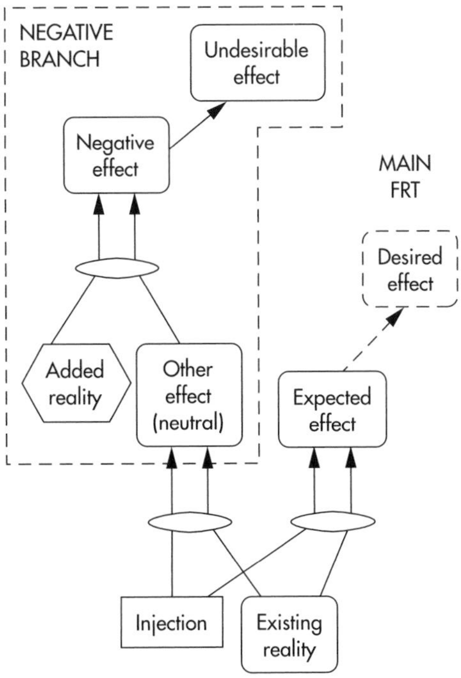

FIGURE 5.30. Developing the Negative Branch.

Your injection may not directly produce an undesirable effect. Instead, it may lead through some intermediate effects that are neutral, or perhaps slightly negative, before reaching something that is definitely undesirable on its own merit. The same is true of the relationship between injections and desirable effects. So be prepared for your negative branch to be more than just one or two entities—possibly even very complex.

Note: Numbering Your Negative Branch Entities. It can be very confusing to number entities in complex trees. This is especially true of Future Reality Trees, where you may have several negative branches on other pieces of paper. To help keep your entities sorted out, you might want to use a different numbering scheme for negative branches. In Figure 5.35, for example, we've used "NB" to indicate that these entities are unique to the negative branch and don't belong in the final FRT.

Added Realities

Note, too, in Figure 5.35 that several "added realities" also appear in the negative branch. These are other statements about reality that exist but that were not necessary for our Future Reality Tree. It was not necessary to display them until we started working with the negative branch. These, too, are confined to the negative branch and are necessary for it to be logically sound, but they don't usually appear in the final FRT.

8. Identify the "Turning Point" of the Negative Branch

When the negative branch seems complete, trace its development from the injection to the undesirable effect (see Figure 5.31). Identify the entity that shows the first sign of being negative—where the branch seems to turn from positive or neutral to decidedly negative. The actual transition occurs between

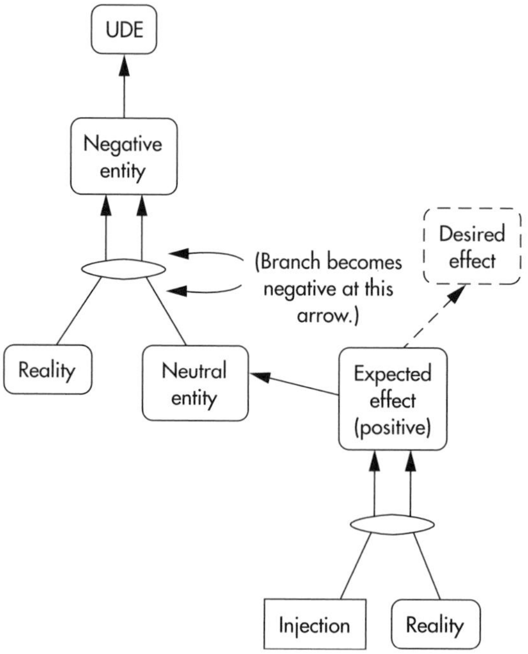

FIGURE 5.31. Identifying the "Turning Point."

entities—that is, with a causality arrow. Find the arrow that connects the last positive or neutral entity with a negative one. It's at this point that the negative branch must be trimmed.

9. Develop Injections to Break Assumptions

As with any TOC logical tool, a causality arrow implies underlying assumptions. On a separate piece of paper, list as many assumptions as you can that might be underlying the arrow where the branch begins to turn from positive or neutral to negative. These underlying assumptions are *critical.* It is here that the problems arise, and it is here that they will be solved. You must formulate injections to break one or more assumptions. Doing so effectively trims the negative branch from the Future Reality Tree. In actuality, the injection at this point prevents undesirable effects from ever arising.

You may also use the "alternative environment" technique described earlier (refer to chapter 4, "Conflict Resolution Diagram") to trim negative branches (see Figure 5.32). In this case, however, your requirement is the desired effect in the Future Reality Tree (or, alternatively, the opposite of the undesirable effect in the negative branch). The prerequisite you're trying to "live without" is the last entity before the negative branch begins to turn sour.

For example, let's look at the negative branch in the first part of Figure 5.38 (at the end of this chapter). The UDE of this branch is "Our friendship suffers." The last neutral entity (working upward from the bottom) before the branch starts becoming negative is "I let you borrow my car." The opposite of the UDE might be "Our friendship remains strong." Make this your requirement for the alternative environment. The prerequisite becomes "I let you borrow my car." Work out an injection to let you satisfy the requirement without needing the prerequisite.

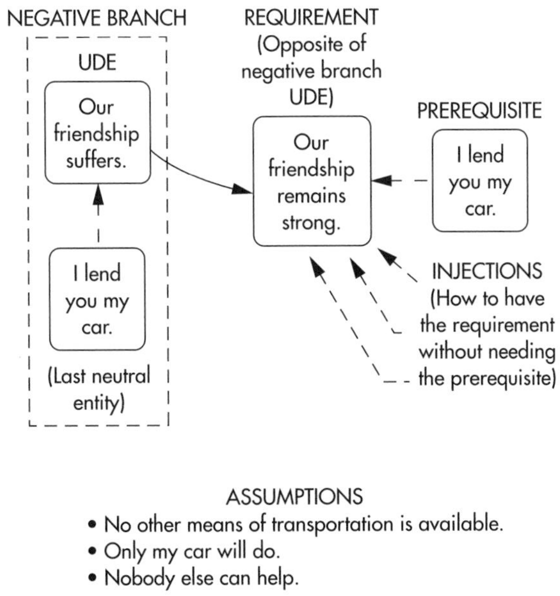

FIGURE 5.32. Developing Branch-Trimming Injections.

10. Validate the Injection

On a separate piece of paper, logically project the consequences of your branch-trimming injection (see Figure 5.33). Combine it with appropriate reality entities. These may come from the Future Reality Tree itself, or they be other previously unstated realities (enclosed in hexagons) that you've had to add.

When you have logically reached the opposite of the negative branch's UDE, scrutinize the new construction using the Categories of Legitimate Reservation (CLR). (Refer to Figure 5.38.) Make sure your new injection doesn't create adverse effects of its own.

11. Incorporate the "Branch-Trimming" Injection into the FRT

This step doesn't apply if you're using the negative branch as a stand-alone tool, without having a Future Reality Tree. If your negative branch is part of a FRT, combine the branch-trimming injection with the entity that prompted it, through an ellipse, and add it to your tree at the appropriate place. Write a reference to your negative branch, which should be completely developed on a separate page (see Figure 5.34).

Derive the consequences of your new addition. This means (a) check to be sure it doesn't affect the logic you originally developed to reach the Future Reality Tree's desired effects, and (b) check to be sure it doesn't create other negative branches.

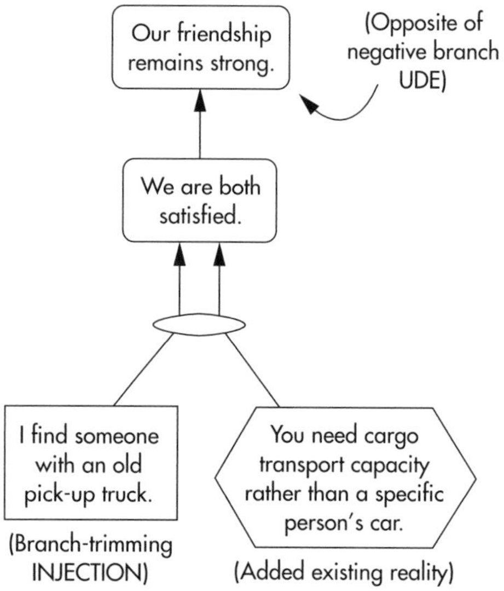

FIGURE 5.33. Validating the Injection.

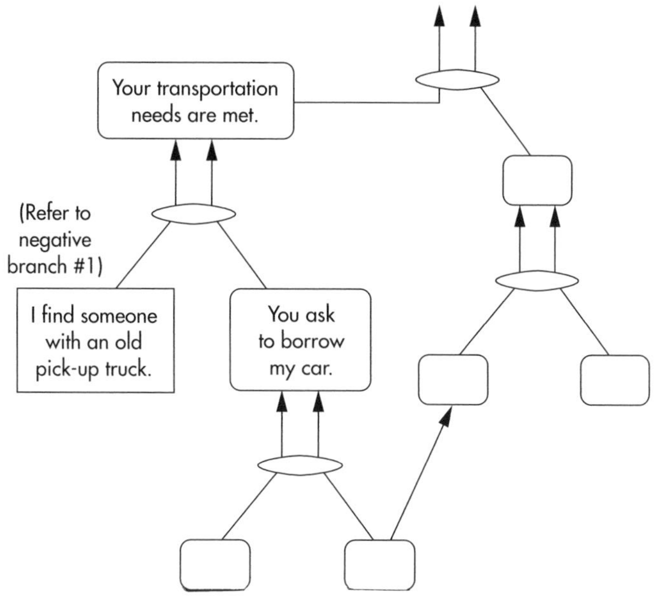

FIGURE 5.34. Incorporating the Branch-Trimming Injection into the FRT.

12. Scrutinize the Future Reality Tree

Once all negative branches have been identified and trimmed, reread and scrutinize the entire tree using the CLR. This is a good time to bring in someone else to help. Helpers don't need to fully understand the CLR to the extent that you do; they just have to have intuitive knowledge about the situation. As part of the scrutiny process, determine whether any parts of the FRT are unnecessary to attaining the desired effects. If so, trim those parts from the tree; the fewer superfluous entities, the more readable your tree will be.

Note: Recall that in building the Current Reality Tree (see chapter 3), once the tree was completed we looked for superfluous "twigs" that weren't necessary to connect the UDEs. We have to do something similar with the Future Reality Tree. But in this case, we'll be looking for superfluous injections.

In building the Future Reality Tree, we added injections for two reasons: (1) to correct our progress "on course" toward our desired effects, and (2) to trim negative branches. Often one injection can do double duty (that is, fulfill both these functions), but because we inserted injections individually for different purposes, we never noticed this duplication. Scrutinizing the entire FRT, including negative branches, at this step affords us the opportunity to find ways to consolidate injections, thus simplifying the tree.

This step also lets us question whether we have elements in the Future Reality Tree that really don't contribute to achieving our desired effects. If so, these parts of the tree can be eliminated without adverse consequence.

Figure 5.36, "Procedures for Building a Future Reality Tree," contains abbreviated steps for constructing an FRT.

SCRUTINIZING A FUTURE REALITY TREE

The scrutiny of a Future Reality Tree is very similar to that of a Current Reality Tree. The Categories of Legitimate Reservation (refer to this section in chapter 2) are used to test the logical connections between entities of the Future Reality Tree. However, there are a few qualifications to consider when using the CLR in an FRT.

Existence Reservations

In chapter 2, we discussed the second level of the Categories of Legitimate Reservation—existence, both entity and causality. While this level of reservation is important in the Future Reality Tree, there are some definite limitations to its use. Take Entity Existence, for example. One of the tests for Entity Existence is whether it is a valid statement of existing reality. Clearly, this test won't be of much use in an FRT, because *outcomes of actions we haven't taken yet don't currently exist.* They can only exist in the future. So the only parts of the Entity Existence reservation that might apply in an FRT would be completeness (a complete sentence) and structure (no embedded "if–then" statements).

Causality Existence—whether the stated cause does, in fact, lead to the stated effect—likewise must be used with caution. Obviously, in a Future Reality Tree the effect does not exist now. The question is whether it will exist as an expected outcome of an injection; that is, will the injection effectively do the job it's designed to do? The Predicted Effect reservation is likely to be much more useful in verifying outcomes of injections that don't yet exist.

Scrutinizing Injections

The only real scrutiny you can apply concerns whether the injection can actually be done and whether it will eventually produce the desired effects. Be careful about rejecting an injection as "undoable" at face value. So was the electric light, until Thomas Edison did it. Instead, consider the subjective probability of being able to complete the injection. If your intuition tells you that the injection is likely to happen "when pigs fly," you might be well advised to look for another one—or multiple injections to accomplish the same purpose. Whether the injection will produce the desired effect is really a future causality issue.

"Oxygen"

A single arrow always implies unspoken "oxygen"—maybe a lot of it. This is especially true in Future Reality Trees. And the assumptions that people might be willing to make about current reality, they are less likely to accept in projections of the future. So in the FRT, you're usually better off displaying "oxygen" visually as an existing reality entity, which you combine with an injection or an expected effect of an injection. There should be very few single arrows in an FRT.

SUMMARY

By the time we've completed a Future Reality Tree, we will have fairly high confidence that our idea for a solution to our system problem will actually work—that it will give us the results we want. We'll also be reasonably certain that our idea won't cause any new problems. Or, if it does, the negative branches will be clear for everyone to see, and we'll know how to trim them before they even develop.

Only now are we ready to consider the phase of the problem that kills the most promising ideas: how to *cause* the change. "Good" ideas go sour in implementation for two reasons. First, we never verified whether or not they'd really succeed before jumping right into execution. (We've taken care of that with the Future Reality Tree.) Second, we aren't aware of what obstacles stand in our way, or how to overcome them.

Uncovering and overcoming obstacles to implementation is the first part of the final phase, determining how to cause the change. That's the subject of chapter 6.

The time it takes to rectify a situation is inversely proportional to the time it took to do the damage. EXAMPLE: It takes longer to glue a vase together than to break one.

—Drazen's Law of Restitution

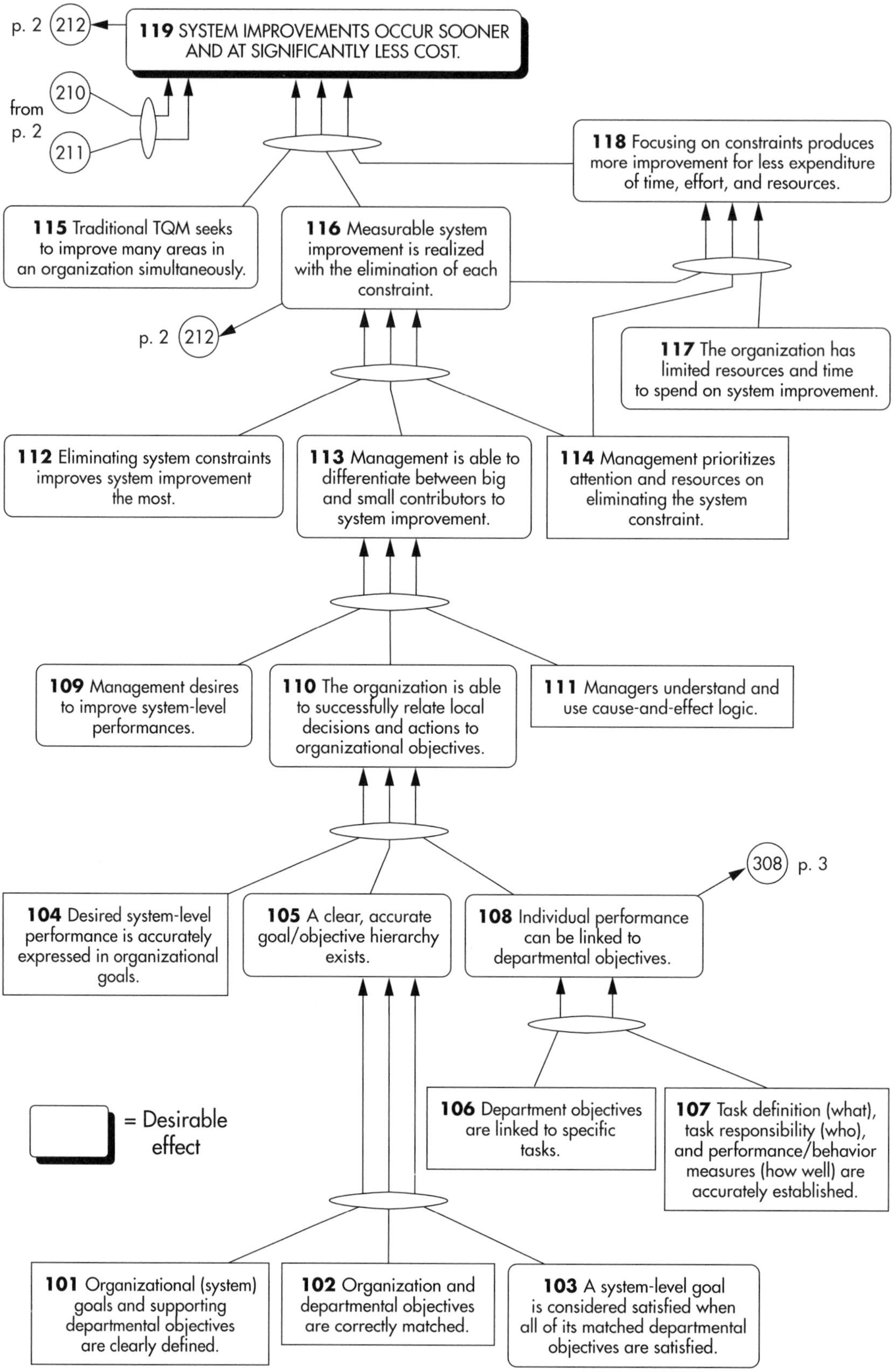

FIGURE 5.35. Future Reality Tree Example.

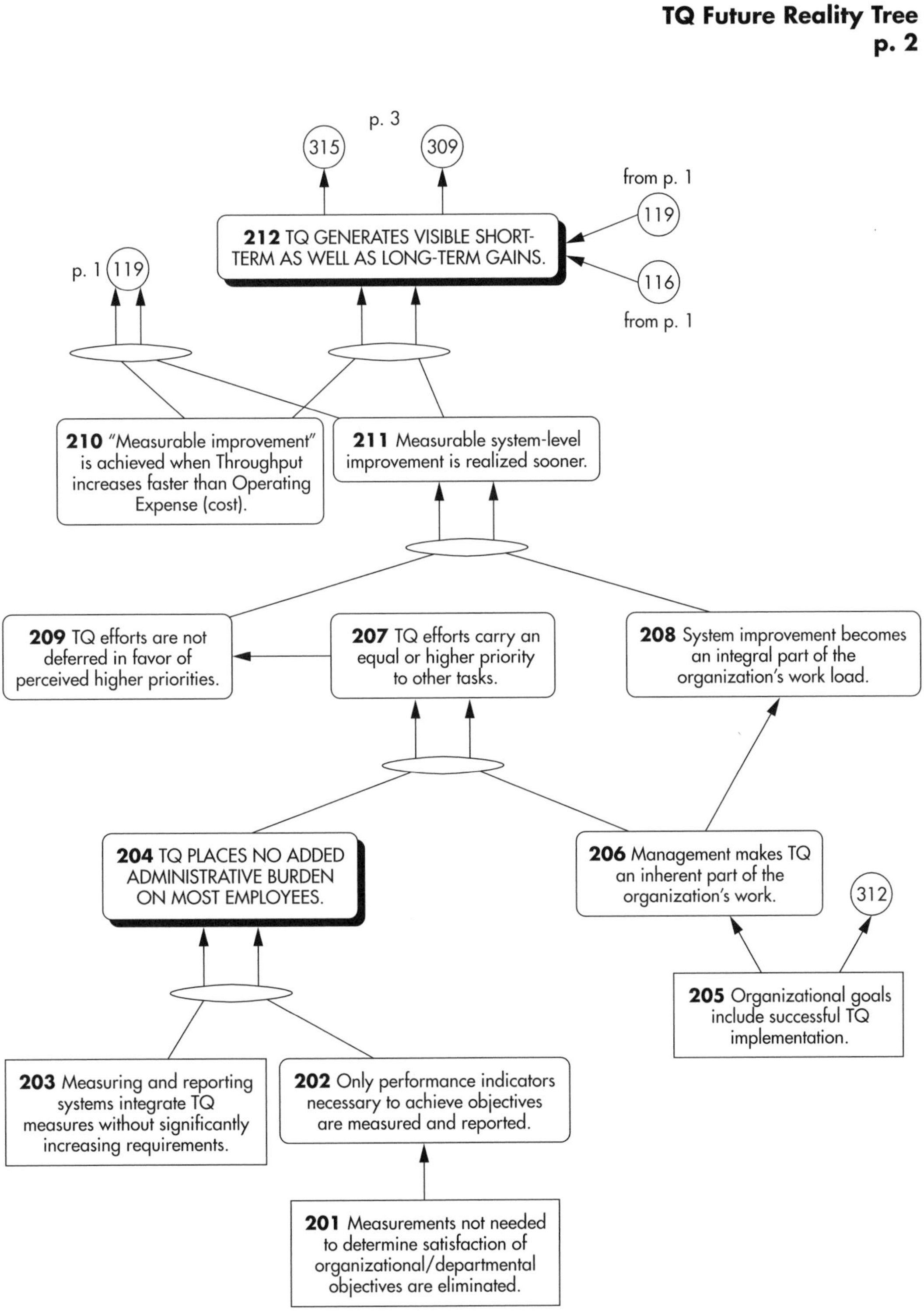
TQ Future Reality Tree
p. 2
p. 3
315
309
from p. 1
119
212 TQ GENERATES VISIBLE SHORT-TERM AS WELL AS LONG-TERM GAINS.
p. 1
119
116
from p. 1
210 "Measurable improvement" is achieved when Throughput increases faster than Operating Expense (cost).
211 Measurable system-level improvement is realized sooner.
209 TQ efforts are not deferred in favor of perceived higher priorities.
207 TQ efforts carry an equal or higher priority to other tasks.
208 System improvement becomes an integral part of the organization's work load.
204 TQ PLACES NO ADDED ADMINISTRATIVE BURDEN ON MOST EMPLOYEES.
206 Management makes TQ an inherent part of the organization's work.
312
205 Organizational goals include successful TQ implementation.
203 Measuring and reporting systems integrate TQ measures without significantly increasing requirements.
202 Only performance indicators necessary to achieve objectives are measured and reported.
201 Measurements not needed to determine satisfaction of organizational/departmental objectives are eliminated.

FIGURE 5.35—*Continued.*

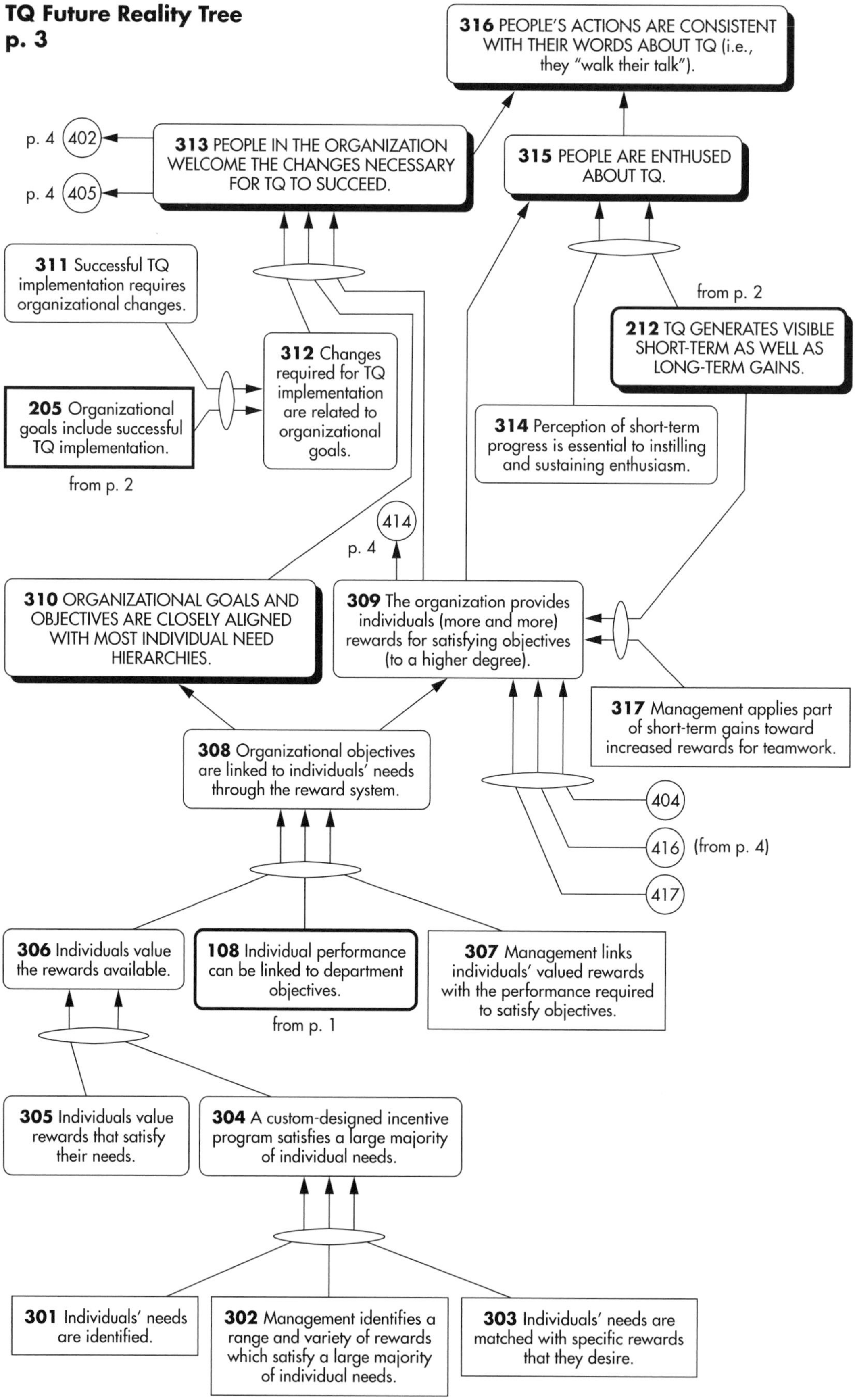
TQ Future Reality Tree
p. 3
316 PEOPLE'S ACTIONS ARE CONSISTENT WITH THEIR WORDS ABOUT TQ (i.e., they "walk their talk").
p. 4 402
p. 4 405
313 PEOPLE IN THE ORGANIZATION WELCOME THE CHANGES NECESSARY FOR TQ TO SUCCEED.
315 PEOPLE ARE ENTHUSED ABOUT TQ.
311 Successful TQ implementation requires organizational changes.
from p. 2
212 TQ GENERATES VISIBLE SHORT-TERM AS WELL AS LONG-TERM GAINS.
312 Changes required for TQ implementation are related to organizational goals.
205 Organizational goals include successful TQ implementation.
from p. 2
314 Perception of short-term progress is essential to instilling and sustaining enthusiasm.
414
p. 4
310 ORGANIZATIONAL GOALS AND OBJECTIVES ARE CLOSELY ALIGNED WITH MOST INDIVIDUAL NEED HIERARCHIES.
309 The organization provides individuals (more and more) rewards for satisfying objectives (to a higher degree).
317 Management applies part of short-term gains toward increased rewards for teamwork.
308 Organizational objectives are linked to individuals' needs through the reward system.
404
416 (from p. 4)
417
306 Individuals value the rewards available.
108 Individual performance can be linked to department objectives.
from p. 1
307 Management links individuals' valued rewards with the performance required to satisfy objectives.
305 Individuals value rewards that satisfy their needs.
304 A custom-designed incentive program satisfies a large majority of individual needs.
301 Individuals' needs are identified.
302 Management identifies a range and variety of rewards which satisfy a large majority of individual needs.
303 Individuals' needs are matched with specific rewards that they desire.

FIGURE 5.35—*Continued.*

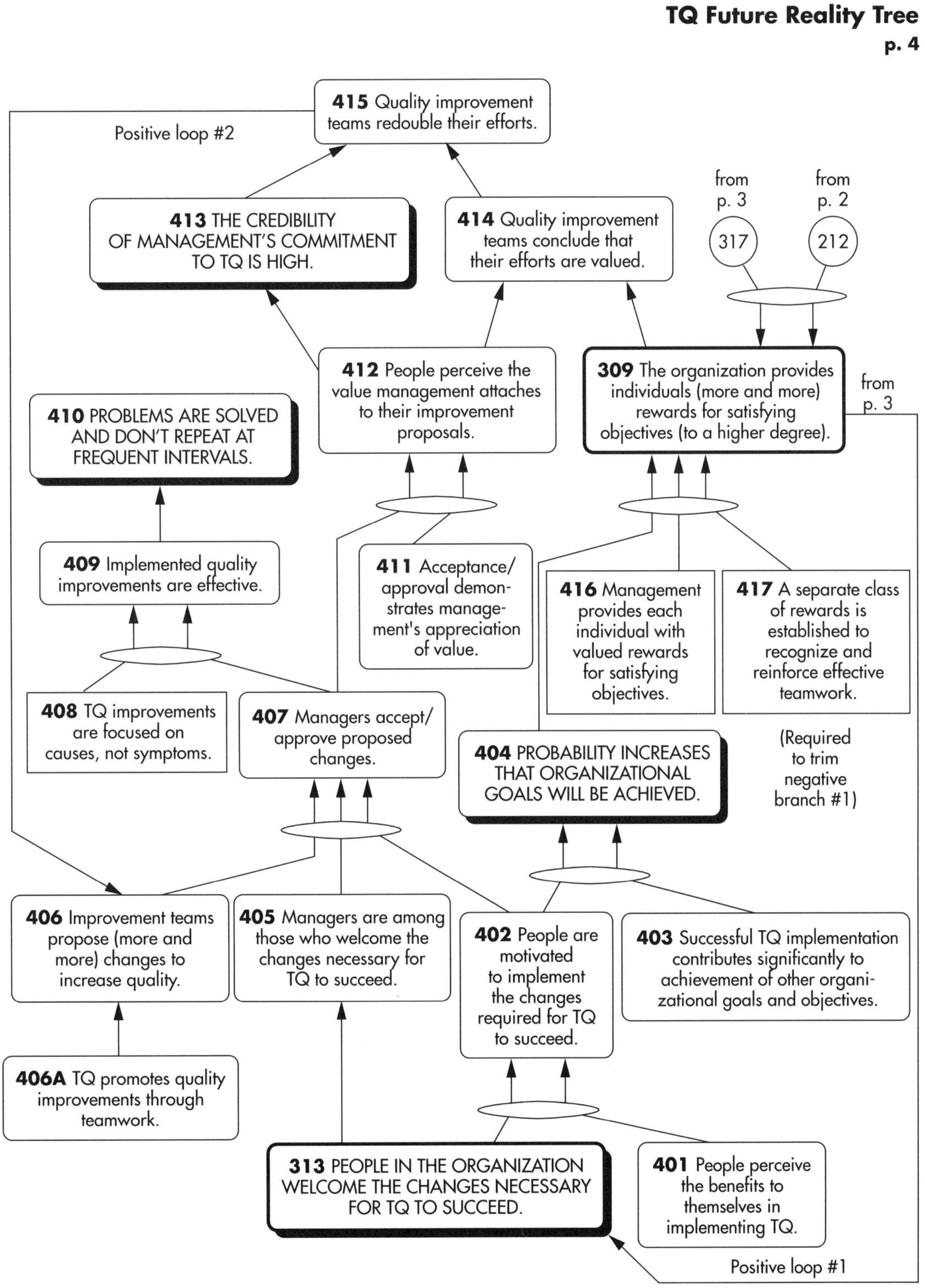

FIGURE 5.35—*Continued.*

NEGATIVE BRANCH #1
TQ Future Reality Tree, p. 5

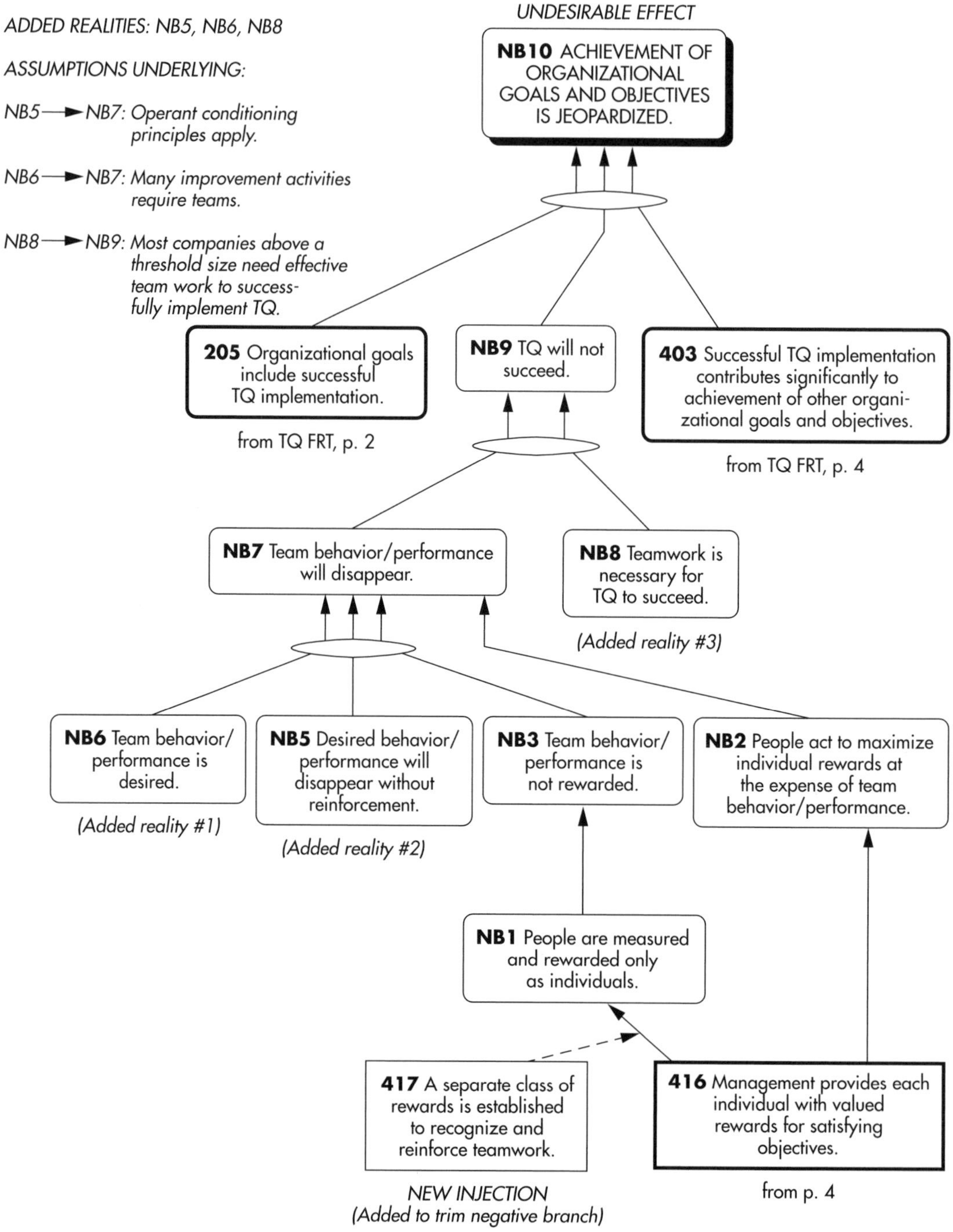

ADDED REALITIES: NB5, NB6, NB8
ASSUMPTIONS UNDERLYING:
NB5 → NB7: Operant conditioning principles apply.
NB6 → NB7: Many improvement activities require teams.
NB8 → NB9: Most companies above a threshold size need effective team work to successfully implement TQ.
UNDESIRABLE EFFECT
NB10 ACHIEVEMENT OF ORGANIZATIONAL GOALS AND OBJECTIVES IS JEOPARDIZED.
205 Organizational goals include successful TQ implementation.
from TQ FRT, p. 2
NB9 TQ will not succeed.
403 Successful TQ implementation contributes significantly to achievement of other organizational goals and objectives.
from TQ FRT, p. 4
NB7 Team behavior/performance will disappear.
NB8 Teamwork is necessary for TQ to succeed.
(Added reality #3)
NB6 Team behavior/performance is desired.
(Added reality #1)
NB5 Desired behavior/performance will disappear without reinforcement.
(Added reality #2)
NB3 Team behavior/performance is not rewarded.
NB2 People act to maximize individual rewards at the expense of team behavior/performance.
NB1 People are measured and rewarded only as individuals.
417 A separate class of rewards is established to recognize and reinforce teamwork.
NEW INJECTION
(Added to trim negative branch)
416 Management provides each individual with valued rewards for satisfying objectives.
from p. 4

FIGURE 5.35—*Continued.*

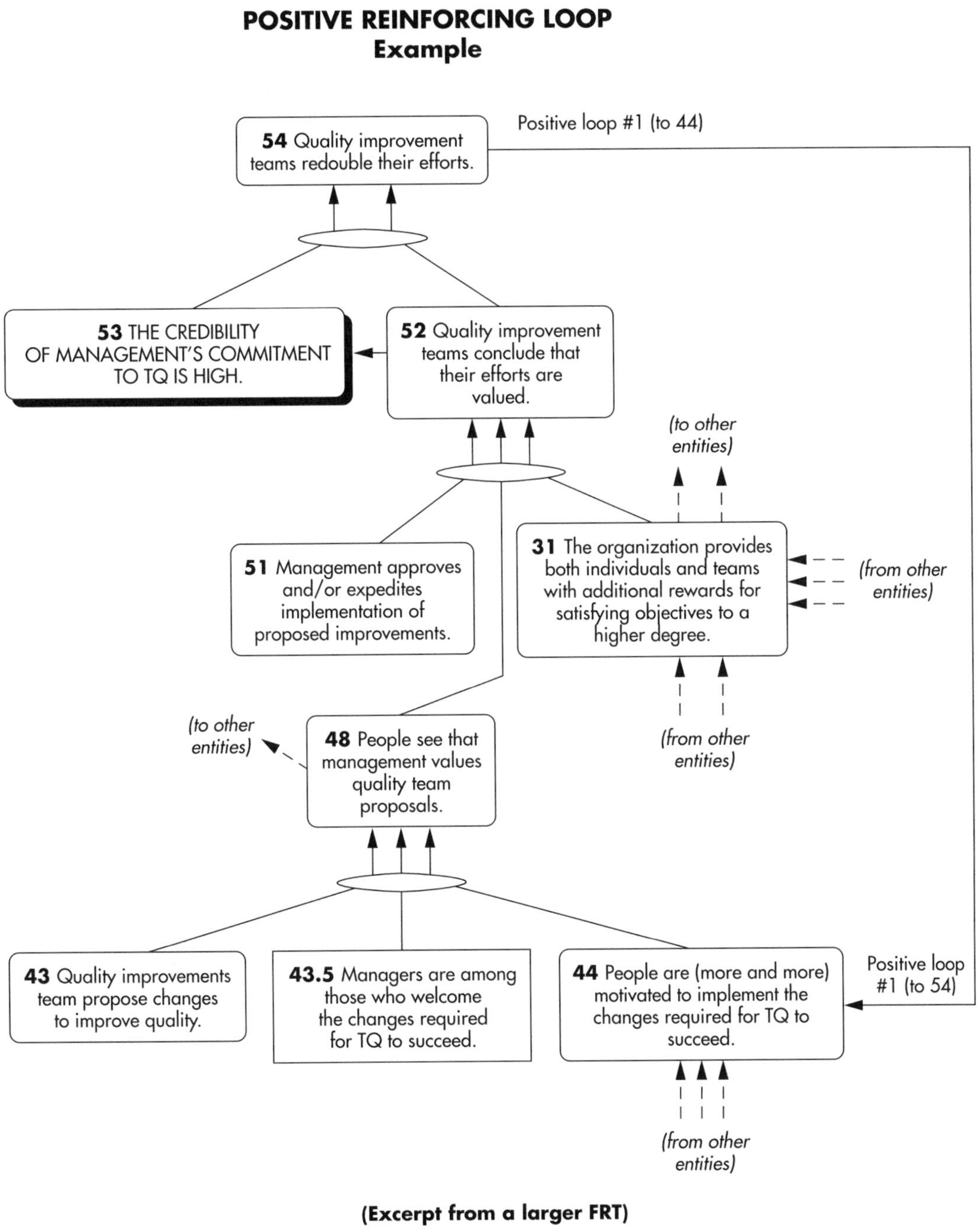

FIGURE 5.35—*Continued.*

1. GATHER ALL NECESSARY MATERIALS.
- Large paper, pencils, pens, Post-it™ notes
- Current Reality Tree (if applicable)
  - Undesirable effects (UDE)
  - Core problem
  - Root causes
- Conflict Resolution Diagram (if applicable)
  - Objective
  - Injections

2. FORMULATE DESIRED EFFECTS.
- Write desired effects on Post-it™ notes.
- Rephrase UDEs from CRT (if applicable).
- If no CRT, develop desired effects independently.
- Use positive, not neutral, wording.
- Use present tense.
- Lay out desired effects near top of page.

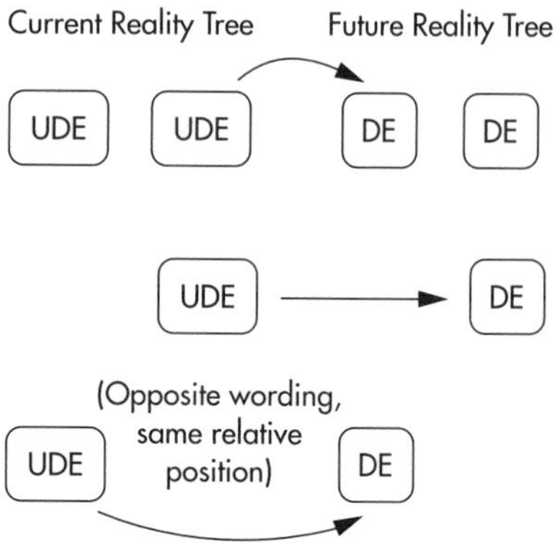

3. ADD THE INJECTION(S).
- Collect injections from the CRD (if applicable).
- Use "idea generators."
- Phrase injections as *conditions.*
- Position injections at the bottom of the page.
- Incorporate the objective from the CRD (if applicable).
- Incorporate the opposite of the core problem (if a CRT is available).

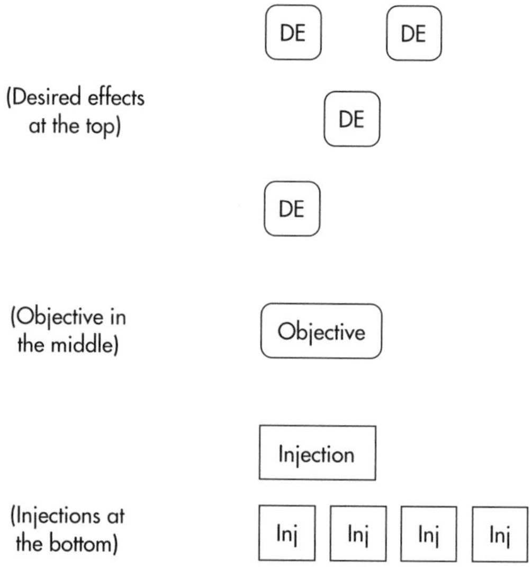

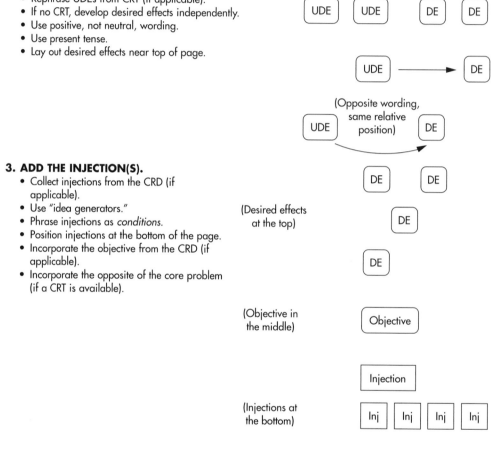

FIGURE 5.36. Procedures for Building a Future Reality Tree.

4. FILL IN THE GAPS.

- Build upward from injections and existing reality entities to expected effects.
- Build upward from one level of expected effects to the next, working consistently toward desired effects.
- Add injections as required.

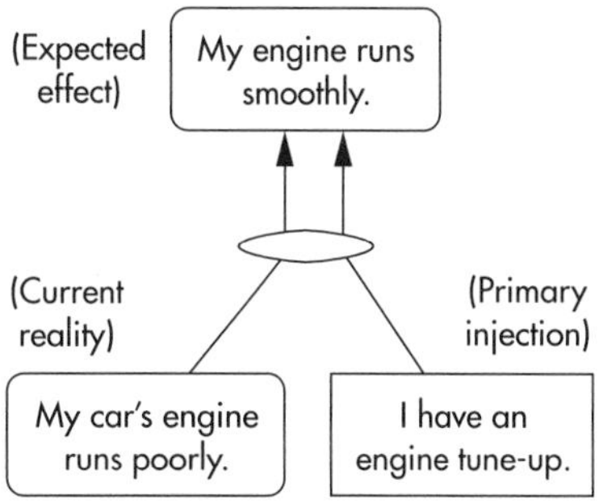

5. BUILD IN POSITIVE REINFORCING LOOPS.

- Find desired effects that might amplify positive expected effects lower in the tree.
- Identify the expected effects they amplify.
- Connect the desired effects to the expected effects with an arrow.
- Add injections, reality entities, and ellipses as required.
- Check to be sure the reentry entity can withstand an additional cause reservation.

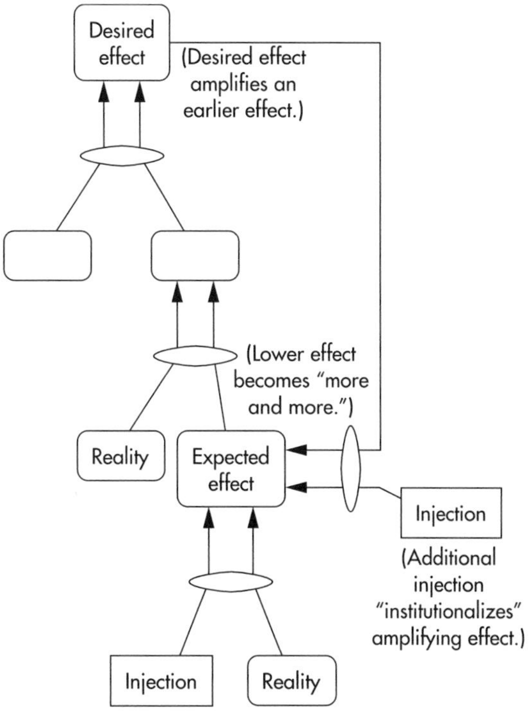

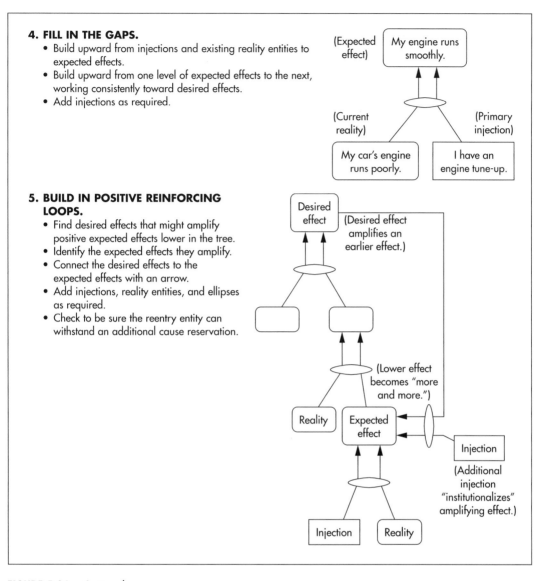

FIGURE 5.36—*Continued.*

6. LOOK FOR NEGATIVE BRANCHES.
- Look after the FRT is completed.
- Solicit outside help if necessary.
- Evaluate each expected effect.
  - "Besides *this* outcome, what *else* could result?"
- Don't overlook negative branches that might originate from desired effects.

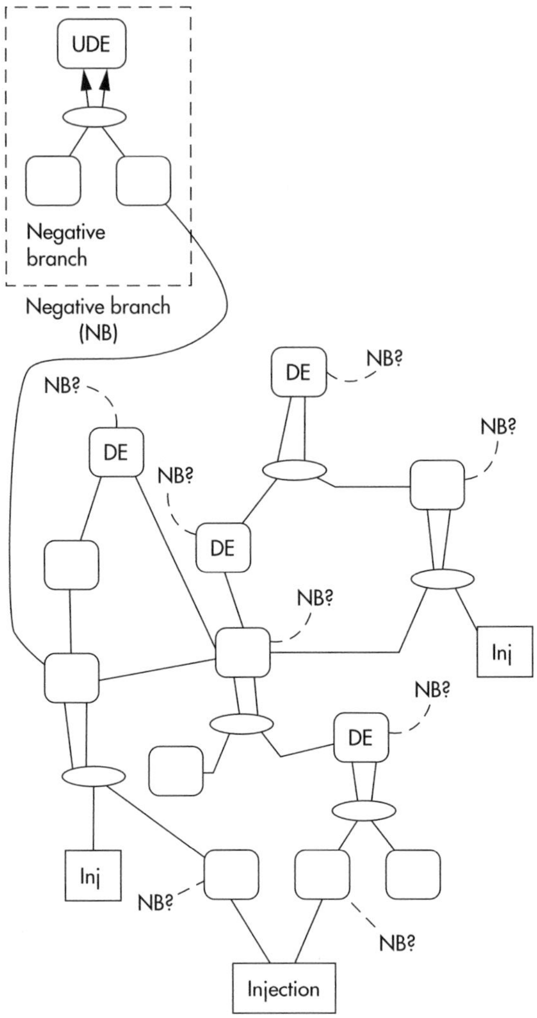

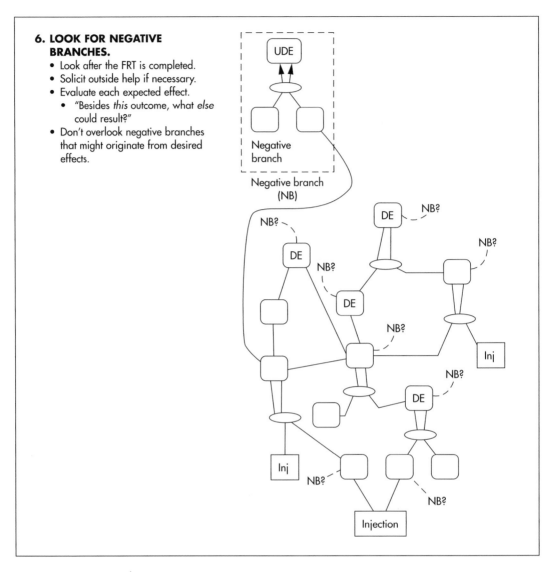

FIGURE 5.36—*Continued.*

7. DEVELOP THE NEGATIVE BRANCH.

- Use a separate piece of paper to develop the negative branch.
- Build upward from the originating injection to one or more undesirable effects.
- Add previously unstated reality entities as required.

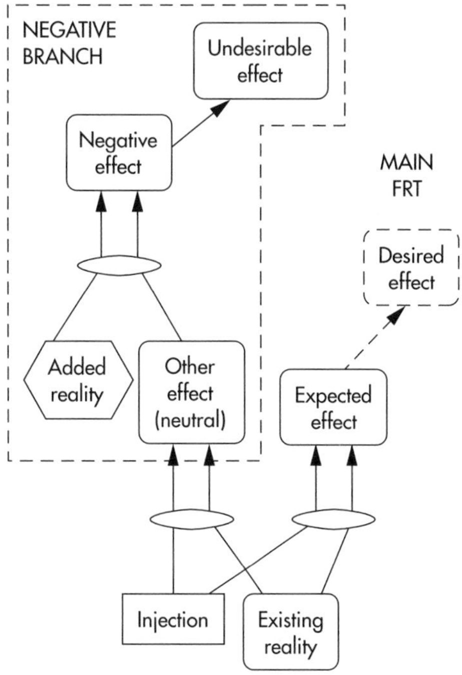

8. IDENTIFY THE "TURNING POINT."

- Find the causality arrow connecting the last positive or neutral entity to the first negative one.
- Identify all assumptions underlying the arrow.
- List the assumptions to one side of the negative branch.

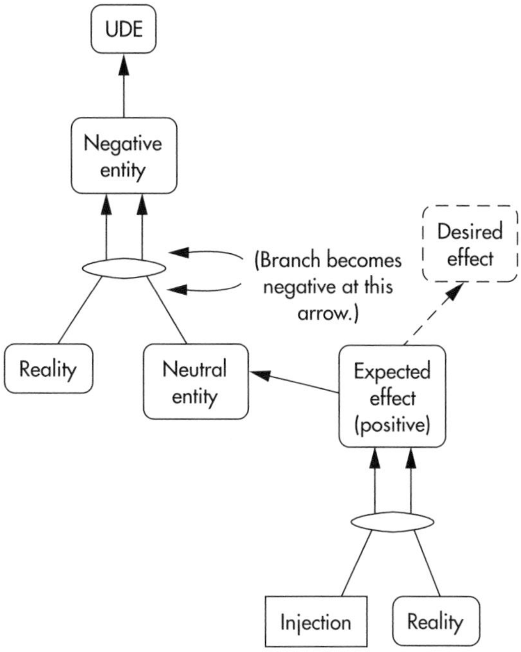

FIGURE 5.36—*Continued.*

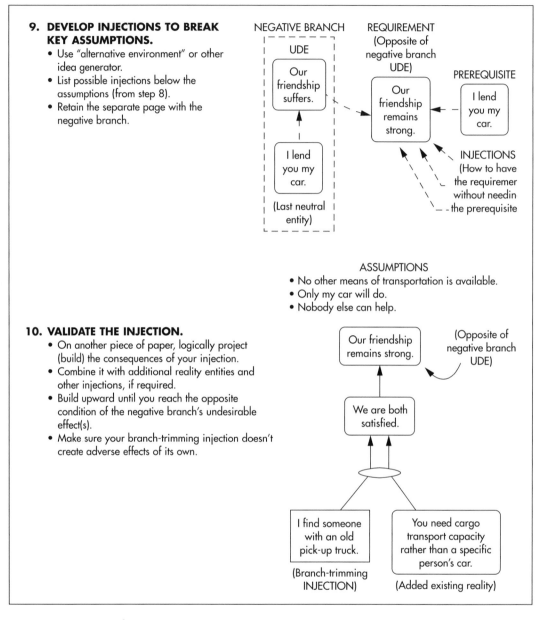

9. DEVELOP INJECTIONS TO BREAK KEY ASSUMPTIONS.

- Use "alternative environment" or other idea generator.
- List possible injections below the assumptions (from step 8).
- Retain the separate page with the negative branch.

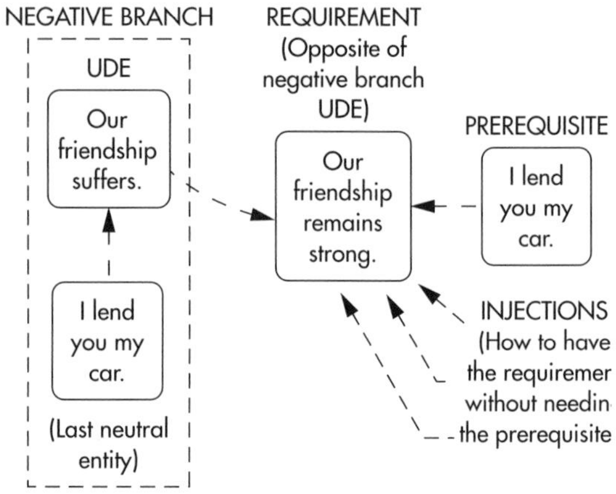
NEGATIVE BRANCH
UDE
Our friendship suffers.
I lend you my car.
(Last neutral entity)
REQUIREMENT
(Opposite of negative branch UDE)
Our friendship remains strong.
PREREQUISITE
I lend you my car.
INJECTIONS
(How to have the requiremer without needin the prerequisite

ASSUMPTIONS

- No other means of transportation is available.
- Only my car will do.
- Nobody else can help.

10. VALIDATE THE INJECTION.

- On another piece of paper, logically project (build) the consequences of your injection.
- Combine it with additional reality entities and other injections, if required.
- Build upward until you reach the opposite condition of the negative branch's undesirable effect(s).
- Make sure your branch-trimming injection doesn't create adverse effects of its own.

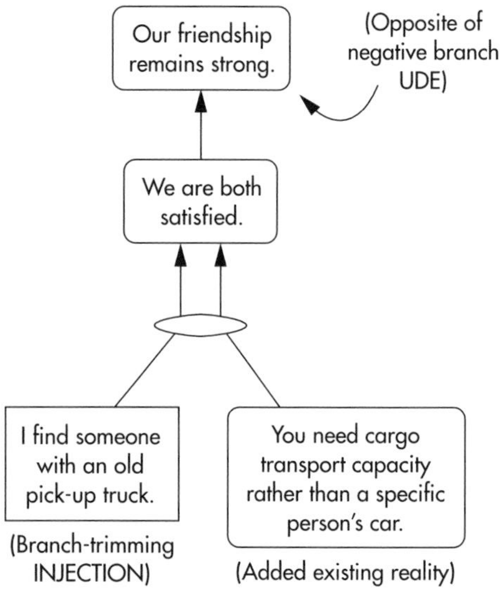
Our friendship remains strong.
(Opposite of negative branch UDE)
We are both satisfied.
I find someone with an old pick-up truck.
(Branch-trimming INJECTION)
You need cargo transport capacity rather than a specific person's car.
(Added existing reality)

FIGURE 5.36—*Continued.*

11. INCORPORATE THE "BRANCH-TRIMMING" INJECTION INTO THE FRT.

(Not applicable if using the negative branch in a stand-alone capacity)

- Combine the branch-trimming injection with the effect entity from the original FRT that produced the negative branch.
- Write a reference to the negative branch beside the branch-trimming injection.
- The *revised* future reality developed in step 10 may be abbreviated when you incorporate it into the original FRT, provided you save the page from step 10 and attach it to the tree.
- Derive the consequences of your new addition:
  - Be sure it doesn't adversely affect the original logic leading to the desired effects (modify as necessary).
  - Check to ensure it creates no new negative branches above it.

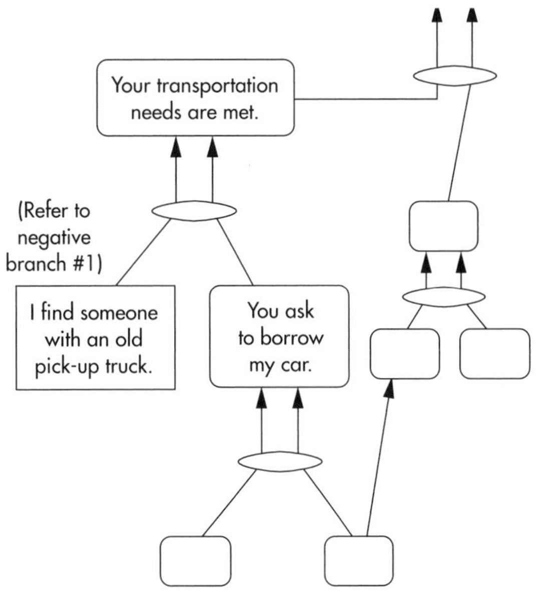

12. SCRUTINIZE THE ENTIRE FRT.

- Reread and scrutinize the entire tree.
- Use the Categories of Legitimate Reservation (CLR).
- Enlist someone else to assist you.
  - Understanding of CLR not required.
  - Intuitive knowledge of the situation *is* required.
- Identify any parts of the FRT not needed to reach the desired effects or trim negative branches.
  - Trim superfluous entities from the FRT.

FIGURE 5.36—*Continued.*

Ask for time to consider the request or decision ("Let me think about that for a while . . .")

Request for decision:
"Dad, can Bonnie and I go to a rock concert in Los Angeles?"

1. ON A SHEET OF PAPER, IN TWO COLUMNS:
- List all possible POSITIVE outcomes that might result.
- List all possible NEGATIVE outcomes that might result.

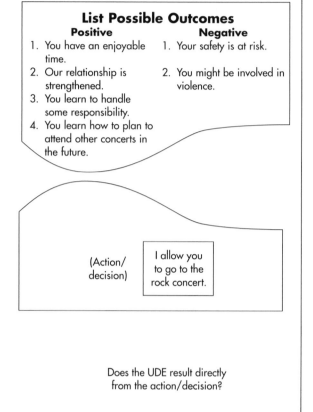

List Possible Outcomes

Positive	Negative
1. You have an enjoyable time.	1. Your safety is at risk.
2. Our relationship is strengthened.	2. You might be involved in violence.
3. You learn to handle some responsibility.	
4. You learn how to plan to attend other concerts in the future.	

2. WRITE THE PROPOSED ACTION/DECISION at the bottom of a separate sheet of paper.

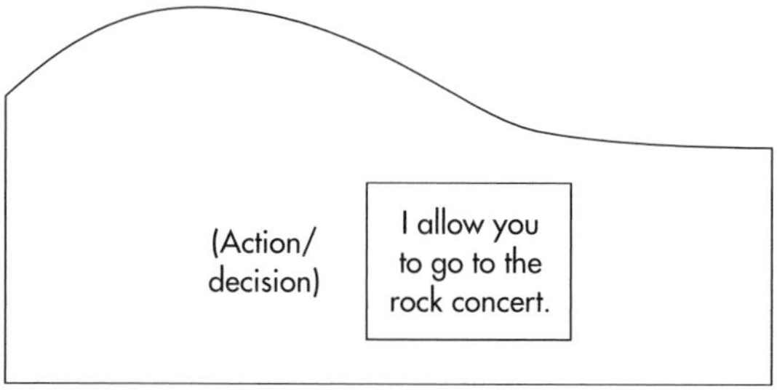
(Action/
decision)
I allow you
to go to the
rock concert.

3. ANALYZE THE ACTION/DECISION.
- Does a UDE result directly from the action/decision?
- If so, write it as a cause-effect relationship on the second sheet. The negative branch is complete.
- If not, begin building the cause-and-effect chain upward from the action/decision to the UDE(s)

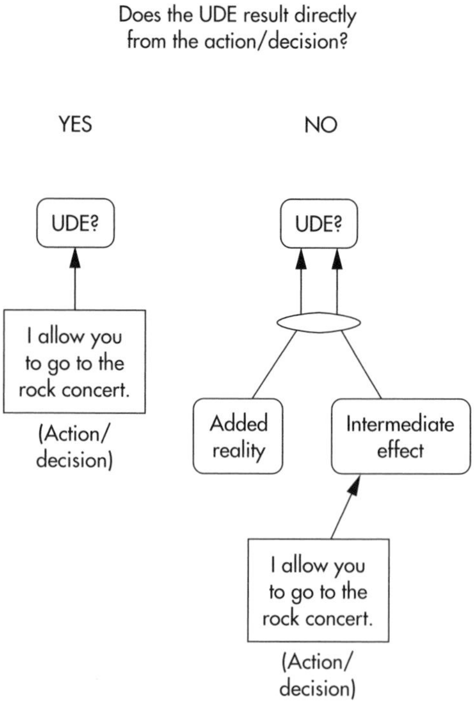
Does the UDE result directly
from the action/decision?
YES
NO
UDE?
I allow you
to go to the
rock concert.
(Action/
decision)
UDE?
Added
reality
Intermediate
effect
I allow you
to go to the
rock concert.
(Action/
decision)

FIGURE 5.37. Procedures for Building and Trimming a Stand-Alone Negative Branch.

4. SCRUTINIZE EACH UPWARD CONNECTION.

- Check each connection for cause sufficiency, using the CLR.

5. INCORPORATE ADDED REALITIES (AS REQUIRED).

- Add statements (entities) about reality as required to produce sufficiency.

6. STOP BUILDING WHEN YOU REACH THE UDE(s).

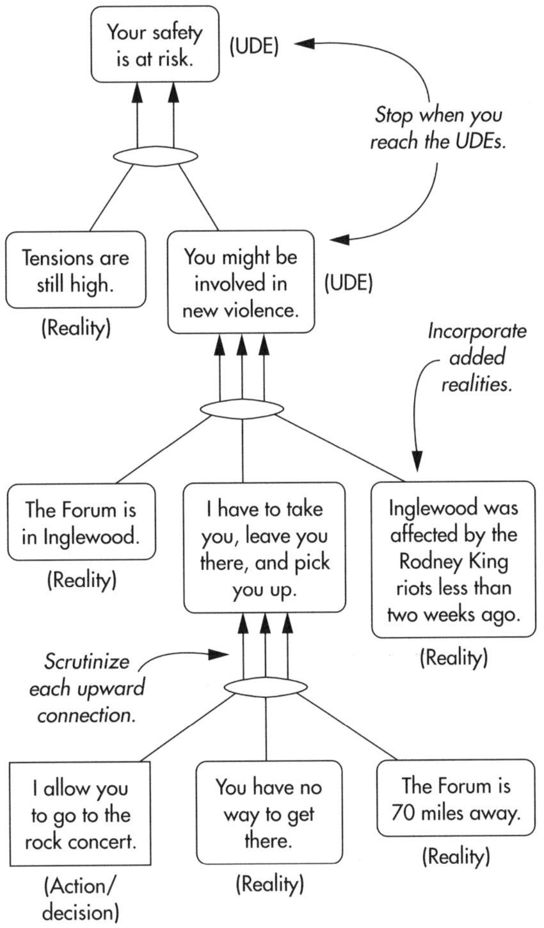
Your safety is at risk.
(UDE)
Stop when you reach the UDEs.
Tensions are still high.
(Reality)
You might be involved in new violence.
(UDE)
Incorporate added realities.
The Forum is in Inglewood.
(Reality)
I have to take you, leave you there, and pick you up.
Inglewood was affected by the Rodney King riots less than two weeks ago.
(Reality)
Scrutinize each upward connection.
I allow you to go to the rock concert.
(Action/decision)
You have no way to get there.
(Reality)
The Forum is 70 miles away.
(Reality)

7. IDENTIFY THE TURNING POINT.

- Find the transitional causality arrow, the one connecting the last positive or neutral entity to the first negative one.

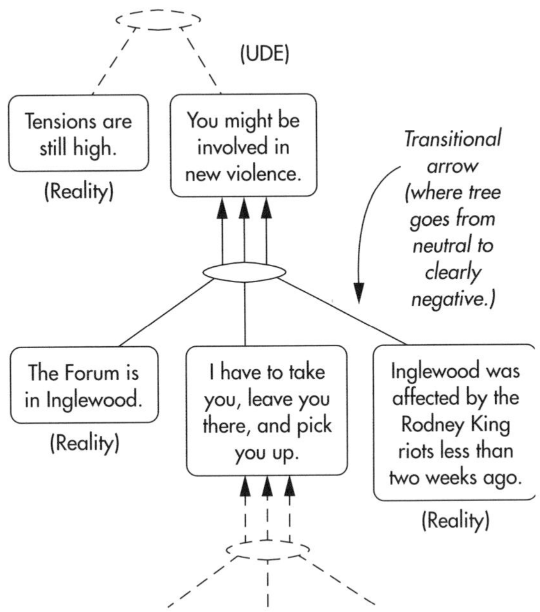
(UDE)
Tensions are still high.
(Reality)
You might be involved in new violence.
Transitional arrow (where tree goes from neutral to clearly negative.)
The Forum is in Inglewood.
(Reality)
I have to take you, leave you there, and pick you up.
Inglewood was affected by the Rodney King riots less than two weeks ago.
(Reality)

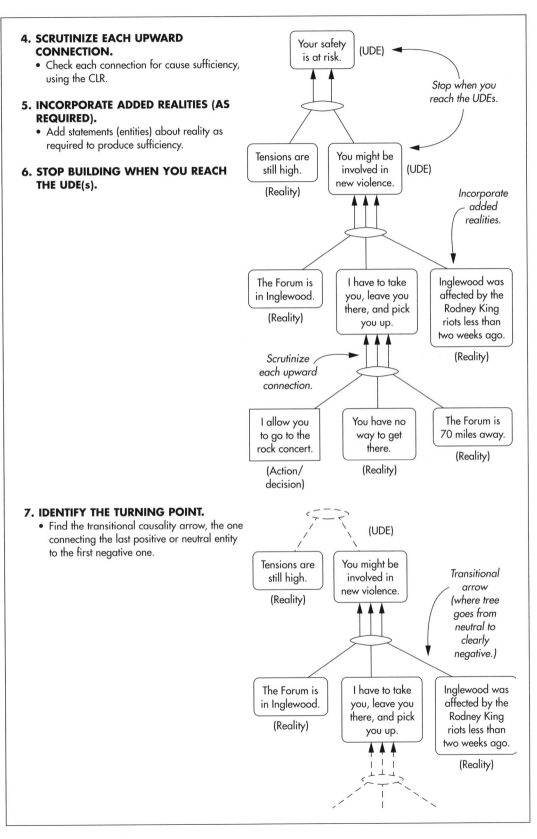

FIGURE 5.37—*Continued.*

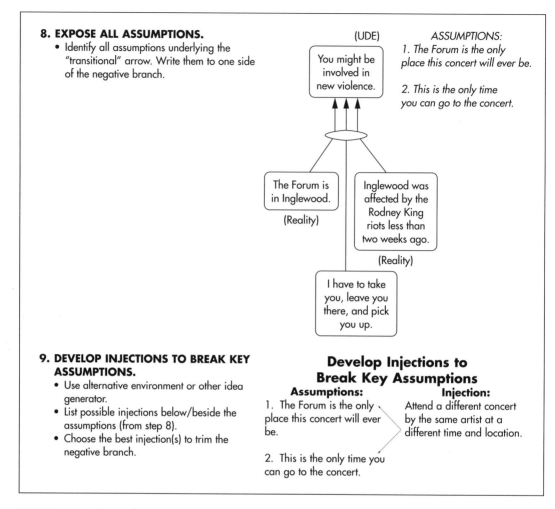

8. EXPOSE ALL ASSUMPTIONS.

- Identify all assumptions underlying the "transitional" arrow. Write them to one side of the negative branch.

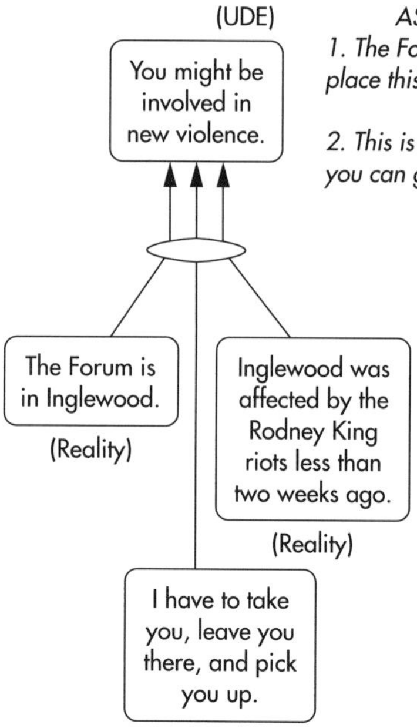
(UDE)
You might be involved in new violence.
The Forum is in Inglewood.
(Reality)
Inglewood was affected by the Rodney King riots less than two weeks ago.
(Reality)
I have to take you, leave you there, and pick you up.

ASSUMPTIONS:

1. The Forum is the only place this concert will ever be.

2. This is the only time you can go to the concert.

9. DEVELOP INJECTIONS TO BREAK KEY ASSUMPTIONS.

- Use alternative environment or other idea generator.
- List possible injections below/beside the assumptions (from step 8).
- Choose the best injection(s) to trim the negative branch.

Develop Injections to Break Key Assumptions

Assumptions:

1. The Forum is the only place this concert will ever be.

2. This is the only time you can go to the concert.

Injection:

Attend a different concert by the same artist at a different time and location.

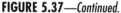

FIGURE 5.37—*Continued.*

10. VALIDATE THE INJECTION. On a new piece of paper:

- Rewrite the last entity before the transitional arrow (i.e., before the first NEGATIVE entity).
- Write your chosen injection(s) beside it.
- Develop the logical effect of combining the injection with the last entity.
- Add other reality entities as necessary (i.e., ones that may not have been included in the original negative branch).
- Continue to build upward until you're certain the UDE has been neutralized or turned into a desirable effect.
- Check to be sure the new injection doesn't create any new negative branches of its own (repeat steps 1–9, as required).

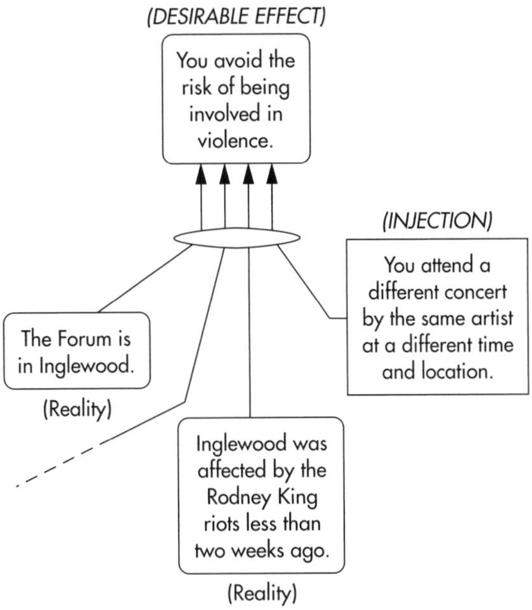
(DESIRABLE EFFECT)
You avoid the risk of being involved in violence.
(INJECTION)
You attend a different concert by the same artist at a different time and location.
The Forum is in Inglewood.
(Reality)
Inglewood was affected by the Rodney King riots less than two weeks ago.
(Reality)

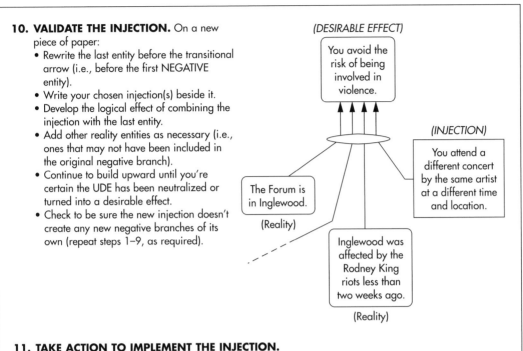

11. TAKE ACTION TO IMPLEMENT THE INJECTION.

Note: If you constructed the negative branch in response to someone else's request for you to do something, meet with that person and do the following:

- Review the POSITIVE outcomes of the decision/action (from the original list).
- Say "I have some concerns about this. . . ," and present the negative branch you build, completely and without interruption, all the way to the undesirable effect(s).
- Do NOT offer YOUR injection as remedy. Hold it in reserve. STOP TALKING and wait for a response from the requestor.
- Allow the requestor to offer a workable alternative (injection).
- If the requestor's suggestion is as good or better than yours, accept it (as long as you can live with it).
- If not, steer the discussion toward your alternative, but give the requestor every opportunity to become part of the solution FIRST.

FIGURE 5.37—*Continued.*

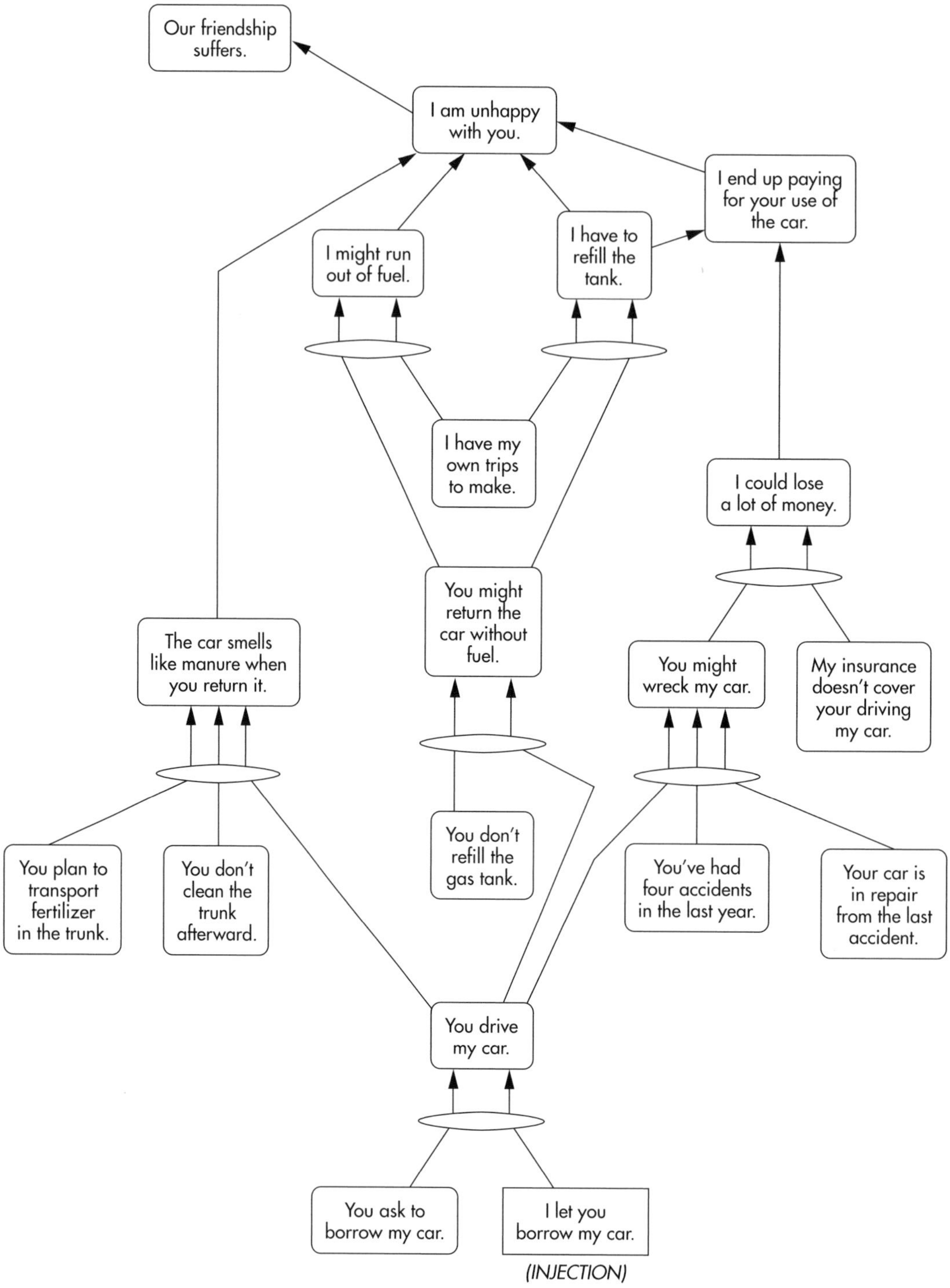

FIGURE 5.38. Negative Branch Example: "May I Borrow Your Car?"

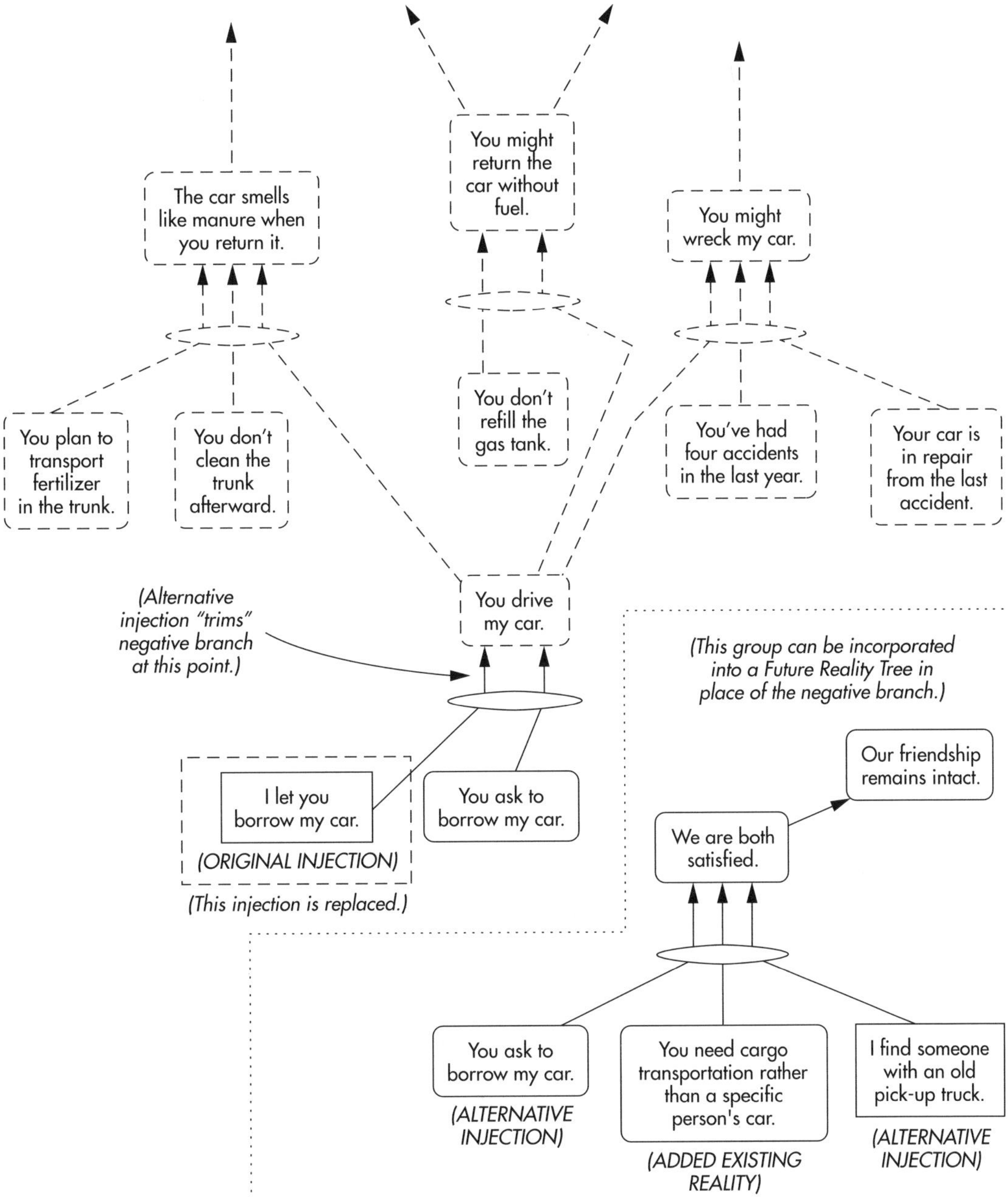
The car smells like manure when you return it.
You might return the car without fuel.
You might wreck my car.
You plan to transport fertilizer in the trunk.
You don't clean the trunk afterward.
You don't refill the gas tank.
You've had four accidents in the last year.
Your car is in repair from the last accident.
(Alternative injection "trims" negative branch at this point.)
You drive my car.
(This group can be incorporated into a Future Reality Tree in place of the negative branch.)
I let you borrow my car.
(ORIGINAL INJECTION)
(This injection is replaced.)
You ask to borrow my car.
Our friendship remains intact.
We are both satisfied.
You ask to borrow my car.
(ALTERNATIVE INJECTION)
You need cargo transportation rather than a specific person's car.
(ADDED EXISTING REALITY)
I find someone with an old pick-up truck.
(ALTERNATIVE INJECTION)

FIGURE 5.38—*Continued.*

Chapter 6
PRERQUISITE TREE

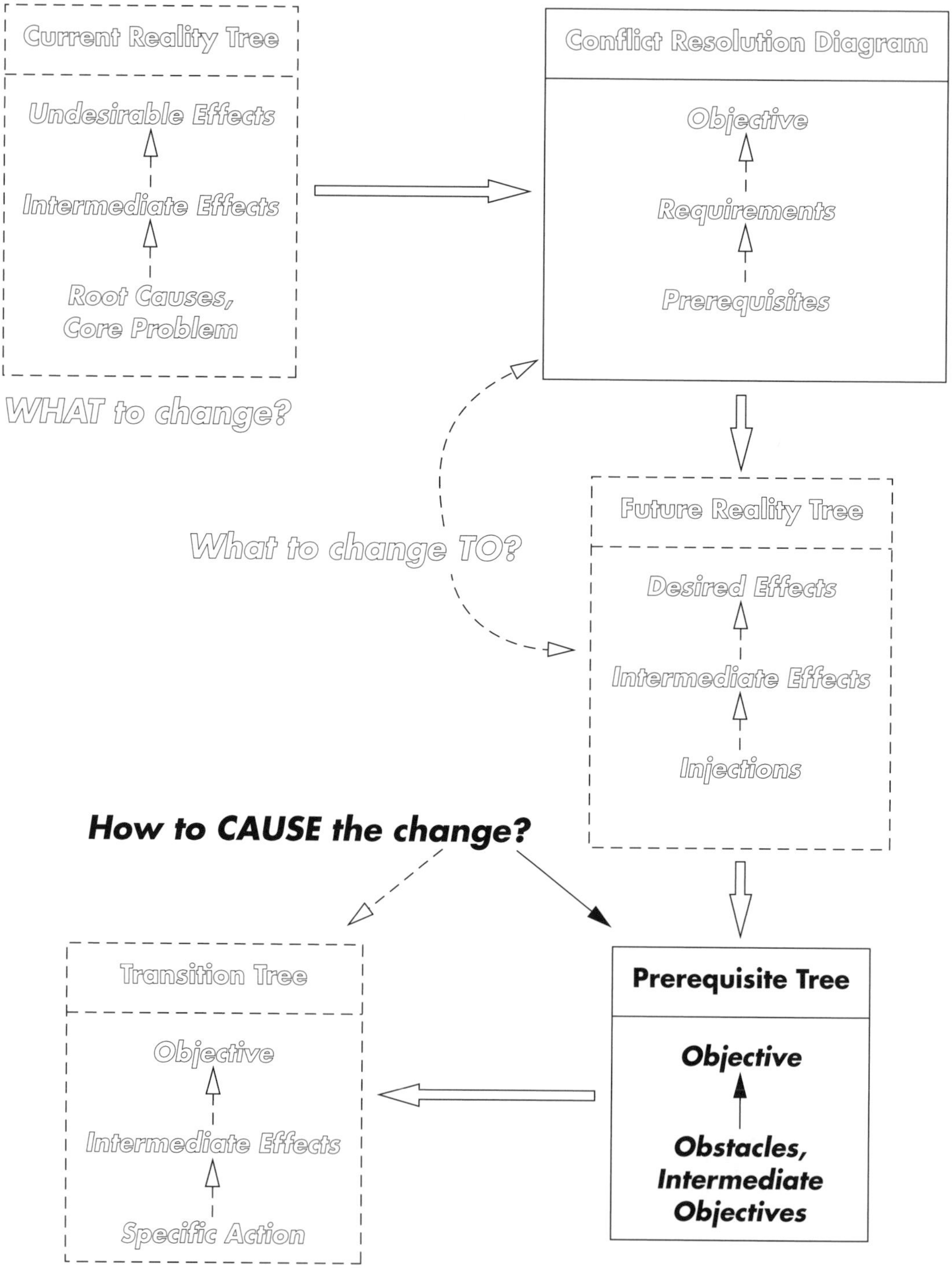

Chapter Outline

Nothing is more difficult to carry out, nor more doubtful of success, nor more dangerous to handle than to initiate a new order of things.
—Niccolò Machiavelli

Good ideas often founder when we try to put them into effect. It's one thing to come up with an idea for a solution to a problem; it's another thing entirely to make it happen. Wanting to do something doesn't get it done. That's why one of the Theory of Constraints principles discussed in chapter 1 says, "Ideas are not solutions." It's not a solution until it's implemented and doing what it's supposed to do.

We might have generated an excellent idea with a Conflict Resolution Diagram, and we might have proven its worth in a Future Reality Tree. But without effective execution, it's a good idea "on paper" only. How can we ensure that our idea will be effectively implemented? A Prerequisite Tree (PRT) can be the first step.

What do we need to know when we consider execution of change? Basically, three things: We need to be sure that what we contemplate doing will work the first time—that there will be no false starts or failures. We also need to know what obstacles stand in our way and what to do about them. And we need to know in what sequence the obstacles must be overcome. The Prerequisite Tree is capable of answering all of these questions.

DEFINITION

The Prerequisite Tree is a logical structure designed to identify all obstacles and the responses needed to overcome them in realizing an objective. It identifies minimum necessary conditions without which the objective cannot be achieved (see Figure 6.1).

PURPOSE

The Prerequisite Tree is used to achieve the following objectives:

- To identify obstacles preventing achievement of a desired course of action, objective, or injection.
- To identify the remedies or conditions necessary to overcome or otherwise neutralize obstacles to a desired course of action, objective, or injection.
- To identify the required sequence of actions needed to realize a desired course of action.
- To identify and depict unknown steps to a desired end when one does not know precisely how to achieve it.
- To bridge the gap between a Future Reality Tree, which identifies major accomplishments or milestones in complex problem solutions, and the Transition Tree, which provides a step-by-step, time-sequenced implementation plan.

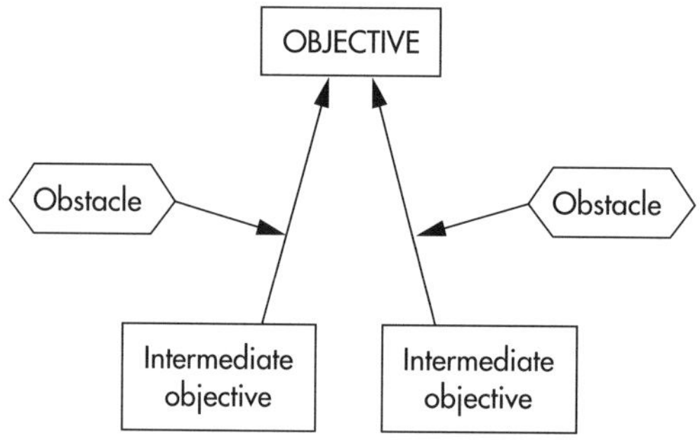

FIGURE 6.1. The Prerequisite Tree.

ASSUMPTIONS

The effectiveness of the Prerequisite Tree is based on the following assumptions:

- Obstacles to a desired end actually exist in reality.
- Obstacles are usually perceived as negative.
- It is not necessary to eliminate obstacles—only to overcome them (that is, it isn't necessary to drain the river, only to get across it).
- There is at least one alternative, or intermediate objective, capable of overcoming each obstacle. In all probability, there will be several alternatives. Some obstacles may require more than one intermediate objective to overcome them.
- Obstacles and their associated intermediate objectives usually have a time-dependent relationship (that is, some must logically precede or follow others).
- The Prerequisite Tree is not static; it is likely to need changing as it is implemented. New obstacles and intermediate objectives may crop up.

HOW TO USE THIS CHAPTER

- Read "Description of the Prerequisite Tree," below. This section describes what a Prerequisite Tree is and how it works.
- Review Figure 6.39, "Procedures for Building a Prerequisite Tree," p. 271, and the associated examples. This section explains in detail each of the steps in building a Prerequisite Tree and why they're necessary.
- Read "Scrutinizing a Prerequisite Tree," p. 259. This section tells how to ensure that your Prerequisite Tree is logically sound and accurately depicts real obstacles and what must be done to overcome them.
- Review Figures 6.37 and 6.38, Prerequisite Tree examples. One of two examples shows how to overcome obstacles to realizing an injection from the Future Reality Tree on "How Organizations Can Succeed at Total Quality."
- Practice with the "Prerequisite Tree Exercise" provided in Appendix F.

DESCRIPTION OF THE PREREQUISITE TREE

The purpose of the Prerequisite Tree is to help overcome obstacles that keep you from doing what you want to do. It answers the question, "What must I do to achieve 'the impossible'?" Your objective—what you want to do—might be as limited as tuning up your car. Or it may be only one step in the solution of a complex problem. For example, you might want to know how to gain admission to a certain college as one step in embarking on a professional career. Either way, the Prerequisite Tree will help you determine what would keep you from successfully reaching your objective and how you can work around it. Using a

PRT, you can map obstacles and determine what to do about them, without regard for *who* is responsible for taking action.

Necessity vs. Sufficiency Logic

The Prerequisite Tree is not like the Current Reality Tree (CRT) or the Future Reality Tree (FRT). The big difference is the type of logic used in the PRT. While the CRT and FRT use sufficiency logic ("Is this enough?") to establish cause-effect connections, the PRT uses necessity logic. That is, it identifies the critical elements (obstacles) that stand in the way of reaching our objective. The overcoming of these obstacles is necessary but may not be sufficient alone to do the job.

For example, you may have the tools, the plans, the skill, and the time to build a house, but maybe you don't have the materials—or the money to buy them. And maybe you don't have ownership of a lot to build on. So to reach your objective of having a house built, you need a lot, money, lumber, nails, roofing material, drywall, electrical wiring, plumbing, cement, reinforcing bars, and paint. These obstacles stand in your way, and to reach your objective they must be overcome. But having them alone isn't sufficient to have a finished house. You still have to include the other factors (tools, skill, time, and so forth) to say, "This is sufficient to build a house."

REMEMBER: The necessity logic in a Prerequisite Tree answers the question, "What stands in the way of my having the objective (or IO)?" Continuing the analogy from above, "To build this house, what must I have that I don't have now?" The answer is the obstacle that you must overcome.

Where does sufficiency figure into the implementation of a solution? In the Transition Tree, which is covered in detail in chapter 7. For now, in the PRT, we'll focus on the obstacles we face in accomplishing our mission, the intermediate objectives we'll need to overcome those obstacles, and the order in which they must happen.

A Single Tool or Part of a Set

Consider the Prerequisite Tree as you would a hammer in a toolbox. You can use the hammer just to drive a nail to hang a picture. Or you can use it in concert with all the other tools in the box to build an entire house. Similarly, the PRT either can be used by itself to overcome routine obstacles in your daily life, or it can be used as an integral part of the entire TOC Thinking Process to resolve some complex problem and implement the solution.

Objective

Whether or not you need a Prerequisite Tree depends on your answer to two questions:

a. Is my objective a complex condition?
b. Do I already know exactly how to achieve it?

If your objective is a complex condition, you may need a Prerequisite Tree to help you sequence the intermediate steps you'll have to complete to achieve it.

If you don't already know exactly how to achieve your objective, you may also need a PRT to help you figure that out. But if neither of these situations applies, you may not need a PRT.

> ***Obstacles are those frightful things you see when you take your eye off the goal.***
>
> ***—Hannah More***

Obstacles

Obviously, before you can overcome an obstacle, you have to know what it is—that is, what stands in your way (see Figure 6.2). If what you're trying to do is complex, or if it happens in a complex environment, you, personally, may not know what all the obstacles are. It may be necessary to enlist the help of people more knowledgeable than you in identifying as many obstacles as possible. The Prerequisite Tree lends itself to group as well as individual effort. Moreover, don't be too concerned if you haven't identified all the obstacles. The beauty of the PRT is that as you and others scrutinize it, any obstacles you might have overlooked will probably jump right out at you.

Once you have a reasonably complete list of obstacles, you're ready to start thinking of ways to overcome them. The entities that overcome obstacles are called intermediate objectives (IO), because they're either actions required or conditions necessary to reaching the overall objective of the Prerequisite Tree.

Actions or Conditions?

The objectives and intermediate objectives in a Prerequisite Tree can be either actions or conditions. If the PRT's objective is an action, most of the IOs are likely to be actions. If the objective is a condition, the IOs may be predominantly conditions (see Figure 6.3).

Obstacles, however, should always be worded as conditions, using such words as "is" or "have," but not as needs. For example, the obstacle might be phrased "We don't have . . ."; it should not be "We need . . ." .

For example, "Take an alternate route to work" is an action that might overcome the obstacle "Traffic is congested." The obstacle "Labor is limited" can be overcome by the condition "We have enough people" (see Figure 6.4). It isn't

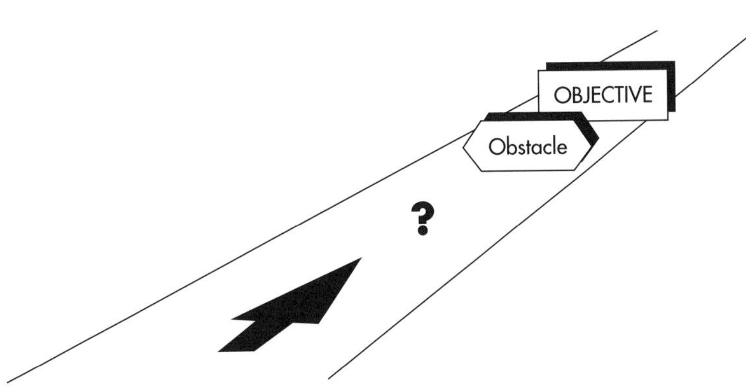

FIGURE 6.2. What Stands Between You and the Objective?

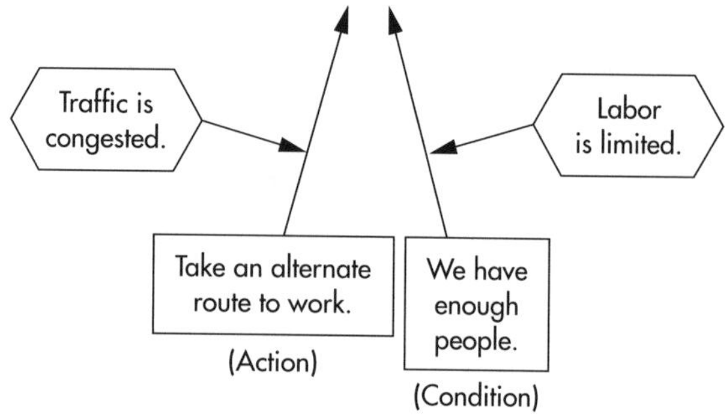

FIGURE 6.3. Intermediate Objectives: Actions or Conditions.

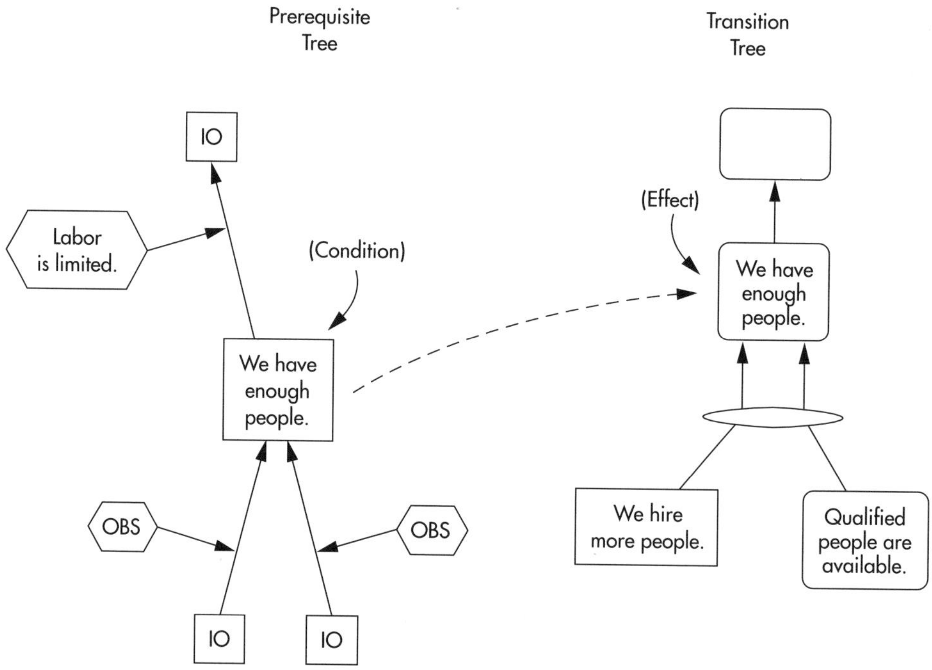

FIGURE 6.4. A Condition Becomes an Effect.

necessary to have every IO be an action. It's especially likely that IOs will be conditions if you're not sure exactly how to go about achieving them. The detailed actions you'll need in order to achieve a condition can be fleshed out in a Transition Tree, if required. If you take this approach, the IOs that are conditions in the Prerequisite Tree will become effects in a Transition Tree.

However, in a typical Prerequisite Tree the IOs nearer the top are predominantly conditions. As you go lower in the tree, the IOs can become more specific. Ideally, each branch of a PRT should terminate with an action you know how to take, or at least a straightforward condition you know how to achieve.

If you review your completed Prerequisite Tree and find that most or all of your IOs are conditions, with few actions, you may not have enough intuition about your original objective to work out a realistic plan to achieve it. You may need some outside help (for example, research, or advice from others).

Intermediate Objectives

Why are intermediate objectives referred to as "intermediate"? They're intermediate because they constitute transitional steps, either conditions or actions, that must be completed before we can attain our ultimate objective.

Different Alternatives

As you develop your intermediate objectives (IO), you'll undoubtedly find that there's more than one way to skin the cat (see Figure 6.5). In other words, two completely different and independent IOs might each effectively overcome the obstacle in question. For example, if your objective is to get to the opposite bank of a river (the obstacle), you might consider swimming, rowing a boat, or building a bridge as possible IOs. Each alone might overcome the obstacle. Which of them you select should be determined by evaluating each against four criteria:

- Which IO does the job most effectively?
- Which IO is the easiest to do?
- Which IO incurs the least expense?
- Which IO produces the fewest negative or collateral side effects?

REMEMBER: Your objective in using a Prerequisite Tree is to work around or to neutralize an obstacle, not to eliminate it. You don't need to drain the river dry—you only need a way across it.

Multiple IOs

Sometimes an obstacle may require two or more completely separate but simultaneous (that is, parallel) IOs to overcome it (see Figure 6.6). This is a highly unusual—even rare—circumstance. While it does happen, watch out in such situations. Every time you think that two or more IOs are necessary, examine the OBSTACLE–IO relationship very carefully. It is much more likely that there is an additional, time-sequenced obstacle that you haven't yet realized is there. If so, the IOs are not really parallel; they're sequential and must be depicted as such.

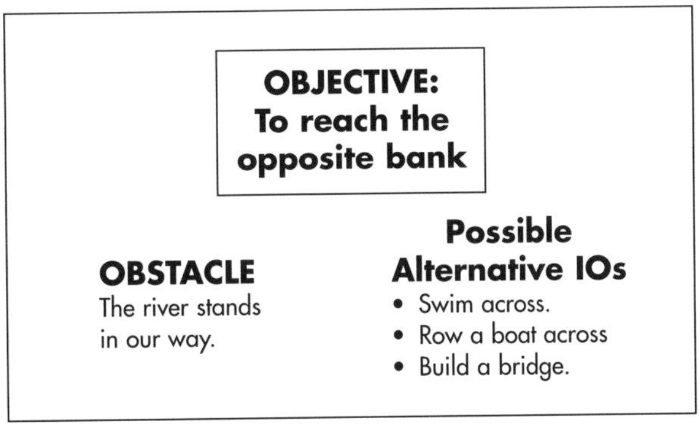

FIGURE 6.5. Different Alternatives.

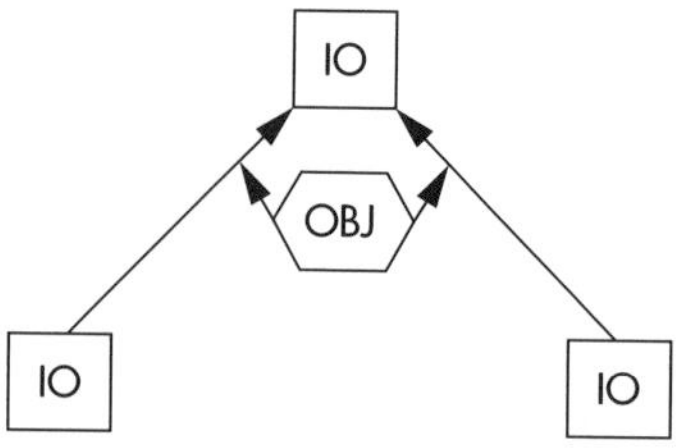

FIGURE 6.6. An Obstacle Needing More Than One IO.

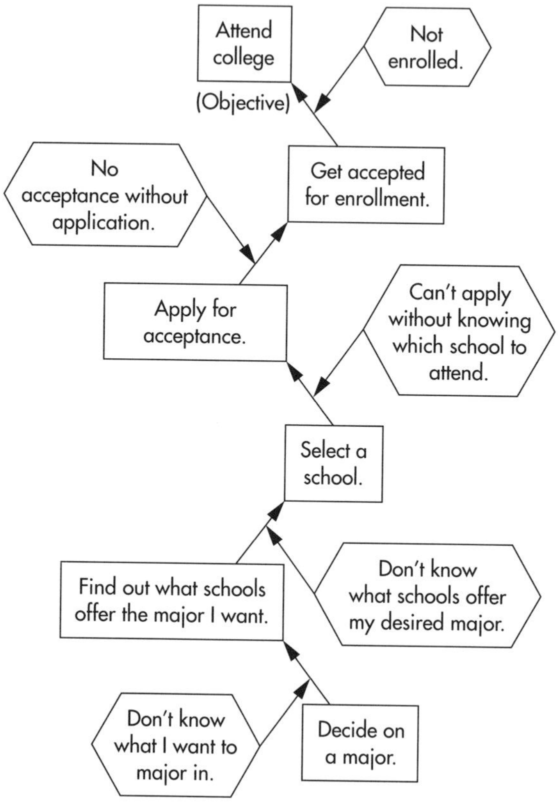

FIGURE 6.7. Time Dependency.

Time Dependency

In solving any complex problem one of the critical questions is "What do we do first?" The Prerequisite Tree answers this question. After identification of obstacles and ways to overcome them, the next most important function a PRT serves is sequencing these ways (intermediate objectives) in the right order.

For example, if your objective is to attend college, you must first be accepted for enrollment (see Figure 6.7). Before that can happen, you must apply to the college. Before you can apply, you must decide which college you want to attend. Before you can decide which college to attend, you must know whether it offers the course of study you desire. Before you can determine that, you have to know what subject you wish to pursue. Before that can happen, it would be nice to have some kind of career goal in mind.

It should be clear from this example that there is a time dependency among intermediate objectives. The more complex the problem you're trying to solve, the more important it will be to identify and properly sequence time-dependent events. This will occur as a matter of course as you construct the PRT.

Prerequisite Tree Symbology

Prerequisite Trees use two symbols and normal arrows to connect them (see Figure 6.8).

- Square-cornered boxes are used to depict the goal of the Prerequisite Tree—the objective that you're trying to achieve. When the PRT is used in concert with the Future Reality Tree, this objective may be an injection (see chapter 5, "Future Reality Tree"). Square-cornered boxes are also used to depict intermediate objectives.
- Hexagons are used to depict obstacles.
- Arrows indicate the relationships between obstacles, intermediate objectives, and the Prerequisite Tree's overall objective. Conditions or actions that occur earlier in time (that is, prerequisites) are depicted at the tail of an arrow.

Arrows connect IOs to the Prerequisite Tree's objective or injection (see Figure 6.9). Obstacles associated with the two IOs have arrows pointing to the approximate midpoint of the arrows connecting the IOs. *Once an obstacle and the IO needed to overcome it have been connected by the obstacle's arrow, they are effectively paired and treated (that is, moved or rearranged) as a single entity.*

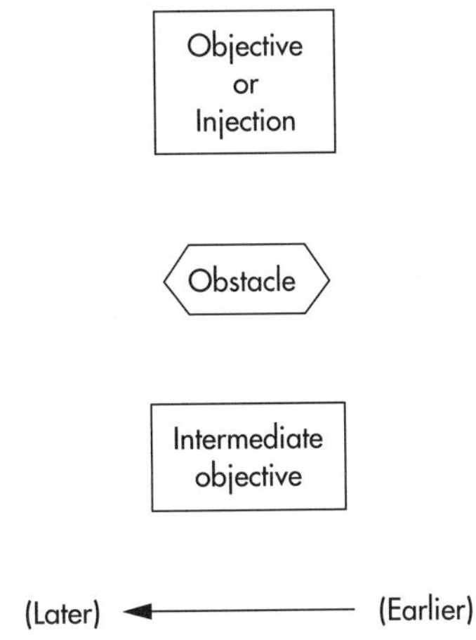

FIGURE 6.8. PRT Symbology.

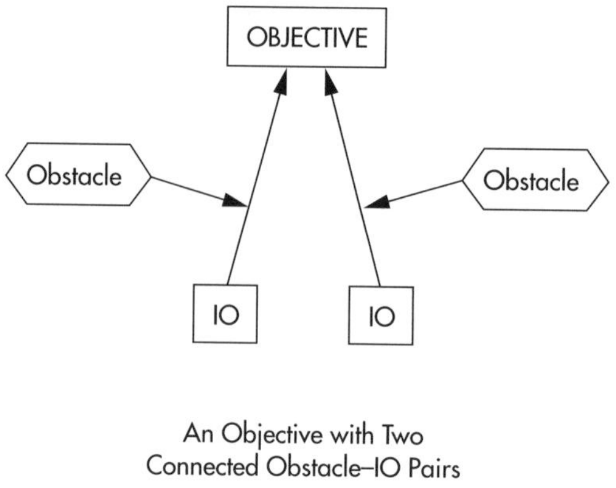

FIGURE 6.9. The Beginning of a PRT.

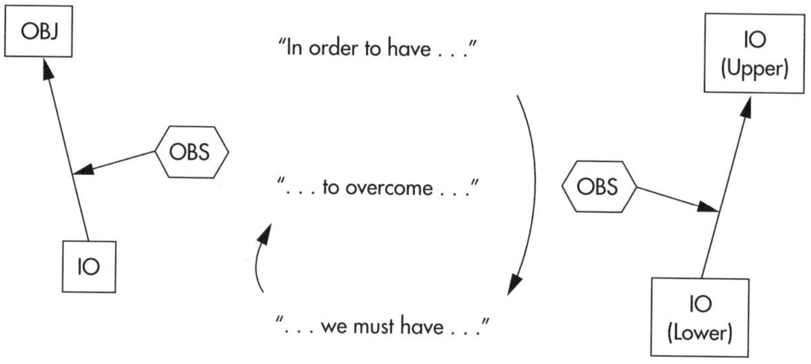

FIGURE 6.10. Reading a PRT, Top to Bottom.

Reading a Prerequisite Tree

Prerequisite Trees can be read from bottom to top, or from top to bottom, depending on your personal preference.

Top to Bottom

If you like to start at the top, with the Prerequisite Tree's objective, and work downward to the earliest prerequisite, read the tree this way (see Figure 6.10):

In order to have [OBJECTIVE], we need to do (or have) [IO] to overcome [OBSTACLE].

or

In order to have [UPPER IO], we must do/have [LOWER IO] to overcome [OBSTACLE].

Another way to read the Prerequisite Tree from top to bottom—one that "flows" a little more easily—is this:

We want [UPPER IO], but [OBSTACLE] stands in our way, so we must do/have [LOWER IO].

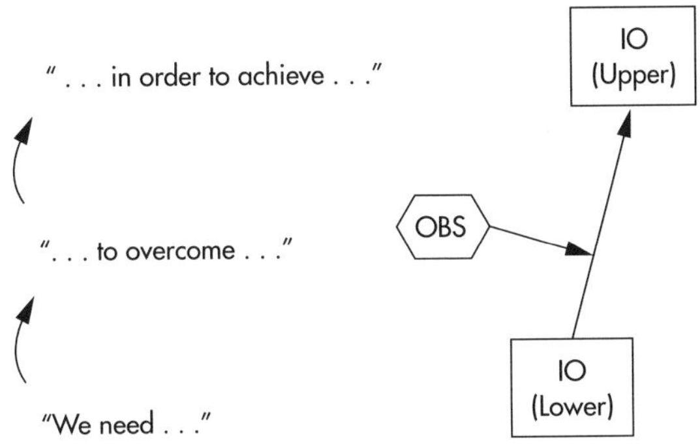

FIGURE 6.11. Reading a PRT, Bottom to Top.

Bottom to Top

If you're more comfortable working forward chronologically, start from the bottom, reading the tree this way (see Figure 6.11):

We need [LOWER IO] to achieve [UPPER IO], because [OBSTACLE] blocks us.

or

We need [LOWER IO] to overcome [OBSTACLE] in order to achieve [UPPER IO].

BUILDING A PREREQUISITE TREE

The procedure that follows assumes you're using the Prerequisite Tree as a stand-alone tool, for a purpose that's not an element of a higher level, complex problem that may require other parts of the TOC Thinking Process (for example, Current/Future Reality Trees, Conflict Resolution Diagram). If you are using the rest of the thinking process, be sure to read the additional advice in "Using the Prerequisite Tree with the Other TOC Thinking Process Tools," p. 262.

Where to Begin?

You're ready to start constructing a Prerequisite Tree. How do you begin? Before you actually get to the tree itself, start with a list of obstacles and intermediate objectives (IO).

1. Create a List

Start with a blank piece of paper. At the top of the page, in the center, write your objective—the purpose of your tree—in a complete sentence (see Figure 6.12). Put a square-cornered box around it.

2. Make Two Columns

Divide the rest of the page into two columns. Label the left one "OBSTACLES" and the right one "INTERMEDIATE OBJECTIVES."

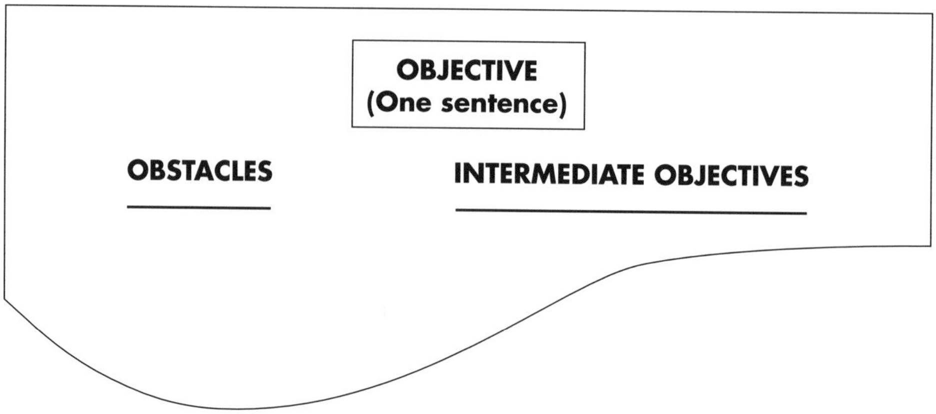
OBJECTIVE
(One sentence)
OBSTACLES
INTERMEDIATE OBJECTIVES

FIGURE 6.12. Creating a List.

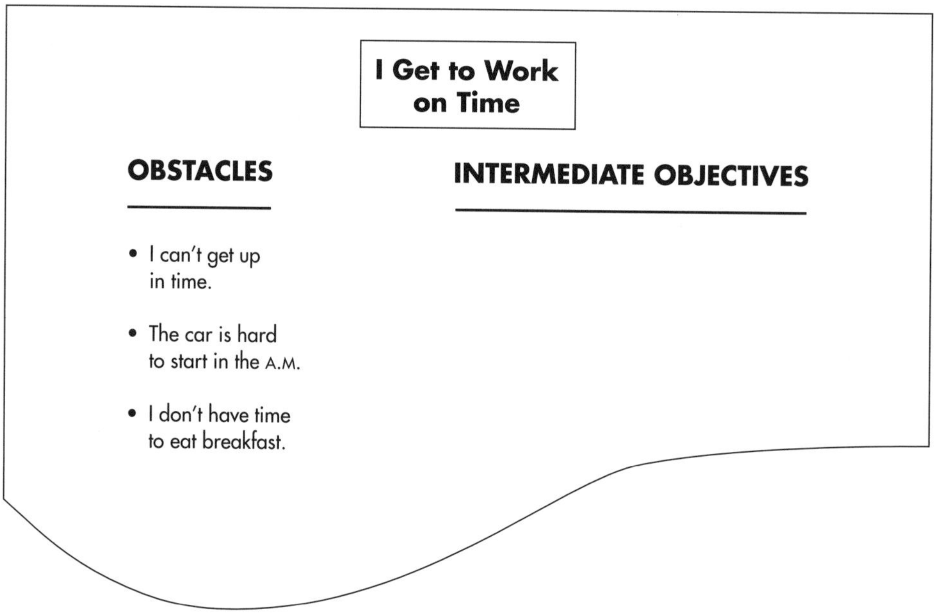
I Get to Work on Time
OBSTACLES
INTERMEDIATE OBJECTIVES
• I can't get up in time.
• The car is hard to start in the A.M.
• I don't have time to eat breakfast.

FIGURE 6.13. Listing the Obstacles.

3. List the Obstacles

Think of all the potential obstacles that could stand in the way of your achieving your objective (in the box at the top). Start writing them down in the left column (see Figure 6.13). Don't number them, and don't worry about sequence. At this point it's a free-form exercise—just generate them in whatever order they come to mind. Don't worry, either, if you think you might be missing something vital. Any critical obstacles you've overlooked will surface as you construct the tree, or during subsequent scrutiny by someone else.

4. Develop Intermediate Objectives

In the right column, beside each obstacle, write an IO that will overcome the obstacle (see Figure 6.14). In fact, if you can think of more than one way to overcome the same obstacle, write them all down. Check each IO for its effectiveness in overcoming the obstacle by inserting it in the following statement:

If [IO], then [OBS] doesn't obstruct me.

If the statement sounds valid to you, the IO will probably be effective.

On the other hand, if you can't immediately think of any specific action that would overcome the obstacle, don't let that slow you down. Write the IO as the opposite condition of the obstacle, and continue on. For example, your obstacle might be "I am delayed by traffic." If, within about a minute, you can't think of a way to beat the traffic, write the IO as "I am NOT delayed by traffic," and go on to the next obstacle. However, you should always strive to find IOs that aren't opposites—that is, they don't contain ". . . not . . ." in their statement. If less than half your IOs are specific conditions or actions, you may not know enough about your problem. You may need assistance from someone who knows more about the situation than you do.

If all you can think of is one specific IO, but you're not sure how you'll get it done, write it down anyway. The "how" will eventually work out as you build the tree. This is also true of "opposite condition" IOs.

Note #1: At some point, you will have to come up with one or more specific actions to replace your opposite condition IO. One method of doing this is to use a Conflict Resolution Diagram as a creative device, rather than as a conflict resolver, to generate a specific action IO. Refer to chapter 4, "Conflict Resolution Diagram," for details on how to construct one. "The Conflict Resolution Diagram and the

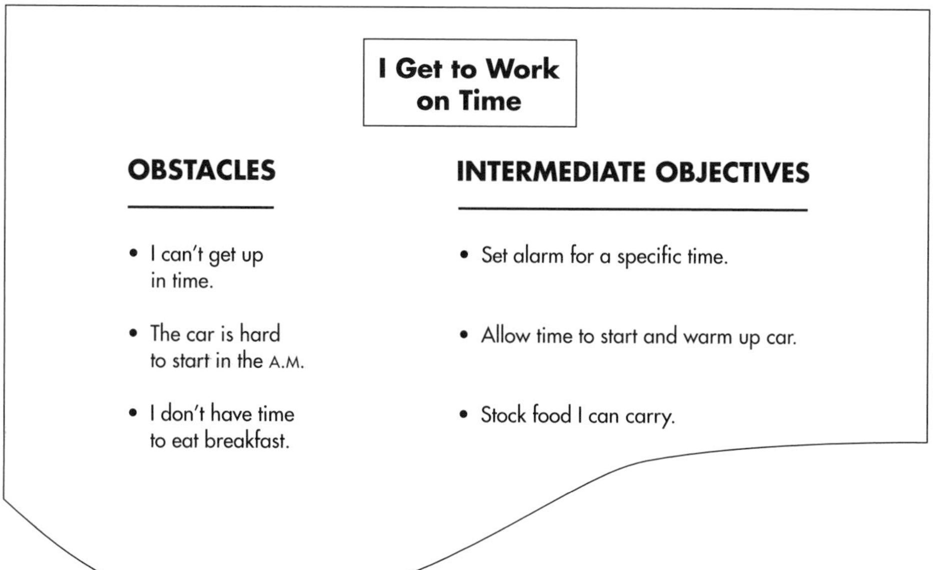
I Get to Work on Time
OBSTACLES
INTERMEDIATE OBJECTIVES
• I can't get up in time.
• Set alarm for a specific time.
• The car is hard to start in the A.M.
• Allow time to start and warm up car.
• I don't have time to eat breakfast.
• Stock food I can carry.

FIGURE 6.14. Developing Intermediate Objectives.

Prerequisite Tree," p. 264, describes how to use the Conflict Resolution Diagram to create specific action IOs to replace opposite condition IOs.

Note #2: If the purpose of your Prerequisite Tree is to figure out how to do a complex injection in a Future Reality Tree, after reading this section refer to "The Future Reality Tree and the Prerequisite Tree," p. 263.

A helpful technique for surfacing obstacles and creating IOs is summarized in Figure 6.40, "Constructing Obstacle–IO Pairs," at the end of this chapter.

5. Refine the Completed List

After you have one or more IOs for every obstacle, review the list.

a. When you have more than one alternative IO for a particular obstacle, the preferred IO is the easiest, the least expensive, or the one that creates the fewest undesirable side effects (see Figure 6.15).

b. If two IOs are required to overcome the obstacle, group them with the obstacle for inclusion in the Prerequisite Tree (see Figure 6.16). If you think more than two IOs are required to overcome the same obstacle, reexamine the IOs and the original obstacle. There may be another hidden obstacle and IO that you have failed to identify. In any event, you should try not to have more than two IOs to overcome any one obstacle.

c. If you've expressed half or more of your IOs as opposite conditions of their paired obstacles, you should now try to develop specific actions to replace those opposite conditions (see Figure 6.17). Try simple brainstorming first. If that doesn't work, refer to chapter 4, "Conflict Resolution Diagram," for details on how to construct a CRD. Figure 6.41, at the end of this chapter, describes how to use the Conflict Resolution Diagram to create specific action IOs to replace opposite condition IOs.

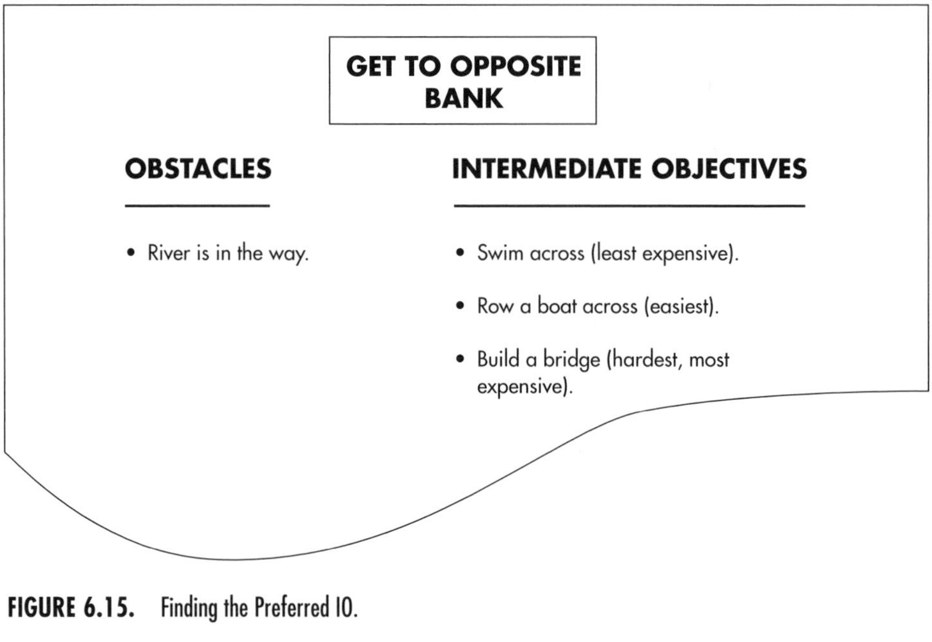

FIGURE 6.15. Finding the Preferred IO.

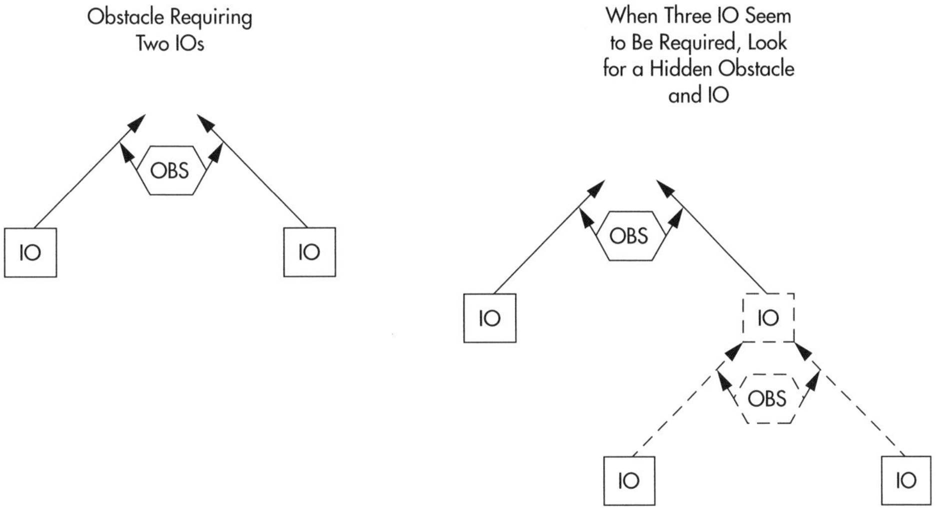

Obstacle Requiring Two IOs
OBS
IO
IO
When Three IO Seem to Be Required, Look for a Hidden Obstacle and IO
OBS
IO
IO
OBS
IO
IO

FIGURE 6.16. Grouping Obstacles.

OBSTACLE	**IO (First cut)**	**IO (Second cut)**
I am delayed in traffic.	I am NOT delayed in traffic. (Condition)	Find alternate, less congested route. (Specific action)

FIGURE 6.17. Converting Opposite Conditions to Actions.

d. Refine the wording of obstacles and IOs. Don't state your obstacles as requirements or needs. They should be stated as conditions (see Figure 6.18). Consider the "river crossing" example. You might be tempted to word the obstacle this way:

I need to cross the river.
or
I must cross the river.

Using the word "need" implies something more basic driving the need—a deeper, underlying condition. If you phrase your obstacle as a need, at some point you'll find your obstacles looking more like IOs than obstacles. A better way to word the obstacle would be as a condition, rather than a need:

The river is in the way.

Intermediate objectives can be worded either as actions or conditions. Clearly, some kind of action is usually required to change a condition, so at some point IOs will have to be phrased as actions. It's more likely, however, that IOs nearer the top of the tree will be stated as conditions, while those closer to the bottom will probably be more specific actions. This is especially true in complex situations, or when you aren't quite sure how to go about accomplishing the tree's

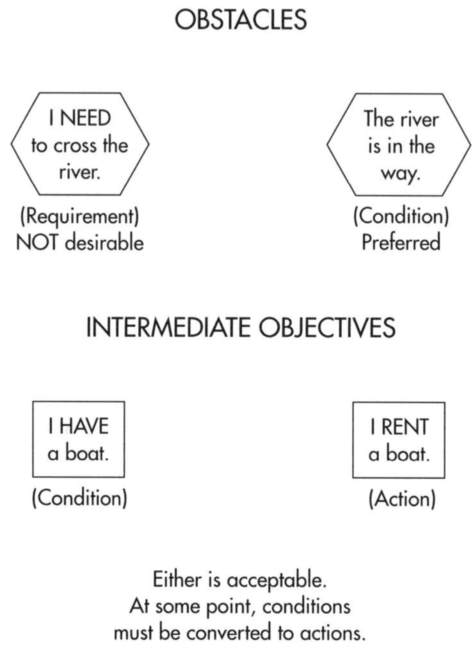

FIGURE 6.18. Wording Obstacles and IOs.

objective. If there's any doubt in your mind about which way to go (action or condition), go for the action. That's really what you're trying to get from a Prerequisite Tree: the actions you need to take to achieve your objective. Thorough scrutiny after the tree is completed will usually show you if you've overlooked something by going to an action too quickly.

6. Begin the Prerequisite Tree (Figure 6.19)

Start a new page, on a larger sheet of paper. If you don't have paper larger than 8½″ × 11″, tape several of these together from behind. Rewrite the Prerequisite Tree objective at the top of the page (see Figure 6.19).

7. Create Obstacle–IO Pairs (Figure 6.20)

Rewrite your obstacles and their paired IOs on one-inch square Post-it™ notes. Use different-colored notes for obstacles and IOs, or draw appropriate distinguishing figures (hexagons for obstacles, square-cornered rectangles for IOs) on the notes. Keep the obstacle and IO notes together by sticking them to one another.

Note: The use of Post-it™ notes is more important for the Prerequisite Tree than for any of the other trees. It's possible to construct any of the other trees sequentially using any of a number of computer graphics programs, because the Current Reality Tree, Conflict Resolution Diagram, Future Reality Tree, and Transition Tree are created (as well as constructed) from top to bottom, or from bottom to top. The PRT is the only one in which you first create a large number of entities, then piece them together, like a jigsaw puzzle. For this reason, the flexibility of being able to move Post-it™ notes around is invaluable.

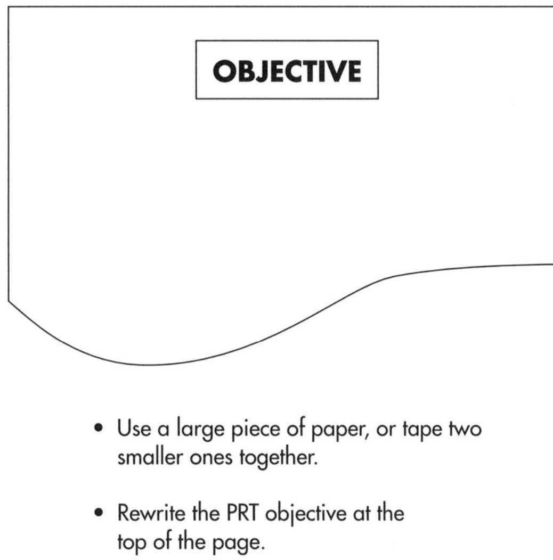

FIGURE 6.19. Beginning the PRT.

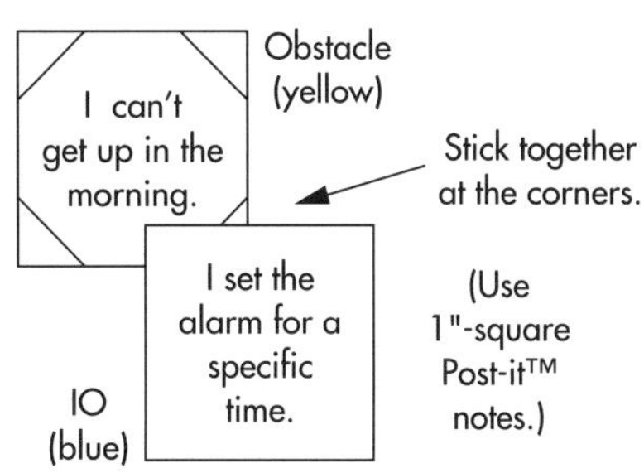

FIGURE 6.20. Using Post-it™ Notes.

8. Array the Obstacle–IO Pairs

Arrange the obstacle–IO pairs on the new page horizontally beneath the objective (see Figure 6.21). At this point no precedence among obstacle–IO pairs has been established—they're all considered equal. So even if you need two or more rows to arrange them, don't attach any significance to their physical locations; virtually all of them will be repositioned at least once before you're done.

9. Time-Sequence the Obstacle–IO Pairs

Review all the obstacle–IO pairs on the new page. Look for obvious time dependencies—one pair that clearly must come before another in time (see Figure 6.22). Examine every obstacle–IO pair with this in mind.

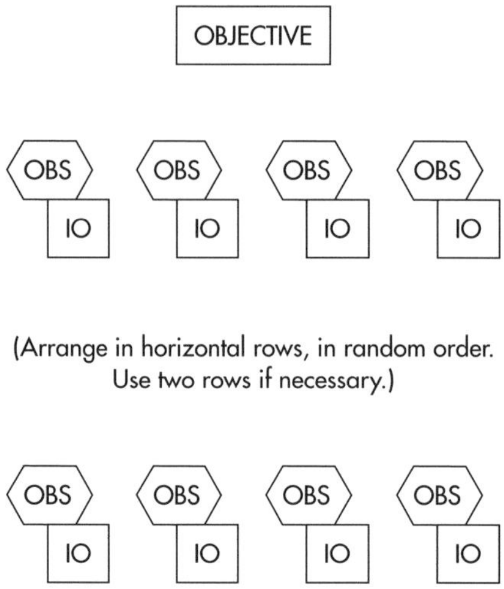

FIGURE 6.21. Starting Layout.

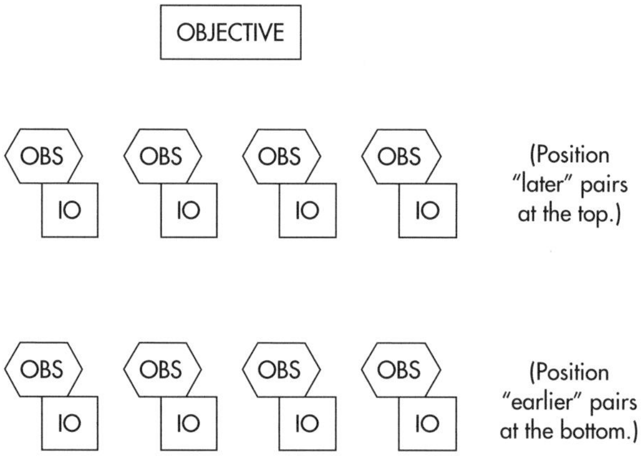

FIGURE 6.22. Segregating "Earlier" from "Later."

a. Group the earlier pairs at the bottom of the page, and the later ones near the top, just below the objective.

Ask yourself the question, "Does this pair come before or after that pair?" The answer tells you whether a particular obstacle–IO pair belongs in the group at the bottom or at the top.

b. Look for pairs in the lower group that might lead to pairs in the upper group. Align them in vertical "branches" and connect them with a dotted line (use an erasable pencil) (see Figure 6.23). The dotted lines are like "bookmarks." They hold your place in connecting IOs until you can sort out and confirm time dependencies ("Is this really first?") and sufficiencies ("Does this really block us?"). Dotted lines are most useful in Prerequisite Trees with a lot of IOs.

c. Review the new vertical alignments. Look for branches that might be consolidated by inserting one into another in the right chronological order.

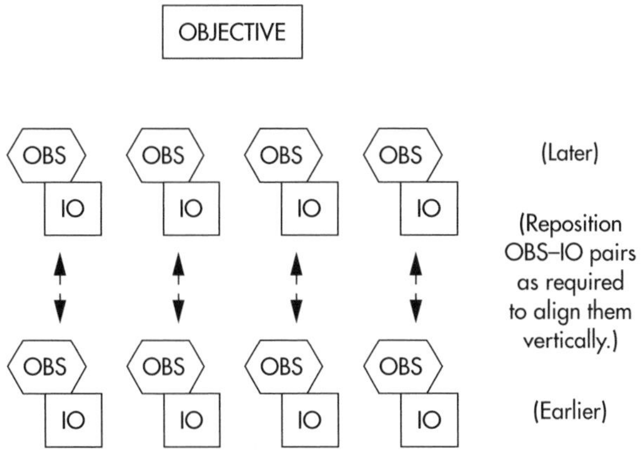

FIGURE 6.23. Looking for Vertical Connections.

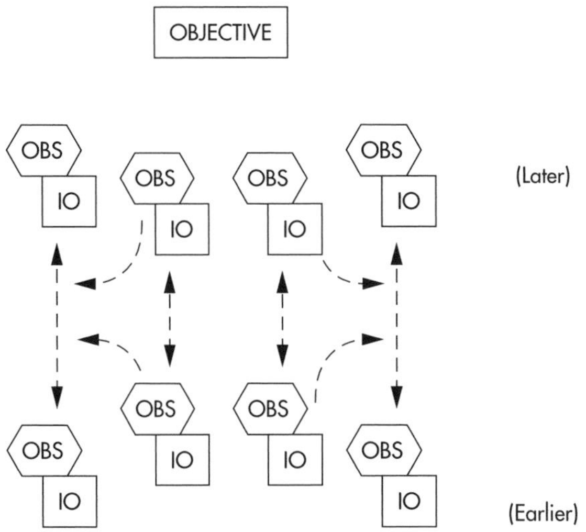

FIGURE 6.24. Consolidate Branches If Possible.

Rearrange pairs as required (see Figure 6.24). Focus on sequencing the IOs rather than the obstacles. The IOs represent necessary conditions that must be satisfied to realize the objective.

Again, ask yourself, "Does this pair come before the upper pair, or after the lower pair?"

10. Fill in the Gaps

Scrutinize each connection between two IOs and their intervening obstacle for entity existence, cause sufficiency, and additional cause (see Figure 6.25) (see "Scrutinizing a Prerequisite Tree," p. 259, for guidance on how to do this). If your scrutiny reveals gaps (for example, obstacles that don't logically obstruct, or lower IOs that don't logically lead to a higher-level IO), identify additional

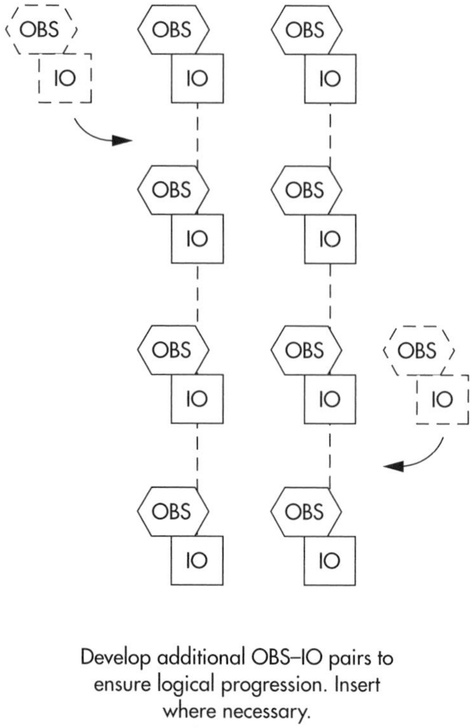
OBS
IO
OBS
IO
OBS
IO
OBS
IO
OBS
IO
OBS
IO
OBS
IO
OBS
IO
OBS
IO
OBS
IO
Develop additional OBS–IO pairs to ensure logical progression. Insert where necessary.

FIGURE 6.25. Filling in Logical Gaps.

obstacles and IOs to fill the gaps. You should be striving for a smooth, unbroken flow of logic, from bottom to top.

11. Remove Dotted Lines

When you have a logically sound progression of obstacles and IOs running from the bottom to the top of a particular branch, erase the dotted line you drew in step 9b (see Figure 6.26).

12. Look for Horizontal Connections

If you have more than one branch of obstacle–IO pairs leading toward your objective, compare the obstacles and IOs in each branch with those in the other branch(es). Look for an obstacle in one branch that might also obstruct an IO in another. Also, look for IOs in one branch that might overcome obstacles in another (see Figure 6.27). If you find such relationships, modify the tree by connecting the appropriate IOs with arrows and repositioning IOs and obstacles as necessary.

13. Make the Final Connections

If you haven't already done so, scrutinize the link between the topmost obstacle–IO pair in each branch and the tree's objective. Can they be logically connected

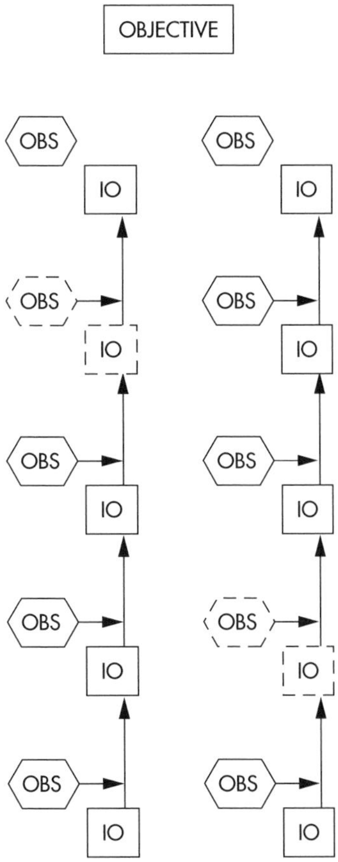
OBJECTIVE
OBS
IO
OBS
IO
OBS
IO
OBS
IO
OBS
IO
OBS
IO
OBS
IO
OBS
IO
OBS
IO
OBS
IO

FIGURE 6.26. Replacing Dotted Connections with Solid Arrows.

directly? Or do intervening obstacle–IO pairs exist that you haven't yet identified? If you can, connect the top layer directly with the objective (see Figure 6.28). Otherwise, develop the missing links and then make the final connections.

14. Review the Modified Tree

After you complete all vertical and horizontal connections, and after all additions or modifications are done, scrutinize the entire tree one more time for entity existence, cause sufficiency, and additional cause deficiencies, using the guidance in "Scrutinizing a Prerequisite Tree," p. 259. Correct any that you find. If there are none, you're done.

> **Note:** There are no minimum or maximum configuration requirements for Prerequisite Trees. Each one will be unique. PRTs may have only one vertical branch. Or they may have two, three, or more. Some branches may have only one obstacle–IO pair. Let the tree "grow" naturally. Don't force it to conform to a preconceived notion of how you think it should look. This is *not* "bonsai"!

Figure 6.39, "Procedures for Building a Prerequisite Tree," at the end of this chapter, constitutes an abbreviated checklist of these steps for quick reference.

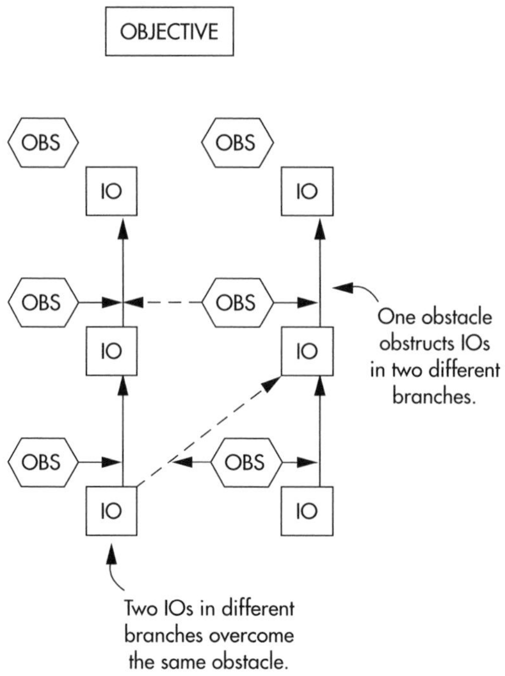

FIGURE 6.27. Looking for Appropriate Horizontal Connections.

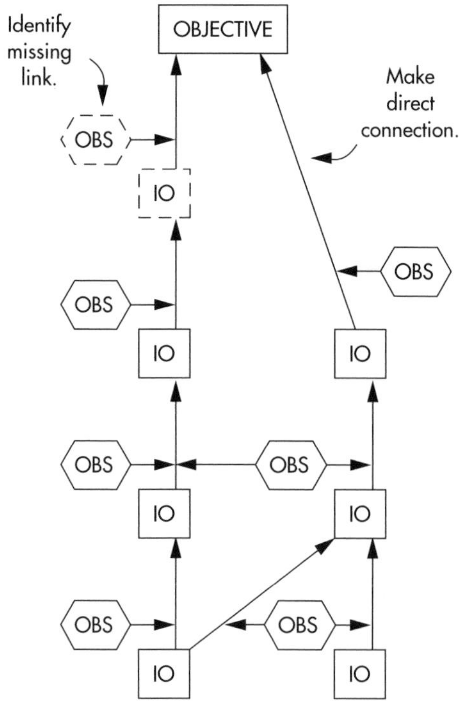

FIGURE 6.28. Making the Final Connections.

However, it should be used only after the supporting material in this section has been thoroughly understood.

> **Note:** Some people may have difficulty using the 14 steps as described in building a Prerequisite Tree, particularly with the time-sequencing and gap-filling. Figure 6.42, at the end of this chapter, offers an alternative sequence of the same steps. Use whichever procedure you feel the most comfortable with.

SCRUTINIZING A PREREQUISITE TREE

How do we know whether the IO–obstacle relationship we (or someone else) created is valid? Does an obstacle really prevent the intermediate objective above it? Does a lower intermediate objective really overcome the obstacle above it? The answer is, "Scrutinize it," much as you would a Current or Future Reality Tree.

Unfortunately, the Categories of Legitimate Reservation (Chapter 2) were designed to verify sufficiency-based logic trees. That is, they ask, "Is the cause adequate, or sufficient, to produce the effect?" But the Prerequisite Tree, like the Conflict Resolution Diagram, is a necessity-based structure: It identifies the conditions necessary to obstruct an objective or to overcome the obstruction. A sufficiency-based logical relationship is expressed:

If. . . [CAUSE], then . . . [EFFECT].

But a necessity-based logical relationship is expressed:

In order to have . . . [OBJECTIVE], we must have . . . [CONDITION], because of. . . [REASON/OBSTRUCTION].

Here's another way of looking at it. In the case of sufficiency, we're asking, "Is this enough to conclude that 1 + 1 = 2?" In the case of necessity, we're asking, "What could prevent 1 + 1 from equaling 2, and what is the minimum we have to do to overcome it?" While this may be a subtle distinction, it forces us to examine Prerequisite Trees in a slightly different way. In scrutinizing a PRT, you're questioning whether an obstacle exists and whether the proposed IO is likely to neutralize it.

Entity Existence

First, there is an Entity Existence issue with respect to any obstacle. Does it really exist, or is it somebody's negative fantasy? Take, for example, the fear of getting fired for expressing your true opinions to your boss (see Figure 6.29). Undoubtedly, some people have been fired for speaking their minds, but is this a realistic probability in the situation at hand? If so, then it is a legitimate obstacle. If not, it isn't.

Cause Sufficiency

Second, each IO pair and its intervening obstacle can be separated into two cause sufficiency relationships, which, taken together, can support or refute the validity of the IO–obstacle relationship.

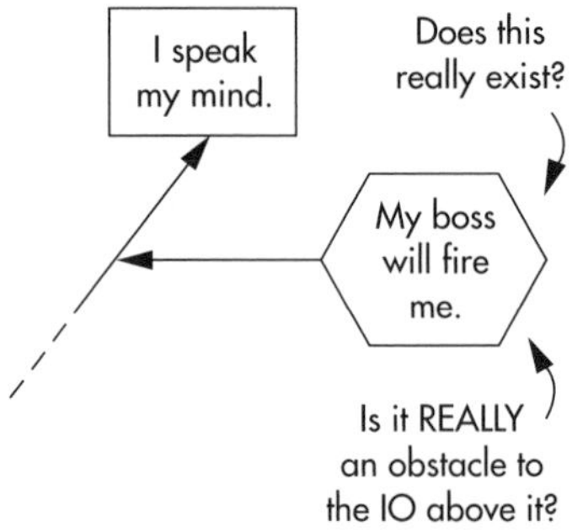

FIGURE 6.29. Entity Existence in a Prerequisite Tree.

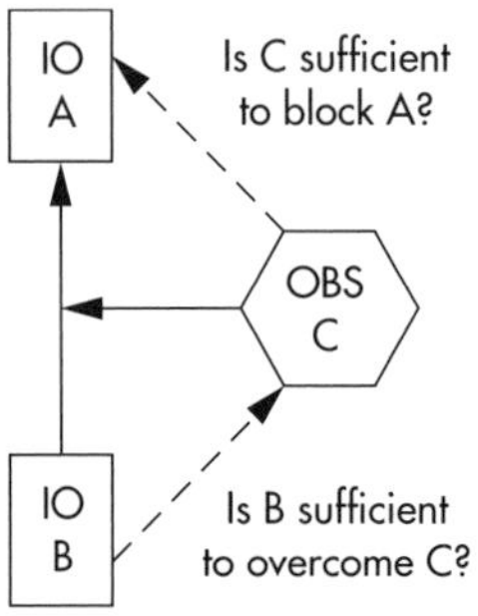

FIGURE 6.30. Cause Sufficiency in a Prerequisite Tree.

In Figure 6.30, for the relationship to be valid, you must be able to make a convincing case that

1. If *C,* then *A is blocked.*

and

2. If *B,* then *C is overcome.*

Another way to check cause sufficiency is to ask two questions:

1. Is C sufficient to block A?

and

2. Is B sufficient to overcome C?

If you can't answer "yes" to either of these questions, the IO–obstacle–IO relationship isn't valid. If you don't really have an obstacle, you'll be wasting your time trying to overcome it. If the lower IO is ineffective, you'll never realize the upper IO.

Additional Cause

Third, you have to ask yourself, "Is there something else?" It's important not to overlook the possibility of an additional cause (obstacle)—one you haven't already thought of—completely independent of the first one, which might also effectively block the higher IO. These less-apparent obstacles may occur to you (or to someone else) only while you're examining the most obvious one. If you find such additional obstacles, you must decide how to incorporate them into your Prerequisite Tree. These additional obstacles don't directly affect the validity of your primary one, but they merit examination in their own right for their capacity to prevent you from reaching your objective.

"Looking for Loops in All the Wrong Places"

What if you find a "feedback" loop in your Prerequisite Tree—an IO at a higher level in the tree that seems to be necessary to overcome an obstacle lower in the same branch? (See Figure 6.31.) In a Current Reality Tree it's not uncommon to find a negative loop. And a Future Reality Tree is always better if you can build a positive loop into it. But a loop in a PRT is always a "catch-22" situation: something to be avoided whenever possible.

If you think your Prerequisite Tree has a such a loop, examine the higher IO and lower obstacle carefully. Look for:

- A different interpretation of what the IO means—one that does not generate a loop
- A different IO to overcome the lower-level obstacle
- The possibility that the lower obstacle is misplaced—that it should actually be located somewhere above the IO where the loop seems to originate

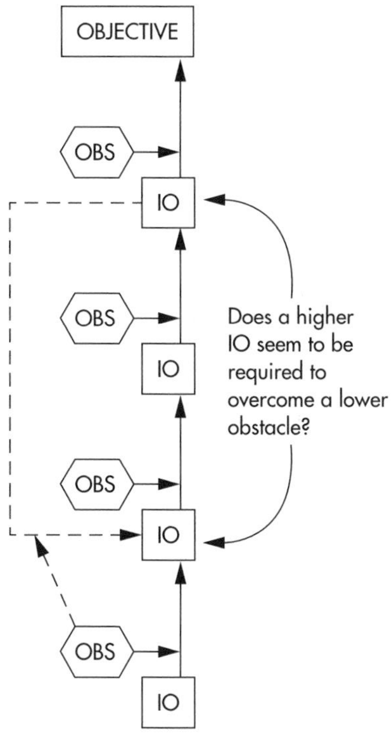

FIGURE 6.31. Avoid "Loops" in the Prerequisite Tree.

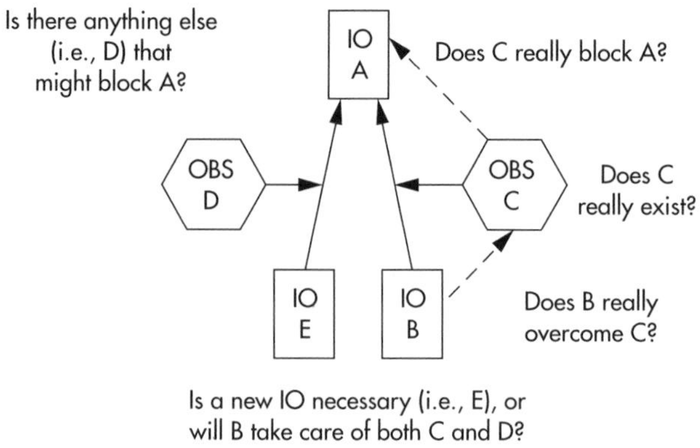

FIGURE 6.32. The Obstacle–IO Validity Test.

The IO–Obstacle Validity Test

In summary, here's how to test your obstacles and IOs for validity (see Figure 6.32):

- Does the primary obstacle really exist?
- Does the primary obstacle really block the higher IO–objective?
- Does the lower IO really overcome its paired obstacle?
- Is the lower IO alone enough to overcome the primary obstacle? Is another lower IO needed?
- Is there anything else (that is, a second obstacle) that might prevent achieving the higher IO?
- Is the original lower IO enough to overcome any new secondary obstacle? Is another lower IO needed?

USING THE PREREQUISITE TREE WITH OTHER PARTS OF THE TOC THINKING PROCESS

While the Prerequisite Tree is extremely useful in stand-alone daily applications, it becomes a very powerful link in a systemic chain when used in concert with other tools of the TOC Thinking Process to improve complex systems. Chapter 1 discusses this integration in more detail.

From the illustration in Figure 1.18 (p. 28), you can see that the Prerequisite Tree is one of five tools in the thinking process. The Current Reality Tree identifies core problems and root causes. The Conflict Resolution Diagram surfaces underlying conflicting interests that may be perpetuating the core problem. It also functions as an "idea generator," a creative engine to help you invent new ideas to solve old or nagging problems. The Future Reality Tree enables you to model and test your ideas for effectiveness in solving problems. Once this is done, the Prerequisite Tree gives you the means to identify and overcome obstacles to implementation. And finally, the Transition Tree allows you to develop the detailed sequence of interdependent steps necessary to put the idea into effect—an implementation plan.

Obviously, the opportunities you have to go through the entire five-stage process may be few or infrequent. But the Prerequisite Tree can be used in concert with some of the other tools without going through all five tools in sequence. Specifically:

- The Prerequisite Tree can help you completely expose the obstacles to an injection from a Future Reality Tree, then identify the intermediate objectives needed to overcome them.
- The Prerequisite Tree can help you identify, organize, and sequence all the actions or conditions necessary to achieve an injection (condition) in a Future Reality Tree, even when you don't know exactly what they might be or how to do them.
- The Conflict Resolution Diagram can be used to convert intermediate objectives that you stated as conditions into specific actions.
- The Prerequisite Tree can provide the detail you need to start transforming a Future Reality Tree (a projection of the future) into a Transition Tree (a specific action plan).

The Future Reality Tree and the Prerequisite Tree

A Future Reality Tree needs a Prerequisite Tree to support it when one or more injections is a condition you aren't sure how to achieve. In such a case, the Future Reality Tree injection in question becomes the objective of the PRT. The PRT is then used to determine the obstacles to achieving that condition, as well as the IOs you'll need to overcome those obstacles.

For example, the objective of your Prerequisite Tree might be "Rebuild the engine," as one of a number of future conditions which must be satisfied in order to restore a classic car to "mint" condition (see Figure 6.33). The larger problem is to restore the car. "Rebuild the engine" is only one injection, and you might not be sure exactly how to go about it. What would you do first? One obstacle might be "Don't have a complete engine." The intermediate objective for that obstacle might be "Locate original or replacement parts for a 70-year-old car."

If your Prerequisite Tree is an outgrowth of a Future Reality Tree, you may already have some useful intermediate objectives, written as injections into your Future Reality Tree. Start by taking a look at all the injections in your FRT. There will usually be several—maybe even a lot. Some, like rebuilding an engine, may be complex states of future reality which you need to make happen. Others may just be simple actions you need to steer the logical path of the FRT toward its desired effects. Others may be injections you need to prevent the growth of negative branches in the Future Reality Tree. (Refer to chapter 5, "The Future Reality Tree," for a comprehensive description of negative branches).

In any case, in achieving the Prerequisite Tree's objective (your "mother of all injections"—the one at the top of your PRT), you may find that some of the other injections in your Future Reality Tree can serve as intermediate objectives (IOs) in your PRT (see Figure 6.34). If so, why reinvent the wheel? You may be able to get "two for the price of one." By accomplishing a different injection from your Future Reality Tree first, as part of the PRT process, you may make it

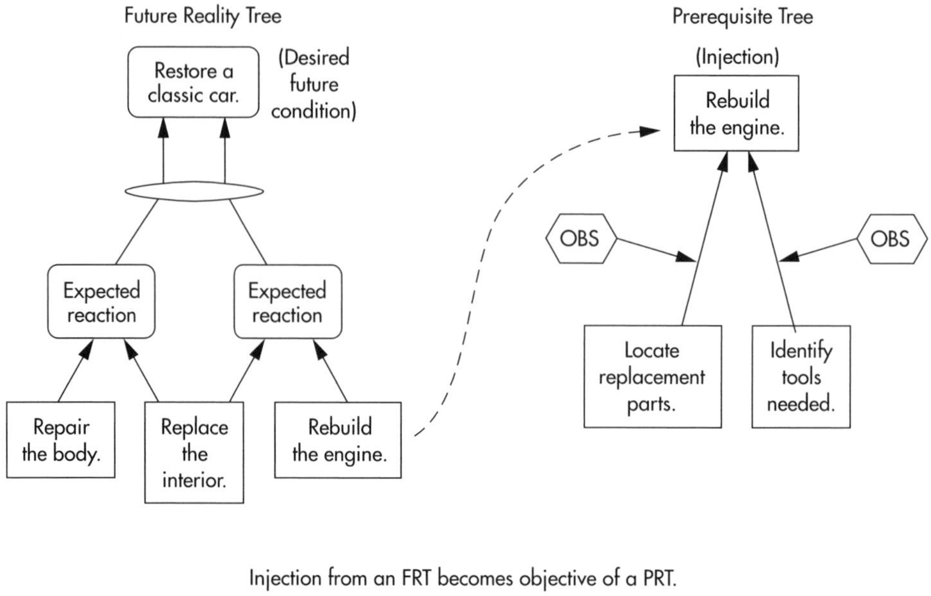

FIGURE 6.33. Building a PRT from an FRT.

easier to accomplish your most important injection, while still doing something that would eventually need doing anyway. So if possible, bring as many injections from your Future Reality Tree into your PRT as you can.

The easiest way to do this is to write all the Future Reality Tree's injections in a column on a separate piece of paper, with the "mother of all injections"—the most important one—at the top. Using your intuitive knowledge, compare each Future Reality Tree injection with the "mother" and determine if it's a necessary condition, at some point, to achieving that injection at the top of the Prerequisite Tree. If so, write it as an IO on a Post-it™ note and set it aside for incorporation into the PRT at the proper time.

The Conflict Resolution Diagram and the Prerequisite Tree

Sometimes, as you're building a Prerequisite Tree, you may run into difficulty trying to come up with an intermediate objective to overcome a specific obstacle. Usually this problem first arises in step 4, before you've even started work on the tree itself. You'll recall that step 4 suggests that if you can't come up with a specific IO to overcome the obstacle, you should word the IO as the opposite condition from the obstacle and press on. At some point, though, you'll need to deal with this opposite condition by converting it into a positive condition or an action. The creative mode of the Conflict Resolution Diagram can help you here.

Build a Conflict Resolution Diagram

One of the ways to use the Conflict Resolution Diagram, described in chapter 4, is as a "creative engine" to develop new potential solutions to difficult problems (see Figure 6.35).

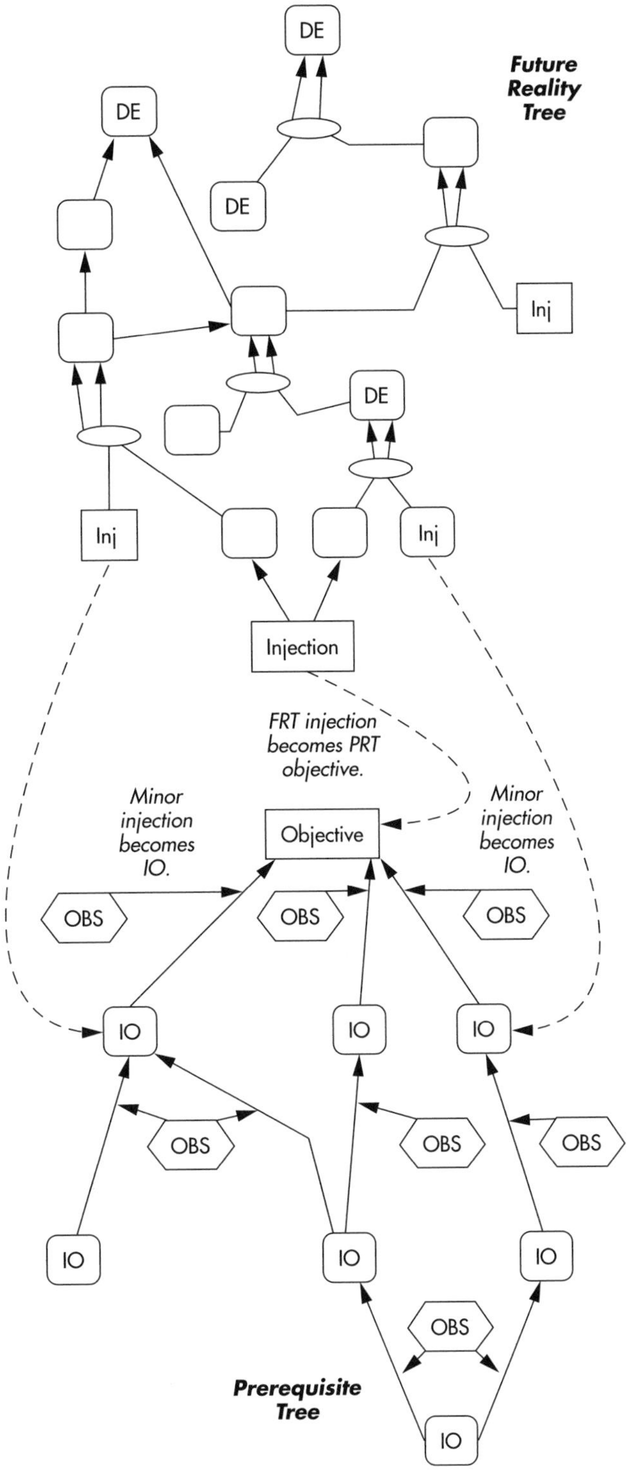

FIGURE 6.34. Using FRT Injections in a PRT.

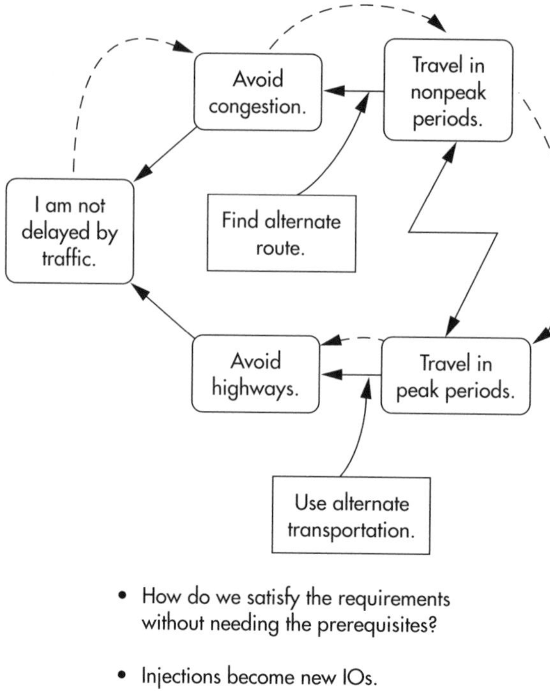

FIGURE 6.35. Using a CRD to Create an IO.

a. Write your previously stated opposite condition—the one you're trying to replace—as the objective of a Conflict Resolution Diagram.

b. Begin building the Conflict Resolution Diagram, from left to right across the upper limb, to the Conflict Resolution Diagram's prerequisite.

c. Write a prerequisite on the lower limb that is the opposite of the one on the upper limb.

d. Work back across the lower limb from right to left, developing a requirement that results from the lower prerequisite and is a necessary condition for achieving the Conflict Resolution Diagram's objective.

e. Using the procedures described in chapter 4, create an injection to "evaporate" the conflict. That injection will replace the opposite condition as the IO needed to overcome the obstacle.

Converting Conditions to Actions

We have seen that an IO can be either an action or a condition. As you get closer to the bottom of the Prerequisite Tree, IOs should be predominantly actions rather than conditions. If you have some conditions you'd like to convert into actions, or if you're not sure how to achieve the condition, the Conflict Resolution Diagram can help you. The same procedure just described applies. Figure 6.41 provides an abbreviated checklist for this purpose.

The Transition Tree and the Prerequisite Tree

The Prerequisite Tree is the logical predecessor of the Transition Tree. If you needed a PRT to sequence intermediate objectives in order to overcome obstacles, you may find that you need a Transition Tree to provide a step-by-step implementation plan. Why can't you just use the PRT itself? If overcoming the obstacles is straightforward enough, you probably would be able to do the job with a PRT alone.

But if your Prerequisite Tree is, itself, composed of a number of complex actions, you may need a Transition Tree to break the implementation down into manageable bites (see Figure 6.36). The more intermediate objectives you have that are conditions, the greater the likelihood that you'll benefit from a Transition Tree. You may recall that the PRT identifies obstacles and actions to overcome them *without regard for who is responsible for taking these actions.* However, at some point you need to establish who's going to have to do what—accountability. A Transition Tree can reflect every action that anybody needs to take to achieve the PRT's objective.

Another benefit the Transition Tree gives you is a sufficiency check. You'll recall that the Prerequisite Tree is necessity-based, not sufficiency-based. This

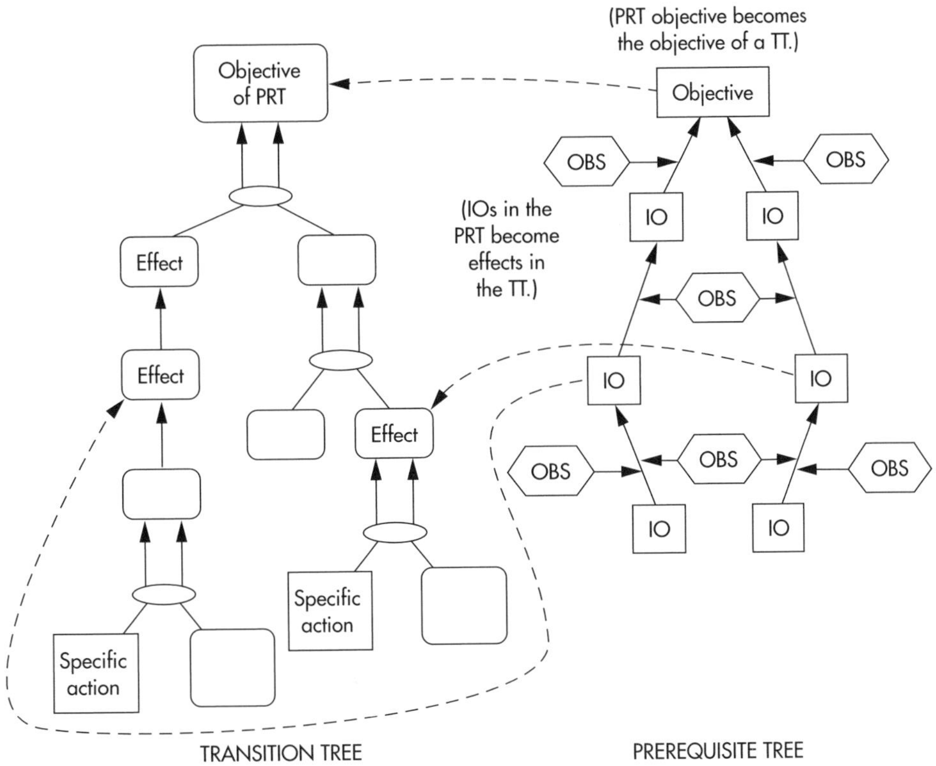

FIGURE 6.36. Integrating a PRT into a TT.

means that while it identifies conditions necessary to overcome each individual obstacle, it won't necessarily include those other conditions—not related to obstacles—that are needed to achieve a desired effect.

If you do follow your Prerequisite Tree with a Transition Tree, the intermediate objectives will become either initiator actions or effects in the Transition Tree. Chapter 7, "Transition Tree," discusses the integration of PRTs and Transition Trees in more detail.

SUMMARY

Now that our Prerequisite Tree is completed, we're ready to enter the final stage of the thinking process: developing detailed, sequential steps to implement our solution.

The Current Reality Tree showed us what to change; the Conflict Resolution Diagram proposed ideas for what to change to: and the Future Reality Tree verified that those ideas would do what we expected them to do. The Prerequisite Tree has shown us the first part of how to cause the change: the obstacles that must be overcome.

But that's just the "framework" for action. Now we're ready to flesh out that framework by adding what the Prerequisite Tree doesn't give us: sufficiency. In chapter 7, we'll learn to use a Transition Tree to answer the question, "Is each step enough to get us to the next implementation milestone?"

The desire to do something good doesn't get it done.

—Unknown

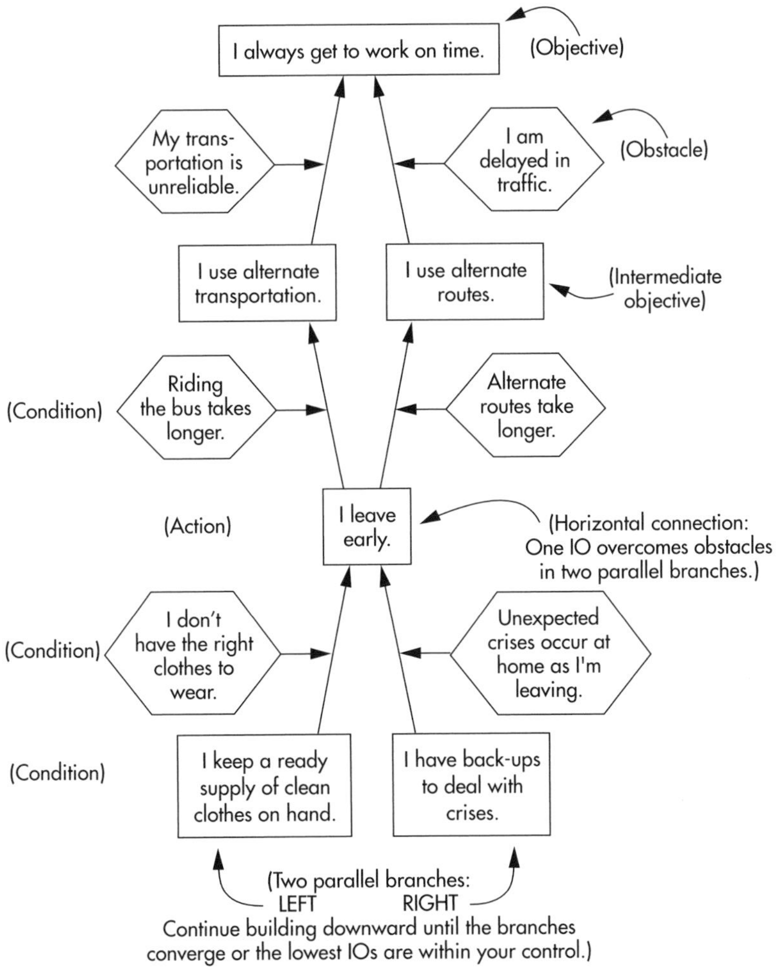

FIGURE 6.37. Prerequisite Tree Example: "I Always Get to Work on Time."

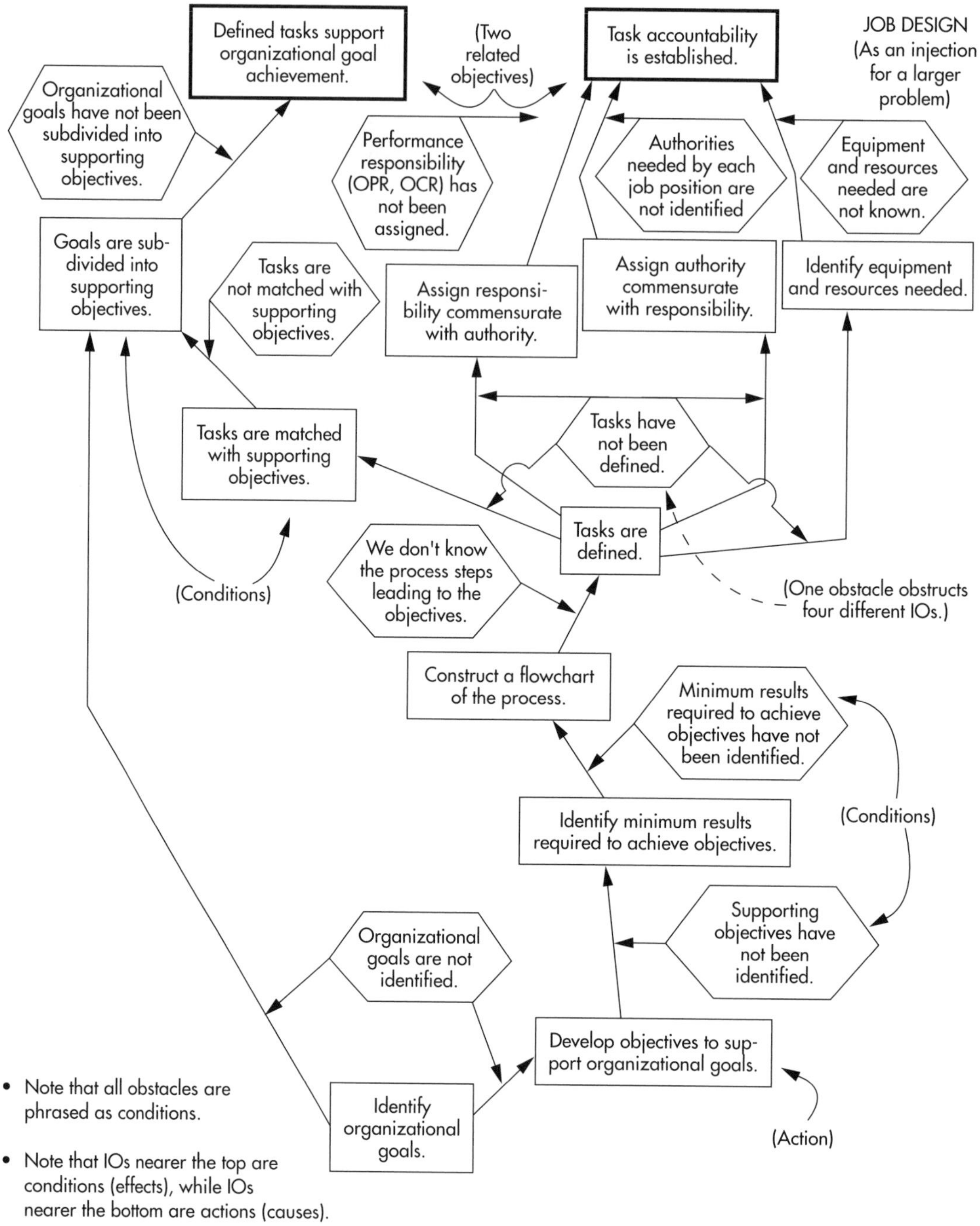

FIGURE 6.38. Prerequisite Tree Example: "Job Design."

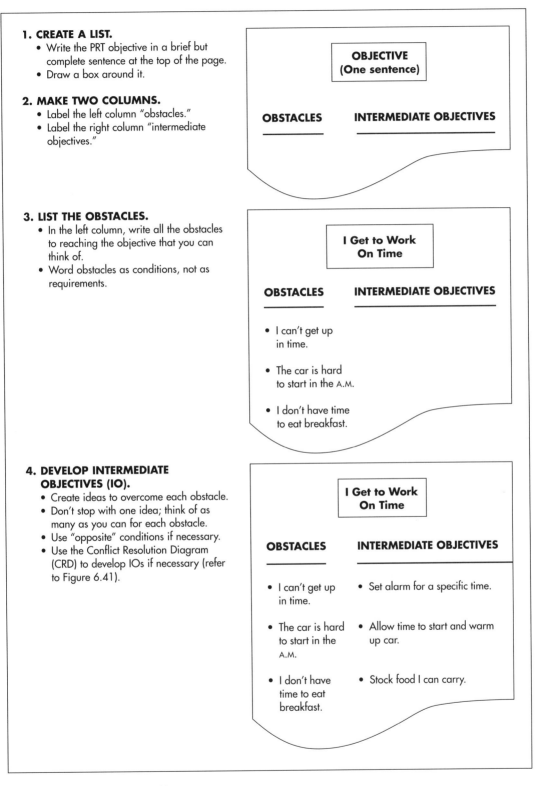

1. CREATE A LIST.
- Write the PRT objective in a brief but complete sentence at the top of the page.
- Draw a box around it.

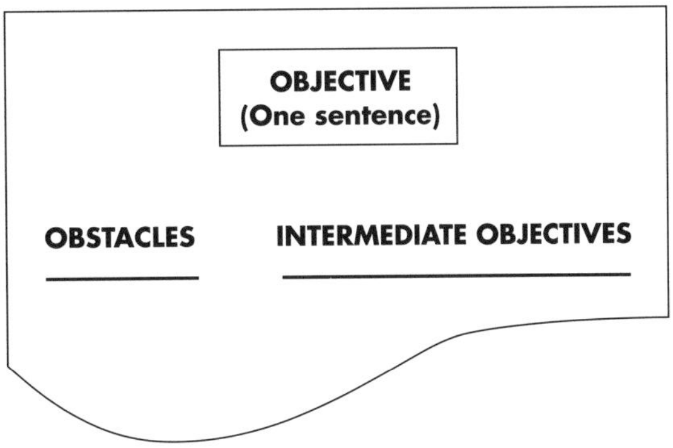
OBJECTIVE
(One sentence)
OBSTACLES
INTERMEDIATE OBJECTIVES

2. MAKE TWO COLUMNS.
- Label the left column "obstacles."
- Label the right column "intermediate objectives."

3. LIST THE OBSTACLES.
- In the left column, write all the obstacles to reaching the objective that you can think of.
- Word obstacles as conditions, not as requirements.

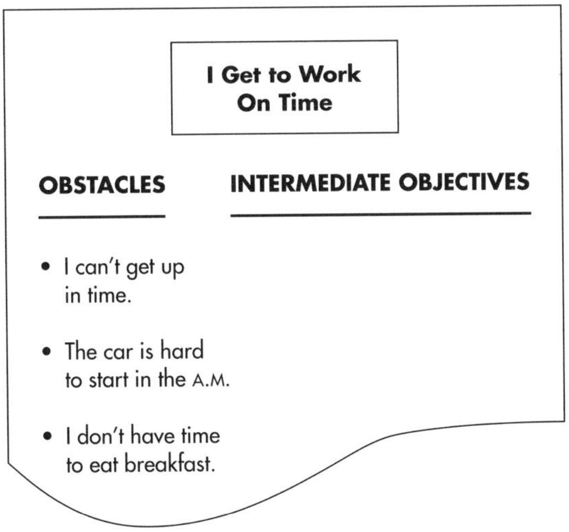
I Get to Work
On Time
OBSTACLES
INTERMEDIATE OBJECTIVES
• I can't get up in time.
• The car is hard to start in the A.M.
• I don't have time to eat breakfast.

4. DEVELOP INTERMEDIATE OBJECTIVES (IO).
- Create ideas to overcome each obstacle.
- Don't stop with one idea; think of as many as you can for each obstacle.
- Use "opposite" conditions if necessary.
- Use the Conflict Resolution Diagram (CRD) to develop IOs if necessary (refer to Figure 6.41).

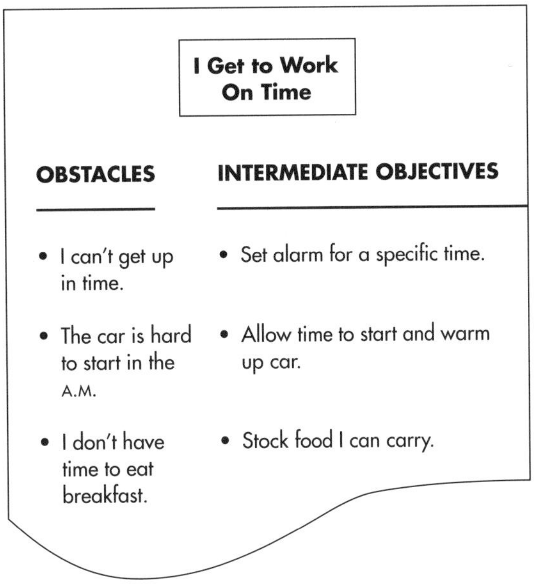
I Get to Work
On Time
OBSTACLES
INTERMEDIATE OBJECTIVES
• I can't get up in time.
• Set alarm for a specific time.
• The car is hard to start in the A.M.
• Allow time to start and warm up car.
• I don't have time to eat breakfast.
• Stock food I can carry.

FIGURE 6.39. Procedures for Building a Prerequisite Tree.

5. REFINE THE COMPLETED LIST.

- Select the easiest or least expensive IO among several choices.
- Identify any obstacles requiring two IOs to overcome.
- Look for hidden obstacles if you think three or more IOs are required.
- Minimize the number of IOs worded as "opposite" conditions; use CRD if necessary (refer to Figure 6.41).

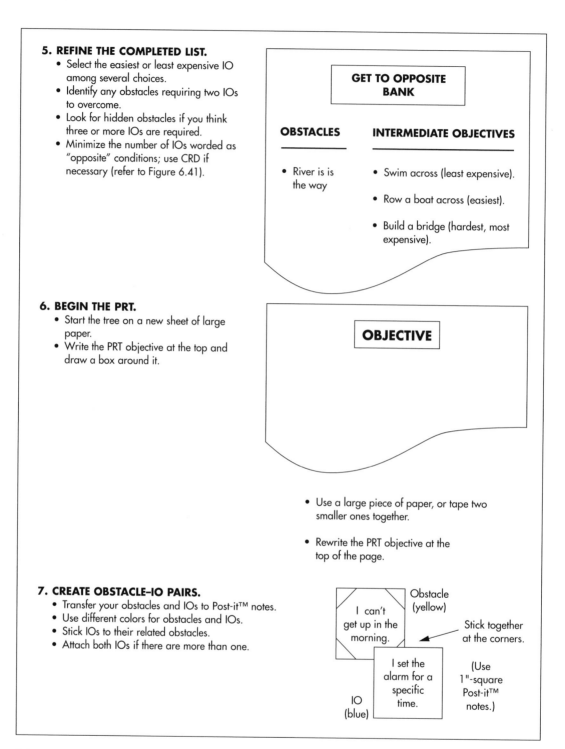

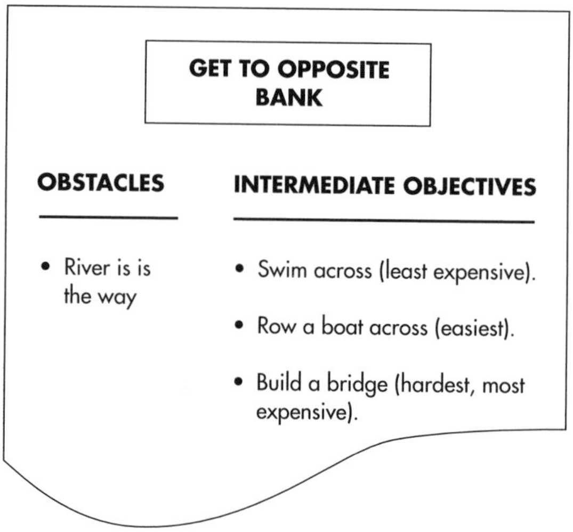
GET TO OPPOSITE BANK
OBSTACLES
INTERMEDIATE OBJECTIVES
• River is is the way
• Swim across (least expensive).
• Row a boat across (easiest).
• Build a bridge (hardest, most expensive).

6. BEGIN THE PRT.

- Start the tree on a new sheet of large paper.
- Write the PRT objective at the top and draw a box around it.

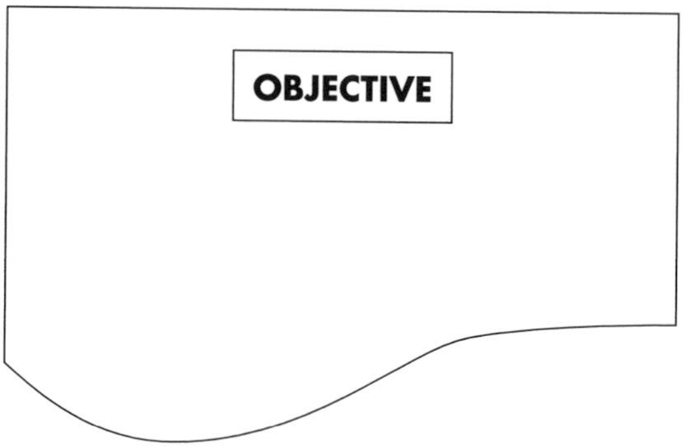
OBJECTIVE

- Use a large piece of paper, or tape two smaller ones together.
- Rewrite the PRT objective at the top of the page.

7. CREATE OBSTACLE–IO PAIRS.

- Transfer your obstacles and IOs to Post-it™ notes.
- Use different colors for obstacles and IOs.
- Stick IOs to their related obstacles.
- Attach both IOs if there are more than one.

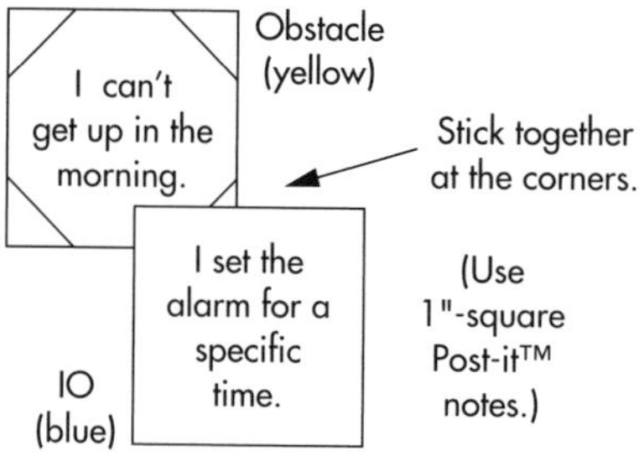
I can't get up in the morning.
Obstacle (yellow)
Stick together at the corners.
I set the alarm for a specific time.
IO (blue)
(Use 1"-square Post-it™ notes.)

FIGURE 6.39—*Continued.*

8. ARRAY THE OBSTACLE–IO PAIRS.

- Arrange obstacle–IO pairs horizontally below the PRT objective.
- Lay them out in random order.
- Use two rows if necessary.

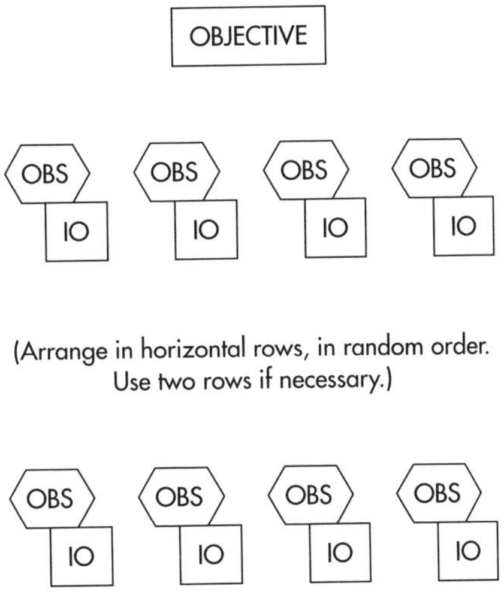

9. TIME-SEQUENCE THE OBSTACLE–IO PAIRS.

- Place "later" pairs near the top, "earlier" pairs near the bottom.
- Focus on sequencing the IOs, rather than the obstacles (i.e., in what order must the IOs be completed?).
- Look for obvious "vertical" connections; align them and connect with dotted lines.
- Look for opportunities to consolidate vertical groupings in fewer "branches."

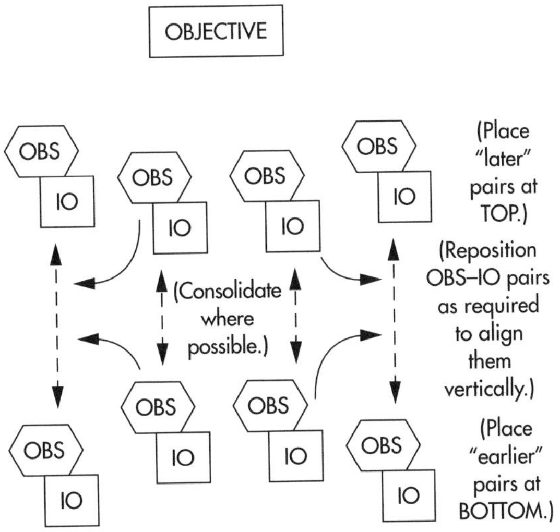

FIGURE 6.39—*Continued.*

10. FILL IN GAPS.
- Examine each branch for logical progression, from bottom (earlier) to top (later).
- Fill in logical gaps by developing more obstacle–IO pairs.

11. REMOVE DOTTED LINES.
- Scrutinize all proposed connections. (Use the obstacle–IO validity test in Figure 6.43.)
- Replace dotted lines with solid lines when the progression is complete, "seamless," and logically sound.

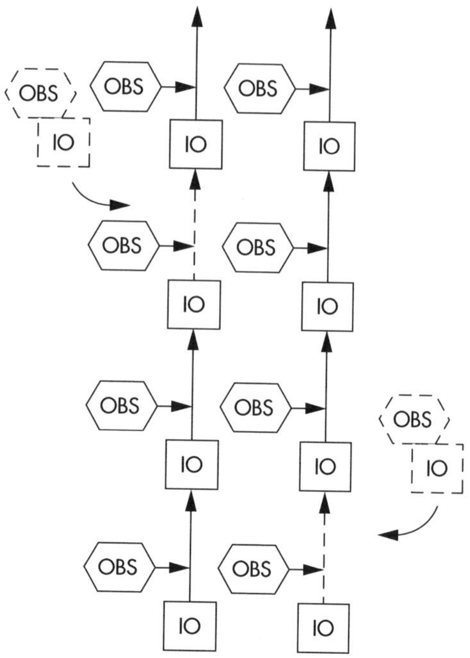

12. LOOK FOR HORIZONTAL CONNECTIONS.
- Search for possible network-type connections between the straight-line vertical branches.
- Connect obstacles and IOs in one branch to obstacles and IOs in another branch, if appropriate.
- Rearrange branches as required to reduce visual confusion after making horizontal connections.

13. MAKE FINAL CONNECTIONS.
- Link the uppermost IOs to the PRT's objective.
- Add/insert obstacle–IO pairs if a logical link to the objective is missing.

14. REVIEW THE MODIFIED TREE.
- Scrutinize: Top to bottom, or bottom to top. (Refer to "Scrutinizing a Prerequisite Tree," p. 259, and "Scrutinizing a PRT: The Obstacle–IO Validity Test," Figure 6.43.)
- Do all obstacles really block the objective/higher IO?
- Do all lower IOs really overcome the obstacle above them?
- Are there as many actions as possible in IOs near the bottom of the tree?

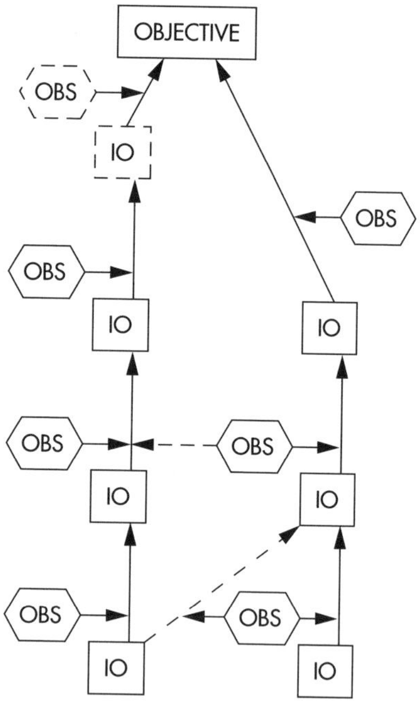

FIGURE 6.39—*Continued.*

Procedure	**Verbalize**	**Depiction**
1. State the objective, injection, or uppermost intermediate objective.	"I want A."	
2. State the first obstacle you can think of.	"One of the first (next) obstacles is C."	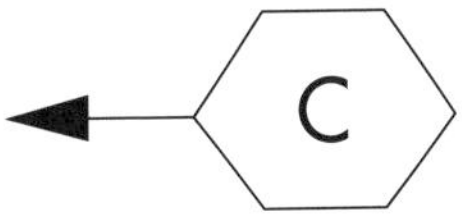
3. State the IO necessary to overcome the obstacle.	"If I have B, then C no longer blocks me from A."	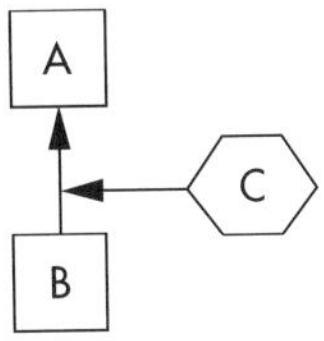
4. Repeat the process until all obstacles to A have been identified and the IOs to overcome them.	"What else keeps me from realizing A? What do I need to do to overcome it?"	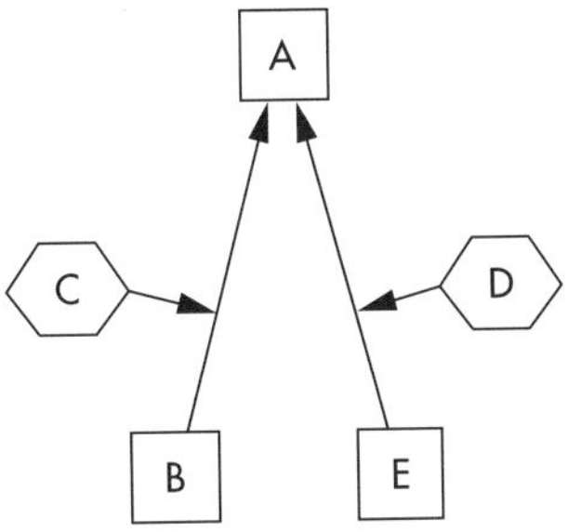
5. Repeat steps 1–4 for each IO (B, E, etc.). Continue DOWN through the hierarchy until there are no more obstacles.	"I want [B, E, etc] . . ."	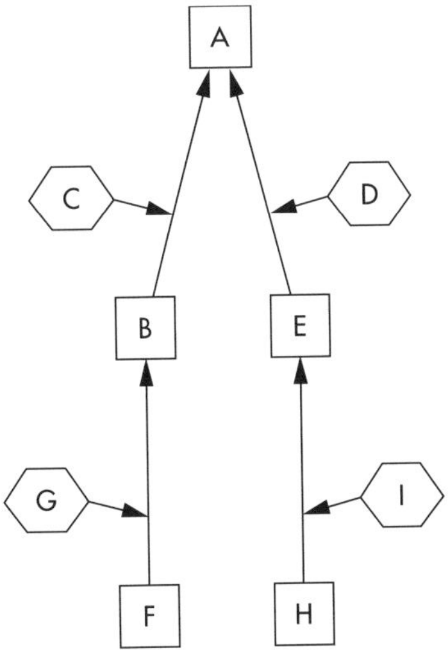

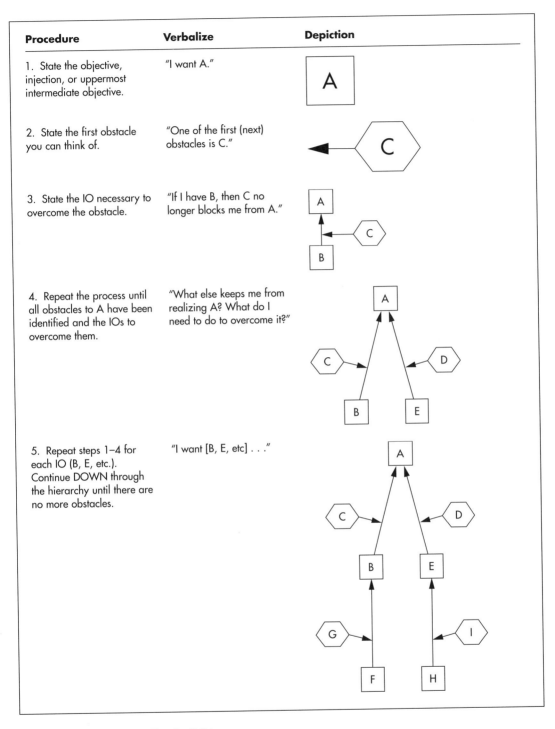

FIGURE 6.40. Constructing Obstacle–IO Pairs.

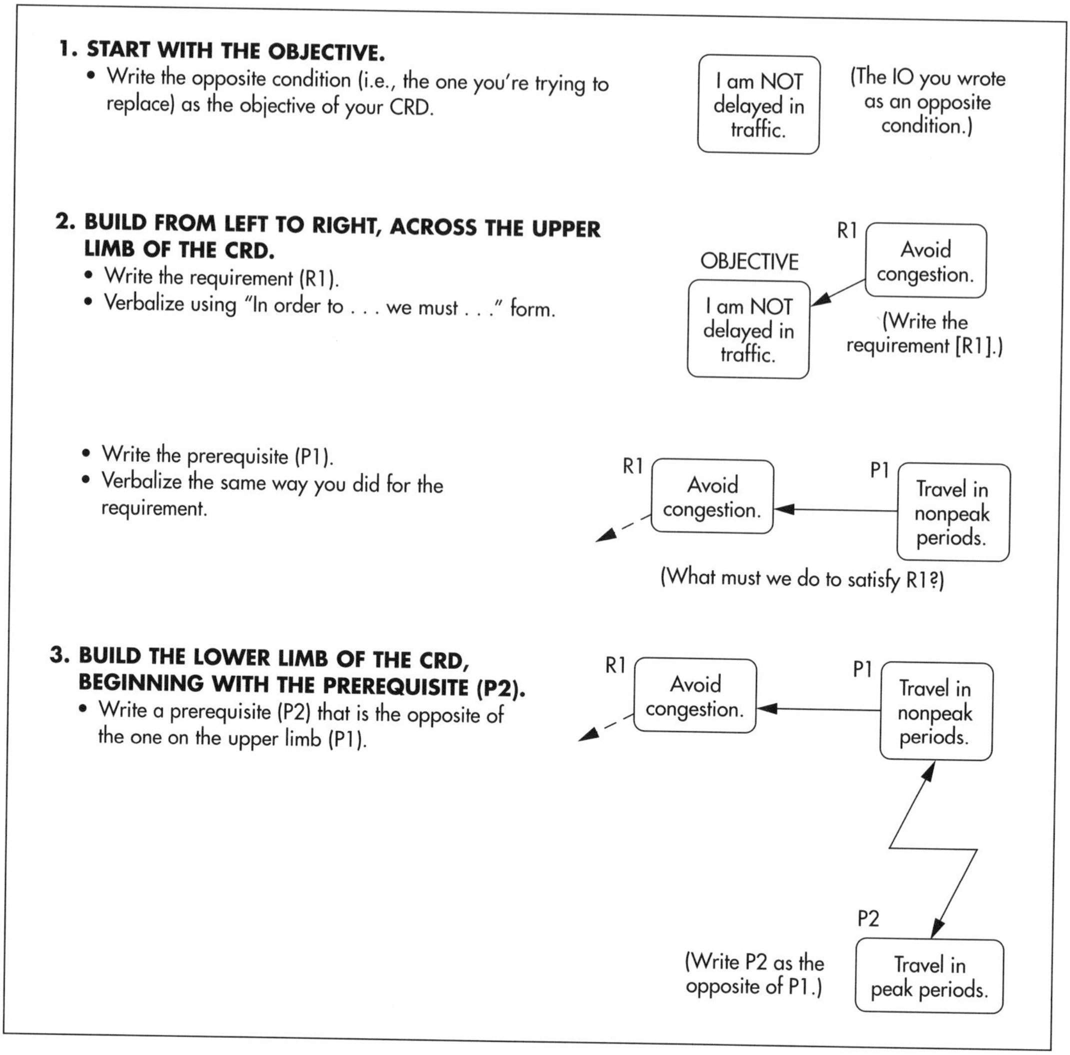
1. START WITH THE OBJECTIVE.
• Write the opposite condition (i.e., the one you're trying to replace) as the objective of your CRD.
I am NOT delayed in traffic.
(The IO you wrote as an opposite condition.)
2. BUILD FROM LEFT TO RIGHT, ACROSS THE UPPER LIMB OF THE CRD.
• Write the requirement (R1).
• Verbalize using "In order to . . . we must . . ." form.
OBJECTIVE
I am NOT delayed in traffic.
R1
Avoid congestion.
(Write the requirement [R1].)
• Write the prerequisite (P1).
• Verbalize the same way you did for the requirement.
R1
Avoid congestion.
P1
Travel in nonpeak periods.
(What must we do to satisfy R1?)
3. BUILD THE LOWER LIMB OF THE CRD, BEGINNING WITH THE PREREQUISITE (P2).
• Write a prerequisite (P2) that is the opposite of the one on the upper limb (P1).
R1
Avoid congestion.
P1
Travel in nonpeak periods.
P2
Travel in peak periods.
(Write P2 as the opposite of P1.)

FIGURE 6.41. Using a Conflict Resolution Diagram to Create Specific IOs.

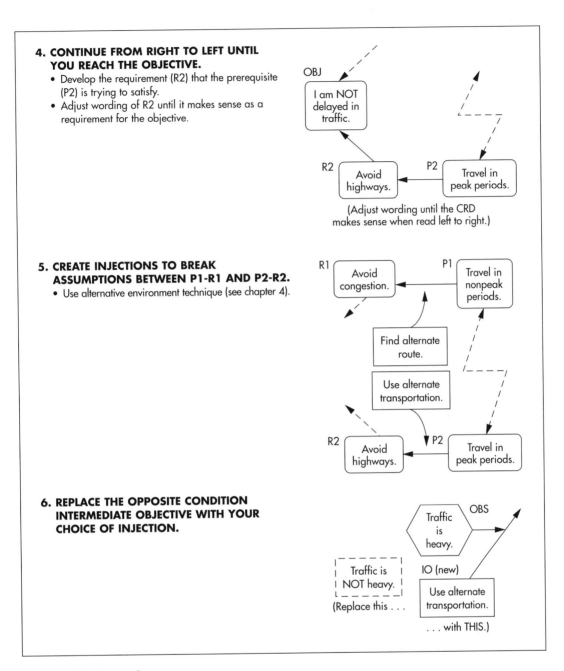

4. CONTINUE FROM RIGHT TO LEFT UNTIL YOU REACH THE OBJECTIVE.

- Develop the requirement (R2) that the prerequisite (P2) is trying to satisfy.
- Adjust wording of R2 until it makes sense as a requirement for the objective.

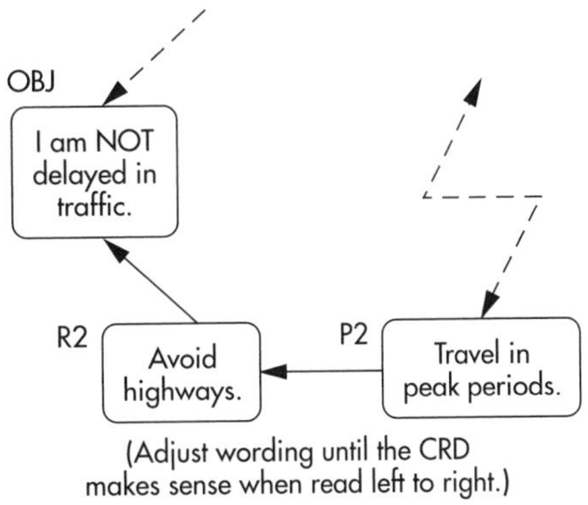
OBJ
I am NOT delayed in traffic.
R2
Avoid highways.
P2
Travel in peak periods.
(Adjust wording until the CRD makes sense when read left to right.)

5. CREATE INJECTIONS TO BREAK ASSUMPTIONS BETWEEN P1-R1 AND P2-R2.

- Use alternative environment technique (see chapter 4).

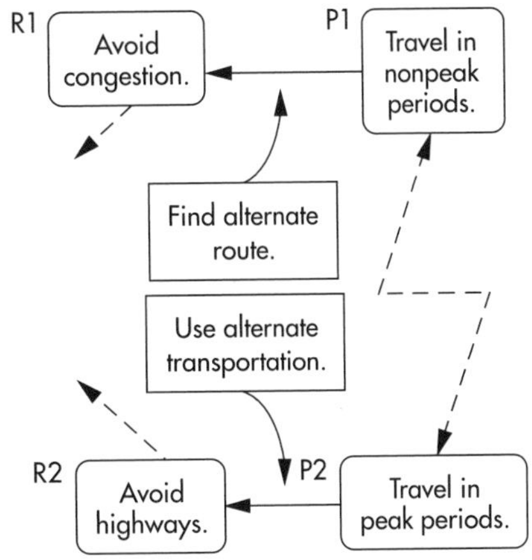
R1
Avoid congestion.
P1
Travel in nonpeak periods.
Find alternate route.
Use alternate transportation.
R2
Avoid highways.
P2
Travel in peak periods.

6. REPLACE THE OPPOSITE CONDITION INTERMEDIATE OBJECTIVE WITH YOUR CHOICE OF INJECTION.

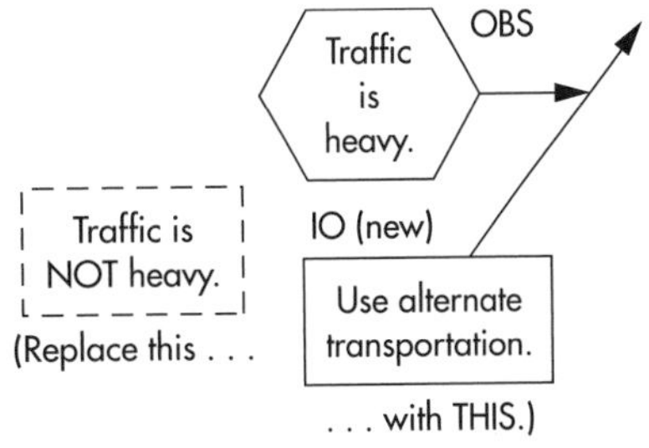
Traffic is heavy.
OBS
Traffic is NOT heavy.
(Replace this . . .
IO (new)
Use alternate transportation.
. . . with THIS.)

FIGURE 6.41—*Continued.*

1. **WRITE THE PRT'S OBJECTIVE.**
   - Write it as the condition you want to achieve.
   - Write it in a complete sentence.

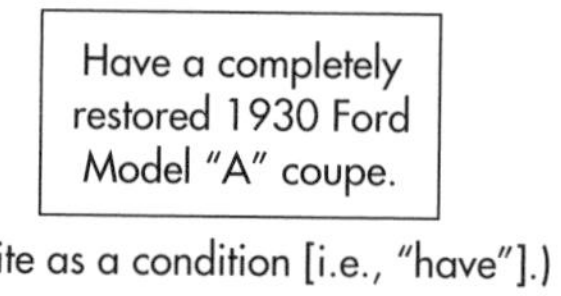
Have a completely restored 1930 Ford Model "A" coupe.
(Write as a condition [i.e., "have"].)

2. **IDENTIFY THE FIRST LEVEL OF OBSTACLES (OBS).**
   - What's the first, most immediate thing that stands in the way of your objective?
   - Ask: "Why can't we have the objective?"
   - What's another immediate obstacle to your objective?
   - Continue until all first-level obstacles are identified.
   - Review the objective and all obstacles until you are sure you've identified all obstacles.
   - You must be able to say: "If we overcome these, there's nothing else to prevent us from having the objective."

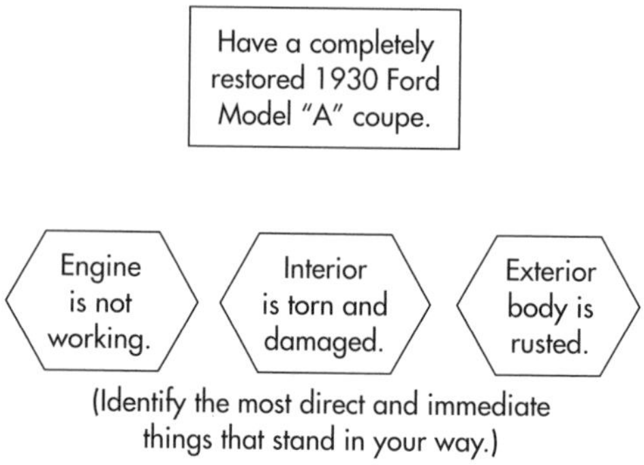
Have a completely restored 1930 Ford Model "A" coupe.
Engine is not working.
Interior is torn and damaged.
Exterior body is rusted.
(Identify the most direct and immediate things that stand in your way.)

3. **DETERMINE THE FIRST-LEVEL INTERMEDIATE OBJECTIVES (IO).**
   - Take each first-level OBS in sequence.
   - Ask: "What condition (or action) must be created to overcome (not necessarily eliminate) the OBS?"
   - Or, ask: "What do we need to beat the OBS?"
   - Does the OBS require more than one IO?
   - Can the same IO overcome more than one OBS?
   - Repeat for each first-level OBS, until all OBS have IOs sufficient to overcome them.

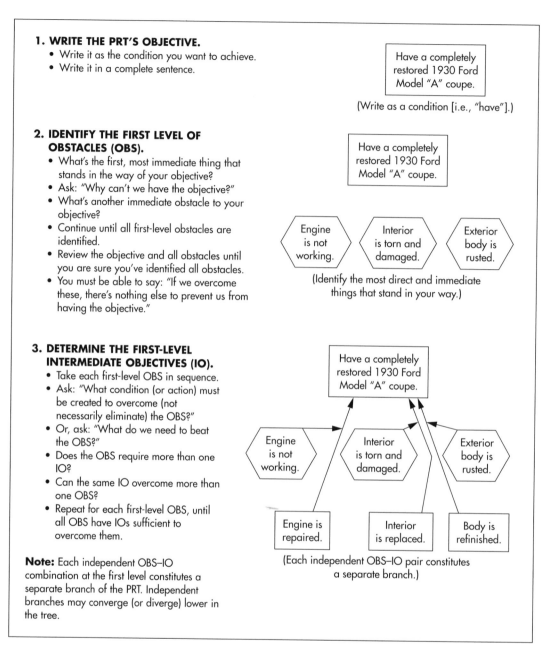

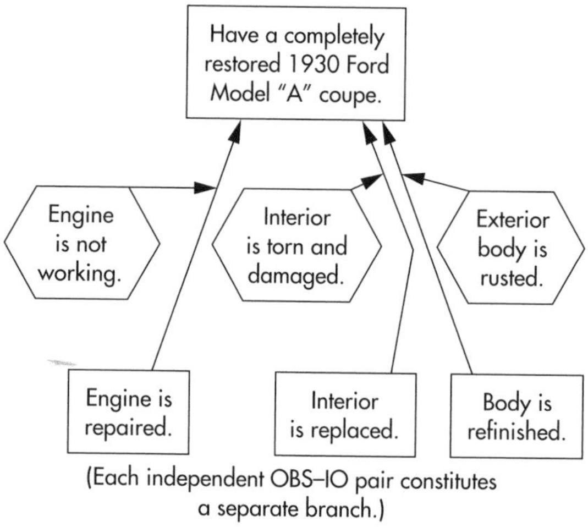
Have a completely restored 1930 Ford Model "A" coupe.
Engine is not working.
Interior is torn and damaged.
Exterior body is rusted.
Engine is repaired.
Interior is replaced.
Body is refinished.
(Each independent OBS–IO pair constitutes a separate branch.)

Note: Each independent OBS–IO combination at the first level constitutes a separate branch of the PRT. Independent branches may converge (or diverge) lower in the tree.

FIGURE 6.42. Alternative Procedures for Building a Prerequisite Tree.

4. SCRUTINIZE EACH CONNECTION CAREFULLY *AS YOU MAKE IT.*

- Does the OBS really prevent you from achieving the OBJ/IO above it?
- Will the IO(s) really be enough to overcome the OBS?

Note: Refer to "Scrutinizing a Prerequisite Tree," p. 259, for a review on how to scrutinize a PRT.

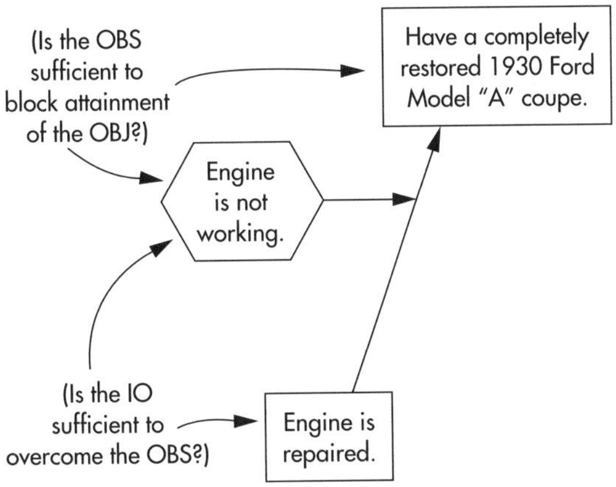
(Is the OBS sufficient to block attainment of the OBJ?)
Have a completely restored 1930 Ford Model "A" coupe.
Engine is not working.
(Is the IO sufficient to overcome the OBS?)
Engine is repaired.

5. REPEAT STEPS 2, 3, AND 4 FOR EACH SUCCESSIVE LEVEL OF OBSTACLE(S) AND INTERMEDIATE OBJECTIVE(S).

- Continue building downward.
- Look for opportunities to cross-link, i.e.:
  - One OBS obstructs IO in more than one branch.
  - One IO overcomes OBS in more than one branch.

Note: If you think you need more than two IOs to overcome a given OBS, look carefully to see if you have overlooked a hidden OBS and its associated IO.

- With each successive level, look for opportunities to employ specific actions, rather than conditions, as IOs.

Note: IOs nearer the top of the tree (closer to the objective) are more likely to be conditions. Toward the bottom of the tree, more IOs should be specific actions.

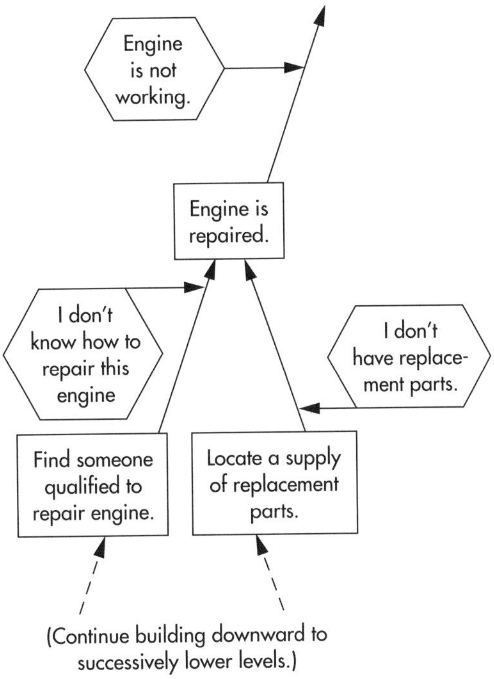
Engine is not working.
Engine is repaired.
I don't know how to repair this engine
I don't have replacement parts.
Find someone qualified to repair engine.
Locate a supply of replacement parts.
(Continue building downward to successively lower levels.)

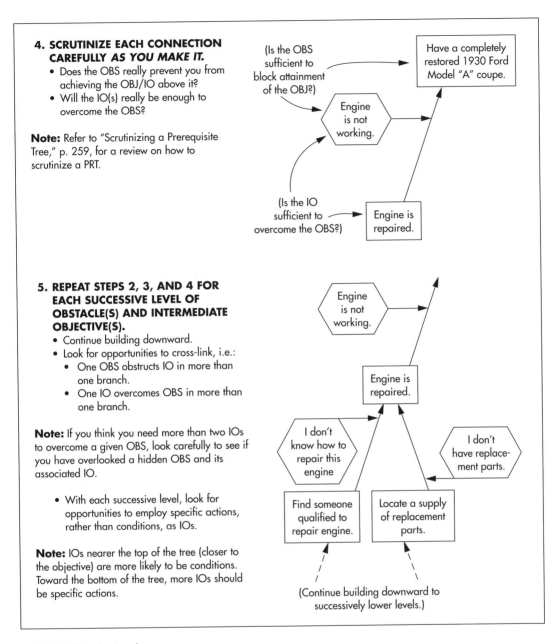

FIGURE 6.42—*Continued.*

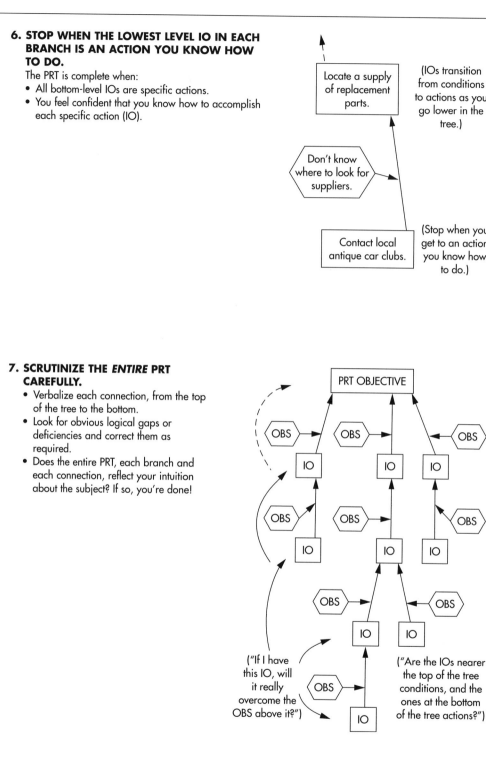

6. STOP WHEN THE LOWEST LEVEL IO IN EACH BRANCH IS AN ACTION YOU KNOW HOW TO DO.

The PRT is complete when:

- All bottom-level IOs are specific actions.
- You feel confident that you know how to accomplish each specific action (IO).

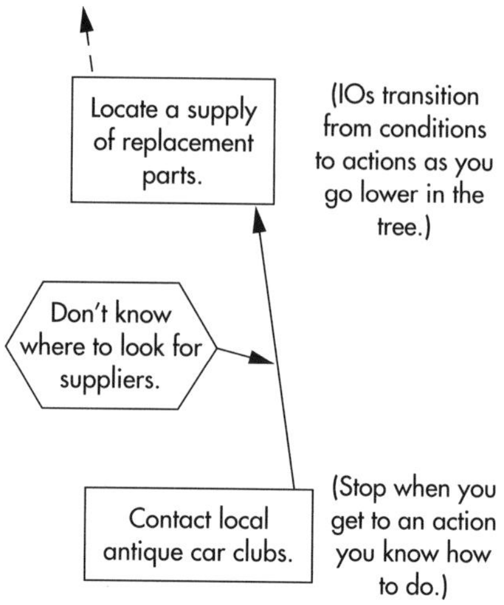
Locate a supply of replacement parts.
(IOs transition from conditions to actions as you go lower in the tree.)
Don't know where to look for suppliers.
Contact local antique car clubs.
(Stop when you get to an action you know how to do.)

7. SCRUTINIZE THE *ENTIRE* PRT CAREFULLY.

- Verbalize each connection, from the top of the tree to the bottom.
- Look for obvious logical gaps or deficiencies and correct them as required.
- Does the entire PRT, each branch and each connection, reflect your intuition about the subject? If so, you're done!

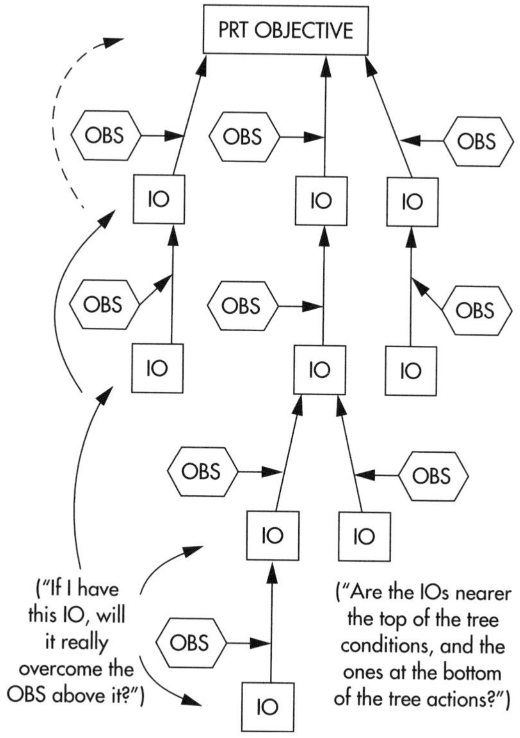
PRT OBJECTIVE
OBS
IO
("If I have this IO, will it really overcome the OBS above it?")
("Are the IOs nearer the top of the tree conditions, and the ones at the bottom of the tree actions?")

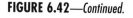

FIGURE 6.42—*Continued.*

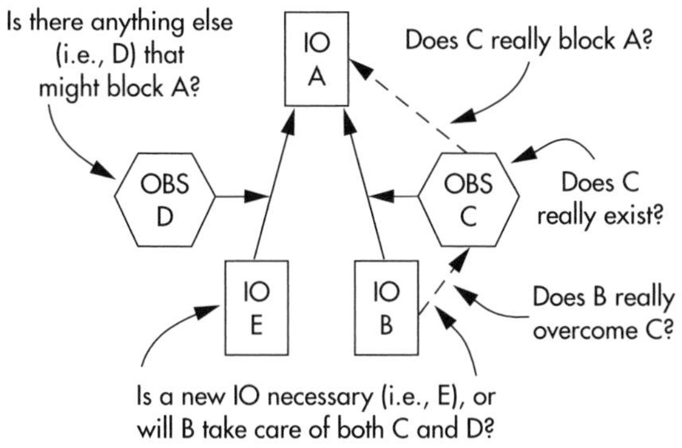

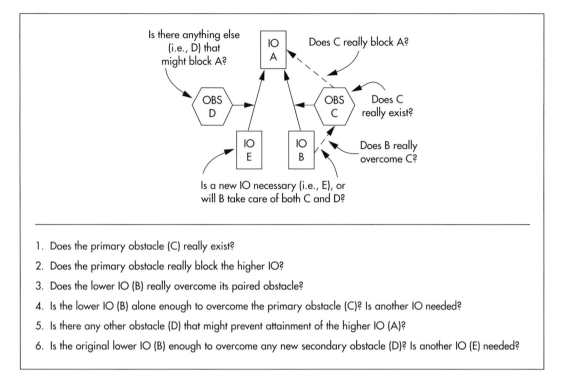

1. Does the primary obstacle (C) really exist?
2. Does the primary obstacle really block the higher IO?
3. Does the lower IO (B) really overcome its paired obstacle?
4. Is the lower IO (B) alone enough to overcome the primary obstacle (C)? Is another IO needed?
5. Is there any other obstacle (D) that might prevent attainment of the higher IO (A)?
6. Is the original lower IO (B) enough to overcome any new secondary obstacle (D)? Is another IO (E) needed?

FIGURE 6.43. Scrutinizing a Prerequisite Tree: The Obstacle–IO Validity Test.

Chapter 7
TRANSITION TREE

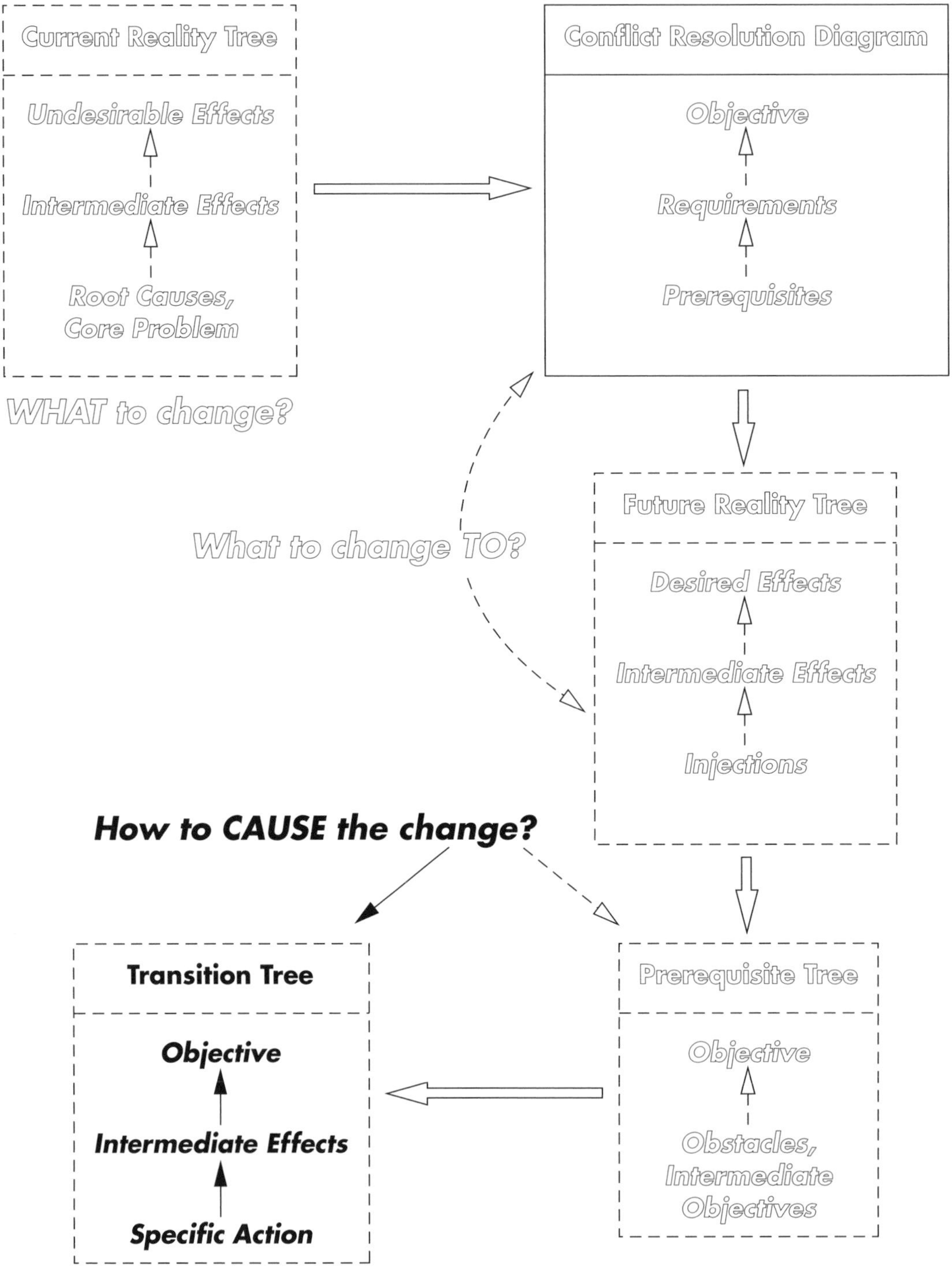

Chapter Outline

An ounce of application is worth a ton of abstraction.
—Booker's Law

The final stage of the Theory of Constraints Thinking Process is the Transition Tree (TT). It permits us to build a cause-effect relationship that will lead from each specific implementation step to a direct and unavoidable outcome. As we add successive actions, we'll come closer to our objective, until the final action delivers it to us.

What the Transition Tree gives us that the Prerequisite Tree doesn't is sufficiency. The Prerequisite Tree told us only what obstacles stood in our way and how to overcome them. With the Transition Tree, for the first time in the implementation stage, we find out whether the actions we plan to take are sufficient to move us progressively toward our objective. If not, we'll see immediately where we need to take additional action and what that action should be.

DEFINITION

A Transition Tree is a cause-and-effect logic tree designed to provide step-by-step progress from initiation through completion of a course of action or change. It's an implementation tool, combining specific actions with existing

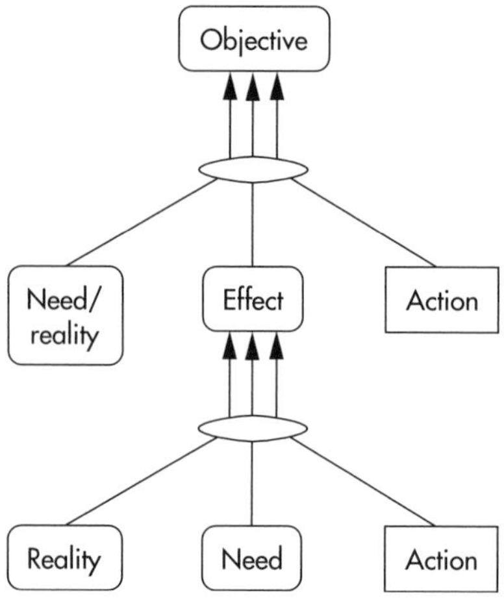

FIGURE 7.1. The Transition Tree.

reality to produce new expected effects (see Figure 7.1). The Transition Tree is an "additive" process, combining each successive expected effect with subsequent specific actions to produce new effects. The objective of a Transition Tree is usually limited in scope.

PURPOSE

The Transition Tree serves nine basic purposes.

- Provide a step-by-step method for action/implementation.
- Enable effective "navigation" through a change process.
- Detect deviation in progress toward a limited objective.
- Adapt or redirect effort, should plans change.
- Communicate the reasons for action to others.
- Execute the injections developed in a Conflict Resolution Diagram or Future Reality Tree.
- Attain the intermediate objectives identified in a Prerequisite Tree.
- Develop tactical action plans from conceptual or strategic plans.
- Preclude undesirable effects (UDE) from arising out of implementation action.

ASSUMPTIONS

The effectiveness of the Transition Tree is based on the following assumptions.

- A definite chain of cause-and-effect governs the functioning of all systems.
- Cause-and-effect logic applies equally effectively to the future as it does to the present or past.

- Any action initiated by someone to execute a decision will have new effects (not currently existing).
- New effects represent change.
- Change has both intended and unintended effects.
- All effects, intended and unintended, will be either beneficial, neutral, or detrimental.
- It is possible to anticipate the unintended effects of change.
- Detrimental effects can be anticipated, located, and prevented before they happen.
- Some changes can cause more problems than they solve.
- The ultimate objective of any action may be several steps removed from the original action.
- Several actions, in sequence, may be required to achieve a desired effect.
- Ideas do not become solutions until they have been validated as effective and implemented.
- Cause and effect is governed by the Categories of Legitimate Reservation (CLR) and is verifiable through the CLR.
- Unstated assumptions about reality underlie all cause-and-effect relationships.

HOW TO USE THIS CHAPTER

- Read "Description of the Transition Tree," p. 286. This section describes what a Transition Tree is and how it works.
- Read "How to Build a Transition Tree," p. 297, and the associated examples. This section explains in detail each of the steps in building a Transition Tree and why they're necessary.
- Read "Scrutinizing a Transition Tree," p. 306. This section tells how to ensure that your Transition Tree is logically sound and accurately depicts each sequential step you must take in making a change.
- Review Figures 7.29 and 7.30, examples of Transition Trees. The first of two examples is a complete four-element Transition Tree on how to achieve one major change (injection) from the Future Reality Tree "How Organizations Can Succeed at Total Quality" (Figure 5.35). It shows in a typical real-world example how complex conditions of future reality can be realized in a step-by-step way.
- Review Figures 7.31 and 7.32, procedures for building a TT. These are abbreviated checklists you can use to guide you in constructing your own Transition Tree. Figure 7.31 addresses four-element trees, and Figure 7.32, five-element trees. The checklist contains brief instructions and illustrations for each step. Detailed explanations for each step in the checklist are provided in the chapter itself, under "How to Build a Transition Tree," p. 297.
- For your convenience, blank five-element Transition Tree worksheets are provided in Figure 7.34. For situations that call for a five-element format, you may reproduce or reconstruct these forms for use in building your own Transition Trees.
- Practice with the "Transition Tree Exercise" provided in Appendix G.

DESCRIPTION OF THE TRANSITION TREE

The Transition Tree is an "action" tool. Through a sequence of cause-and-effect logic, it permits you to map every detailed step between your current status and your objective. For example, if you're unemployed and your objective is to secure a job, the Transition Tree can help you create a step-by-step action plan to follow through the entire process.

The Transition Tree and the Future Reality Tree

There are similarities between the Transition Tree and the Future Reality Tree. For example, the rules of logic are essentially the same for the Transition Tree as for the FRT. In fact, the Transition Tree might be considered a specialized variety of FRT.

Both deal with realities that don't yet exist. Both require *you* to make some change in the status quo. Both start with existing reality, add changes that you initiate, and produce expected effects. Both are based on sufficiency, rather than necessity, rules of logic. (Refer to chapter 4, "Conflict Resolution Diagram," for an explanation of the differences between sufficiency-based and necessity-based logic trees.) Both can have negative branches and positive reinforcing loops, and both take you from where you are to where you want to be.

It begins to sound as if there's no difference between Transition Trees and Future Reality Trees. Actually, there are two significant, related distinctions: purpose and level of detail.

Purpose

If you recall from chapter 5, the Future Reality Tree is designed to "bench test" a proposed course of action—to determine (a) whether it will actually produce the ultimate desired effect, and (b) whether (and where) it will produce undesirable side effects. But the purpose of the Transition Tree is

- Implementation of action: It deals with how to do something you've already decided to do, rather than determining whether it's the right thing to do.
- Providing step-by-step guidance.
- Showing time-sequenced order.

Level of Detail

As a consequence of its purpose—action—the Transition Tree ends up being much more detailed than a Future Reality Tree. In a Future Reality Tree you may summarize a complex action, reality, or effect in a single entity (enclosed block). In the Transition Tree, however, you need much more detail—specific, sequential actions you must take to proceed toward your eventual goal.

Look at Figures 7.2 and 7.3.* The Future Reality Tree and Transition Tree deal with the same subject: finding a job. But on close examination, you can see that the Future Reality Tree is more like "concept testing," while the Transition Tree

*The author is indebted to Jennifer Nikcevic for the use of her Future Reality and Transition Trees in Figures 7.2, 7.3, and 7.30.

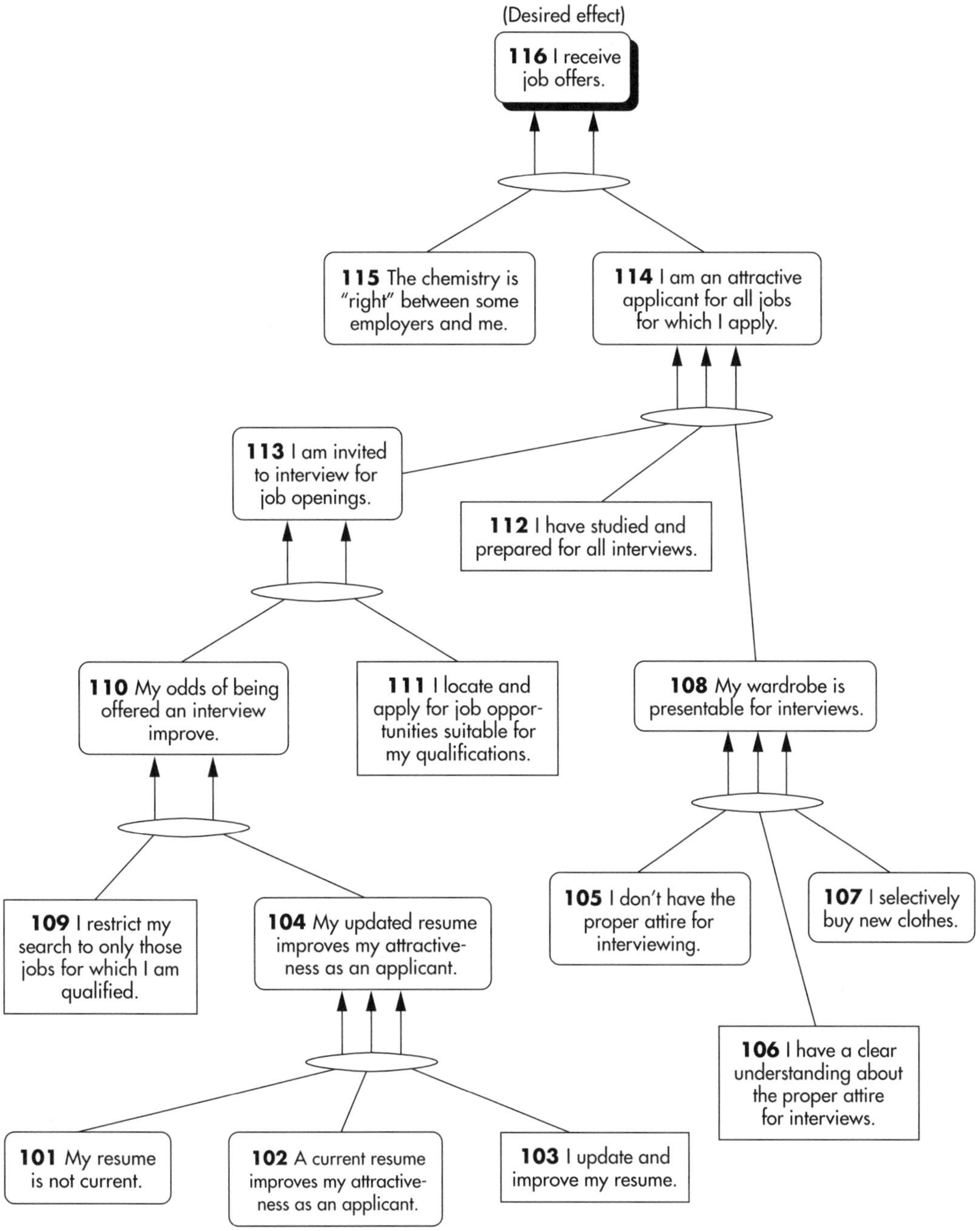
(Desired effect)
116 I receive job offers.
115 The chemistry is "right" between some employers and me.
114 I am an attractive applicant for all jobs for which I apply.
113 I am invited to interview for job openings.
112 I have studied and prepared for all interviews.
110 My odds of being offered an interview improve.
111 I locate and apply for job opportunities suitable for my qualifications.
108 My wardrobe is presentable for interviews.
105 I don't have the proper attire for interviewing.
107 I selectively buy new clothes.
109 I restrict my search to only those jobs for which I am qualified.
104 My updated resume improves my attractiveness as an applicant.
106 I have a clear understanding about the proper attire for interviews.
101 My resume is not current.
102 A current resume improves my attractiveness as an applicant.
103 I update and improve my resume.

- The Future Reality Tree is less detailed, tests effectiveness of overall strategy.
- The FRT identifies major *conditions*, not yet existing, that are necessary to realize the objective.

FIGURE 7.2. Jennifer's Future Reality Tree: "Finding a Job."

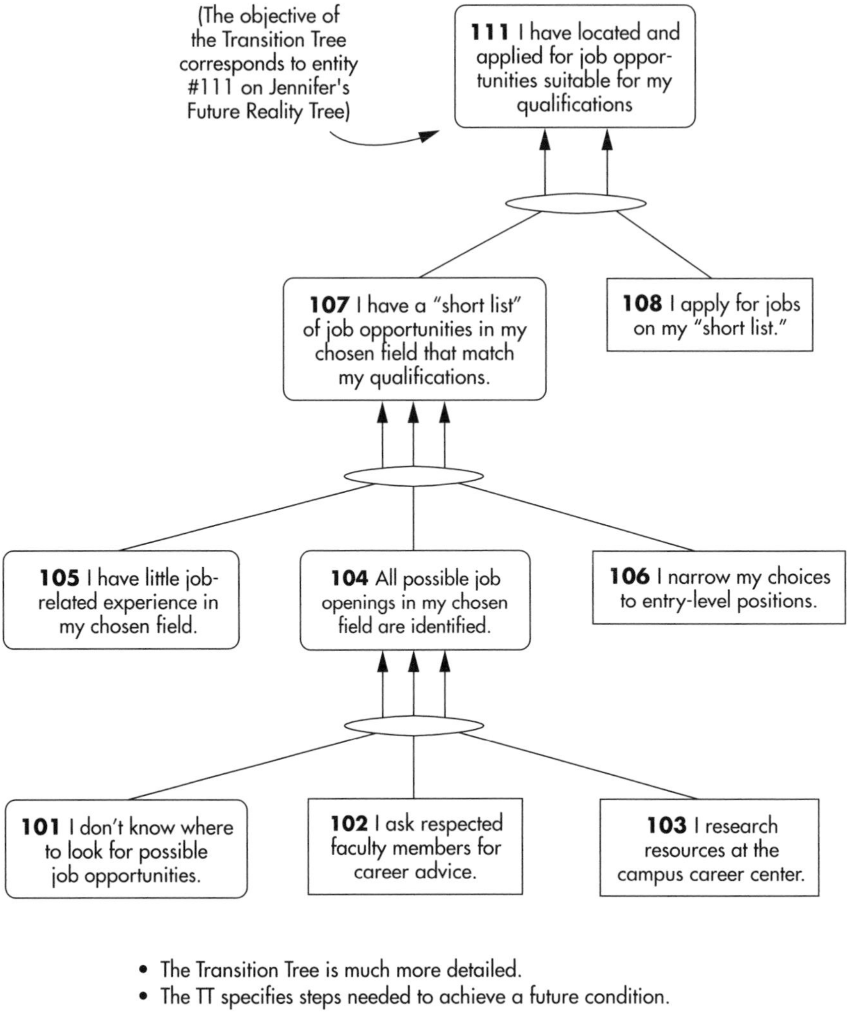
(The objective of the Transition Tree corresponds to entity #111 on Jennifer's Future Reality Tree)
111 I have located and applied for job opportunities suitable for my qualifications
107 I have a "short list" of job opportunities in my chosen field that match my qualifications.
108 I apply for jobs on my "short list."
105 I have little job-related experience in my chosen field.
104 All possible job openings in my chosen field are identified.
106 I narrow my choices to entry-level positions.
101 I don't know where to look for possible job opportunities.
102 I ask respected faculty members for career advice.
103 I research resources at the campus career center.
• The Transition Tree is much more detailed.
• The TT specifies steps needed to achieve a future condition.

FIGURE 7.3. Jennifer's Transition Tree: "Locating Job Opportunities."

is more like "project planning." In fact, that's a good analogy, because a TT can be a potentially valuable project planning tool.

The Transition Tree and the Prerequisite Tree

There is also a significant shared characteristic between the Transition Tree and the Prerequisite Tree. The Transition Tree is sensitive to time sequence, just as the Prerequisite Tree is. It ensures that the "horse precedes the cart" for each stage of action; it will help make certain that you open the door before trying to pass through it. As such, it can be a valuable aid for building procedural tasks or checklists.

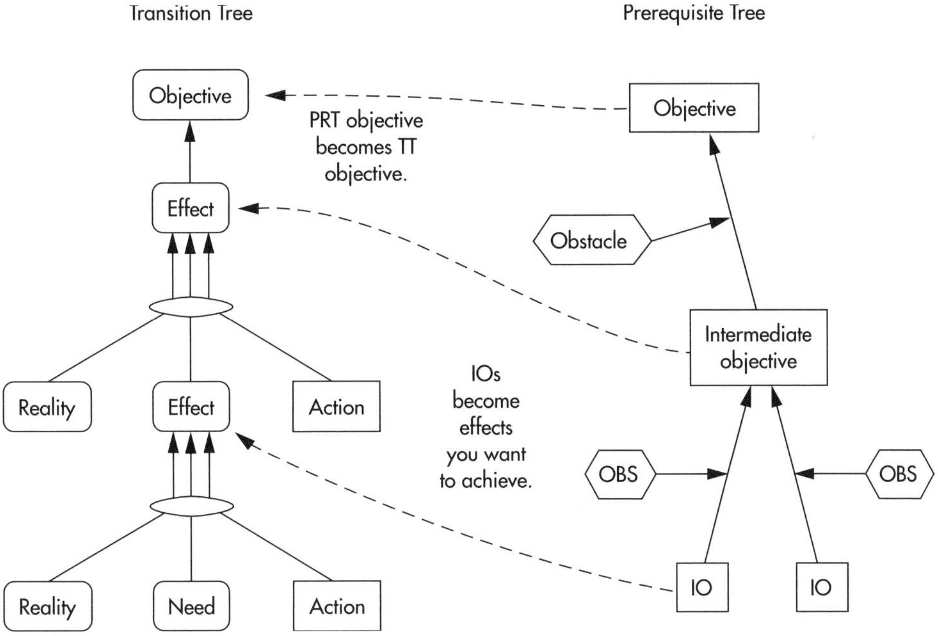

FIGURE 7.4. The Prerequisite Tree as a Basis for a Transition Tree.

In some situations, a Prerequisite Tree provides the basis for building a Transition Tree, although it isn't necessary in all cases (see Figure 7.4). Since a Prerequisite Tree identifies the necessary conditions for achieving an objective (and time-sequences them), these conditions (the intermediate objectives in the Prerequisite Tree), when transferred to the Transition Tree, become the expected effects of the specific actions you initiate. The TT details the specific step-by-step actions and outcomes needed to achieve these necessary conditions.

Consequently, the Prerequisite Tree functions much like a PERT (Program Evaluation and Review Technique) chart in project management, while the Transition Tree serves almost as a checklist for project completion. Clearly, these two tools together offer great potential for improving the planning and management of projects.

Applications for a Transition Tree

Since a Transition Tree is designed to convert concept into action, the possible applications for it are almost unlimited. Generally, however, they'll fall into two broad categories: (1) limited, task-oriented jobs that you might do each day, and (2) conversion of complex plans or ideas into action.

Task-Oriented Applications

Let's say your boss has given you the job of arranging a conference among people from both your own workplace and out of town. You may have to schedule, produce, or coordinate a conference facility, audiovisual equipment, an agenda, conference materials, guest speakers, hotel accommodations, meals, local transportation, message or phone service, or any of a number of other details. How do you tackle all this and make sure you haven't forgotten anything important? (See Figure 7.5.)

Here's another possible use. Let's say your company has a complex procedure for which there aren't any written instructions. You haven't needed any in the past, because you have an experienced employee who's done it for 30 years, who knows exactly what to do, when, and how. You've never had to worry about it before—until now. Your 30-year veteran just retired, to be replaced by a newly minted high school graduate who says, "Show me what to do—and I'll do it!" But you're not even sure what to do yourself.

Or perhaps you're faced with finding a job, and you don't know what to do first. Do you call friends, create a resume, send out letters, or answer newspaper ads? Or do you first decide what kind of career you'd like to pursue? Obviously, you might do any or all of these, but in what order for best effect? (See Figure 7.6.)

All of these situations are prime candidates for a Transition Tree. The conference is a one-time project for which there may not be recurring requirements. The second, formulating a procedure, might require construction of a step-by-step checklist, complete with conditional paths (such as, "If A happens, do X; if B happens, do Y."). And the third, a job hunt, is likely to be unique to your situation, too, just as the first one was: What's right for someone else may not be for you.

Complex Plan Implementation

Before anyone ever considered using a Transition Tree as a stand-alone tool for day-to-day jobs, Goldratt conceived of it as the culmination of the preceding

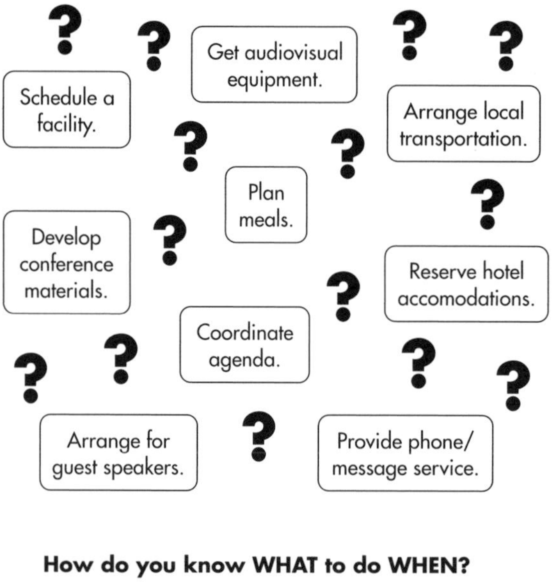

FIGURE 7.5. A Task-Oriented Application: Arranging a Conference.

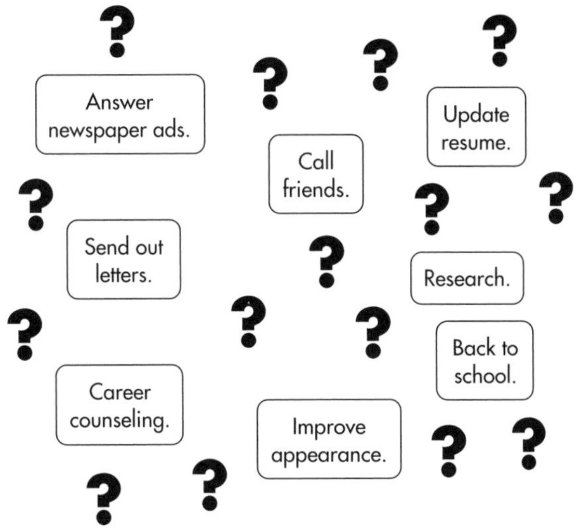

FIGURE 7.6. Another Task-Oriented Application: Finding a Job.

three stages (Conflict Resolution Diagram, Future Reality Tree, and Prerequisite Tree) in his Thinking Process.

The Transition Tree provided the means to formulate the specific actions, and their sequence of completion, required to put into effect the changes identified by the Conflict Resolution Diagram, Future Reality Tree, and Prerequisite Tree. In Goldratt's concept of a process of ongoing improvement, you must first decide *what* to change. Then you have to figure out what to change it *to*. Once these decisions are made, you have to determine *how* to put the change into effect. The Transition Tree is the final element of the "how" part of the process. Figure 7.7 illustrates this relationship.

You should note, however, that if you use the Transition Tree as an implementation tool in this way, you're likely to need more than one Transition Tree. A Future Reality Tree might have three or four major changes (injections) that you must implement. Since most of these will probably be complex conditions resulting from detailed steps, you might find it easier to have separate smaller Transition Trees for each injection, rather than one massive Transition Tree incorporating all of them.

Here's an example. Let's say the objective of your Future Reality Tree is to have a fully restored, "mint condition" 1930 Ford Model "A" automobile. One of your injections might be "Rebuild the engine." Another might be "Restore the body." A third might be "Replace the interior." Each of these alone might be the objective of an individual Transition Tree that lays out the steps needed to achieve them (see Figure 7.8).

You might even use a Prerequisite Tree to sequence major intermediate objectives leading to the overall objective, then build the Transition Tree from the Prerequisite Tree to "flesh out" the details. In a case like this, each intermediate objective would be translated over to the Transition Tree, but as an effect of more detailed, specific actions.

Application: The Transition Tree as a Tactical Planning Aid

In chapter 5, we saw how a Future Reality Tree might be used in strategic planning. But at some point, operational or tactical plans must be developed to

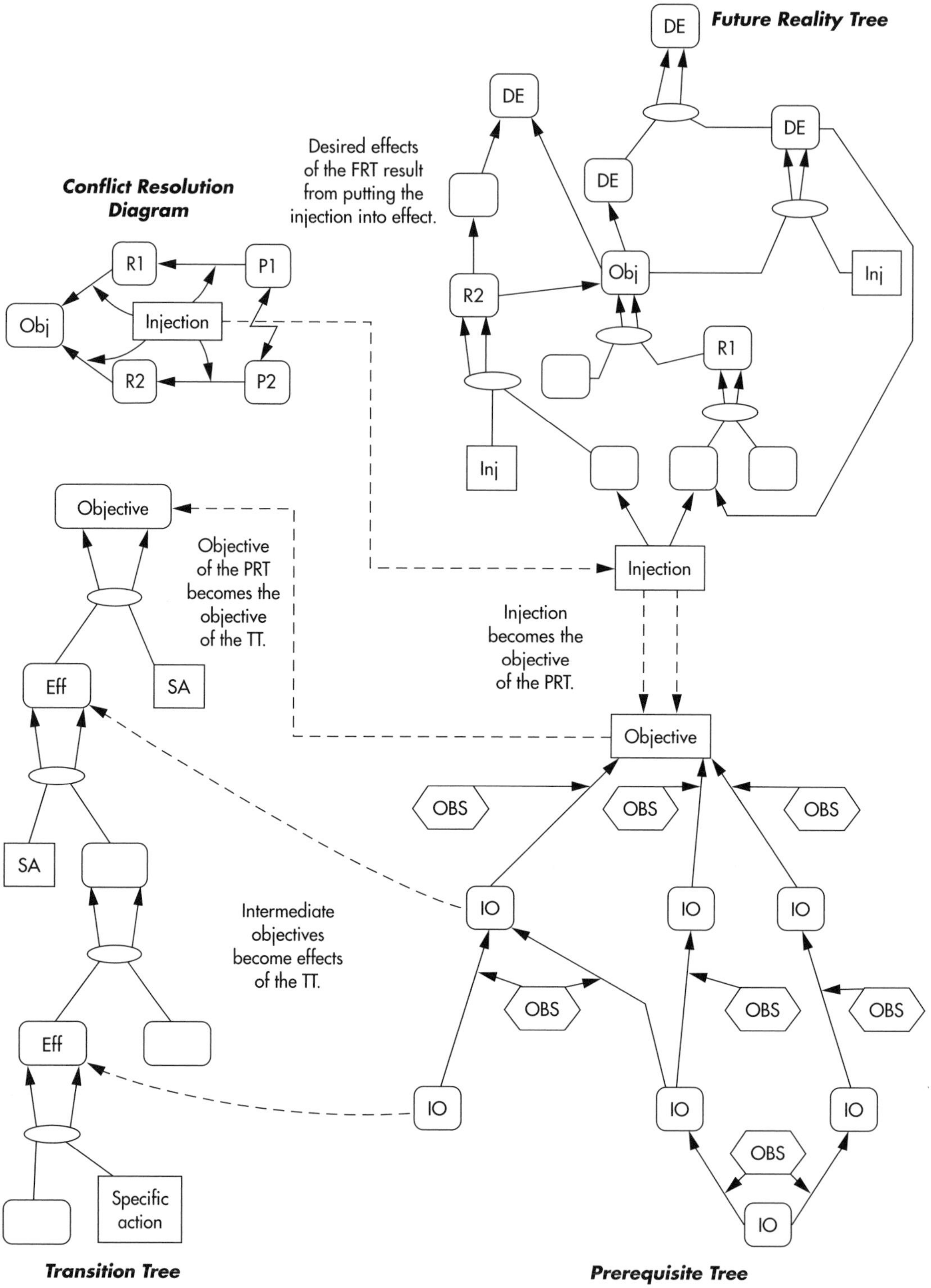

FIGURE 7.7. Complex Plan Implementation: The Transition Tree Implements Change.

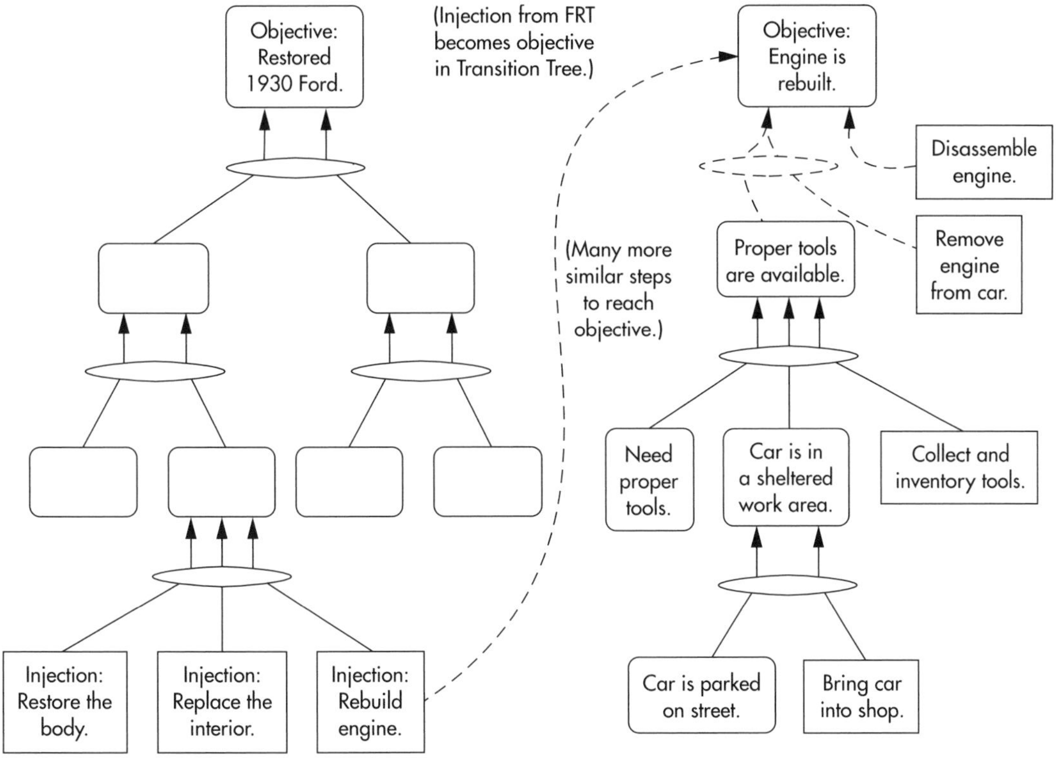

FIGURE 7.8. Complex Plan Implementation: Restoring an Antique Automobile.

advance the goals specified in the strategic plan. Much like the automobile restoration just described, a Transition Tree can be a way to turn strategic plans into tactical operations.

Consider a really large-scale example: war planning (see Figure 7.9). If the strategic mission is to defeat an enemy, one of the supporting goals might be "To achieve air superiority." Let's say that, as with the Persian Gulf War of 1991, the theater of operations lies several thousand miles away from the Air Force's main operating bases in the United States. One injection in the Future Reality Tree might be "1st Tactical Fighter Wing is deployed to the combat theater." Despite the fact that this is summed up in one short sentence, this is no simple task. In fact, it might be the equivalent of moving a small town halfway around the world. But a Transition Tree might make planning such a deployment considerably easier, especially if an effective Prerequisite Tree pointed the way by time-sequencing the most critical actions. In fact, a thorough Transition Tree could produce a step-by-step deployment checklist. Figure 7.9 shows in a general way how a Transition Tree might be used in support of a strategic plan.

Structure of the Transition Tree

The Transition Tree has undergone an evolution over the years.

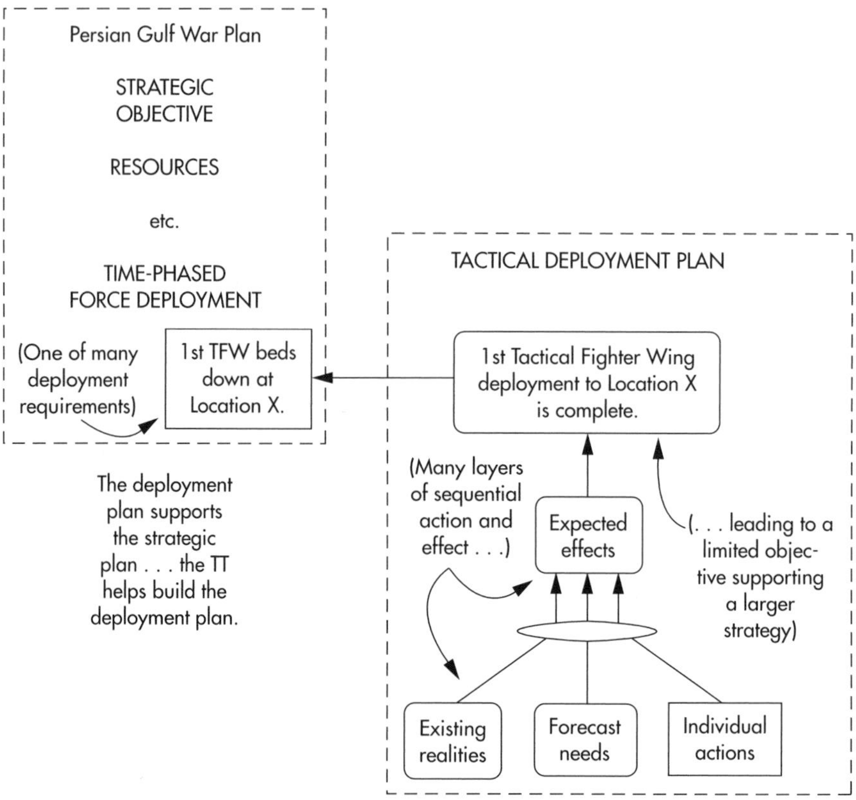

FIGURE 7.9. Tactical Planning with a Transition Tree.

The Four-Element Transition Tree

The first incarnation of the Transition Tree as we now know it had four basic elements: (1) a condition of existing reality, (2) an unfulfilled need, (3) a specific action to be taken, and (4) an expected effect of the integration of the preceding three (see Figure 7.10).

Each succeeding level of the tree was built upon the previous level, with the expected effect taking the place of the unfulfilled need (in the bottom level) (see Figure 7.11). As each successive effect was combined with subsequent actions, new effects resulted, leading progressively upward to an overall objective or desired effect.

This variation of the Transition Tree could have many diverging branches and be somewhat free-form, like the Future Reality Tree. But eventually the diverging branches will converge near the top, at the objective of the tree.

The Five-Element Transition Tree

More recently, Goldratt devised a modification of the Transition Tree's structure by adding an element to better integrate each successive level of the tree with the one below it. The new element is the rationale for a need at the next higher level of the tree (see Figure 7.12).

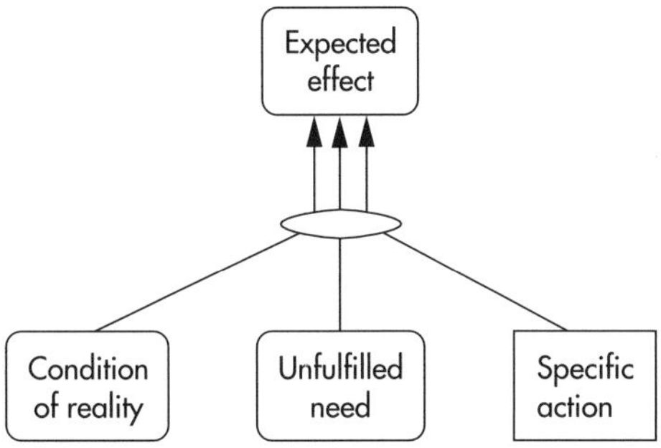

FIGURE 7.10. The Four-Element Transition Tree.

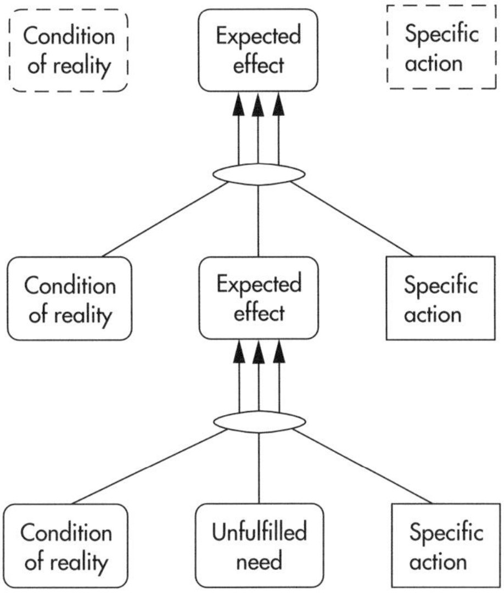

FIGURE 7.11. A Vertical Progression.

Why did Goldratt add this element? To facilitate communication and persuasion. Remember that the purpose of a Transition Tree is to implement change. As we discussed in chapters 1 and 3, many of the changes we might want to make are outside our span of control (that is, we don't have unilateral change authority). Rather, they're in our sphere of influence. This means we need the help, or approval, of others to make the changes. Since people often resist change without a good explanation why, in the five-element Transition Tree Goldratt has given us the means to provide the rationale (need) for the action at every level of the Transition Tree where an action occurs. The four-element tree doesn't always fill this gap.

So the five-element Transition Tree is a fairly rigid, repeating structure. This makes it especially useful for preparing step-by-step checklists and explaining the reason each step is needed—an invaluable aid in training (see Figure 7.13).

Does this mean that the four-element tree is obsolete? Not really. There are some situations in which the rigid, repeating structure of the five-element tree

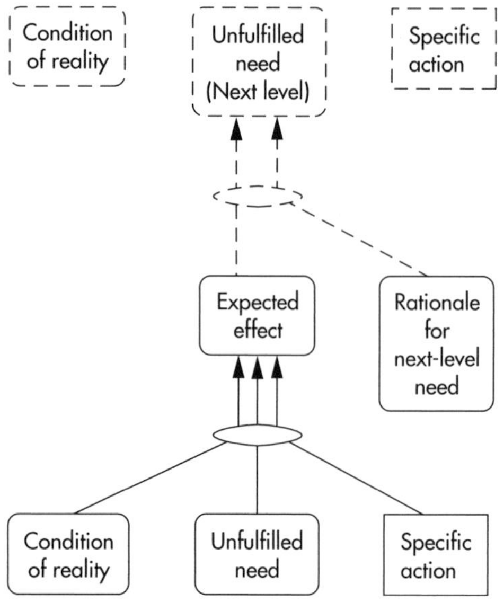

FIGURE 7.12. The Five-Element Transition Tree.

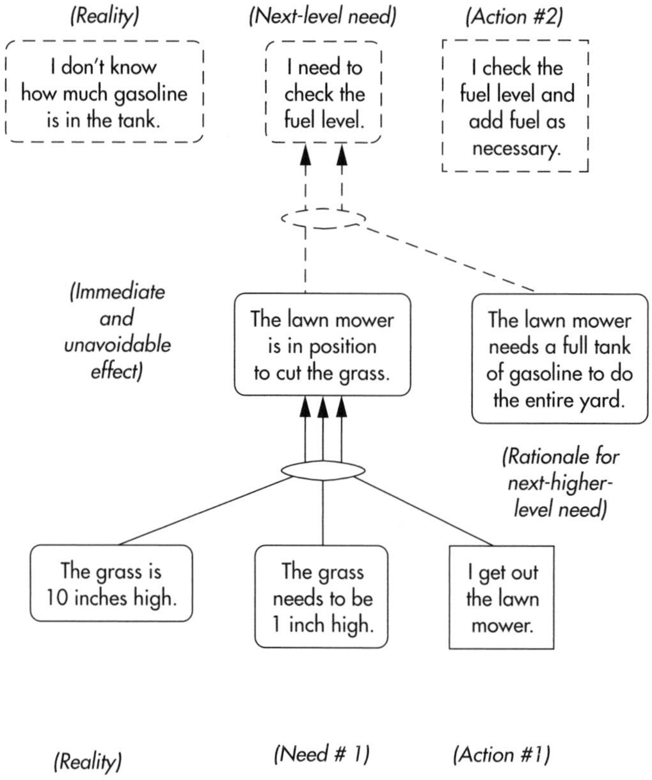

FIGURE 7.13. A Five-Element Transition Tree Example.

is neither necessary nor desirable. Not all change is accomplished in rote checklist fashion. Sometimes several intermediate levels of successive effects must occur before the next action. The four-element tree still allows a kind of free-form development that would be more cumbersome with the five-element tree.

How to Know Which to Use?

If you're constructing step-by-step procedures and need to explain to others why each step is required, the five-element Transition Tree is the "weapon of choice." However, if your Transition Tree grows out of a Prerequisite Tree in a full "Thinking Process analysis," the four-element tree may be adequate for your needs. The "KISS" principle applies: Keep It Simple, Stupid!

TRANSITION TREE SYMBOLOGY

The symbols used in visually displaying a Transition Tree are the same as those used in a Future Reality Tree: round-cornered boxes, square-cornered boxes, ellipses, and arrows (see Figure 7.14).

The round-cornered boxes indicate conditions of existing reality, needs or requirements for change, and expected effects. The square-cornered boxes indicate specific, detailed actions that must be taken to begin the change process. Ellipses are used to show sufficiency—that is, absence of any cause whose arrow passes through the ellipse is enough to invalidate the cause-effect relationship.

HOW TO BUILD A TRANSITION TREE

The procedures that follow describe how to build a four-element Transition Tree. For instructions on building a five-element tree, refer to Figure 7.32, at the

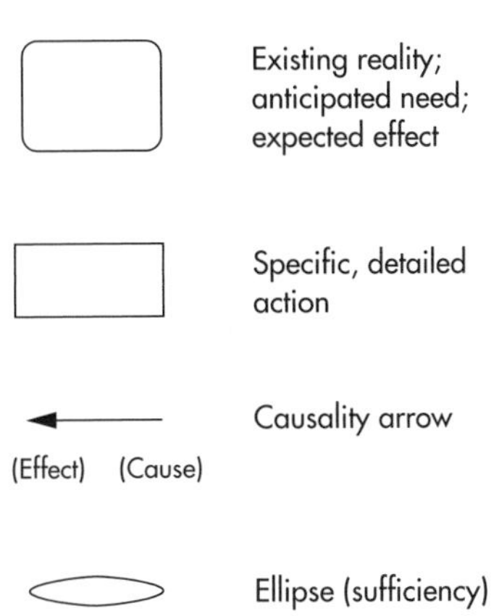
Existing reality;
anticipated need;
expected effect
Specific, detailed
action
Causality arrow
(Effect) (Cause)
Ellipse (sufficiency)

FIGURE 7.14. Transition Tree Symbology.

end of this chapter. As with other trees, begin by assembling the materials you'll need:

- A large sheet of paper
- A pencil
- Post-it™ notes, if desired

Like a Future Reality Tree, the Transition Tree is built from the bottom upward. And, like a Future Reality Tree, you don't necessarily have to start "cold" at the bottom.

1. Determine the Objective

What are you trying to achieve with your Transition Tree? The answer to this question should be written at the very top (in present tense), in a round-cornered box (see Figure 7.15). Why round-cornered? Even if it's an injection from a Future Reality Tree or the objective of a Prerequisite Tree (both normally depicted with square corners), when transferred to the Transition Tree the objective becomes an effect you're trying to achieve.

Make sure that your wording is as specific as you can make it. Vaguely worded objectives leave room for questions about whether they've been achieved—and how you know it.

2. Determine the First Action

What do you think is the first step you should take in reaching your Transition Tree's objective? Write it near the bottom of the page in a square-cornered box (all actions in a Transition Tree are square-cornered) (see Figure 7.16).

3. Identify the Reality and the Need

a. You normally take an action to change an existing condition (reality). Your reality is likely to be a current condition that you're not satisfied with. Decide

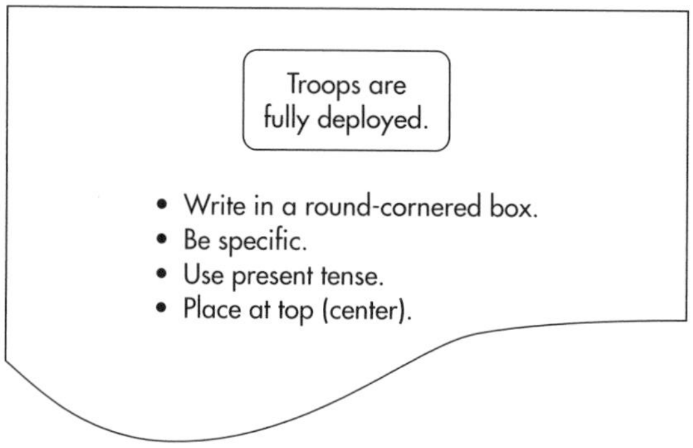

FIGURE 7.15. Determining the Objective.

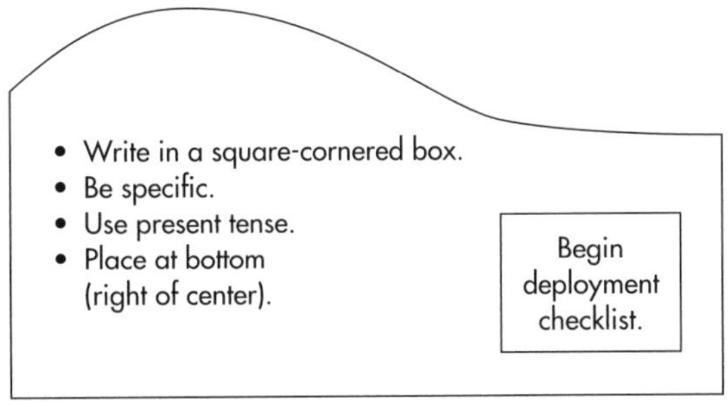

FIGURE 7.16. Determining the First Action.

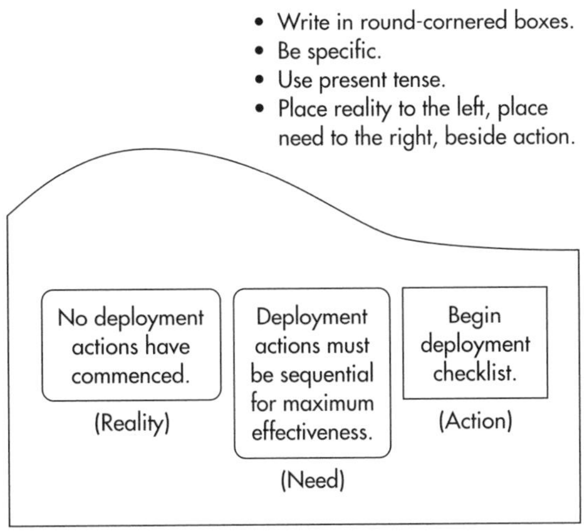

FIGURE 7.17. Identifying Reality and Need.

what that reality or condition is and write it succinctly in a round-cornered box positioned at the same level as the action created in step 2 (see Figure 7.17).

b. The action (defined in step 2) is usually taken to satisfy a need or requirement that must be met to realize a future condition (one that doesn't exist yet). At some point, that future condition will be the Transition Tree's objective, but at first it's usually just the next step toward that objective. Identify that need, and write it in a round-cornered box. Position that box at the same level as the reality entity and the action.

4. Determine the First Effect

What is the direct and unavoidable outcome of combining the reality, the need, and the action? This will be the effect of the first action. Write this effect in a round-cornered box, positioned at the next level up from the reality-need-action trio (see Figure 7.18). Connect the lower-level entities to the effect with three arrows passing through an ellipse (this is, after all, a sufficiency-based tree).

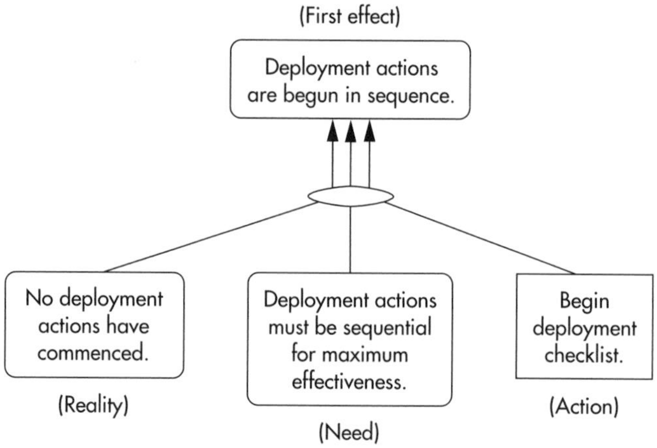

FIGURE 7.18. Determining the First Effect.

Use caution when formulating your effect. Everyone has a natural tendency to look ahead a step or two to where you'd like to be. The result, of course, is that you may overlook (or not consider significant enough) an intervening effect that is the real "direct-and-unavoidable outcome" of the first reality-need-action group. Two possible problems arise from this deficiency. First, you may create clarity or causality reservations in the minds of people to whom you present your tree. But most important, you may overlook the fact that the effect you skipped over needs some other small but critical action to really move you to the following level.

5. Scrutinize the Connections

Before going on to the next level, carefully examine the connections between the reality-need-action and the effect (see Figure 7.19). Try to do this with a "fresh eye." Keep the Categories of Legitimate Reservation in mind. (Refer to chapter 2, "Categories of Legitimate Reservation," if necessary.) Ask yourself these questions:

- Are all entities clear and comprehensible?
- Do the causes *really* produce this effect?
- Does this effect *really* move me closer to my objective? (If not, consider a different action.)
- Is there anything missing (at the cause level)?

Note: While we can't completely ignore additional causes (see chapter 2), we're less concerned with them in a Transition Tree. If you're trying to achieve an objective, what do you care if something else causes the effect you're looking for, as long as you know your action will? That's one less action you may have to take. Your only real concerns about an additional cause are: (a) knowing that it caused your effect, and (b) if it *did* cause the effect, whether you need to ensure that the effect will remain if that additional cause goes away.

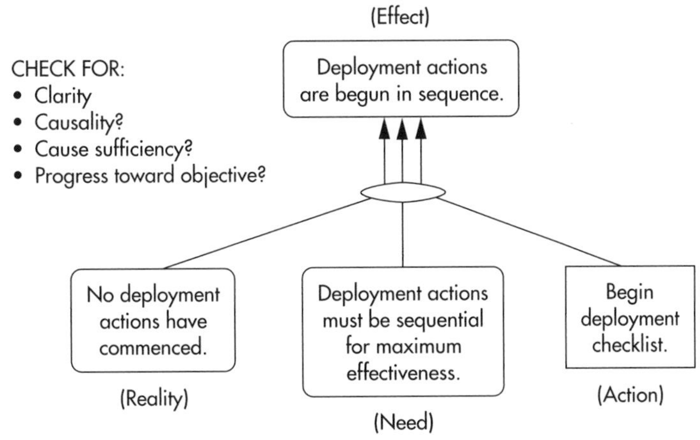

FIGURE 7.19. Scrutinizing Connections.

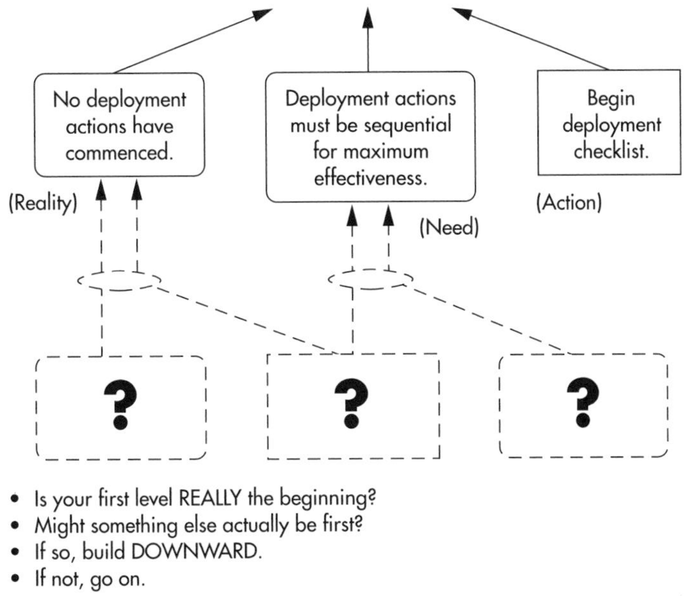

FIGURE 7.20. Verifying the First Level of Causation.

For example, if you think you need to set up a light for visibility in the dark, but a security floodlight is already lighting your area, you may not need your light—unless the security light burns out.

6. Verify the First Level of Causation

Before going on to the next-higher level, take a good look at the reality-need-action again (see Figure 7.20). Is this really an origin, or do you have to make something else happen first in order to have either the reality or the need? If you do, the reality or the need are actually effects of some causes at a lower level. Reenter the checklist at step 2 and build downward, if necessary, to the real root cause level. Reaccomplish steps 2 to 5 for this new lower level. Note, however, that at step 4 your only decision should be where to make vertical connections (including an ellipse)—to the "reality" or to the "need" entity of the original first level. If no lower level is necessary, go on to the next step.

7. Determine the Next Action

From the first effect (step 4), we now have to move closer to the objective. Study the first effect. Ask yourself, "What action, when combined with that effect, will move me closer to my objective?" Or another way to say it might be, "What's the next thing I have to do to get closer to the objective?" Write your next proposed action in a square-cornered box, just as you did in step 2, and position it to one side of the first effect (from step 4) (see Figure 7.21).

8. Determine the Next Reality or Need

This step may not be necessary. If it's intuitively obvious that combining your new action (from step 7) with the first effect (from step 4) will produce the next effect, you won't need to depict any other entities. But if the new action and last effect seem incomplete, decide whether you need a supporting statement about reality, or a statement of need to get you to the next level of effect. Add this in a round-cornered box, opposite the new action but on the same level (see Figure 7.22).

9. Determine the Next Effect

What is the direct and unavoidable outcome of the most recent action, combined with the previous effect and associated reality or need? Repeat step 5 to

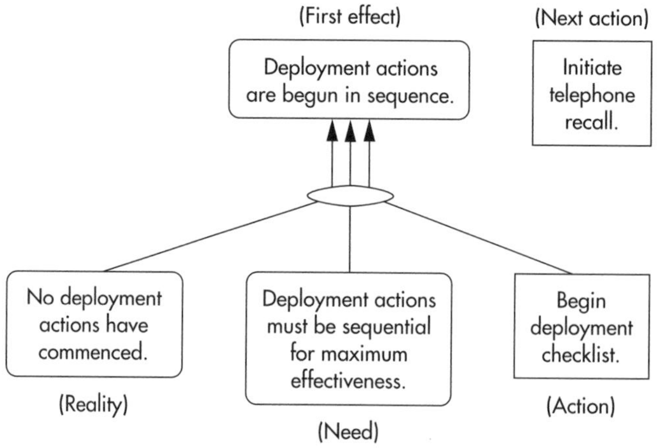

FIGURE 7.21. Determining the Next Action.

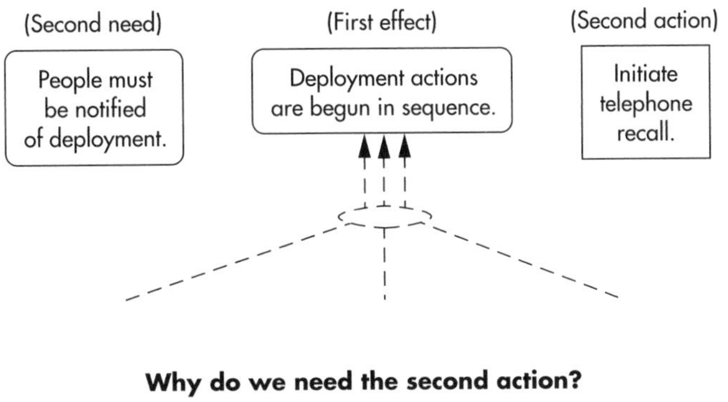

FIGURE 7.22. Determining the Next Reality or Need.

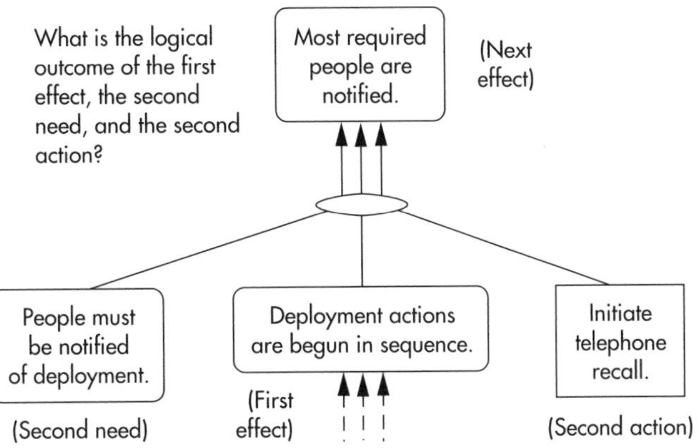

FIGURE 7.23. Determining the Next Effect.

determine this (see Figure 7.23). Be sure this effect moves you closer to the objective, or select a different action.

Note #1: Some actions have more than one effect. Sometimes you want this to happen, other times you don't. When you want this to happen, your tree will diverge into discrete branches (see Figure 7.24). Such branches indicate parallelism—several activities that may be accomplished at the same time. Keep in mind that, eventually, diverging branches must converge again at some point to reach the objective. If they don't, you'd better ask yourself, "Why not? Do I really need this branch to achieve my objective?"

Note #2: If your actions can have effects *other* than the ones intended and these effects are neutral, no harm is done. But sometimes these effects can be negative (see Figure 7.25). In this case, if the action producing the negative effect is really necessary to get you to your objective, you must take some additional action to preclude or mitigate the negative effect. Failure to recognize such negative effects and do something about them ahead of time is the primary reason that otherwise excellent plans fail. See "Negative Branches" in chapter 5, "Future Reality Tree," for a detailed description of how to handle unintended adverse effects.

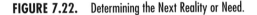

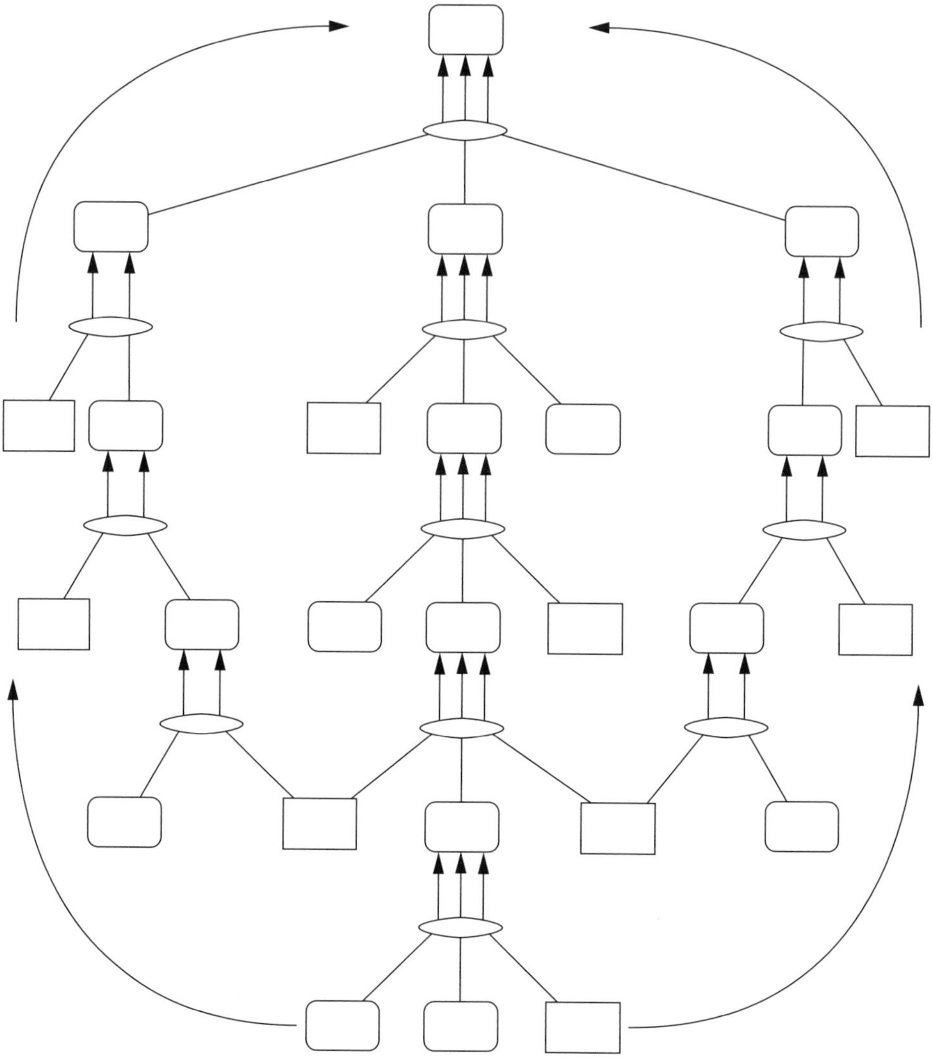

FIGURE 7.24. Branches Can Diverge and Converge.

By now it should be apparent that the Transition Tree assumes the general shape of a fir tree: Each layer usually tapers to converge in the center of the next layer (see Figure 7.26). Try to maintain this structure, even with diverging branches, all the way to the objective.

10. Scrutinize Connections

Repeat step 5 in its entirety, but confine your scrutiny to the level you're currently working on.

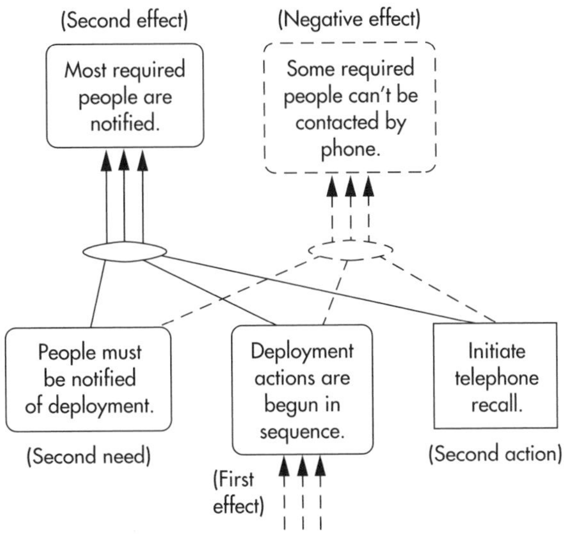

FIGURE 7.25. Multiple Effects of the Same Action.

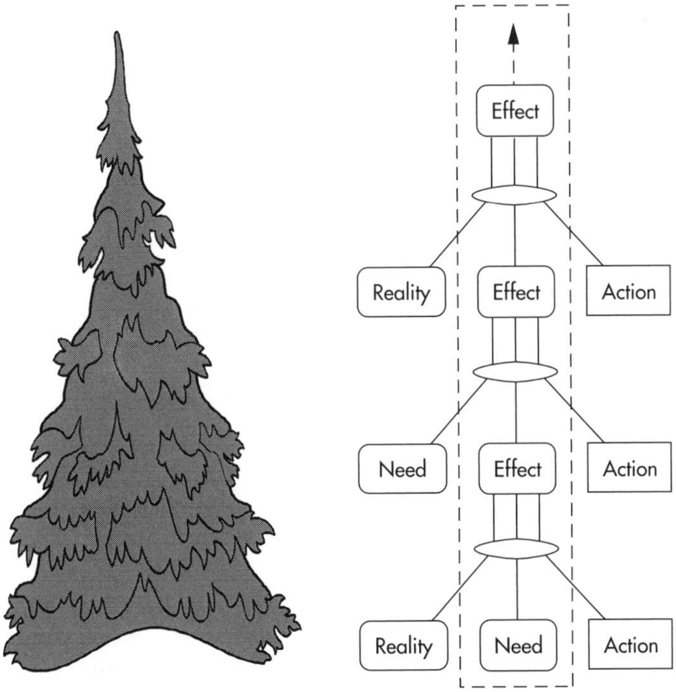

FIGURE 7.26. The "Fir Tree" Effect.

11. Repeat Steps 7 to 10

Continue repeating steps 7 to 10 until you reach the point where your next effect will be the Transition Tree's objective. If your path diverged into more than one branch, be alert at each successive iteration of steps 7 to 10 for an opportunity to converge to a single path again. In some cases this may not happen until you connect to the objective. In others it may occur farther down. Once you've connected all the branches to the objective, the tree is complete—but it still needs "bulletproofing."

12. Review the Completed Tree

The basic structure is now in place. With care on your part, the logic will probably be fairly tight, too. You only need to do three things to bulletproof your tree:

- Search for negative branches (refer to chapter 5) (see Figure 7.27).
- Look for opportunities to build in positive reinforcing loops (see Figure 7.27).
- Get someone else to review the tree—someone who has some knowledge of its subject.

Human frailties being what they are, even a consummate logician has some personal "blind spots." Depending on how important this tree is to you, you might want several people to review it and suggest ways to improve it.

SCRUTINIZING A TRANSITION TREE

The scrutiny of a Transition Tree is very similar to that of a Future Reality Tree. The Categories of Legitimate Reservation (refer to chapter 2, "Categories of Legitimate Reservation") are used to test the logical connections between entities of the Transition Tree. However, as with the Future Reality Tree, there are a few qualifications to consider when using the CLR in a Transition Tree.

Existence Reservations

In chapter 2, we discussed the second level of the Categories of Legitimate Reservation—existence, both entity and causality. While this level of reservation is important in the Transition Tree, there are some definite limitations to its use. Take Entity Existence, for example. One of the tests for Entity Existence is whether it is a valid statement of existing reality. Clearly, this test won't be of much use in a Transition Tree, because *outcomes of actions we haven't taken yet don't currently exist.* They can only exist in the future. So the only parts of the Entity Existence reservation that might apply in a Transition Tree would be completeness (a complete sentence) and structure (no embedded "if–then" statements).

Causality Existence—whether the stated cause does, in fact, lead to the stated effect—likewise must be used with caution. Obviously, in a Transition

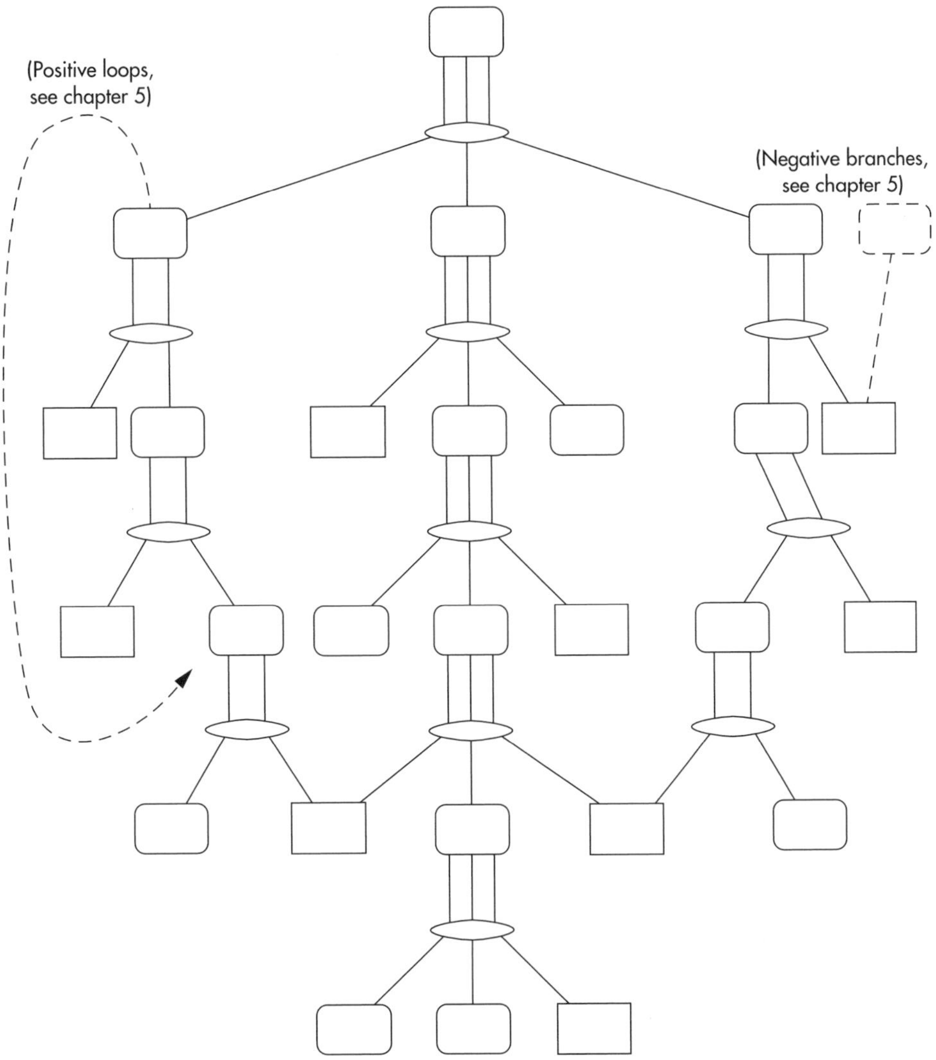

FIGURE 7.27. Looking for Negative Branches and Positive Loops.

Tree the effect does not exist now. The question is whether it will exist as an expected outcome of an action on your part, that is, will your action effectively do the job it's designed to do? The Predicted Effect reservation is likely to be much more useful in verifying outcomes of initiated actions that don't yet exist.

Scrutinizing Actions

The only real scrutiny you can apply to actions you initiate concerns whether the action can actually be done, and whether it will eventually produce the desired effects. Be careful about rejecting an action as "undoable" at face value: So was the electric light, as we have seen, until Thomas Edison did it. Instead, consider the subjective probability of your being able to complete that action. If your intuition tells you that the action you want to take is likely to happen "when pigs fly," you might be well advised to look for another one—or for multiple actions to accomplish the same purpose. Whether the action will produce the desired effect is really a future causality issue.

"Oxygen"

Remember the concept of "oxygen" (refer to chapter 2, "Categories of Legitimate Reservation")? "Oxygen" is an assumption about reality that, though not explicitly stated, applies to the cause-effect relationship.

A single arrow always implies unspoken "oxygen"—maybe a lot of it. This is especially true in Future Reality and Transition Trees. And the assumptions that people might be willing to make about current reality, they're less likely to accept in projections of the future. So in the Transition Tree, you're usually better off displaying "oxygen" visually as an existing reality entity, which you combine with an initiated action, or an expected effect of an action. That's why we incorporate statements of need or reality. This is how we ensure that the only unspoken "oxygen" is that which is really obvious or implied at face value. There should be very few, if any, single arrows in a Transition Tree.

USING THE COMPLETED TRANSITION TREE

Each action (square-cornered box) now represents a sequential (or parallel, if branches diverged) step in the implementation process. If you like, you can extract these actions and make them steps in a checklist (see Figure 7.28).

Readers familiar with project management may notice the similarity between a Transition Tree and a PERT chart. PERT charts invariably contain additional quantitative data about expected, optimistic, and pessimistic completion times, as well as slack time at each node. But the basic structure of a PERT chart is very similar to that of a Transition Tree. You could even use the Transition Tree to create the basic relationships for a PERT chart, filling in the quantitative data afterward. Figure 7.33 shows how the Transition Tree might be used to lay out a PERT chart.

SUMMARY

The five-stage Thinking Process is now complete. We began with a Current Reality Tree, which told us what needed to be changed. Then we used a Conflict Resolution Diagram to begin the design of a new reality—what to change to. We used a Future Reality Tree to verify that the idea we created would, in fact, solve our problem without creating other new ones that we couldn't handle. Then we searched out obstacles to implementation and determined how to overcome them using a Prerequisite Tree. Finally, we constructed a step-by-step implementation plan to guide us in causing the change to happen.

One of the recurring messages throughout this book is worth reiterating here: These five logical tools can be used individually or in concert, depending on the situation you face. Some problems are not complex enough to warrant a Current Reality Tree, Conflict Resolution Diagram, or Future Reality Tree. In cases like

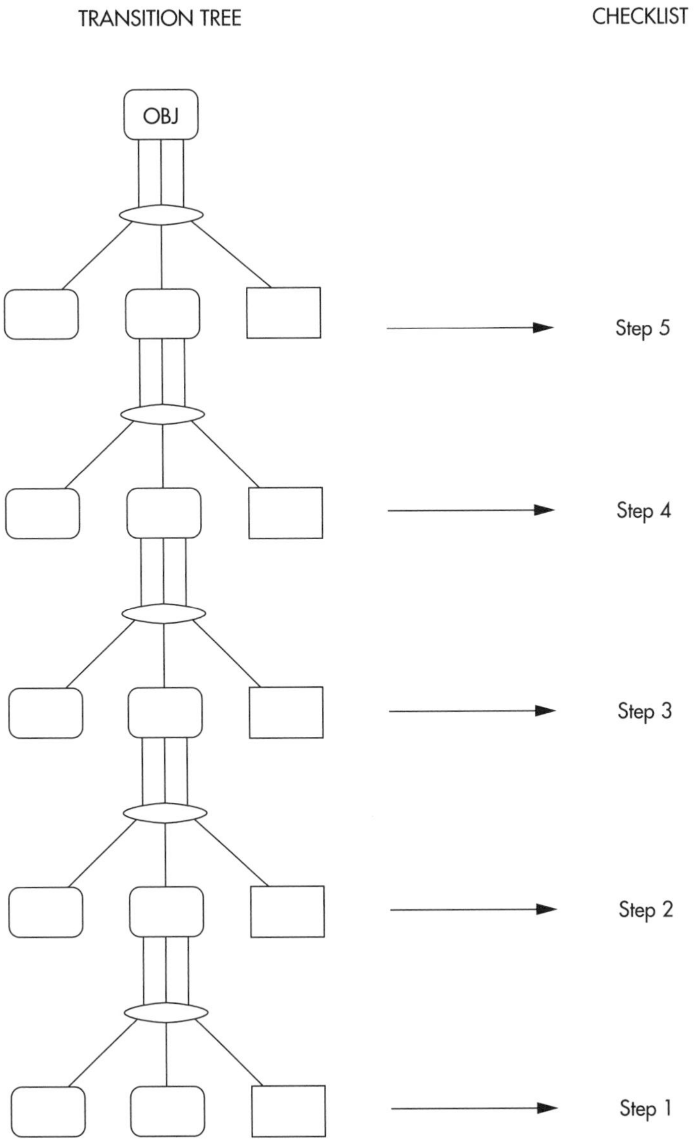

FIGURE 7.28. Using a Transition Tree to Build a Checklist.

that, there's nothing wrong with proceeding directly to a Prerequisite Tree, or even a Transition Tree. Remember that you can use a hammer to hang a picture on a wall or as part of a complete toolbox to build an entire house.

In each of the preceding chapters, the unstated assumption has been that we're using these logic tools by ourselves, as single individuals. That's often an effective way to learn how to use them. But in the "real world," we live in a society that includes other people, and in fact our success in using the logic trees usually depends on including others in the process. In chapter 8, we'll see how to use this thinking process in groups of two or more. We'll find out how we can integrate the help of others in building our trees, even if they don't know very much about the process.

Transition Tree (Partial)
p. 1

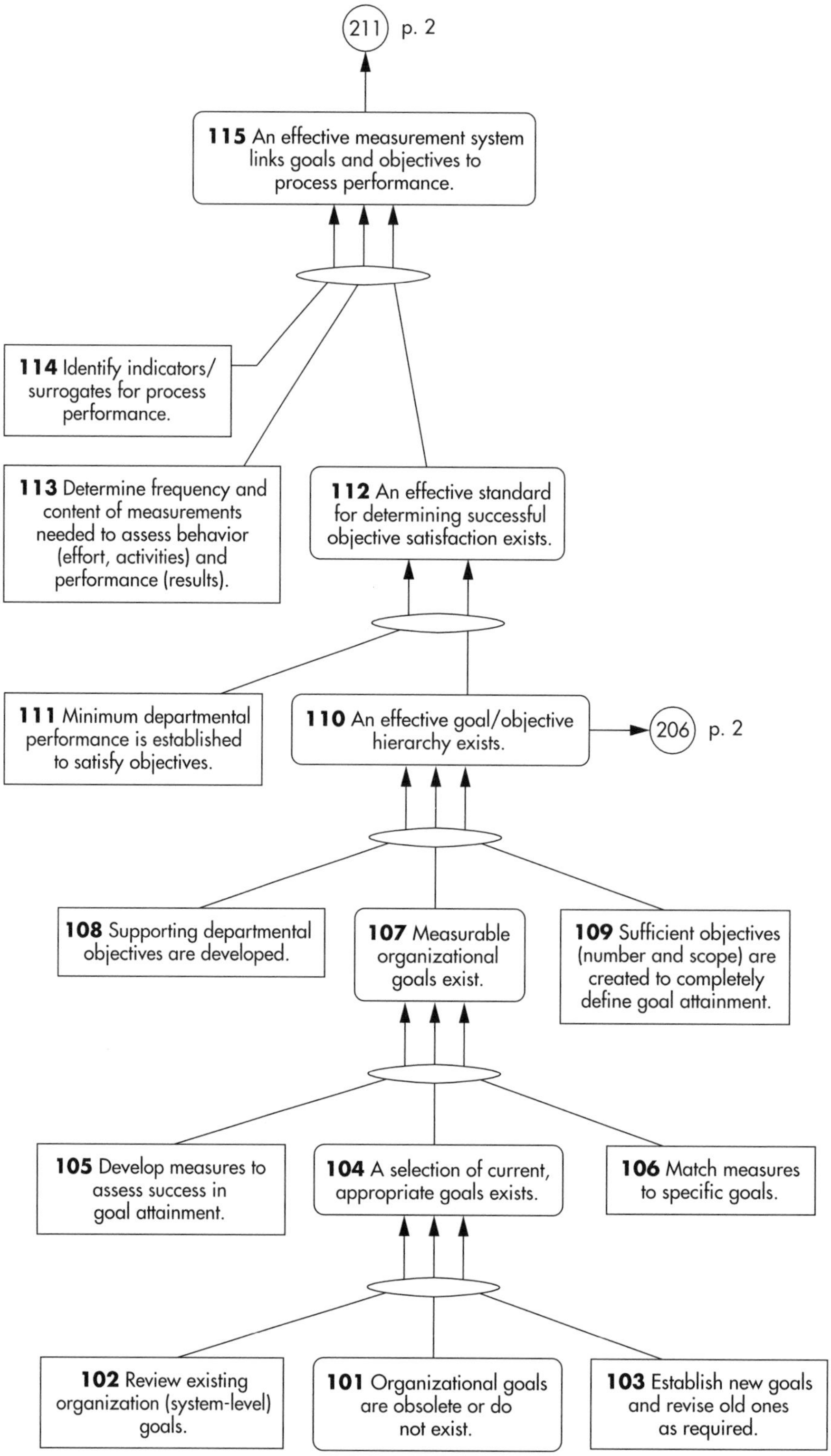

FIGURE 7.29. Partial Transition Tree: "How Organizations Can Succeed at Total Quality."

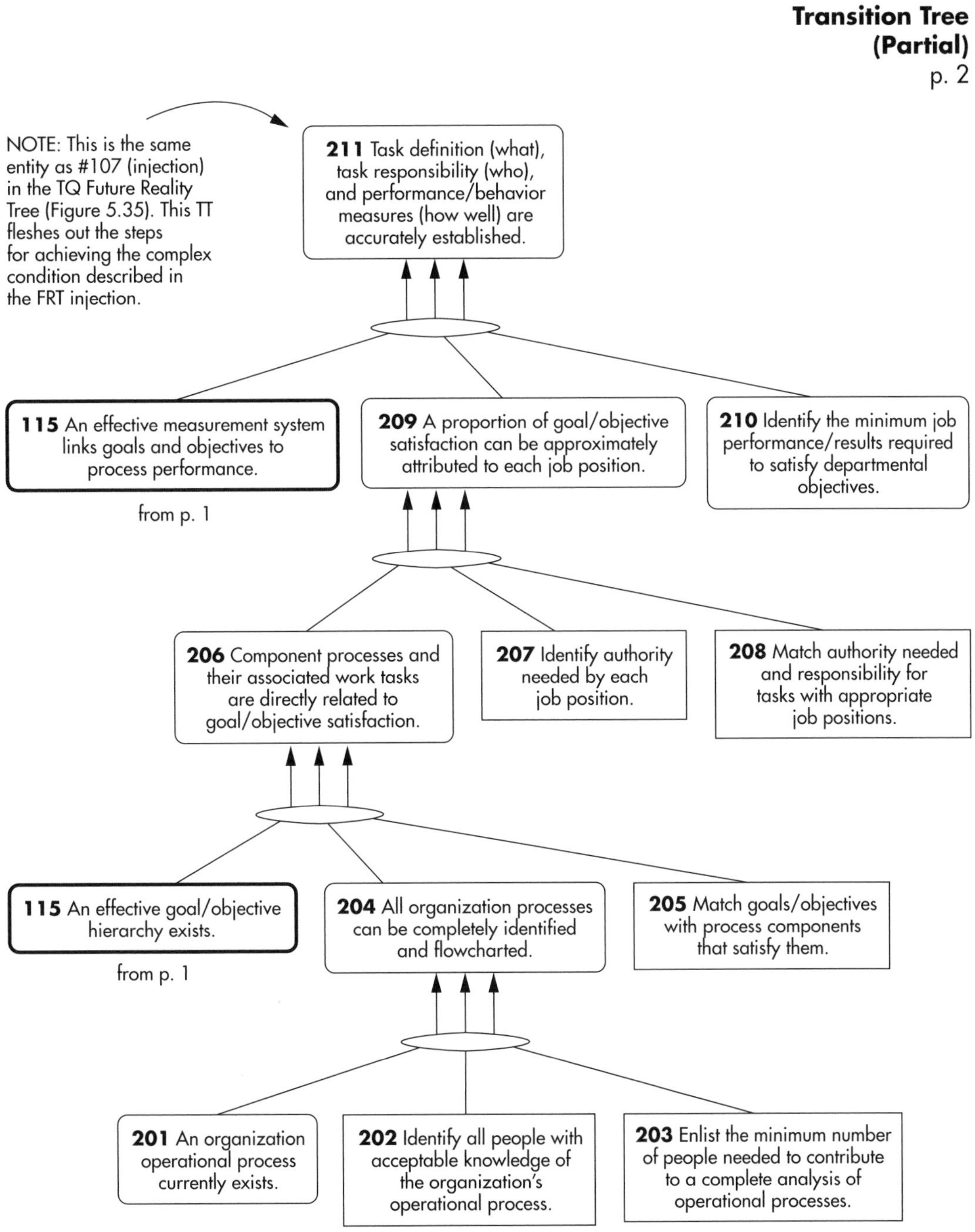
Transition Tree
(Partial)
p. 2
NOTE: This is the same entity as #107 (injection) in the TQ Future Reality Tree (Figure 5.35). This TT fleshes out the steps for achieving the complex condition described in the FRT injection.
211 Task definition (what), task responsibility (who), and performance/behavior measures (how well) are accurately established.
115 An effective measurement system links goals and objectives to process performance.
from p. 1
209 A proportion of goal/objective satisfaction can be approximately attributed to each job position.
210 Identify the minimum job performance/results required to satisfy departmental objectives.
206 Component processes and their associated work tasks are directly related to goal/objective satisfaction.
207 Identify authority needed by each job position.
208 Match authority needed and responsibility for tasks with appropriate job positions.
115 An effective goal/objective hierarchy exists.
from p. 1
204 All organization processes can be completely identified and flowcharted.
205 Match goals/objectives with process components that satisfy them.
201 An organization operational process currently exists.
202 Identify all people with acceptable knowledge of the organization's operational process.
203 Enlist the minimum number of people needed to contribute to a complete analysis of operational processes.

FIGURE 7.29—*Continued.*

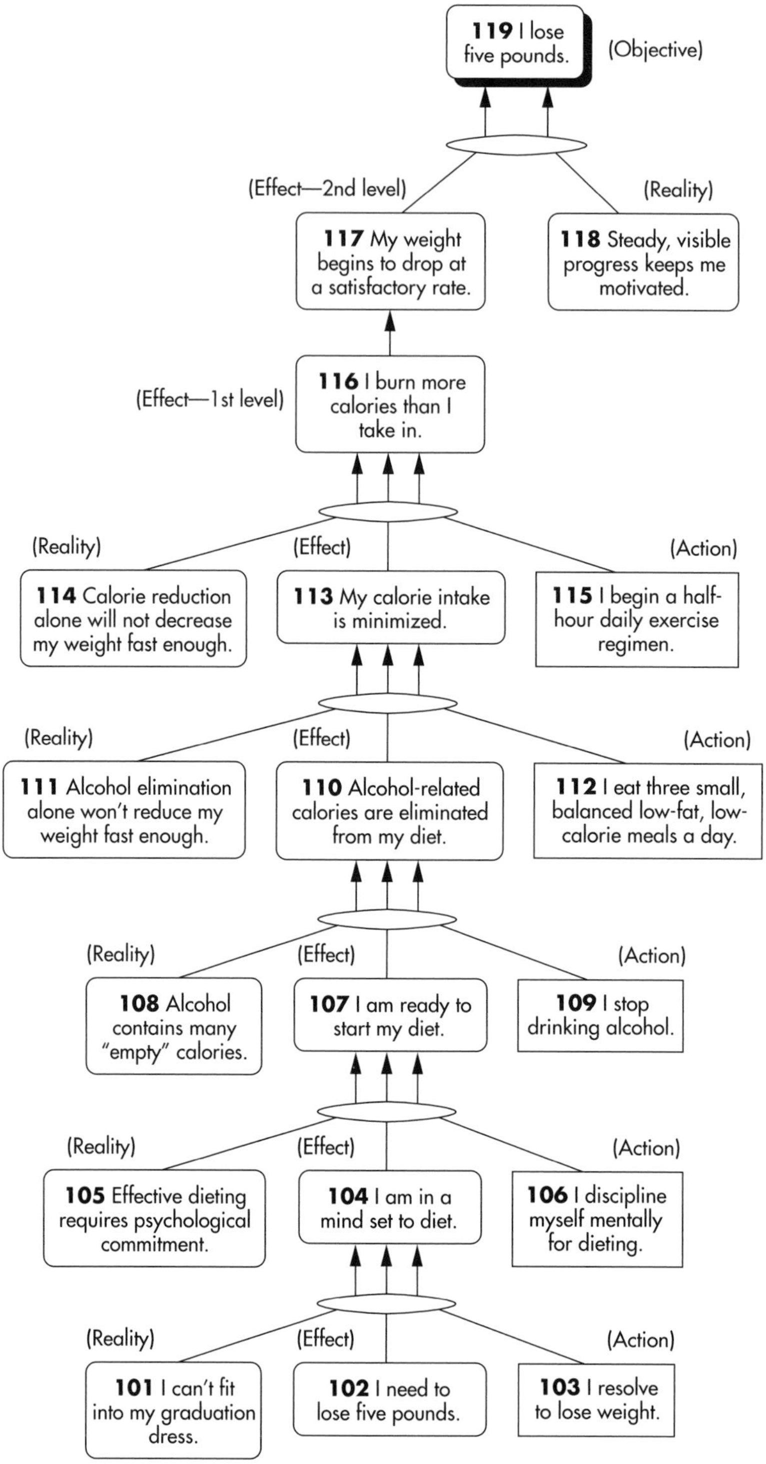

FIGURE 7.30. Jennifer's Transition Tree #2: "How to Lose Five Pounds in a Hurry."

1. GATHER ALL NECESSARY MATERIALS.

- Large paper, pencils, pens, Post-it™ notes
- FRT or PRT (if applicable)
  - Objective (FRT or PRT)
  - Injections (FRT)
  - Intermediate objectives (PRT)

2. DETERMINE OBJECTIVE.

- What's the purpose of the TT?
- Write it in a succinct sentence.
  - As specific as possible
  - Present tense
  - In a round-cornered box
- Center it at the top of the page.

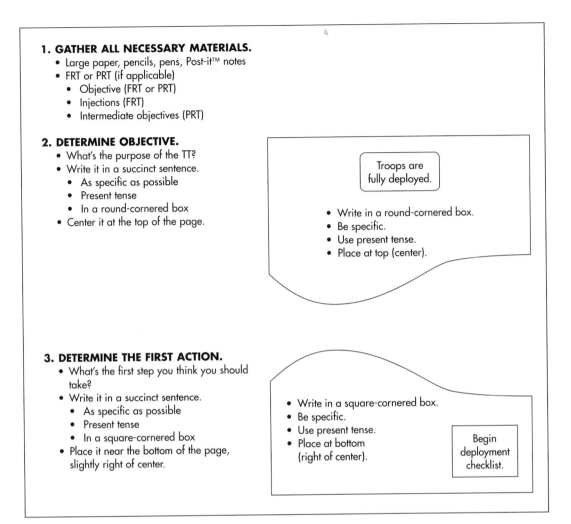

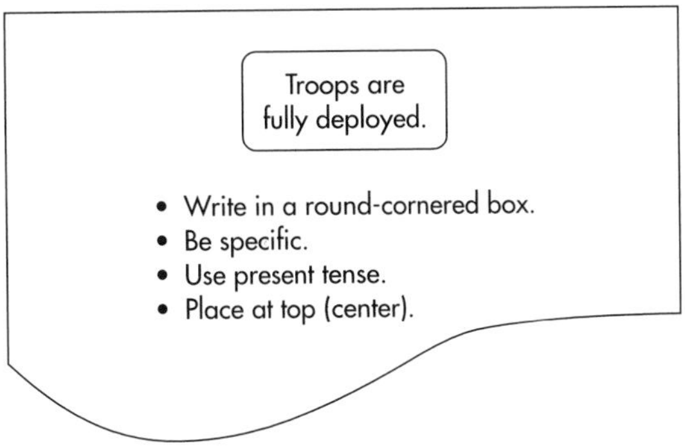
Troops are fully deployed.
• Write in a round-cornered box.
• Be specific.
• Use present tense.
• Place at top (center).

3. DETERMINE THE FIRST ACTION.

- What's the first step you think you should take?
- Write it in a succinct sentence.
  - As specific as possible
  - Present tense
  - In a square-cornered box
- Place it near the bottom of the page, slightly right of center.

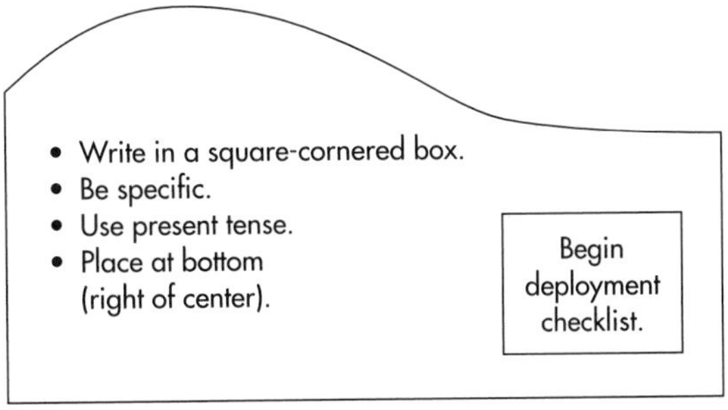
• Write in a square-cornered box.
• Be specific.
• Use present tense.
• Place at bottom (right of center).
Begin deployment checklist.

FIGURE 7.31. Procedures for Building a Four-Element Transition Tree.

4. IDENTIFY THE REALITY AND THE NEED.

- What condition of existing reality are you trying to change?
- Write it in a succinct sentence.
  - As specific as possible
  - Present tense
  - In a round-cornered box
- Place it near the bottom of the page, slightly left of center.
- What is the immediate need you're trying to satisfy by your action?
- Write it in a succinct sentence.
  - As specific as possible
  - Present tense
  - In a round-cornered box
- Place it near the bottom of the page, between the reality and the action.

- Write in round-cornered boxes.
- Be specific.
- Use present tense.
- Place reality to the left, place need to the right, beside action.

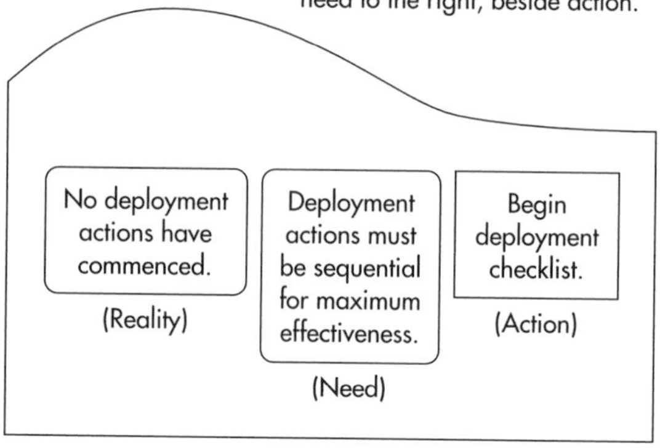

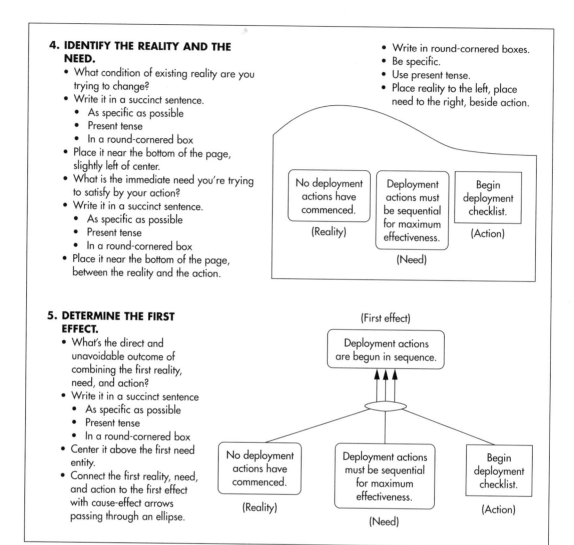

5. DETERMINE THE FIRST EFFECT.

- What's the direct and unavoidable outcome of combining the first reality, need, and action?
- Write it in a succinct sentence
  - As specific as possible
  - Present tense
  - In a round-cornered box
- Center it above the first need entity.
- Connect the first reality, need, and action to the first effect with cause-effect arrows passing through an ellipse.

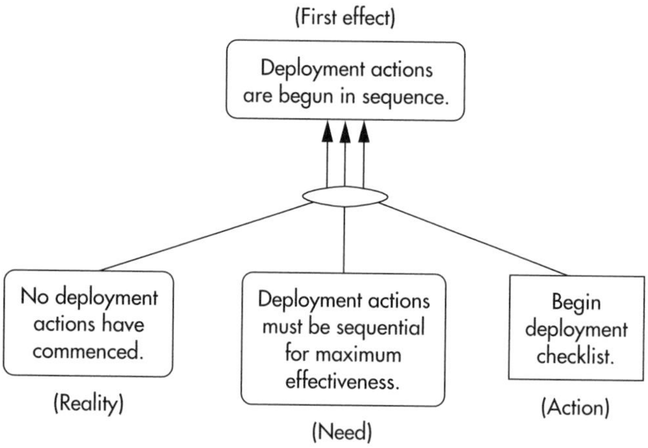

FIGURE 7.31—*Continued.*

6. SCRUTINIZE THE CONNECTIONS

- Use the "Categories of Legitimate Reservation" (chapter 2)
- Look particularly for:
- Clarity—Clear and comprehensible?
- Causality—Do the causes *really* produce this effect?
- Insufficiency—Is any cause missing?
- Progress—Does this really move me closer to my objective?
- Negative branches—Possible undesirable effects of the action? (Refer to chapter 5 for more on negative branches.)

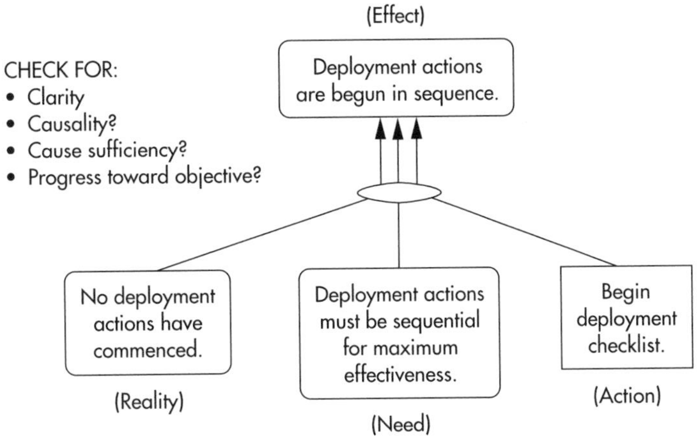
CHECK FOR:
• Clarity
• Causality?
• Cause sufficiency?
• Progress toward objective?
(Effect)
Deployment actions are begun in sequence.
No deployment actions have commenced.
(Reality)
Deployment actions must be sequential for maximum effectiveness.
(Need)
Begin deployment checklist.
(Action)

7. VERIFY THE FIRST LEVEL OF CAUSATION.

- Determine whether you're *really* starting from the bottom of your TT.
- Is your stated reality actually in existence now, or must something else have happened first to give you the first reality?
- Is your stated need really the first one, or is there a more basic one you must satisfy first?
- Does the first action really originate the initial change to reality? Or do you have to do something else first?
- If not, build downward using steps 2–4. Remember that what you thought was reality in your original first layer will now become the effect of your new lower level.
- When your intuition tells you that you're really at the bottom of your tree, go on to the next step.

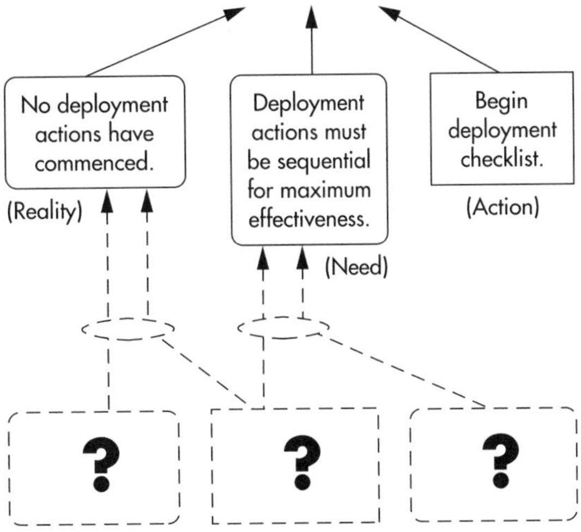
No deployment actions have commenced.
(Reality)
Deployment actions must be sequential for maximum effectiveness.
(Need)
Begin deployment checklist.
(Action)
?
?
?

- Is your first level REALLY the beginning?
- Might something else actually be first?
- If so, build DOWNWARD.
- If not, go on.

FIGURE 7.31—*Continued.*

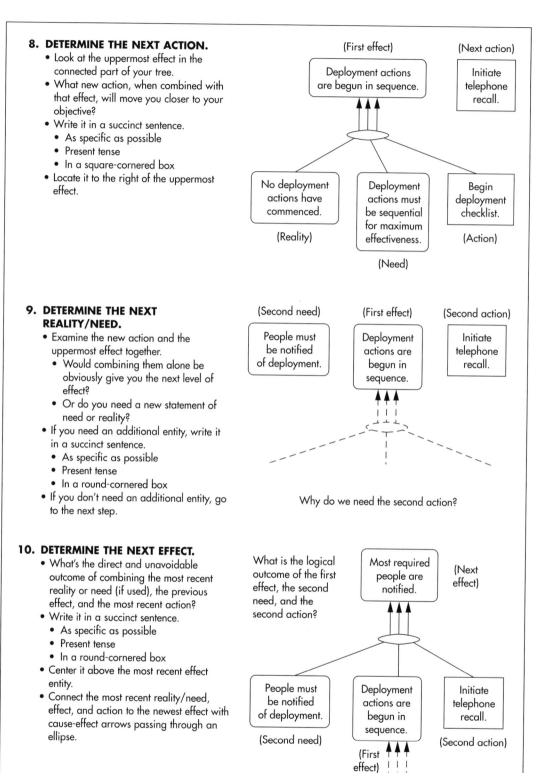

8. DETERMINE THE NEXT ACTION.

- Look at the uppermost effect in the connected part of your tree.
- What new action, when combined with that effect, will move you closer to your objective?
- Write it in a succinct sentence.
  - As specific as possible
  - Present tense
  - In a square-cornered box
- Locate it to the right of the uppermost effect.

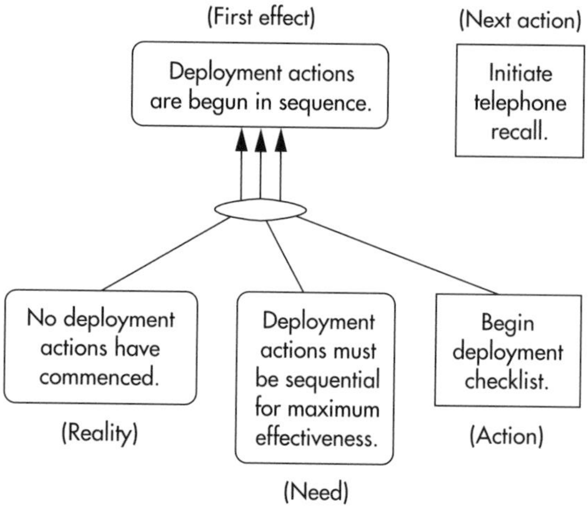

(First effect)
(Next action)
Deployment actions are begun in sequence.
Initiate telephone recall.
No deployment actions have commenced.
(Reality)
Deployment actions must be sequential for maximum effectiveness.
(Need)
Begin deployment checklist.
(Action)

9. DETERMINE THE NEXT REALITY/NEED.

- Examine the new action and the uppermost effect together.
  - Would combining them alone be obviously give you the next level of effect?
  - Or do you need a new statement of need or reality?
- If you need an additional entity, write it in a succinct sentence.
  - As specific as possible
  - Present tense
  - In a round-cornered box
- If you don't need an additional entity, go to the next step.

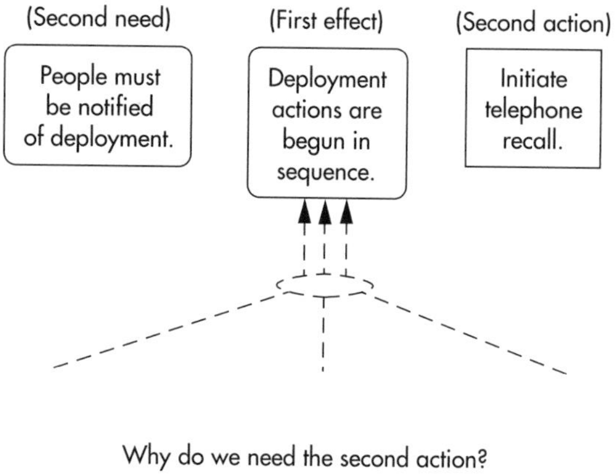

(Second need)
(First effect)
(Second action)
People must be notified of deployment.
Deployment actions are begun in sequence.
Initiate telephone recall.
Why do we need the second action?

10. DETERMINE THE NEXT EFFECT.

- What's the direct and unavoidable outcome of combining the most recent reality or need (if used), the previous effect, and the most recent action?
- Write it in a succinct sentence.
  - As specific as possible
  - Present tense
  - In a round-cornered box
- Center it above the most recent effect entity.
- Connect the most recent reality/need, effect, and action to the newest effect with cause-effect arrows passing through an ellipse.

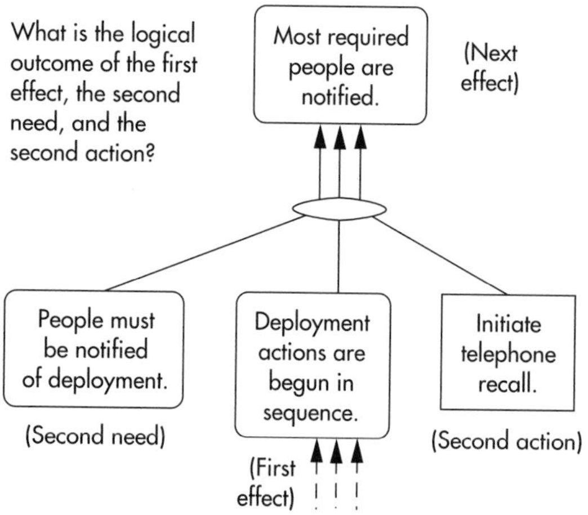

What is the logical outcome of the first effect, the second need, and the second action?
Most required people are notified.
(Next effect)
People must be notified of deployment.
(Second need)
Deployment actions are begun in sequence.
(First effect)
Initiate telephone recall.
(Second action)

FIGURE 7.31—*Continued.*

11. SCRUTINIZE THE LATEST CONNECTIONS.

- Use the "Categories of Legitimate Reservation" (chapter 2).
- Look particularly for:
  - Clarity—Clear and comprehensible?
  - Causality—Do the causes *really* produce this effect?
  - Insufficiency—Is any cause missing?
  - Progress—Does this *really* move me closer to my objective?
  - Negative branches—Possible undesirable effects of the newest action? (Refer to chapter 5 for more on negative branches.)

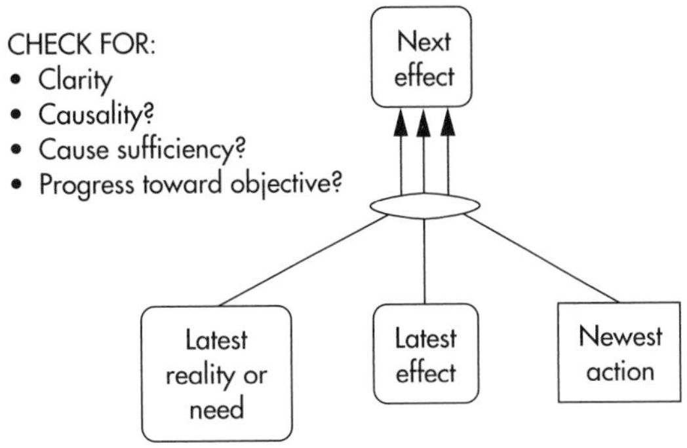

12. REPEAT STEPS 8–11.

- Continue repeating steps 8–11 until you can connect a level of reality/need-effect-action directly with your TT's objective.
- Be alert for diverging branches.
  - Your tree may need them to get you to your objective.
  - If branches do diverge, be alert for opportunities to converge them again.

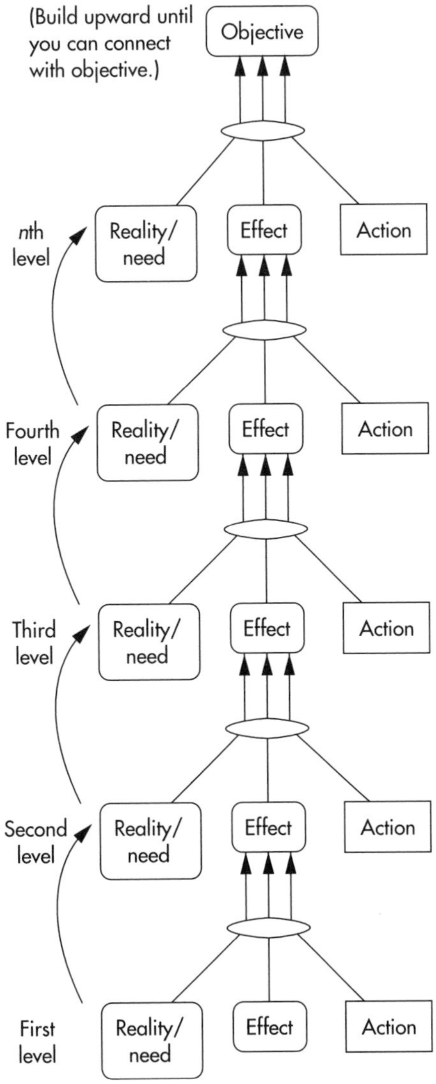

FIGURE 7.31—*Continued.*

13. REVIEW THE COMPLETED TREE.

- Read through the tree in its entirety.
  - Does it make sense?
  - Does it agree with your intuition about what should be done and in what sequence?
  - Is everything there that should be there?
  - If the answer to any of these questions is "No," modify the tree as necessary.
- Review each action again, this looking for possible negative branches. "Trim" with supplementary actions as necessary.
- Look for opportunities to build in positive reinforcing loops, if applicable.
- Review your tree with someone else who has knowledge of the subject; modify as necessary.

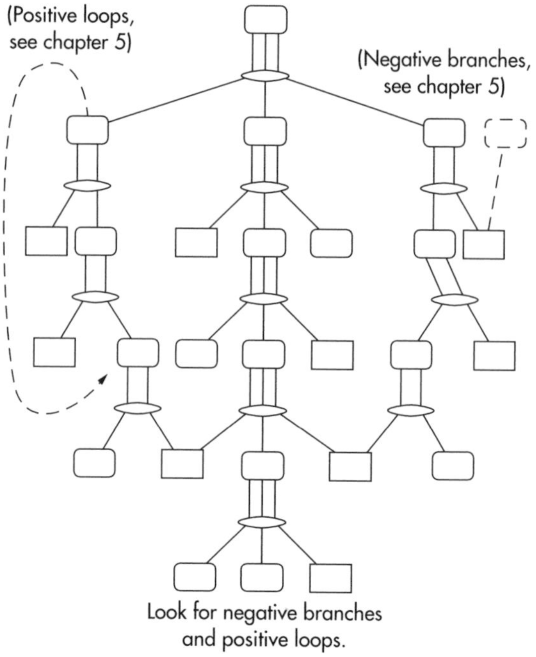
(Positive loops, see chapter 5)
(Negative branches, see chapter 5)
Look for negative branches and positive loops.

FIGURE 7.31—*Continued.*

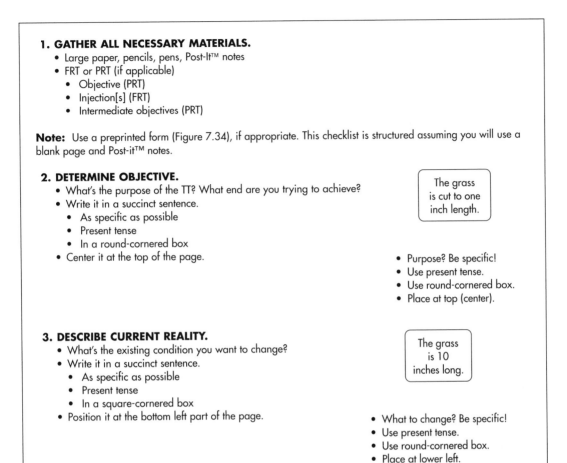

1. GATHER ALL NECESSARY MATERIALS.

- Large paper, pencils, pens, Post-It™ notes
- FRT or PRT (if applicable)
  - Objective (PRT)
  - Injection[s] (FRT)
  - Intermediate objectives (PRT)

Note: Use a preprinted form (Figure 7.34), if appropriate. This checklist is structured assuming you will use a blank page and Post-it™ notes.

2. DETERMINE OBJECTIVE.

- What's the purpose of the TT? What end are you trying to achieve?
- Write it in a succinct sentence.
  - As specific as possible
  - Present tense
  - In a round-cornered box
- Center it at the top of the page.

The grass is cut to one inch length.

- Purpose? Be specific!
- Use present tense.
- Use round-cornered box.
- Place at top (center).

3. DESCRIBE CURRENT REALITY.

- What's the existing condition you want to change?
- Write it in a succinct sentence.
  - As specific as possible
  - Present tense
  - In a square-cornered box
- Position it at the bottom left part of the page.

The grass is 10 inches long.

- What to change? Be specific!
- Use present tense.
- Use round-cornered box.
- Place at lower left.

FIGURE 7.32. Procedures for Building a Five-Element Transition Tree.

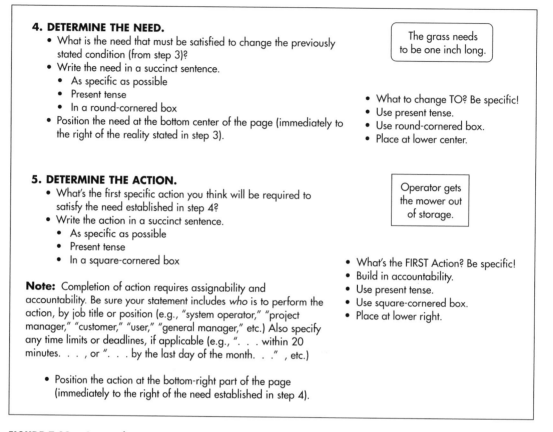

4. DETERMINE THE NEED.

- What is the need that must be satisfied to change the previously stated condition (from step 3)?
- Write the need in a succinct sentence.
  - As specific as possible
  - Present tense
  - In a round-cornered box
- Position the need at the bottom center of the page (immediately to the right of the reality stated in step 3).

The grass needs to be one inch long.

- What to change TO? Be specific!
- Use present tense.
- Use round-cornered box.
- Place at lower center.

5. DETERMINE THE ACTION.

- What's the first specific action you think will be required to satisfy the need established in step 4?
- Write the action in a succinct sentence.
  - As specific as possible
  - Present tense
  - In a square-cornered box

Note: Completion of action requires assignability and accountability. Be sure your statement includes *who* is to perform the action, by job title or position (e.g., "system operator," "project manager," "customer," "user," "general manager," etc.) Also specify any time limits or deadlines, if applicable (e.g., ". . . within 20 minutes. . . , or ". . . by the last day of the month. . ." , etc.)

- Position the action at the bottom-right part of the page (immediately to the right of the need established in step 4).

Operator gets the mower out of storage.

- What's the FIRST Action? Be specific!
- Build in accountability.
- Use present tense.
- Use square-cornered box.
- Place at lower right.

FIGURE 7.32—*Continued.*

6. DETERMINE THE EFFECT.

- What is the direct and unavoidable outcome of combining the reality, need, and action from steps 3–5?
- Write the effect in a succinct sentence.
    - As specific as possible
    - Present tense
    - In a round-cornered box

Note #1: Be careful not to skip any intervening effects. Write the first, most immediate effect. If that produces a second effect (before you accomplish the next action), display the two effects separately.

Note #2: Remember that branching can occur in a Transition Tree. If this happens, it will most likely occur at the effect (i.e., more than one effect of the same action).

- Center the effect above the need established in step 4.
- Connect the reality, need, and action to the effect with three arrows enclosed by an ellipse.

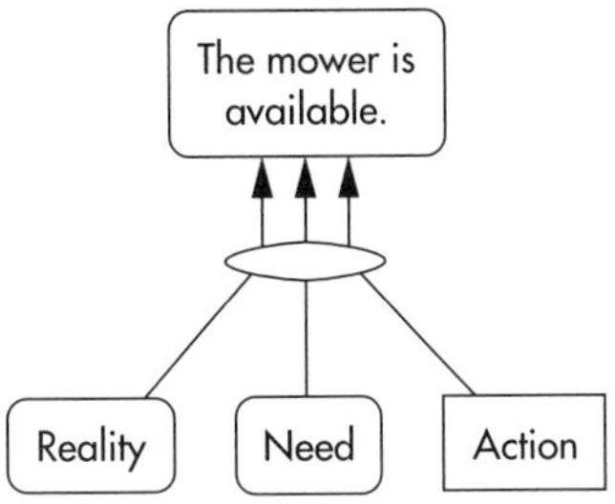

- What's the DIRECT AND UNAVOIDABLE outcome of the action? Be specific!
- Use present tense.
- Don't skip intervening effects.
- Use round-cornered box.
- Look for possible branches.
- Center the effect above the need.
- Connect need with reality, need, and action.

Intervening Effects

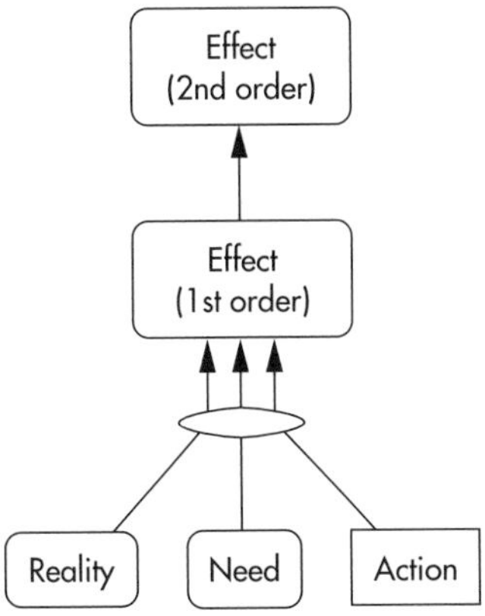

Branching

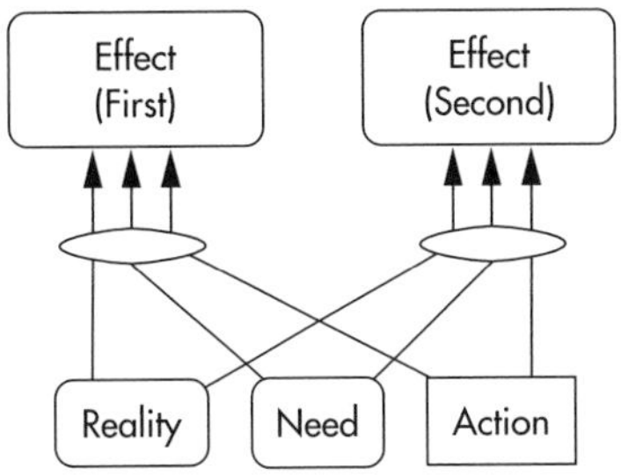

FIGURE 7.32—*Continued.*

7. SCRUTINIZE THE CONNECTIONS.

- Verify the logical connections between the reality-need-action and the effect.
- Use the "Categories of Legitimate Reservation" (chapter 2).
- Look particularly for:
  - Clarity—Clear and comprehensible?
  - Causality—Do the reality, need, and action really produce this effect?
  - Insufficiency—Is any cause missing?
  - Progress—Does this effect *really* move me closer to my objective?
  - Negative branches—Possible undesirable effects of the action? (Refer to chapter 5 for more on negative branches.)

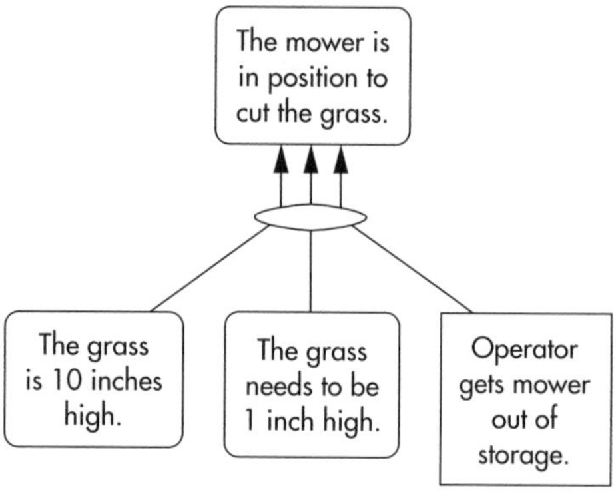

- Use the CLR.
- Clarity?
- Causality?
- Insufficiency?
- Progress?
- Negative branch?

8. IDENTIFY THE RATIONALE FOR THE NEXT NEED.

- What characteristic of the situation makes the most recent effect not enough to produce the desired objective by itself?
- What is the next most important condition of reality that generates the need for the next action?
- Write it in a succinct sentence.
  - As specific as possible
  - Present tense
  - In a round-cornered box
- Position the rationale to the right of the effect identified in step 6.

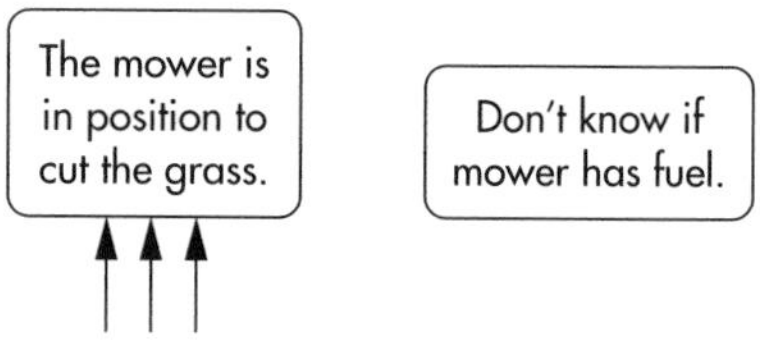

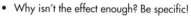

- Why isn't the effect enough? Be specific!
- Use present tense.
- Use round-cornered box.
- Place to right of effect.

9. DETERMINE THE NEXT NEED.

- What is the next immediate and unavoidable need for action generated by combining the results of steps 6 and 8?
- Write it in a succinct sentence.
  - As specific as possible
  - Present tense
  - In a round-cornered box
- Center the need directly above the effect identified in step 6.
- Connect the preceding effect (from step 6) and the rationale (from step 8) with this need, using two arrows enclosed by an ellipse.

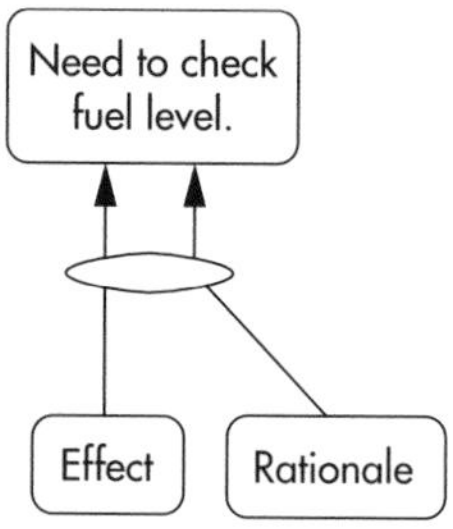

- What is the next need? Be specific!
- Use present tense.
- Use round-cornered box.
- Center need above effect.
- Connect need with effect, rationale.

FIGURE 7.32—*Continued.*

10. SCRUTINIZE THE CONNECTIONS.

- Verify the logical connections between the effect-rationale and the next-level need.
- Use the "Categories of Legitimate Reservation" (chapter 2).
- Look particularly for:
  - Clarity—Clear and comprehensible?
  - Causality—Do the effect and rationale really produce this new need?
  - Insufficiency—Is any cause missing?
  - Progress—Does this connection *really* move me closer to my objective?
  - Negative branches—Possible undesirable effects of the action? (Refer to chapter 5 for more on negative branches.)

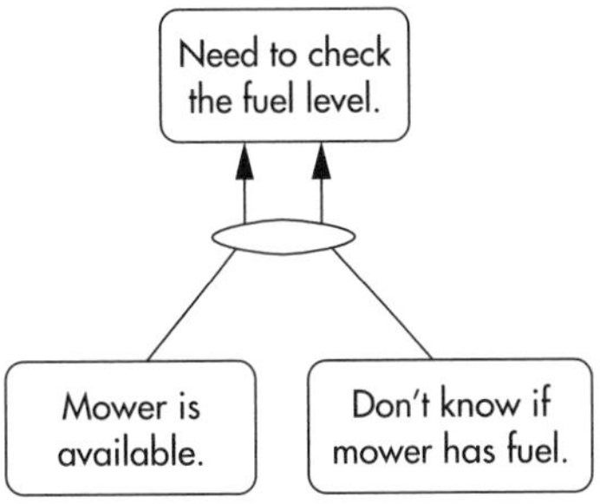

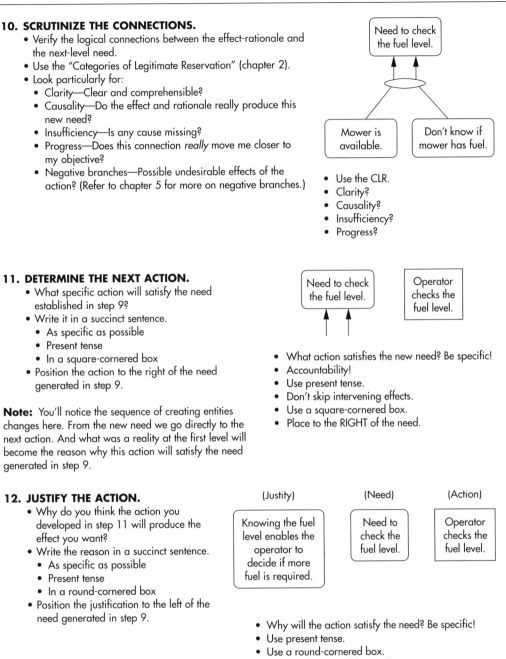

- Use the CLR.
- Clarity?
- Causality?
- Insufficiency?
- Progress?

11. DETERMINE THE NEXT ACTION.

- What specific action will satisfy the need established in step 9?
- Write it in a succinct sentence.
  - As specific as possible
  - Present tense
  - In a square-cornered box
- Position the action to the right of the need generated in step 9.

Note: You'll notice the sequence of creating entities changes here. From the new need we go directly to the next action. And what was a reality at the first level will become the reason why this action will satisfy the need generated in step 9.

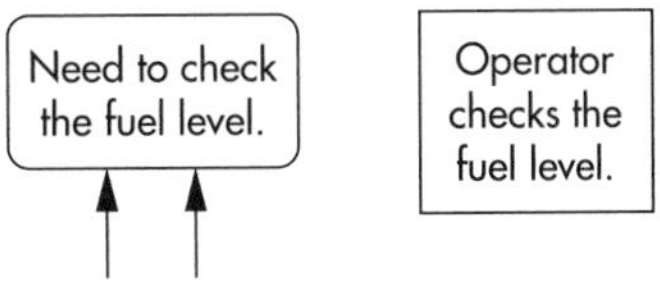

- What action satisfies the new need? Be specific!
- Accountability!
- Use present tense.
- Don't skip intervening effects.
- Use a square-cornered box.
- Place to the RIGHT of the need.

12. JUSTIFY THE ACTION.

- Why do you think the action you developed in step 11 will produce the effect you want?
- Write the reason in a succinct sentence.
  - As specific as possible
  - Present tense
  - In a round-cornered box
- Position the justification to the left of the need generated in step 9.

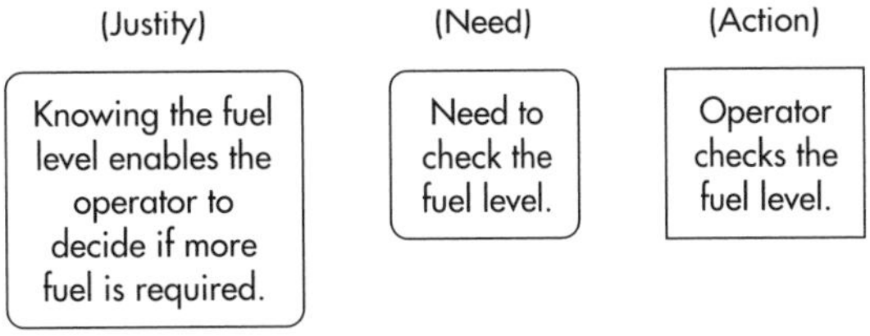

- Why will the action satisfy the need? Be specific!
- Use present tense.
- Use a round-cornered box.
- Place to the LEFT of the need.

FIGURE 7.32—*Continued.*

13. REPEAT STEPS 6–12.

- Continue building the Transition Tree by repeating steps 6–12 until the objective you established in step 2 is the next logical effect.
- Be sure that any branches that diverged reach a point of final completion or converge at the objective.

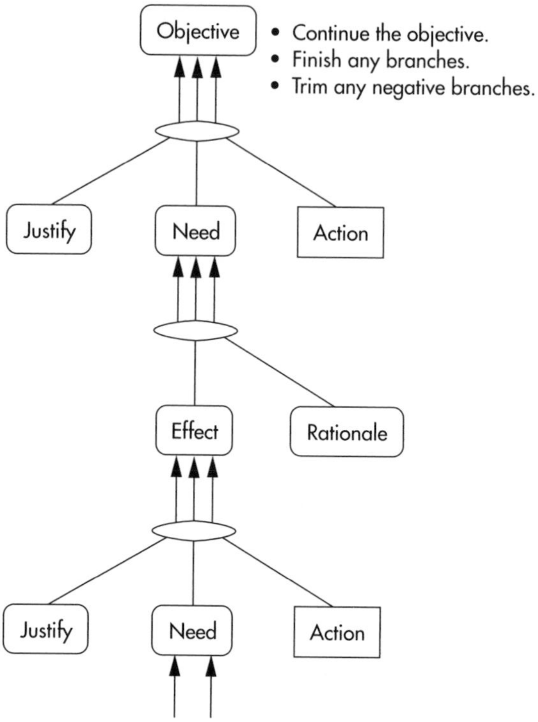

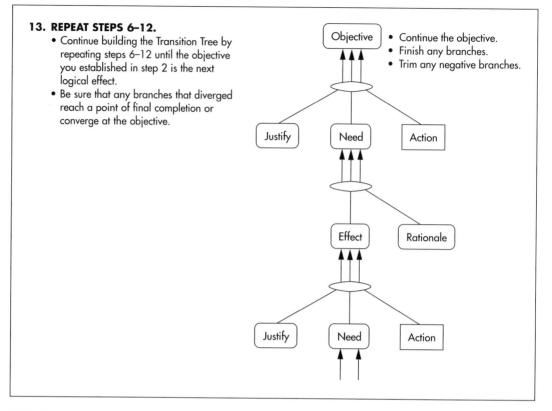

FIGURE 7.32—*Continued.*

14. REVIEW THE COMPLETED TREE.

- Read through the tree in its entirety.
  - Does it make sense?
  - Does it agree with your intuition about what should be done and in what sequence?
  - Is everything there that should be there?
  - If the answer to any of these questions is "No," modify the tree as necessary.
- Review each action again, this time looking for possible negative branches. "Trim" with supplementary actions as necessary.
- Look for opportunities to build in positive reinforcing loops, if applicable.
- Review your tree with someone else who has knowledge of the subject; modify as necessary.

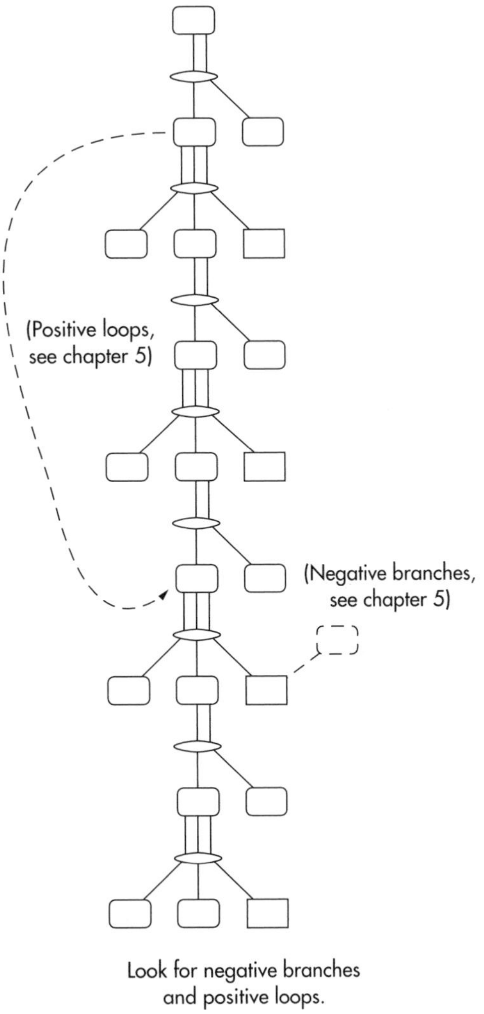
(Positive loops, see chapter 5)
(Negative branches, see chapter 5)
Look for negative branches and positive loops.

FIGURE 7.32—*Continued.*

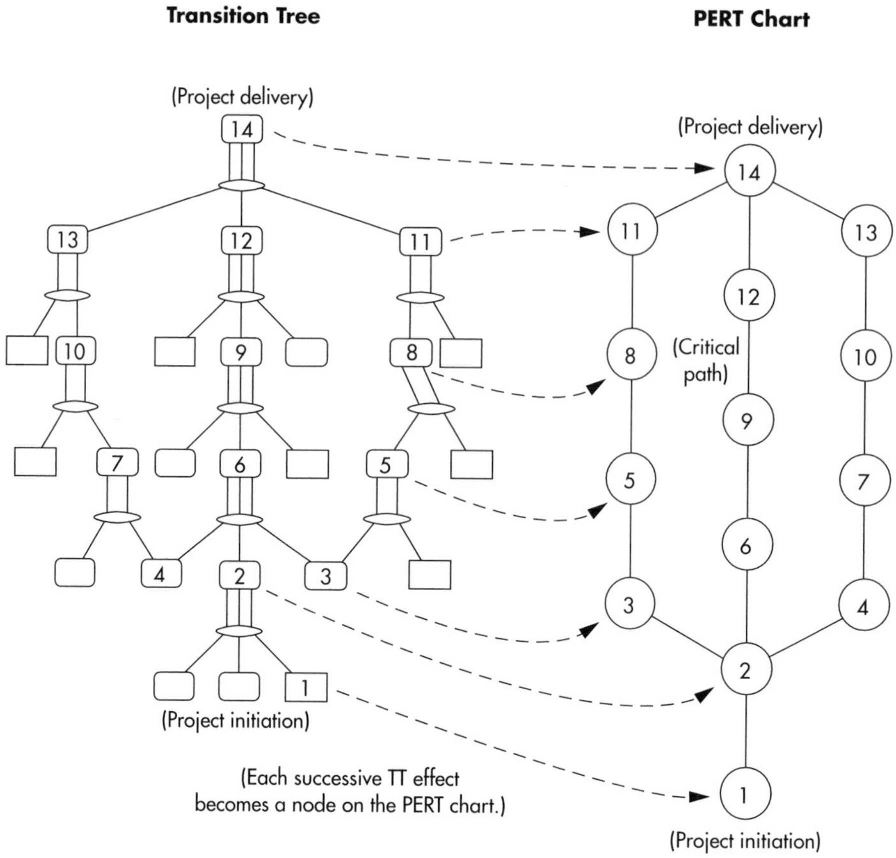

FIGURE 7.33. Similarities Between Transition Trees and PERT Charts.

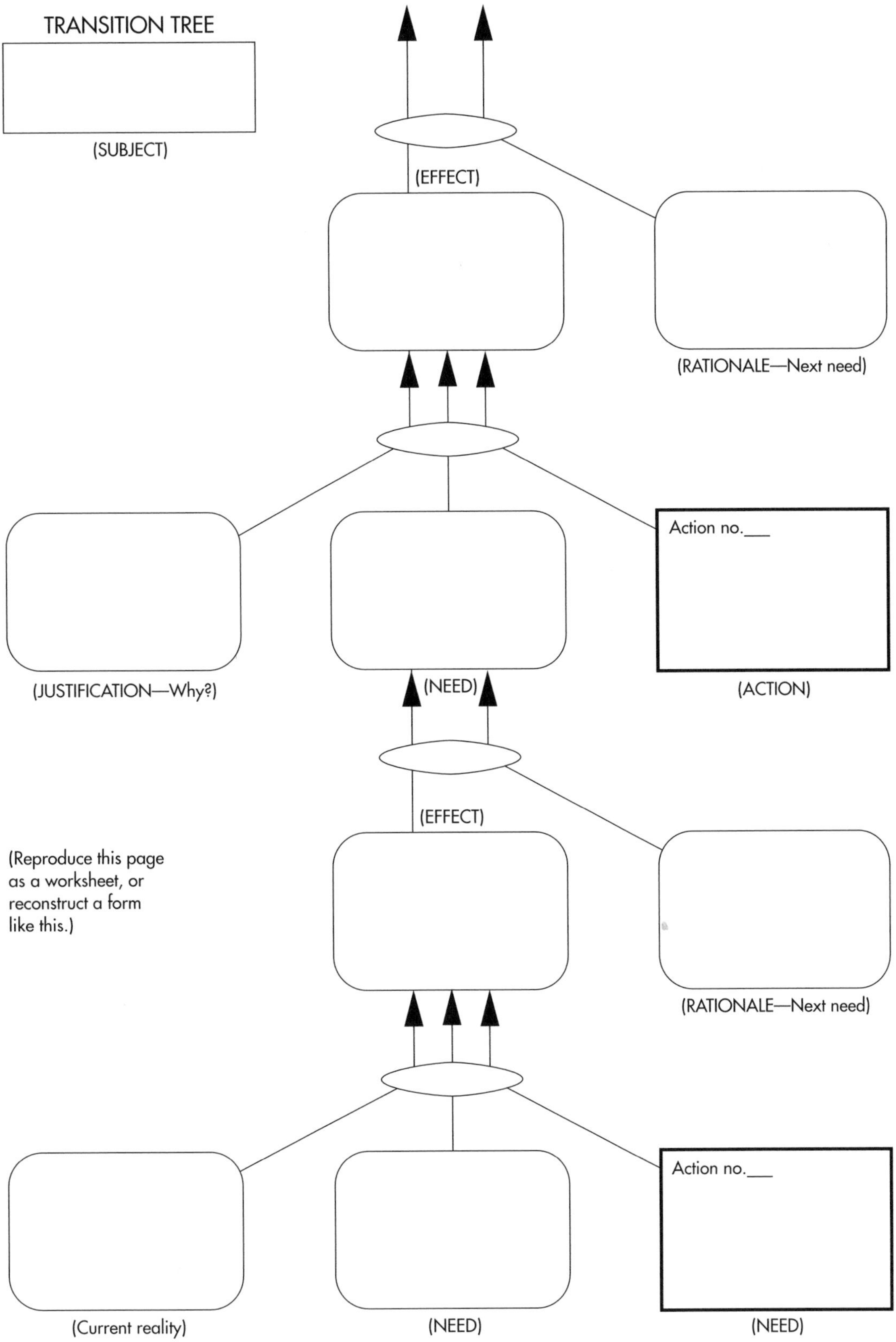

(Reproduce this page as a worksheet, or reconstruct a form like this.)

FIGURE 7.34. Blank Form for a Five-Element Transition Tree.

Chapter 8
GROUP DYNAMICS AND THE TOC THINKING PROCESS

Chapter Outline

To beat the bureaucracy, make your problem their problem.
—Principle of Displaced Hassle

"Group dynamics" refers to the use of the TOC tools by two or more people working together. There are several different ways that groups can use the logical tools as a basis for interaction.

One person might construct a tree on his or her own, while a second person might scrutinize it. A third person might observe to be sure that the rules of logic (the Categories of Legitimate Reservation) are being followed by the first two. Groups of two or more might collaborate in the construction of a tree as a team. Or, one person might use the tree as a vehicle of persuasion, to logically structure a presentation to a second party in order to gain commitment or approval for a new idea—to convince others to "buy in" on the idea.

Up to this point, we've talked about each of the logical tools as if we were using them by ourselves. But none of us lives or works in complete isolation. We're all parts of various complex systems that invariably include other people. And the problems we face in these systems usually involve other people, or at least their solution requires the cooperation of others.

So it's worth devoting some time to examining the ways two or more people might effectively use these logical tools together. Why would you want to do this? There are several distinct reasons:

- To overcome personal biases or "blind spots." Everyone has them. We overlook or "see through" things every day. A different set of eyes can often see things we alone might miss.
- To promote synergy in the creative process—"two heads are better than one."

- To enable instant scrutiny of one's own logic, ensuring better quality on the first pass.
- To overcome a shortage of expertise—no one person might have all the requisite knowledge.
- To engender a sense of cohesiveness, teamwork, and unified commitment.
- To communicate disagreement in a way that averts conflict. In this instance, the Categories of Legitimate Reservation can be used without resorting to trees to help others discover their own logical inconsistencies and correct them without embarrassment.

ASSUMPTIONS

The effective use of the logical tools in a group is based on several key assumptions:

- No one person is likely to have all the required knowledge on a complex subject to analyze it comprehensively.
- Better system solutions result from a wider range of inputs.
- People gain a sense of commitment from participation; involvement satisfies affiliation and esteem needs.
- Implementation is easier when participation is broader.
- Everyone has personal biases that can compromise logical examination of problems.
- All individuals, to some degree, have a pride of authorship, or pride of the inventor, which can color their objectivity in analyzing their "brain children" and any ideas that might be perceived to compete with them.
- People often defend their ideas because of an emotional commitment to them.
- People in any system are sensitive to "turf control" and resist infringement on it.
- People are more open to other points of view if these other viewpoints are presented in a nonthreatening way.
- Most people would rather discover their own mistakes than have someone else point them out.
- Most people, at heart, want the system to succeed.

HOW TO USE THIS CHAPTER

This chapter is intended to be used in concert with the five logical tools and the Categories of Legitimate Reservation. It is not primarily an "ode to teamwork," though team effort is a significant part of this chapter. A suggested approach is to:

- Read the section that applies to the type of group use you would like to employ.

- Review the earlier chapters that apply to your situation.
- Thoroughly review the Categories of Legitimate Reservation, especially Figure 8.4, "Communicating Using the Categories of Legitimate Reservation."
- Practice in a "safe" (nonthreatening) environment.

DESCRIPTION OF THE GROUP PROCESSES

Perhaps the best way to introduce the concept of group dynamics in the TOC Thinking Process is to examine the different "roles" you might play. Here's an overview of these roles, which are discussed in detail a bit later.

Presenter

The most frequent role you're likely to play is presenter. In this role, you'll be showing a tree you've constructed to someone else—maybe to a number of people at the same time. Your presentation may be informal—a private meeting with one other person whose advice you seek in bulletproofing the logic of your tree. Or your presentation might be formal—a meeting or briefing at which you're offering a proposal or trying to enlist support or approval for an idea. In either case, as a presenter your most important function is to lead your audience, whether it's one person or a group, through the unbroken chain of cause and effect (or necessary conditions) from origin to conclusion. Specific guidance on how to present a tree follows in "Presenting the CRT, FRT, and TT," p. 333.

Scrutinizer

At times you might be a scrutinizer. In this role, you watch and listen as someone else presents a tree. Using your understanding of the Categories of Legitimate Reservation, you assess the quality of the logical connections between causes and effects, or between necessary conditions. When you identify a causal or necessary condition connection that doesn't seem to conform to the rules of logic, you raise one or more of the eight reservations (refer to chapter 2, "Categories of Legitimate Reservation"). As the presenter explains his or her rationale for the connection, you assess the logic of the explanation and suggest ways to tighten the logic. A scrutinizer needs two basic qualifications to scrutinize well: (1) an understanding of the subject matter under consideration, and (2) an understanding of the Categories of Legitimate Reservation. Specific guidance on how to scrutinize follows in "4. Scrutinize the Tree as the Presenter Reads Each Layer," p. 334.

Facilitator

The facilitator is the guardian of the logical process—no more, no less. As a facilitator, your only concern should be with the correct application of the Categories of Legitimate Reservation and the protocol for introducing reservations, described in Figure 8.4, at the end of the chapter. The facilitator need not be an expert, or even knowledgeable, in the subject matter of the tree, because the facilitator's function is more like an umpire, not a participant. Facilitators must be very well qualified in the use of the Categories of Legitimate Reservation. Specific duties of facilitators follow in "Small-Group Scrutiny," below.

Communicator

The role of communicator is similar, and related, to that of scrutinizer. One of the things a scrutinizer does is to communicate disagreement with what a presenter says, though in a nonconfrontational way. But the communicator role is not limited to the scrutiny of trees alone. What happens if you're in a meeting, and a speaker makes a statement that you suspect to be in error, or composed largely of nonsense? You could challenge the speaker about it directly, and earn his or her undying displeasure in the process. (In some cases, this might be your objective!) Or you could communicate your disagreement in a way that doesn't alienate the speaker or belittle him or her in everyone's eyes. In this instance, your knowledge of the Categories of Legitimate Reservation will enable you to zero in on the logical deficiencies in the speaker's statement. But it will be your deft use of the protocol for introducing those reservations that will avert confrontation and ill feelings. "Communicating Disagreement," p. 33b, tells specifically how to use the communication protocol.

Persuader

The persuader is a presenter with a purpose—to obtain "buy in." The presenter typically offers up his or her tree for someone else's scrutiny primarily to have the scrutinizer help tighten its logic. Normally, however, presenters do this because they anticipate taking the next big step into persuasion; they want to show their trees to someone of influence whom they hope to persuade on the subject of the tree. So a persuader is part presenter and part communicator. But a major difference lies in the requirement for the persuader to listen and watch for feedback from the decision maker—both verbal and nonverbal—and adjust accordingly. In addition, the persuader must understand some aspects of psychology that dictate variations in how the trees are presented if the persuasion is to succeed. "Persuading Others with Your Logic," p. 343, discusses how to use the Categories of Legitimate Reservation and logic trees for persuasion.

GROUP APPLICATIONS OF THE TOC THINKING PROCESS

Once you appreciate the different roles that make up the group dynamic, you can think about ways to apply it. The applications described here are a sampling—by no means inclusive—intended to stimulate your thinking about new ways to use the logical tools. By all means, let your imagination run loose on this one.

Small-Group Scrutiny

The most common group application is scrutiny of one person's tree in a small group—usually three or four. In such a situation, a presenter takes the group through his or her tree while a scrutinizer and a facilitator watch and listen. Presenters may begin with a brief synopsis of the issue that prompted their construction of the tree. They then make it clear that they are looking for rigorous, constructive criticism—the more, the better.

1. Self-Scrutinize Ahead of Time

As a courtesy to the person who's scrutinizing your work, make sure your trees are as tight, or "dry," as you can make them before you show them to someone else. This means that after you've constructed your tree, you should set it aside for some period of time—perhaps a day or so—then examine it again with a "fresh eye," using the Categories of Legitimate Reservation (refer to chapter 2).

2. Get Your Worst Enemy to Help

This is a shock to many people, because most of us are used to soliciting approval, approbation, or agreement, rather than criticism. In most instances, when we say, "What do you think about this?" the answer we're really seeking is, "Boy, that's just great!" In real, productive scrutiny, however, we shouldn't shrink from the "slings and arrows" of frank evaluation. In fact, this is what we want. Remember that one of our assumptions for this chapter was that we all have personal biases, or "blind spots," that prevent us from seeing some of the weaknesses in our own logic. We need a logical devil's advocate to help us find the holes in our tree.

The best scrutinizer is one who has no emotional ties to you, one who doesn't really care about hurting your feelings but who knows the subject of the tree like a book. The more blood the scrutinizer leaves on the floor in an informal setting, the less blood you're likely to leave when the chips are on the table.

Who is best able to do this kind of job for you? Your own worst enemy, though if that person really doesn't like you, he or she might not be inclined to help! If this arrangement works, a third party acting as a facilitator can help keep the blood-letting from becoming emotionally charged. Seriously, though, you're better off having a scrutinizer who is not emotionally attached to you as a friend or to the subject of your tree. The exception to this rule would be a scrutinizer who is equally trained in the TOC tools and the Categories of Legitimate Reservation, and who can set aside personal biases toward you or the issue in order to assess your tree objectively.

3. Present Trees Without Explanation

You should briefly explain the subject and the purpose of your trees to a scrutinizer and facilitator, but once you begin reading your trees, don't amplify what's already there. One of the things you're checking for is to see whether the tree can stand on its own, at face value. Use the following guidelines when reading your trees.

Presenting the CRT, FRT, and TT

a. Starting at an entry point, read aloud verbatim the content of the first cause entity (at the tail of an arrow).

b. Pause briefly to allow time for scrutinizers to raise Clarity or Entity Existence reservations. Watch for nonverbal feedback that might indicate confusion or an unasked question. Try to draw out the question. Address any reservations using the communication protocol and responses described in Figure 8.4. If no reservations are raised, go on to step c.

c. Read the first entity again, preceding it with "If . . .". Follow up immediately by reading the effect preceded by ". . . then . . .". If the cause includes multiple entities (indicated by an ellipse), read all cause entities consecutively before reading the effect.

d. Pause briefly to allow scrutinizers time to raise Clarity or causality reservations. Watch for nonverbal feedback, as in step b. Use the communication protocol in Figure 8.4 to respond to reservations. Modify your tree if you need to as you go along.

e. After you make each modification to your tree, ask if there are any other reservations. If so, address them. If not, go on without delay.

f. Read the most recent effect as the cause for the next effect. Repeat steps a through e. Continue this way until you have finished the entire tree.

Note: It won't help your presentation if your audience is leapfrogging ahead to read entities higher in your tree. You might want to consider covering part of the tree you haven't presented and "unfolding" it as you move on to each new level.

Presenting the CRD and PRT

a. Read the CRD aloud from left to right, and the PRT from top to bottom.

b. Read the objective of each tree first. Pause briefly to allow scrutinizers time to raise clarity reservations. Watch for nonverbal feedback that might indicate unasked questions, and try to draw them out. Explain as necessary, and modify if you see a need to do so. If not, go on.

c. Reread the objective preceded by "In order to have . . . ," followed immediately by the first requirement (for a CRD) or the first intermediate objective (for a PRT). Pause briefly to allow scrutinizers to raise reservations. Watch for nonverbal feedback, as in step b. If no reservations are raised, continue.

d. Read the next "In order to have . . . we must have . . ." relationship. Pause to allow reservations to be raised. Watch for nonverbal feedback, as in step b. Address reservations as required, and modify your tree if you see a need to do so.

e. Repeat step d until you've read the entire tree.

4. Scrutinize the Tree as the Presenter Reads Each Layer

If you're the scrutinizer, review the Categories of Legitimate Reservation (chapter 2) beforehand, and familiarize yourself with the sequence for offering reservations shown in Figure 8.3, at the end of the chapter. This protocol requires that you adhere to the following sequence:

Level 1: Seek first to understand before seeking to be understood. In other words, always raise a Clarity reservation as the first step. Give the presenter an opportunity to help you understand exactly what he or she is trying to say, even if you're relatively certain you already know what that might be. The presenter's explanation will clarify the issue.

Level 2: If you still have a reservation after the clarification, raise the entity or Causality Existence reservation, as appropriate, but don't explain or specify the concern you have. *Allow the presenter the opportunity to find his or her own deficiency first.*

Level 3: If the presenter doesn't explain the entity or causality existence to your satisfaction, or if the presenter asks you to help him or her understand the nature of your reservation, you are now obligated to specify your reservation as one of the following:

- Cause Insufficiency
- Additional Cause
- Cause-Effect Reversal
- Predicted Effect Existence
- Tautology

You must also justify your reservation by providing the missing cause (if a Cause Insufficiency or Additional Cause), an explanation of the Cause-Effect Reversal or of the circularity of logic (Tautology), or the Predicted Effect that is or is not present. A word of caution: Don't nit-pick excessively unless the presenter asks you to do so. Not only does this slow the process down, it tends to increase presenters' blood pressure! Your ultimate test of whether to press an issue or let it go should be twofold:

- Would an average reasonable listener see and understand the logical connection? If the answer is "no," be a "bulldog" about it! If "yes," let it go.
- Will the presenter's credibility be compromised later if I let this go unchallenged now? If the answer is "yes," keep the pressure on. If "no," let it pass.

5. Facilitate the Logical Process

If your role is facilitator, your job is to be the "logic traffic cop." Make sure the presenter follows the communication protocol for reading trees and responding to reservations. Make sure scrutinizers follow the protocol for raising reservations. Don't inject any comments concerning content of the subject matter of the tree unless specifically asked to do so by the presenter. As a facilitator, you should:

- Check to be sure that all reservations have been surfaced before allowing the presenter to move on.
- Raise your own reservations only as a last resort—and confine them to logical issues, not content issues.
- Watch for miscommunication between presenter and scrutinizer. Paraphrase either the presenter's entity or the scrutinizer's reservation if necessary.
- Keep a record of term definitions the presenter provides when Clarity reservations are raised, and watch to be sure that later uses of those terms are consistent with earlier definitions. Challenge the presenter when they seem not to be.
- Summarize any modifications to the tree suggested by the scrutinizer and agreed to by the presenter. Keep a record of these changes if requested by the presenter.

• Evaluate the presenter's progress through his or her tree. If the presenter seems to be hammered with logical reservations at every turn, suspend the process. Obviously he or she needs to go back and work on the tree some more, because it's not "dry" enough for effective scrutiny without wasting other people's time. A perceptive presenter might recognize the need to do this without being told. But if not, you, as facilitator should suggest it.

Criticism, like rain, should be gentle enough to nourish one's growth without destroying one's roots.

—Unknown

Communicating Disagreement

One of the most difficult things anyone can try to do is to voice an opinion that someone else isn't going to want to hear—especially in a public gathering. It's akin to "telling the emperor he's not wearing any clothes." For instance, if someone in a group makes a statement you know to be erroneous, not factual, or not logical, what can you do about it?

Obviously, one choice is to let it pass without comment. There are times when this might be politically advisable—if it's your boss or your company's CEO, for example. As long as there are no immediate adverse consequences to the erroneous statement, necessary corrections can be delayed until a more private moment.

But if the speaker's error will compound problems, correction probably should not be delayed. What if the erroneous assertion is to be the basis for subsequent action? In good conscience, you might not be able to let the error slide. You might have to resolve it immediately. Here's an example.

The Plant Expansion Example

Let's say you're a member of a team planning an expansion of your company's plant. In the course of a team meeting, the team leader says, "If we double the size of the construction team, we can finish the job in 40 percent less time." You're reasonably sure that this assertion is not supported by logic or facts. And if you let the issue pass without comment, the team might decide to commit a lot of money toward increasing the workforce without any real hope of reducing the schedule. You could embarrass the team leader by contradicting him or her in front of everybody, or you could follow the TOC communication protocol, which might sound like this.

You: "Could you clarify what you mean by 'finish the job in 40 percent less time'?" (Clarity reservation.)

Leader: "Sure. It means we can begin plant operations three months earlier than we expected."

You: "I have a question about that. I'm not sure I see how doubling the workforce alone will speed completion by that much. Could you explain it?" (Causality reservation.)

(Leader explains that the additional workers will allow most tasks to be worked in parallel rather than sequentially.)

You: "I still have a reservation about the schedule reduction. It seems to me that there might be other factors that would affect it besides size of workforce alone (Cause Insufficiency). One of those might be the purchasing of long lead-time items like the milling and machining equipment. Another might be the sequential dependency of major parts of the job. (Provide the missing elements.) Each of these might negate the effects of increasing the workforce. How can we get around these obstacles?"

(Leader reconsiders the original statement and modifies the schedule reduction to 20 percent, which, considering workforce alone, is acceptable to you.)

Benefits of the Communication Protocol

What have you accomplished? You've communicated your disagreement to the team leader in front of colleagues without incurring resentment. In fact, everyone is probably more comfortable because the new time estimate is more realistic. How did you do it? You used the TOC communication protocol to focus the disagreement *on the issue rather than on the person making the statement.*

1. Nonthreatening. You began with an innocent enough question, one that threatens nobody: "Could you clarify what you mean . . . ?" You allowed for the possibility that you might have misunderstood what was said, so you confirmed it before risking "foot-in-mouth" syndrome. Once you were sure you really heard what you thought you did, you escalated your disagreement by raising a Causality Existence reservation—again, keeping the focus on the logic of the issue rather than on the person making the statement. More important, by saying "I'm not sure I see how . . . ," you keep the perception of fault away from the person who made the statement.

2. Allows People to Find Their Own Errors. By asking for an explanation of causality, you increase the chance that people will find and correct their own logical deficiencies without your having to rub their noses in them. When the speaker still didn't find the fallacy in the statement regarding productivity, you took it a step farther by raising the Cause Insufficiency reservation, and made your position clearer by providing the cause you thought might be missing. Again, your focus was on the construction planning process, not on the leader's fallacious reasoning.

3. Engenders Cooperation. By concluding with a question that includes everyone ("How can we get around these obstacles?"), you save the leader's pride by allowing that a 40 percent schedule reduction still might be possible, and you put the initiative for solving the problem on the whole group, rather than dumping it back in the leader's lap alone. Using the TOC communication protocol enables you to protect the interpersonal relationship while you're registering your disagreement—an invaluable benefit if you're going to have to work with the same people in the future!

The moral of this story:

Asking dumb questions is easier than correcting dumb mistakes.
—Launegayer's Observation

How to Use the TOC Communication Protocol

So, how does this communication protocol work? Essentially, it's much like scrutinizing a tree. It uses a three-level hierarchy.

Level 1: You begin by asking for clarification, to be sure you understand what was said. Many times that will resolve the issue without having to go farther.

Level 2: If not, you begin with the Entity Existence and Causality Existence reservations, but you let the speaker explain. You continue seeking to understand before you try to make yourself understood.

Level 3: If you're still not satisfied with the explanation, then you have to make yourself understood by specifying the precise nature of your reservation and providing the missing or inverted elements—Cause Insufficiency, Additional Cause, Tautology, or Cause-Effect Reversal. And you support your contention using an additional Predicted Effect. Figure 8.1 provides a road map through the three levels.

Don't lose sight of one very important factor, however. Remember that when scrutinizing a logic tree, you can assume that those present are conversant with the TOC rules of logic—the Categories of Legitimate Reservation—and the communication protocol. You can use shorthand terminology ("I have a Causality Existence reservation."), and people will understand what you mean. But in any other circumstances, you must assume that people won't understand—and might resent the brusque appearance of your use of this shorthand. In just about every setting except tree scrutiny, you'll have to translate the reservations into normal, conversational English. Figure 8.2 provides some suggestions on how to do this.

Building Trees in Teams

By the time you've read this far, the idea of two or more people working together in building a tree has undoubtedly crossed your mind. As with almost anything, it has its advantages and disadvantages.

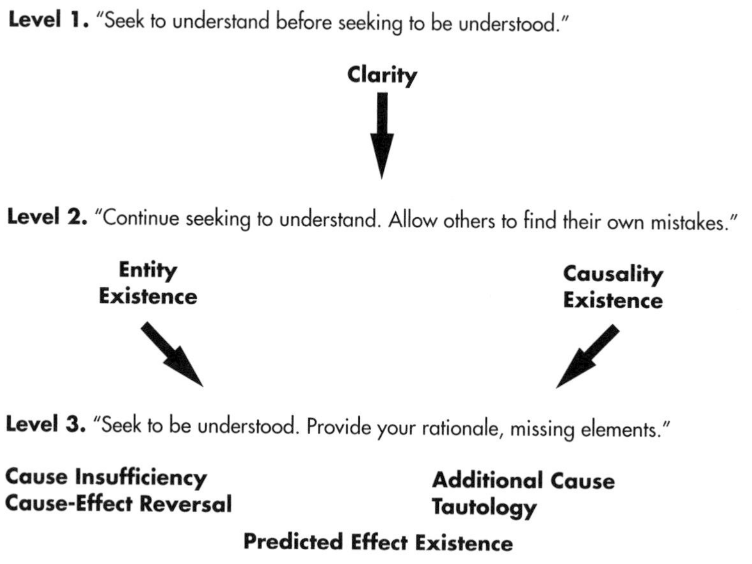
Level 1. "Seek to understand before seeking to be understood."
Clarity
Level 2. "Continue seeking to understand. Allow others to find their own mistakes."
Entity Existence
Causality Existence
Level 3. "Seek to be understood. Provide your rationale, missing elements."
Cause Insufficiency
Cause-Effect Reversal
Additional Cause
Tautology
Predicted Effect Existence

FIGURE 8.1. The TOC Communication Protocol.

Scrutinizing Trees with Others Knowledgeable in CLR	In Casual (or Formal) Conversation
1. "I have a CLARITY reservation on . . . [specify]."	1. "I'm not sure I understand something. Could you CLARIFY what you mean by . . . [specify]?"
2. "I have an ENTITY EXISTENCE reservation on . . . [specify entity]."	2. "Maybe I still don't understand. How do we know that [specify] EXISTS? What evidence is there to support it?"
3. "I have a CAUSALITY EXISTENCE reservation on the connection between [specify]."	3. "I'm not sure I see how [CAUSE] leads to [EFFECT]. Maybe you could explain it to me."
4. "I have a CAUSE INSUFFICIENCY reservation about [specify EFFECT], and I think the missing element is [specify]."	4. "It seems to me there's something missing. Besides [specify CAUSE], you'd also need [provide contributing CAUSE] to get [EFFECT]."
5. "I have a CAUSE-EFFECT REVERSAL reservation. It looks like [specify CAUSE] is really the effect, and vice versa."	5. "I think you definitely have a connection there, but could [specify CAUSE] really be the effect? And [specify EFFECT] really be the cause?"
6. "I have an ADDITIONAL CAUSE reservation about [specify EFFECT], and the Additional Cause is [specify independent CAUSE]."	6. "What you have there looks good. But could there be something completely separate that could give that same effect? I'm thinking of [specify ADDITIONAL CAUSE]."
7. "I have a PREDICTED EFFECT EXISTENCE reservation. If [CAUSE] really leads to [EFFECT], then we should also see (or not see) [specify PREDICTED EFFECT]. But we do not (or do)."	7. "The cause you're proposing is a little hard to verify. It seems to me that if what you say is true, we should also see [specify PREDICTED EFFECT]. But as far as I know, it's not there."
8. "I have a TAUTOLOGY reservation about [specify CAUSE and EFFECT]. The absence or presence of [specify EFFECT] alone doesn't confirm [specify CAUSE]."	8. "Wait a minute. Are you saying that [EFFECT] is the justification that [CAUSE] exists? That sounds like circular logic. Maybe you can explain it to me."

FIGURE 8.2. Translating Reservations into Conversational English.

Advantages

The most obvious advantages of team tree-building are:

1. *Expanded Knowledge Base.* Clearly, in many situations two or more heads are better than one. It's highly likely that others with knowledge of the situation will be able to help you think of things to include in your tree on the first pass that you might otherwise overlook. The more complex your challenge, the more benefit you might derive from assistance in building your tree.

2. *Avoiding "Mental Block."* Sometimes we just hit a dead end, not knowing what to do next. Or maybe we're fresh out of ideas—our creativity "well" is temporarily dry. In such cases, other team members might be able to take up the slack and continue.

3. *Instant Scrutiny.* In a group, when one person comes up with a cause-effect relationship, invariably someone else will question it, perhaps before it's even written down. Answering such questions often takes you through Level 1

(Clarity) and into Level 2 (Existence—either Entity or Causality) before you're even aware of it. As a result, the logic of a group tree might be tighter to begin with than that produced by one person alone. Formal scrutiny time after tree completion can be reduced significantly.

4. *Automatic "Buy-In."* As we'll see later, persuasion is one of the most difficult of skills. Building trees in a group takes care of that. By virtue of participation and consensus with each cause-effect relationship in the tree, everyone contributes to the construction. This imbues each person with a sense of ownership of the tree, or pride of authorship. Goldratt calls this phenomenon the "pride of the inventor." The basic premise is, "How can anyone disagree with something he or she had a direct hand in building?"

Disadvantages

The most obvious disadvantages of building trees in groups are:

1. *Schedule Conflicts.* It's often difficult to get all the people you need together at the same time—even if that's only *two.* It also becomes very frustrating when people must leave to attend to other commitments right in the middle of work.

2. *Time Requirement.* Tree-building in a group takes longer than one person doing it alone. Part of the reason for this is the "instant scrutiny" mentioned above. Every logical connection will undoubtedly elicit some comment from somebody as it's added to the tree. It's an example of the philosophy that "there's no such thing as a free lunch." What you gain in quality on the first pass you pay for in time spent doing it.

3. *Digression.* This is an insidious pitfall of any group activity—brainstorming, group problem solving, or even routine meetings. Put two or more people together, and there will be a natural tendency for them to develop side conversations or to go off on tangents. The classic digression is jumping ahead to the next stage too early: speculating on ideas for solutions before determining core problems, or worrying about implementation before validating the idea's effectiveness. For this reason, every group tree-building effort needs a dedicated facilitator to keep the group on course.

When Is Team Tree-Building Appropriate?

As in almost any other situation, teamwork is appropriate when a problem is complex—perhaps crossing several organizational lines—or obviously requires more knowledge than one person alone is likely to have. It's appropriate for use by task forces or project teams, especially for structured problem solving. Anytime your organization is faced with a constraint, obstacle, or problem, a team can use TOC logical tools to determine:

- What's wrong with the system? (CRT)
- Why is it a problem, and what can be done about it? (CRD)
- Will a new idea work? (FRT)
- What obstacles do we face in implementing the new idea, and how do we overcome them? (PRT)
- What steps must we take—in sequence—to mobilize the solution? (TT)

Procedures for Building Trees in a Group

Here are some simple guidelines for team tree-building:

1. *Determine the players.* Who should participate? Who has the required knowledge? Who can we stand to work with in a group? (And who can't we stand to work with? Friction and personality conflicts don't contribute to unemotional logic any more than they do to other kinds of teamwork.) Limit the total number to between two and five. Any more makes for too cumbersome a group. The disadvantages mentioned above become amplified.

2. *Agree on a quiet, undisturbed meeting place.* The location should include seating around a table and a means of displaying the tree—the visual aid—for all to see as you develop it. Some possible ways to do this include:

- Overhead projector and screen (write on blank transparencies)
- Black or white board (write in chalk or dry-erase marker)
- Flip-chart and easel (write in dark pencil or marking pen)

3. *Select a "scribe" and a "facilitator."* One person should be designated to record "if–then" statements or necessary condition statements on the visual aid. This role as scribe doesn't preclude the person from offering ideas. Another person should serve as facilitator, the primary "keeper of the logic." This person may also offer ideas, but his or her primary role is to monitor and arbitrate the logic process using the Categories of Legitimate Reservation and the Communication Protocol. A secondary role is to record working definitions of terms on which the group agrees. Refer to "Small-Group Scrutiny," p. 332, for the specific duties of facilitators. Be sure to select someone knowledgeable in both the Categories of Legitimate Reservation and the communication protocol for this role.

Everyone else alternates as both tree-builder and scrutinizer. One person offers an idea, and the rest scrutinize it.

4. *Follow the procedures for tree-building.* Refer to the appropriate chapter for the steps in building the tree you need. Be aware that these will only be general guidelines, since building trees in a group is somewhat different than doing it alone.

- Chapter 3—Current Reality Tree
- Chapter 4—Conflict Resolution Diagram
- Chapter 5—Future Reality Tree
- Chapter 6—Prerequisite Tree
- Chapter 7—Transition Tree

5. *Group tree-building protocol.* As you refer to the specific tree-building procedures, use the following sequence to maximize group effectiveness.

a. *Agree on Purpose.* One person begins with a statement of why the group is meeting: "What problem are we attempting to solve?"

b. *Decide on the Tree.* When consensus is reached on the nature of the problem, the group must agree on the appropriate tree to use. The problem might require more than one type of tree, so the group must agree on which tree should be built first.

- If you're not sure of the root cause or core problem (what to change), start with a Current Reality Tree.
- If you already know the root cause or core problem, decide if there's anything preventing you from fixing it right now. If so, start with a Conflict Resolution Diagram. If not, start with a Future Reality Tree.
- If you don't know whether the idea you have for fixing the problem will do the job (what to change to), start with a Future Reality Tree. If you already know what to do, start with a Prerequisite Tree. *But be very careful about jumping to this step.* It assumes that you know with absolute certainty that you've (a) correctly identified the problem and (b) selected the right solution, that is, one that will work. This is not a casual assumption to make!

c. *Formulate the opening statement.* One person begins with an opening statement for the tree. This will vary, depending on the type of tree.

If the tree is:	Start with:	Scribe records:
Current Reality Tree	Statements of undesirable effects	On a separate list
Conflict Resolution Diagram	1. Statement of the conflict or 2. Statement of the objective of the CRD	1. On the right side of the diagram 2. On the left side of the diagram
Future Reality Tree	Statement of injections	At the bottom of the tree
Prerequisite Tree	Statement of the objective of the PRT	At the top of the tree
Transition Tree	1. Statement of the objective of the TT or 2. Statement of the first expected action	1. At the top of the tree 2. At the bottom of the tree

d. *Scrutinize the opening statement.* Everyone scrutinizes the first entity, suggesting modifications or additions until the group reaches consensus.

e. *Build on the opening statement.* One person offers the next logical statement for the tree. Anyone may offer this statement, but some first-time groups need a little more structure. In this situation, let one specific person offer the statement for others to scrutinize. The scribe can designate this person. ("Jean, why don't you start us off? What's next?") As group interaction matures, others will naturally step in with their own ideas.

f. *Continue and scrutinize.* Continue building the tree, one entity at a time, scrutinizing by consensus as you go along. From this point on, use the Categories of Legitimate Reservation aggressively to "dry out" each logical connection as it is made, rather than after the tree is completed.

g. *Review the entire tree.* After group consensus is reached that the tree is completed, have the scribe "present" it aloud, in its entirety, for one final scrutiny by the group. Refine the tree as necessary. If it passes muster, the group should designate someone to convert the tree to some final form for its eventual use.

h. *Decide on the next action.* If this tree needs to be followed with another tree, the group should decide on the next meeting time and that tree they will work on. For example, if the first meeting was dedicated to finding a core problem with a Current Reality Tree, the group might decide that the second meeting should be devoted to building a Conflict Resolution diagram to identify the underlying conflict perpetuating the core problem and to develop an injection to resolve it.

If you want to make enemies, try to change something.

—Woodrow Wilson

Persuading Others with Your Logic

The power of logic is hard to argue with. The TOC logical tools and the Categories of Legitimate Reservation offer you that power. Human behavior is often based on emotion, but even in these cases it might be rational, which implies a degree of predictability. Consequently, the rules of logic—that is, cause and effect—can apply even to what appears to be an emotional or illogical situation. Contrary to Mr. Spock's assertion in *Star Trek,* humans are very logical, even predictable, despite their emotional sides. Logic can be applied to human behavior, but it does require some knowledge of individual and organizational behavior.

Human behavior is comprehensively described in any number of psychology books and will not be addressed in detail here. A short list of such books is included at the end of this chapter.[1] For our purposes, we'll talk about human behavior only to the extent that it applies to our use of the TOC logical tools and the Categories of Legitimate Reservation.

Selling a decision is as important as making a decision. Decision makers must take time to develop selling strategies that turn ideas into action.

—Philip Marvin

"Buy-In"

The concept of "buy-in" is critical to your success in persuading someone to do what you want. Buy-in isn't telling someone to do something. It's not even persuading someone to do something that he or she might not want to do. You achieve buy-in when the target of your persuasion internalizes your objective as his or her own—that is, assumes "ownership" of your initiative. The advantage to buy-in is that the person who buys in is now self-motivated to help you further your objective. You probably won't have to watch over or prod the individual to action.

Buy-in works because of one very basic human behavioral principle: People will usually act in their own self-interest. If you can show them what's in it for them, your chances of achieving buy-in increase. If you can show them that they have a *lot* to gain, their commitment increases exponentially. Such prospective gains can be either positive or avoidance of the negative. A possible positive gain: "You'll get a lot of money." Or, "You'll get a lot of positive visibility with the boss." A possible negative avoidance: "Our plant won't be shut down. We'll all keep our jobs." Or, "Your job will become much easier, and it will cost you less of your departmental budget."

Goldratt has observed that what is *improvement* to one person (usually the person who thinks of an idea) is *change* to another (usually everyone else—or at least the one who has to do something about it). While "improvement" is generally perceived to be good, "change" often is not. You might be able to support the idea logically that your proposal is an improvement from the organization's standpoint (increases Throughput, decreases Inventory, decreases Operating Expense). But unless you can simultaneously create the perception in others that it will somehow benefit them personally, it'll never be more than change to anyone else—and possibly an inconvenience to be avoided.

So in using the TOC logical tools, we must also apply logic—and display it in our trees—to the human behavioral situation. This means incorporating some people's personal undesirable effects in our Current Reality Trees. It means including the personal interests of some people in the assumptions of our Conflict Resolution Diagram. It means prominently displaying people's personal desired effects in our Future Reality Tree and Transition Tree. The trees might be focused primarily on organizational problems and solutions, but they can't ignore personal ones. Okay, whose personal issues must we include? We can't put everybody's in—our tree would be too confusing. To answer this question, we have to know the major players in our scenario.

The Buy-In Players

Besides yourself, there are three kinds of people involved in the buy-in issue.

Players	**Interest/Role**
Intimately Involved People (IIP)	People who are directly affected by the problem or solution; people whose tasks, responsibilities, or authorities might change as the problem is solved. These people have a direct, personal interest—a "stake"—in the problem or its solution.
Outside People (OP)	People *not* directly affected by the problem or solution, but who have some interaction with the system. Effect of problem or solution on them is largely neutral.
Directly Responsible People (DRP)	People who have the responsibility *and* the authority to change the system in order to solve the problem. These people also are exposed to higher visibility and risk in any policy action that they take. As such, they might also be Intimately Involved People—especially if their personal tasks, responsibilities, or authorities are affected.

Each of these players is likely to see the problem or issue from a different perspective. It will occupy a different place in each one's perception of the system and how it ought to be. Consequently, you must consider your audience when preparing a buy-in presentation of logic trees.

Examples of Buy-In Situations

Let's look at some examples of each type of player. First, a family situation. Let's say your son asks to go to an all-night party at the beach. He wants to drive the family's second car and take two friends. Your son and his friends are Intimately Involved People, by virtue of their stake in your decision. So is your spouse, since that's the car he or she usually drives. You are the Directly Responsible Person. To the extent that you and your spouse jointly agree on such decisions, your spouse might also be a Directly Responsible Person. Because you both have a vested interest in the safety of your children, you're both Intimately Involved People as well. The parents of the friends who have already agreed to let their children ride with your son, provide gasoline money, and lend beach equipment are Outside People (to your decision or buy-in).

Here's an organizational situation. Assume you're part of a continuous improvement team in your company. You have a proposal to improve Throughput, which you're ready to present to your boss. Because this proposal has cross-functional implications (it affects more than just your department), your boss's boss has final decision authority on the idea: She's the Directly Responsible Person. Your boss and his contemporary department heads whose people and functions are affected are Intimately Involved People. As such, their activities—and maybe their "empires"—will change to some extent. The purchasing and shipping departments are Outside People, because their cooperation is necessary but the effects of the proposal are largely neutral on them; it's no skin off their noses either way.

Because the Directly Responsible Person isn't likely to decide in your favor without an affirmative recommendation from your boss and his contemporaries (Intimately Involved People), you have to persuade them that your team's idea is beneficial. You might also have to persuade subordinates in each department to buy into the idea, especially if their influence over their boss is significant. In other words, anyone with the power to torpedo your proposal must be "bought in."

Obviously, in the family situation mentioned earlier, your son isn't likely to present you (the Directly Responsible Person) with a logic tree. But in the organizational situation just described, logic trees could prove invaluable for inspiring buy-in of the broad spectrum of people involved.

Using the Logical Tools to Achieve Buy-In

How do you go about persuading a Directly Responsible Person (DRP) to do what you want? There are a couple of approaches, each of which might be appropriate at different times. You'll probably construct the related logic trees in the usual sequence (that is, CRT to define the core problem, CRD to resolve the conflict perpetuating the problem, FRT to validate the proposed solution, and so forth). But for best effect, it's advisable to change the sequence of these trees when you're actually presenting the situation to a Directly Responsible Person.

Why? Because it's a lot like telling the emperor he's not wearing any clothes—it might not be something he's going to be thrilled to hear. It's a natural reaction for everybody who's been told they're directly responsible for a problem to become defensive about it—maybe very defensive. Think how you'd feel if someone came to you with a detailed, logical analysis showing that you're at the root of their problems! So in presenting a logic tree analysis, it's a good idea to first demonstrate that you've considered the Directly Responsible

Person's needs and motivations. It's also a good idea to avoid blaming the DRP for the problem. Instead, try to demonstrate how the *system* has put you both in this undesirable position. In other words, your approach should not be "you against me," but rather "you and I against the system."

Define the Conflict First Begin by first presenting a Conflict Resolution Diagram to describe the conflict relationship. Be sure to read across the limb that represents the Directly Responsible Person's current position first, from left to right. Indicate all the assumptions under each segment of that limb of the CRD. This conveys to the Directly Responsible Person that you understand what he or she is doing and why. Then present the other half of the CRD, the one that shows the conflict and the requirement your position is trying to satisfy. Review those assumptions in detail also. At this point, if your logic is sound, you should have the Directly Responsible Person's agreement that there is, in fact, a conflict.

Then show how you tried to resolve the conflict by thinking of ways to satisfy your requirement without needing your prerequisite. This should convince the Directly Responsible Person that you've done everything in your power to resolve the issue before coming to the DRP. Then show the Directly Responsible Person all the ways you thought of to satisfy his or her requirement without needing his or her prerequisite. Solicit the Directly Responsible Person's input at every step. ("Does this sound like the right objective to you?"; "Would you agree that both these requirements are necessary?"; "Can you see any assumptions I've overlooked?"; "Can you think of any alternatives to either of these prerequisites (injections) that I might have overlooked?") Many Directly Responsible People will have suggestions on how to improve the CRD or assumptions they might want to add. They might even come up with additional injections you hadn't thought of. *Include them in the CRD.* By the time you've done this, in most cases you'll find that the Directly Responsible Person has assumed a degree of ownership for both the conflict and its resolution.

Define the Directly Responsible Person's Current Reality After you have the conflict defined, you need a clearer picture of the cause-effect relationship that makes the Directly Responsible Person act as he or she does. If knowledge truly is power, the Directly Responsible Person's thorough understanding of the cause-effect relationship generating the problem is essential to obtaining a commitment to solve it. Once you've co-opted the Directly Responsible Person using a Conflict Resolution Diagram, you're ready to show how a core problem lies at the root of the undesirable effects (UDE) you want to get rid of. Since that core problem really lies within the DRP's span of control (or at least his or her sphere of influence), you again must be careful not to focus too early on the negatives (UDEs). So rather than presenting the Current Reality Tree the way you constructed it—from the top down—walk through it from the bottom up. Ask for feedback at each step ("Can we agree on this so far?"; "How does that strike you?"; "Any problems with the logic so far?"). Accept any comments or suggestions from the Directly Responsible Person. Those that clearly reinforce the direction your tree is going in help your case. Those that seem to contradict it might actually help you to strengthen your logic. Be sure to slow down as you are about to derive the undesirable effects for the Directly Responsible Person.

Propose the New Future Reality With the Directly Responsible Person co-opted by the Conflict Resolution Diagram and convinced by the Current Reality

Tree, you're ready to show how the solution you propose is a winner for everybody. Present your Future Reality Tree from the bottom up, beginning with the change you want to make. Follow the trunk of the tree logically to the desired effects, just as you did in the Current Reality Tree with the core problem and the undesirable effects. Be sure to show where you anticipated negative branches, how you trimmed them, and where the trimming injection is incorporated into the FRT. Emphasize any positive reinforcing loops you can build into the tree. If you've done your homework well, the Directly Responsible Person should be right with you every step of the way, assuming co-ownership for the solution.

Implementation In many cases, you'll be able to stop with the Future Reality Tree; the job of persuasion will be done. But as we learned in chapter 1, "Ideas are not solutions." If your problem or change is sufficiently complex, and especially if you've never attempted the kind of solution you're proposing, a Directly Responsible Person might want to be convinced that this new idea won't die in execution. This is particularly true if your solution depends on overcoming some critical obstacles to success. You might also have to be prepared to present a Prerequisite Tree (PRT) and a Transition Tree (TT).

These presentations should be considerably easier if you've followed the buy-in approach described above. You'll have the Directly Responsible Person already in your corner, seeking to help you succeed. You should still strive to present the tightest, most logically sound trees that you can. And even if your PRT and TT aren't completely "fleshed out," you're likely to find the Directly Responsible Person helping you by scrutinizing them and suggesting things you might have overlooked. *Accept these suggestions enthusiastically.* Besides helping you with your work, the DRP is reinforcing his or her ownership of your solution by offering them.

CONCLUSION

The scope of this book has been confined to explaining the "basics" of how to use the five Thinking Process tools Goldratt created. I've provided a lot of examples of the use of each tool, but I haven't even touched on the permutations and combinations of ways that the logic tools can be applied. For example, could the Current Reality Tree and the Future Reality Tree be combined into a single tree? Certainly! Such an "integrated" tree could be a powerful persuasion tool. And the Conflict Resolution Diagram can be used in concert with the negative branch during dispute negotiations to quickly assess the effectiveness of proposed solutions.

Applications of this powerful, flexible Thinking Process are the subject of another book. Until that book is written, I challenge the readers of this one to think of creative new ways to apply the process on their own.

In closing, let me recall one of the basic principles of the Theory of Constraints, from chapter 1: Even good solutions deteriorate over time, as the environment and circumstances change. Or, as an anonymous farmer once said:

The hardest thing about milking cows is that they never stay milked.

NOTE

1. The following psychology books may help you to understand why people behave as they do, either singly or in groups. Understanding human behavior provides the basic knowledge foundation needed to build a logic tree about what, at face value, might appear to be a nonlogical subject.

James L. Gibson, John M. Ivancevich, and James H. Donnelly Jr., *Organizations: Behavior, Structure, Process,* 7th ed. (Homewood, Ill.: Richard D. Irwin, 1991).

John Gray, *Men, Women, and Relationships: Making Peace with the Opposite Sex* (Hillsboro, Oreg.: Beyond Words Publishing Co., 1990).

David Keirsey and Marilyn Bates, *Please Understand Me: Character and Temperament Types* (Delmar, Calif.: Prometheus Nemesis Book Co., 1984).

Otto Kroeger and Janet M. Thuesen, *Type Talk* (New York: Delta Books, 1988).

Andrew D. Szilagyi Jr. and Marc J. Wallace Jr., *Organizational Behavior and Performance,* 4th ed. (Glenview, Ill.: Scott, Foresman and Co. 1987).

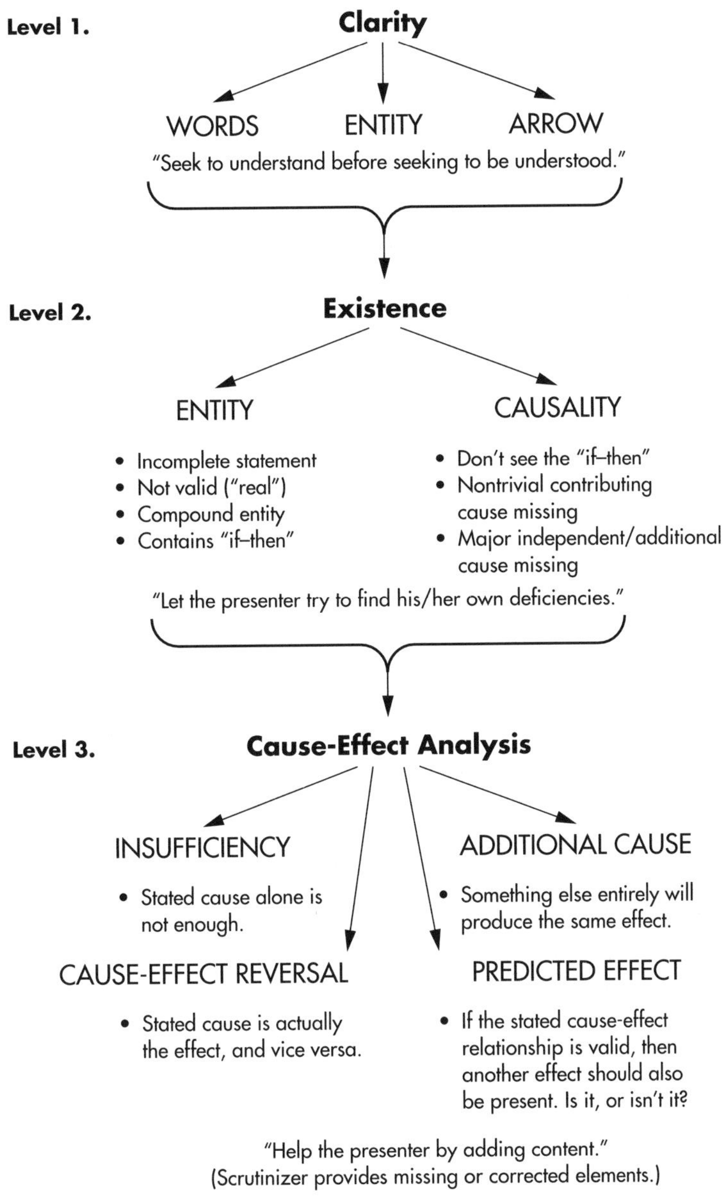
Level 1.
Clarity
WORDS
ENTITY
ARROW
"Seek to understand before seeking to be understood."
Level 2.
Existence
ENTITY
• Incomplete statement
• Not valid ("real")
• Compound entity
• Contains "if–then"
CAUSALITY
• Don't see the "if–then"
• Nontrivial contributing cause missing
• Major independent/additional cause missing
"Let the presenter try to find his/her own deficiencies."
Level 3.
Cause-Effect Analysis
INSUFFICIENCY
• Stated cause alone is not enough.
ADDITIONAL CAUSE
• Something else entirely will produce the same effect.
CAUSE-EFFECT REVERSAL
• Stated cause is actually the effect, and vice versa.
PREDICTED EFFECT
• If the stated cause-effect relationship is valid, then another effect should also be present. Is it, or isn't it?
"Help the presenter by adding content."
(Scrutinizer provides missing or corrected elements.)

FIGURE 8.3. Categories of Legitimate Reservation: Sequence of Introduction.

Level I. CLARITY (Seek to Understand the Presenter)

THE SCRUTINIZER SAYS:

"Could you CLARIFY for me the:

- **Word [specify]."** (definition)

  (TRANSLATION: "Please define that word for me—no more, no less.")

- **Entity [no.] ."** (what it means)

  (TRANSLATION: "I don't understand the *idea* you're trying to convey with this entity.")

- **Arrow between [entity no.] and [entity no.]."** (where *each* part of the effect derives from)

  (TRANSLATION: "I don't see how the effect you're proposing results from the cause you stated.")

  or

  "I have a CLARITY reservation on the [WORD, ENTITY, or ARROW]."

THE PRESENTER RESPONDS:

Possible responses:

- **"The word ___ means . . ."** (Give a synonym or short phrase)

- **"[Subject] means . . ."** (Give definition)

  "[Verb] means . . ." (Give definition)

  "[Object] means . . ." (Give definition)

- **"[Subject of Effect Entity] comes from . . ."** (Specify which part of Cause Entity)

  "[Verb of Effect Entity] comes from . . ." (Specify which part of Cause Entity)

  "[Object of Effect Entity] comes from . . ." (Specify which part of Cause Entity)

  Note: A part of an effect may be *implied* by the cause.

Level II-A. ENTITY EXISTENCE (Enable Presenter to Discover and Correct)

THE SCRUTINIZER SAYS:

a. "I have an ENTITY EXISTENCE reservation on (entity no.)."

(TRANSLATION: "I don't think that entity is valid because:

- It's not a complete statement,
  or
- It contains an 'if–then' relationship,
  or
- It's too exclusive (*all* or *none*),
  or
- It doesn't exist for me.")

THE PRESENTER RESPONDS:

- Pause and reread the entity. The Scrutinizer clearly thinks you've missed something.
- Check for:
  - Complete statement
  - Improper "if–then" structure (CLUE: Look for ". . . in order to . . .")
  - Possible invalid "all," "none," "some," "many," or "most" statements.
- Change entity if you see a reason to do so.

Possible responses:

- **"I think I understand your reservation."** (Make changes as appropriate.) **"Does this change resolve it? If not, could you clarify your Entity Existence reservation?"**

  or

- **"I don't understand your Entity Existence reservation. Could you help me?"**

FIGURE 8.4. Directions for Communicating Using the CLR.

Level II-B. CAUSALITY EXISTENCE (Enable Presenter to Discover and Correct)

THE SCRUTINIZER SAYS:

b. "I have a CAUSALITY EXISTENCE reservation between [entity no.] and [entity no.]."

(TRANSLATION: "I don't think an 'if–then' condition actually exists, because:

- The cause, as stated, doesn't lead to the effect,
  or
- The cause, as stated, isn't sufficient alone to produce the effect,
  or
- Another independent cause, which you have not indicated, can produce the same effect.")

THE PRESENTER RESPONDS:

- Pause and reread the cause-effect. The scrutinizer clearly thinks you've missed something.
- Check for:
  - "Oxygen" you may have omitted
  - Another entity you may have overlooked (either going through an ellipse or separate from it)
- Change or add entities only if you see a reason to do so.

Possible responses:

- **"I agree with you."** (Make changes as appropriate.) **"Does this resolve your reservation?"** (If not, modify as necessary.)

  or

- **"I can't understand your reservation without some additional clues. Can you help me?"** (If you don't see the point the scrutinizer raised, or if the entity seems okay to you as written.)

FIGURE 8.4—*Continued.*

Level III-A. MODIFY THE TREE (Seek to Be Understood)

THE SCRUTINIZER SAYS:

a. "I have a CAUSE INSUFFICIENCY reservation, and the missing entity is [state it word-for-word]."

Note: It's a good idea to work out the wording before you speak.

(TRANSLATION: "I think that your stated cause needs to be combined [i.e., arrow through an ellipse] with something else to produce the effect you're proposing.")

THE PRESENTER RESPONDS:

- Write down the added entity, and pause to consider it.
- Decide whether, like "oxygen," it's obvious and likely to be understood by everyone as being present without having to specifically state it, or whether it's really a significant, but overlooked, contributor to the effect.

  Note: If you plan to present your tree to others, and they might not see it as "oxygen," consider adding it to your tree.

Possible responses:

IF YOU ACCEPT THE RESERVATION:

- **"I agree with your reservation. The entity you propose is part of the causality and needs to be there."**

  or

  "It's 'oxygen' to me, but it might not be to someone else." (Either way, add it, through an ellipse.)

IF YOU *DON'T* ACCEPT THE RESERVATION:

- **"I agree with your reservation, but I consider that to be 'oxygen.' For now I'll leave it as it is."** (Don't change it.)

  or

- **"I can't accept your reservation. For me, that entity is not part of the cause, because [explain your reasoning]."** (If you don't agree that the proposed additional entity is part of the cause, don't change it.)

FIGURE 8.4—*Continued.*

Level III-B and C. MODIFY THE TREE (Seek to Be Understood)

THE SCRUTINIZER SAYS:

b. "I have an ADDITIONAL CAUSE reservation, and the additional cause is [state it word-for-word]."

Note: It's a good idea to work out the wording before you speak.

(TRANSLATION: "I think that there is *another* independent cause that you haven't stated that will produce the same effect.")

c. "I have a CAUSE-EFFECT REVERSAL reservation."

or

"I have a 'HOUSE ON FIRE' reservation." [EXPLAIN WHY YOU BELIEVE THAT THE STATED CAUSE-EFFECT RELATIONSHIP HAS BEEN REVERSED.]

(TRANSLATION: "I think you've got the arrow going in the wrong direction. What you show for the cause is really the effect, and vice versa.")

THE PRESENTER RESPONDS:

- Write down the additional cause, and pause to consider its magnitude. Is it:
  - A possible cause *but not* significant? [REJECT]
  - A possible cause *and* significant? [ACCEPT]

Possible responses:

- **"I accept your Additional Cause reservation."** (Add it to your tree.)

or

- **"I can't accept your Additional Cause reservation. For me, this is *not* an additional cause, because . . ."** (YOU *MUST* EXPLAIN WHY YOU'RE NOT ACCEPTING THE RESERVATION. One common reason is that the magnitude of the effect would be negligible.)

- Pause and reread your proposed cause and effect.

- See if the relationship makes more sense with the arrow pointing the other way. If, by adding "We know that . . ." to the beginning of your effect, it makes sense, the reservation is probably valid.

Possible responses:

- **"I agree with your cause-effect reversal reservation."** (Make appropriate changes.)

or

- **"I can't accept that reservation, because . . . [explain]."** (No changes.)

FIGURE 8.4—*Continued.*

Level III-D. MODIFY THE TREE (Seek to be Understood)

THE SCRUTINIZER SAYS:

d. "I have a PREDICTED EFFECT reservation. If I accept that [stated cause] leads to [stated effect], then [stated cause] will also lead to [separate predicted effect]. Since this means that [predicted effect] is:

- **in direct conflict with your stated effect,**

or

- **of greater or lesser magnitude than expected,**

the two cannot exist simultaneously."

(TRANSLATION: "If your cause leads to the effect you claim, it should also lead to a different predicted effect which is:

- Not there
- In direct conflict with the effect you propose
- The same as your proposed effect, but greater or less than expected in magnitude

Any of these is enough to invalidate your proposed effect.")

THE PRESENTER RESPONDS:

- Write down the predicted effect, and pause to consider it.

Possible responses:

- **"I accept your Predicted Effect reservation."** (Change the entity or causality, as appropriate.)

or

- **"I can't accept your Predicted Effect reservation because . . ."**

(YOU *MUST* EXPLAIN WHY YOU'RE NOT ACCEPTING THE RESERVATION. Some common reasons: statistics, differences in environment, etc.)

FIGURE 8.4—*Continued.*

Appendix A
CONVENTIONS FOR ALL TREES

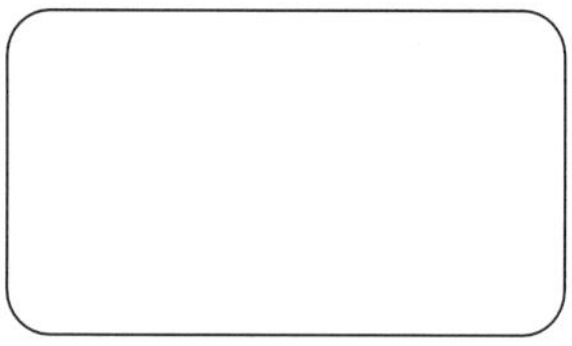

ENTITY (Round corners). An event (cause, effect, or condition of reality). The basic element of cause-and-effect trees. Connected by a single-barbed arrow to another entity. Used in the CRT, FRT, and TT. Also used in a CRD to indicate pre-requisites, requirements, and objective. In a negative branch, an added reality; that is, one that did exist but was not necessary to the FRT from which the negative branch grew.

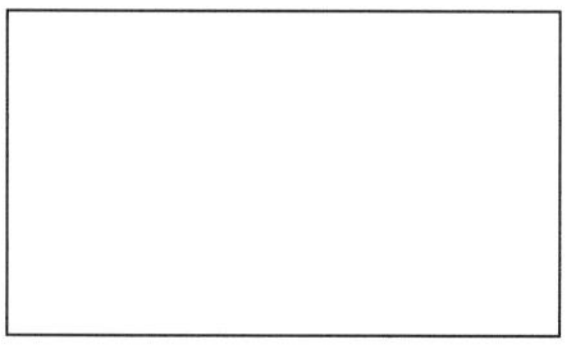

INJECTION, OBJECTIVE, INTERMEDIATE OBJECTIVE, INITIATOR ACTION (Square corners). A condition or action initiated by someone intended to result in some effect. Used in FRT to change future reality. Used in a PRT to overcome obstacles. Used in a TT to indicate specific action someone must take.

OBSTACLE (Hexagon). A situation or condition that prevents the accomplishment of an injection or the objective of a PRT. Appears *only* in the PRT. Overcome by an intermediate objective (square-cornered rectangle).

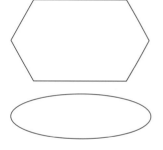

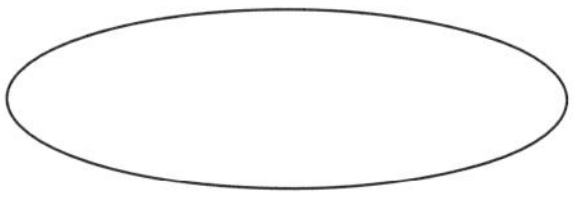

ELLIPSE. Denotes sufficiency. Identifies a situation where two or more causes of approximately equivalent magnitude are necessary to produce the indicated effect. Loss of any one cause passing through an ellipse invalidates the entire cause-effect relationship. Used in CRT, FRT, and TT.

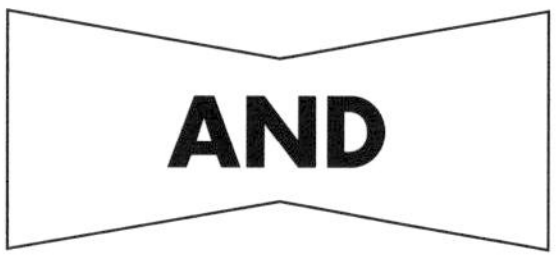

MAGNITUDINAL "AND" (Bow tie). Denotes an additive condition. Identifies a situation where each of the causes passing through the symbol adds more incrementally to the effect. Loss of any one cause does not eliminate the effect, but rather reduces it by some substantial amount. Used in the CRT, FRT, and TT.

CAUSE-EFFECT ARROW; NECESSARY CONDITION ARROW. In A CRT, FRT, and TT, indicates a direct and immediate cause-effect relationship. Cause lies at the tail, effect at the barb (head). In CRD and PRT, indicates a necessary condition relationship. Necessary condition lies at the tail, objective at the barb. One or more unspoken (invisible) assumptions underlies every arrow.

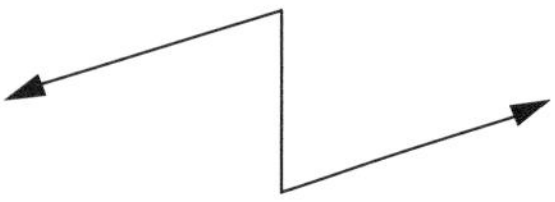

CONFLICT ARROW. Indicates two conflicting conditions or prerequisites. Used in CRD to indicate the lowest essential level where conflict occurs.

Appendix B
GLOSSARY OF TOC TERMS

Action. Something performed. In logical usage in trees, an action is something done by someone, as opposed to a condition of reality, which simply exists. An action is an entering argument (for example, "I wash the dishes"). In contrast, a condition is a resulting effect (for example, "The dishes are washed"). In logic trees, certain entities are phrased as actions, rather than conditions. Example: In the Conflict Resolution Diagram, conflicting prerequisites may be worded as actions (for example, "Do this/Don't do this"). Some injections in a Future Reality Tree and a very few intermediate objectives in a Prerequisite Tree may also be worded as actions. All specific actions in a Transition Tree are phrased as actions.

Assumption. A statement or condition accepted as valid without substantiation or proof. Assumptions sometimes are used because proof is not possible or available. Frequently based in tradition rather than logic. Represented by cause-and-effect arrows in the Conflict Resolution Diagram (CRD) and the various trees. The primary targets for refutation in searching for an idea (injection) to break through the conflict between prerequisites. Invalidation of any assumption in a CRD "evaporates" the cloud and its attendant conflict.

Capacity Constrained Resource (CCR). A resource whose capacity is less than the demand placed upon it. Sometimes referred to as a "bottleneck."

Categories of Legitimate Reservation (CLR). Eight rational tests of a stated cause-effect relationship in a tree. A nonconfrontational way of expressing nonacceptance of cause and effect. The eight categories are: Clarity, Entity Existence, Causality Existence, Cause Insufficiency, Additional Cause, Cause-Effect Reversal, Predicted Effect Existence, and Tautology.

Cause-and-Effect Arrow. An element of all TOC trees that indicates a cause-effect relationship. The visual depiction (→) connects the cause (tail) with the effect (head). Expressed verbally as "If [condition at tail], then [condition at head]."

Condition. A state of nature or being. A statement about existing or future reality (for example, "The light is on"). Different from an action, which implies that somebody does something (for example, "I turn the light on"). Conditions can be results of actions or, in a Current or Future Reality Tree, existing environmental reality. In a Future Reality Tree an effect you're trying to achieve would be worded as a condition. So would the obstacles and most intermediate objectives in a Prerequisite Tree. In a Conflict Resolution Diagram, the requirements and objective are worded as conditions.

Conflict Resolution Diagram (CRD). A logical technique for identifying conflicts and opposing assumptions that underlie core problems and objectives. Composed of an objective (the stated opposite of the core problem), requirements (the conditions most essential to obtaining the objective), and prerequisites (mutually exclusive conditions that define the conflicting requirements).

Constraint. Any element of a system or its environment that limits the output of the system. Analogous to the weak link in a chain. The entity that will ultimately prevent increases in Throughput regardless of improvements made to any other part of the system. May be physical (equipment, facilities, and so forth) or policy. If the capability of the system is not constrained internally (such as by physical means or policy), the constraint may lie outside the system, in the environment (for example, market demand).

Core Problem (CP). The single underlying root cause of a majority (that is, approximately 70 percent) of undesirable effects (UDEs). The core problem, when effectively solved, automatically eliminates all resulting (downstream) UDEs. The opposite condition of an objective (see Conflict Resolution Diagram; Objective). The prime target of improvement efforts.

Correlation. A dependent relationship between two variables. Correlation is the observation that one thing changes in concert with the changes in something else. Differs from cause and effect, because no causality is rigorously and logically established. Example: "The team has a winning record; attendance is higher." No cause-effect relationship is established.

Current Reality Tree (CRT). A visual depiction of current cause and effect. Beginning with undesirable effects (UDEs), the Current Reality Tree integrates UDEs, necessary conditions, and intermediate statements until all UDEs are linked and root causes and core problems are identified. A diagram that, through the bonds of cause and effect, connects all of the existing UDEs. Answers the question, "What's the core problem?"

Desirable Effect (DE). A result or outcome that is, in and of itself, positive, desirable, or beneficial. The direct or indirect result of an injection. The opposite of an undesirable effect (UDE).

Entity. A collective term referring to graphical blocks in a logic tree. Any statement of condition or action enclosed in a geometric figure is an entity. Effects, causes, actions, conditions, injections, intermediate objectives, and obstacles are all entities.

Expected Effect. A new condition, not previously existing in current reality, that results from an injection. Depicted as a reality entity (round-cornered rectangle) because it is an outcome of an artificially constructed condition (injection).

Future Reality Tree (FRT). A visual depiction of future cause and effect. A means to logically test the efficacy and validity of solutions/actions (injections) before embarking on implementation. Answers the question, "Does the proposed injection take us where we want to go?"

Goal. The purpose for which the system is created. Should be stated in a way that implies continuum, not absolute destination, in order to facilitate a Process of Ongoing Improvement (POOGI). The goal is determined solely by the owner(s) of the system. Any other influence exerted by internal or external forces other than the system's owners may be considered necessary conditions, but they will not be the goal.

Injection. A new or not yet existing condition that must be created in order for future reality to unfold in the desired manner. A breakthrough idea that neutralizes conflict. A means of converting undesirable effects (UDEs) into desirable effects (DEs) through a chain of cause and effect. A primary element of the Conflict Resolution Diagram (CRD), the Future Reality Tree (FRT), and the Prerequisite Tree (PRT). An action or condition that invalidates assumptions underlying the requirements and prerequisites of a CRD.

Intermediate Objective (IO). A lower-level condition or requirement that is used to overcome obstacles. An element of the Prerequisite Tree (PRT). An action or change that is necessary to the effectiveness of an injection.

Intuition. The ability to recognize and understand patterns and interactions of a system. The ability to see or connect patterns out of a few data points. Not "flying by the seat of your pants." Convergence of knowledge and experience.

Inventory (I). All the money a system invests in things it intends to sell. Includes raw materials, but also includes items traditionally considered assets, such as facilities, equipment, land, and so forth (things that can depreciate). Inventory is not an asset. Inventory is not subject to value added (no value is added to inventory until the moment of sale).

Necessary Condition (NC). A condition or state of nature that must be satisfied in order to realize a system's goal. Necessary conditions are imposed by power groups, both internal and external to the system. Without satisfying the necessary condition, the system will fail to realize its goal. EXAMPLE: The goal may be to make more money. But necessary conditions may be product quality, customer satisfaction, regulatory compliance, production safety, and so on.

Negative Branch (NB). An undesirable or unfavorable development in a Future Reality Tree (FRT) that results from an injection. May be a side effect deleterious to realizing desired effects (DEs), or may be a significant negative outcome that compromises the effects of a proposed problem solution (injection). Requires an additional injection at the point where the tree branch starts turning negative in order to trim the branch.

Objective (O). The stated opposite of a core problem (CP). The focus of an Conflict Resolution Diagram (CRD). The outcome that an injection is designed to achieve.

Obstacle (OBS). A condition or opposing reaction that may prevent successful application of an injection. An element of a Prerequisite Tree. Usually conceived (that is, brainstormed) by the tree-builder to anticipate possible complications in implementing the injection. Requires the creation of an intermediate objective (IO) to neutralize.

Operating Expense (OE). All the money the system spends turning Inventory (I) into Throughput (T). A system-level measurement, not an individual product unit cost allocation. As Inventory is depreciated, it becomes an Operating Expense.

Power Group. An individual or group, internal or external to the system, that exerts influence on realization of the system's goal by imposing necessary conditions. Examples are unions, government regulatory agencies, Congress, special interests, and so on.

Prerequisite (P). An element of the Conflict Resolution Diagram (CRD) and the Prerequisite Tree (PRT). In the CRD, one of two mutually exclusive conditions that embody a conflict. In the CRD, a prerequisite is considered a "want" rather than a "need." In the PRT, the prerequisite is called an intermediate objective and constitutes the condition or action, not yet existing, necessary to overcome an obstacle.

Prerequisite Tree (PRT). A logical technique used to identify potential obstacles to proposed solutions (injections) and ways to overcome them (intermediate objectives).

Process of Ongoing Improvement (POOGI). A cybernetic, repeating cycle of effort to continuously improve a system by increasing Throughput and decreasing Inventory and Operating Expense.

Requirement (R). An element in a Conflict Resolution Diagram (CRD). A nonnegotiable need that must be satisfied to realize the objective of a CRD. A necessary condition.

Reservation. A nonconfrontational means of qualifying acceptance of a cause-effect statement represented by a cause-effect arrow. Indicates that the cause-effect relationship, as depicted, is insufficiently clear to the observer. A request for more information. Expressed verbally as, "I have a reservation . . ." Must be followed by citing one of seven reasons (see Categories of Legitimate Reservation).

Root Cause (RC). An original cause, through a chain of cause and effect, of an undesirable effect (UDE). Any statement in a Current Reality Tree (CRT) that does not derive from another statement. An entry point into a CRT. Depicted as an entity from which cause-effect arrows lead away but do not enter. If a root cause results in approximately 70 percent or more of the UDEs, it is considered a core problem (CP). Otherwise, it is only a root cause.

Subject Matter (SM). The information content pertaining to an issue. In logic trees, the topic about which the tree pertains, as differentiated from the logic process itself.

Throughput (T). The rate at which the system generates money through sales (profit-making systems). Throughput does not occur with the transfer of money internally (within the company). It can only occur through the infusion of new money from outside the system. Throughput and sales are not synonymous; Throughput is concerned with the rate at which money is generated through sales.

Transition Tree (TT). A logical technique for projecting and time-sequencing injections, intermediate objectives, and their resultant effects to realize an objective (eliminate a core problem). A variation of the Future Reality Tree (FRT). In essence, an implementation plan that structures management action (injections), obstacles to such action, and the intermediate objectives (IO) necessary to neutralize those obstacles.

Undesirable Effect (UDE). A visible symptom of a deeper, underlying core problem (CP). An effect that, in and of itself, is negative or undesirable, without dependence on any other factor. ("Undesirability" must be defined in relation to the system's goal.) A major entity on a Current Reality Tree (CRT).

APPENDIX C
CURRENT REALITY TREE EXERCISE

For Want of a Nail

For want of a nail, the shoe was lost.
For want of a shoe, the horse was lost.
For want of a horse, the rider was lost.
For want of a rider, the message was lost.
For want of a message, the battle was lost.
For want of a battle, the war was lost.
For want of a victory, the nation was lost.
All for want of a horseshoe nail.

The poem above is believed to date back to the time of the American Revolution. It clearly reflects a worst-case scenario involving cause and effect. Consider it an expression of an actual situation. Obviously, there would be much more to this scenario than the poem itself indicates—details such as organizational relationships, tactical and strategic situation, resource availability, leadership, and so forth. Use your imagination to flesh out some of the details of the circumstances under which this poem might have been written. Using the guidelines you have for building trees and the Categories of Legitimate Reservation:

- Identify the undesirable effects (UDE) inherent in this situation, beginning with those indicated in the poem. Add any others you think apply.
- Using the procedures outlined in Figure 3.44, build a Current Reality Tree that accurately reflects the situation, and from it identify a core problem.
- You may make any assumptions you need to about the situation in order to fill in gaps and develop entities for your tree.

APPENDIX D
CONFLICT RESOLUTION DIAGRAM EXERCISE

The Situation. The XYZ School District has a problem. Because of an increasing trend in violence at high schools and middle schools, the district, with Board of Education approval, has instituted a stringent disciplinary policy. It is an automatic expulsion offense if a student brings drugs or a weapon to school (or onto a school bus). Students can also be expelled for fighting or assault on other students or teachers. Communicating threats, intimidation, and disrespect to teachers or administrators are grounds for suspension on the first offense and expulsion for a second offense.

After six months, the results seem to be mixed. Most parents support the tighter discipline policy. And although incidents have decreased to some extent, they have not gone away completely. Moreover, a new problem faces the school district. A vocal group of parents and community activists has been protesting expulsions and suspensions at Board of Education meetings. They charge the district with ethnic and racial discrimination, because a disproportionate number of students expelled or suspended are from ethnic or racial minorities.

The district denies the discrimination charges, saying that the students expelled or suspended are the ones causing the trouble, regardless of their race or ethnicity. The Board has emphasized its commitment to a safe, secure school environment for all students. They refuse to allow a few disruptive, violent students to compromise the learning environment for the majority of "good" kids.

The protesters counter that the students expelled are the very ones most in need of schooling, because they are the ones most at risk of dropping out of society's mainstream and into lives of crime, poverty, or homelessness. They criticize the school district for not doing enough to save the "at risk" youth, aggravating the problem through expulsion, and creating more of a burden on society.

Things have come to a head. The activists organized a walk-out of about 300 students from two of the district's four high schools. Along with about 150 parents, they marched two miles through city streets to the school district offices, where they picketed for several hours. Besides the high visibility and adverse publicity associated with this walkout, the district has suffered financially. The state provides funds to local school districts based on percentage of registered attendance and withholds a fixed amount when a student is absent. Every day a student is absent from school, the district loses money. The protesters have promised many more walk-outs, until the school district agrees to negotiate on their demands.

Your Assignment. Consider yourself an arbitrator called in to help resolve the conflict.

1. What are the conflicting positions?
2. What are the requirements the positions of each side are intended to satisfy?
3. What is the common objective of both parties?
4. What type of conflict is embodied in this situation (mutually exclusive conditions, or differing alternatives)?
5. Using the worksheets at the end of chapter 4, construct a Conflict Resolution Diagram (CRD) to describe the situation.
6. Identify as many underlying assumptions as you can for each arrow of the CRD.
7. Using the "alternative environment" technique, develop as many injections as you can to break the conflict.
8. Select one (or more) injection(s), based on a decision rule of your choice (easiest to do, least expensive, most effective, and so forth).

APPENDIX E
FUTURE REALITY TREE EXERCISE

The Situation.* You are a 35-year-old person with a highly successful professional career. You're financially independent and want for nothing—except the personal fulfillment of a love relationship. You have never been married, but you have had a moderately active social life, though until now your career has always come first.

After nearly two years dating the same person, you are inclined to finally get married. Clearly, there are benefits to be derived from marriage, both personal and professional. There may also be some difficulties as well.

The Challenge. Because marriage will require a major emotional commitment and involve a significant change in lifestyle, you want to be certain that you're doing the right thing. You also have some concerns about whether you might regret it later. As a result, you want to carefully consider all the pros and cons before committing yourself and your prospective life partner to such a decision.

Your Assignment. Referring to chapter 5, construct a Future Reality Tree (FRT) that grows out of the following decision (injection):

I AM MARRIED TO (person).

1. Determine the desired effects of your decision. Come up with at least five.
2. Identify and incorporate any additional injections required in your FRT to reach the desired effects.
3. Build in positive reinforcing loops, wherever possible.
4. Search out and develop negative branches that may result from the original or any subsequent injection. Create "branch-trimming" injections to eliminate the negative branches, and incorporate them into your FRT.

*The author is indebted to Lisa Scheinkopf for the idea of creating a Future Reality Tree on the decision to marry.

APPENDIX F
PREREQUISITE TREE EXERCISE

The Situation. You have just inherited a house and property as part of a deceased relative's estate. You don't plan to move into it yourself. Instead, you intend to sell the house and property for as much as you can get for them and invest the proceeds in a stock portfolio.

When you make your first visit to the property, you are dismayed by what you find. Although the house and property reside in a prosperous, well-established, middle class neighborhood, the place has deteriorated significantly since your relative died.

While the will was tied up in probate, freezing weather caused plumbing to crack. The basement and first floor absorbed large amounts of water damage. Windows and door locks have been broken by vandals, who also spray-painted graffiti on all interior walls and punched holes in the wallboard. Many light fixtures have been torn out, and the porcelain bathroom fixtures have been cracked. Carpeting throughout the house has been damaged or destroyed by water leakage, squirrels that entered through broken windows, and the vandals.

Burning embers from a nearby brushfire damaged the wooden shake roof of the house, causing significant holes before firefighters were able to put out the blaze. The resulting holes in the roof admitted significant rainwater to the upper floor. The central heating and air conditioning has been cannibalized and major parts stolen. One post holding up the porch roof is cracked and another is completely broken through.

The overhead garage door has been pulled off its tracks and is lying in a heap on the garage floor. The yard has gone completely to weeds, and all the grass has died from lack of regular watering and fertilizer. All the ornamental shrubbery has become overgrown. Trash and junk litters the yard. The septic tank has obviously backed up, and all the toilets and drains in the house are inoperative.

Adding insult to injury, a group of nine homeless squatters have taken up residence in the house. They've been burning fires in a 55-gallon drum in the living room for heat, and using homemade kerosene lamps for light, which have embedded large amounts of hydrocarbon deposit on all the ceilings and walls. Finally, the place reeks.

The Challenge. You have to restore the house and property to a condition that will bring a maximum selling price. You also have to find a buyer and transact the sale.

Your Assignment. Referring to chapter 6, construct a Prerequisite Tree that identifies all the obstacles to selling the house for top dollar. Identify the intermediate objectives needed to overcome the obstacles and the sequence in which they must be accomplished. Begin your PRT with the following objective:

Conclude a successful sale of the house for "top dollar."

APPENDIX G
TRANSITION TREE EXERCISE

The Situation. You have decided to run for election to the office of representative to the state legislature. Although you're familiar with local politics, this is your first attempt to run for elective public office. You have some capable advisors, many willing volunteer workers, and some initial campaign contributions (but not enough to carry you through the election). You also have a reasonably good idea of the major tasks that need to be done and the general sequence in which they must be completed (refer to list, below, and the flowchart on p. 367).

The Challenge. What you don't have is a detailed plan that divides work, assigns responsibilities, and identifies the specific steps needed to fulfill them. Time is a factor—the election is only four months away, and you're just getting started. Resources are also a concern. Because your campaign contributions and staff are limited, it's critical for you to be sure you get the most "bang for your buck," or for the limited time your volunteers have to give. There's no room for false starts, no time to go down "blind alleys," and no money to waste nonproductively. You have to do everything right the first time—which means you need a plan, or road map.

Your Assignment. Construct a Transition Tree detailing the steps you and your campaign staff must take, starting today, in the sequence you must take them. The end (top) of your Transition Tree should be your key "desired effect"—your election to office. Consider the tasks listed below to be the objectives you must satisfy enroute to that desired effect.

DESIRED EFFECT: I win the election.

Major Tasks:

- Build an effective campaign organization.
- Create a campaign strategy.
- Finalize a campaign platform.
- Assign campaign work to volunteers.
- Raise campaign funds.
- Develop a public relations program.
- Win campaign debates.
- Achieve comprehensive, effective media exposure.

Major Task Flowchart

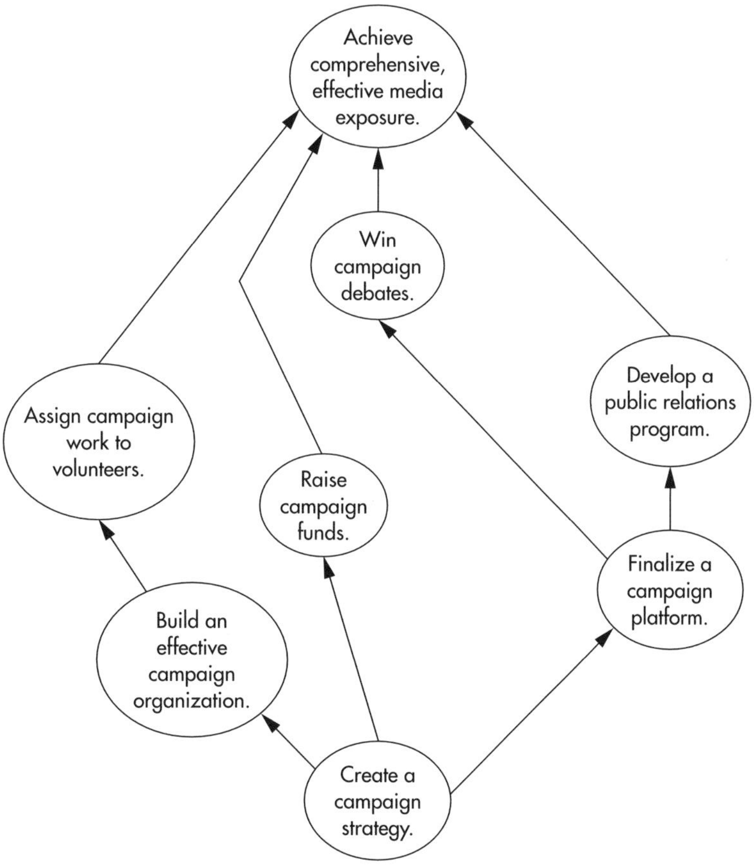

INDEX

D

E

F

G

P

V

W